The Global Challenge

The Global Challenge

Frameworks for International Human Resource Management

Paul Evans
INSEAD

Vladimir Pucik
IMD

Jean-Louis Barsoux
INSEAD

Boston   Burr Ridge, IL   Dubuque, IA   Madison, WI   New York   San Francisco   St. Louis
Bangkok   Bogotá   Caracas   Kuala Lumpur   Lisbon   London   Madrid   Mexico City
Milan   Montreal   New Delhi   Santiago   Seoul   Singapore   Sydney   Taipei   Toronto

McGraw-Hill Higher Education 🖭

*A Division of The **McGraw-Hill** Companies*

3 4 5 6 7 8 9 0 DOC/DOC 0 9 8 7 6

ISBN: 978-0-07-239730-7
MHID: 0-07-239730-6

Publisher: *John E. Biernat*
Sponsoring editor: *Marianne C. P. Rutter*
Editorial assistant: *Tammy Higham*
Senior marketing manager: *Ellen Cleary*
Project manager: *Jean R. Starr*
Senior production supervisor: *Lori Koetters*
Coordinator of freelance design: *Mary E. Kazak*
Associate supplement producer: *Joyce J. Chappetto*
Producer, Media technology: *Melissa Kansa*
Cover design: *Mark Gerardot*
Typeface: *10/12 Times Roman*
Compositor: *Carlisle Communications, Ltd.*
Printer: *R. R. Donnelley & Sons Company*

Library of Congress Cataloging-in-Publication Data

Evans, Paul, 1946–
    The global challenge: Frameworks for international human resource
        management/Paul Evans,
Vladimir Pucik, Jean-Louis Barsoux.
        p. cm.
    Includes bibliographical references and index.
    ISBN 0-07-239730-6 (alk. paper)—ISBN 0-7-112114-5 (international: alk. paper)
    1. International business enterprises—Personnel management. I. Title: International human resource management. II. Pucik, Vladimir. III. Barsoux, Jean-Louis. IV. Title.
HF5549.5.E45 E93 2002
658.3—dc21

                                                              2001054432

www.mhhe.com

Contents

v

2 Three Faces of Human Resource Management in the International Firm   47

PART 2

Strategies for International Growth 99

3 Exploiting Global Integration 101

4 Becoming Locally Responsive 157

Preface

The focus of *The Global Challenge* is on the human resource management challenges that accompany the process of internationalization and how to operate in an interconnected world where people are the source of sustainable competitive advantage.

As we headed toward the new century, globalization surfaced as the buzzword of the times. Many ingredients of globalization had actually been around for several decades without making more than a modest impact on our thinking. The progressive dismantling of trade barriers, the availability of global capital, advances in computing and communications technology, and the gradual convergence of consumer tastes had all been underway for some time. These trends reached a threshold where they became mutually reinforcing. The tragic events of September 11th will create as yet unpredictable consequences and challenges for the global economy, but the process of internationalization is not likely to stop. For better or worse, we have moved into an era when it makes less and less sense to consider any aspect of management without taking into consideration its international context.

Internationalization has a particularly strong impact on our understanding of human resource management. Few factors have sensitized us more to the importance of human resource management than the rise of postwar Japan, a nation with only intangible assets, while its "fall" reinforced our awareness that when competitive success factors change so must these management practices. The issues that gave birth to international human resource management remain important—expatriation and the adaptation of practices to different cultures—but globalization has brought new challenges. Its tensions have increased the complexity of organizations, captured by the notion of matrix. As the complexity grew, we realized that structure alone cannot deal with the tensions—matrix must be built into the minds of managers. Looking to the future, there is a broad agreement that a firm's competitive advantage will increasingly come from its ability to transfer know-how not just from the parent country to the developing world, as in the past, but between subsidiaries in an international network. While information and communications technology can assist, the challenges are largely those of people and organizational culture. And eternal human resource questions such as leadership development take new shape. If our future depends on leaders who can respond to these global challenges in socially responsible ways, then the obvious question for human resource management is how we today should develop the leaders of tomorrow.

Some years ago, the scholar Karl Weick queried the distinction between *international* human resource management and the "regular" human resource management field. Now the boot is on the other foot. In a global era, the most relevant insights into management processes will come from studying human resource management in an international context.

Our teaching, research and consulting has taken place more or less equally over the years in North America, Europe and Asia, and to a lesser extent South America and Australia. We wanted to write a book on such issues that would be genuinely international in its orientation, building on the voluminous research of the last decade.

In framing these challenges and the responses, we also wanted to address the criticisms of human resource management (HRM) that have been building up in the world of scholarship. The point was well made by the chair for the Human Resource Division of the Academy of Management when he recently noted:

> We are still viewed by many as being too myopic and functional, dissecting what we do into the traditional domains of selection, training, compensation and so forth. One of my colleagues has even added "HR strategy" as another functional area of HR . . . . We need to start thinking in terms of organizational problems (e.g. How can we improve organizational productivity? How can we enhance innovation? How can we deal effectively with foreign competition?) that may be approached from a variety of HR perspectives rather than HR content domains.[1]

Much of the field of human resource management is focused on functional human resource activities, and we have not yet fully digested the fact that the performance value of HRM comes not from the practices themselves but from the way in which they fit consistently together. When the word "international" is appended to HRM, the focus narrows even further, from managing "people" in general to managing "expatriates" in particular. Our experience of international human resource management is that the challenges are far wider than those of expatriation. The field has to be extended to cover localization of management, international coordination, global leadership development, cultural due diligence and integration in cross-border acquisitions, and the emerging cultural challenges of global knowledge management, to name but a few of the issues we discuss in this book.

We also wanted to combine the leading edge of practice with the state-of-the art in theory. The consistency argument is one of myriad examples of how practice needs theory, and the reader will find him or herself exposed to many different theoretical perspectives in this book. Indeed we argue that what is exciting about the international human resource field is that it must be interdisciplinary in its orientation.

Writing this book has been an opportunity to develop a particular theoretical perspective that has its heritage in the work of some of our colleagues and friends in the in-

---

[1]Luiz Gomez-Mejia (2000), "Moving forward," HR Division Newsletter, Academy of Management, *24*:1.

ternational strategy field—Sumantra Ghoshal and Chris Bartlett, Yves Doz, C.K. Praha-lad, and the late Gunnar Hedlund—all of whom were drawn into the field of HRM be-cause human resource management is a matter of managing and getting things done in the global economy.

The distinctive feature of the "transnational enterprise," to use the concept coined by Bartlett and Ghoshal, is that it is characterized by contradictions such as having to be both local and global in its orientation, capable of exploiting resources today while de-veloping resources for tomorrow. We are concerned with the question of how to thrive in a world of contradiction, and the perspective running through this book is that of du-ality theory.

This is a perspective that will be new to most executive, MBA and even academic readers—new and yet familiar. It is increasingly obvious that we live in a world of par-adox. Organizations are becoming more and more similar, but competitive advantage comes from being different. We need to understand cultural stereotypes, but it is dan-gerous to use them in practice. The performance advantage of HRM comes through con-sistent alignment, but this in turn leads to "the failure of success." We have to make sure that subsidiaries and people are clearly accountable, and then focus on building team-work where it will add value. In this age of discontinuity, the future may be quite un-predictable. While some despair, we hope to show that an understanding of duality helps us to build the future into the present.

Our audience is both the reflective practitioner and the postgraduate student. We be-lieve that a book is rich if it helps people to make sense out of their own experience, and it is not intended for the neophyte. *The Global Challenge* is designed for use on MBA and executive programs at business schools. We provide practical advice, built on the ex-perience of leaders and organizations as well as research, but we aspire to more than that. Our aim is to help people understand the mindset, the deeper set of attitudes, that are needed to thrive in a world increasingly characterized by paradox and duality.

We hope that human resource professionals will find this book to be helpful in pro-viding new insights and inspiration for action as they face up to the paradoxes of their field. We also hope that our academic colleagues will be stimulated by the way we have attempted to frame this field.

Instructors will find guidance, references to cases and exercises, and many other forms of assistance in designing courses for MBA and executive participants on the following website: *www.mhhe.com/business/management/evanspucik/.* This website is designed to be a state-of-the-art hub in the field of international human resource management.

Each chapter in this book is a stand-alone guide to a particular aspect of international human resource management—from the history of international human resource man-agement in the first chapter to the functional implications for human resource profes-sionals in the last; from managing the human side of cross-border acquisitions to build-ing multinational coordination without falling into the traps of stultifying bureaucracy. A version of the book can be tailor-made for a particular course using McGraw-Hill's Primis service, using selected chapters with appropriate case and reading material.

OVERVIEW

Part 1, "Challenges, Concepts, Frameworks," sets the stage for *The Global Challenge* by reminding the reader of our historical context, tracing how the domain of international human resource management has evolved. The challenges are situated, and our basic framework for thinking of human resource management in an international context is introduced, with its three roles of the builder, the change partner, and the navigator who steers through the dualities.

Part 2, "Strategies for International Growth," reviews the human resource management implications of four paths for international development. These are the routes of global integration, local responsiveness, alliances, and cross-border acquisitions. Each chapter reviews in depth the challenges that are associated with these strategies, such as those of managing expatriation in the globally integrated firm and adapting to different cultures in the multidomestic firm.

Part 3, "The HRM Agenda in the Transnational Firm," addresses the role of human resource management in resolving the contradictions of the transnational enterprise, with its challenges of local entrepreneurship and global coordination. We focus on how human resource management can build the necessary "glue," on talent and leadership development, on how to build "a global mindset." And we discuss some of the frontiers for this domain—building global knowledge management and steering the process of change that underlies everything else.

Part 4, "Organizing Human Resource Management," consists of a final chapter that addresses the implications, above all for the professional human resource manager. It focuses on how corporations are organizing the vital basics of human resource management so as to free up energies to focus on the emerging challenges of social architecture such as procedural justice and contention management.

The philosophy behind this book can be neatly summarized by Henri Bergson's advice: "Think like a man of action. . . and act like a man of thought."

ACKNOWLEDGEMENTS

A book such as this builds on the insights, experiences, and research of many people. First, we would like to thank executives from companies that we have worked with over the last twenty-five years who have shared their experiences and views during teaching seminars, research studies, consulting projects, forums and conferences. If we were to single out a few, they would include ABB, Apple Computers, PT Astra, Avon, British Airways, Citibank, Canon, Daimler-Chrysler, Danfoss, DHL, Exxon, General Electric, Hewlett Packard, Hitachi, Huhtamäki, Kodak, Lafarge, Marks & Spencer, Nokia, Royal Bank of Canada, Samsung, San Miguel, Shell, Sony, 3M, Unibank, Unilever, and Whirlpool. We extend particular thanks to Johann Brongers, Luis Cabrera, Federico Castellanos, Glenn Heidenreich, John Herbert, John Hofmeister, Phil Kirkby, Thorleif Krarup and Steen Kristensen, Brian McNamee, Bob Muir, Masa Murakami, Arne Olsson, Timo Peltola, Cal Reynolds, Minoru Sakurai, Yasuo Sekijima, Betania Tanure, Roy Williams, and Yukari Yomo.

We have intellectual debts to pay to many academic colleagues and friends. Some of the foundation concepts underlying this book were laid down by Chris Bartlett and Sumantra Ghoshal, as well as Yves Doz, C.K. Prahalad and Gunnar Hedlund, and also Charles Hampden-Turner. In the human resource management field, we owe particular thanks to Nancy Adler, Ingmar Björkman, Wayne Brockbank, John Boudreau, Chris Brewster, Lee Dyer, Lynda Gratton, David Guest, Martin Hilb, Susan Jackson, Gareth Jones, Steve Kerr, Ed Lawler, Mark Mendenhall, George Milkovich, Dan Ondrack, Randy Schuler, Noel Tichy, Dave Ulrich, Theresa Welbourne, and Pat Wright. Thanks also go to Henri-Claude de Bettignies, Michael Brimm, Charles Galunic, Martin Gargiulo, Xavier Gilbert, Charles Handy, Peter Killing, André Laurent, Stefanie Lenway, Tom Murtha, Phil Rosenzweig, Ed Schein, and Susan Schneider.

Craig Beytien at McGraw-Hill/Irwin is the grandfather of this project, and we are indebted to him. Thanks also for the encouragement and patience of our able editor Marianne Rutter, as well as Jean Starr, Tammy Higham, Tracy Jensen and the rest of the crew. We take this opportunity to express our profound appreciation to Nathalie d'Aboville at INSEAD and Anne-Marie Tassi at IMD who have shared all the trials, tribulations, and joys of this project, and also to Ranu Capron and Hee Jae Cho.

And finally there is the deepest of thanks for the patience of Bente, Hoan, and Astrid who have lived with this project, now come to fruition, for more years than they would care to remember.

About the Authors

Paul Evans is Professor of Organizational Behavior at INSEAD in Fontainebleau, France. Raised in Africa, he has an M.A. in law from Cambridge University, a Danish business diploma, an MBA from INSEAD, and his Ph.D. is in Organizational Psychology and Management from the Sloan School at M.I.T. He is also Titular Professor at the European Institute for Advanced Studies in Management in Brussels, and he has been visiting professor at the University of Southern California and London Business School, also teaching management courses at many universities on three continents. His research interests focus on human resource management, leadership and the management of change, while his long-standing intellectual interest is in the dualities that underlie human and organizational behavior. Among his books are a pioneering international study of the relationship between professional and private life of executives, *Must Success Cost so Much?* (translated into seven languages), and the first book on international HRM, *Human Resource Management in International Firms: Change, Globalization, Innovation.* Former board member of the Human Resource Planning Society, he is the founding board member of the European Human Resource Forum (EHRF), a project-oriented network with 150 corporate members, and he directed a project for Royal Dutch/Shell to reorient their approach to management training and development.

Vladimir Pucik is Professor of International Human Resources at IMD, the International Institute for Management Development, Lausanne, Switzerland. Born in Prague, Czech Republic, where he studied international economics, law, and political science, he received his MIA in international affairs (specializing in East Asia) and Ph.D. in business administration from Columbia University in New York. Before joining IMD, Dr. Pucik was Associate Professor and the first Academic Director of International Programs at the Center for Advanced Human Resource Studies at the Industrial and Labor Relations School, Cornell University, and a faculty member at the Graduate School of Business, University of Michigan. He has held a number of visiting appointments in universities around the world, including INSEAD and three years as a visiting professor at Keio and

Hitotsubashi University in Tokyo. During his career he received numerous research awards in particular for his work on HRM in Japan and has published extensively in academic and professional journals in the area of international business and human resource management. His previous major works include *Accelerating International Growth, Globalizing Management: Creating and Leading the Competitive Organization* and *Management Culture and the Effectiveness of Local Executives in Japanese-owned U.S. Corporations.* His current research interests focus on international human resources, strategic alliances, and cross-border mergers and acquisitions.

Jean-Louis Barsoux is Senior Research Fellow at INSEAD in France. Born in France and raised in Britain, he received his Ph.D. in comparative management from the University of Loughborough in England. Before joining INSEAD, he worked with Rosemary Stewart at Templeton College, Oxford, on two studies—a comparison of management in Britain and Germany and one on the nature of managerial work. He is the author of several books, including *Managing Across Cultures* (with Susan Schneider), *INSEAD: From Intuition to Institution, The Diversity of Management* (with Rosemary Stewart), *Management in France* (with Peter Lawrence). His book on the uses of humor in business, *Funny Business,* won the Management Consultancies Association Prize for Book of the Year, and he is the co-author of several award-winning cases (Rank Xerox, British Airways, Air France). He is currently working with INSEAD colleague Jean-Francois Manzoni on a book about "The Set-Up-to-Fail Syndrome," following a Harvard Business Review article on how bosses create their own poor performers.

PART 1

Challenges, Concepts, Frameworks

The first part of the book provides a historical and conceptual understanding of the challenges facing human resource management in international firms. Beginning with a narrative history of internationalization in the first chapter, the aim is to help the reader understand how the concept of human resource management (HRM) has evolved, and notably how ad hoc concerns with international personnel matters have developed into vital competitive challenges associated with globalization. This narrative will help in understanding the emergence of the transnational firm, where HRM issues are of paramount importance.

The defining feature of the transnational enterprise is its ability to cope with contradiction—what is called *duality*—notably the need to be both locally responsive and globally integrated. Another important duality is the pressure to leverage and develop resources simultaneously, experienced as a tension between short-term and long-term interests. We assess in broad terms how human resource management can meet these challenges.

In Chapter 2, the question of how human resource management contributes to the performance of firms spells out the conceptual framework underlying this book. The relationship between HRM and organizational performance must be separated into three different faces or roles. The first role is that of the *builder* who gets basic HRM foundations into place. Internationalization involves a lot of building activity, and we examine the forces that influence this process. The evidence suggests that attention should be focused on ensuring consistency between practices while recognizing that the impact of specific human resource practices will depend on the context.

Since markets, technologies, and competitive conditions all change with time, the second contribution of HRM to performance is as a *change partner*, facilitating organizational realignment in response to changes in strategy. Finally, as the need for change increases, it becomes necessary to anticipate future changes, guided by an awareness of the dynamics of tension between opposing sides of dualities. Here we introduce the third face of HRM, the role of the *navigator* who steers through the dualities and paradoxes that international firms increasingly face.

A recurrent critique of the human resource management field is its lack of a theoretical base. In this first part of the book, we also set out to introduce different theoretical perspectives, and link them to their practical implications. We draw on fit and contingency theory, the resource based view of the firm, different contextual schools (comparative management, institutional theories from political science, etc.), as well as building links to social capital and network theories, postmodernism, theories of organizational learning, and other perspectives.

The Challenges of International Human Resource Management

BORN TRANSNATIONAL

In 1990, the French engineer Bernard Liautaud and a colleague set up a software firm to develop a product acquired from a third party. The software in question helped companies use information stored in their databases to analyze, for example, sales trends and inventory levels. Aware that their strategic window of opportunity would not be open for long, the founders knew they would have to build an international presence quickly and at the same time attend to the next generation of products.

The founders consciously eschewed the traditional path of starting small and developing the domestic market. They opted instead for what they called the "Silicon Valley model": raising venture capital, attracting senior level people with stock options, and going public early. At the same time, in order to compete head-on with American rivals, the company had to do something else different—it had to adopt a global approach from the outset. Although they incorporated in France, the founders gave the firm the English name Business Objects for marketing purposes. In France it was widely assumed to be the subsidiary of a U.S. firm (even French firms prefer to buy software from the United States!). And the company's employees and finance and business partners would be drawn from around the world.

To attract foreign talent, they immediately set up a stock-option plan, although the French tax legislation was not especially conducive to such measures. Naturally enough, the company preferred to locate executives who had heavy option grants in the United States or options-friendly Britain. Very quickly recruitment was decentralized internationally to the unit heads.

Within two years of its launch, the company had set up offices in California, New York, and elsewhere in the United States, as well as in the U.K., Germany, and Singapore. It deliberately split the head office from the French subsidiary so as to emphasize to employees that Business Objects was not "a French company." English became the working language and financial statements were in U.S. dollars from the outset.

In order to launch the product simultaneously across markets, the company developed English, French, Spanish, German, and Japanese versions of the product. This R&D work was conducted in France, where there was lower turnover and less pressure on salaries. However, selected headquarter functions were relocated to the United States, including corporate finance, business development, and public relations.

In 1994, when the firm needed extra capital for growth, it decided to go public in the United States, believing that the company might be severely undervalued on the French Bourse. It thus became the first French company listed on the Nasdaq. Again, this meant breaking with the local model. According to the CEO Bernard Liautaud: "There is a fallacy in France that unless you retain 51 percent of the company, you don't control it anymore."

Besides bringing in $26 million to finance further growth, the flotation helped the company's development in other ways: It trumpeted the firm's resolve to compete head-on with the best in the field, providing instant credibility and visibility. This had a rapid impact on sales and marketing activities, as well as on recruitment and business partnerships.

The company was able to sign distribution agreements with large hardware manufacturers in key markets (AT&T, Fujitsu, and Bull) and with consulting partners (Price Waterhouse) to provide customer education and training. It also started to attract higher caliber executives with experience in larger firms. The problem with rapid growth was that qualified recruits could quickly become underqualified, as had already happened with the first chief financial officer. As Liautaud observed in 1995, this placed "a tremendous pressure on top management to think ahead. Our leitmotif is 'anticipate, anticipate, anticipate'—the financial needs, the internationalization needs, the recruitment needs, the product needs."

This was easier said than done. After announcing record profits of $8.5 million in 1995, the company ran into major difficulties as revenue growth slowed while marketing and R&D costs continued to rise. The share price tumbled as the company tried to tweak its core product while simultaneously developing the next generation. Many analysts foresaw that the company's products would be rendered obsolete by the technological developments associated with the Internet. But in 1998, the company bounced back with a new Web-based product that not only allowed clients to analyze their own data but also gave them access to customers and suppliers. In 1999, the company's record 1995 profit was surpassed.

In the same year, Business Objects for the first time appointed a corporate level human resource executive to guide the increasingly complex challenges of global coordination.

CONFLICTING PRESSURES

Firms competing globally face a multitude of demands on their organization and people. Often they are pushed simultaneously in several contradictory strategic directions. As we will see later, this is the hallmark of what is called "the transnational organization."

The above case illustrates many of the dilemmas faced by international firms today. To survive and prosper in the software industry, Business Objects needed to serve global markets. The costs of developing and marketing the product were simply too great to be amortized over only one market. At the same time, the firm had to be flexible and responsive to local market needs. For example, when developing different versions of its software, Business Objects had to take into account some fairly subtle requirements. The size of the windows needed to be tailored to the language (English is more compact); similarly the icons had to be carefully adapted across cultures. In order to penetrate the Japanese market, the firm had to spend time developing a version of the software that accommodated different reporting formats and a radically different character set.

The company also needed to gain access to resources dispersed throughout the world—venture capital, technical and managerial talent, and sources of complementary products. While this meant that the company had to be dispersed, the whole organization needed to be coordinated in the interests of efficiency and collective learning, encouraging the free flow of ideas across all boundaries. The accompanying corporate culture had to be open and empowering, but also tightly focused and competitive. To guide development of its culture, six values were formulated, including that of "transnational identity."

Part of Business Objects' ability to achieve rapid global coverage as well as local understanding came from the international partnerships and alliances that it forged. Such alliances raised a further set of challenges. Much of the writing on multinational companies assumes that the parent owns its foreign subsidiaries. The reality today for many firms is that growth, indeed survival, forces them into joint ventures as well as other kinds of alliances in research, manufacturing, or distribution. Managing an international organization with dozens, even thousands, of such alliances raises new dilemmas regarding how to manage without full control over one's people and other resources.

The need to exploit a product quickly on global markets is partly spurred by the necessity to raise cash to fund major R&D investments, reflecting another tension that is acutely evident in the case of Business Objects. New technologies or industry standards can rapidly make one's product obsolete. If one moves too slowly, foreign competitors with imitations can undermine the market. So the company has to invest scarce funds both in marketing its existing products abroad *and* in developing new products and new technologies capable of providing platforms for the future. Business Objects very nearly failed to manage the transition—highlighting the difficulty of what we will call "managing the future in the present."

Reviewing the history of international business in this opening chapter, we will see that these dilemmas have always existed. Traditionally, they were resolved in pendulum fashion. When it came to internationalization, one route was to build up the home base, and then to set up foreign sales subsidiaries as a pipeline to exploit market opportunities abroad—what we will call the *meganational strategy*. When the centralized meganational company started to experience difficulties in adapting its products to local needs and in attracting and retaining good local people, the pendulum would swing back toward greater decentralization.

Another route was to hire entrepreneurs in foreign countries who would build up autonomous local operations—a *multidomestic strategy* which had the advantage of strong local responsiveness. However, the decentralized multidomestic company found that its products were becoming uncompetitive because of the costs of duplication around the world. It would now be forced to tighten the reins of control.

Licensing, joint-ventures with foreign partners, and other forms of *alliance* were a third route to internationalization, sometimes as a path on their own and sometimes complementary to other means. While alliances could allow quick entry into new markets, firms that internationalized through such ventures found that, as business evolved, necessary changes were slow or impossible to implement because of conflicting interests of partners. So some firms favored a fourth path to enter a foreign market—outright *acquisition* which would, in theory, avoid the constraint of lack of control embedded in many alliances. But this seemingly quick route to internationalization often hid the protracted difficulties of merging cultures and operations across borders.

In the past there was time for companies to work through such dilemmas. Today, time has become a source of competitive advantage—and the need to do things faster is rewriting the rules of multinational competition. Companies can no longer afford to "muddle through." They need to address all dilemmas simultaneously, and Business Objects is an example of the new wave of twenty-first century organizations that are having to learn how to do this.

The multinational corporation today faces many contradictions—of being simultaneously local and global in scope, of being both centralized and decentralized, of delivering short-term results while developing tomorrow's assets, of managing hundreds (even thousands) of alliances where one does not have full control, of responding to market pressures to do things better AND cheaper AND faster. Indeed, at the heart of the concept of *transnational organization,* as developed by Bartlett and Ghoshal, is the notion of contradiction or what they call the need to maintain "a dynamic balance."[1]

In this book, we discuss the *people implications* of traditional strategies for internationalization and how such strategies get executed through human resource management. We consider how to manage expatriates from the parent country, how to go about adapting management practices to circumstances abroad, and how to localize management. We explore the human obstacles in joint ventures and how to avoid them, as well as how to expand across borders through acquisitions. This leads us inexorably to the critical role that human resource management (HRM) has in responding to the contradictory pressures on the transnational firm, in enabling managers to resolve these paradoxes in innovative ways. We also discuss the way in which global competition is changing the nature of management and organization, even for firms operating in domestic markets.

To illustrate our discussion, we present many practical examples of companies that have taken these paths and experienced these dilemmas and we draw on research studies from different disciplines—from personnel/human resource (HR) management to organizational theory, from cross-cultural analysis to strategic management. To illuminate the lessons, we make use of well-known theoretical perspectives—from the contingency theory of fit, to institutional theories from sociology and political science, to emerging theories of social capital—and also new theoretical perspectives, notably that of duality or dilemma theory.

In order to understand the challenges of HRM in international firms, it helps to have some understanding of the history of internationalization and of the evolution of HRM. This chapter sets the stage by providing a chronological narrative, which also highlights some of the significant theoretical advances. The aim is to sensitize readers upfront to perspectives and paradigms with which some may be unfamiliar and to establish links between theoretical streams—in short, to frame the domain.

DEFYING BORDERS: WHAT'S NEW?

International business is not a recent phenomenon; nor is international HRM a product of the twentieth century. The Assyrians, Phoenicians, Greeks, and Romans all engaged in extensive cross-border trade. There is evidence that Assyrian "commercial organizations" shortly after 2000 B.C. already had many of the traits of modern multinational companies (MNCs), complete with head offices and branch plants, clear hierarchy, foreign employees, value adding activities in multiple regions, and the search for new resources and markets.[2] Roman organizations spanning Asia, Africa, and Europe are heralded as the first "global" companies in that they covered the whole of the then known world.

Empire building was the primary goal of Roman-style international expansion, commerce being a by-product so as to clothe and feed the dispersed garrisons.[3] For centuries the dividing line between conquest and exchange remained fuzzy, as it was with the Viking raids from Scandinavia to the east and west in the early Middle Ages. Even in the first half of the twentieth century, internationalization was still closely associated with empires and colonization, often with the gunboats behind. So when can we situate the birth of international companies?

While economists typically view the growth and expansion of multinational firms as an American phenomenon of the post-1950 period, business historians refer to the European and American companies of the nineteenth century as the early versions of today's multinationals.[4] Some go further back, arguing that the real precursors were the sixteenth- and seventeenth-century trading companies—the English and Dutch East India companies, the Muscovy Company, the Hudson's Bay Company, and the Royal African Company.[5]

International Operations in the Preindustrial Era

These early trading companies exchanged merchandise and services across continents and had a geographical spread to rival today's multinational firms. They signed on crews and chartered ships; they engaged the services of experts with skills in trade negotiations and foreign languages, capable of assessing the quality of goods and determining how they should be handled and loaded. They had numerous outposts or warehouses in far-flung countries. The volume of transactions forced them to delegate considerable responsibility to local representatives. It also created a new challenge, precursor to modern expatriate dilemmas: How could the local managers be encouraged to use their discretionary powers to the best advantage of the company? The trading companies had to develop control structures and systems to monitor the behavior of their scattered agents.

Distance makes control more difficult. This was particularly the case in an era when the means of transport and communication were both slow and inseparable. The risks of opportunistic behavior loomed large.[6] Initially, this meant demanding not just accounts but also written records of decisions as well as notification of compliance with directives from home. But the high volume of transactions quickly overwhelmed the processing capabilities of the owners, which led to the creation of subcommittees to process receipts and accounts and to handle correspondence, staffed by salaried employees from the home office. By the mid-eighteenth century the Dutch and English East India companies each employed over 350 head office administrators.

Establishing formal rules and procedures was one way of exercising control, but it did not eliminate the attractions of personal opportunism. Other measures were developed. For example, the employment contract stipulated that managers would work hard and in the interests of the company. Failure to do so would be reprimanded and could lead to dismissal. Managers' actions were monitored in two ways. On the one hand, performance measures were established: These included the ratio of capital to tonnage, the amount of outstanding credit on advance contracts, whether ships sailed on time, and the care taken in loading mixed cargoes. On the other hand, systems were installed to supply additional information on behavior and outcomes. Pursers were assigned on ships, vessels were searched, ships' captains were rewarded for detecting illegal goods, and private correspondence was read to minimize the risk of violations.

There were also financial incentives. For example, bonds were often required from managers as insurance against private trade. But there were also generous remuneration packages comprising a fixed component and a sizeable bonus for those abstaining from private trade. Such approaches can be seen as precursors to modern methods used to evaluate managerial effort in large multinationals.

The Impact of Industrialization

The Industrial Revolution, starting in Britain in the late eighteenth century with the emergence of the factory system, had a dramatic impact both on international business and on the management of people.

The spread of industrialization in Europe and the United States provided growing markets for minerals and foodstuffs and prompted a global search for sources of supply. Technological advances such as in mining equipment also permitted the profitable exploitation of new territories. The exploitation of raw materials fueled the growth of multinational service companies—trading and shipping companies, banks and utilities—to support the expansion of world trade. British banks were already establishing branches and financing foreign trade in Australian, Canadian, and

West Indian colonies in the 1830s.[7] These international companies were distinct from the trading companies described previously in that they invested and controlled assets in foreign countries, a strategy known as foreign direct investment (FDI).

Cross-border manufacturing began to emerge by the mid-nineteenth century. An early forum for international benchmarking, the Great Exhibition of 1851 in London, exposed visitors to a number of U.S. products whose parts were built to such exacting standards that they were interchangeable.[8] Among these products were the Singer sewing machine and the Colt repeating pistol. Not surprisingly these firms went on to establish two of the earliest recorded U.S. manufacturing investments in Britain: Colt set up a plant in 1853 and Singer did so in 1867.

Given the state of transport and communications, it was difficult to exercise meaningful control over distant operations. The rare manufacturing firms that ventured abroad often used family members to manage their international operations. For example, when Siemens set up its St. Petersburg factory in 1855, a brother of the founder was put in charge. In 1863 another brother established a factory for the production of sea cables in Britain. This was the best guarantee that those in distant subsidiaries could be trusted not to act opportunistically.

The international spread of rail networks and the advent of steamships in the 1850s and 1860s brought new speed and reliability to international travel. More significantly still, long distance communication was uncoupled from transportation with the advent of the telegraph. London was joined by cable to Paris in 1852, and over the next twenty years successively to the US, Bombay, and Australia. The improved communication and transportation opened up new markets and facilitated access to resources in distant locations. It became possible for firms to manufacture in large batches and to seek volume distribution in mass markets. The rapid growth in firm size provided a domestic platform from which to expand abroad, paving the way for a decisive surge in international business activity in the last decades of the nineteenth century.[9]

In parallel with these developments, industrialization had a significant impact on the organization of firms, which were reshaped by new manufacturing techniques and by the division of labor. With the infusion of unskilled agrarian workers unaccustomed to such requirements of industry as punctuality, regular attendance, supervision, and the mechanical pacing of work effort, factories experienced discipline and motivation problems. To alleviate these problems, some individuals started to pay more attention to working conditions and the welfare of employees.

An early pioneer in this effort was Robert Owen, a British entrepreneur who reproached his fellow manufacturers for spending heavily on the best machines yet failing to invest in the human element. Owen proposed a number of labor policies and even put them profitably into practice in a Scottish cotton-spinning factory in the 1810s. Under his direction, workers were provided with housing and eating facilities, the minimum working wage for children was increased, working hours were reduced, workers were systematically trained, schooling was introduced, and evening recreation centers were opened. For these reasons, Robert Owen has been referred to as the father of modern personnel management.[10]

Owen's message took hold in United States in the 1870s. Partly inspired by religious motives and partly motivated by growing labor management difficulties, a generation of prominent industrialists sought to apply a philosophy known as *industrial betterment* in their businesses. Cornelius Vanderbilt and other railroad magnates founded Young Men's Christian Associations (YMCAs) along trunk lines to minister to the rail workers' physical and spiritual needs in the hope that the YMCAs would stem drunkenness and foster a more reliable workforce.[11]

Prelude to the Modern Era

A number of developments in international business and people management practices in the late nineteenth century and early twentieth century that warrant the label "modern," led to a golden age of internationalization the world would not see again until it had climbed out of the pit of two world wars.

The Pre–World War I Golden Age

In international business, there was the first cross-border merger, between Britain's Shell and Royal Dutch, in 1907. Singer opened a second sewing machine factory in Scotland in 1885 that was actually bigger than its domestic factories in the United States, and then went on to open plants in Canada, Austria, Germany, and even Russia.

By 1914, the list of companies with foreign subsidiaries was starting to have a modern look about it (see Figure 1–1). The growth in international manufacturing sustained the flourishing service sector that provided the global infrastructure—finance, insurance, transport—to permit the international flow of goods. Multinational activity had become an important element in the world economy. It was a kind of golden age for multinationals, with direct foreign investment accounting for about 9 percent of world output, but set to decline. Indeed, it was not until the mid-1990s that direct foreign investment was to rally back to the level reached in 1914.[12]

Meanwhile, in management practice, the period was dominated by the emergence of *scientific management,* seen by some as a reaction to excesses of the paternalistic industrial betterment philosophy (see box "The Pendulum of Management Thought"). One concrete legacy of the industrial betterment movement had been the emergence of welfare secretaries.[13] Initially concerned with health and safety, education, and social issues, these welfare specialists quickly appropriated line responsibilities such as handling grievances or arranging transfers for dissatisfied workers. Their role changed with the advent of scientific management in the 1910s, requiring them to conduct time-and-motion studies, prepare job specifications, and create wage incentive programs.[14] In this respect, the emergence of personnel management can be regarded as having a dual heritage in the industrial betterment and in the scientific management movements.

War and Economic Depression

World War I, the period of economic depression that followed, and then World War II transformed management practices on the one hand and multinational activity on the other in very different ways.

FIGURE 1–1. Large Multinational Manufacturers in 1914

Company	Nationality	Product	Number of Foreign Factories in 1914	Location of Foreign Factories
Singer	U.S.	Sewing machines	5	U.K., Canada, Germany, Russia
J&P Coats	U.K.	Cotton thread	20	U.S., Canada, Russia, Austria-Hungary, Spain, Belgium, Italy, Switzerland, Portugal, Brazil, Japan
Nestlé	Swiss	Condensed milk/baby food	14	U.S., U.K., Germany, Netherlands, Norway, Spain, Australia
Lever Brothers	U.K.	Soap	33	U.S., Canada, Germany, Switzerland, Belgium, France, Japan, Australia, South Africa
St Gobain	French	Glass	8	Germany, Belgium, Netherlands, Italy, Spain, Austria-Hungary
Bayer	German	Chemicals	7	U.S., U.K., France, Russia, Belgium
American Radiator	U.S.	Radiators	6	Canada, U.K., France, Germany, Italy, Austria-Hungary
Siemens	German	Electrical equipment	10	U.K., France, Spain, Austria-Hungary, Russia
L. M. Ericsson	Swedish	Telephone equipment	8	U.S., U.K., France, Austria-Hungary, Russia
Accumulatoren Fabrik	German	Batteries	8	U.K., Austria-Hungary, Spain, Russia, Poland, Romania, Sweden

Source: G. Jones, *The Evolution of International Business* (London: Routledge, 1996), 106.

For the development of people management practices these successive external shocks had a stimulating effect, hastening the spread of new thinking. To service the war needs after 1914, there was a sudden influx of inexperienced workers into factories and pressure to improve productivity. Tasks had to be simplified and redesigned for novices. To contain labor unrest more attention was paid to working conditions and employee demands, which also meant training first line supervisors. These initiatives served to centralize many aspects of employment previously discharged by line managers—effectively laying the foundations for the first of what we will call three faces or roles of HRM (see Chapter 2).

The history of management thought shows pendulum swings in the attention paid to *people*. There have been successive movements, with alternating focus on the "hard" and "soft" aspects of people management.[A] For example, industrial betterment was concerned with the impact of industrialization on people, rejecting the laissez-faire indifference to working conditions and remuneration levels, even showing concern for employees' social, educational, and moral needs outside the work environment.

Scientific management, proposed by Frederick Taylor and embraced by the growing body of engineers in industry, emerged in the 1910s as a reaction to the underlying sentimentalism of this welfare orientation. Taylor was highly critical of welfare programs, and his recommendations were well attuned to the needs of employers who wanted to make more efficient use of a poorly educated labor pool containing many immigrants. Taylor described how employees could be trained for the repetitive tasks, making them easy to replace. *The Principles of Scientific Management*[B] became the first management best-seller, and with it, the social gospel gave way to the gospel of efficiency.

Although scientific management proved successful particularly during the period when industry was straining to meet the production demands of World War I, it was widely criticized for treating the worker as a "living tool" with little discretion or variety in work. The excesses of scientific management, sometimes leading to industrial unrest, are invoked to explain the emergence of the human relations movement.[C] Elton Mayo's classic experiments at Western Electric's Hawthorne plant in Chicago led to the conclusion that human interaction and the attention paid to the workers by the researchers caused their productivity to increase. This contravened Taylor's dour philosophy of self-interest, suggesting that social factors and the relationship of working groups to management were keys to performance. This linked personnel management with the field of psychology, thus giving personnel management an academic credibility it had so far lacked.

At the level of practice, initiatives to enhance loyalty, motivation, and satisfaction flourished after World War II. These went beyond the basics of counseling and supervisory training proposed by Mayo. There were corporate experiments with innovative shop floor compensation systems, schemes for participatory decision-making and job enrichment, and attitude surveys which have since become standard practice in large firms such as IBM. For personnel managers, these developments made a change from the staple work of hiring, record keeping, administration of pay and benefits, basic training, safety, and manpower planning—and helped to bolster the legitimacy of personnel departments.

For human relations, the backlash started in the mid-1960s. Systems rationalism—characterized by operational research methods such as critical path analysis and Program Evaluation and Review Technique (PERT)—was a reaction to the "touchy-feely" approaches introduced under the human relations umbrella (including T-groups and psychodrama). Personnel systems made a comeback, with MBO (management-by-objectives), pay-for-performance, and manpower planning leading the way. More recently, the organizational culture movement can be seen as a response to the mechanistic excesses of systemic management, with its strong belief in planning. And in turn the emergence of business process reengineering in the 1990s can be seen as a reaction against the "culture craze."

Looking back over time, we can detect waves of alternating ideologies. The "soft" rhetorics of industrial betterment (1870–1900), human relations (1925–55), and organizational culture (1980–90) have emphasized normative control, arguing that organizations are collectives held together by shared values and moral involvement. Control is exercised by shaping the identities and attitudes of workers. These movements were interrupted by surges emphasizing the "hard" rhetoric of rationalism, focusing on productivity improvement from the careful application of methods and systems to individuals who are assumed to have an instrumental rather than affective orientation to work—scientific management (1900–23), systems rationalism (1955–80), and reengineering (1990–98).[D]

These swings reflect the underlying tension between views of the organization as a "market," in which people are resources, and as a "community," in which people are team members and assets.[E] The HR function often finds itself at the center of this contradiction in that it is supposed to represent the interests of the employees while at the same time serving the instrumental needs of the firm.

[A]Barley, 1992; Ouchi, 1989.
[B]Taylor, 1911.
[C]Child, 1969; Donaldson, 1995; O"Connor, 1999.
[D]Barley, 1992.
[E]Legge, 1999.

During World War I, the number of companies with "employment managers" increased dramatically. By 1920, the National Personnel Association had been formed in the United States and the National Civic Federation had started to refer to "personnel directors" instead of "welfare secretaries."[15] This institutionalized a tension that had previously been resolved tacitly by line managers—the competing demands of short-term efficiency (the production department) and employee morale (the personnel department).

In the interwar years, economic depression increased the attractions of union membership. At the same time, the pendulum began to swing back as the Human Relations movement gained ground to counterbalance the harsh face of scientific management and industrial "progress."

The Great Depression was the start of a bifurcation in employment practices in the United States and Japan. Moriguchi shows how leading firms in both the U.S. and Japan were experimenting with corporate welfarism in the 1920s.[16] The depth of the Depression in the United States meant that firms had no option except to repudiate these implicit welfare arrangements, turning to a path of explicit and instrumental contracts between employee and employer (performance management, pay-for-performance, and short-term contracts). Because of the militarization of the Japanese economy, the impact of the Depression was much less severe on the other side of the Pacific. Under legislation fostering "social peace" in the name of national unity, firms maintained these welfare experiments, leading step-by-step to an HRM orientation built around implicit contracts (life-time employment, corporate responsibility for the development of staff, low emphasis on formalized performance evaluation). Endorsed by the strong labor unions that emerged in postwar Japan, these practices became institutionalized, reinforcing and reinforced by cultural differences.

In the West the advent of World War II intensified interest in the systematic recruitment, testing, and assignment of new employees so as to leverage their full potential. Psychological testing used by the military spilled over into private industry.[17] Moreover, the desire to avoid wartime strikes led the U.S. government to support collective bargaining, further strengthening the role of the personnel function.

If these external shocks had some salutary consequences for the development of personnel practices, they had quite the opposite effect on multinational activities. With the World War and the loss of direct investments in Russia in the wake of the 1917 communist revolution, firms began to think twice about foreign investment. In an environment of political uncertainty and exchange controls, this caution was reinforced by the Great Depression at the end of the 1920s, followed by the collapse of the international financial system. Indeed, the adverse conditions during the interwar years encouraged firms to enter cross-border cartels rather than risk foreign investments. By the late 1920s, a considerable proportion of world manufacturing was controlled by these agreements—the most notorious being the "seven sisters" controlling the oil industry.[18] Similarly in pharmaceuticals, electric light bulbs, steel, and the engineering industries, elaborate arrangements were established among national champions allowing them to focus on their home markets and suppress international competition.[19]

World War II dealt a crushing blow to these cartels, and after the war the United States brought in aggressive antitrust legislation to dismantle those that remained. But by then there was little incentive for American firms to enter into cartels. European competition was devastated and the Japanese corporations known as *zaibatsu* were dismembered, while U.S. firms emerged from the war in relatively good shape. Moreover, technological innovation had been stimulated by the demands of the war. American corporations had no desire to confine their geographic activities.

THE MODERN MULTINATIONAL

Although, as we have pointed out, Europe had a long tradition in international commerce, it was the global drive of the U.S. firms after World War II that gave birth to the multinationals as we know them today. U.S. firms that had hardly ventured beyond their home markets prior to the war began to flex their muscles abroad. By the early 1960s, U.S. companies had built an unprecedented lead in the world economy: "American companies have spent the past decade running a helter-skelter race to get located overseas. . . . What U.S. business is seeing, in the words of Chairman Frederic G. Donner of General Motors, 'is the emergence of the modern industrial corporation as an institution that is transcending national boundaries.' "[20] Throughout the 1960s, U.S. industrial productivity was the highest in the world, accounting for 40 percent of world manufacturing output.[21] The United States accounted for almost 70 percent of the R&D undertaken in the OECD.[22]

American firms also found faster ways of entering new markets. Many now moved abroad through acquisitions, followed by investment in the acquired subsidiary in order to benefit more fully from the economies of scale and scope.[23] This was the approach taken by Procter & Gamble, which acquired an ailing French detergent plant in 1954 so as to establish a presence in continental Europe.[24] An alternative strategy was to join forces with a local partner, as in the case of Xerox, which entered into two joint ventures, in 1956 with the English motion picture firm, the Rank Organisation, and in 1962 with Fuji Photo Film in Japan.

American service firms followed their clients abroad. The advertising agency J. Walter Thompson had an agreement with General Motors that it would open an office in every country where the car firm had an assembly operation or distributor.[25] But the internationalization strategies varied. In professional services, McKinsey and Arthur Andersen opened their own offices in foreign countries in a scramble through the 50s and 60s. Others such as Price Waterhouse and Coopers & Lybrand built their international presence through mergers with established national practices in other countries. For most others, the route was via informal federations or networks of otherwise independent firms.

Advances in transport and communications facilitated this rapid internationalization—the introduction of commercial jet travel, the first transatlantic telephone link in 1956, then the development of the telex. More significant still was the emergence of computers as business tools in the late 1950s. By the mid-1970s computers had become key elements in the control and information systems of industrial concerns, paving the way for later complex integration strategies. Taken together, the jet plane, the new telecommunications technology, and the computer contributed to a "spectacular shrinkage of space."[26]

Alongside these technological drivers of internationalization, there were also powerful economic forces at work. The Marshall Plan to support the rebuilding of war-tattered Europe set the tone. Barriers to trade and investment were progressively dismantled with successive GATT trade agreements. Exchange rates were stabilized following the Bretton Woods Agreement, and banks started to play an international role as facilitators of international business. Then the 1957 Treaty of Rome established the European Community. U.S. firms, many of whom perceived Europe as a single entity, were the first to exploit the regional integration which laid the foundations for a European market of a size comparable to that of the United States. European companies were spurred by "the American challenge" (the title of a European call-to-arms book by France's Servan-Schreiber in 1967 which became an instant best-seller), encouraging them to expand beyond their own borders.

Staffing for International Growth

The largest 180 U.S. multinationals opened an average of six foreign subsidiaries each year during the 1960s.[27] This rapid international expansion opened up new job possibilities, including foreign postings. While U.S. firms in the immediate postwar period had been "flush with veterans who had recently returned from the four corners of the globe [and who] provided a pool of eager expatriates,"[28] more managers were now urgently needed. People had to be persuaded to move abroad—both those with needed technical skills and managers to exercise control over these expanding foreign subsidiaries.

The focus of the expanding international personnel departments was on expatriation. In most companies at this time, this meant paying people generously as an incentive to move abroad. Consequently compensation expertise tended to be the background of the top executive running the international personnel function at this time. The intricacies of expatriate compensation were such that there was little interest either in line management or in academia for this highly specialized task.

In the late 1970s, horror stories of expatriate failure started to widen the interest—the technically capable executive sent out to run a foreign subsidiary, brought back prematurely as a borderline alcoholic, having run the affiliate into the ground. Academic surveys seemed to confirm this problem,[29] which for some companies started to become a major handicap to international growth. It was no longer just a question of persuading people to move abroad—it was a question of "how can we help them to be successful?" The interest was boosted by concern over the growing costs of expatriation, dramatized by some controversial studies. There was increasing resistance to moving abroad, partly for family reasons but also because of the mismanagement of reentry to the home country.

At the same time, back home (particularly in the United States and Scandinavia), the initiatives in the people management domain continued to multiply in the postwar years—participative management, training initiatives going from "sensitivity training" to the "Managerial Grid," the organizational development (OD) movement with its focus on planned organizational change, work redesign, the socio-technical and industrial democracy movements in northern Europe, to name but a few. While some academics argued that people were resources rather than just labor costs, what led to use of the term "HRM" in the United States was as much as anything the need to find a home in the firm for these burgeoning initiatives.[30] AT&T created a new role of senior vice president in human resource development in 1971 with that intention. Others followed suit, although this was often initially no more than a relabeling of the personnel department with a more fashionable term.

The field of international business as a domain of academic study also came into being during this period. In the early 80s the challenges of expatriation started to attract the attention of these researchers (reinforced by this newly found HR legitimacy) as well as of senior managers concerned with growth prospects abroad. While it was too early to talk of an international HRM field, international growth was leading to new challenges beyond expatriation that were to shape this emerging domain.

Organizing for International Growth

Growth brought with it structural problems of coordination and control. Attempts to find alternative structural solutions proved to be disappointing. Some companies started to find solutions to the coordination problem through lateral teamwork and to the control problem via management development. The awareness that international HRM is crucial not just for international staffing but also for building corporate cohesion was to grow and mature during the period between the 1960s and 1990s as it became increasingly apparent that structure could not cope with the growing complexities of coordination. Let us look at how this awareness developed.

In April 1963, a special report in *Business Week* heralded a growing "phenomenon" in international business: "Shaped in the crucible of complex foreign competition, the largest of U.S. corporations have found themselves changing into a new form: the multinational corporation. . . . The term serves as a demarcation line between domestically oriented enterprises with international operations and truly world-oriented corporations."[31]

This transition was captured by research on the Harvard Multinational Enterprise Project, initiated in 1965,[32] which raised the question of how to organize effectively for international growth. Two researchers reviewed data on how multinationals expand abroad, proposing a stage model of structural evolution.[33] At an early stage, when foreign sales were of limited volume and scope, an export department tacked onto sales could handle this. As sales grew, the export department would become an international division within the divisional structure (which was replacing the functional organization to become the predominant organizational form).[34] But when this international division reached a certain size, it triggered a wholescale transformation of the company into a "multinational structure."[35] Firms selling a wide range of products abroad were expected to opt for a structure of worldwide product divisions, whereas those with few products but operating in many countries would typically organize themselves around geographic area divisions, as did IBM (see Figure 1–2).

The tricky question was how to organize when the firm had many different products that were sold in many different geographic markets. It was not at all clear how companies should deal with this zone of maximum complexity. In practice, two responses were emerging. Some firms implemented matrix organizations involving both product and geographic reporting lines (see the box "The Origins of the Matrix Concept"), as the Harvard researchers advocated. An alternative response was to have more headquarters staff in coordinating roles. Both of these routes were ultimately to show their limits, but the paths gave rise to a growing understanding of the potential role of HRM in dealing with these fundamental problems of coordination and control which, as we saw, have existed since the dawn of international trade. We will discuss these two routes in turn.

FIGURE 1–2. Alternative International Strategies

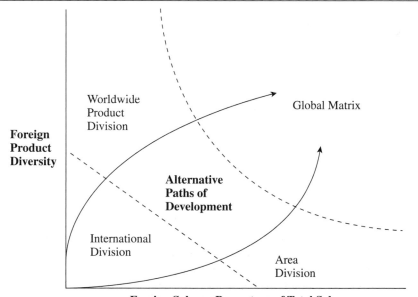

Foreign Product Diversity

Worldwide Product Division

Global Matrix

Alternative Paths of Development

International Division

Area Division

Foreign Sales as Percentage of Total Sales

Source: J. M. Stopford and L. T. Wells, *Managing the Multinational Enterprise (New York: Basic Books, 1972),* 65.

The Origins of the Matrix Concept
Practice Box

In May 1961, John F. Kennedy announced that the United States would aim to put the first man on the moon. At the time, Congress was not inclined to put up much money to achieve this ambitious objective. This placed NASA under tremendous pressure to perform, but with limited resources. To solve the complex coordination and scheduling challenges of this huge project, NASA's engineers, mathematicians, and scientists came up with a gridlike organization they called a matrix. The idea was to leverage people two ways—they would report to both a project boss and a functional boss. Eight years later, Neil Armstrong became the first man on the moon.[A]

Awareness of the matrix concept seeped into industry via the aerospace industry and was quickly heralded as an idea which might be of interest to firms engaged in multiple short-term projects.[B] Of course, NASA's dramatic and highly visible success with this novel structure stimulated further interest. Indeed, *Fortune* speculated that the managerial competence developed by NASA in sending a man to the moon might turn out to be its greatest contribution to a better world.[C] Industries such as chemicals, banking, insurance, packaged goods, electronics, and computers decided to reorganize in a similar fashion.

This was a radical departure from the "one boss" model enshrined in Fayol's classic principle of unity of command (one-person-one-boss). For this reason, it has been regarded by some as the only totally new twentieth-century form of organization.[D] By the same token, it was a form of organization that met with resistance in cultures which were particularly attached to hierarchy or to functional specialism, or which had low tolerance for uncertainty.[E]

[A]One might speculate on why the matrix structure worked for NASA but encountered problems with large industrial firms. Two immediate explanations suggest themselves: first, the NASA personnel benefited from a dramatic mission which contributed to a strong sense of shared values and surely made matrix conflicts easier to resolve; and second, the geographical dispersion of the large firms add an extra dimension of complexity to the matrix challenge.
[B]Mee, 1964.
[C]*Fortune* (1969). "The Unexpected Payoff of Project Apollo." June, p. 114.
[D]Bell, 1976; Davis and Lawrence, 1978.
[E]Laurent, 1981.

The Matrix Structure Route

By the early 1970s, several U.S. and British companies (Citibank, Corning, Dow, Exxon, Shell) that were quite diversified in terms of products and international activities had grabbed the idea of matrix. Right from the start, scholars advised caution. One empirical study of nine British matrix organizations demonstrated that implementation was hindered by traditional management behavioral styles,[36] while Peter Drucker asserted that matrix was "a fiendishly difficult" structure to operate and would therefore "never be a preferred form of organization."[37] Others pointed out that matrix was not just a question of reporting lines and structural coordination—it was much more complex than that. Matrix had to be built into leadership development, control and evaluation systems, teamwork, conflict resolution mechanisms, relationships and attitudes—this anticipated the later insight that matrix has more to do with HRM than it has to do with structure.[38] Few of the companies that opted for the matrix solution had such "matrix cultures." But the warnings fell on deaf ears.

In practice, companies indeed found matrix structures difficult. Managers were uneasy about the separation of authority and accountability. The new arrangements generated power struggles, ambiguity over resource allocation, passing the buck, and abdication of responsibility. Resolving differences involved intensive communications that slowed decision-making.

Worse still, many multinationals found that competitive pressures to do things better, cheaper, and faster were forcing them to multiply matrix dimensions. The traditional dimensions of product and geography were now overlaid with functions, market segments, customer accounts, global suppliers, and other dimensions. In theory, matrix structures operated on a diamond principle—a manager reported to two bosses, and conflicts between them would be reconciled at the apex of the diamond one level further up. But in some companies, such as Exxon Chemicals, managers were reporting to four or five bosses, so that reconciliation or arbitration could happen only at a very senior level. The matrix initiative that had been introduced to help cope with complexity seemed to be contributing to it.

The importance of time-based management in certain industries sounded the death knell of matrix structure. While matrix might ensure the consultation necessary for sound decision-making, this was a painfully slow process. By the time the firm had decided, say, to build a new chemical plant in Asia, faster competitors would already have done this.

By the early 1980s, influential management observers such as Peters and Waterman were proclaiming that matrix was dead: "It has particular difficulty executing the basics. . . . It also regularly degenerates into anarchy and rapidly becomes bureaucratic and noncreative."[39] The call was for clearer accountability, a notion that was becoming increasingly present in the management jargon. Many firms reverted to business-driven structures with clear accountability lying with the product divisions— though some retained matrix features.[40]

But if matrix structures were going out of fashion, the matrix problem of organization was more alive than ever. All but the most simple international organizations faced three, four, or five dimensional matrices. Both practitioners and researchers turned their attention to how lateral relations (coordination and teamwork) can provide the flexibility of matrix without its disadvantages. Indeed research reviews had shown that there were two dimensions of matrix management:[41]

- First, the dual or multiple authority relationships (formal reporting lines) reflected in the structure.
- Second, the horizontal communication linkages and teamwork (for example, between product and country managers) that matrix organization intends to foster.

Most of the disadvantages appeared to stem from the former dimension, while most of the advantages originated from the latter. This observation was supported by new ideas in organizational theory concerned with the growing demands of information processing and decision-making in complex firms.[42] The argument here was that the traditional hierarchic tools of coordination and control (rules, standard operating procedures, hierarchical referral, and planning) could not manage the growing complexity of information processing. Organizations required strong capabilities in two areas: first in information processing (computers) and second in lateral coordination and teamwork. There was an explosion of interest in how to improve lateral coordination while keeping the reporting relationships as clear and simple as possible.[43]

It was starting to become clear that the matrix challenges of coordination in complex firms, such as multinationals, were essentially challenges for HRM and the emerging information technologies rather than for structure and strategy. How can one build more effective horizontal coordination and teamwork (what we call *organizational glue*) through the application of human resource technology? Matrix, as two leading strategy scholars were later to say, is not a structure—it is a "frame of mind" nurtured more than anything else by careful human resource management.[44]

The Headquarters Coordination Route

Only a small number of leading edge companies had adopted matrix. Faced with the growing complexity of international coordination, the majority of organizations took a more well-trodden path—initially successful but leading to paralysis in recent decades. Their staff functions at corporate and divisional levels expanded to cope with the growing coordination needs. This was particularly true for German and Japanese companies, but also the dominant pattern in Anglo-Saxon firms.[45]

It took a long time to work through the decisions in the German *Zentralebereiche* (central staff departments), and particularly in Japan with their *nemawashi*[46] (meaning negotiation) processes of middle-up consultative decision-making. However, both these countries were largely export oriented with sales subsidiaries abroad, and the disadvantages were initially outweighed by the quality of decision-making and by the commitment to implementation that accompanied such consensus-oriented structures of decision-making. Moreover, the complex consultative processes worked reasonably well as long as everyone involved was German or Japanese, respectively.[47]

The strains of staff bureaucracy began to show up in the early 1980s in the U.S. Increasing globalization obliged companies to acquire or build integrated subsidiaries abroad, necessarily implying a greater degree of responsibility for local staff. With localization, the coordination of decision-making by central staff became more difficult, slowing down the process of decision-making at a time when speed was becoming more important. Local managers in lead countries argued for more autonomy and clearer accountability, impossible when the responsibility for coordination and control lies with headquarters. The costly overhead of the heavy staff structures contributed to the erosion of competitiveness.

The Americans were the first to begin the process of downsizing and delayering of these staff bureaucracies, followed by Europeans in Nordic and Anglo-Saxon countries. Between one-third and one-half of all medium-sized and large firms in North America and Western Europe restructured between the 1980s and the early 1990s. The Japanese and Germans followed more slowly, and then other Asian corporations as the Asian crisis took hold in the late 90s.

After decades of postwar international growth, attention in human resource management shifted back home to painful new challenges—learning how to deal with outplacement, organizational streamlining, and job redesign, or how to manage change under situations of crisis. At a deeper level, this was an apprenticeship in how to master a new contradiction—maintaining loyalty and commitment at the same time as one engages in successive rounds of layoffs.[48]

Downsizing was not just limited to the developed world—the consequences of failure to manage this effectively could be much more dramatic in the developing countries, where there were no sophisticated buffers provided by national social security systems. For example, Tata Steel in India came to the conclusion in the early 1990s that it could not compete with foreign competition unless it invested in a modern and highly automated steel plant, one that required 2,000 skilled staff instead of 20,000 in their antiquated traditional steel mill. However, in the surrounding community in India, there were a million direct and indirect dependants. The delicate downsizing operation was managed well, thus preempting a real risk of discontents taking machine guns into the hills and guerilla warfare that would undermine any future for the company. As China modernizes today, this is a challenge that the Chinese communist party faces on a grand scale; if mismanaged, it could conceivably lead to the disintegration of the Chinese nation.

The pain of restructuring focused the attention of HRM back at home, though the consequences spilled over to the subsidiaries in pendulum swings. The pendulum would swing from central bureaucracy to decentralized accountability. Foreign subsidiaries would start to create their own independent kingdoms, the "not-invented-here" syndrome would take hold, and then a few years later the pendulum would swing back to centralization. Why? Because the underlying problem of how to coordinate foreign subsidiaries remained. These firms were led slowly to the same conclusion as the matrixed firms, that they had to develop nonbureaucratic coordination technology by building lateral relationships and by investing in new information technologies. The only clear answer was through horizontal teamwork, facilitated by human resource management.[49]

Along with expatriation, the coordination problem has been another important strand in the development of international HRM during the last thirty years. Meanwhile, there were other developments in the human resource management field that were calling the attention of general managers as well as of the personnel specialists.

HRM Goes International

As we moved into the 80s, conceptual developments were starting to deepen the interest in HRM, born initially as an umbrella for people initiatives. The idea that HRM might be of strategic importance was gaining ground (see box "HRM Hitches Up with Strategy"). Chandler's insight that strategy gets implemented through structure had taken hold, and it was logical to argue that strategy also gets implemented through changes in selection criteria, reward systems, and other HR policies. In turn, this shook up the notion that there might be a "best approach" to HRM. It started to become clear that the approach all depends on one's strategy.

And maybe what is appropriate in HRM practice also depends on the national culture of the firm? The difficulties that expatriates had consistently experienced in transplanting management practices abroad had raised this question. Now this was supported by growing research on cultural differences, pioneered by Geert

HRM Hitches Up with Strategy
Research Box

There were two significant conceptual developments in the United States in the early 1980s that were to give HRM an identity as a field, rather than just as an umbrella for multiple initiatives that had something to do with people and the HR department. They suggested in different ways that HRM could contribute to the performance of the firm. Underlying both of these is the idea from emerging contingency theory that there is no "right" way of organizing or managing people—it all depends on the fit with one's strategy, the specific tasks, and the environment. The two concepts are known as "internal" and "external" fit, respectively.[A]

The first development was the Harvard model of managing human assets, which emphasized the importance of configuring different HRM policies so as to ensure internal consistency.[B] Between the mid-80s and mid-90s, a great deal of research evidence accumulated to show that strong internal fit is associated with organizational performance, even convincing Europeans who were initially skeptical about this American evangelical rhetoric.[C]

The second development was the birth of "strategic human resource management," based on the concept of "external fit" between the strategy of a firm and its HRM policies and practices. The origins lay in the idea of *implementing* strategy through changes in reward and other systems. Building on this, Fombrun, Tichy, and colleagues developed the notion that strategy should guide the selection, appraisal, reward, and development activities of the firm, thereby influencing performance in a future-oriented direction.[D]

Strategic HRM was eagerly embraced in the United States, at least within the professional HRM community. In the battleground for status it provided a rationale for elevating the influence of the HR function. Human resource planning, involving methodologies to link HR planning with strategy formulation, came into being.[E] During the next ten years, all self-respecting American firms spent considerable efforts

on developing their "human resource strategies." The idea of strategic HRM was reinforced and popularized by the 7-S model that underpinned the all-time management best-seller, *In Search of Excellence.*[F] The authors set out to distil the characteristics of the leading American firms. They concluded that competitive success stemmed from a tight configuration between the people side of the organization (style, skills, shared values, and staff) and the hard side (strategy, structure, and systems). In making this "fit" argument, they were implicitly placing the HRM dimension on a par with the dimensions of strategy and structure that had dominated organization theory since the earlier writing of Chandler.[G]

Though intuitively appealing, the notion of external fit proposed by strategic HRM had a number of flaws, and its operationalization proved to be difficult. The human resource planning movement was short-lived. Indeed in an age of increasing discontinuities, the whole notion of strategic planning was being questioned.[H] "Strategic" HRM had perhaps more to do with change than with planning. And the focus of practical attention in personnel and human resource management shifted in the mid-1980s from such grandiose ideas to the painful nitty-gritty of downsizing and restructuring.

[A]These two concepts of "internal" and "external" fit are discussed in Chapter 2, along with their implications for international HRM.
[B]Beer, Spector et al., 1984.
[C]Legge, 1995.
[D]Galbraith and Nathanson, 1979; Fombrun, Tichy, and Devanna, 1984.
[E]Walker, 1980.
[F]Peters and Waterman, 1982.
[G]Chandler, 1962.
[H]Mintzberg, 1994. In North America the Human Resource Planning Society emerged as the first strategic human resource professional association and was later to regret its choice of name. While the idea of linking strategy and HRM initially generated a lot of enthusiasm among HRM scholars, one article in 1985 accurately described the outcome as "somewhere between a dream and a nightmare" (Golden and Ramanujam, 1985).

Hofstede's study based on the IBM opinion survey, which showed highly significant differences in the meaning of management and organization, even within the same company.[50]

The emergence of "the Japanese challenge" as both threat and icon further highlighted the issue of cultural differences, as well as the strategic importance of "soft" issues such as HRM. There were numerous efforts to explain how the Japanese, destroyed and occupied after World War II, had managed to rebound with such vigor, successfully eroding America's market share in industries such as automobiles, consumer electronics, and the emerging computer-based industry. How had they managed to pull this off without any natural resources except people? A large part of the answer seemed to lie in distinctive HRM practices that helped to provide high levels of skill, motivation, and collective entrepreneurship, as well as organizational interconnections.[51] This was a culture shock for Western managers, who suddenly realized that very different approaches to management could be equally successful. The assumption that a company that was spreading abroad necessarily had superior management practices came into question.

New human resource challenges of an international nature were emerging. Many local governments began to apply pressure on foreign firms to hire and develop local employees. The combination of local government pressures and the cost of expatriation persuaded some multinational firms to start aggressively recruiting local executives capable of running their foreign subsidiaries. Often this required extensive training and development, but as one observer pointed out: "The cost [of improving the managerial and technical skills of its foreign employees] must be weighed against the cost of sending an American family to the area."[52] At Unilever, for example, the proportion of expatriates in foreign management positions dropped from 50 percent in 1950 to 10 percent twenty years later.[53]

There was a catch-22, however, in trying to localize: The greater the talent of the local person, the more likely he or she was to be poached by other firms searching for local skills. Consequently, localization remained the concern of a minority of multinational firms until well into the 1990s, except for operations in highly developed regions such as North America, Europe, and Japan.[54]

Another factor added to the difficulties. Local managers were typically appointed to take charge of the HR function in their subsidiaries. This made sense regarding the blue-collar workforce because it was important to be familiar with local employment legislation, wage norms, working conditions, and labor practices—and to advise expatriates on cultural idiosyncrasies. But these local managers were ill equipped to deal with the more political task of developing indigenous managers to run local operations while maintaining coordination with other parts of the corporation.

There were exceptions, and these tended to be firms that used expatriate assignments for developmental reasons rather than just to solve an immediate job need. In these corporations, high potential executives would be transferred abroad in order to expose them to international responsibilities. The assumption was that with growing internationalization *all* senior executives needed international experience, even those in domestic positions. For example, the vice president of Procter & Gamble pointed out in 1963: "We never appoint a man simply because of his nationality. A Canadian runs our French company, a Dutchman runs the Belgian company, and a Briton runs our Italian company. In West Germany, an American is in charge; in Mexico, a Canadian."[55] This meant that P&G was able to attract the very best local talent, quickly developing an outstanding reputation around the globe, and not just in the United States, for the quality of its management. For local firms in France, Singapore, Australia, and Brazil, Procter & Gamble was the benchmark for management in fast moving consumer goods. Other firms started to adopt the P&G approach, though this created new challenges for international human resource management. How does one manage the identification, development, transfer, and repatriation of talent spread out across the globe?

The link between international management development and the problems of coordination and control (the matrix/staff bureaucracy dilemma) was established by a landmark study. Edström and Galbraith studied the expatriation policies of four multinationals of comparable size and geographic coverage in the mid-70s, including Shell.[56] The research showed that these companies had quite different levels and patterns of international personnel transfer.[57] There were three motives for transferring managers abroad. The first and most common was to meet an immediate need for particular skills in a foreign subsidiary. The second was to develop managers through challenging international experience, as mentioned above. But the study of Shell revealed a third motive for international transfers—as a mechanism for control and coordination. The managers sent abroad were steeped in the policies and style of the organization so that they could be relied on to act appropriately in diverse situations. Moreover, frequent assignments abroad developed a network of personal relationships that facilitated coordination.

It appeared that Shell was able to maintain a high degree of control and tight coordination while at the same time having a more decentralized organization than other firms. Indeed, one of the basic principles of the "Royal/Dutch Shell Group of Companies" (the official title of the corporation) was to allow subsidiaries a high degree of "local autonomy." This suggested that appropriate HRM practices could allow a firm to be globally coordinated and relatively decentralized at the same time—an impossible act when viewed through the structural lens of centralization-decentralization. Global integration or coordination, it appeared, could be provided through socialization (what academics call "normative integration"), minimizing the necessity for centralized headquarters control or bureaucratic procedures.

These findings drew attention to expatriation, mobility, and management development as vital parts of the answer to the "matrix/ bureaucracy" problem of coordination. In truth, the concept was not entirely new. The Romans had come up with a similar approach many centuries before.

By the mid-1990s, when globalization had taken hold, surveys consistently showed that global leadership development was one of the top three HRM priorities in major U.S. corporations.[58] In some companies in Europe and the United States, international management development was seen as so critical that this department was separated from the corporate HR function, reporting directly to the office of the corporate president.

The findings also lent substance to earlier research by Perlmutter suggesting that the "multinational corporation" (MNC) label covered various postures or "states of mind."[59] The first was the *ethnocentric orientation,* in which each subsidiary was required to conform precisely to parent company ways regardless of local conditions. The second was the decentralized *polycentric corporation,* in which each subsidiary was allowed to develop with minimal interference, providing it remained profitable. The third was the *geocentric orientation,* in which "subsidiaries are neither satellites nor independent city states, but parts of a whole whose focus is on worldwide objectives as well as local objectives, each making its unique contribution with its unique competence."[60] Perlmutter anticipated that it was HRM practices that build this geocentric orientation. The hallmarks were that the skill of the person counts more than the passport, as with Procter & Gamble; and there was a high degree of mobility not only from headquarters to subsidiaries, but also from subsidiaries to the HQ and between the subsidiaries, as with Shell. Perlmutter saw an inevitable but tortuous route from initial ethnocentrism to geocentrism.

The research of Perlmutter, along with Edström and Galbraith, suggested that international HRM is not just a question of sending expatriates abroad and getting "the right person in the right place" in foreign environments, important though these tasks may be. Their ideas provided a framework for understanding the role of HRM in the strategic and organizational development of the multinational corporation. However, until the early 90s, the focus of attention in the United States at least was on the home problems of restructuring. Most of the research (and indeed business school teaching) in international HRM remained heavily functional in its orientation, focused until well into the 90s on managing expatriate and international assignments.

Accelerating global competition in the 1990s was to change that. Then the seeds of another important idea were sown: that the competitive advantage of a corporation lies in its ability to learn across its geographic and other boundaries.[61]

ENTER GLOBALIZATION

By the end of the 1980s the traditional distinction between domestic and multinational companies had started to become blurred. International competition was no longer the preserve of industrial giants. It was affecting everybody's business. Statistics from the 1960s show that only 6 percent of the U.S. economy was exposed to international competition. By the late 1980s, the corresponding figure was over 70 percent and climbing fast.[62]

In 1985, Hedlund had noted: "A radical view concerning globality is that we are witnessing the disappearance of the international dimension of business. For commercial and practical purposes, nations do not exist and the relevant business arena becomes something like a big unified 'home market.' "[63] By the early 1990s, this was no longer a radical proposition.

Globalization surfaced as the new buzzword at the turn of the 1990s. Many of the ingredients of globalization had actually been around for several decades without making much more than a modest impact on the world's economy. The steady dismantling of trade barriers in Western Europe and in North and South America, the increasing availability of global capital, advances in computing and communications technology, and the progressive convergence of consumer tastes had all been under way for some time. What made a difference was that these trends now reached a threshold where they became mutually reinforcing.

Economic barriers such as national borders now became less relevant as governments dismantled the barriers to trade and investment that once segmented the world economy, though many people argued that human and cultural barriers would not disappear. At the same time, widespread deregulation and privatization opened new opportunities for international business in both developing and developed countries. The multinational domain, long associated with the industrial company, was shifting to the service sector, which by the mid-90s represented over half of total world foreign direct investment (FDI). Problems of distance and time zones were further smoothed away as fax gave way to e-mail and as fixed phone networks ceded to mobile telephony.

Globalization was further stimulated by the unexpected fall of communism in Russia and Eastern Europe. Taken together with China's adoption of market-oriented policies, huge new markets were opened up to international business. Most of the world was drawn into the international economy. Back in the 1970s, world trade was already growing nearly 20 percent faster per annum than world output. This intensified in the 1980s, growing 60 percent faster than world output. That period also saw the U.S. share of world FDI decline from 50 percent to 26 percent, which was much more in line with the weight of the United States in the world economy. Meanwhile Japan, with a strong international rather than domestic focus, increased its share of world FDI from 1 percent to 20 percent during the period 1967–90.

International business was not just growing in volume. It was also changing in form. Much of the early theorizing depicted a step-by-step progression to international status, as mentioned earlier.[64] Already by the early 1980s, there was evidence that market entry by Swedish firms into Japan, for instance, was faster than incremental theories would have predicted.[65]

Indeed by the late 1980s, many companies were learning to jump ahead through alliances which took different shapes and forms—international licensing agreements, cross-border R&D partnerships, international consortia such as Airbus, and the joint ventures that were increasingly used to expand fast into emerging markets. The creation of the Single European Market in 1992 had triggered, through anticipation, an unprecedented wave of cross-border mergers and acquisitions.

Today companies like our case example at the beginning of this chapter, Business Objects, would never get off the ground if they followed the logic of the past. Innovation in organization has become vital for prosperity, changing the shape of organizations. After the waves of restructuring and downsizing, formerly hierarchic companies with clean-cut boundaries are giving way to complex arrangements and configurations, often fluctuating over time. The new buzzword from GE in the 1990s was "the boundaryless organization."[66] There is much greater flexibility for multinationals to locate different elements of their value added activities in different parts of the world.

With increasing cross-border project work and mobility, the image of an organization as a network is rapidly becoming as accurate as that of hierarchy. For example, a European pharmaceutical corporation might have international R&D partnerships with competitors in the United States and manufacturing joint ventures with local partners in China, where it also has outsourced sales of generic products to a firm strong in distribution and local HRM. The new arrangements mean that companies might cooperate along some segments of the value chain and compete along others.

Another characteristic of the emerging competitive environment has been the democratization of historic sources of strategic advantage, leading to the search for new ways of competing. Traditionally, the only distant resources that multinationals had to seek out were raw materials or cheap labor. Everything else was at home: sources of leading-edge technology, world-class suppliers, pressure-cooker competition, the most sophisticated customers, and the best intelligence on future trends.[67] The home base advantage was so strong that multinationals could maintain their competitiveness while they gradually learned to adapt their offerings to fit better with local needs (thus supporting an incremental approach to international expansion).

Global competition has now dispersed some of these capabilities around the world. India, for example, developed its software industry using a low-cost strategy as a means of entry, but then quickly climbed the value chain, just as Japan had done previously in the automobile industry that had been dominated by Detroit. The implication of such developments is that multinational firms, especially U.S. ones, can no longer assume that all the capabilities deemed "strategic" are available near home. Recent studies suggest that enterprises with a long domestic history face a legacy that handicaps the way in which they confront the tensions of international growth. Firms like Business Objects that internationalize early are likely to grow faster than "domestic" enterprises, particularly if they compete on the basis of technological knowledge.[68]

With the erosion of traditional sources of competitive advantage, such as access to finance or technology, multinationals needed to change their perspective. To compete successfully, they had to do more than exploit scale economies or arbitrage imperfections in the world's markets for goods, labor, and capital. Toward the end of the 80s, a new way of thinking about the multinational corporation came out of studies of how organizations were responding to these challenges. The concept of the "transnational organization" provided a roadmap for how to respond to this new world.

The Roadmap for Managing Globalization

If there is a single perspective that has shaped the context for our understanding of the multinational corporation and its HRM implications, it is probably the research of Bartlett and Ghoshal on the *transnational organization.*[69] To this we can add Hedlund's related concept of *heterarchy* and the studies of Doz and Prahalad on the *multi-focal organization,* all with origins in Perlmutter's *geocentric organization.*[70] We will be referring frequently to their findings and concepts in this book, for all of these strategy researchers were led to believe that human resource management is perhaps the single most critical domain for the multinational firm. None of them had any interest in HRM by virtue of their training, but all were drawn toward the field of HRM by their research findings.

Doz and Prahalad began to link the fields of multinational strategy and HRM when researching the patterns of strategic control in multinational companies.[71] As they saw it, multinational firms faced one central problem: responding to a variety of national demands while maintaining a clear and consistent global business strategy. This tension between strong opposing forces, dubbed *local responsiveness* and *global integration,* served as a platform for much of the subsequent research and came to be seen as the central challenge for the multinational company. It was captured by Sony's "act local, think global" aphorism, adopted by the newly created Swedish-Swiss ABB as its guiding motto.

These concepts were picked up and developed by Bartlett and Ghoshal in their study of nine firms in a cross-sample of three industries (consumer electronics, branded packaged goods, and telephone switching) and three regions (North America, Europe, and Japan).[72] They discovered that these companies seemed to have followed one of three internationalization paths that they called "administrative heritages":

- One path emphasized responsiveness to local conditions, leading to what they called a "multinational enterprise" (we prefer to call it *multidomestic*). This led to a decentralized federation of local firms led by entrepreneurs who enjoyed a high degree of strategic freedom and organizational autonomy. Close to its customers and with strong links to the local infrastructure, the subsidiaries were seen as indigenous companies. The strength of the multidomestic approach was local responsiveness, and some European firms such as Unilever and Philips as well as ITT in the United States embodied this approach.

- A second path to internationalization was that of the "global" firm, typified by U.S. corporations such as Ford and Japanese enterprises such as Matsushita and NEC. Since the term "global" is generic, we will call this the *meganational firm* in this book. Worldwide facilities were typically centralized in the parent country, products were standardized, and overseas operations were considered delivery pipelines to access international markets. There was tight control of strategic decisions, resources, and information by the global hub. The competitive strength of the meganational firm was its global integration, seen in efficiencies of scale and cost.

- Some companies appeared to have taken a third route, a variant on the meganational path. Like the meganational, their facilities were located at the center. But the competitive strength of these *international firms* was their ability to transfer expertise to less advanced overseas environments, allowing local firms more discretion in adapting products and services. They were also capable of capturing any learning from such local initiatives and then transferring it back to the central R&D and marketing departments. The international enterprise was thus a tightly coordinated federation of local firms, controlled by sophisticated management systems and corporate staffs, with a particular competitive strength in learning and knowledge management. Some American and European firms such as Ericsson fitted this pattern, heralding the growing concern with global knowledge management.

It was apparent to Bartlett and Ghoshal that specific firms were doing well because their internationalization paths matched closely with the requirements of their industry. Consumer products required local responsiveness, so Unilever thrived while Kao in Japan, centralized and meganational in its heritage, was hardly able to get outside its Japanese borders. But it was a different situation in consumer electronics, in which the centralized meganational heritage of Matsushita (Panasonic and other brands) fitted much better than the more localized approaches of Philips and GE's consumer electronics business (the latter was subsequently sold to France's Thomson). And in telecommunications switching, the international learning heritage of Ericsson led it to dominate the respectively multidomestic and meganational strategies of ITT and NEC.[73]

Whereas different organizational orientations matched different industry requirements in the early 1980s, at the beginning of their study, the most significant observation of Bartlett and Ghoshal was that accelerating global competition was changing the stakes. In all of these three industries, it was clear that the leading firms had to become more locally responsive AND more globally integrated AND better at learning between headquarters and subsidiaries. Increasing competition was shifting the competitive positioning of these firms from "either/or" to "and/and." The challenge for Unilever was to maintain its local responsiveness, but at the same time to increase its global efficiency by eliminating duplication and integrating manufacturing. Conversely, the challenge for Matsushita was to keep the economies of centralized product development and manufacturing, but to become much more local and responsive to differentiated niches in markets around the world. These firms had to become more *transnational,* both local *and* global in their orientation.

It is important to note that the defining characteristic of the transnational enterprise is its capacity to steer between the contradictions that it confronts. As Ghoshal and Bartlett put it:

> [M]anagers in most worldwide companies recognize the need for simultaneously achieving global efficiency, national responsiveness, and the ability to develop and exploit knowledge on a worldwide basis. Some, however, regard the goal as inherently unattainable. Perceiving irreconcilable contradictions among the three objectives, they opt to focus on one of them, at least temporarily. The transnational company is one that overcomes these contradictions.[74]

This early research on transnational enterprise focused on one major contradiction, that of local versus global (the box "From Taiwanese Fisherman to Global Market Opportunity" illustrates the advantages of being both local and global). But with their "international" firm Bartlett and Ghoshal also implicitly identified a second contradiction that we mentioned earlier, that of leveraging resources for the present versus developing resources for the future (academics call this the exploitation versus exploration dilemma). Although we will highlight these two contradictions in this book, we believe that they are simply the tip of an iceberg of competing values,

From Taiwanese Fisherman to Global Market Opportunity
Practice Box

A story often told at Nokia, the Finnish mobile phone manufacturer, communicates clearly the transnational spirit and what it means to be both global and local.

When product penetration of mobile phones was still fairly low, a sales manager of the company, on holiday in Taiwan, noticed that the local fishermen all carried mobile phones. It dawned on him that this might be the clue to a neglected market. Perhaps the greatest potential for the firm's products was not sophisticated urbanites, as the central marketing people thought, but rather people in remote areas where the cost of laying a network of telephone cables was prohibitive (or impossible, in the case of fishermen).

The Taiwanese fishermen themselves did not represent much of a marketing opportunity. The strategy only makes sense on a larger scale, if the company focuses on clusters of users with similar needs scattered internationally. It is therefore a good example of the transnational challenge. The company has to be sensitive to local needs in order to spot such opportunities in the first place; but then it needs to be global in order to exploit the opportunity across all sorts of other different markets.

or what we call *dualities,* that twenty-first century organizations will have to confront, if they want to stay afloat.

In many ways, the transnational concept drew its inspiration from the matrix concept discussed earlier. But its focus was different. Whereas the matrix concept was a structurally dominated solution, the transnational concept is neither a particular organizational form, nor a specific strategic posture. Rather it is an "organizational model," a "management mentality," and a "philosophy."[75] The crux is to create balanced perspectives[76] or a "matrix in the mind of managers,"[77] as mentioned earlier. In this book, we will discuss how human resource management can help to achieve this.

The Transnational Solution

Readers should not misinterpret the so-called transnational. It is not clear that all international firms are destined to move in a transnational direction. While all companies are forced to contend with the dimensions of responsiveness, integration, and learning, and while intensified competition heightens the contradictory pressures, these features are not equally salient in all industries. Moreover, these pressures do not apply equally to all parts of a firm. One subsidiary may be more local in orientation, whereas another one may be tightly integrated. Even within a particular function such as marketing, pricing may be a local matter whereas distribution may be controlled from the center; selection decisions in HR may be more integrated whereas reward systems may be left to local discretion. Indeed another aspect of the complexity of the transnational is this *differentiation*—one size does not fit all.

Transnational pressures have been strongest in certain industries, such as pharmaceuticals and automobiles, in which firms must be close to local authorities and consumers while at the same time harnessing global efficiencies in product development, marketing, and manufacturing. In other industries, such as steel, paper, and printing, the pressures to be locally responsive or globally integrated have been less strong, at least in the past. In certain environments, developing a differentiated transnational approach would not be appropriate. Indeed, the researchers demonstrated that "unnecessary organizational complexity in a relatively simple business environment can be just as unproductive as unresponsive simplicity in a complex business environment."[78] In terms of theory, it is the principle of *requisite complexity* that underlies the appropriate fit between organizational environment and form— the internal complexity of the firm should reflect the complexity of the external environment.[79]

Whereas some research[80] suggests that industry characteristics influence the strategic approach of the firm—local, globally integrated, or transnational— companies have some degree of choice. For example, among the best-known names in retailing is Wal-Mart, with its strong globally integrated strategy. Yet Ahold, a Dutch retailer, is far stronger in the United States than Wal-Mart is in Europe. So why have so few people heard of Ahold? Because it pursues a highly local strategy. In the United States, Ahold is better known by the names of its subsidiaries, such as Stop & Shop, Tops Markets, Giant-Carlisle, Giant-Landover, and BI-LO. We could speculate that different cultural heritages have pushed two firms in the same industry to pursue different strategies, but other examples suggest that it is more than that.

Take the case of the brewing industry, in which two nearby firms of the same size, boasting similar financial performance, have also taken contrasting paths. Everyone has heard of Holland's Heineken with its one brand worldwide. But how many readers have heard of Interbrew? Based just across the border in Flemish-speaking Leuven (Belgium), it is the owner of over forty local brands worldwide, including Stella Artois, Sol, and Rolling Rock. In the energy sector, the success of the highly centralized U.S. firm CMS Energy is matched by the success of internationally decentralized AES, also American. In such cases, we might invoke different administrative heritages to explain the differences. Notwithstanding industry imperatives, companies may still have a fair degree of strategic choice. Different models may be equally viable provided that there is good execution, consistency in implementation, and alignment between HRM and competitive strategy—some of the basic principles that we will be exploring later.

Sustainable Competitive Advantage through HRM

Ghoshal and Bartlett argue that the role of top management in the transnational is not so much to manage strategy, structure, and systems, as it was seen to be in the past. Structure cannot cope with the complexity, as discussed earlier, and strategic initiatives come increasingly from the entrepreneurial activities of local businesses around the globe, not from top management planners. The challenge for senior management is to build a common sense of purpose that will guide local strategic initiatives, to coordinate through a portfolio of processes rather than via hierarchic structure, and to create a behavioral context that will shape people's attitudes across the globe (what is called *social architecture*). [81]

This is part of the changing landscape of thinking about the sources of competitive advantage. Globalization has meant an increase in competition that is felt not just by multinational players but also by those who operate on domestic markets, threatened by new players from abroad. Although our focus is on international HRM, it is useful to outline at the start of this book four new ways of thinking about how to achieve competitive advantage that emerged during the 90s. They are improved operational effectiveness; investment in invisible assets such as human capital; the development of core organizational capabilities; and the transfer and recombination of knowledge. The idea is to clarify concepts that are often used loosely, sometimes interchangeably, and to outline how these relate to HRM.

Operational Effectiveness

In the wake of the wave of downsizing and restructuring that started in the United States in the mid-80s, HR's immediate contribution to competitive advantage was in terms of operational effectiveness. Downsizing itself would confer only short-term advantage. Firms had to find new ways of organizing themselves so that they could resolve another contradiction, namely, doing things better, cheaper, *and* faster. Top management attention switched from its traditional emphasis on strategic positioning to the issue of internal organization.

This was a big challenge and a big change. Porter had suggested as recently as 1985 that strategy meant choice. His data, collected in the 1970s, suggested that firms had a choice between three generic strategies: cost leadership (doing things *cheaper*), market differentiation (doing things *better*), and niche orientation.[82] Firms that did not make a clear strategic choice were "stuck in the middle," as he put it. His data showed that they ended up less profitable. However, one can argue that his conclusions were dated by the time of their publication, even a dangerous guide to the future. Accelerating competition was obliging firms to find ways of doing the impossible.

The evolution at Shell is a good example. The strategic value that had previously guided Shell's development around the globe was professionalism (quality) in everything that they did. Until the early 1980s, Shell did not pretend to be the lowest cost producer and marketer of petrochemical products. Its strategy followed Porter's advice, opting for a strategic focus on market differentiation. Trading on its quality reputation, customers were for decades willing to pay a premium. But by the middle of the 1980s, Shell's strategic values had changed. With increasing global competition, also from national oil firms in emerging countries, Shell's new directive to its managers around the world was "reinforce quality, safety and professionalism . . . and drive down your costs dramatically!" This launched a wave of outsourcing, restructuring, and a reorientation in its HRM practices. Over the next decade, while revenues climbed, the headcount came down from 140,000 people to 90,000.

Then in 1993 the strategic values at Shell underwent a further shift. Top management became aware that they were losing out because the corporation was too slow in decision-making. The directive to managers around the globe was now, "Find ways of reinforcing professionalism, cutting costs . . . and becoming more responsive." Three years later, the biggest obstacle to speed was identified as the consensual matrix structure of business areas, geographic zones, and management functions that steered the group of companies. In order to be better, cheaper, and faster, Royal Dutch/Shell decided to bite the bullet and break itself into four different companies.

Much of the mainstream of human resource management during the last fifteen years has focused on this challenge of reorganization so as to meet the needs for improved operational effectiveness. This has brought HRM more to the center stage of management thought and practice. It has stimulated new techniques and developments—from competency-based management to 360° feedback, from salary broad-banding to the team building that accompanies reengineering. It has reinforced the importance of classic principles of HRM such as getting the right people into the right places at the right times. It has stimulated research in many domains, from high performance management to handling downsizing to new reward systems.

The Intangible Assets of Human Capital

The second new source of competitive advantage relates to the firm's *invisible assets,* such as consumer trust, brand image, control of distribution—and corporate culture, the talent of people and leadership skill.[83] These are gradually replacing the traditional and tangible resource factors of capital and labor. As Microsoft's Bill Gates puts it: "Our primary assets, which are our software and our software-development skills, do not show up on the balance sheet at all." The growing gap between the book value and the stockmarket value of a firm reflects this.

A 1995 American report on the relationship between education and productivity at 3,100 U.S. workplaces suggests that a 10 percent increase in workforce education leads to, on average, an 8.6 percent gain in productivity. In comparison, a 10 percent investment in the traditional capital stock of equipment increases productivity by only 3.4 percent. In other words, the marginal value of investing in human capital is about three times greater than the value of investing in machinery. Smart people simply work smarter![84] By way of further example, ABB's Percy Barnevik believes strongly that competence in international management development, developing a pipeline of leaders with global experience who are selected for their skill rather than their passport, is a major source of competitive advantage. His view is that it takes at least a decade to develop such an asset and thereby puts a firm far ahead of its competitors who have not invested in such competence.[85]

The idea of "people as assets" caught on quickly, and not just within the professional HRM community where this view had long been held. There was new evidence that firms with unusually high return on investment pay great attention to the selection of people and then invest heavily in the development of that human capital.[86] The notions of human and intellectual capital have been popularized as the "new wealth of organizations."[87]

In this process of popularization, however, the important concept of *firm specificity* sometimes got lost. As Gary Becker, the Nobel prize–winning father of human capital theory, had emphasized, investment in training and education does not confer any long-term advantage to an organization if it is "general purpose." Individuals can simply sell their new skills to another employer, or use this threat as a bargaining tactic to obtain an increase in wages.[88]

Distinctive Organizational Capability

This leads to a third and related source of competitive advantage, *core organizational capability* or *core competence.*[89] Such a capability is a highly firm-specific bundling of technical systems, people skills, and cultural values.[90] Such capabilities are developed by iterative experimentation over decades. Well-known examples would be Canon's capability in new product development or American Express's core competence in the rapid processing of mass information.

What is the difference between a core capability and an invisible asset such as human skill or consumer trust in a brand? The distinguishing feature of a capability is the *integration* of skills, technologies, systems, managerial behaviors, and work values. For example, Federal Express has a core competence in package routing and delivery resting on the integration of bar-code technology, mobile communications, systems using linear programming, network management, and other skills.[91] The capability of INSEAD or IMD in executive education depends on faculty know-how integrated with program design skills, marketing and address lists, the competence of support staff, the attitude of deans, reward systems, and a host of other interwoven factors that have evolved over the years. Being highly firm specific, such organizational capabilities are difficult to imitate because of the complex configuration of elements.

These capabilities can be a major source of competitive advantage (though their very success can also create dangerous rigidities). Usually, they get built up step-by-step in the home country. The challenge for the transnational firm is how to transfer such complex capabilities to other countries. How can Toyota, for example, transfer its capability in production technology from its plants in Japan to the other plants that it wishes to build as it localizes operations around the world? This is much more than a "technology transfer," a misnomer because one can rarely transfer the hard technology without the underlying people skills, management approaches, and deeper values that often underpin such a capability.

Let us single out two observations concerning HRM that stem from this concept of capability. The first is that narrow functionally oriented concepts of human resource management as embodied in many textbooks may be of steadily diminishing value except to the personnel specialist. The capabilities that confer significant competitive advantage are complex, and one cannot separate the practice of HRM from the specifics of the technical, business, and organizational context. In the recent HRM literature, this is known as the concept of "bundling," or fitting things together, and we will discuss this further in the next chapter.

A second observation is that the capability literature has tended to reinforce a traditional HRM bias toward internal labor markets and firms that nurture their own resources. One visible HRM book by a well-known scholar has recently argued in no uncertain terms that organizations with the highest returns on investment are those that practice employment security, carefully building the skills of their staff, and nurturing capabilities.[92] We would be more cautious in our conclusions. This may be an example of the Porter-type danger of extrapolating lessons from the past and applying them to the discontinuous future. It may well be that fast moving "instant transnationals" such as our case firm Business Objects, or firms operating in hypercompetitive environments, will have to be much more flexible in recruiting and outplacing talent to keep pace with their fast moving markets.

Transferring and Recombining Knowledge

Knowledge is what underlies both human capital and core competence—the codified or tacit knowledge embedded in people's skills and the complex tacit know-how anchored in an organizational capability (see box "Collections and Connections: Codified and Tacit Knowledge"). A fourth source of competitive advantage comes from the firm's ability to create, transfer, and integrate knowledge. In a world where

---

Collections and Connections: Codified and Tacit Knowledge
Research Box

It was reputedly Peter Drucker back in the 1960s who spread the idea that we are entering the knowledge society, built on knowledge as a basic resource rather than capital or labor.[A] During the 1990s this quickly became reality in the developed world. The practical interest in "knowledge management" (KM) exploded after 1995.

At the heart of KM lies the distinction between "explicit" and "tacit" knowledge.[B] *Explicit* or *codified knowledge* is knowledge that you know that you have—objective, formal, systematic, incorporated in texts and manuals, and easy to pass on to others. On the other hand, *tacit knowledge* is knowledge that you do not know that you have—personal, context specific, hard to formalize and communicate. Tacit knowledge often underlies complex skills—you have a set of skills in teaching or in merger and acquisition analysis, but it is built on intuitive feel acquired through years of experience and is hard to put into words.

One of the major domains of KM involves *building collections*—simply collecting all the explicit knowledge (on patents, customer contacts, presentation overheads, etc.) using software systems and making that knowledge available internally via an intranet. Driven by software companies, this is the domain of KM that has attracted the most practical attention.[C]

On the other hand, *building connections* or contacts between people can better transfer tacit knowledge. Many professional service firms have gone down this route. Yellow-page directories on the intranet allow the consultant to find out who else has experience on a particular type of assignment, and to call that person so as to tap into that experience.

Although attention typically focuses on technology (software systems, intranets, Web-based approaches), all studies have shown that KM is "10% hardware and 90% software"—the software of cultural norm building, developing the leadership infrastructure, and providing focus.[D] The majority of Western companies do not have a culture of sharing, and knowledge is still widely seen as a personal asset to be hoarded, increasing bargaining power over status and salary, rather than something to be shared for general corporate use.

KM is certainly not a "quick fix." However, we and other scholars expect that knowledge management is with us for the long term.

[A]Drucker, 1992.

[B]The distinction between explicit and tacit knowledge was first made by the epistemologist Michael Polanyi, and developed by the Japanese management scholar Nonaka (Polanyi, 1966; Nonaka and Takeuchi, 1995).

[C]See the special issue on Knowledge Management in *Management Review*, April 1999.

[D]For some of the studies and reports highlighting the importance (and neglect) of the "software" of knowledge management, see O'Dell and Grayson (1998), Pfeffer and Sutton, (1999), as well as *Management Review*, April 1999.

the retention of people is more difficult, what is important is to retain and transfer their knowledge.

New knowledge gets created through social processes of combination and exchange.[93] Combination, which can be either incremental or radical, means linking elements that were previously unconnected or developing novel ways of recombining associated elements. The elements may be technologies, areas of expertise, or people skills. Examples of combination go from Schumpterian radical innovation in which a new technology is combined with existing know-how in a process of "creative destruction," to the interaction between two functional groups in a multinational firm brought together by a project, to new ideas that are transferred through the mobility of people from one division to another.

Indeed, Kogut and Zander have argued cogently that *the* source of advantage for multinational firms is this ability to transfer and recombine knowledge across borders.[94] Corporations that do not have the capacity to do this will inevitably run into problems and be taken over by those who have. This perspective will lead us in this book to some of the frontiers of human resource management in multinational organizations, exploring different aspects of the social and cultural technology of knowledge management.

It should be added that these emerging ideas concerning the source of competitive advantage, with the exception of the first (operational effectiveness), all stand under the umbrella of a new strategic view of the firm called the *resource-based perspective*. This influential view, based largely on research on multinational corporations, has come to dominate strategic thinking at the turn of the century (see box "The Resource-Based View of the Firm").

Beyond the Transnational Model: Emerging Front-Back Organizations

You cannot get competitive advantage from doing simple things. Anyone can do them. In response to the complexities of the market environment, some firms are trying to gain competitive advantage by creating new organizational architectures, going beyond the transnational model in the pursuit of efficiency, speed, and responsiveness to customers.[95]

Building on the difference between the customer-oriented "front office" and the production-oriented "back office," one of the most interesting organizational forms today is the front-back organization, recently adopted by Hewlett-Packard, ABB, and Citibank. In all cases, the aim is to resolve a contradiction—combining customer focus (the front end) with global scale-economies (the back end). It is a dual structure in which both halves are multifunctional units. The front end is organized around customer segments, while the back end is built around products or product lines.[96]

Some form of matrix is used to tie both parts together, and there is the hitch. A very high degree of coordination and skill in contention management is needed to implement this form of organization. Conflicts are normal and everyday because virtually every issue has the potential to be contentious. Most corporations who are trying to implement such forms have prior experience with matrix organization and the forms of coordination that come from effective HRM.

The Resource-Based View of the Firm
Research Box

The field of corporate strategy is as young as that of HRM. Porter developed a first systematic framework in the early 80s for understanding how firms create and sustain competitive advantage.[A] During the 80s, strategy meant competitive positioning.

The resource-based view of the firm that came into prominence in the early 90s provided a different view, more in tune with the shifting environment of global competition. It drew its inspiration from the writings of the economist Edith Penrose, who pioneered the view of the firm as a bundle of resources—including tangible *and* intangible assets.[B] Competencies, capabilities, and "stocks" such as technological expertise and invisible assets are the source of competitive advantage, as opposed to positioning.

Barney (who had suggested that organizational culture could be a source of competitive advantage) proposed that to provide the basis for superior economic performance, the resources in question should be valuable to the customer, rare, and difficult to purchase or imitate.[C] This is today a widely accepted view, also captured in the idea of "firm specificity."

This view of strategy quickly attracted the attention of HRM scholars because its broad defini

tion of resources could be applied to HRM-related capabilities, such as training and development, teamwork, and culture. Drawing on the distinction made by Dierickx and Cool between resources as either asset stocks or asset flows, Boxall argues that firms should build both their "human capital advantage" and their "human process advantage."[D] This means employing people with valuable knowledge (human capital advantage) and applying sophisticated processes to them, such as cross-departmental cooperation and executive development (human process advantage).

Resource-based theory helped to reinforce the interrelationship between HRM and strategy. It provides a direct conceptual link between an organization's more behavioral and social attributes and its ability to gain a competitive advantage.

[A]Porter's "five forces" model of industry attractiveness and his framework for competitive positioning within an industry provided a paradigm for the emerging strategy domain (Porter, 1980).
[B]Penrose, 1959.
[C]Barney, 1991.
[D]Dierick and Cool, 1989; Boxall, 1996.

Here we are at the absolute frontiers of our know-how. Commenting on HP's bold attempts to implement such an organization, *Business Week* notes that its CEO Carly Fiorina "is betting on an approach so radical that experts say it has never been done before at a company of HP's size and complexity."[97] Behind the gamble (with disappointing results at the time of writing) lies a conviction that HP must become "ambidextrous"—local and global, excelling at short-term execution while pursuing long-term visions that create new markets. "There isn't a major technology company in the world that has solved the problem she's trying to address, and we're all going to learn from her experience," says a Stanford business school professor.[98] Organization and international HRM are at the edge of paradox.

INTERNATIONAL HRM ON THE EDGE OF PARADOX

The aim of this chapter has been to help the reader understand how the domain of international human resource management has developed, in parallel with the evolution of the multinational enterprise. This provides the context for our book.

FIGURE 1–3. The Evolution of International HRM

Dates	Developments in International Business	People Focus	
		Practice	Theory
1870s	Early manufacturing FDI	Welfare programs—first experiments with working conditions, training schemes, and wage policies.	Industrial betterment
1900s		Appointment of welfare or social secretaries to handle grievances, arrange transfers of dissatisfied workers, run the sick room, provide recreation/education.	
1910s	The "Golden Age" of international business	Time and motion studies, fatigue studies, job analysis, and wage administration emerge as new tasks for the employment manager.	Scientific management
1920s	International cartels	Employment policy is increasingly centralized as a staff function responsible for hiring and firing, keeping performance records, and handling disciplinary problems.	
1930s	Multidivisional organizations	Personnel managers introduce due process disciplinary procedures and complaint systems, replicating the protective structures proposed by labor unions.	Human relations
1950s	U.S. companies expand abroad	The recruitment, testing, and assignment of employees becomes more systematic with practices spilling over from wartime experience. Manpower planning is introduced.	
1960s–1970s	Focus in U.S. on expatriation; matrix structures and staff bureaucracies	Personnel starts to pay attention to the managerial population as well as workers. Managers expect careers, not just jobs. Succession planning and expatriation policies are developed. HRM becomes the umbrella for flourishing people management initiatives.	Systems thinking about organization
1980s	U.S. faces stronger competition from Japan and Europe. Rationalization and consolidation.	"HR planning" grows and dies. Corporate restructuring, with handling of layoffs, outplacement. Greater attention to talent development. Increasing attention to HR implications of international alliances.	Strategic HRM—Organization Culture
1990s	Globalization	Greater localization. Growing awareness of the role of HRM in providing corporate cohesion. Global leadership development becomes vital. Attention to cross-boundary merger integration. Focus on developing "human capital" leads in turn to a focus on "social capital" underlying innovation and knowledge management.	Resource-based view of the firm. "Transnational concept."
2000s	Beyond globalization	Competitive advantage comes from speed and adaptation, differentiation rather than imitation. Increasing emphasis on global knowledge management. Internet-based solutions drive reengineering of HR foundations. Contradictory pressures—advancing global integration versus the backlash against the consequences of triumphant capitalism. Social architecture becomes the frontier challenge for HRM.	Tension, paradox, and duality.

As we have seen, the challenges of foreign assignments and adaptation to practices abroad and those of coordination and control of distant operations have existed since antiquity. It was only during the last fifty years that specialized personnel managers assumed a responsibility for these tasks. With the recent acceleration of globalization, these and other international HRM issues have developed into a central competitive challenge (see Figure 1–3, which traces the developments in practice and theory over the last 130 years). As Floris Maljers, former co-chairman of Unilever, put it: "Limited human resources—not unreliable or inadequate sources of capital—has become the biggest constraint in most globalization efforts."[99] Most scholars studying the multinational firm, whatever their discipline or background, would today agree.

The centrality of these issues has increased step-by-step. With the postwar boom in internationalization, the problems of persuading people to go abroad led specialists in international compensation to be tacked onto the personnel function. The concern with expatriation broadened with the awareness that this was not just an issue of sending bodies abroad but of helping expatriates (and thereby their companies) be successful—the bottom line consequences became more visible. As foreign markets moved from developing to developed status, localization became a new imperative, also leading to the complex task of tracking and developing a global talent pool. It became clear that even local executives needed to have international experience as globalization started to have an impact on domestic operations. Awareness of the implementation problems in the growing number of ventures, alliances, and cross-border mergers further spurred the strategic importance of international HRM.[100]

Until recently, HRM was seen essentially as a task of helping get strategy executed. But the links between HRM and strategy really came together with the transnational concept that helped to dissolve many of the traditional boundaries in organizational thinking. HRM started to be seen as an integral element of the multinational organization, spurred by the failure of structural solutions to the problems of coordination and control, and by the fact that strategic innovations increasingly came from local units rather than central planners. This led to a focus on how HRM management practices might assist in providing cohesion to the multinational firm. HRM is at the crux of today's challenges of knowledge management that may be so vital to keeping up with a future that is rushing toward us.

As these issues become more important, the boundaries between the HR function and line management become fuzzier, as do the boundaries with other management functions such as planning, information and communications technology, and operations. Throughout this book, we take a broad managerial perspective, addressing "the manager," regardless of whether that person works as a professional in the HR function or as a line or general manager. From time to time, we address implications or challenges that in most firms are more functional tasks. The convention that we will use is to refer to HR whenever we mean the functional domain. When we talk about HRM or human resource management, we are adopting the generalist perspective.[101]

The increasing centrality of these international HRM issues has also resulted in a blurring of the boundaries between this domain of academic study and others.[102] Once no more than an appendix to the field of personnel/HR management, international HRM has become a lens for the study of the multinational enterprise, the form of organization that dominates the world's economy. Understanding the complex challenges of transnational organization and knowledge transfer/creation calls for interdisciplinary work with scholars of strategy, institutional economics, organization, cross-cultural management, leadership, change management, organizational culture, and others.

Scholars of HRM in general and international HRM in particular are generally united in calling for broader theoretical perspectives.[103] Indeed this book will expose the reader to many different theoretical perspectives on issues related to international HRM, drawn from multiple disciplines:

- The resource-based perspective on strategic management, bringing the fields of HRM, strategy, and organization under one umbrella, united by the search for sources of competitive advantage.
- Fit and contingency theory that underlies much of traditional HRM reasoning, including the issue of how to align HR to other aspects of organization.
- Emerging duality and dilemma perspectives, responding to the increasingly apparent contradictions of complex organization in a competitive environment.
- Institutional theories that help us understand how organizations copy each other and how knowledge of practice gets adopted around the globe.
- Network theories that help us to understand nonbureaucratic coordination, including the theory of social capital underlying knowledge creation.
- Postmodernism with its insights into how HRM practices are social constructions of reality and into the ethical dilemmas of organization.
- Cross-cultural theories of management and organization, with their implications for the adaptation of management practice.
- Socio-political institutional theories that help us understand how organizations are influenced by their context.
- Socialization theories that facilitate understanding of how the "matrix" of multinational operations can be built into minds rather than structures.
- Organizational learning theories that illuminate facets of the exploitation-exploration dilemma.
- Other elements of organizational theory, including design, agency, evolution, and configuration.
- Theories of knowledge transfer and creation through combination and exchange.

As we have seen in this chapter and as we shall see throughout this book, there is perhaps one perspective that characterizes the multinational corporation in general and the international HRM area in particular. The manager experiences this perspective as paradox, as contradiction, as the need for balance. From a theoretical perspective, it is that of duality, the tension created by opposites. We are not alone in this view—it is at the heart of Bartlett and Ghoshal's notion of the transnational. Other writers on strategic HRM in multinational enterprises have been struck by the fact that the terrain is marked by these tensions between opposites.[104] We will develop this idea further in the next chapter, where we look at the different faces of human resource management in the international firm.

These contradictions are not exclusive to transnational firms. However, transnational firms are currently at the forefront of these pressures, and therefore it is by understanding such organizations that we may best comprehend how to thrive in a world of paradox. For multinational start-ups like Business Objects, the ability to negotiate the gap between these contradictions, described in this chapter and throughout the book, may be the difference between prosperity and extinction.

TAKEAWAYS

1. To know why international business evolved in the way it did, we need to understand how our predecessors resolved dilemmas such as exercising distant control before modern transport and communications developed.

2. Industrialization drove both internationalization and the precursors to personnel management, both of which enjoyed a boom in the early decade of the century. World War I had a negative impact on internationalization but a stimulating effect on personnel practices.

3. With the emergence of the modern multinational in the expansion years after World War II, international personnel departments were set up to manage international assignments. Until the 90s, different aspects of expatriation have remained the dominant focus.

4. Increasing geographical spread allied to a growing product range led some multinationals to adopt the matrix solution, a big conceptual advance but ultimately unmanageable as a structural solution. Firms started to realize that IIRM could help them combine local autonomy with a high degree of coordination.

5. In most firms, the headquarters bureaucracies grew to cope with these increasingly complex problems of international coordination and control. With localization and time-based competition, these bureaucracies were restructured, accompanied by downsizing and delayering.

6. The emergence of the Japanese challenge represented a culture shock for Western managers, leading to the realization that there were actually "two best ways"—and if there were two best ways, then there might be more.

7. International firms have always muddled through dilemmas and contradictions, often in a pendulum fashion. These contradictions started to become apparent as firms were pushed to be simultaneously responsive to local needs and globally integrated. Such contradictions are the hallmark of the so-called "transnational organization."

8. All multinationals face transnational pressures but not with equal force—there is considerable discretion in the choice of strategy. We are seeing firms going beyond the transnational—today's "front-back organization" that poses big challenges for coordination and contention management.
9. As the resource-based perspective on strategy took hold, HRM came to be seen more and more as one of the keys to building sustainable competitive advantage.
10. What distinguishes international HRM is its interdisciplinary perspective.

NOTES

1. Bartlett and Ghoshal, 1989, p. 174
2. Moore and Lewis, 1999.
3. Ibid., p. 230.
4. Wilkins, 1988.
5. Carlos and Nicholas, 1988. On the other side of the world, southern Chinese clans spread their hold across South East Asia in the fourteenth and fifteenth centuries.
6. In academic terms, this is known as "agency theory" and concerns the extent to which self-interested agents will represent their principal's interest.
7. Jones, 1996.
8. Wren, 1994.
9. Wilkens, 1970.
10. George, 1968.
11. Barley, 1992.
12. Jones, 1996.
13. In Britain, the first industrial welfare worker was appointed by Rowntree in 1896 (Crichton, 1968). In the United States, the National Cash Register Company established an office for welfare work in 1897. For some, these appointments mark the official start of the history of HRM (Springer and Springer, 1990).
14. Tead and Metcalf, 1920.
15. Baritz, 1960.
16. Moriguchi, 2000.
17. Jacoby, 1985.
18. Sampson, 1975.
19. Vernon, Wells and Rangan, 1997. Of course, not all sectors were equally amenable to such collusion. Cartels were rare in industries with a wide variety of products or a large number of producers, such as most finished consumer goods—or in dynamic industries such as automobiles (Jones, 1996).
20. "Multinational Companies: Special Report," Business Week, April 20, 1963, p. 69.
21. Jones, 1996.
22. Dunning, 1988.
23. Chandler, 1990.
24. Schisgall, 1981.
25. Jones, 1996, p. 173.
26. Vernon, 1977.
27. Vaupel and Curhan, 1973.
28. Hays, 1974.
29. Tung, 1982.

30. Use of the term "human resources" began to creep into the vocabulary in the 1960s—perhaps the earliest systematic use of the term was in Japan, where the word Jinzai (combination of characters for "human" and "material") gained currency in the 1950s. The Japanese did not have the capital or physical resources of the Americans—all they had was Jinzai. Economists had for some time spoken of the productive "resources" or "factors" of the firm, though attention focused more on capital and physical resources. Edith Penrose was particularly influential, arguing that both intangible assets such as people as well as tangible assets such as capital or machinery are the basis for productive output (Penrose, 1959). The research on human capital by the Nobel prize–winning economist Becker reinforced the focus.

31. "Multinational Companies," Business Week, p. 63.

32. This Harvard project was initially inspired by Raymond Vernon's seminal product life cycle model of stages in the internationalization of the firm (Vernon, 1966).

33. Stopford and Wells, 1972.

34. The transition from the functional to the M-form divisional structure was assessed by Alfred Chandler (Chandler, 1962, 1977). Between 1949 and 1969, the number of Fortune 500 U.S. firms organized along functional lines dropped from 63 percent to 11 percent (Rumelt, 1986). As Chandler put it: "Although not all integrated industrial enterprises became multinationals, nearly all industrial multinationals evolved from such enterprises" (Chandler, 1986, p. 409).

35. The threshold as a percentage of sales that would trigger this transformation from a divisional to a multinational structure was hotly debated.

36. Argyris, 1967.

37. Drucker, 1973.

38. Davis and Lawrence, 1977.

39. Peters and Waterman, 1982, p. 314.

40. It would be misleading to say that matrix structure is dead. Some organizations introduced matrix organizations in the late 80s and 90s. The matrix structure that ABB employed until 1998 is perhaps the most well-known example. But as we will see in Chapter 7, this was a different form of matrix from those introduced in the 70s—a matrix built around a structure of clear accountability. Research suggests that matrix structure can be appropriate as a transition organization, facilitating the development of a "matrix culture," though typically it will ultimately lead to a more unitary structure now made flexible by coordination mechanisms that matrix introduced (Ford and Randolph, 1992).

41. Ibid., 1992.

42. Galbraith, 1977.

43. Martinez and Jarillo, 1989.

44. Bartlett and Ghoshal, 1990.

45. Take AT&T as one example. At the time of the split-off of Lucent as a separate company in 1996, AT&T had 4,800 people in its central HR function in New Jersey (excluding the HR staff in divisional and business unit roles). In comparison, their European competitor Alcatel, with roughly the same number of employees, had between 8 and 12 persons in corporate HR. To take a German example, the pharmaceutical firm Bayer today has 1,800 people in its corporate personnel function.

46. The nemawashi process in Japanese firms is explained on page 20.

47. Many German international firms had an unusual structure abroad where the sales subsidiary was run jointly by a local general manager with a German commercial manager on a primus inter pares basis, facilitating this consensual approach.

48. This fueled a new question for HRM around the world: Since the old psychological contract of "a-fair-day's-pay-for-a-fair-day's-work . . . with a generous pension at the end" was now

under threat, what is the nature of the new psychological contract for the future (Greller and Rousseau, 1994; Rousseau and Robinson, 1994)?

49. Although we know of no research directly on the point, our observation is that firms that took the matrix route generally learned more quickly the importance of lateral relations and "normative integration" than those who took the headquarters coordination route. Indeed, researchers have described matrix structures as an apprenticeship in building lateral teamwork (Ford and Randolph, 1992). For example, when Dow Chemicals abandoned its matrix structure, it was partly because it no longer needed it since the necessary "matrix culture" mechanisms were solidly in place to ensure coordination. Companies taking the headquarters route appear more typically to gyrate from centralization to decentralization and back, sometimes getting stuck in protracted pendulum swings.

50. Hofstede, 1980a. See discussion in our Chapter 4.

51. See Pucik and Hatvany (1981) and Pucik (1984). The success of Japan threw the spotlight on HR ingredients such as long-term employment, intensive socialization, team-based appraisal and rewards, slow promotion and job rotation. Certain distinctive features of Japanese management that were given attention in the West were continuous improvement, commitment to learning, quality management practices, customer focused production systems, and consultative decision-making. Some observers saw these HRM practices as amounting to a third way of organizing, based neither on "command-and-control" (Theory X) nor on "participative management" (Theory Y) and which were dubbed "Theory Z" (Ouchi, 1981).

52. Oxley, 1961.

53. Kuin, 1972.

54. Localization, discussed in Chapter 4 (how to develop the talent of local staff), remains today one of the most neglected areas of international human resource management.

55. "Multinational Companies," Business Week, p. 76.

56. Edström and Galbraith, 1977.

57. "Three times the number of managers were transferred in Europe at [one company rather than the other], despite their being of the same size, in the same industry, and having nearly identical organization charts" (Ibid., p. 255).

58. See the SOTA (State of the Art) surveys run annually since 1955 by the Human Resource Planning Society, reported each year in the journal Human Resource Planning; see also a survey undertaken in Fortune 500 firms by Gregersen, Morrison et al. (1998).

59. Perlmutter, 1969.

60. Ibid., p. 13.

61. Kogut and Zander, 1993.

62. Prescott, Rothwell and Taylor, 1999.

63. Hedlund, 1986, p. 18.

64. Vernon, 1966; Stopford and Wells, 1972; Johanson and Vahlne, 1977.

65. Hedlund and Kverneland, 1984.

66. Ashkenas, Ulrich et al., 1995.

67. Such clusters of critical factors helped particular nations to develop a competitive advantage in certain fields—such as German firms in chemicals or luxury cars, Swiss firms in pharmaceuticals, or U.S. firms in personal computers, software, and movies.

68. This empirical study covered 57 electronics firms in Finland (Autio, 2000). See also a study on the international expansion of 25 Dutch firms, which similarly finds that learning on internationalization is handicapped by the prior domestic success of the enterprise (Barkema and Vermeulen, 1999).

69. Bartlett and Ghoshal, 1989.

70. See Hedlund (1986), Prahalad and Doz (1987), and Perlmutter (1969).

71. Doz and Prahalad, 1981, 1984, 1986.
72. Bartlett and Ghoshal, 1989.
73. Although NEC clearly had the grand vision, with its notion of combining computers and communication (long before the emergence of Cisco), it was unable to implement that vision. A big part of the problem is that they were never able to globalize and go where the talent was.
74. Ghoshal and Bartlett, 1998, p. 65.
75. Bartlett and Ghoshal, 1989.
76. Doz and Prahalad, 1986.
77. Bartlett and Ghoshal, 1989.
78. Nohria and Ghoshal, 1997, p. 189.
79. Requisite complexity is a concept borrowed by management theorists from the field of cybernetics (Ashby, 1956). Nohria and Ghoshal (1997) argue that for effective performance, the multinational firm's internal complexity should reflect the external complexity of its environment.
80. See Nohria and Ghoshal (1997) for a classification of the business environments of multinational firms.
81. Ghoshal and Bartlett, 1997.
82. Porter, 1985.
83. Itami, 1987.
84. This study by Robert Zemsky from the University of Pennsylvania and the National Center on the Educational Quality of the Workforce is outlined in Stewart (1997). It controls for parameters such as organizational size and industry.
85. "A Multinational Cadre of Managers Is the Key," S. Wagstyl, Financial Times, October 8, 1997, p. 19.
86. This is discussed in Chapter 2 (see Becker, Huselid et al., 1997).
87. Stewart, 1997.
88. See Baron and Kreps (1999), Chapter 15, for a good analysis.
89. Hamel and Prahalad, 1994; Leonard, 1995.
90. This is discussed further in Chapter 9, pp. 421–423,
91. This example is taken from Hamel and Prahalad (1994) who provide in their chapter 9 a more complete definition, emphasizing that core competencies should be gateways to the future.
92. Pfeffer, 1998.
93. For research on the concept of combinatory capacity, see Kogut and Zander (1992) and Galunic and Rodan (1998). The concept of coevolution refers to the same phenomenon at the level of organizational design—see Eisenhardt and Galunic (2000) and the special issue on coevolution of strategy and new organizational forms in Organization Science, (1999) 10: 5.
94. Kogut and Zander, 1992.
95. See Galbraith (2000) for a good review of organizational designs for global corporations until and beyond the transnational form.
96. Ibid. provides examples in these different industries.
97. "The Radical: Carly Fiorina's Bold Management Experiment at HP," Business Week, February 19, 2001. See also the commentary on ABB in The Economist, January 12, 2001.
98. Robert Burgelman, cited in "The Radical," Business Week.
99. Cited by Bartlett and Ghoshal, 1992.
100. Even in the mid-1980s there was speculation as to whether international HRM was "fact or fiction" (Morgan, 1986).
101. It is only in our final Chapter 10 that we will be focusing on the functional HR manager and how the forces described in this book are changing that role.

102. At the same time as the importance of HRM and international HRM is beyond question, whether it is or should be a "field" is an open question, one that can engender hot debate among academics. We recently organized a workshop for the leading scholars of HRM in Europe and the United States, and this issue came up for discussion. There were strongly divided views, about half of the 40 scholars arguing that "HRM" is clearly a field, whereas the other half saw it more as a focus of attention.

103. See McMahan, Virick and Wright (1999), as well as other papers published in this edited book.

104. See for example De Cieri and Dowling (1999), p. 321.

CHAPTER 2

Three Faces of Human Resource Management in the International Firm

The hundred-year-old Ohio-based Lincoln Electric Company has long been a favorite case of business schools to show how human resource management can contribute to sustainable business performance. The largest manufacturer of welding equipment in the world, Lincoln motivates its American employees through a distinctive compensation system and a culture of cooperation between management and labor based on the fervent beliefs of one of the founders in self-reliance, the necessity of competition for human progress, and egalitarian treatment of managers and employees. Introduced by family management in the 1930s, the incentive system replaced hourly wages and salary with piece rates and an annual bonus linked to profits that typically amounts to over half of the employees' income. To determine the bonus, production employees are appraised twice a year on four criteria: output, quality, dependability, and ideas/coop eration. The company had enjoyed unrivaled and much-acclaimed growth and prosperity, driving strong competitors such as GE out of the business—until Lincoln Electric, led by a management team who had never worked outside the United States, decided on a bold strategy for internationalization.[1]

After the deep U.S. recession of the early 1980s, Lincoln Electric decided to expand abroad, spending the equivalent of over half its sales on building greenfield plants in Japan and Latin America and on nineteen acquisitions in various European countries and Mexico. Tremendous opportunities were envisaged to leverage their manufacturing expertise and HRM system internationally, transferring their now famous motivational and incentive system which worked well in operations that had been built up earlier in Canada, Australia, and France. Combining the lowest cost manufacturing operation with the highest quality, they seemed destined to dominate the global market.

The rapid international expansion brought Lincoln Electric to the brink of bankruptcy. Lacking managers with international experience, the firm was forced to rely on acquired managers who wanted to maintain their own autonomy. The tight link of sales with manufacturing—another pillar of Lincoln's success—disintegrated, and inventory ballooned while sales stagnated in the recession of the early 90s. The only new country where its incentive system and culture took gradual hold was Mexico. In Europe and Japan, where piece rate payments are viewed with deep suspicion, Lincoln's approach was totally rejected. In Germany, with a 35-hour work week, no one would consider working nearly 50 hours as was the case in the United States.

In fact the firm was saved only by the willingness of the U.S. workforce to deliver on stretch goals to save the company. Senior managers who had track records of strong international experience and yet who admired the culture of Lincoln were recruited from the outside. Lincoln sold off or restructured most of its acquisitions, turning successfully to an export strategy that local Europeans had earlier said would never work. Lincoln's international venture was a lesson in the disastrous consequences of poor transfer of high performance work technology abroad, in spite of the phenomenal success of its approach at home.[2]

The Lincoln Electric drama raises many issues of importance for us. How can companies maintain control over the process of internationalization, and how can management practices that are successful in one country be adapted to another? What are the HRM risks and challenges in internationalization? How should cross-border acquisitions be assessed and integrated? How can problems of coordination be best managed? And how should one go about developing international leaders? Above all, Lincoln Electric's experience raises the general question of how human resource management contributes to organizational performance as a company goes international.

CHAPTER OVERVIEW

In this chapter, we lay out the conceptual framework that underlies this book. We start with the chapter's central question: How does human resource management contribute to the performance of international firms? Not surprisingly, there is a great deal of controversy about this issue, given the enormous variation in HR practices from one firm to another and from one culture to another. Some firms, nevertheless, are much more successful than others, as we know, not only in the short but also in the long term. Are there any patterns demonstrating a relationship between such success and HRM that apply across cultural and institutional settings? And what are the implications for internationalization? Our reading of the research, our own studies, and our experience on various continents lead us to argue that the issue of the relationship between HRM and organizational performance must be explored in the light of three different HRM faces or roles, which are the focus of this chapter.

The first role is the *builder* who gets basic HRM foundations into place. We do not see any evidence to suggest that specific HRM practices have the same impact in all situations—it very much depends on the context. There is evidence, however, that careful attention to the basics and above all to the consistency between practices does pay off. Consistency is the strength of Lincoln in the United States. It was not its incentive system (others have tried to copy such systems with disappointing results) but the finely tuned interrelationship of its practices that contributed to its performance, a coherence that was lost when it moved abroad. With this in mind, we will review the important debate over "high performance work systems" (HPWS).

Since internationalization involves a lot of building activity, we will examine the forces that influence this process.

Builders tend over time to become administrative custodians, and this is a handicap when it comes to the second face or phase of HRM, that of the *change partner.* Markets, technologies, and competitive conditions all change with time, and so does the strategy of the firm. The contribution of HRM to performance is now to facilitate organizational realignment so as to respond to changes in strategy and the external environment. This is a more complex and less understood process (at least from the HR perspective). We draw on some principles of change process theory and practice as we introduce some of the realignment challenges confronting the international firm.

As the need for change speeds up, it becomes necessary to anticipate future changes—for example, swings of the pendulum between centralization and decentralization, between evolutionary progress focused on exploiting resources and revolutionary progress focused on developing new resources. There is a dualistic pattern in change reflecting the tension between opposing forces, leading us to explore emerging theoretical perspectives on organizational dynamics. Understanding these dynamics allows leaders to "build the future into the present." The third role of HRM is as the *navigator* who steers through these dualities and paradoxes. This aspect of HRM is particularly important for the transnational, defined by the contradictions that it confronts.

We conclude the chapter with a section on the implications for managerial roles. Instead of trying to deal with the dynamics of operational performance versus long-term change via structural mechanisms, as in the past, this tension now gets built into the role of the manager, leading us to what we call the "split egg" or matrixed role, critical to understanding how HRM works in the transnational firm.

HOW DOES HRM CONTRIBUTE TO THE PERFORMANCE OF INTERNATIONAL FIRMS?

There is no disguising the controversy about the question of HRM's contribution to performance. While some scholars have collected data on shareholder returns over the decades convincing them of a strong and direct relationship between the quality of human resource practices and return on shareholder investment,[3] others remain skeptical, questioning the robustness of the evidence. Even more fundamental criticism comes from postmodernists who argue that the rhetoric outstrips the reality, that the focus on performance only masks the manipulation of people in the interest of management (see the box "Critical Views of HRM").

Despite European Union, there is a bewildering variety in human resource practices across European countries and industries.[4] Culture and context, which are important given our international focus, make the issue of how HRM contributes to performance even more complex. Companies such as Lincoln Electric in the United States and Marks & Spencer in Britain regarded their human resource practices as a major source of competitive advantage. Yet these practices failed when transferred abroad, jeopardizing the prosperity of these corporations.[5]

In addition to the diversity, there is considerable flux over time in what is regarded as successful practice. Japanese HR practices were thought to be a source of competitive strength in the early 80s, only to go out of favor as the Japanese economy declined in the 90s. The "Japanese" approach to management may today be significantly impeding the globalization of Japanese enterprises.[6] The pendulum swings. American management practices are enjoying a heyday today, but who knows about the future?

Our research and our experience over three decades with multinational firms lead us to believe that one reason for the controversy and confusion is that we are looking at different aspects of the proverbial elephant as experienced by a blind man. We have said that there are three different faces to the contribution that HRM can make to organizational performance, as shown in Figure 2–1. These faces can be thought of as stages, because development in most organizations goes from the simple to the complex (though this is not always the case).

We have called the first face *building HRM,* getting the basics of human resource management into place and ensuring their internal coherence. While this role is often the responsibility of a specialized personnel or HR department, it may be assumed by line management. In both cases, the strategy of the firm is taken for granted, and the builder may over time become a custodian.

The second face or stage is *realigning HRM* so as to meet the needs of the changing external environment. Shifts in the marketplace or in the structure of competition or the advent of new technologies call for a strategic realignment within the firm. The focus of attention is on reconfiguring and changing the approach to HRM so as to implement new strategies effectively. Typically this involves a partnership between line management and the professionals within HR, and we call this role the *change partner.*

The third face may be described as *steering via HRM.* Whereas many will recognize the first two roles, visible both in the literature and in practice,[7] this third role may be less familiar. Here strategic and HR factors cannot be separated; both are completely interlinked. The focus is on developing the capabilities of the organization and its people to thrive in a world of continuous change, which in fact means constructively managing the tensions between opposing forces such as short-term operating results and long-term growth, global integration and local responsiveness, the need for change and the continuity required by execution. Indeed these contradictions are at the heart of what is called the transnational firm. We call this third role of HRM that of the *navigator* who steers between opposing forces.

Each of these faces or phases of HRM and their underlying roles reflect a different set of assumptions about the link between HRM and organizational performance. Each face corresponds to a different theoretical perspective, and each has particular implications for international HRM that are reflected in the structure of this book.

In building HRM foundations, the link between HR practices and organizational performance is direct in the sense that attention to human resource management may pay off in terms of increased performance if those practices are internally consistent. We will discuss the extent to which this is true, though the Lincoln Electric story reminds us that successful practices in one cultural context can fare differently elsewhere. The theoretical perspective behind the builder role is that of *fit,* focusing on

Critical Views of HRM
Research Box

"Big hat, no cattle!" This Texas idiom taken from the title of an article expresses the criticism of HRM in the United States,[A] which has focused on the conflicting messages of human relations, labor relations, personnel management, and industrial engineering; the lack of influence of the personnel or HR function; and questions about the empirical evidence for some of its assumptions.[B] But it is from European and particularly British academics of the critical and postmodernist schools that there has been the strongest critique.[C]

Postmodernists reject the rationality, elitism, and linear progress that was epitomized by the industrial era of Henry Ford, arguing that this is still strongly present in today's society. They are suspicious of excessive order and consensus, which they view as suggesting acceptance of a power structure that removes individual choice and freedom. Influenced by French sociologists and philosophers, they argue that society, as we perceive it, is not objective but socially constructed. Language (or "discourse") plays an important role, masking power structures and domination.

In their view, what is typically presented as a body of knowledge should be seen as an ideology or a system of control. Traditional or modernist social scientists (the worst variety being those from business schools) provide an aura of legitimacy to social structures through "scientific studies" based on these linguistic concepts, acting as agents to socialize people into accepting such power structures. For example, the term "strategic management" is never questioned by traditional positivist researchers, even though it institutionalizes the domination by those who manage the organization-environment interface, reducing others in the firm to the troops who merely "implement." Concepts such as value-based management are attempts to impose domination by certain interest groups in society, suppressing conflict and dissenting views.

The language of HRM is seen as masking the harsh face of managerialism in the service of capitalism, reducing people to mere productive "resources." The rhetoric of TQM (Total Quality Management) disguises the reality of doing more with less, training

and development hides manipulation, empowerment implies making someone else take the risk and responsibility, team work means reducing the individual's discretion.[D] An influential argument is that HRM is a way of coping with the indeterminate, open-ended nature of employment contracts, a way of organizing time, space, and movement by means of language (rhetoric), taxonomies, and codes of ranking, grading, and measurement.[E] Thus distinctions such as manual versus nonmanual, core versus periphery are ways of classifying people so as to bring about order; job evaluation, competence schemes, and appraisal systems are ways of ordering people through ranking on positive/negative scales, all reflecting the machinelike order of the Fordist modernist era in order to make employees governable and predictable, thereby reducing human freedom. Such views have begun to have an influence on academics elsewhere, including in the United States.[F]

Critical scholars often focus on unmasking contradictions in modernist or managerial thinking, notably within HRM—between "hard" and "soft" schools of thought, between HRM's rhetoric and its reality. The functional IIR professional is portrayed as a victim of these contradictions.[G] Others point out that these are really complementary polarities (dualities) rather than contradictions[H]—indeed the view that we take in presenting our third face of HRM.

[A]Skinner, 1981.
[B]Nord and Durand, 1978; Ulrich, Losey, and Lake, 1997; Wright, Dyer, Boudreau, and Milkovich, 1999.
[C]See Legge (1995) for a fine review of the field of HRM from critical and postmodernist perspectives. See Alvesson and Deetz (1996) for an overview of Critical Theory and Postmodernism (though not in the context of HRM), which constitute two related but different schools of thought. While there are massive bodies of literature in these areas, Alvesson and Deetz concede that much is difficult to read, and sometimes esoteric in nature—that some of the insights remain of great importance, reminding us that our reality is indeed socially constructed rather than objective.
[D]Sisson, 1994.
[E]Townley, 1994.
[F]Jermier, 1998; Zbaracki, 1998.
[G]Legge, 1995.
[H]Keenoy, 1997.

FIGURE 2–1. **Three Faces of Human Resource Management**

	Activity	Focus of Attention	Theoretical Perspective	Role
BUILDING HRM	Foundations— getting the basics in place	Internal coherence	FIT (internal)	THE BUILDER
REALIGNING HRM	Adjusting to environmental change; strategy implementation; reconfiguring	Change	FIT (external as well as internal)	THE CHANGE PARTNER
STEERING VIA HRM	Organizational capability development; managing context	Constructive tension between opposites	DUALITY/ PARADOX	THE NAVIGATOR

internal coherence between the elements of HRM and with other parts of the work system. Specific methods of selection, compensation, and development are not necessarily effective in and of themselves. What is important is how these are linked together and with the work technology, supervisory system, measurement system, and other elements of organization. It is an inward-looking perspective on the firm. From an international perspective, cultural differences, local labor market patterns, and legislative constraints are an important influence on *internal fit.*

Realigning HRM is, in contrast, a more externally oriented perspective on the firm. The theoretical perspective behind the change partner role is that of *external fit,* the fit of contingency theory between an organization and its competitive environment. The payoff in terms of performance comes only if HRM is closely linked to a strategy that appropriately reflects the industry and competitive context. If the environment changes and HR practices remain rooted in the past, the contribution of HRM to performance may be negative. However, for many reasons the impact of HRM is difficult to demonstrate or prove empirically: the payoff lies in the future, and it assumes that the underlying strategy is valid and indeed that a strategy exists (which may not be the case).

There is a potential contradiction between these first two roles and their underlying theoretical perspectives. Surely the achievement of external fit will mean destroying the internal coherence? That is indeed correct; there is a tension between these two perspectives—any process of change will involve tension. The focus is on the dynamics of change, realigning for the future while managing the immediate needs of the present.

Scholars have emphasized how the credibility of the HRM field in general and HR managers in particular has often been undermined by such contradictions. This leads us to the third face of HRM, that of steering: the task of the navigator is to steer between such contradictions. We call them dualities, and one example of a duality is the tension between the internal coherence that may be needed for short-term performance and the external fit that may be needed for longer-term organizational survival. Strategy itself is both planned and emergent, and the tension between planning and opportunism is another such duality. The navigator cannot resolve or eliminate such tensions. But an organizational context can be created so that such tensions between opposites act as motors for development rather than as sources of conflict. This perspective, duality/paradox theory, is still being defined, and it will be explained later in this chapter. The third, steering face of HRM is particularly relevant to the challenges of the transnational organization described in Part III of the book. We now return to the builder's role, the first face of HRM.

BUILDING HRM: FOCUS ON FOUNDATIONS

A few years ago one of the authors of this book was invited to participate in a panel advising an international organization on its HR policies. The other panelists consisted of a few academics and the senior HR executives from companies such as 3M, Gannett Publishing, and GE. The participants were grappling with some of the intricacies of strategic human resource management and its role in managing change when GE's Frank Doyle brought us down to earth. "This is all well and good," he said. "But do you know what Jack Welch [CEO of GE] would fire me for? It would not be for some failure in 'strategic human resource management,' but it might happen if we ever had serious problems with the pension fund."

This is the spirit of the first face of HRM. Every organization has to cope with a number of basic and vitally important human resource tasks, those of attracting, motivating, and retaining people. People have to be recruited for changing job needs or to fill vacancies. Their work has to be planned, and this is the task of performance management. They do not necessarily have the skills for the job, so these must be developed through coaching or training. They have to be paid and rewarded, and their pension rights must be respected. There are also many legislative constraints and societal pressures to be satisfied which differ significantly between countries.

These are the basic tasks of HRM—"getting the right people into the right place at the right time." It is the facet that is most familiar to us, dealt with in myriad books on personnel management and HRM. It is a vital task, and organizational performance will suffer if it is not executed well.

Most texts on personnel and HRM are organized around frameworks for these basic activities.[8] A simple framework is shown in Figure 2–2. When we discuss the functional foundations of HRM in this book, this is the framework that we will use. The key activities in building HR are recruitment and selection, development and training (including career management), and performance management (including commitment management and rewards). However, with our focus on managers, professionals, and "knowledge workers," we will rarely consider the area of labor and industrial relations except in passing.

An organization that has not built up solid basic HRM foundations in these areas will be severely handicapped when it ventures abroad. It does not have the codified

---

FIGURE 2–2. HRM Foundations: The Framework Used in this Book

RECRUITMENT AND SELECTION
- Manpower or HR planning
- Recruitment
- Equal opportunity management
- International transfers
- Termination and outplacement

TRAINING AND DEVELOPMENT
- Induction
- Job training (on-the-job and off-the-job)
- Auditing performance and potential
- Leadership development
- CAREER MANAGEMENT[*]
  - Career planning
  - Coaching and mentoring
  - Succession management

PERFORMANCE MANAGEMENT
- Managing employee motivation and commitment (including policies such as open door and attitude surveys)
- Job evaluation
- Goal/standard setting and budgeting
- Performance measurement
- Appraisal
- REWARD MANAGEMENT[*]
  - Compensation and benefits
  - Informal rewards

LABOR AND INDUSTRIAL RELATIONS[†]

---

[*]Sometimes this will be separated as a category in its own right.
[†]This will rarely be considered, except in passing, in this book.

experience either to avoid making mistakes or to learn from its experiences. It will find it difficult to manage the mobility of expatriates to foreign affiliates and their reentry into home positions because it does not have the basic systems and processes in place. Companies without solid HRM foundations may be disadvantaged in joint venture negotiations, finding that foreign partners are wary of entering an alliance with a firm that does not have the proven sophistication in people management to make the joint venture work. Acquisition integration is likely to be a nightmare. Differences in approach to management, including HRM, between two firms that are to be merged can be worked through if they are clear and transparent—what is difficult to merge is two firms that lack clearly articulated approaches.

Getting the right people into the right places is also vital for the individual. Our research into the managerial lifestyles of over 50,000 managers in most major countries of the world shows that no less than 45 percent of people feel dissatisfied with their lifestyles in terms of the relationship between their professional and private lives. The most important reason is 'misfit.' If people do not do their jobs well, do not enjoy them, and do not feel proud of what they are doing and whom they are working for, there is a high probability that the stress they experience will spill over into their private lives.[9] The consequence of poor HRM in this sense is that everyone suffers—the organization, the individual, and that person's wider family.

The Importance of Consistency

How does one judge the quality of such foundations? Partly, and only partly, by the quality of individual practices—for example, in compensation or recruitment. More important, especially from an organizational or general management perspective, is the consistency of the elements, the way in which they fit together. The traditional activity-based view of HRM shown in Figure 2–2 misses what is perhaps the most important issue at the building stage—the whole is much more than the sum of the parts. Objective-setting, appraisal, and reward practices may contribute separately to performance. But they contribute much more when they are considered as parts of an overall performance management system. The activity-based treatment of personnel management in most texts targeted toward HR specialists may be useful when taking a detailed administrative point of view, but this misses the vital interrelationships, how they hang together.

Consistency is important for performance reasons. For example, if a firm invests a great deal of money in skill development, it should pay attention to retention through feedback practices, above average compensation, and careful attention to career management. Policies of long-term employment do not make sense unless people have valuable skills that are worth retaining. But consistency is also psychologically important the performance, motivation, and retention of staff suffers when they experience policies as inconsistent, or when they feel unfairly treated in comparing themselves to others.

Some scholars argue that consistency is one of the only nostrums in the domain of HRM. Baron and Kreps note that successful firms have systems of HR practices that display consistent themes or messages, often embodied in some philosophy of management or value system that provides the coherence.[10] They distinguish between three aspects of consistency. First, there is *single-employee consistency,* reflecting whether employees experience different HR elements such as appraisal, promotion, and compensation as complementary or conflictual. Studies of the impact of HRM on employees show that it fails to live up to its frequent hype when staff experience these practices as an inconsistent mix of policies owing to poor design and conflicting management priorities.[11] Second, there is *consistency among employees,* referring to whether employees in similar roles but working in different departments or units feel that they are treated fairly. This type of consistency is particularly important in the international firm. Finally, there is *temporal consistency* or continuity over time. If practices and policies are constantly changing, this drains away productive energy and leads to dysfunctional frustration.

Underlying the idea of consistency is the concept of fit. The concept of fit is clearly the most important theoretical perspective underlying HRM (see the box "Fit Theory"), together with associated notions of matching, coherence, congruence, consistency, complementarity, and contingency.[12]

This means that practices have to be tailored to specific circumstances. In one firm they might be built around network properties that foster long-term skill development. Recruitment is highly selective, oriented more to fit with company values and long-term potential than with immediate job skills. There is heavy emphasis on training both on and off the job, while teamwork reinforces the development of broad skills. Salaries are above the industry average to ensure retention of those skills. Extrinsic rewards linked to short-term performance may be downplayed so as to encourage a long-term orientation, though benefits are generous to lock people in. There may be a heavy component of seniority-based pay that encourages experienced people to share their know-how with others. Career development is a major priority. This might be a consistent set of HRM practices for a firm in an industry with a long cycle whose strategy is to nurture capabilities.

The strategy of another firm might be built around strengths in responding quickly to market shifts. Its approach to HRM is more mercenary. Extrinsic rewards are the hub of its approach to HR—the pay of general managers is linked to their achievement of the quantified objectives of the business plan, while the compensation of professionals is based on peer comparisons on a bell-shaped curve. People are recruited for jobs, not careers, and there is an understanding that they can be terminated at will. Benefits are downplayed, available in "cafeteria" form. The approach to HRM is quite different though equally consistent.

Lincoln Electric has a very consistent approach to HRM that worked well in the U.S. context. The widely publicized piece rate and bonus systems are only one part of a finely tuned set of practices that evolved over a fifty-year period.[13] The incentive system goes hand in hand with a radical belief in the equality of management and employees—no-holds-barred consultative mechanisms, open door practices, and total transparency regarding company results. The same bonus compensation principles apply equally to the chief executive officer (CEO) and to the factory worker. The appraisal system evolved step-by-step over the decades to meet a more demanding environment; guaranteed employment goes hand in hand with an agreement to switch to lower paid jobs in event of difficulties; and the role of the few supervisors is more mediation and appraisal than control.

Good books on HRM help people to understand the necessary contingencies and configurations of these elements, providing analytic frameworks and case examples rather than recipes. One frequently used framework suggests that one is attempting to optimize the four Cs of Competence (the skill and attitudinal element), Commitment (the motivational or energy element), Cost effectiveness, and overall Congruence.[14] There are obviously other frameworks for assessing effectiveness, but the key point is that it is not a mechanical task but one involving trade-offs.

Two Versions of the Building Model

There are two approaches to building HRM: a universalist and a relativist model. Between the two is an argument about whether various HR practices supposedly associated with high performance are universally applicable.

The Universalist Approach to Building HRM Foundations

The universalist approach to building HRM foundations argues explicitly or implicitly that there is a one-best-way of managing and organizing people, embodied in specific functional best practices in recruitment, appraisal, compensation, and the like. A more nuanced version would claim this to be so "in our sector," though perhaps not across all industries.

The academic field of HRM, perhaps more than any other field of management, has tended to ignore context, often implicitly adopting this universalist perspective. But this is not limited to the world of academia. Successful companies, particularly those that have operated unchallenged for long periods of time on home markets, sometimes adopt the universalist approach. Lincoln Electric is a case in point, assuming that the transfer of its special approach to incentives would give it competitive advantage abroad. The British retailing concern Marks & Spencer set up operations in France and Belgium—"the French and Belgians come to London to buy at Marks & Spencer, so why don't we profit from the European Union to set up shop there." Personnel practices that were seen in Britain as a key component of their success were transferred lock, stock, and barrel to continental Europe. Even the shopping bags in their first Paris store were the same as those used in Britain—a union jack flag with the label "Buy British, Keep British Jobs!" Needless to say, their early steps at internationalization were not successful.[15]

The universalist approach of Marks & Spencer may seem naïve, but many other firms have at times walked the same path with great enthusiasm. For example, benchmarking or best practice modelling is one commonly used (or abused) manifestation of universalism. The firm identifies exemplary and successful firms, then surveys their HRM practices and attempts to imitate them, irrespective of circumstances. This piecemeal approach is unlikely to add much value except at the most basic stages of building foundations.[16]

In our view, the universalist approach ignores the consistency/fit argument. Differences in legislative context as well as culture require at least some reconfiguration of practices to be effective.[17]

The Relativist Approach

The relativist approach to building HR foundations recognizes that there are few objective rights and wrongs in terms of these basic activities. The context is all important and the only objective statements that one can make are generalities such as "Pay close attention to how you select and develop people and how you manage performance." The relativist school has many adherents especially among HR scholars in Europe.[18]

Fit Theory
Research Box

The idea of "fit" is perhaps the most important concept in the organizational design and strategy literature of the latter half of the twentieth century. It first appeared in the 1960s, associated with developments in systems theory and as a reaction against previous "one-best-way" thinking about management.[A] The basic idea from systems theory is that nothing is right unless it fits with other elements of a system. Other concepts that are associated with fit theory are matching, coherence or consistency, complementarity, and contingency.

In the 1960s, fit theory started to take two different forms. One form, born out of the Human Relations movement, focused on the *internal fit* between the elements of what constitutes an organization. The Stanford scholar Hal Leavitt emphasized the importance of assessing the fit between structure, people, and technology in order to try to understand organizational effectiveness.[B] In Europe, a school of thought called Socio-Technical systems theory was developing in England and in Scandinavia, based on the analysis in coal mines, factories, and the shipbuilding industry of how changes in technology implied necessary changes in work system management (including HR).[C] The growing HRM movement adopted this perspective in the applied psychology focus on person–job fit and in the Harvard general management model, in which the four HRM policy areas of work systems, human resource flows, reward systems, and employee influence must be optimized against the criteria of commitment, congruence, competence, and cost effectiveness).[D]

The other form of fit theory focuses on the *external interface* between an organization and its environment, particularly the competitive environment. The pioneering historical studies of Chandler showed that structural change follows change in strategy, giving birth to the field of business strategy.[E] Another series of studies indicated that the degree of differentiation and integration inside an organization must match its environmental complexity, leading to the birth of structural contingency theory.[F] Although attention focused initially on structure, it was soon pointed out that reward systems should also follow strategy,[G] and then it was argued that all aspects of HRM (selection, development, etc.) should also flow from strategy, giving birth to the concept of "strategic human resource management" that is associated with the second face of HRM.[H]

These two aspects of fit, internal and external, were brought together in theories of HRM in the late 80s,[I] though they remain largely separate. They were widely popularized by the McKinsey 7-S model underlying *In Search of Excellence,* emphasizing that effectiveness is the fit between the hard Ss of strategy, structure, and systems, and the soft Ss of staff, style, skills, and superordinate values. Porter's recent reformulation of the concept of strategy is built on the con-

---

In the extreme, the argument that everything depends on the specific context and on everything else is sterile for pragmatic managers.[19] Relativists might argue with glee that the failure of Lincoln Electric abroad supports their view. However, this story should not be interpreted as implying that reward and appraisal systems linked to individual and company performance will not work in Germany. Such a conclusion would be as naïve as the "the one-best-way." After careful analysis, an appropriate conclusion might be that such an approach to HRM might work in Germany IF people can be selected who find such a reward system to be attractive; and IF there are no legal problems with the underlying metrics in the code of German labor legislation; and IF the work system can be designed so that individual performance can be measured; and IF internal transfer pricing does not modify profits of the German unit; and IF appropriate practices can build and maintain employee

cept of fit—"strategy is creating fit among a company's activities."[J] He distinguishes between three levels of fit: first, simple consistency; second, self-reinforcement of activities; and third, optimization of effort. He also emphasizes that a high degree of strategic fit takes time to develop and is costly to change. Additionally, the notion of fit and coherence is at the heart of one of the most influential models of managing change, known as the *punctuated equilibrium model*. Put simply, organizations go through cycles of evolution (where tight coherence develops) and revolution (where external changes lead to radical reconfiguration of fit).[K] This underlies theories of transformational change and has been used to analyze how technological innovation leads to strategic, structural, and organizational revolutions in industries.[L]

While its advocates would regard it as common sense, there are severe methodological problems with the conceptualization and measurement of fit.[M] The nature of the theory is such that with all the infinite angles of fit, it is doubtful that it could ever be proven scientifically, though there is convincing evidence for certain propositions.[N]

A school of thought that is influential in the United Kingdom and increasingly in the United States goes beyond fit theory. *Contextualism* argues that contingencies are so complex that they should be the object of study (the content of HRM can only be understood in the external context of the firm, its internal context, the business strategy context, the HRM context).[O]

[A]For an account of changing management paradigms this century, see Evans and Doz (1992).
[B]Leavitt, 1965. The landmark study that is often seen as launching the concept of fit and its implications for contingency theory is that of Burns and Stalker (1961), which suggested that mechanistic organizations suit stable environments, while complex and turbulent environments require organic structures.
[C]Trist and Bamforth, 1951; Thorsrud, 1976; see also the British studies of Woodward and the empirical work by the Aston school in Birmingham, England.
[D]Beer, Spector et al., 1984. See Hanna (1988) and Nadler and Tushman (1988) for similar frameworks.
[E]Chandler, 1962.
[F]Lawrence and Lorsch, 1967. See Donaldson (1996) for a review of contingency theory.
[G]Galbraith and Nathanson, 1979.
[H]Fombrun, Tichy, and Devanna, 1984.
[I]Meshoulam and Baird, 1987; Lengnick-Hall and Lengnick-Hall, 1988.
[J]Porter, 1996.
[K]Tushman, Newman, and Romanelli, 1986.
[L]Tushman and O'Reilly, 1996.
[M]See Wright and Snell (1998) for a recent review focusing on the HRM field.
[N]Donaldson, 1996.
[O]Hendry and Pettigrew, 1990. See also Sorge (1991); Sparrow, Schuler, and Jackson (1994); and Jackson and Schuler, 1995.

trust in management; and IF . . . Some of these "ifs" might rule out the use of such a system or render it excessively expensive.

The "High Performance" Approach

Between the universalist and the relativist approaches to building HR foundations lies a hot debate that has been raging for some years. There are many credible scholars (mostly of American origin) as well as a number of firms who strongly argue that although there may not be a single best way of managing people, there are common features to what are called *high performance work systems* (HPWS).[20] This belief grew out of research and practice on participative and enabling management (in contrast to Theory X "command-and-control") and was reinforced by the success of Japanese management practices in the 1980s.

There are many different versions of the HPWS argument, and different labels are used, such as "high commitment HRM" (the term preferred by British researchers)—we refer readers to the literature and commentaries.[21] Typical features include highly selective hiring of new personnel and a focus on skill development, training, and teamwork. To retain skills, there is premium compensation (often linked to team, unit, or organizational performance) as well as attention to career management, some employment security, and extensive job rotation. Some form of explicit management philosophy ensures the necessary consistency.

Some of these researchers take a universalist position, arguing that the empirical evidence suggests that this configuration of HR practices always lead to better performance, regardless of the context. In other words, they believe that there is a universal "best practice" set. The most influential of these studies was undertaken by Huselid and Becker, exploring the payoff from careful selection of staff, investment in training and development, and performance management.[22] They collected data on HR practices and on economic and accounting performance from 968 large and medium firms in thirty-five U.S. industries. The researchers controlled for variables that affect firm performance such as industry, firm size, union coverage, sales growth, and R&D intensity so as to accurately measure the independent effect of HR practices. One standard deviation in such practices enhanced profitability by more than $4,000 per employee and increased market value by more than $18,000 per employee.[23]

Similarly, Pfeffer examined the characteristics of firms with the highest return on shareholder investment over the last twenty years, leading him to identify seven interdependent HR-related dimensions that characterize "most if not all of the systems producing profits through people."[24] In a study of American banks, Delery and Doty found strong support for a universal relationship between financial performance and best practice in result-oriented appraisal, profit sharing, and employment security.[25] Other studies provide similar support for the universalist view of high performance.[26]

This evidence intrigues but does not convince skeptical culturalists.[27] They point out that these studies are mostly U.S.-based. From a descriptive viewpoint, such HPWS are clearly not prevailing management practice in many if not most other cultures (and indeed noncapitalist cultures may be hostile to such practices), though this may be changing. Take Korea for example.[28] A recent study of 138 firms in Korea found strong empirical evidence for a link between HPWS practices and perceptual and objective market-oriented measures of firm performance.[29] Other studies have found evidence that HPWS lead to better firm performance in other Asian cultures such as Hong Kong, though there are significant differences in the shape of these practices depending on the origin of the parent company.[30]

Much more research is needed. First, the configuration of elements constituting an HPWS is not clearly defined or researched, and indeed there may be multiple variants (or HR "bundles" as they are often known).[31] There is, however, general agreement that the "Fordist" bundle of low wages, no investment in human capital, and little career mobility is associated with lower than average financial performance. Second, the verdict is out until there is wider empirical research on the relationship between these HR practices and financial performance in different cultural contexts.[32]

There may also be a bias in the HPWS hypothesis toward firms that nurture their own resources and capabilities through attention to their internal labor markets. We would certainly be more cautious than, for example, Pfeffer in suggesting that all high performing organizations feature a particular constellation of HR practices. There is a danger in extrapolating lessons from the past and applying them to the discontinuous future. It may well be that fast moving "instant transnationals" in hypercompetitive environments, such as our case study in Chapter 1, Business Objects, will have to make much more use of external recruitment and decruitment to keep pace with their rapidly changing markets, having to confront new paradoxes in the process.

Other researchers agree that companies with a record of long-term financial success who have a strategy of building firm-specific capabilities will tend to have the properties of high commitment or HPWS. They rely on resources developed internally—for example, McKinsey in consulting, Coca-Cola in beverages, Chubb in property and casualty insurance. But they point out that others in the same industries who are equally profitable have different strategies focused on flexibility and responsiveness (examples in the same respective sectors being Boston Consulting, Pepsi, and AIG). These firms tend to rely on external labor markets, moving fast by bringing in needed talent and weeding out the obsolete.[33] However the evidence for such a contingent relationship (it depends on the strategy) is mixed.[34]

In fact, consistency between external strategy and internal HRM may be what is important. As contingency theory would predict, there is a great deal of evidence to suggest that there are different configurations of HRM, organization, and strategic orientation, and indeed configurational research is an important area for future study.[35, 36]

In summary, we would tentatively conclude that there is evidence to suggest that firms that pay careful attention to the selection of people and to their skill development, that worry about how to retain people with valuable skills, and that try to find an appropriate way of linking performance to individual rewards will indeed yield superior financial results—as long as these practices are internally consistent and consistent with their strategies. This, in our experience, seems so plausible and supported by the data that one can accept it as a hypothesis that applies universally, regardless of context. Indeed, this is what we mean by "foundations." However, it is important to emphasize that it is not the specific practices that are important—these do very much depend upon context.

The International Context

Of all the contingencies applying to HRM, those relating to national and institutional context are the least mapped out, except perhaps in the domain of comparative labor law (see the observations in the earlier box "Fit Theory"). While some general foundation principles may apply universally, the specifics of HR practice vary enormously with national context: working hours, the motivating power of money, the structure of labor markets, whether personnel information is secret or public, the social significance of titles, the difficulty and cost of laying people off, the degree to which terms of employment and benefits are passed on to the acquiring firm in an acquisition, the very concept of management. The list is long and growing, and various books have begun the task of cataloguing these differences across countries and regions of the world.[37] Indeed, HRM is probably the function that is most sensitive to context, in contrast to finance or engineering where figures, formulas, and calculations have intrinsic meaning stripped of their context.[38]

"When in Rome, do as the Romans do" is one polar strategy for internationalization, the multidomestic strategy which places emphasis on local responsiveness. The other polar strategy is to export what is successful at home via expatriates, who undertake the necessary local modifications—the global integration strategy.

For most firms, internationalization involves finding a differentiated path between these two extremes. In fact there are at least four different contextual effects on international HR practices: the influence of the mother *country;* that of the mother *company* and its distinctive culture; the influence of the local business context; and the influence of other international companies[39] (see Figure 2–3). These constitute different "isomorphic" influences. While internal consistency pushes toward a particular configuration of policies, work systems and practices, it is subject to the pushes and pulls of these four different forces.

1. *Country-of-origin effect* (cross-national isomorphism): Companies develop HR and other management practices which reflect their national conditions and then transfer these practices to foreign environments. Thus U.S. multinationals may tend to place more emphasis on pay for performance wherever they operate than say European or Asian MNCs. Such country-of-origin effects may reflect differences in the governance structures of corporations rather than cultural differences. Take for example time perspective. U.S. firms where top managers' tenure depends on annual if not quarterly results reported to shareholders are likely to have a shorter-term perspective than traditional German firms where bankers and employee representatives may have a controlling influence on the external board of directors.[40] Whether senior management looks only for short-term results or takes a long-term view will have a profound effect on the orientation of HRM within the firm, at home and abroad.

   The establishment of greenfield sites abroad is a good opportunity to explore the impact of the country of origin. One such study expected U.S. firms setting up operations in the U.K. to emphasize careful selection and socialization so as to promote American values of individualism and high commitment; Japanese subsidiaries in Britain would emphasize single-status, security of employment, team working, and in-house representation linked to a single union; German firms would emphasize the German-style representative system and rigorous staff training. Selecting sixty U.K. sites that were strictly greenfield establishments, researchers found little evidence for such country-of-origin effects. However other studies report strong differences in practices according to the country of origin.[41]

FIGURE 2–3. Isomorphism: Four Ways in Which a Multinational Corporation Can Adapt to Local Conditions

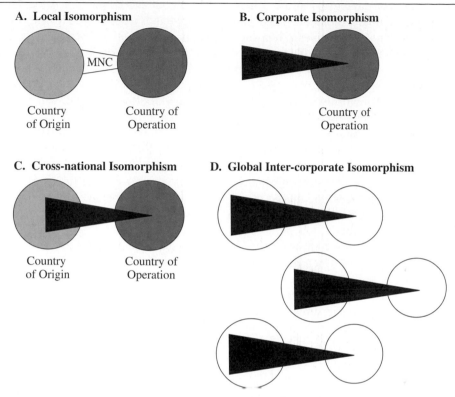

Source: Adapted from A. Ferner and J. Quintanilla, *"Multinationals, National Business Systems and HRM: The Enduring Influence of National Identity or a Process of 'Anglo-Saxonization,' "* International Journal of Human Resource Management 9:4 (1998), 710–31.

2. *Company-of-origin effect* (corporate isomorphism): Companies develop distinctive HRM practices and then transfer these to foreign environments. Lincoln Electric's story in the late 1980s would be a less successful case in point, though there are many examples of the successful transfer of company culture. Hewlett Packard has a distinctive culture that is embodied in the "HP Way." When HP is looking to recruit a French engineer for its operations in Grenoble, it is not looking for a typical French engineer who might be interested in joining Thomson or Matra. Rather it is looking for a qualified engineer who deviates from the French norms, someone who is likely to thrive in the more loosely structured environment of Hewlett Packard.

3. *National business systems effect* (local isomorphism): Here companies adopt HR and management practices that reflect institutional and cultural conditions in the place of local operations. To some degree, all organizations must conform to local practices. Hofstede's classic study showing significant cultural differences in

management conceptions was based on IBM data, at that time a company with a strong corporate philosophy in the HRM area.[42] Some firms adopt local isomorphism as a strategy—"Strategy may be global, but everything else is local implementation." Ahold, the global Dutch retailer that is a competitor to Wal-Mart, is one of many examples. Companies that expand internationally via acquisition and alliance are more likely to experience the pressures of local isomorphism than those that grow by setting up greenfield sites.

4. *Multinational corporation effect* (global intercorporate isomorphism): In this recent era of worldwide diffusion of technology, footloose capital, widespread intercontinental travel, and global accessibility to information via the Internet, knowledge flows easily from one region of the globe to another. International companies compare themselves with other companies that have international experience and model their practices on these, as well as on their own experience with their different subsidiaries. Technology diffusion, diffusion of management practices, and the use of greenfield sites means that national effects become less important than this globalization effect, which the Internet may further accelerate.

   The automobile industry is often used as an example of global intercorporate isomorphism, in which manufacturers not only sell the same model in different countries across a continent but also use common platforms across continents, sharing the same equipment and process technology. The message of convergence was reinforced by the MIT international automobile project. The observation that the lean production system can be practiced in any national environment was justified by the performance of Japanese transplants in Europe and the United States. In advanced transnational companies, the source of innovation is less the mother company and more its leading affiliates throughout the world.

There is an old debate about whether management practices around the world, including HRM practices, are converging or diverging. In fact, as we realize today, different forces or "effects" exist simultaneously. How should a company that is internationalizing design its HR practices? What are the trade-offs, what is the evidence? This important issue is considered throughout Part II of this book.

Given these different influences, the driver of HRM policy at the foundation stage is "single employee" consistency as well as consistency across employee groups. The globally integrated firm wants a high degree of consistency across national affiliates, and so policies and practices will tend to reflect those of the mother firm (strongly influenced by mother company and mother country effects). On the other hand, the locally responsive firm downplays the need for consistency across geographic units. Units are quite separate, and so each national affiliate is free to develop its own practices. Policy making in the transnational firm is obviously the most difficult—allowing for local variation but attempting to ensure cross-unit consistency so as to allow transfers of know-how, joint collaboration on projects, and transfers of personnel.

An interesting argument emerging recently is that companies in which there are strong country- and/or company-of-origin effects may be at a disadvantage in this era of accelerating globalization. For companies with big home markets such as

American and Japanese firms, it is not surprising to find strong country/company-of-origin effects. However, there is new evidence that the success of firms with big domestic markets may handicap their adjustment as they grow internationally. One Finnish study showed that companies that internationalize early are likely to grow faster overall and in foreign markets; not being prisoners of their domestic heritage, they may adjust more quickly to international environments.[43]

How the Builder Can Turn into a Custodian

Building solid and consistent foundations can take years, even decades. Lincoln Electric is an example. But like the foundations of a building, the approach to HRM is difficult to modify without changing the entire structure. There are powerful forces for consistency over time. There is a danger that if you change one important element in the approach, then you have to reconsider everything else. And employees get frustrated when the rules of the game are changed.

Pushed by the need for internal fit, structures, systems, and practices tend to crystallize into a particular configuration (this is indeed the meaning of the term "isomorphism").[44] Once policies and practices in selection, performance management, and the like become established, they often become rigid—a deep structure that regulates people's lives far more than the superficial structure of reporting lines. The orientation of functional professionals consequently tends over time to become transactional or administrative rather than proactive. For example, personnel managers may resist arguments for moving to a reward system linked to competence rather than to the job in order to attract people with valuable skills.[45] Not only would this undermine a finely tuned salary system, it might also threaten the job evaluation/ranking system linked in turn to titles that give people status in the outside community. It would threaten the employee's concept of a career as climbing the ladder, the authority structure of the firm, norms about relationships between boss and subordinate, and so on—many of the elements of the hidden structure of working life. It is far easier to change the surface structure of reporting lines than it is to modify these parameters of daily life.

As a consequence, some HR professionals have a tendency to get stuck at the stage of HR foundations, becoming administrators of their systems, attempting to refine or patch over the holes, rather than trying to anticipate changes in markets, technology, and strategy. *The builder becomes a custodian*—sometimes in the pejorative sense of an administrative janitor. Maintaining internal fit or consistency becomes an end in itself, at the expense of commitment, competence, cost, or strategic performance. The orientation of HR becomes transactional, and the hallmark of success is "no news is good news." This is a widely discussed and well-known phenomenon, as true of Japan and Korea as it is of the United States and Germany.

This expresses itself in one of the many paradoxes in this field. While the rhetoric of today's human resource management emphasizes change and development, the reality is that practices may be based on antiquated assumptions reflecting a bygone era, yet immensely difficult to change. HRM may be critical to the success of the business, yet HRM practices may constitute the biggest obstacle to necessary changes.

While it is easy to criticize the HR function,[46] it is often a victim of its own success in the past—a paradox that we will meet regularly in this book. For example, the IBM crisis in 1991 was partly attributed to the conservatism of its arrogant HR function. As noted earlier, Japanese personnel management is another example.

There is nothing wrong with this first face of HRM. Solid foundations are the basics of good management. The Finnish group Nokia sought our advice in the early 90s. They were already a fast moving "shoot-before-you-aim" culture, and the HR professionals were not sure about the role that they should play. We advised them to focus first on building solid HR foundations rather than trying to play strategic partner or change agent. Recently, they came back to us and told us how sensible that advice had been.

But it can be dangerous to remain tinkering with the foundations that one has built. The reader might like to guess how many people were employed in the corporate HR function in New Jersey in 1994—fifteen years after the breakup of the AT&T monopoly, the decentralization of responsibility to business units within the new divisions, and the internationalization of the firm. The answer is over 4,500 staff out of a total workforce of 320,000, including 2,500 people in corporate training at a time when responsibility for training had been decentralized. A "small" corporate HR department consisted of 50 people. In contrast, their European competitor Alcatel, slightly smaller in overall size, had between 8 and 12 people in the corporate HR office in Paris.

This heavy structure made sense when AT&T was a telephone monopoly whose profits could be eroded by discontented employees, hostile unions, or negative public image. Training was a good investment—it keeps people happy, it is socially legitimate, budgets can be adapted to cash flow, and it even develops people professionally. But the logic behind AT&T's approach to HRM evaporated in the different environment since the 1980s. As with many successful firms, it is difficult to modify a formula associated with so much historic success.

HRM scholars also tend to focus on the foundations. Research attention has been so focused on issues such as the impact of HPWS that the role of HRM in managing change has been largely neglected. As Purcell puts it, "We need to be much more sensitive to processes of organizational change and avoid being trapped in the logic of rational choice. A fruitful line of research is analysis of how and when HR factors come into play in strategic change. This would enable us to gain a better understanding of the synergistic combinations of HR policies (internal fit) and the link between HR system and business and operational strategies (external fit) in dynamic contexts."[47]

The difficulties of changing approach have implications for international HRM. When a company expands internationally in an organic way, it may have some degree of control over the selection and development of people. However, organic growth is often slow. Rapid international growth may demand joint ventures or alliances, in which one faces the difficulty of negotiating an approach reflecting two different cultures. Acquisitions may lead to even faster growth but pose even greater challenges of integrating different HR foundations.

The need in our dynamic and competitive business environment for proactive human resource management moves us on to the second face of HRM, the focus of which is on managing change.

REALIGNING HRM: FOCUS ON STRATEGIC CHANGE

Companies organizing an international HR workshop sometimes contact us. They tell us that they are trying to become more strategic in their orientation to human resource management and they want input on the topic of "strategic HRM." Then they inform us about all the interesting change projects that they have under way in terms of competency management, succession planning, 360° feedback, appraisal system development, and the new seminars they have launched on managing change. "That's fine," we say, "But tell us about the strategy of your company and its business units." There is a long pause. "Well, we'll have to get back to you about that," they reply.

As we discussed, there is a tendency for HR foundations, even those oriented toward high performance aims, to become ends in themselves. In contrast, the focus of the second face of HRM is on the changes required in order to achieve new strategic goals and the implementation of strategy by facilitating change, including necessary changes in the deep structure of HRM foundations. A recent popular book calls this "results-based leadership," which means always returning to the "so that . . ." question—the need to invest in human capital SO THAT . . . *fill in the desired result;* leadership development is important SO THAT . . . *fill in the desired result.*[48]

The theoretical framework behind the second face of HRM remains that of fit. But achieving this is more complicated since the need for internal consistency must be complemented by a new focus on matching to the demands of the external environment. This is external fit, often called *strategic HRM.*[49]

The Evolution of Strategy in "Strategic" Human Resource Management

Even if there is a relationship between HR investment and financial performance, as some U.S. studies have found (see the discussion on HPWS in the previous section), this relationship is not linear. Investing in HR foundations may bring a performance payoff, but the impact quickly levels off. Investing more in perfecting HR practices brings little. There is only a continued payoff if the investment in HRM is closely and coherently linked to strategy (where strategy refers to the link between the internal and external environment).[50] When strategies change, so must the corresponding configuration of HRM.

But what is strategy and how does one measure it in order to test the hypothesis that a tight link between HRM and strategy leads to better performance?[51] Early studies used Porter's concepts of "generic strategies"[52] (cost-based leadership, market differentiation, and niche strategies), or the classification of strategic postures by Miles and Snow[53] (defender, prospector, and analyzer strategies). High performing firms pursuing cost-based strategies should emphasize short-term results in their appraisals, use detailed job descriptions, and have narrowly defined specialist career paths. Firms pursuing differentiation strategies should emphasize training much more, blending individual and group criteria in appraisals and paying more attention to long-term career development.[54] The results were mixed,[55] raising doubts about these definitions of strategy. Indeed, as the field of strategic management moved to the resource-based view, scholars began to argue that what confers competitive advantage is not generic strategic positioning in the marketplace but something that is difficult to copy. Even Porter was to reformulate his concept of strategy as creating fit between internal activities of the firm and the external competitive and resource environment.[56]

This fit between activities can constitute an organizational capability, a bundling or configuration of technical systems, managerial systems (including those in HRM), skills, and attitudes. It is impossible to separate one element from another. If one analyzes the capability of American Express in data processing, that of Toyota in manufacturing, or INSEAD or IMD in executive education, it is difficult to separate the logistic system from the human skills or the customer service interface from the reward system. Careful analysis by MIT researchers of "lean production" capabilities in the automobile industry showed how the tight bundling of technical, managerial, and human elements builds a capability. Such a capability is specific to the requirements of that industry, and it is not transferable without substantial modification to a different industry.[57] As Huselid put it:

> HRM systems only have a systematic impact on the bottom line when they are embedded in the management infrastructure and help the firm achieve important business priorities such as shortening product development cycle times, increasing customer service, lowering turnover among high-quality employees, etc.[58]

This leads to a broader and more complex concept of fit, and there are many different frameworks. We like that of Baron and Kreps. They emphasize that HRM has to strive for internal coherence on the one hand, as discussed in the previous section, and more externally oriented coherence on the other hand, with five different factors in mind:[59]

- *The organization's strategy:* Its objectives (financial aims such as return on investment or economic value added and strategic aims such as growth, market share, cost effectiveness); the balance between short- and long-term objectives; its basis for achieving competitive advantage (superior quality, customer service, technical innovation, low cost production).
- *The external institutional environment:* The external social, political, and legal norms and constraints.
- *The workforce:* The implications of demographics (age, gender, ethnic profiles) and heterogeneity or diversity.
- *The organization's culture:* For example, whether work is viewed as instrumental or as fun; whether relationships are egalitarian or hierarchic; whether collaboration or competition is valued in peer relationships.
- *The technology and work organization:* The skills required by the technology; the degree of independence imposed by the work system; the degree to which

the technology and work design require judgment and creativity on the part of employees; and related factors.

At the building stage, these various elements are given and often taken for granted. The founding team has a particular strategy, the institutional environment is that of the home country or region, the technology and work organization are set. But all of these factors change over time and with expansion. The demographics of the internal workforce change—for example, big skill gaps appear between the founders who have broad experience and more narrow specialists and executors who follow them. The external demographics change as the labor market moves from an ample supply of baby boomers to a tighter market for professional talent, more diverse in terms of gender and ethnic background. Legal and social norms evolve over time, and with internationalization, that diversity grows exponentially. Technologies change, both the core technologies as well as the back office technologies, the impact of the Internet on recruitment being one example. And obviously the organization's strategy changes with competitive shifts.

All these changes and shifts compel a process of *realignment*—the word is used because it captures the necessity to reconfigure the different elements.[60] One current example is realignment to respond to changing demographics and changes in recruitment technology in the Western world (see the box "Realigning HRM to Meet the Need for Talent").

The process of realignment is more than a technical task of implementing change by modifying HR practices, in isolation from business strategy and each other. This was often the case in early approaches to human resource planning in the 1980s. The implications of strategies such as cost reduction or market differentiation were spelled out for appraisal practices, for career development, for performance management, and for rewards—each one as a separate initiative, sometimes disseminated by HR as a new "global policy." When HR practitioners attempted to develop "human resource strategies," these were often too general to be useful since the HR managers were not involved in the business.

The shortcomings of the fragmented approach to realignment can also be seen in the HRM practices of some highly externally oriented firms, where new strategic objectives are rapidly put into place with centralized corporate initiatives, often in response to the latest management fad, without considering the relevant linkages and consequences. External fit is the focus of attention at the expense of internal fit. As a result, HRM practices are seen as inconsistent, and in due time as irrelevant. Even sophisticated companies such as Shell can fall into this trap. In the mid-90s they introduced open job posting systems across the world, creating rampant confusion and frustration since they did not realize that this demanded a fundamental reconfiguration of their entire approach to HRM.

It is important to recognize that adjustment to new demographic trends, to new market needs, or to technological change is a process of change and reconfiguration that often takes quite some time to achieve. Gratton makes the point well when emphasizing the temporal dimension of HRM.[61] It took Glaxo-Welcome ten years to meet their goal of rapid product development by creating cross-functional teamworking,

Realigning HRM to Meet the Need for Talent
Practice Box

Demographic changes during the last decade have triggered major changes in the recruitment process in the Western world. Though the economic downturn has slackened the pressure, companies now desperately seek educated professionals to meet the demands of the knowledge-based economy, while the number of 35–45-year-olds on the labor market has dropped by 15 percent. There are deep qualitative changes. Talent is more mobile across companies, there is less loyalty, the idea of a long-term career holds less appeal, retention is more difficult, small companies are seen as offering more opportunity than the larger firm.[A] The basic HR area of recruitment has clearly become more important.

But this does not imply doing more of the same. Internet and digital processing are revolutionizing the recruitment process at both supply and demand ends. Job candidates seek information on opportunities, make applications, and receive notification through the Internet. A majority of leading corporations are wholly or partially e-centric in their administration of recruitment.[B] Filters screen out relevant applicants who then are asked to complete online questionnaires and simulations to ascertain fit with company competencies and values. Short-listed candidates are passed by Intranet to managers who meet with the candidates, along with internal candidates who apply through internal intranet job posting. The cycle time is reduced from 12 to 6 weeks or less. Companies are even talking about a one-week benchmark.

Leaving aside the more specialist issues, responding to the potential of Internet recruitment involves facing up to many challenges:[C]

1. *Competencies?* Does the firm have a clear map of the competencies it requires, allowing it to filter out applications? Without this, the Internet world overloads the firm with information.

2. *Outsourcing?* Given the rapid developments in websites and software, should an outsourcing partnership be considered, as with many Microsoft subsidiaries? Or should the firm maintain control over software to exploit future possibilities for HR integration (with online Intranet induction, training, appraisals and salary adjustments, with the online auditing of the internal bench strength on key competencies—all of which are a reality in many firms)?

3. *A global recruitment process?* What about the opportunity to develop a global process for recruitment, standardized through external websites and the internal intranet?

Global firms also have to confront the reality of greater transparency of information on what it is like to work for the firm available through websites used by candidates. As the administrative side of recruitment is streamlined, the recruitment task becomes more akin to brand management—monitoring and promoting the reputation of the firm (what it offers as a company, in terms of jobs and in competitive compensation), dealing intimately with the problems that lead to excessive turnover, knowing well the different segments of the employment market. Firms with a fine recruitment image often use referral systems (a majority of Cisco employees are hired on the basis of such internal referrals).

[A]See Tulgan, 2001.
[B]One 2000 survey suggests that 80% of the global 500 corporations are Internet recruiters including all high tech enterprises (90% of the Americans, 73% in Europe, and 68% in Asia) ("Global 500 website recruiting," info@recruitsoft.com, 2000).
[C]See Kanter, 2001. Many of these issues will be discussed later in this book. The issue of global processes is explored in Chapter 7, while that of competencies is discussed in Chapter 8. The whole issue of the impact on the HR function is the topic of Chapter 10.

requiring changes in performance management, selection and development, technology, workflows, careers, and deeper cultural norms and values. Similarly, it took Motorola nearly a decade to build a premier local management cadre for its operations in China.

Some of the dualities that are central to the next face of HRM become apparent in the process of realignment. A notable dilemma is the need to manage today's operational requirements at the same time as one realigns toward future needs, and we will meet this dilemma in different shapes and forms throughout this book. One of the basic laws of change is that there is always a cost to change—upheaval, disruption, internal preoccupation, as well as big investments of time and energy. One is always better off in the short term by not changing, simply doing better what one did yesterday. But this logic would lead to change and realignment happening only through crisis.

Over the last fifteen years we have discussed the following proposition with thousands of line and HR managers across the globe: "The ultimate (though perhaps unattainable) objective of every human resource professional is to do him or herself out a job." The responses vary, more from one firm to another than from country to country. Overall, roughly half agree and half disagree, with little difference between line and professional managers. A summary of the ensuing debates would be the following: If the world were static, the ideal indeed might be to cut back radically on the HR function once good foundations have been built. Routine matters can be automated, those requiring expertise can be outsourced, and line managers can decide on strategic matters concerning HRM. But the world is *not* static. We face continuous and never-ending change, the need for constant realignment. This requires a dedicated HR focus, to manage the continuous process of realignment in a world of accelerating change.

The Elements of Strategic Realignment

Following a framework developed by Ulrich, it has become common to separate the strategic roles of HR into those of the *business partner* and those of the *change agent*.[62] From a functional perspective, the idea of the business partner makes some sense as a precondition for tackling the challenges of realignment. However, the two roles are difficult to separate, as Ulrich's own empirical evidence suggests.[63] The content and process of change are indivisible. It is very difficult to manage change if content and process are separated, if there is not a healthy partnership between line and HR management, if processes such as business planning and people planning are not closely linked. Indeed, this is the reason why we use the term "change partner" to describe the role associated with this second face of HRM.

Preconditions for Change Partnership

One of the implications of the fit argument is that realignment involves a very close relationship between the strategic and business factors involved in fit and the people and HR aspects. Indeed human resource, organizational, strategic and other factors become not just linked, elements to be matched, but quite inseparable. One of the obvious implications is that HR professionals have to be credible business partners, familiar with the external changes that will drive realignment and involved in the business planning process.

Organizations with a long custodial history such as AT&T (to use the example in the previous section) develop functional cultures in which the HR specialists have little involvement with the ongoing business issues. Line managers may also be content to leave those HR specialists to deal with the people matters, freeing themselves up to focus on the technical aspects of business management.

In the era of relative stability that characterized the Western world until the 1980s, the custodial pattern was the norm. While the rhetoric about the importance of "devolution" of HRM responsibility to line managers grew rapidly—making "every employee a manager," as Texas Instruments put it in 1970 when this idea was radical—HR professionals were often reluctant to cede responsibility for HRM to the line. Even recent studies show that this continues to be an uphill struggle in many firms.[64] In addition to reluctance on the part of the HR professionals to give up budgetary control, there are real and substantive concerns on two fronts. First, there is a fear that line managers will overreact to external changes, resulting in a loss of internal consistency. And second, there is a concern that short-term operational considerations will drive out attention to long-term development.

How then can HRM be linked to business strategy? During the 1980s, the emerging field of strategic HRM focused initially on the involvement of the HR function in the business planning process (the first American professional association in the strategic HRM field was called *The Human Resource Planning Society*).[65] Early studies focused on how HR was integrated into the strategic and business planning process. One survey of practice in U.S. firms showed different types and degrees of linkage.[66] The first level of linkage is *interpretation:* HR and other functions are asked to consider the functional implications after the plan has been decided. A second level is *inspection:* the draft business plan is considered by functions such as HR before it is finalized. The third level is *insertion:* initial functional inputs are made in the business planning process, also leading to inspection. The highest linkage is full *integration:* now the HR manager is an integral and respected member of the senior management team and all management team members are sensitive to HR aspects of implementation. In that way, the linkages are managed in an ongoing way. This is seen as an ideal, though practice is often far removed.[67]

Today the notion of human resource planning seems rather dated, as does that of traditional strategic planning.[68] More attention is paid to performance management as a way of linking strategic goals to the objectives. On the basis of studies with a consortium of eight international firms operating in the U.K. such as BT and Hewlett-Packard, most of whom were undergoing strategic reorientation, Gratton and her colleagues see the realignment task as focusing on two cycles, short-term and long-term.[69] The short-term cycle links annual business objectives to the performance of individuals through performance management—objective setting, performance measurement, rewards, and short-term training. At the heart of the cycle is the analysis of the gap between current capabilities and the strategic vision for the future, leading to appropriate corrective changes.[70] The long-term cycle focuses on linking long-term strategy to its people implications, with an emphasis on leadership development, wider workforce development (e.g. skills that will be needed to manage future technologies), and organizational development (e.g. greater needs for flexibility and responsiveness). We will be discussing the need for such a global process of performance management in transnational firms later in the book.[71]

Managing Realignment

When the environment or strategy changes, the process of realigning people involves a delicate unfreezing of an organizational configuration that may be finely tuned. In larger and complex firms, such a transformation may take many years to work through. GE's Jack Welch is the architect of one highly publicized transformation that began in 1981 when he took over as CEO for General Electric. We sat in on a session with his key troops in 1990. GE had just launched its process of "Work Out" of the cultural barriers to change. "We started nine years ago," said Welch, "and we're about thirty percent of the way there. We've done the easy part—the difficult challenge of culture change still lies ahead."

The starting point for realignment is the external changes in customer needs, technology, competition, resources and the like, leading to a new strategy. However, one cannot assume that there is a common understanding of these external changes and their strategic implications, even on the part of the management team itself. Research has showed that in over a third of 3,000 management teams in Europe, there were serious differences of view about strategic goals that are not discussed, hidden under the table.[72] While differences in view are the basis for sound decision-making, what is striking is that they are so often not discussed, although everyone in the organization may know that the management team is divided.

Longitudinal research on the transformation of ICI, the major British pharmaceutical and chemical concern, showed that its strategic transformation took decades.[73] The process started with a foresighted minority who believed that change was needed. While the weight of the existing configuration suppressed overt dissent, small coalitions undertook experimental changes that led to greater confidence. A crisis triggered a change in leadership and a restructuring of top management as the new coalition took over. This led first to new strategic objectives, then to restructuring, and then to a long working through of changes in people processes and underlying culture. Although some American academics have argued that there is a step-by-step logic to this,[74] most researchers and observers would see this as a more iterative process.

With a few exceptions, strategic HRM researchers have tended to focus on the functional implications of strategic orientations rather than on the HRM interface with change processes. Since our focus in this book is on internationalization, we do not intend to provide a comprehensive overview of the people aspects of managing change, referring the reader to the existing literature.[75] Some of the pitfalls are briefly indicated in the box "Why Is Managing Change So Difficult?"

Gratton captures well the process of realignment with her concept of "living strategy."[76] In contrast to former concepts of strategic planning, driven by numbers, analysis, and top-down processes (much criticized by Mintzberg and others),[77] Gratton sees strategy as something that must be brought alive though the careful design

Why Is Managing Change So Difficult?
Research Box

In the myriad books and articles written on managing change, especially during the last thirty years, various consistent reasons come back time and time again as to why change and realignment are so difficult: lack of clarity on the goals or objectives of change, or incorrect goals; lack of clear commitment on the part of the management teams; lack of support of external stakeholders; employees who do not understand why change is necessary; failure to confront people resistance; lack of follow-through and the continuity that change requires.

One of the reasons why managers fall so often into these traps is that they learn a methodology for managing change early in their careers that leads to them to get promoted. And they continue to apply this methodology, which we call *solution-oriented management,* even in senior leadership positions in which the challenges of managing change are fundamentally different in nature.

Solution-oriented change (called technical leadership by others)[A] is appropriate in professional or lower management positions in which the problems or opportunities are relatively clearly defined and the success criteria or goals are also reasonably clear. Attention is focused on the analytic work, coming up with a solution or a way of getting from A to B.

However, managing organizational change at senior leadership levels requires a very different methodology. Problems and opportunities are now highly ambiguous—"We know that we have problems, but no one is sure what they are, and there are strongly divided views." The vision, goal, target, or desired end-state is also ambiguous. There are typically conflicting views from different stakeholders as to what should be the goals and priorities; there are conflicts between short- and long-term priorities.

The temptation is to fall back on the change technology in which one has been trained earlier. The management team does not agree on the problems, the goals are unclear—but the world is full of solutions: lean management, value-based management, TQM, pay-for-performance—just talk with the consultants or business school professors! The solution is analyzed and worked out by experts, and then announced to an organization that does not understand the problem ("why change?") or the intended goals or vision ("in what direction?").

Effective realignment focuses attention on the problems, the reasons for change, and the goal, vision, or destination to be reached. As for the actual solutions, these will be best developed by the people in lower level managerial and professional positions. They will be far more committed to implementing their own solutions rather than those of others.

[A]Evans calls these two change methodologies solution-oriented and problem-oriented management (Evans, 1994), while Heifetz (1994) calls this technical and adaptive leadership.

of appropriate processes in order to manage realignment. Conventional strategic planning ignores the time dimension of realignment, as well as the search for meaning and the fact that realignment is an emotional process that must appeal to the soul. The role of HRM is to design and facilitate processes that will result in effective realignment, a task that can take many years.

Gratton views realignment (or the creation of a living strategy, as she calls it) as a process that can be broken down into six steps:

Step 1: Building a guiding coalition. Unless there is a strong coalition of key stakeholders committed to the need for change, this will not happen. Indeed, GE developed a change acceleration process (CAP) with the help of leading experts, and one of its ground principles is that change does not happen unless there is what we call "act-with-one-voice" commitment on the part of that leadership team.

Step 2: Imagining the future. Realignment is driven by a vision or imagined end-state. One of the major reasons why change processes do not produce change is because the vision was unclear or wrong. There are many techniques such as backward imaging (listing the characteristics of the future state) to help a management team to construct a vision. Such a vision statement should then be amplified by testing it out in discussions with key stakeholders, from shareholders to staff to customers.

Step 3: Understanding the gap with current capabilities. The vision then needs to be contrasted with current capabilities so as to highlight the gaps. Benchmarking, surveys, focus groups, and the like can assist here, with particular focus on identifying the risks that are involved.

Step 4: Creating a map of the change system. Realignment then involves building a meaningful map of the systemic linkages, leading to an understanding of the key levers for change. Again this is a process of developing understanding of complex interrelationships.

Step 5: Building commitment to change. Whereas previous steps are largely cerebral, here the challenge is to build wider commitment to the change path. Techniques such as force field analysis can be useful in assessing resistances. There will typically be some restructuring at this stage so as to bring champions into the fore, but a danger is to confuse reorganization with change.

Step 6: Bridging into action. Finally action plans need to be developed and roll-out processes designed, typically involving multifunctional taskforces.

There are of course other models of this realignment process,[78] the basic tenets of which were established by the Organizational Development movement in the 1960s and 70s.

HRM also plays a key, indeed essential, role in the implementation of change. In implementation, as in the preparation of change, it is the *sequencing* of steps that is important.[79] Beer, Eisenstat, and Spector argue cogently that implementation is a process of learning, typically following a sequence of four steps: (1) redefinition of roles and responsibilities (often associated with restructuring); (2) training and coaching, developing new skills on the part of the large number of people who are willing but lacking the necessary skills; (3) formalization of new appraisal and succession criteria, leading to the replacement of people who cannot adjust, accompanied by recruitment of people with the desired new competencies; and (4) formalization of the new organization in new criteria for measurement, compensation, and the like. The point to emphasize here is that the formalized new alignment is one of the later steps in the process of change, building on informal changes in behavior—and not one of the early steps. Formalizing organizational arrangements that have not been tried and tested is exceedingly risky.

Internationalization as a Change Process

Obviously the process of managing change in a multinational enterprise is exceedingly complex. In Part III we will be discussing what we know about the sequenced phases in complex change as companies with strategic orientations toward local responsiveness or global integration struggle to develop transnational capabilities.[80]

To the extent that a firm can adopt a clear, consistent polar strategy toward internationalization, the problems of realignment and strategic change are minimized. Firms adopting a strategy of global integration take a consistent stance—policies and practices are determined by the center, interpreted and adjusted locally by trusted expatriates. Locals who are entrusted with responsibility are socialized into the global mold. Any realignment, from changes in recruitment strategy to technological change, will also be managed by the center. Those adopting a strategy of local responsiveness take the opposite, but equally consistent, stance of allowing each local unit to develop its own distinctive approach to the management of people. How strategic changes are worked through is a matter for local management to figure out. However, reality these days rarely follows these two extremes since most firms experience some degree of transnational pressure.[81] Consequently we will be meeting practical and conceptual issues concerning realignment and strategic change throughout this book. The following are just a few examples.

Consider the issue of expatriation. In the early stages of internationalization, expatriates may be sent abroad partly because they have skills that are not locally available, and partly because only they can be entrusted to run and control local operations. But the need to attract and retain talented local managers leads to changes in policy so that expatriates become responsible for localization, resulting in dilemmas that will be discussed in later chapters. As transnational pressures to be both global and local increase, this leads in turn to a reconfiguration of the corporation's approach to leadership development so as to open leadership responsibilities up to the best managers, regardless of national background. This may be a difficult reorientation that takes time to achieve, as Percy Barnevik, former CEO of ABB, points out :

> Too many people think you can succeed in the long run just by exporting from America or Europe. But you need to establish yourself locally and become, for example, a Chinese, Indonesian or Indian citizen. You don't need to do this straightaway but you need to start early because it takes a long time. It can take 10 years.
>
> Globalisation is a long-lasting competitive advantage. If we build a new gas turbine, in 18 months our competitors also have one. But building a global company is not so easy to copy.
>
> ABB has virtually finished building its global structure. The main task now is to bring more executives from emerging countries in Eastern Europe and Asia into the higher levels of the company. We have 82,000 employees in emerging economies. We have to bring the best of these to the top. This takes time.[82]

International development typically leads to alliances and acquisitions, which also constitute interesting examples of strategic change. Each alliance or partnership involves a delicate process of alignment reflecting the strategic aims of the parent company, those of the alliance partner, and the needs of the venture itself. To the extent that the partnership is oriented toward learning, this should lead in turn to realignment within the parent company itself, though as we shall see this is often not the case. Indeed partnerships such as joint ventures are excellent training grounds for developing skills in this second face of HRM. In turn, cross-border mergers and acquisitions are doomed to failure without strong skills in alignment and strategic change.

Another change accompanying internationalization that we will be discussing in subsequent chapters concerns the transfer of know-how within the firm. Initially, the corporation faces the challenge of transferring know-how from the mother company to new subsidiaries abroad. But as these subsidiaries gradually develop their own capabilities, this leads to the need to transfer know-how between subsidiaries and to the development of global knowledge management capabilities. Again, this involves multifaceted change—deciding what know-how is of strategic importance, building the network of relationships that facilitate transfer, harnessing electronic communications technology, and above all overcoming the cultural barriers that block the transfer of know-how. This in turn facilitates the transfer of complex capabilities in, say, manufacturing technology from one part of the world to another.[83]

These are all specific facets of the overall challenge of realignment so as to develop stronger capabilities in managing the contradictions of the transnational world.

The Dangers of Fixation on Change

If there was a danger of getting stuck in a custodial orientation at the building stage, as discussed earlier, there is a corresponding danger of getting fixated on change.

Fixation can stem from poor change management that is excessively focused on solutions (see the earlier box "Why Is Managing Change So Difficult?"). Each new management team scrambles around to find new solutions to the challenges. Since employees do not understand the problems and since goals are not clear, these solutions fail to yield the expected results. A new management team is brought in, under greater pressure to come up with new solutions, and the cycle repeats itself. Gradually a cynicism concerning change programs and initiatives builds up among employees. They learn to ignore the rhetoric of change, quietly carrying on with their work and their own lives—until real change is brought about only through crisis. The lesson is that real change requires continuity (one of the steering dualities in the next face of HRM). This continuity can be provided only if top management has a clear focus on long-term vision and goals, leaving the solutions to those who will implement them.

Excessive mobility under the guise of international management development can exacerbate the fixation on change. Each new expatriate leader will start off a new change initiative, driving the local unit toward cost reduction, for example. Just as the change is beginning to take hold, the expatriate is transferred and a new successor is appointed. Since there are few brownie points for implementing what someone else has started, the new expatriate will take the unit off in a different direction, say toward improved customer service. The focus of that person's successor is morale boosting and teamwork, and after that the goal returns to cost reduction. There is accountability for change, but not for execution.

The damaging parallel at the corporate level is violent swings in the change pendulum, gyrating from centralization to decentralization. Among other consequences, this undermines any consistency in international HRM policy.

In some firms, the focus of top management attention is exclusively on change, improvement, stretch, and constant realignment, exploiting strong but short-term performance management systems. The danger is that foundations may get neglected, leading the firm to become unstable. Each year, the targets are stretched further. Last year's achievements justified a good bonus, and now these represent the base line for further achievements this year. This creates a treadmill atmosphere where more and more is being squeezed out of an existing organization. Attention to longer-term strategic and organizational development is shunted aside. No one takes time to listen to people. There is no time to be concerned with traditional matters such as morale, loyalty, climate, whether these highly paid people are having fun and enjoying their lives. No one tracks the turnover and retention rates that herald the dangers.

In the 1980s, Apple Computers scorned traditional personnel management. Caught up with the spirit of "strategic human resource management" in a fast moving technology sector, the HR function was closely involved in strategic decisions such as the acquisition of distributors and manufacturing policy. Led by the Europeans, they developed an innovative approach to management built on the need for change.[84] They pioneered the concept of the corporate university as a learning center and were exemplary in many aspects of realignment. There was a strong orientation to performance management, driven in part by HR—everyone in the business unit down to the lowest assistant was familiar with the current "BizPlan."

However, the neglect of traditional basics had its price. For example, Apple's headquarters in California took a decision to restructure the manufacturing area, closing a plant in Ireland, and the local plant manager heard of the decision via the local Irish press, as did his staff! That story ricocheted around Europe as confirmation that management, particularly at the HQ and in the HR function, could not be trusted. By 1987, employees were grumbling that no one was listening to them. While high potentials were nurtured, the average employee felt neglected. The staff in one European subsidiary started to unionize. That entire generation of HR professionals was swept away, replaced by solid personnel managers who could put the basics into place. The pendulum swung from one extreme to the other.

Continuous change has become a reality in many sectors, and with accelerating global competition there are no signs that the pressures for change will go away. This leads us to the third face of HRM, which from a theoretical perspective takes us into frontier territory.

STEERING WITH HRM: FOCUS ON DUALITIES

In many industries, and particularly in the new high tech, software, professional service and e-based sectors, the process of change is accelerating. Technological and product life cycles get shorter, one competitive change succeeds another in waves. As the process of change speeds up, it becomes necessary to anticipate future changes and to "build the future into the present."

An organization cannot go through constant realignment. As noted earlier, some measure of temporal consistency is important for employees. And every process of realignment exacts a cost. However, there is a dualistic pattern in change, seen for example in swings of the pendulum between centralization and decentralization, between evolutionary progress focused on exploiting resources and revolutionary progress focused on developing new resources. Why not exploit the advantages of decentralization while anticipating tomorrow's needs for greater coordination? Why not try to find a way of balancing the focus on today while investing in tomorrow? This is the role of the *navigator,* steering through the dualities and paradoxes. It is a role that is particularly important for the transnational, defined by the contradictions that it confronts.

The Paradoxical Nature of Organizational Effectiveness

Much of the early work on organizational dualities originated with research on the ultimate though elusive dependent variable in organizational studies—organizational effectiveness. A series of studies since the early 1980s suggested that the concept is difficult to pin down, first because organizational effectiveness is a multidimensional concept, and second because those dimensions involve opposites. For example, Quinn's data led him to suggest that multiple opposing dimensions underlie thinking about effectiveness—control and flexibility, internal and external focus, focus on both means and ends.[85] To be effective, an organization must possess attributes that are simultaneously contradictory, even mutually exclusive.

We will refer to such opposites as *dualities,*[86] although other terms are used such as *competing values,*[87] *dilemmas,*[88] and *dialectics.*[89] They express themselves as paradoxes (see the box "Duality/Paradox Theory"). These opposites are not "either/or" choices, the appropriateness of which depends on a particular context (as in contingency theory), but dualities that must be reconciled or dynamically balanced. Some of the many dualities facing organizations and groups are shown in Figure 2–4.

Lincoln Electric itself is a good example of duality-based management at work. What gets the publicity and outside attention is Lincoln's renowned reward system—the apparent success of "pay-for-performance" taken to an extreme, built around unfashionable piecework payment that for many people represents an exploitative remnant of the early industrial revolution. However, what the superficial observer does not notice and what Lincoln feels is equally important is the attention paid to maintaining trust between management and employees—a principle that is anchored in the value system of the founders as much as the principle of self reliance. There can be few firms at which the CEO and top managers pay as much attention to working through any employee grievance at regular meetings of the Employee Advisory Board as at Lincoln. Equally important, incentive pay goes hand in hand with employment security.

How many CEOs would accept being paid on the same bonus basis as the workers, as at Lincoln?[90] Arguably, it is not incentive-based rewards alone that lie behind Lincoln's success in the U.S., but the awareness of its founders and subsequent generations of management that incentive rewards are only powerful if they go hand in hand with trust and very careful attention to employee relations. Moreover, it is this subtle dualistic combination that has to be transferred abroad if the Lincoln system is to work in other countries.

The notion of duality is ancient. It can be traced far back in philosophy (seen in similar concepts such as dialectic); it is strongly present in Asian religious and philosophical concepts (yin and yang, the Chinese *I Ching* (or *Book of Changes*), Taoism, Japanese Zen-Buddhism); it is a cornerstone of modern post-Jungian personality theory; duality features strongly in the work of the social philosopher Gregory Bateson.[A] But the awareness of duality in organizational life dates back only twenty years. While we refer to duality theory, it is still not a codified paradigm.[B]

One of the essential postulates of this emerging school of thought is that opposites and contradictions are not "either-or" choices but "both-and" dualities that must be reconciled. The proponents of duality theory emphasize the limits of fit theory, arguing that excessive concern with fit or consistency leads to pendulum or see-saw pathologies, cycles of complacency alternating with crisis/transformation. Fit or contingency theories are too static for the fast moving modern age, and they leave little room for understanding organizational dynamics.[C]

An important postulate is that positive qualities taken too far become negative or pathological. Instead of trying to maximize anything, an organization should try to ensure that it maintains at least a *minimal* level of attention to a desirable attribute. An organization requires a minimal degree of consensus, but not so much as to stifle the dissension that is the life blood of innovation, and a minimal degree of contentment, sufficient to ensure that key people remain with the firm, but not so much as to allow arrogance or complacency.[D]

This implies that the key dependent variable in organizational analysis is *tension*—for example, the tension between short-term profitability and longer-term investment in renewal, or the tension between centralization and decentralization.[E] An important issue for research concerns the conditions under which tension becomes destructive or constructive. When does tension lead to dysfunctional outcomes such as fragmentation, political infighting, conflict avoidance, or complacency? And when does tension lead to innovation and organizational development? Contention management is thus another important issue.[F] Indeed, constructive tension is a better term than the often used idea of "balance" between opposites. Another important concept is that of *interpenetration,* a state in which two differentiated poles become part of a larger whole.[G]

Duality theory is implicit (rather than explicit) in many theoretical and empirical studies, particularly in much work on innovation[H] and organizational learning.[I] A review of studies on organizing for hypercompetition concluded that "organizations must develop languages and models that encourage the achievement of constantly contradictory goals when coping with adversity (flexibility through stability, diversification through focus, freedom to break rules in the context of a strong culture, etc.)."[J] The notion of duality figures in work on understanding national cultural differences,[K] leadership,[L] teamwork,[M] organizational culture,[N] strategic styles,[O] debates on whether strategy is planned or emergent,[P] organizational flexibility,[Q] diffusion of innovation,[R] the firm-level implications of strategic similarity,[S] and strategic renewal.[T]

Many popular management books in the last two decades have also highlighted duality issues. Peters and Waterman suggested that "excellent" companies have learned how to manage paradox, possessing both loose and tight properties, a "soft" concern for people and a "hard" bias for action, both entrepreneurship and focus.[U] Similar concepts were introduced by Handy[V] and others.[W]

[A]Bateson, 1972.

[B]Evans and Doz, 1992.

[C]Quinn and Cameron, 1988.

[D]Hedberg and Starbuck, 1976.

[E]Evans and Génadry, 1998.

[F]Pascale, 1990; Brown and Eisenhardt, 1998.

[G]Quinn, Spreitze et al., 1992.

[H]Nonaka, 1988; Burgelman and Grove, 1992; Cheng and Van de Ven, 1996; Mastenbroek, 1996; Tushman and O'Reilly, 1996; Nohria and Ghoshal, 1997.

[I]March, 1991.

[J]The review of studies is found in Brown and Eisenhardt (1998), while the citation is from Ilinitich et al. (1996, p. 214).

[K]Hampden-Turner and Trompenaars, 1993; Trompenaars, 1993, and notably Hampden-Turner and Trompenaars, 2000.

[L]Kets de Vries and Miller, 1984.

[M]Belbin, 1981; Smith and Berg, 1987; Katzenbach and Smith, 1993.

[N]Goffee and Jones, 1998.

[O]Goold and Campbell, 1987.

[P]Mintzberg and Waters, 1985.

[Q]Bahrami, 1992; Volberda, 1998.

[R]Zbaracki, 1998.

[S]Deephouse, 1999.

[T]Baden-Fuller and Volberda, 1997.

[U]Peters and Waterman, 1982.

[V]Handy, 1994.

[W]Cannon, 1996; Price Waterhouse Change Integration Team, 1996; McKenzie, 1996; Fletcher and Olwyler, 1997.

FIGURE 2–4. Some of the Dualities Confronting Organizations

---

managing today's assets — building tomorrow's assets
satisfying customer needs — being ahead of the customer
short term — long term
exploitation — exploration

competition — partnership

low cost — high value-added

differentiation — integration
decentralization — centralization
unit performance — corporate integration
individual accountability — team responsibility

loose — tight
opportunistic — planned
entrepreneurship — control/accountability
flexibility — efficiency

change — continuity
speed of responsiveness — care in implementation

professional — generalist
technical logic — business logic

taking risks — avoiding failures

task orientation — people orientation

It is the pace of change that has recently highlighted these paradoxical features of organization. In the past, dualities expressed themselves as leisurely swings of the proverbial pendulum.[91] On the wider ideological stage, the Lincoln duality expressed itself in swings between "hard" rationalism and "soft" human involvement, as noted earlier.[92] There was the ebb and flow of centralization and decentralization, there were long periods of evolution within an existing product life cycle alternating with short periods of revolutionary crisis when the technology changed.[93] A manager could work for an entire career in an organization without experiencing a swing in this pendulum.

Fueled by the pressures of globalization, these pendulum swings have become more frequent as competition compresses time frames.[94] As product life cycles speed up, as swings between undercapacity and overcapacity shorten, so speed of responsiveness becomes vital. This is reflected in changing organizational structures—the life cycle of a division at Hewlett-Packard is now less than three years before its charter and resource base are renegotiated.

The pendulum swings from one opposite to the other, from centralization to decentralization, from managing growth to managing decline, not just within the course of a career but often within the cycle of a single job. The oscillations become visible as dualities, and the limits of fit theory become apparent. Whereas the notion of fit may allow us to capture the match with a specific context at a particular point in time, duality theory recognizes that this context is likely to change in predictable ways in the future. Since organizational realignment may take considerable time, as discussed in the previous section, that change must be anticipated. *The future must be built into the present.*

Opposing forces such as differentiation and integration, external and internal orientation, hierarchy and network, short term and long term, planning and opportunity, rational analysis and human involvement, change and continuity can never be reconciled once and for all. They create *tensions* that the navigator must anticipate and manage.[95] The navigator or helmsman on a yacht is a useful metaphor for understanding such tensions.[96] The navigator is one who steers the vessel through continuous change. The job of the navigator at the helm is to manage a constant but varying tension between the need to maintain a particular course and the changing winds and currents. Steered by a skilled navigator, the path of the boat toward its destination is a series of controlled zigzags according to wind and current. The unskilled helmsman fights to maintain a course, overcorrecting the path when the boat is blown off route, failing to anticipate the storms and calms that lie ahead. The resulting path is a series of excessive pendulum zigzags as the boat sails from crisis to crisis.

Charles Hampden Turner, one of the pioneers of duality theory (or dilemma theory as he calls it) shows how this can lead to virtuous or vicious circles of organizational development.[97] Most firms have to steer between opposing forces such as functional excellence and interfunctional coordination, low cost and high flexibility, mass and niche marketing. Some firms focus on a fixed strategy, for example, aligning the firm around the development of functional excellence. This might lead to initial success. But when that success is threatened by opposing pressures (for example, slow decision-making caused by lack of coordination among functions), the leaders often respond by reinforcing what led them to be successful in the first place, increasing the pressure for functional excellence. In the extreme, this leads to a vicious circle of threat, reinforced efforts, and further threat, culminating in crisis. In contrast, the leaders of other firms appear to anticipate the need for a change in course, gently steering specialized functions toward greater teamwork before the problems of slow decision-making show up. Alternating between one course and the other, they steer toward their aims of higher profits and better return on investments in a virtuous spiral of increasing capabilities in *both* functional excellence *and* integrated teamwork. We have called this process of capability development "sequenced layering."[98]

Dualities and Transnational Management

Understanding dualities is a cornerstone for effective transnational management since the defining characteristic of the transnational enterprise is its capacity to steer between the contradictions that it confronts. As Ghoshal and Bartlett put it:

> [M]anagers in most worldwide companies recognize the need for simultaneously achieving global efficiency, national responsiveness, and the ability to develop and exploit knowledge on a worldwide basis. Some, however, regard the goal as inherently unattainable. Perceiving irreconcilable contradictions among the three objectives, they opt to focus on one of them, at least temporarily. The transnational company is one that overcomes these contradictions.[99]

Thus the duality perspective that lies behind this third face of HRM goes hand in hand with the management of the transnational enterprise—or rather the *steering* of the transnational firm.

There are two particular dualities confronting the transnational enterprise that we will highlight in this book—the duality of local responsiveness versus global integration, and that of resource leverage versus resource development.[100]

Centralization-Decentralization : The Local Responsiveness–Global Integration Duality

Many firms decentralize responsibilities to their subsidiaries and local business units. Decentralization is very powerful. It has many advantages—being close to customers, a heightened sense of accountability, more local innovation and entrepreneurship, better employee morale. The trouble is that decentralization has a shadow side. After initial success, it often leads to reinventing the wheel, the not-invented-here syndrome, duplication of back office functions, slowness in responding to technology change, difficulties in dealing with matrix pressures, lack of shared resources to respond to emerging needs. These "handmaidens of decentralization," as Bartlett and Ghoshal have called them, often lead firms to swing the pendulum back to centralization, until bureaucracy, loss of responsiveness, and the inability to retain good people swings the pendulum again to decentralization.

After several swings of the pendulum, organizations begin to realize that decentralization (local autonomy) and centralization (global integration) are a duality. Even though there may be an immediate advantage to, for example, local responsiveness, it is necessary to anticipate a future swing in the pendulum. One executive expressed this in terms of advice to senior management: "Organize one way, manage the other way." If the structure is currently being decentralized, the focus of senior management attention should be on building coordination linkages across the units. If the structure is centralized, the focus of attention is on preventing the loss of local entrepreneurship. An example of the latter is a recent worldwide recentralization at Otis Elevators. There were too many plants and engineering units around the world, and it was necessary to recentralize so as to close plants and develop a more rational structure for engineering. But Otis recognized that the centralized reorganization must be undertaken in such a way as to redecentralize responsibilities smoothly to local units after the restructuring, appointing as leader of the change process a person with a strong international sales background.

All firms maintain corporate integration through rules, central procedures and planning, and hierarchy. But as the needs for integration grow, more rules, more control, and more bosses at the center simply will not work, but instead will only kill local entrepreneurship and drive away good people. So these classic tools need to be complemented with more informal mechanisms for coordination: lateral relationships, best practice transfer, project management, leadership development, shared frameworks, and the socialization of recruits into shared values. These tools of "glue technology," as we call them, are to a large degree the application of human resource management.

This changes the roles of local leaders, who while acting as local entrepreneurs also need to have a clear understanding of global strategy. Strategic management becomes a process that involves all key leaders around the world, and local managers need to have a global mind-set. The role of people in central staff positions, including corporate HR, is not to tell local people what to do or to solve their problems for them, for this would be incompatible with needs for local autonomy. Instead, central staff must act as network leaders, getting people together to face up to common problems.

These challenges are of crucial relevance to HRM, and they will be discussed at greater length in Part III of this book.

The Failure of Success : Leveraging versus Developing Resources

Around 1980 Peters and Waterman studied the best companies in the United States as a way of figuring out how to respond to the Japanese challenge. Their book *In Search of Excellence* remains the biggest management best-seller of all time. However, eleven years later in 1991, all but a few of these 50 firms were performing below their industry averages. Some of them like IBM, the bluest of the blue league a decade before, were now in the throes of crisis.[101]

This illustrates a now well recognized phenomenon with which the transnational must also cope, called the "failure of success." Put simply, it says that the more successful you are, the higher the probability that necessary changes will happen only through crisis. Success creates complacency, arrogance, and obstacles to innovation and change. Unless they recognize dualistic logic, success pushes firms to take what led them to be successful in the first place to the pathological extreme.

Miller describes this as the "Icarus phenomenon," referring to the Greek myth of Icarus who having learned how to fly got carried away by the success. He soared across the Aegean Sea, only to have the wax holding his wings melt, plunging to his death.[102] The rise and fall of corporations such as ITT, Litton, and A&P (as well as the crises at firms such as IBM and TI) illustrates how outstanding firms will extend their orientations until they reach dangerous extremes, with increasing momentum that ultimately leads to trajectories of decline. Miller maps out four success strategies: the focused Craftsman (with a single-minded orientation on cost leadership (TI) or quality (Digital)); the venturing Builder (ITT, Dome); the inventive Pioneer (Apple); and the Salesman with genius in marketing and image management (IBM, P&G).

Each of these corporations brilliantly executed an appropriate strategy, developing a distinctive competence that propelled their initial success. But when the winds began to change and that success came under threat, their steersmen or women intensified the focus on that capability rather than turning to develop complementary strengths. The cost leadership of the Craftsman becomes miserly obsession that drives away any talent in marketing or design. Quality focus becomes worship of irrelevant engineering standards. Admiration for the diversified empire of the Builder fosters reckless expansion. The Pioneer becomes an escapist who is mesmerized by the game itself, and the Salesman becomes a drifter with image replacing substance. As the vicious circle accelerates, pride gradually becomes obsession, focus becomes machinelike order with the suppression of any dissent, strategy becomes recipe, leading to a polarization that is associated with impending crisis.

Behind this "failure of success" paradox lies another duality that is becoming important in our accelerating world. Firms have to *leverage their existing resources* so as to make profits today, and at the same time *develop new resources* that will be the source of their profits tomorrow. Leverage (called *exploitation* by academics) involves the concern for efficiency, execution, production, and short-term success, but excessive focus leads to the failure of success. Resource development (or *exploration*) involves innovation, learning, risk-taking, experimentation, and focus on long-term success.[103] However, an excessive focus on development is risky, compromising the survival of the firm. Indeed, the duality behind resource leverage and development is at the heart of the resource-based view of the firm.[104] While the transnational firm faces the local-global dilemma, it also faces this leverage-development dilemma.

Some firms grow internationally via *leverage strategies*. They exploit capabilities developed at home through export pipelines to new markets. Growth through wholly owned subsidiaries is preferred since control is maintained, maximizing leverage and maintaining a hold on core competences. Other firms may expand internationally for a period of time via *learning strategies* to develop new know-how, typically involving joint ventures and other forms of alliance. A historic example that we will meet in a later chapter is the expansion of Japanese firms into the United States from 1976–89 through carefully selected joint ventures in which they could initially learn the U.S. market but later acquire the control necessary for leverage.[105] Currently, many Internet-based firms must develop their capabilities in global markets from the outset, using such global learning strategies. The *transnational strategy* involves managing both leverage and development, resolving the potential contradictions.[106] Indeed one of its hallmarks is the capacity to leverage the learning that comes from its local subsidiaries. This is particularly true of technology intensive firms that must exploit global markets so as to recover the massive investments that they make in products and technologies with short life cycles.

We will meet many other dualities in this book—the competition versus partnership duality underlying alliances, the need for change versus the continuity that execution requires, teamwork versus accountability. This perspective allows us to understand many of the management challenges of the transnational organization.

Duality and Organizational Longevity

Let us end our discussion of the third face of HRM by pointing to work on organizational longevity by Porras and Collins.[107] They were interested in what is special about organizations that appear to be "built to last." Many firms do well under a particular leader or in one product life cycle, only to head for crisis after the succession or change in product life cycle. Only a few seem to have enduring properties.

The researchers selected eighteen enterprises founded before 1950 with such enduring characteristics, enterprises which were also widely admired and which had left an indelible imprint on our world. These were compared to a group of solid competitors which had not shown the same resilience to shocks and changes. So 3M was paired with Norton Abrasives, General Electric with Westinghouse, Hewlett-Packard with Texas Instruments, Sony with Kenwood, Marriott Hotels with Howard Johnson. The latter "bronze medal" firms had outperformed the stock market over a 65-year period by a factor of two-to-one, while the enduring "gold medal" companies had outperformed the market by twelve-to-one.

The comparison exploded a number of popular myths, such as the belief that it takes great charismatic leadership to build a great company (some leaders were, but many were not). The overriding feature of the enduring companies in contrast with those in the bronze medal category was their ability to thrive on paradox, the way in which duality characterized their cultures. On the one hand, strong corporate philosophies impregnated their cultures, providing the consistency we discussed earlier. On the other hand, they pragmatically pursued profit and financial goals as necessary for survival. Visionary thinking was combined with superb attention to nuts-and-bolts execution; bold long-term investments went hand in hand with strong demands for short-term performance on the part of their staff. The managers promoted were steeped in the core values, yet they handled succession by selecting those who would induce necessary change.

L'Oréal is another of those enduring companies, founded well over a hundred years ago. The world's leading firm in the toughly competitive cosmetics industry, l'Oréal is the most consistently profitable corporation in France. It is also a company that recognizes the importance of duality and tension. Its culture is based on the foresighted values of the founding family last century, "Etre poête et paysan en même temps"—to be the passionate and creative poet, and at the same time the conservative peasant who dislikes risk and counts the last centimes. The belief that growth and profits will come if creativity can be combined with sound financial management manifests itself in practices of tension management. Reminiscent of King Arthur's Round Table, l'Oréal uses "confrontation rooms" where all parties can gather around the table to freely argue about important decisions, such as the launch of a new product. Like GE's Jack Welch, l'Oréal managers believe that the only way of making sound decisions in a world of dualities is through constructive conflict.

L'Oréal recognizes that one of the most important tensions to manage is the short-term bottom line versus long-term development. It is not easy. There is a natural tendency in decision-making to privilege the short term since it is so immediate and concrete. This hurts many companies in the area of people development. Faced with an immediate profit squeeze, the budgetary valve on recruitment, training, and team development is turned off. Consequently the major constraint in boom times later is that there are no skilled people in the pipeline to exploit those opportunities. Similarly, local business unit managers are tempted to cling to their best people for the sake of today's results rather than releasing them to other units—even though the longer-term price may be that these people ultimately get bored at lack of opportunity and leave to seek challenges elsewhere.

There are no magic policies that will resolve such dilemmas. Since the short term typically drives out the long term, the role of the human resource function at l'Oréal is to act as the guardians of the strategic and long-term perspectives, especially concerning decisions about recruitment, promotion, and the development of people. This is recognized by all. But it does not give HR the right of veto, waving some policy blue book. It gives them the right to stop the music, to say, "Time out folks! Let's look at the long-term arguments before we decide." Sometimes the decision may favor the short term, sometimes the long term, and sometimes a creative solution favoring both may be found.

Take another international corporation that satisfies the "built-to-last" criteria. The A.P. Møller Group is a Fortune 100 company that is indisputably Denmark's leading and most admired corporation. It is arguably the leading shipping company in the world, in container transport, shipbuilding and chartering, and it has a broad line of industrial and consumer businesses. The company is family owned, and Mr. Maersk McKinney Møller, the son of the founder and now aged 88, is Denmark's most influential businessman.

The Human Resource vice president for the Group recalls how the firm experienced a conflict between short- and long-term interests. A few years ago, he was under pressure from the business heads at a time of recession to halt the graduate recruitment and training program. Since the owner of the company keeps a close eye on such matters, he went to Mr. Møller with the request. "It was embarrassing," he said. "A look of horror went across the face of Mr. Møller. 'Don't people understand how you make money? Because of the recession, everyone will be cutting back on training and recruitment. We are *not* going to do that, we are going to recruit and train with more care than ever before! This means that we will be the only firm in the business seven years from now to profit from the boom times that certainly lie ahead!' "

Managing Context

In one enduring firm, Hewlett-Packard, the founders note that they wrestled for decades with the issue of making their management philosophy explicit. "We thought that if we could get everybody to agree on what our objectives were and to understand what we were trying to do, then we could turn them loose and they would move in a common direction," said David Packard.[108] The result of their reflections developed gradually to become "the HP Way."

The same idea applies more than ever to the transnational corporation, in which it is impossible to control the employees spread across the world who have to respond to constant change. More and more scholars view institutional leadership as the task of creating a context in which desired behaviors are more likely to occur. This is particularly clear when it comes to innovation and value creation. The idea of commanding or ordering innovation makes no sense whatsoever. All one can do is create a context in which people are more likely to behave in innovative ways.

An alternative metaphor for the navigator would therefore be that of the *social architect,* responsible for the management of this context. If the hallmark of the transnational organization is contradiction, this implies that a deep understanding of duality should guide the architect. When the structure of the firm is built to foster decentralized initiative, this has to be counterbalanced with close management attention to the needs for coordination across boundaries. Challenging stretch goals go hand in hand with know-how sharing so as to generate the means to attain them. A culture of experimentation and networks needs to be combined with the discipline and focus that come from rigorous performance management and shared values (what is known as normative integration). Short-term operational focus needs to be combined with longer-term focus on change and improvement projects. And so on. It is through the design of context that institutional leaders steer the firm. We will be meeting many examples of dualistic context management in this book.

LEARNING HOW TO WORK IN "SPLIT EGG" WAYS

Duality thinking brings temporal dynamics and the concept of time onto the center stage of management and organization. The conflict between the needs of today and the different needs of tomorrow is becoming one of the fundamental dilemmas of leadership. Today's needs for internal consistency have to be met at the same time as one attends to tomorrow's needs for realignment. The operating results of this year's local business plan have to be pursued at the same time as wider and longer-term global priorities.

Over the years, there has been an important change in the way that these dilemmas get worked through. Instead of building the dilemma into the structure of the organization through matrix, today it gets built into the role of the individual manager. In the past, the traditional line-staff organization met these conflicting temporal needs through the structural separation of responsibilities. The focus of line managers and employees out in the business units was operational. Their attention was centered on local targets and budgetary constraints that invariably had a one-year time horizon. The responsibility for long-term change and development lay with senior leaders and their staff at corporate headquarters. These staff people were responsible for such change projects, typically global in nature: externally oriented projects such as strategic planning and business development; internally oriented projects such as cost reduction and the introduction of new IT systems; and lateral projects such as best practice transfer or new product development. This was judged to be the natural order of things. Research on "the time span of discretion" (maximum target completion time in a job) showed that department heads and senior professionals had a one-year horizon, whereas corporate vice presidents or heads of global functions had a five-year horizon.[109]

However, the neat distinction between line people out in the units responsible for annual operations and staff people at headquarters responsible for longer-term development created a bureaucracy in which much fell into the cracks between the two. Some of the difficulties in managing realignment stemmed from this structural separation—the responsibility for planning change lay with people who were not responsible for the implementation of those changes. At the time of writing, the authors are working with one major international firm at which senior management does not want managers at the subsidiary level to worry about the need for change since this will distract them from their focus on delivering the operating results. Top management and its staff views its role as figuring out the strategic problems and coming up with solutions that are then announced and implemented in the shape of new policies. Ten years ago, new policies were issued to meet the needs for a more international management profile, to respond to cross-border client pressures, and to speed up decision-making. However, the management team is forced today to recognize that little has changed during the past decade. New people who were brought in from the outside as part of the change have nearly all left the organization.

As we saw in the previous chapter, what started to happen in the early 1980s was a cutback in corporate staff functions and decentralization of responsibilities to the line, initially driven by the competitive need to cut costs but increasingly by the need to become more responsive. In a world of accelerating change and competition, however, the long-term project needs for change and realignment were not disappearing; they were growing exponentially. A healthy response was to deal with this duality in a different way, through managerial roles rather than through the structure. The responsibility for change was added to the operational responsibilities of the manager. The local manager in the business unit now had two roles, operational and project, as shown in the matrixed "split egg" in Figure 2–5. The local manager is now expected to spend, say, 30 percent of his or her time or work on change or improvement projects with a longer-term development perspective.

This was not a radically new role concept (McKinsey used the metaphor of the T-shaped manager back in the 1970s).[110] In most firms, it had always applied to high potential managers who were expected both to deliver on their operational targets and to earn visibility by working on broader development projects. Many organizations would sanction people if they did not meet their operational targets, but people would be promoted only if they showed leadership ability in the project role.[111] This concept is now being extended to all managerial and professional staff.

The split egg concept builds the responsibility for *both* short-term and long-term results, for solid foundations *and* for change, into the role of all professionals, and thereby into the whole organization and its culture. Conceptual differences between "management" and "leadership" start breaking down. The person is expected to be both an effective manager—doing things right in the operational role—and an effective leader—doing the right things in the project role. The former is built into the job description or organized through performance management. The latter requires initiative, guided by the long-term strategic priorities of the firm. The duality is managed at the interface between the two roles (shown by the wavy line in the middle of the "egg" in Figure 2–5), leading to a process of continuous improvement and change.

The split egg role actually beefs up the quality of HRM foundations. How do you free up 30 or 40 percent of your time for project initiatives when you are also accountable for delivering on tough operational targets? Having good people to whom you can delegate becomes a matter of personal survival. Line managers learn to pay rigorous attention to getting the right people into the right places, and to the negotiation of performance objectives, in their own interests. In short, they learn that one of their most important tasks is human resource management. Paradoxically, attention to basic foundations is strengthened when managers come under pressure to work in split egg ways.

FIGURE 2–5. The Matrixed "Split Egg" Role of the Manager

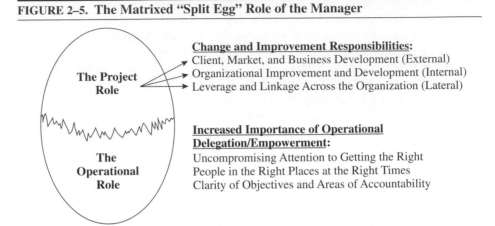

Change and Improvement Responsibilities:
Client, Market, and Business Development (External)
Organizational Improvement and Development (Internal)
Leverage and Linkage Across the Organization (Lateral)

Increased Importance of Operational Delegation/Empowerment:
Uncompromising Attention to Getting the Right People in the Right Places at the Right Times
Clarity of Objectives and Areas of Accountability

The same reasoning applies to professional human resource managers. The operational and custodial tasks of recruitment and selection, training and development, and performance management do not go away. They are the bottom of the egg. But the top of the egg, which tends to be more fulfilling as well as leading to rewards and promotion, is the project role—that of acting as a partner in the management of change.

Most managers today clearly recognize this split egg or matrixed role. In effective firms in fast moving environments, we find that virtually all leaders, managers, and high level professionals see themselves as working in this manner. In more stable environments, in which there are fewer competitive pressures, it is only a few people who work in this way, typically those in key leadership positions and some others with leadership potential.

Simple as it may be, this split egg role concept is fundamental for the international firm. For example, managers, and professionals are expected to be local and entrepreneurial in their operational roles, but by working on cross-boundary teams in their project role they are closely involved in the broader global challenges. Corporate staff roles shift from being providers of policies and solutions to being network leaders, roping in individuals with the appropriate expertise from around the world to work on coordination or change projects. As we will discuss in Part III of the book, working in split egg ways is one of the key mechanisms that help the transnational firm to meet the conflicting needs of local responsiveness and global integration.

TAKEAWAYS

1. HRM contributes to organizational performance in three different ways: through sound functional basics; through effective realignment when the external environment changes; and by building an organizational context so that the organization can cope with the dualistic forces that it confronts.

2. The theoretical perspective behind the builder role is that of internal fit and consistency. The perspective behind the change partner role is that of external fit (associated with strategic HRM). The perspective behind the navigator role is that of duality or paradox theory.

3. There are dangers of getting stuck in specific HR roles. Builders may become administrative custodians, losing the business credibility that is necessary to act as a change partner. Change partners may neglect the importance of internal consistency and solid foundations.

4. The universalist model of HRM, maintaining that certain practices are universally associated with high performance, is not realistic. However, there is evidence that companies who adopt certain configurations, such as that of "high commitment" or "high performing" practices, have better financial returns.

5. There are many potential influences on a firm's approach to HRM as it expands internationally—the influences of the mother country, the company's culture, the local country, and other multinational corporations. To maintain consistency, firms tend to adopt one of two polar strategies in HR, either global integration or local responsiveness. Transnational pressures, however, may threaten such strategies.

6. One of the ways in which HRM contributes to organizational performance is in helping the firm to adjust to environmental change and to implement new strategies. However, since change involves realignment or reconfiguration, this often takes much more time (continuity) than people expect.

7. An important aspect of the realignment process is open constructive debate on the nature of the problems or opportunities and the intended goals—a difficult task in many cultures.

8. Organizational effectiveness is inherently paradoxical, requiring opposing capabilities. In the fast moving, complex, and competitive environments facing most international firms, the future has to be built into the present by managing the context.

9. Two dualities of particular concern to the transnational firm are centralization versus decentralization (reflecting the global-local dilemma), and resource leverage versus resource development (often known also as exploitation versus exploration).

10. One of the underlying challenges of realignment is managing long-term change while facing short-term operational pressures. Integrating this duality into individual roles in the form of "split egg" responsibilities is more effective than structures of line and staff responsibilities.

NOTES

1. Berg and Fast, 1983; Hastings, 1999; Bartlett and O'Connell, 1998.
2. Lincoln Electric learned its lessons and was again enjoying record profits by the late 1990s, as described by Björkman and Galunic (1999), continuing to expand abroad, but more cautiously.
3. Pfeffer, 1998.

4. Sparrow and Hiltrop, 1994; Brewster and Hegewisch, 1994.
5. See Evans and Farquhar (1986) for an account of the difficulties that Marks & Spencer faced when they expanded internationally to Europe and North America.
6. Bartlett and Yoshihara (1988) argue that once-lauded Japanese HRM practices have become the Achilles heel of Japanese management. See also Porter, Takeuchi, and Sakakibara (2000).
7. Many readers will be familiar with David Ulrich's so-called Four Box Framework (Ulrich, 1997), a framework that matches well the results of our own research. Ulrich's operational roles of the "administrative expert" and the "employee champion" are directly equivalent to what we call the Builder role. His strategic/long term roles of the "strategic partner" and the "change agent" are also equivalent to our Change Partner role. However, the Navigator role does not feature in Ulrich's framework.

   There are also some similarities (and some important differences) between our three face framework and that of Tyson and Fell (1986). Their focus is more on functional personnel management, with a typology consisting of three roles, that of the clerk of works, the contract manager, and the architect.
8. Among the many good basic personnel and HRM textbooks are Torrington and Hall (1995); Milkovich and Boudreau (1997); Jackson and Schuler (1999); and Noe, Hollenbeck et al., 1999.
9. Evans and Bartolomé 1979; Bartolomé and Evans, 1980.
10. See Baron and Kreps (1999) for a detailed discussion of the importance of consistency between HR practices, notably chapter 3.
11. One example is a collection of studies by British researchers on employee experiences of HRM (Mabey, Skinner, and Clark, 1998). A reviewer commented on how these studies show that HRM fails to live up to its rhetoric, showing that employee attitudes are negatively affected by an inconsistent mix of policies (Bacon, 1999).
12. Researchers should note however that "fit" can be operationalized in different ways—as moderation between two variables, as matching, as gestalts, as covariation, etc. See Venkatraman (1989), and Wright and Sherman (1999).
13. For details on the evolution of Lincoln Electric's approach to HRM, see Berg and Fast (1983), Björkman and Galunic (1999).
14. Beer, Spector et al., 1984. Another interesting framework looks at how approaches to career and development management vary with the nature of the internal labor market, mapping out four models called, respectively, clubs, fortresses, academies, and baseball teams (Sonnenfeld and Peiperl, 1988).
15. Evans and Farquhar, 1986.
16. This does not invalidate appropriate use of benchmarking. As Ellen Glanz from Digital put it, "Benchmarking for us was most useful when it was understood as a vehicle to see 'outside the box.' We learned that there was no one right answer, but many approaches that might work. And we learned the value of balance and duality—strengths when carried to the extreme might turn to weaknesses" (Glanz and Bailey, 1993, p. 15).
17. This issue is the focus in Chapter 4 of this book.
18. Whitfield and Poole, 1997; see also Godard and Delaney (2000) for a review from an industrial relations perspective. See Clark and Mallory (1996) for a particularly critical contextualist stance.
19. See the next section "The International Context." The cultural and institutionalist relativist arguments are discussed further in Chapter 4.
20. Lawler, 1992; Huselid, 1995; Neal and Tromley, 1995; Pfeffer, 1998.
21. The term "high performance management" is used by Nadler and Tushman (1988) as well as by Huselid and Pfeffer (discussed in the text), while Lawler calls this "high involve-

ment management" (Lawler, 1992). Arthur (1994), Neal and Tromley (1995), Baron and Kreps (1999), and Purcell (1999) refer to "high commitment work approaches," while Osterman (1994) and MacDuffie (1995) speak of flexible work systems. See Becker and Gerhart (1996) for a comparison of different definitions of high performance. See also Dyer and Reeves (1995) for a review of different configurations of HPWS. For reviews, see Whitfield and Poole (1997), Varma, Beatty et al. (1999); and Godard and Delaney (2000)—the latter two written from a more critical perspective.

22. Huselid, 1995; Huselid, Jackson, and Schuler, 1997; Becker, Huselid et al., 1997.

23. Huselid and Becker also found that sales per employee increased by more than $27,000 for each standard deviation in the use of high performance work practices. Overall, consider a firm with 10,000 employees that is quite sophisticated in selection, training, and performance management, scoring say two standard deviations higher than its competitor. One would expect it to be making $80 million more in annual profits, with a superior market capitalization in the order of $360 million.

24. See Pfeffer, 1998; Pfeffer, 1994. The seven dimensions are (1) highly selective hiring of new personnel; (2) focus on skill development and extensive training; (3) use of self-managed teams and decentralization of decision making; (4) reduced status distinctions and barriers (including dress, language, office arrangements, and wage differentials); (5) employment security (to retain those skills); (6) comparatively high compensation contingent on organizational performance (also to retain those skills); (7) extensive sharing of financial and performance information throughout the organization.

25. Delery and Doty, 1996. It should be added that they also found empirical support for the contingency and configurational hypotheses underlying our second face of HRM, as well as for the universalist hypothesis.

26. MacDuffie, 1995; Welbourne and Andrews, 1996; Arthur, 1994; Youndt, Snell et al., 1996. See Gerhart (1999) for a critical review of this research; also Delery and Doty (1996) and Varma, Beatty et al. (1999).

27. See references in note 18, especially Clark and Mallory (1996) for a critical contextualist stance to the debate. Contextualists also question the causality—successful companies may adopt HPWS, though this may not have been what led them to be successful in the first place (Purcell, 1999).

28. Driven by globalization and the need to restructure after the Asian crisis, Korean firms are introducing what they call "new human resource management" systems that emphasize teams, employee empowerment, performance-based evaluation and pay, and selective recruitment (Bae, 1997; Ungson, Steers, and Park, 1997).

29. Bae and Lawler, 2000. This study included Korean-owned firms as well as subsidiaries of American, European, and Japananese multinationals.

30. See Ngo, Turban, Lau, and Lui (1998) for a study of the link between some elements of HPWS and firm performance in Hong Kong. Bae and Lawler (2000) report similar unpublished studies claiming that this also applies to India and Taiwan.

31. Using empirical data from other studies, Dyer and Reeves (1995) argue that there may be different configurations of HPWS in different settings. Yet the difficulties of modeling and testing all the configurations and contingencies have been noted by many including Boxall (1992) and Purcell (1999).

32. As most empirical studies on the financial returns of HPWS note, it is notoriously difficult to evaluate firm performance—especially given the fact that the concept of firm performance itself may vary from one culture to another (see Redding, 2001; and our discussion in Chapter 4). Large-scale databases are also needed (Purcell, 1999).

33. Cappelli and Crocker-Hefter, 1996.

34. Most researchers would accept the contingency hypothesis to some degree. Studies in various cultural settings have examined the contingency hypothesis that HPWS are associated with firm performance when the strategy is one of market differentiation, though with mixed results (see Bae and Lawler, 2000, for a summary of these studies).

35. One of the important research questions raised by the internal fit or consistency perspective is whether there are identifiable configurations between the different elements. It is possible that configurational fit is equally or more important than contingency fit between an organization and its environment, though perhaps within certain limits. In other words, is "internal fit" more important than "external fit"?

    According to contingency theory, beverages and retailing are viewed as environments in which locally responsive strategies will be most appropriate (Nohria and Ghoshal, 1997). However, as discussed in Chapter 1, one can contrast the more global approach of Heineken with the local approach of Interbrew in beverages, and the global approach of Wal-Mart with the local approach of Ahold in retailing—all four companies being highly successful in performance terms, also having organizations and HR approaches that are consistent with their different strategies. From a theoretical perspective, we would expect the highest performing firms to demonstrate both strong internal and external fit.

    The issue of configuration is not a new question—the sociologist Durkheim distinguished between organizations built around Gesellschaft (the rational division of labor) and Gemeinschaft (common values), with parallels in the latter distinction between mechanistic and organic organizational forms (Burns and Stalker, 1961). Other well-known configurational studies are Mintzberg (1979) (distinguishing between the machine bureaucracy, the professional bureaucracy, divisionalized form, and the adhocracy); Ouchi (1981) (bureaucracy, market, and clan organizations); Miller (Miller, 1996; Miller and Whitney, 1999) (pioneer, salesman, and craftsman configurations); and Miles and Snow (1978) (whose strategic posture configurations of the prospector, defender, and analyzer have been quite widely used by researchers exploring the link between strategy and HRM).

    The study of Delery and Doty investigating evidence for universalistic, contingency, and configuration predictions of performance found evidence for the fact that appropriate configurations lead to higher performance, even though this was more difficult to measure than the hypothesis that certain practices lead universally to better performance. See also Dyer and Reeves (1995).

36. Baron and Kreps are studying configurations in emerging young enterprises such as high tech start-ups, based explicitly on HR-oriented dimensions of attachment, selection, and coordination/control (Baron and Kreps, 1999, chapter 19). They identified five ideal type configurations, called respectively the Engineering, Commitment, Star, Bureaucracy and Autocracy models.

    Concerning the Commitment model, there were two tentative but provocative findings. First, firms founded by CEOs with a high commitment philosophy formalized their HR approach earlier and were subsequently able to economize on HR bureaucracy and administrative overhead. This supports the HPWS argument that there may be long-term advantages to the approach. However, they found that high commitment blueprints were never switched to or adopted after the founding of the company—thereby raising a new question as to whether it is possible to move a firm in this direction unless the values were part of the founding philosophy.

37. For Europe, see Sparrow and Hiltrop (1994), Brewster and Hegewisch (1994); for Asia, see Moore and Devereaux Jennings (1995); Rowley (1998).

38. O'Hara-Devereaux and Johansen, 1994.

39. Mueller, 1994; Ferner and Quintanilla, 1998.

40. Loveridge, 1990.
41. Guest and Hoque, 1996. See Bae, Chen, and Lawler (1998) for a study of American, European, Korean, Japanese, and Taiwanese firms operating in Hong Kong that strongly supports the country-of-origin hypothesis.
42. Hofstede, 1980a; Hofstede, 1980b. This is discussed in Chapter 4.
43. Autio, Sapienza, and Almeida (2000). See also Barkema and Vermeulen (1999).
44. See the earlier note 35 on configurational research.
45. For the substance of the argument that organizations are moving from job-based to competence-based approaches, see Lawler (1994).
46. See the essays in Ulrich, Losey, and Lake, 1997.
47. Purcell, 1999.
48. Ulrich, Zenger, and Smallwood, 1999, p. vii.
49. Meshoulam and Baird, 1987; Lengnick-Hall and Lengnick-Hall, 1988. Sometimes internal fit or consistency is called "horizontal fit" while external fit is known as "vertical fit" (Wright and McMahon, 1992).
50. Becker, Huselid et al., 1997; Huselid, Jackson, and Schuler, 1997. This is their interpretation of correlational data between investment in HR and financial performance. With increasing investment in HPWS there is an initial yield which then levels off, increasing later with further investment (interpreted as HR investment in strategic alignment).
51. See Chapter 1 for a brief history of "strategic human resource management." See also Chadwick and Cappelli (1999) for a useful review.
52. Porter, 1980.
53. Miles and Snow, 1978.
54. As outlined in greater detail by Schuler and Jackson (1987).
55. See Legge (1995, chapter 4) for a critical review of these studies. One banking study referred to earlier that found support for the universalist proposition also found evidence for the idea that firm performance also depends on the linkage between strategy and HR practices (Delery and Doty, 1996).
56. Porter, 1996.
57. MacDuffie, 1995. See also the analysis of Ichniowski, Shaw, and Prennushi (1997) on the effect of HR practices on productivity in the steel industry. This concept of capability is discussed further in Chapter 9, where we discuss how capabilities can be transferred from one country to another.
58. Becker, Huselid et al., 1997, p. 230.
59. The reader who is interested in understanding more about the importance of fit and coherence should consult Baron and Kreps (1999) for a good analysis.
60. We talk of "realignment" rather than "alignment." The word "alignment" captures only one part of the picture (where one wants to go), it does not capture the other half, namely the fact that one is coming from a different place.
61. Gratton, 2000.
62. Ulrich, 1997.
63. Conner and Ulrich, 1996.
64. For a British study on devolution of personnel activities and references to the literature, see Hall and Torrington (1998). The philosophy of Texas Instruments, radical at the time, is described by Scott Myers (1970).
65. Walker, 1980; Fombrun, Tichy, and Devanna, 1984; Schuler and MacMillan, 1984.
66. Dyer, 1984.
67. Golden and Ramanujam, 1985; Brewster and Larsen, 1992.
68. See Mintzberg, 1994.

69. Gratton, Hope-Hailey et al., 1999a; Gratton, Hope-Hailey et al., 1999b.

70. The tightness of the linkage between strategy and individual performance is measured in terms of five levels (Gratton, Hope-Hailey, et al., 1999a). At the weakest level 1, there is no clear articulation of business strategy to the individual. Discussions between individuals and their managers about performance and expectations are ad hoc, often vague, and not linked to clear objectives for the business. Needless to say, the absence of any linkage makes the management of realignment extremely difficult, if not impossible. In contrast, at the strongest level 5, the business objectives of the strategic plan are clearly articulated to individuals and teams, translated into clear objectives that are discussed and agreed upon. Processes exist to ensure that individual objectives are realigned to take account of ongoing changes in business strategy, with clear monitoring.

71. See Chapter 7. The challenges of long-term leadership are discussed in Chapter 8, while those of building the HR-line business partnership are explored in Chapter 10, with particular reference to the international firm.

72. Kakabadse, 1991; Kakabadse, 1993. Kakabadse found that 30% of British teams were divided, 34% of German teams, 39% of the French, and 46% of the Spanish teams.

73. Pettigrew, 1985.

74. See Kotter (1996).

75. Among the few researchers who have undertaken research on the HRM/change interface are Beer and Spector (Beer, Eisenstat, and Spector, 1990; Beer and Nohria, 2000) and Pettigrew and his associates (Pettigrew, 1988; Pettigrew and Whipp, 1993), as well as Tichy (1983). However, the Organizational Development movement in the 1970s focused heavily on these issues—see, for example, Beckhard and Harris (1977), and many current textbooks on OD. Other studies or books of note include Tushman, Newman, and Romanelli (1986), Levy and Merry (1986), Mohrman, Mohrman et al. (1989), Dunphy and Stace (1988); Stace and Dunphy (1991), Mintzberg and Westley (1992), Hambrick, Nadler et al. (1998); and from a more managerial perspective Kanter, Stein, and Jick (1992), Conner (1992), and Kotter (1996).

76. Gratton, 2000.

77. Mintzberg, 1974. The former group planning officer at Royal Dutch/Shell viewed the planning process as one of learning (De Geus, 1988).

78. Conner, 1992; Kotter, 1996. GE's approach (CAP or Change Acceleration Process) is discussed in Chapter 9.

79. Beer, Eisenstat, and Spector, 1990. The concept of sequencing is particularly important in managing complex strategic change processes, such as the process of change in developing transnational properties. This is discussed at length in Chapter 9.

80. See Chapter 9 in particular.

81. Evans and Lorange, 1989.

82. Wagstyl, 1997.

83. See Chapters 7 and 9.

84. Evans and Wittenberg, 1986.

85. Quinn and Rohrbaugh, 1983.

86. Evans and Doz, 1989; Evans and Doz, 1992; Evans and Génadry, 1998.

87. Quinn, 1988.

88. Hampden-Turner, 1990.

89. Mitroff and Linstone, 1993.

90. Though the concept of duality is not used, see Berg and Fast (1983), Björkman and Galunic (1999), for details. To elaborate on one aspect, the current CEO was paid $1.2 million in total in 1998, a far cry from the multimillion dollar salaries of his other U.S. counterparts. On a CBS "60 Minutes" video about Lincoln, a worker was asked what he would feel if his CEO

was to earn $50 million. The worker laughs and says that he would not mind at all—because that would mean that he himself would be earning $45 million!

91. Historians have been well aware of these swings. Indeed Arnold Toynbee's monumental *A Study of History* is built on the insight that the decline of civilizations occurs when a society goes to excesses in its success formula (Toynbee, 1946).

92. See the box "The Pendulum of Management Thought" on p. 12 in Chapter 1.

93. Greiner, 1972; Tushman and O'Reilly, 1996.

94. Stalk, 1988; Fine, 1998.

95. Evans and Génadry (1998) argue that it is tension between opposites that should be the dependent variable in organizational research.

96. Hampden-Turner, 1990.

97. Ibid.

98. Evans and Doz, 1989. Similar examples of steering are provided by Eisenhardt and Brown (Brown and Eisenhardt, 1997; Brown and Eisenhardt, 1998). They show how successful firms in fast moving industries steer between the need for semi-structures (clarity of roles, deadlines, priorities) and for improvisation (opportunism, open communication).

99. Ghoshal and Bartlett, 1998, p. 65.

100. It was awareness of the fomer duality, local-global or responsiveness-integration, that led to the development of the transnational concept, as well as earlier parallel concepts of the multifocal organization (Prahalad and Doz, 1987) and the heterarchy (Hedlund, 1986). Indeed, the notion of the heterarchy was first presented by Gunnar Hedlund at a conference to define the field of international human resource management organized by one of the authors of this book, published in a special journal issue of the proceedings.

  However, the latter duality, resource leverage–development, emerged around 1990 with resource-based views of the firm Dierickx and Cool (1989), though it was outlined earlier in economic theory by Penrose. It is also known as the exploitation-exploration duality (March, 1991), and it is implicit in all concepts of the transnational.

101. Data compiled by S. Makridakis at INSEAD show that 49 out of the 50 "excellent" firms had P/E ratios above their industry averages in 1980, but 47 of them were below that average in 1991.

102. Miller, 1990.

103. March, 1991.

104. Penrose, 1959; Dierickx and Cool, 1989.

105. Tallman and Fladmoe-Lindquist, 1999. See Chapter 5.

106. Tallman and Fladmoe-Lindquist, 1999.

107. Collins, 1994.

108. Packard, 1995, p. 80.

109. Jacques, 1989.

110. See Hansen and von Oetinger (2001) for a recent update on the T-shaped concept, applied to knowledge managers.

111. As we will discuss in Chapter 8, this sometimes led to game playing on how to get ahead. Ambitious managers would focus on their project initiatives at the expense of operational performance, getting visibility with senior corporate leaders. The name of the game was to get promoted quickly so that when the operational problems showed up the individual would have moved on—they are now someone else's responsibility!

PART 2

Strategies for International Growth

There are four strategies for going international—global integration (used by what we call the "meganational" firm), local responsiveness (the strategy of the "multidomestic" firm), joint ventures and other forms of alliances, and cross-border mergers and acquisitions—though many firms use a combination. The four chapters in Part 2 explore successively the human resource management implications of these strategies. Each chapter focuses on a particular challenge: expatriation, the influence of culture and context on HRM, partnership/learning, and human resource aspects of interorganizational integration respectively.

Building on theories of control, Chapter 3 reviews the mechanisms for ensuring global integration since most international firms are too complex for all decisions to be taken at the center. Most of these tools rely on the use of expatriate managers, so we focus on how to manage effectively the expatriation process. Framed by the different stages in the expatriate cycle (going from selection to repatriation), we present the key theories, concepts, and practices, also discussing family adjustment and dual career challenges as well as the implications of emerging trends such as impatriation and the growing number of women and younger expatriates.

Chapter 4 examines the people implications of multidomestic strategies that emphasize local responsiveness. It is often argued that HRM practices in particular should be managed in the local way, and we explore this from the angle of cultural, institutional, and network perspectives. The choices that companies face in responding to cultural and institutional diversity are discussed, along with the issue of developing and retaining local talent, which should be a key pillar of a multidomestic strategy. We close the chapter with the theme of business ethics, where doing things locally may not be the most appropriate approach.

Chapter 5 focuses on alliances as a way to tackle internationalization. We review the motives for entering an international alliance, presenting a framework that helps thinking strategically about alliances and how they may evolve over time. The success of a joint venture or other alliance depends on the alignment of HRM practices with the strategy, so we focus on the major role that HR has to play in planning and negotiating such a venture. Another significant HRM task is to enhance alliance learning, so we review the key obstacles and suggest how human resource processes can help the parent firm develop new competencies from the alliance.

An increasingly popular route to internationalization is cross-border mergers and acquisitions, discussed in Chapter 6. While the number of deals may be soaring, the track record of success is not impressive. Lack of attention to soft factors such as human resources is typically cited as a major reason. We review frameworks that help us understand the why's and how's of mergers and acquisitions, leading us to emphasize HRM's contribution to the acquisition process, from the planning and due-diligence stage to post-merger integration. Key issues requiring human resource involvement such as talent retention and management of change are explored.

CHAPTER 3

Exploiting Global Integration

Who would have anticipated even a decade ago that Nokia, a hundred-year-old Finnish company with origins in the pulp and paper business, would become the world's biggest producer of mobile phones? Today, Nokia handsets are sold in more than 150 countries, and its brand name is a symbol of status and quality among consumers worldwide. It is also one of the leading suppliers of the wireless telecommunication infrastructure for mobile operators around the world.

Nokia entered the telecom business only in 1981 when the company acquired 51 percent in the state-owned phone equipment firm. A hundred years ago the firm had been born as a pulp and paper mill on the Nokia river, later teaming up with rubber and cable companies to form one of the largest business groups in Finland, a big player in the small Finnish market that was heavily dependent on trade with the former Soviet Union. After the oil crisis of 1973, Nokia's leaders decided the company could not grow and prosper in its traditional commodity businesses, initiating a series of divestitures and acquisitions over the next twenty years. Although attempts to become a leading TV and PC manufacturer nearly bankrupted the group, the transformation gained speed when the visionary head of its mobile phone business, Jorma Ollila, became CEO in 1992. Under his leadership, Nokia step-by-step became a global company with a nearly exclusive focus on wireless telecommunications, a market it got to know well as the Finns were among the early and most eager adopters of mobile phones.

Nokia's strategy was to leverage its early R&D investment by rapidly growing international sales. Top management took a gamble, correctly forecasting that GSM technology would become the new global standard outside the United States, and put all available resources behind it. R&D and core manufacturing were concentrated in Finland to maximize efficiency and speed of product development and to exploit the manufacturing economies of scale. Ollila spelled this out even before becoming the CEO: "To succeed in mobile phones means becoming a consumer-driven, marketing-driven business and designing the product in such a way that we can mass produce and lower the price of the product. How cheap and how efficient our production ability is will have a major impact."

As Nokia expanded rapidly around the world, the product groups located in Finland retained full control over major commercial decisions, supervised by a tightly knit group of Finnish senior managers. Responsibility for profit-and-loss was at the center. Foreign subsidiaries, managed in most cases by Finnish expatriates, were responsible for meeting sales and budget targets. The company's culture emphasized quick entrepreneurial decision-making. As Ollila notes, "A prime part of our organization is our policy to give the employees who have shown capability of taking the company forward three times more responsibility than they themselves see reasonable."[1] This culture spread abroad through the expatriate network, facilitating Nokia's global expansion.

By the end of 1999, Nokia had become one of the most valuable companies in Europe, the market leader in mobile handsets, and the second-largest provider of wireless infrastructure.

CHAPTER OVERVIEW

Nokia became a leader in mobile telephony by pursuing a strategy of global integration—leveraging its investments at home into global dominance. Building on this story, we will elaborate on the benefits of global integration strategies and outline the key mechanisms of global integration and their implications for the organization and HRM practices. Our discussion of the specific organizational tools for global integration builds on a "control" perspective. We start by reviewing different control mechanisms relevant to firms operating across national boundaries: direct and explicit mechanisms such as centralization of decision-making or standardization of work processes, as well as indirect and implicit approaches such as performance management and socialization of managers.

All the tools of global integration are associated with a heavy reliance on expatriate managers. The second and main part of the chapter therefore focuses on the challenges in managing expatriation processes effectively. While different aspects of expatriation are explored throughout the book, the core concepts will be introduced here. After a review of the literature on expatriate success and failure, we present the key theories, concepts, and practices concerning the different stages in the expatriate cycle (selection and training, compensation, career development, repatriation). We compare research findings with current practice, discuss particular challenges such as family adjustment and the management of expectations, and highlight learning and action points, emphasizing the inevitable tensions in the expatriate cycle (home/host, global/local, short/long-term, leading/learning) and exploring the implications of trends such as dual careers and the growing number of women and younger expatriates.

In conclusion, the chapter summarizes the benefits that can be derived from well-implemented strategies of global integration, nevertheless pointing to the rigidities that need to be overcome when the company experiences transnational pressures.

THE LOGIC OF GLOBAL INTEGRATION

Global integration means centralized control over key resources and operations that are strategic in the value chain.[2] Many companies choose to expand internationally while maintaining close control over the value chain, that is, the string of primary activities (R&D, manufacturing, logistics, marketing, etc.) and support activities (such as HR and procurement) that are the source of value added, and the linkages between these elements. Decisions are made from a global perspective—in the extreme, the firm operates as if the world were a single market.[3] While Nokia's globalization strategy stands out for its remarkable success, the logic that the company followed is quite common. Nokia's strength came from its focused R&D investments and from control over the linkages between technology, product development, supply-chain management, and marketing, integrating these activities on a global basis.

Key strategic decisions at Nokia involve a fast moving process of data gathering and analysis, consultation, and conflict resolution, involving many different perspectives. Until the late 90s, this was enabled by key players being in the same place—Finland.[4] They shared a common language and cultural background, and they were used to working with each other. In other words, they functioned as a tightly integrated team.

In global integration, the development of new knowledge also takes place mostly at the global hub, usually the corporate headquarters or the worldwide product division. Foreign subsidiaries depend on the center for resources, direction, and information. They act as product delivery pipelines to foreign markets, implementing the parent company strategies. We call the company that focuses on global integration as a way of creating competitive advantage a *meganational* firm.[5]

Gillette, the U.S.-based consumer giant, is another good example of such a firm. Al Zeien, the former CEO who was the architect of Gillette's hugely successful global expansion, put it this way: "We know Argentina and France are different, but we treat them the same. We sell them the same products, we use the same production methods, we have the same corporate policies. We even use the same advertising, in a different language of course."[6] However, not all meganational companies standardize the products and policies to this degree. Global integration does not necessarily imply selling the same product in the same way all over the world. What it does mean is that decisions on how to address local customer needs or market differentiation are made by managers who have an integrated global point of view.

Strategies of export-driven Japanese and Korean manufacturing companies— relative latecomers to internationalization—are typical of this path. Their tightly integrated product development and manufacturing functions at home allowed them to develop economies of scale in cost, quality, and product innovation, flooding the world with automobiles, cameras, copiers, consumer electronics, and other products via their sales subsidiaries abroad. Their products were essentially the same, whether sold in Los Angeles, London, Buenos Aires, or Singapore.

The meganational approach is not limited to companies that compete globally by exporting standardized low cost consumer products. Meganational companies can be found across the spectrum of industries, from high tech to fast foods, in particular where products are naturally relatively standardized across the world, where there are only limited benefits of local responsiveness, or where maintaining key activities in the value chain at the central hub can create a competitive advantage in terms of speed of product development, cost reduction, or quality improvement.[7]

Some companies such as Nokia use a meganational strategy of global integration as a first step to internationalization, moving to a different strategic posture as they progress. Indeed, elements of meganational strategy can be detected in most cases of early internationalization when resource constraints require careful central control. Other firms maintain their meganational orientation for an extended period of time because it fits with their products and/or markets.

The Business Advantages of Global Integration

There are a number of reasons why companies may choose to follow the global integration route. For Nokia, doing so allowed them to carefully manage their investments in R&D and to maximize economies of scale in manufacturing. For other companies, brand management may be the driving force. The box "Strategic Drivers of Global Integration" reviews the major reasons why companies pursue global integration and the benefits derived from it.

Global integration does not mean centralization of all aspects of a company's operations. It may be limited to a particular product, function, or value chain segment. For example, P&G standardizes the formulation of products worldwide because P&G's key success factor is technological innovation and its rapid application to all markets. Packaging and advertising, on the other hand, are adapted to local needs.

With increased global competition, an argument can be made that global integration is becoming a competitive necessity in a number of markets in which decentralized strategies were dominant in the past. Among the factors favoring integration are the emergence of global consumers owing to greater homogeneity of tastes; the diminishing importance of country borders with regional integration in Europe, Latin America, and Southeast Asia; and the increasing importance of fast decision-making in our rapidly changing competitive environment.

THE "SOFT" FACTORS MATTER. Although "hard" factors such as industry and market characteristics may be the most important reasons for global integration, they are not the only determinants. Meganational firms can be found even in industries in which the forces for local responsiveness are supposedly high—Coca Cola and Heineken in beverages, McDonald's in fast foods, and Wal-Mart in retailing. Within the same industry, companies may pursue different strategies of internationalization, as the choice of strategy is also influenced by the corporate heritage on "soft" issues, such as the company's culture and management style.

When firms go abroad, they may naturally follow the path that led them to be successful in their home markets. So when after deregulation U.S. utilities began to expand abroad, Virginia-based ASE adopted the same approach it had used to build its successful U.S. operations—granting its foreign units a high degree of autonomy. In the same industry, the foreign subsidiaries of the Detroit-based CMS are tightly controlled from the headquarters—just like their domestic counterparts.

Strategic Drivers of Global Integration
Practice Box

Global integration can provide a firm operating internationally with a number of important benefits derived from a worldwide optimization of resources:

Economies of scale. A company can lower its unit costs by centralizing critical value chain activities, such as manufacturing or logistics. This may involve having a small number of large facilities to make products for export, or creating a network of specialized and focused operations spread around the world that are tightly controlled by the central hub.

Value chain linkages. Sometimes competitive advantage comes from tight linkages between value chain activities—between R&D, manufacturing, and marketing in the home country which is a technological leader (for example Silicon Valley in the Internet equipment business); or between manufacturing and logistics. Tight integration allows the firm to stay ahead of technological and competitive changes.

Serving global customers. To the extent that customers are integrated and operate on a global basis, their suppliers may be forced to adopt a similar structure. Subsidiaries do not have their own stand-alone customers; prices, quality standards, and delivery terms are determined globally.

Global branding. Consumer product companies such as Coca Cola or Gillette promote a unified brand image around the world. Coke standardizes both its formula and advertising themes (its two critical success factors), gaining efficiencies in utilization of marketing tools such as advertising and merchandising.

Leveraging capabilities. Some companies expand globally by transferring capabilities developed in the home market. The international expansion of both IKEA and Wal-Mart depends on supply-chain management skills that allow these companies to pursue their traditional low price strategies around the world.

World-class standardization. Key processes are standardized and centrally controlled so as to maintain competitive advantage. The pharmaceutical giant Merck manufactures locally to meet government requirements. Its manufacturing processes are complex, however, and these are standardized in order to maintain high quality.

Competitive platforms. Tight control of local subsidiaries by central headquarters may allow rapid response to competitive conditions and redeployment of resources so as to facilitate expansion worldwide. For example, tightly centralized Japanese multinationals penetrated new markets in the past through price subsidization funded by profitable operations elsewhere.

Information advantage. Prime examples of meganational firms—Japanese trading companies (*sogo shosha*)—are located in every corner of the world. Through the network of local offices, staffed primarily by Japanese expatriates, they optimize global business opportunities by tapping into pricing and delivery information about thousands of products.

Because its aim is to maximize the interests of the center, a meganational firm is sometimes perceived as ethnocentric. This may be particularly visible in the composition of the top management team, typically composed exclusively of mother country nationals. Expatriates from the mother country often have key roles on local management teams to maintain the necessary close linkage with the head office. Not surprisingly, Japanese multinationals, with their historical preference for a meganational approach, consistently have more expatriates per subsidiary and a greater presence of Japanese in local management than multinationals from other countries.[8]

The Tools for Global Integration

The levers of global integration are primarily those that enable centralized control over operations.[9] Companies have a wide range of control tools at their disposal—planning systems, goal setting mechanisms, accounting and budgetary systems, measurement and evaluation systems, IT-based information systems to monitor and disseminate information, central decision-making on the location of key functions or facilities, management development systems, many types of steering boards and councils, project committees, business reviews, sign-off procedures on investments and new product introductions, performance appraisal policies, and so forth. Is there a pattern to the use of these tools?

Five Ways of Exercising Control

There is an extensive literature on control in organizations, much of it focused on the microeconomic debate about the respective virtues of markets and hierarchies as governance mechanisms.[10] More pertinent to our focus are the frameworks in organizational theory. The idea underlying these control frameworks is that as the degree of complexity and uncertainty of tasks increases, a progressively wider range of control mechanisms will be employed. Simple mechanisms such as rules and procedures can manage simple tasks, but as the complexity of the task increases, direct supervision, planning, and more complex levers of control will come into play.[11]

These mechanisms of control can be classified broadly into five types, each with a different quality:[12]

- Centralization, or personal control.
- Standardization, based on control through formalization.
- Contracting, focused on control of outputs.
- Socialization, built around control over norms and values.
- Mutual adjustment, or control through informal interaction.

These mechanisms are referred to sometimes as tools of control, sometimes as co-ordination. *Control* and *coordination* are two closely related concepts that are difficult to separate.[13] Reflecting popular usage, we use the term "control" when the mechanism is visible and hierarchic in nature, as with centralization and standardization. The element of power is overt. We use the term "coordination" when control or power is exercised in more indirect ways, such as through socialization and in the design of sophisticated forms of mutual adjustment such as project groups or knowledge sharing networks.

Personal control through centralization. This control mechanism is reflected in the managerial hierarchy of roles and responsibilities, in which decision-making authority is concentrated at the center of the organization. This is the most direct and personalized form of control. The center takes key decisions, supported by direct supervision—visits to foreign operations by senior executives and personalized control by expatriates as emissaries. Since all organizations are organized in a hierarchy, some degree of personal control is universal.

Expatriation, discussed later in this chapter, is typically a form of direct, hierarchic, personal control[14]—companies trust their expatriates more than they trust their locals. However, trusted expatriates are also likely to have gone through intense socialization, their networks may allow them to achieve much through mutual adjustment, and they may be levers for standardization.

Formalized control through standardization of work rules, procedures, and processes. In its simplest form, standardization involves specifying rules and procedures, typically in written form. These procedures can come to constitute an internal governance system, mandating the processes for recruitment, for signing external contracts, or concerning safety measures. The promulgation of what is expected from the employees is generally impersonal and indirect. Scholars sometimes use the Weberian term "bureaucratic" control.

Standardization can take more sophisticated forms, as in the development of global work processes. Standardization can also apply to skills (training people in how to approach customers or handle a performance appraisal) as well as knowledge (codifying new knowledge on customer solutions so that it can be diffused across operations).[15]

Output control through performance contracting. In contrast to the other types of control, the focus here is on results rather than on behavior or a course of action. Control is exercised through the negotiation of and agreement on objectives or targets. This is analogous to market ways of governance as opposed to hierarchic means. Targets that have been agreed upon constitute quasi-contractual obligations, backed up by explicitly stated rewards and sanctions. There are bonuses linked to the achievement of the results, and the ultimate sanction for nondelivery may be replacement of the individual, equivalent to termination of the contractual relationship.

The broad trend in some companies toward greater rigor in performance management (objective setting, evaluation and appraisal, and rewards) reflects a beefing up of the quasi-contractual nature of output control. However, in many firms the market nature of output control is guided by some form of planning system that focuses on working through the trade-offs between long-term strategic objectives and short-term outputs (financial targets and budgets).[16] Otherwise output control can lead to an excessively short-term orientation.

Normative control through socialization. In comparison with hierarchic supervision, socialization is a more informal and subtle form of control. Socialization means learning important corporate values and norms so that they become internalized. People are recruited on the basis of their potential fit with these values, they are trained and rewarded according to these norms, and those who demonstrate their adherence are likely to be candidates for positions of responsibility. To the extent that employees share common norms and values, they can be trusted to exercise discretion without the necessity for rules, procedures, and supervision. Socialization can be viewed as the standardization of norms, reflected in a strong culture. In its extreme, this can become indoctrination, creating strong conformity.

Informal control through mutual adjustment. The last form of control is both the most basic and the most sophisticated. It is the informal process of communication and consultation that takes place between people who form natural networks. In an organization, relationships reflect respect and friendship as well as hierarchy. Relationships cut across hierarchic lines—for example, people who are gatekeepers or brokers of contacts may be frequently consulted regardless of their formal position in the hierarchy.

Especially when combined with socialization, mutual adjustment can be influenced through social architecture. This means bringing selected people together in a project group, committee, or team to decide what to do about problems and opportunities. In organizational theory, this is known as lateral coordination, also reflected today in an increasing focus on understanding networks.

These different control mechanisms are complementary, not substitutes. Almost all organizations have some hierarchy, some formalized procedures, some shared norms, some degree of output negotiation and associated planning, and some attention paid to mutual adjustment through teams and committees. Firms tend to employ some levers of control more than others, however, leading to different organizational configurations.[17] Research tentatively suggests that globally integrated companies tend to rely on hierarchic mechanisms, notably via expatriates. On the other hand, locally responsive firms rely more on output control (see box "Control Strategies during Early Internationalization"). Research also shows cross-cultural differences according to the country of origin with respect to the type of control exercised by the headquarters.[18]

Implementing Global Integration

Building upon this review of control theory, let us discuss three ways of implementing globally integrated strategies. These build upon personal, formalized, and normative control respectively:

- The *alignment* of decision-making to ensure that local decisions reflect a global perspective, particularly through personal control exercised by expatriates. Performance management also plays an important role in the process of alignment.
- The *standardization* of processes to achieve desired efficiencies and uniform behavior, using formalized control.
- The *socialization* of key individuals in central and expatriate leadership positions to ensure that they have a global orientation (normative control).

Again, these are complementary rather than alternative ways of achieving integration, each connected with specific HRM tools and techniques that we will examine here. What they have in common is a dependence on expatriation, and much of this chapter will be devoted to the underlying policies and practices concerning *international transfers*.

Alignment

When one thinks of meganational firms, the first characteristic that usually comes to mind is centralized decision-making at the all-powerful HQ, or at the central office

Control Strategies during Early Internationalization
Research Box

As a company begins to internationalize, it faces a lot of uncertainty. Lacking information on how to expand and operate abroad, it can basically choose between two alternative control strategies.

One strategy is to rely on *personalized central control,* built around the network of key players of the parent nationality who have successfully led the growth of the company. For example, despite its sales across the globe, Microsoft remains not just a U.S. firm but a Seattle-based firm. The parent decision-makers may travel widely to keep an eye on foreign operations and exercise control. Holderbank, one of the world's leading cement companies, was long led by a trio of executives who spent much of the year traveling to their operations around the world. The arms of the headquarters are extended by means of mother country expatriates who have been carefully socialized into the central culture.

The alternative control strategy is focused on *performance contracting on local output objectives.* In order to expand internationally, the company finds entrepreneurs who are attracted by the opportunity to create their own local company. Or it acquires distributors and foreign companies. Here the control over the subsidiaries is exercised primarily by negotiating strategic and operational objectives with the management of local affiliates. Top management does not concern itself with the uncertainties and ambiguities of operational management abroad since this is the responsibility of the local management team. This strategy allows for greater local responsiveness, though at the expense of corporate integration.[A]

The dichotomy between these two strategies is supported by empirical evidence. Harzing studied the relationship between HRM and control in more than 100 multinational corporations.[B] One of her clearest findings was that the higher the percentage of expatriates in the workforce of a subsidiary, the lower were the levels of output control used with respect to that subsidiary. In other words, "output control and expatriate control appear to be seen as alternative ways to control subsidiaries."[C] Output control is associated with local responsiveness, while central and expatriate control is linked to global integration.

[A]This locally responsive strategy for internationalization is discussed in Chapter 4.
[B]Harzing, 1999. This sample of MNCs had headquarters in nine different countries and subsidiaries in 22 nations. The quotation is from page 351.
[C]Harzing, 1999, p. 351.

of the worldwide product group in the case of a more diversified firm. This is misleading. Senior managers at the headquarters would become overloaded with operational details, taking their attention away from the important strategic issues. As the scope of international operations expands, decision-making would break down— everything stops until HQ decides. It would be difficult to attract and retain local staff who would feel alienated at slow decision-making by distant bosses with no understanding for their local circumstances.

Global integration is not about dictatorship by headquarters; it is about alignment. In fact, as Gillette's Al Zeien argues, it would be impossible to run a worldwide operation effectively without a lot of delegation. The trick is to make sure that managers worldwide are on the same wavelength.[19] One way to ensure alignment is expatriate staffing, shifting the locus of decision-making to the affiliates while assuring that a global view prevails. A second way is through a performance management system that rewards global rather than local objectives.

IT IS NOT "WHERE" BUT "WHO." Decentralizing decisions to affiliates does not necessarily mean increasing their autonomy. There is a lot of confusion here since autonomy in multinational companies is often measured in terms of the locus of decision-making.[20] If decisions are made at headquarters, subsidiaries are said to have little autonomy; if decisions are made locally, then they have high autonomy. In fact, taking decisions locally does *not* necessarily imply autonomy if the decisions are taken by expatriates rather than local managers. Who makes the decision may be as important as where the decision is made!

The typical pattern in meganational firms is that mother country expatriates, well socialized into the parent company norms, occupy key positions in the subsidiaries. Companies typically staff positions they deem strategic with an expatriate. For many firms this may be the key post of either general manager or financial comptroller. For others, it may be a critical technical position, such as the brew master at Heineken.[21] Indeed, several authors suggest that sending expatriates to subsidiaries can have the same results as centralizing decisions at headquarters.[22] Reinforced by the network of relationships with colleagues at the HQ, local decisions may be similar to those made at the center.

For example, research has shown that a large Japanese presence in subsidiaries is associated with more "local" decision-making.[23] However, this merely indicates that the Japanese are pursuing global integration through informal networks. Local executives may not like centralization (critical decisions are made in Tokyo), but they also find it hard to live with this more subtle pseudo-decentralization (decisions are made locally by Japanese executives). No matter how hard some Japanese companies try to open and enlarge their management pool, skeptical observers doubt the impact of such efforts.[24]

ALIGNMENT THROUGH MANAGING AND MEASURING PERFORMANCE. Another essential part of alignment is a performance management process that fosters decisions and behaviors consistent with a global orientation, independent of location.[25] As pointed out earlier, in a meganational firm the subsidiary acts as a pipeline of products or services to the local market. Under such circumstances, the performance management process should reflect global objectives and common standards. While all international firms face tensions in balancing global and local performance criteria, it is the global result that counts in a meganational organization.

Take the early stages of Nokia's internationalization as an example. As with many globally oriented companies, profit-and-loss was measured only at a worldwide level, while local subsidiaries operated on the basis of budgets, with cost and sales targets. For fiscal reasons, business results may have been reported for local subsidiaries; but these local profitability figures were arbitrary owing to transfer pricing and cross-border cost allocations.

When local business results are subordinated to global results, it is meaningless to hold local managers responsible for performance in the sense of profit-and-loss output. Corporate expectations of a subsidiary may be quite inconsistent with local financial interests. For example, a meganational firm may adopt aggressive pricing policies in a particular country, leading this subsidiary consistently into the red. The aim may be to tie up the resources of a competitor who is the market leader in that country so as to allow substantially higher returns elsewhere. Consequently, the performance of the whole is not equal to the sum of the parts. This is just one example of the difficulties facing multinational firms in measuring subsidiary performance. There are other obstacles to measuring subsidiary performance, such as noncomparability of data, separation by distance and time, variability in market conditions, and transfer pricing.[26]

Approaches to performance management that emphasize *both* local responsibility for financial results and alignment with global strategy are fraught with difficulty. For the firm that is internationalizing, the risk is confusion and inconsistency. Consequently, performance management and the use of expatriates are closely linked. These parent company expatriates usually set and reinforce global standards and measurements (we will discuss the performance appraisal of expatriates later).

Performance measures in the globally integrated firm are often linked to business processes based on quality and customer satisfaction data. For example, global ball-bearing leader SKF uses a single product quality measurement system worldwide to maintain high standards in all of its factories around the world. Coca-Cola, P&G, and Citibank maintain worldwide customer satisfaction measurement systems, controlled by headquarters, so as to obtain comparable, nonbiased feedback from local customers. In this manner, performance management is linked to process standardization, which is another way of promoting global integration.

Standardization

The second facet of organizational control in meganational firms concerns standardization of processes to achieve both efficiencies and uniform performance in the delivery of product and services. This can be accomplished in two ways. The first is through the development of shared global standards so as to drive the transfer of know-how and to ensure consistent performance (for example, in terms of quality as well as conformity to environmental/safety standards). The other is to focus on the work organization as a complete system, in which standardization is achieved by a full transfer of home country practices to a foreign location. Both of these control strategies are closely linked to specific HRM tools and techniques. Let us start with an example of the former approach.

MAINTAINING GLOBAL STANDARDS. Ask anyone anywhere for a list of companies that deliver the same product around the world, and it is likely that McDonald's, the largest global fast food company operating in more than 120 countries, would be on the list. Be it in Tokyo, Moscow, Paris, or Cincinnati, the experience of ordering, buying, and eating a meal at McDonald's is virtually the same, although menus may vary with local tastes. What attracts customers to McDonald's is the consistently high service level, from product quality to speed of order execution, from the ambiance of the stores to their hygiene. McDonald's operating system has been a model for scores of other businesses in which personal contact is an essential part of delivering value to customers.[27]

Every aspect of McDonald's operations is designed to satisfy customer expectations based on standards that are universal around the world. Nothing is left to chance or individual discretion. A big part of McDonald's success is its ability to transfer expertise developed at home to other markets worldwide. Global standardization of practices through operation manuals is an important tool. Even more critical is a relentless focus on education and training, led by Hamburger University and its regional "colleges" throughout the world.[28]

Another example of process standardization is the Swedish furniture retail chain IKEA. Its well-designed, simple but durable products are sold in more than thirty countries, including the United States and China. IKEA's competitive advantage comes from its ability to optimize work processes worldwide—integrating product design, low cost manufacturing, logistics, and efficient service. As marketing textbooks explain, this is built around a tightly controlled standard marketing concept in an area normally associated with strong cultural preferences. What is less known is how IKEA's approach to HRM supports its global strategy.

Guided by an unwavering commitment to its core values, IKEA standardizes its approach to people management in the same way it standardizes its approach to markets. Wherever it operates, the company carefully recruits people who will blend well into the IKEA culture of humility, simplicity, and cost-consciousness. It prefers to hire people without much previous experience, developing them quickly by delegating responsibility and frequent rotations. During the 1980s, specially trained "IKEA ambassadors" were assigned to key positions in all units, charged not only with the transfer of know-how but also with inculcating "IKEA's way" among its staff around the world.

Such a focus on homogeneity may border on the ethnocentrism that characterizes some meganationals. In the words of IKEA's former CEO: "I would advise any foreign employee who really wants to advance in this company to learn Swedish."[29] This way of thinking has created problems in adapting to local markets,[30] although IKEA continues its successful global expansion with a strategy in which the standardization of processes goes hand in hand with "standardization of behaviors."

TRANSPLANTING THE WORK SYSTEM. The success of manufacturing practices in Japan has been well studied.[31] Human resource practices play an important role—factors such as team-based production, worker participation in problem solving, job rotation, few job classifications, single status, and high levels of training. Japanese firms transferred these practices to their U.S. plants, although not blindly and with considerable adaptation.[32] On the one hand, the use of comprehensive methods for employee selection and socialization reduced the impact of being in a different cultural and institutional environment. On the other hand, while job rotation practices were similar to those in Japan, problem solving team methods were substantially adjusted, and the compensation remained more comparable to U.S. rather than Japanese norms. Overall, the progressive transfer and adaptation led to levels of performance similar to those in Japan.[33]

Probably no other foreign investment site has received more coverage in the media and in academic literature than NUMMI—a joint venture created by General Motors and Toyota in 1982 to manufacture a small car on the site of a closed GM plant in Fremont, California. The box "Transferring the Toyota Production System to NUMMI" focuses on the transfer of Toyota's manufacturing system to Fremont.[34] Many in the U.S. automobile industry expected that the transfer would fail since Japanese manufacturing methods were assumed to be deeply dependent on Japanese

Transferring the Toyota Production System to NUMMI
Practice Box

In 1963, General Motors opened an automobile assembly plant in Fremont, California. By the late 70s the plant employed over 7,000 workers but ranked lowest in productivity in the entire GM system, and one of the worst in terms of quality. Distrust, even fear, marked relations between management and the union. Daily absenteeism was almost 20 percent, drug abuse and alcoholism were rampant, and first line supervisors were known to carry weapons for personal protection. The plant was closed in the 1982 recession.

Under an agreement between Toyota, GM, and the United Autoworkers' Union, the plant reopened in 1984 as NUMMI, a joint venture between the two automakers. Toyota accepted the same 25-person union bargaining committee that existed under the old GM system. Eighty-five percent of the initial workforce of 2,200 was hired from the original pool of laid-off GM employees (employment reached 4,000 by the early 1990s). By 1986 the plant was 60 percent more efficient than a comparable plant fully owned by GM. How did this happen? Part of the change came from integrated HR and manufacturing processes, using intensive involvement of the workforce in a way that simultaneously empowers and controls them.[A]

Just as important was the deliberate and extensive socialization of NUMMI employees into the new system. First, in deciding whom to rehire there was a heavy emphasis on the selection of employees who had the ability to function within the NUMMI philosophy. Second, Toyota sent no less than 400 trainers from Japan to explain the Toyota methods to the U.S. workforce. At the same time, 600 of NUMMI's blue collar employees were sent to Japan for three weeks to several months for training at Toyota factories. This included classroom training and working alongside Toyota workers. As part of the training, NUMMI employees were asked to suggest improvement to the famous Toyota manufacturing system. The approach was not "Now you have to learn to work this way!" but instead "Can you help us all to improve?"—cross-cultural action learning at its best.

The whole transplant effort was headed by a bicultural leadership group combining expatriates from Toyota in key plant positions, a small number of GM managers (mainly finance and procurement), and other Americans recruited from the outside (including HR).[B] The plant itself was organized around teams, with a three-level hierarchy (in contrast to five or six levels in traditional GM plants). Most of the original team leaders went through the training in Japan, and many of them were subsequently promoted to managerial positions at the Fremont plant.

By 1996, after a decade of improvements in the U.S. automobile industry, NUMMI was still 20 percent more efficient and 25 percent higher on key quality indicators than other GM plants and comparable with Toyota's operations in Japan.

[A]Pil and MacDuffie, 1999; O'Reilly and Pfeffer, 2000; Adler, 1999.
[B]The small number of General Motors managers assigned to the JV seriously impeded transfer of learning back to GM—see the discussion on alliance learning in Chapter 5.

---

culture. However, the venture was an instant success, becoming the U.S. leader in quality and productivity within three years.

While NUMMI's case may be extreme in many ways, including the extensive use of HRM tools, companies routinely attempt to replicate their domestic work environment in foreign locations without much thought to the benefits and costs—"this is how we do things around here."

Socialization

A key factor in Nokia's success has been what outside observers sometimes have called "the secret code": the cohesion and *esprit de corps* of its senior management team. As pointed out earlier, its senior managers have worked together for many years, sharing the same experiences, talking the same language. Most important of all, they share values and behaviors that foster open debate, collaboration, trust, and quick decision-making.[35] Socialization involves selecting and inculcating such a cultural code in others, notably those who will be entrusted with responsibilities either at the center or abroad as expatriates. Some firms such as IKEA extend socialization to the locals they recruit for their foreign operations.

Organizational socialization is defined as the process by which a new member learns the value system, the norms, and the required behaviors of the organization that he or she is joining (see the box "Organizational Socialization"). As mentioned earlier, this is a subtle but powerful form of control, quite the opposite of bureaucratic or hierarchic control, often used as an alternative or at least complementary mechanism of global integration.

Traditional Japanese firms, with their strong meganational orientation, epitomized the use of socialization. They recruited their elite straight from the Japanese universities for long-term careers, choosing people more for their adaptability and potential than for their job skills. The early career years were a period of extensive socialization

Organizational Socialization
Research Box

Socialization, as defined by social scientists, refers to "the process by which individuals acquire the knowledge, skills, and dispositions that enable them to participate as more or less effective members of groups and the society."[A] While psychologists, sociologists, and anthropologists have long been concerned with understanding the way in which individuals are molded by their family, institutional, and cultural contexts, the study of occupational and organizational socialization began only in the 1960s.[B]

Socialization works essentially through a subtle process of reward and punishment. When people behave "in the right way," they are made to feel good. When they behave in the wrong way, they are ostracized, made to feel bad, or even punished. Through this process, members learn a common language and conceptual categories that facilitate communication (for example, what "high quality" means). They come to understand the criteria for inclusion and exclusion in groups, how decisions are reached, and the criteria behind the power structure and the reward/punishment system. They learn the acceptable ways of handling disagreement and conflict, the rules of the game for peer relationships and intimacy, and the ideology that gives meaning to the organization, often expressed through symbols and stories.

The approaches to socialization may be individual or collective (e.g., training), they may be formal (guided by explicit norms or values as at Johnson & Johnson) or informal.[C] In short, it is through socialization that the culture of the firm is learned and maintained. However, while socialization provides social cohesion, it also risks killing innovation and adaptation. Excessive socialization creates cloned individuals. Potentially innovative ideas are labeled as deviant. The theory of socialization argues that when individuals are new to a firm or a job, the pressures of socialization will be strongest. But once they have learned the ropes, there should be room for creative individualism that can lead to innovation.[D]

[A]Brim, 1966.
[B]Schein, 1968; Moore, 1969.
[C]For dimensions of socialization processes see Van Maanen and Schein (1979).
[D]Schein's study of organizational culture and leadership (Schein, 1985) contains the most complete analysis of the how socialization maintains the culture of an organization.

into the norms and values of the firm, where training and job rotation were intended to indoctrinate as well as to develop skills. Such mechanisms became the focus of wider attention with the success of Japanese companies in the 70s and early 80s. Ouchi called such firms "clans."[36] People who moved into top management or key expatriate positions abroad would be those who had successfully internalized the norms and behaviors of the clan. He contrasted clans on the one hand with "bureaucratic" firms that use traditional centralized mechanisms of authority and on the other hand with "market" firms using exchange mechanisms such as output control and rewards.

SOCIALIZATION IN PRACTICE. Socialization is exercised by means of a variety of HRM tools. The process begins with the *selection* of people who will "fit well here," guided by some explicit or implicit set of values and competencies. It is difficult and time consuming to resocialize people who do not have a prior affinity with the corporate culture, so companies pay a great deal of attention to recruitment.[37] In today's fast moving environment, selection on the basis of fit with guiding norms and values becomes important since there is less time for extended socialization, and less career loyalty. In companies such as Honda, Nokia, and Hewlett-Packard, many different people interview candidates—the potential line and the human resource managers, peers from other departments, as well as a senior executive. If several people say, "I don't think that the person will fit well here," then there will be no job offer.

The early career years are a period of extensive socialization through formal and informal *induction and training,* through guidance and instructions from the boss, mentors, and experienced peers, and via role modeling. Powerful traditions, myths and sagas are also tools of indoctrination. German, Japanese, and other companies that recruit for long-term careers often use formalized apprenticeship programs, rotating professional recruits across different departments accompanied by intensive training.[38]

Indeed, as seen in the IKEA example, socialization often involves *the extensive use of mobility* through which individuals learn further the culture of the firm and its nuances. Transfers, especially geographic moves, typically involve some degree of sacrifice of family and personal life, and the experience of sacrifice has long been shown to be part of commitment building, in modern organizations as in primitive tribes. Each transfer is an unfreezing experience by which the individual is remolded. Since the company culture is the constant throughout, that culture progressively becomes internalized.[39] The more frequent the transfers, the stronger the degree of socialization will be. The outcome is a strong informal organization (senior managers or professionals recruited from outside find it difficult to operate effectively), providing coordination and flexibility.

In the context of international firms, the socialization process can be viewed from two perspectives. First, it is important to build a common culture across different subsidiaries, facilitating their alignment with the global priorities. Second, since the culture is transferred abroad in part through expatriates, it is important that these expatriates be well socialized into the parent firm before being dispatched to the subsidiaries. Indeed, in the globally integrated firm, it is unlikely that expatriates will be entrusted with major responsibilities abroad unless they have demonstrated their understanding and commitment to the corporate perspective. This brings us back again to the importance of the role and the process of expatriation.

Expatriation: The Heart of Global Integration

We have examined several organizational tools that international firms can use to enhance global integration: centralization and ways of building alignment, standardization, and socialization. For human resource management, the biggest challenge underlying these tools is that of managing expatriation. This is particularly true at early stages in the internationalization of the firm.

As discussed above, international transfers support global integration in different and complementary ways. First, expatriation allows the firm to avoid the pathologies of excessive centralization. Business decisions can be made locally but with the global perspective in mind. Second, the standards of the parent firm are transferred abroad via expatriates. Third, mobility promotes the diffusion of shared values—a key element in global integration.

The pattern we discuss in the rest of this chapter is the flow of people from the parent firm to the subsidiaries. International transfers are also an important lever of coordination in the transnational firm that we will explore later with a broader scope (from subsidiaries to the parent as well as between subsidiaries). With this in mind, we now turn to this complex and sometimes controversial issue.

MASTERING EXPATRIATION

At a corporate HR conference in the United States in the early 90s, one of the presenters commented that most international HR professionals devoted about 90 percent of their time to expatriate issues, 70 percent of it to compensation. This reflects the historical orientation of American MNCs. Indeed at the early stages of internationalization, the role of expatriates was critical, reinforced by later concern for global integration strategies. Consequently the international HR profession has historically been the domain of relocation specialists, consultants in compensation and benefits, and experts on international taxation. In the academic literature, the field of international human resource management is also to a large extent synonymous with studies on expatriation.

Today the emphasis of international HR has changed dramatically. Nevertheless, the effective management of expatriation—or more broadly of international transfers—remains one of the foundations for the implementation of global strategy.

The Evolution of Expatriate Management

Expatriation is not a new concept. It has been a tool of organizational control since the early stages of civilization. In ancient Rome, as with the Dutch and English trading houses that pioneered international trade in the sixteenth and seventeenth centuries, the art of developing trusted representatives to manage distant subsidiaries often spelled the difference between success and failure in overseas colonization (see the box "Holding the Roman Empire Together").

In the early modern era of expatriation after World War II, foreign business was usually run by an international division that supervised exports, licensing, and sub-

Holding the Roman Empire Together
Practice Box

The geographical reach and longevity of the Roman Empire can be regarded as a prodigious feat of international management. Rome expected those in charge of even the most distant part of the Empire to be more than just representatives—they had to make the right decisions on behalf of Rome. One of the binding forces of the Empire was the careful attention paid to the selection, training, and socialization of Rome's expatriates, the generals and governors entrusted with the governance of far-flung provinces.[A]

Such positions required a long apprenticeship in a highly trained and organized army. Governors were selected exclusively from consuls who had held high state office. By the time they were dispatched abroad, the ways of Rome were so ingrained in their minds that they would not need policy guidance—nor had they means of getting such advice. They were "centralized within."

This policy of administrative decentralization coupled with tight socialization of the local decision-makers created strong, self-contained provinces or "subsidiaries." A tribute to their robustness was that the Roman Empire survived even the fall of Rome (a sort of involuntary divestiture) when the center of the Empire moved east to Byzantium.

[A]Jay, 1967.

sidiaries abroad. The main role of corporate HR was to facilitate the selection of staff for foreign postings, finding employees familiar with the company's products, technology, organization, and culture who were at the same time amenable to the constraints of working abroad.

The parent country employees stationed abroad operated as a viceroy—directing daily operations, supervising the transfer of know-how, communicating corporate policies, and keeping the home office informed about relevant developments in their assigned territory. Assignments were decided on an ad hoc basis, with crash courses in language and foreign culture occasionally being provided. Since foreign assignments often meant being at a distance from the politics of career progression in the parent company, all sorts of financial incentives were used as lures.

During this period, the notion of "expatriate" brought to mind a middle-aged, male executive dispatched from a first world HQ to a third world subsidiary. In fact, this stereotype was not true then, and it is even less so today. Most international transfers were to economically advanced countries. After all, that was where the bulk of foreign direct investment went. Today, the countries with the highest population of resident expatriates are the United States and United Kingdom (see the box "A Portrait of Expatriates in U.S. Multinationals"). And as we will discuss later, the expatriate population is increasingly diverse in its ethnic origins, gender, age, and most important, in the roles expatriates are expected to perform.

A Portrait of Expatriates in U.S. Multinationals
Practice Box

A 1999 survey profiled expatriates in U.S. multinationals:[A]

- 70% came from the home country; 13% were women.
- 69% were married; spouses accompanied 77% of the married expatriates.
- 49% of the spouses were employed before the assignment; 11% during the assignment.
- 44% had previous international experience.
- 38% of the assignments were for two years or less; 39% for two to three years; 23% were expected to last over three years.

Among other findings:

- 68% of the companies expected an increase in total expatriate population; 12% expected a decrease.

- 52% of the companies expected an increase in U.S. expatriates.
- 53% of the companies expected an increase in non-U.S. expatriates.
- The most frequent expatriate locations were U.K., U.S.A. (foreigners assigned to positions with the mother firm), and Hong Kong.
- The most common assignment objective was filling a skills gap.
- The most critical challenge was finding candidates (in 66% of the cases).

[A]Windham International, *Global Relocation Trends 1999 Survey Report,* 1999. www.windhamint.com/html/interpretingsurv.html. This survey was based on responses of 264 major U.S. multinationals with nearly 75,000 expatriates. Similar surveys by other relocation firms such as Cendant International reported comparable results.

Understanding the Expatriate Phenomenon

The roles that expatriates play today are far more varied than in the past. Before looking in detail at specific HRM practices associated with international transfers, we briefly review the range of motives that drive expatriation, and we examine the controversy over whether expatriate failure really is as serious a problem as some people have argued.

The Motives for Expatriation

Much of the literature on expatriation focuses on international assignments of parent (or home country) employees. In a classic article, Edström and Galbraith explored the principal motives.[40] They proposed that expatriates are dispatched abroad for three reasons that sometimes overlap. The first is simply to *fill positions* that cannot be staffed locally because of a lack of technical or managerial skills. The second reason is to support *management development,* enabling high potential individuals to acquire international experience. The third reason is *organizational development,* referring to the control and coordination of international operations through socialization and informal networks.[41]

Pucik differentiates between *demand-driven* and *learning-driven* international assignments.[42] Traditional expatriate jobs fit mainly into the former category: employees who were dispatched abroad to fix a problem or for reasons of control. On the other hand, more and more companies recognize that cross-border mobility is a potential learning tool, thus increasing the number of assignments in which the primary driver is individual or organizational learning. Many assignments combine both elements, but in most cases it is clear which dimension dominates.

In addition, expatriates differ in the time they spend in an assignment abroad. Many assignments are long term, lasting two to four years or more.[43] Others are short term, less than one year, linked to a specific task or need. Figure 3–1 combines the length and purpose of the assignment together into a framework for understanding the nature of expatriate roles.

Traditionally, most expatriates were assigned abroad for a relatively long period of time (usually three years or longer) as agents of the parent firm in order to accomplish a variety of tasks related to operations and/or oversight of the subsidiaries. Here the demand for their services is driven primarily by control or knowledge transfer requirements, and thus the expatriates serve a *corporate agency* role. In other cases, the demand for expatriates is driven by short-term start-up or problem solving needs—the length of the assignment is determined by the the time it takes to address the task. We call this a *problem solving* role. Historically, most expatriate assignments were of these two types. In both cases, the expatriate has knowledge and competencies that are not available locally.

With the development of local managerial and professional capabilities, there is less demand for expatriate assignments to fill a local skill gap.[44] At the same time, companies face an increasing need to develop global coordination capabilities, fostered in part by mobility across borders. The focus of these *competence development* assignments is on learning rather than teaching.[45]

Finally, a rapidly growing type of expatriation today is short-term learning assignments of young high potential professionals who move across borders primarily for personal and *career enhancement.*[46] These jobs generally last less than a year and often involve rotation across several countries or even regions. In a number of global

FIGURE 3–1. The Purpose of Expatriation

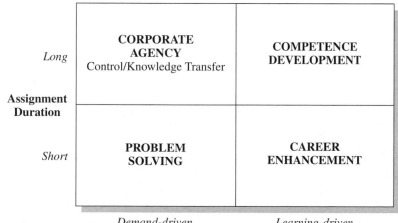

	CORPORATE AGENCY Control/Knowledge Transfer	**COMPETENCE DEVELOPMENT**
Long		
Assignment Duration		
Short	**PROBLEM SOLVING**	**CAREER ENHANCEMENT**
	Demand-driven	*Learning-driven*

Assignment Purpose

firms, such assignments are becoming an integral part of career development planning for young professionals and managers.[47]

While employees take up expatriate positions for different reasons and lengths of time, most companies have dealt with expatriates from a policy point of view as if they were a homogenous group placed abroad for agency reasons. If distinctions were made, they were based on family situation or hierarchic level. As we review the extensive research on expatriation, it is important to bear in mind that the concepts, empirical observations, and practical recommendations of most of the studies are generic across expatriates. And despite growing national diversity in expatriate studies, there still is a strong U.S. orientation.

Studying Expatriation: What Is Failure?

The voluminous research on expatriation is heavily oriented toward the issue of selecting managers for international assignments. This has led to lists of competencies and characteristics that an expatriate manager should have, as well as to personality and psychometric tests that can be used to measure them. Research has also focused on analyzing the causes of failure in overseas assignments, recommending human resource practices that would help organizations to select, develop, and retain competent expatriates.[48] In sharp contrast, practitioner work emphasizes compensation issues, an area in which there is little academic research.

Until recently, a typical study on any topic linked to expatriation was usually framed by an introduction on the high cost of expatriates and the high frequency of failure on such assignments, especially in the case of American multinationals.[49] The direct costs of relocating an expatriate are real, as we shall see later, though there are no studies that have empirically linked failure rates with company or subsidiary performance.

The extent of expatriate failure and the question of defining what "failure" means are controversial issues. There is no shortage of references to high expatriate failure rates, with claims that as many as 40 percent of expatriations are aborted.[50] But does the empirical evidence support these claims? As discussed in the box "Expatriate Failure: How Real Is the Problem?" the current answer is a surprising but unambiguous no.

In fact, the exaggeration of expatriate "failure" may actually slow down the adoption of some useful recommendations. When companies compare their failure rates with the alarming "average" presented in some textbooks, their situation does not look too bad. Why spend resources on what does not seem to be broken? It is also important to note that retention of expatriates after completion of the assignment seems to be more of a problem than failure or recall during the assignment. Most relocation surveys put the turnover among repatriates in American and European multinationals at 20–25 percent in the first two years after re-entry in comparison to 5–10 percent turnover during the assignment itself.[51]

Notwithstanding the limitations of this heritage, the literature on the predictors of expatriate failure provides a rich source of ideas on the effective management of expatriation, leading to some understanding of required personal attributes that may guide selection decisions. The inability to cope with stressful situations and lack of

Expatriate Failure: How Real Is the Problem?
Research Box

Until recently, most publications defined and measured expatriate failure as the percentage of expatriates returning home prematurely before their assignment contract expires, because of poor performance or personal problems. Typically, failure rates that were cited ranged between 15 and 40 percent for U.S. firms, with lower figures for European and Japanese firms, causing substantial cost, productivity, and morale problems for the firms concerned.[A] However, there is little empirical evidence for such high failure rates, and what there is is dated.

Harzing argues that a persistent myth of high failure rates seems to have been created by "massive (mis)quotations" of a handful of articles on U.S. multinationals, some dating back to the 1960s.[B] In her view "the vast majority of the publications [dealing with this subject] do not present any original data at all. The authors simply refer to other publications, which in a large number of cases also do not mention specific research results, referring in turn to yet other publications."

Some recent empirical studies of European multinationals put the rate of expatriate failure defined as premature return at less than 5 percent for the majority of firms, though a few companies clearly have difficulties in managing cross-border transfers. There is also general agreement that U.S. rates are slightly higher, but certainly not as high as reported earlier.[C] However, it is far from certain that expatriate failure rates in most firms are significantly higher than for domestic relocations.

More important, is the simple fact of "premature return" an adequate reflection of expatriate failure? Harzing concludes that expatriate failure should continue to be examined, but using other measures. It may be far more damaging for a company if an expatriate who fails to perform adequately stays until the completion of the overseas assignment. When "underperformance" in the new job as a result of poor cultural adaptation is included, failure rates are typically higher.[D]

[A]For comprehensive reviews of research on expatriate failure rates see Harzing (1995) and Forster (1997).
[B]Harzing 1995. As Harzing emphasizes, major research in this area originated with Tung (1981,1982) with a survey of 80 U.S. firms, 29 Europeans, and 35 Japanese MNCs.
[C]For a discussion of additional data see Forster (1997), and Dowling, Welch, and Schuler (1999, pp. 76–84).
[D]Forster, 1997; PriceWaterhouse, 1997.

skill in communicating with people from a different culture are among the frequent reasons why an expatriate returns prematurely.[52] Some of these personality characteristics will be examined in more detail later in the section on expatriate selection.

Above all, the studies of why expatriates fail have highlighted *the role of the family* in expatriation. The inability of the spouse and the family to adjust to the new country was found in many empirical studies to be a reason, sometimes the main reason, behind premature return.[53] Dual career couples are also more likely to experience stress in international assignments because of the expected negative effects of a career interruption.[54]

The focus of attention of researchers shifted during the 90s from explaining failure to *intercultural adjustment*—how well do expatriates adjust to the work and living circumstances in a foreign environment? Indeed one can argue that failure in the sense of recall is only the extreme of poor adjustment. Moreover, it may be just as important to assess expatriate "success" (with measures such as time-to-proficiency, the time that it takes to master a new role).[55] One recent American survey showed that nearly a third of expatriates who stayed in their position did not perform up to the expectations of their superiors.[56]

Managing International Transfers

Making an expatriate assignment into a success for the individual, the family, and the firm requires paying attention to many factors from the time of initial selection until repatriation. A starting point is the recognition that expatriation is a process, not an event. From an HRM perspective, such a process can be broken down into a set of phases:

- Selecting expatriates.
- Preparing and orienting them.
- Adjusting to the expatriate role.
- Managing the performance of expatriates.
- Compensation.
- Repatriation.

We will discuss each of these activities in the "expatriate cycle" separately, although naturally they are closely linked. The problems of later phases have to be anticipated earlier—for example, repatriation has to be taken into account at the selection phase, while the purpose of preparation is to facilitate role adjustment.

Selecting Expatriates

A lot of research has focused on understanding selection criteria. Surveys show that technical expertise and domestic track record are the most important factors that firms pay attention to (with additional weight among European multinationals given to language skills and international adaptability).[57] But this is not sufficient. Selection processes often fail to consider factors such as the candidate's cross-cultural ability or the family's disposition to live abroad.[58] Indeed, there is broad academic support arguing that stronger efforts should be deployed by organizations to assess other "softer" factors.[59] What do these studies say about the characteristics of successful expatriates?

CHARACTERISTICS OF SUCCESSFUL EXPATRIATES. Together, these factors can be grouped as professional and technical competence, relationship and communication abilities, leadership factors, family situation, and cultural awareness.[60]

Starting with the research of Tung, a number of researchers focused on the competencies of effective expatriates.[61] Mendenhall and Oddou identified four key dimensions in the expatriate adjustment, arguing that expatriate acculturation is a multidimensional process.[62] The *self-oriented dimension* measures the expatriate's personal adaptability. The *others-oriented dimension* measures the expatriate's ability to interact effectively with host country nationals. The *perceptual dimension* refers to the ability to understand why foreigners behave the way they do, and thus reflects the ability to learn. The last, the *cultural-toughness* of the host country, is a contextual dimension that refers to cultural distance from the home country (the likely difficulty or "toughness" of the posting).

Ronen expanded on the previous work and identified five categories of attributes of success: job factors, relational dimensions, motivational state (referring to interest in the assignment and host country), family situation, and language skills.[63] Oddou concluded by stating that while there are never any guarantees in identifying the "right" person for the international assignment, a few indicators enhance a firm's chances of picking a successful person:

- The capacity to adapt to change (new structures, new rules, and new faces).
- The open-mindedness of the candidate.
- Sociability.
- Self-confidence.
- Having a supportive family.
- The capacity to deal with stress.[64]

If one adds up all the characteristics that have been found to be important, the ideal expatriate is close to superhuman! One cross-cultural textbook identified 68 dimensions, 21 of which were deemed to be highly desirable.[65] Which traits and skills are the most relevant depends on the role the expatriate is expected to assume. For agency-type assignments, clear managerial qualifications together with the relevant professional skills are the essential foundation. Expatriates in such roles should also be able to improvise and find new solutions in the face of unexpected changes, impart confidence in their own ability to solve problems in difficult situations, and most of all, motivate all members of the organization to cooperate. In contrast, for learning-oriented assignments, relationship abilities and cultural awareness may become more important since they are the keys that open access to new knowledge.

How do international companies respond to these recommendations? The emphasis is clearly on enlarging the pool of potential candidates for international assignments and on making sure that the international track attracts those with the best potential to succeed in the firm.[66] Assessments for international assignment are becoming closely linked to the overall evaluation of an employee's potential and are also increasingly rigorous.

ASSESSMENT TOOLS. So far, only a minority of multinationals rely on any kind of standardized tests and evaluations, be it psychological profiling, cultural proficiency tests, or family readiness evaluations.[67] For companies interested in formal assessment methods, there is no shortage of expatriate selection tools, though not all are well validated. Some of the desirable expatriate traits such as intercultural adaptability, conflict-resolution style, and willingness to communicate can be assessed using standard psychometric tests. Some companies using formal assessments evaluate candidates only after they have been identified for an international assignment; others such as Nestlé and Lafarge screen all college graduates for future success as "global managers."

When formal assessment is used, it is argued that this should not be applied to screen out unsuitable candidates.[68] The results should instead guide objective feedback to the employee. This allows the potential expatriate (and the family) to carefully consider all the factors that may influence success on the assignment, to consult with experts on how to deal with problematic areas—or to decline the assignment.

By far the most common assessment method is simply to interview the potential candidate, and here appropriate structured interview techniques can increase effectiveness.[69] In addition, people from the intended host firm should be involved in the interview process.

Many experienced international firms send potential expatriates on a preassignment orientation visit. This helps the local hosts to evaluate the candidate's fit with the new environment, and the candidate can review the job and location before agreeing. Such visits can avoid costly surprises later, and they may be valuable even after both sides agree to the assignment. In data collected by GE on global HR best practices, expatriates in a number of firms felt that free time with the family is required upon arrival, prior to starting the new job. This minimizes the need to divide attention between family and work during the demanding period of settling into a new job and getting to know colleagues and the customer network.

WHAT ABOUT THE FAMILY? Family considerations have a critical impact on the willingness to relocate and the outcome of the assignment. Brett and Stroh showed that the decisions of American managers to relocate were influenced by their spouse's feelings about international relocation, by their own attitude toward moving in general, by the number of children at home, and by the employer's transfer policies (one of the major reasons why people are reluctant to relocate is educational considerations for the children).[70] Virtually all research studies highlight the importance of family well-being, both of spouse and children, the lack of which in Western cultures at least emerges as one of the most important explanations for expatriate failure.[71] The stress of a new job in a new culture combined with strong stress on the family front puts people under intense pressure so that the likelihood of effective adjustment is greatly reduced.

The implication? Whenever possible, select a family, not a person. Not surprisingly, a number of international firms involve the candidate's spouse, if not the whole family, in the process of assessment and counseling, and particularly in the predeparture training.

Research shows that when firms actively seek the opinion of spouses about the assignment, spouses are more likely to adjust to living in the new culture.[72] Furthermore, general living conditions (comfort and safety), the availability and quality of education, expected family life-style, and the like all play a role in the acceptance decision. However, "buying off" the family to gain acceptance can be short-sighted, as a temporary increase in standard of living can make a successful repatriation more difficult.

IS IT OK TO SAY NO? We have pointed out that a properly executed assessment can provide a candidate with feedback before making the final decision on whether to accept the assignment. But what happens if the potential expatriate declines the offer?

The answer depends greatly on the culture of the firm. In some, such a refusal could mean the end to a promising career since international mobility at the discretion of the company is considered to be an integral part of the employment relationship. For junior staff in some international British firms, or in the not so distant past in Japan, expatriate assignments were considered an inherent component of executive development—the issue was not if, but when.[73] Part of the socialization lore was the hardships endured when the boss called on the second day of the honeymoon.

However, it is important to note that the expectations were clearly communicated to the staff before they joined the company.

One can make a strong case for the principle that an individual should not be penalized for declining a job, especially if there is a perceived hardship for the family. Lack of commitment or desire to work internationally only increases the likelihood of failure. However, since companies are trying to ensure that senior executives have international experience, some degree of international mobility is fast becoming a necessary prerequisite for career success. One of the arguments for assessment feedback is to facilitate mutual dialogue around assignment planning at an early stage.

Preparing for an Assignment

Not surprisingly, there is strong agreement in the academic and practitioner literature alike about the need to invest in thorough training and predeparture orientation. Good preparation can go a long way to reducing the time it takes to adjust to the new environment. For the increasing number of companies in which international experience is a key component in management development, early planning and training is important.[74]

Insufficient commitment to expatriate training and development emerges as one of the most common criticisms leveled at HRM practice in multinational companies. Studies show that only a minority of firms offer any kind of predeparture training; and training designs reflect relatively few of the recommendations stemming from research.[75] Why is this? Are the normative prescriptions concerning expatriate training unrealistic? Or could it be that the companies, in particular, top executives, do not see the problem in such a dire light as do the academics?[76] There is a healthy debate that is likely to continue as we learn more about the factors that contribute to expatriate success and failure.

Let us focus on certain important questions concerning expatriate training and development. What kind of expatriate training is required or desirable? When should training take place? Is language competence essential? And what about training for the expatriate's family?

WHAT KIND OF TRAINING? Expatriate training has long focused on cross-cultural issues—the greater the cultural distance of the host country and the more the job involves social interaction, the more important this is.[77] Today there is a rich abundance in this domain—cultural briefings, books, videos, case studies, cross-cultural simulations, websites. But not all preparation happens in a classroom—there are preassignment visits, "shadowing" visits while still in previous job, coaching by an experienced manager, open dialogue on key issues that emerged during the selection process.[78] Obviously, no one training methodology will be universally appropriate—the preparation for a European plant manager to be dispatched to China is bound to be different from that of a Japanese bank trainee on the way to the New York branch. What is often missing is a framework that would guide training managers to make rational choices as to what makes sense when.

WHEN SHOULD TRAINING TAKE PLACE? Some companies start this process a long time before the departure so as to ensure solid preparation.[79] Others argue that training about the host culture is best conducted after the start of the assignment, linked to the expatriate's experience, keeping the predeparture orientation brief and practical and leaving more complex cultural issues for later. Early training may build stereotypes, whereas real assimilation involves understanding subtle differences within a culture, which comes only with experience. However, from a practical viewpoint many expatriates, especially those in executive positions, are either too busy to attend a formal training program after the start of their assignments or their time is considered too valuable to allow for off-the-job education. Without company commitment and a specific training plan built into the workload, any formal learning during the assignment will be difficult.

IS LANGUAGE COMPETENCY ESSENTIAL? Everyone would agree that knowledge of the local language is beneficial—but is this a "must" or just something desirable but not essential? The answer depends on the nature of the job. Many expatriate jobs are focused on internal cross-border control and coordination in which English is rapidly becoming the company language. Here local language proficiency may not be essential. However, when the assignment requires extensive interaction with local customers or with local employees who may not speak English or any other "office language," the capacity to speak the local language may be essential.[80]

Our own experience suggests additional dimensions to the language issue. Often it is not mastery of the language that counts but the effort and commitment shown by the expatriate in acquiring the ability to converse. This shows respect for the local culture, and that is appreciated anywhere in the world. Also, learning to speak another language is for most people a humbling experience, at least in the initial stages, leading to more empathy with those speaking a nonnative language.

PREPARING THE FAMILY. Preparation and training for the family, or at least the spouse, deserves the same attention and material support as for the expatriate. The spouse is typically more exposed to the local culture than the expatriate on the job, and learning the language may be important in facilitating adjustment. Again, learning opportunities after the start of the assignment may be more valuable than predeparture training—here the argument is much stronger since there are not the same job constraints. Toyota and General Motors are two companies at which language training is available for the whole family before and during the foreign assignment.

Adjusting to the Expatriate Role

When people move to an unfamiliar environment they have to learn to adjust to new behaviors, norms, values, and assumptions. Most people today are familiar with the notion of *culture shock*. This is a U-shaped process of adjustment in which an initial honeymoon stage of excitement, worry, and adventure leads to a depressive downswing, the phase of shock and unfreezing. Ideally this heralds an upswing of learning and adaptation. Digging further into culture shock, Black and other researchers have spelled out three dimensions of cross-cultural adjustment (defined as the degree of psychological comfort with living and working in the host country)—adjustment to work, general adjustment, and interaction adjustment.[81]

The first dimension is *adjustment to the work* in the new environment. If the job is unclear, if there is conflict inherent in the role, and if there is little discretion in the work, adjustment is likely to be difficult. Some companies schedule an overlap with the job predecessor to ease some of these strains. In the globally integrated firm, this may be the easiest dimension of adjustment because of similarities in procedures, policies, and tasks across the global firm.

The second dimension is *adjustment to the general environment.* Here the difficulties increase with cultural distance—reactions to housing, safety, food, education, transportation, and health conditions. Companies try to minimize the problems via expatriate house and educational allowances. Previous international experience, an effective orientation (including for the family), and spending time with other expatriates prior to the assignment facilitate this aspect of adjustment.

The challenge of *adjustment to interaction with local nationals* is generally the most difficult for the expatriate and the family. Behavioral norms, patterns of communication, ways of dealing with conflict, and other aspects of relationships may be different in the new culture, creating frustration or even anger, which may in turn be counterproductive. How the person adjusts here is linked to the quality of the support network inside the host country, as well as to time spent with other expatriates prior to the assignment and to the linkage with the home office.

Family adjustment matters. Family characteristics, such as family support, communication, and adaptability were found to be related to expatriates' work adjustment.[82] To facilitate this, Honda has "family centers" in their Ohio factory and in Tokyo to help families in the cultural adaptation process. In addition, families of American employees transferred to Japan are "adopted" by Japanese families with similar characteristics (e.g., same age children). Mentors are assigned to each expatriate before departure to keep the expatriate informed of changes in the home organization.

These challenges of adaptation are facilitated if the previously discussed investments in predeparture feedback and training have been made. Then the expatriate and family are better prepared to cope. However, there are limits to what an organization can do. Much depends on the personality of the expatriate, from the motivation to be transferred abroad to the willingness to learn from the new environment. The ultimate indication of cross-cultural adjustment is the ability to express respect for and appreciation of the foreign culture without rejection of one's own roots.[83]

BALANCING MULTIPLE ALLEGIANCES. One of the elements of the adjustment process is finding the right balance of commitment between potentially conflicting allegiances to the parent firm and to the foreign operations. Black and his colleagues have outlined four different patterns of commitment.[84]

Expatriates who are free agents. One group of expatriates is marked by low allegiance to both the parent and the local firm. They see themselves as "free agents" committed to their careers. They do not expect to return home, either because they understand that their careers in the parent firm have already reached a plateau, or because they see their international experience as increasing their value on the external market. Some free agents may do fine in an isolated affiliate, and companies undergoing rapid internationalization may need such "hired guns." As a rule, however, the lack of commitment quickly becomes transparent to local staff, diminishing the credibility of the expatriate.

Expatriates who leave their hearts at home. Another group of expatriates, usually those with long tenure in the parent firm and little previous international experience, remain emotionally attached to the parent firm with little allegiance to local operations. This is reinforced by discomfort with the local culture and strong networks with senior executives back at home. Their behavior is often ethnocentric, which may antagonize employees or customers, though their ability to work easily with the HQ may make them valuable in situations in which close global coordination is required. This group can benefit most from cross-cultural training and other tools facilitating adjustment.

Expatriates who "go native." Some expatriates exhibit the opposite pattern, building a strong identification with the local firm and culture. They are difficult to repatriate, often preferring to leave the firm and remain in their new home. The main challenge facing the parent office here is the difficulty in getting their cooperation for the implementation of corporate policies and programs. They do not fit well into a meganational firm, though they may thrive in one with a multidomestic orientation, capitalizing on their ability to build trust and support with local employees and influential stakeholders.

Expatriates with dual allegiance. Obviously, the ideal outcome would be to develop expatriates who are strong on both dimensions, though research shows that this is the exception rather than the rule (perhaps less than 25 percent of all expatriates).[85] These expatriates see themselves as "dual citizens" and feel a responsibility to serve the interest of both parties. While they adjust well to the local culture, they see their careers in a broader global context and anticipate repatriation. They deal effectively with the local environment, but they are also responsive to the needs of the parent, thus facilitating the coordination of global initiatives. The key factors supporting the development of such ideal "dual citizens" are associated with the work environment. Dual allegiance is fostered by role clarity, job discretion, and a manageable degree of role conflict. The first two sets of factors can be addressed through appropriate job design; the last factor is closely linked to implementation of an effective expatriate performance management system.

Appraising Expatriate Performance

As mentioned earlier, performance management is one of the HRM tools that can facilitate (or hinder) global integration through the subordination of local business results to global objectives and standards. This is just one example of the potential challenges in appraising performance. Conducting performance appraisals is not easy in any circumstances, but the difficulties are compounded in the expatriate context.[86] We will review three key issues concerning the performance management process and examine how they relate to the expatriate situation: What is the purpose of the appraisal, what criteria and standards should be used, and who should conduct the performance evaluation?[87]

WHAT IS THE PURPOSE OF THE APPRAISAL? Typically, managerial performance appraisals have two broad objectives: first, assessing past performance (with the conflicting aims of providing feedback and of assessing the implications for pay and promotion decisions); and second, setting development goals to improve performance in the future. But there is no generic expatriate performance appraisal system. Given the varied roles and responsibilities of expatriates identified above, performance evaluation should be carefully targeted to the specific roles and responsibilities of the expatriate. One of the lessons from Nokia's global expansion is the value of differentiated expatriate performance management.[88]

In many expatriate appraisals, the link between performance and rewards is problematic. The use of traditional financial incentives is often distorted by the constraints of expatriate compensation schemes heavily tilted toward fixed income and benefit-rich packages. With respect to promotional incentives, research shows that relatively few international assignments led to promotion after the return home, even though most expatriates expected them to. And what about the consequences of underperformance? As mentioned earlier, the high cost of international mobility may lead to greater tolerance for substandard performance.

WHAT STANDARDS AND CRITERIA TO USE? Multinationals around the world use fairly similar criteria in evaluating the performance of their *subsidiaries,* though the specific targets and standards will obviously be different.[89] However, when it comes to the performance evaluation process of *managers,* especially expatriates, there are great differences between firms. Some companies keep expatriates in the parent country pool for appraisal purposes, some treat expatriates as they would a local employee in the same job, while others add specific criteria reflecting the nature of the expatriate's job.

If criteria specific to the expatriates are used, should these criteria be customized or standardized?[90] The main reason why some companies use expatriate-specific criteria is to assess competencies unique to international assignments such as cross-cultural and interpersonal skills, sensitivity to local norms and values, understanding of differences in labor practices or customer relations, or ease of adaptation to an unfamiliar environment.

Many environmental factors such as exchange rate fluctuations, local borrowing costs, and changes in the tax regime have an impact on the performance of the subsidiary, which in turn will affect the performance evaluation of its expatriate managers. As mentioned earlier, however, defining performance in multinational firms is a complex issue, going well beyond matters of accounting. Companies often face serious challenges in dealing with some of the obstacles in measuring local performance. How these challenges are operationally resolved can have a major impact on how expatriates act.

In a broader sense, these issues reflect the global/local tension in any multinational firm. However, there is another critical tension that impacts expatriate performance criteria, namely the difference in the time horizon of expatriates and locals—short-term success in the job versus accountability for the long-term performance of the business unit. Indeed, the short-term focus is one of the most frequent criticisms leveled at expatriate managers by their local subordinates.[91] Rightly or wrongly, expatriates are often perceived as caring about results only within the time frame of their expected assignments. This is a generic issue when employees move across intraorganizational boundaries, but it has special significance in the cross-cultural context.

There is one long-term consideration that many observers consider a "must" in most expatriate appraisals, namely, developing a local successor. This is so often a desirable goal that if only some of the train-the-successor schemes had been implemented, there would not be many expatriates left in the world! Reality, however, is a different story. Sometimes the goal is conveniently forgotten as the limitations of local reality set in. At the other extreme, rigid adherence to such a visible target can lead to the appointment of a local successor ("that objective can be checked off"), only to see the performance of the unit collapse in the long term. Then the local successor is removed (often bought out at great expense), and another expatriate parachutes in with the order to fix the performance and groom a successor.

WHO SHOULD CONDUCT THE EVALUATION? A frequent complaint about expatriate appraisal is that many expatriates are evaluated mainly by superiors or HR staff in the home office who may not have much international experience.[92] For example, a study of ninety-nine Finnish companies operating internationally reported that in 79 percent of the firms the expatriate performance evaluation was conducted by the superior located in Finland.[93] Are such raters competent? Only those who can observe the expatriate in action can have anything to say about their developmental needs. Even if they have international experience they may not be in a position to evaluate the performance of a manager in the faraway subsidiary. At the same time, knowing that performance is being judged only in the head office may also induce the expatriate to spend more effort in managing the center rather than the business.

Another important issue in this context is the extent to which local managers and employees can influence the performance appraisal of the expatriate. In meganational firms, this is not likely to happen. For example, in studies of Japanese companies abroad, local managers rarely provided meaningful input to the appraisal of their Japanese subordinates.[94] Some local managers accept this as inevitable because of the ownership structure and strategic orientation of the firm. Others see it as a major obstacle since their impact on subordinate behaviors is limited unless they have an influence on the appraisal process. The extent to which local managers have input into the performance appraisal of expatriates is a good indication of the degree to which the company is following a meaningful localization strategy. Even when it is, this does not eliminate the risk of perverse results. In one major multinational, local staff were politely praiseworthy of even overtly incompetent expatriates. They knew that if they said anything negative, they would be saddled with the individual for a longer period of time!

Part of the justification for excluding the input of local managers is that people from different cultures may often misinterpret one another's behavior.[95] From this perspective, the utilization of 360° feedback in some form or another guarantees multiple points of view on expatriate performance, and this is probably the appropriate direction for resolving some of these dilemmas.

Expatriate Compensation

Surveys often show that the cost of expatriate managers is a major concern of international firms.[96] This is not surprising as the total cost burden for the company is estimated at two to four times an expatriate's salary, depending on the location of the assignment.

The field of expatriate compensation is more the domain of international compensation specialists and consultants than of academic research. Over the years, most international companies have developed elaborate systems to account for cost-of-living differences between countries, to respond to variations in tax regimes, or to provide incentives for employees to work in so-called hardship areas. In most contributions on the topic, however, there seems to be a constant yearning for a more effective model of expatriate compensation. Developing an effective expatriate compensation system is a task that goes far beyond technical analysis and is in fact linked closely to the company's internationalization strategy.

THE EVOLUTION OF EXPATRIATE COMPENSATION STRATEGIES. Historically, during the early stages of globalization, the expatriate pay package was usually the result of individual negotiations. Since foreign assignments were not considered particularly desirable from the point of view of career progression, financial incentives such as relocation premiums were common—mostly dependent on the bargaining skills of the expatriate. The net result was generally high and continuously escalating expatriate costs, accompanied by corresponding difficulties in repatriation after the completion of the assignment.

With the increasing number of expatriates, the ad hoc negotiation-driven approach quickly outlived its usefulness. The next generation of compensation plans attempted to provide at least a common base—usually the home or host country salary, whichever was highest—reducing the size of the added component negotiated on a case-by-case basis.[97] Yet, as the expatriate population continued to grow, so did the need to move away from the traditional location-specific incentive approach to a more generic across-the-board compensation schemes.

Today, a number of generic methodologies have emerged (see the summary of expatriate compensation systems in Figure 3–2).[98] The determination of what kind of specific expatriate compensation plan to select is influenced primarily by three sets of considerations:

- *Cost efficiency*—making sure that the plan delivers intended benefits in the most cost-effective manner (including tax consequences).[99]
- *Equity issues*—making sure that the plan is equitable irrespective of the assignment location or nationality of the expatriate.
- *System maintenance*—making sure that the plan is relatively transparent and easy to administer.

We will examine in more detail the costs and benefits of one method that is commonly used by North American and European firms—the balance sheet approach—and we will also review some of the emerging expatriate compensation trends.

FIGURE 3–2. A Summary of Expatriate Compensation Systems

Compensation System	For Whom Most Appropriate	Advantages	Disadvantages
Negotiation	• Special situations • Organizations with few expatriates	• Conceptually simple	• Breaks down with increasing numbers of expatriates
Localization	• Permanent transfers and long-term assignments • Entry-level expatriates	• Simple to administer • Equity with local nationals	• Expatriates usually come from different economic conditions than local nationals
Headquarters-based Balance Sheet	• Many nationalities of expatriates working together • Very few TCNs	• No nationality discrimination • Simple administration	• High compensation costs • Difficult to repatriate TCNs
Home Country-based Balance Sheet	• Several nationalities of expatriates on out-and-back-home assignments	• Low compensation costs • Simple to repatriate TCNs	• Discrimination by nationality • Highly complex administration
Modified Home Country-based Balance Sheet	• Many expatriates of many nationalities on project assignments	• Moderate costs • Moderately simple administration	• Lack of conceptual purity
Lump-Sum Approaches	• Consistently short assignments (less than three years), followed by repatriation	• Resembles domestic compensation practices • Does not intrude on expatriate finances	• Exchange rate variation makes this unworkable except for short assignments
International Pay Structures	• Senior executives of all nationalities	• Tax- and cost-effective • Expatriates and local nationals may be on the same compensation plan	• Inhibits mobility for lower levels of expatriates • Lack of consistency among locations
Cafeteria Approaches	• Senior executives	• Tax- and cost-effective	• To be effective, options needed for each country • Difficult to use with lower levels of expatriates
Regional Plans	• Large numbers of expatriates mobile within region(s)	• Less costly than global uniformity • Can be tailored to regional requirements	• Multiple plans to administer • Discrimination between regionalists and globalists
Multiple Programs	• Many expatriates on different types of assignments	• Can tailor compensation programs to different types of expatriates • Possible lower compensation costs	• Difficulty of establishing and maintaining categories • Discrimination by category • Highly complex administration

Source: C. Reynolds, *Compensating Globally Mobile Employees* (Scottsdale, AZ: American Compensation Association, 1995).

BALANCE SHEET APPROACH. The term "balance sheet" refers to any compensation system that is designed to enable expatriates to maintain a standard of living roughly equivalent to the standard of living in their own country, irrespective of the location of their assignment. Home country salary is divided proportionately into several components based on norms (see Figure 3–3). A typical breakdown is goods and services, housing, taxes, and a reserve. Home and host country expenses for each component are compared and the expatriate is compensated for the increased cost.

The balance sheet approach is popular, as it is perceived to maintain in a reasonably cost-effective manner the purchasing power of the expatriate (the common HR jargon used is "keeping the employee whole"), thus eliminating most of the direct financial obstacles to mobility. In reality, given that many expatriates complain about reduced compensation upon repatriation,[100] this methodology tends to overcompensate—but probably less so than the alternatives.

While the balance sheet methodology is simple in concept, it is complex to implement. For example, what is the definition of the home country for the purpose of the balance sheet calculations? When expatriates all come from the same country or economic region, work abroad for a single two-to-three-year assignment, and then are expected to return to their home country, there is no ambiguity about what is home. But if expatriates in one foreign location come from different countries with substantially different costs of living, the methodology may result in unacceptably wide discrepancies in compensation. If the company uses the HQ location as "home," then expatriates from countries with lower compensation standards will be difficult to repatriate. Some companies use a modified approach where the real home is the base for goods and services while HQ standards are applied to housing (the most visible component of compensation)(see Figure 3–3).

While the balance sheet approach is a well-accepted methodology, it has further limits. It encourages people to import their lifestyles, thereby creating barriers between expatriates and locals, especially in countries with lower purchasing power. It also eliminates any incentives for expatriates to moderate their spending patterns as they learn to navigate in the new environment. Most important, since a sizeable part of compensation and lifestyle is guaranteed, it is difficult to establish a clear connection between results and rewards.

ALTERNATIVES TO THE BALANCE SHEET APPROACH. Increased heterogeneity of expatriates may require a "global" compensation package in which national origin or home has no impact, at least for senior executives who are regarded as "corporate property." Consider the case of the vice president of a U.S.-based firm, leading a global business unit located in Tokyo. If this person comes from the United States or Europe, it is taken for granted that housing arrangements will reflect the lifestyle back home. If the successor happens to be Japanese (just returning from a senior assignment in the HQ), does this mean that no housing allowance should be paid?

Some version of a cafeteria approach is becoming increasingly more appealing. A weakness of the balance sheet approach (indeed of most compensation methodologies)

FIGURE 3–3. Balance Sheet Approach to Expatriate Compensation

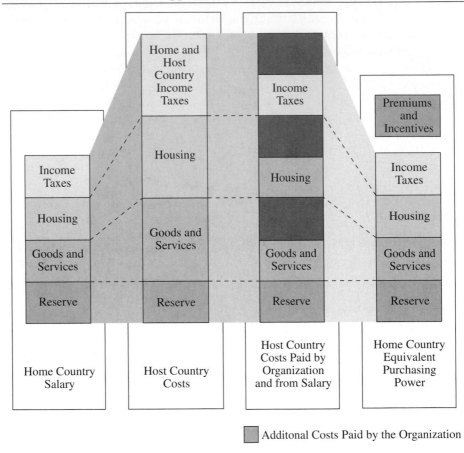

☐ Additonal Costs Paid by the Organization

Source: Adapted from C. Reynolds, *Compensating Globally Mobile Employees* (Scottsdale, AZ: American Compensation Association, 1995), 9.

is its reliance on norms tailored to the "average" expatriate. Again, the increased heterogeneity of the expatriate population is creating havoc with this assumption. For example, the balance sheet approach does not work well for those expatriates whose spouses suspend their own careers. For some expatriates, support for their children's education may top the list of essential benefits, while for others it may be long-term care for parents left behind. The cafeteria approach to benefits, pricing such benefits and permitting choice within a limit, is often essential.

For short-term assignments, it may be more convenient to provide simple lump-sum payments to cover the additional expenses and let the expatriates manage their finances the way they see fit. This avoids unnecessary entitlements or intruding too much into private financial circumstances such as tax status.

In some firms, the vast majority of international assignments are confined to a specific region (e.g., the European Union or ASEAN). In that case, it may be advisable to tailor the policy to the conditions within that region rather than apply a worldwide policy. Again, differences in treatment of "regional" and "global" expatriates have to be carefully monitored. Whenever employees in similar jobs are treated differently, morale and commitment are bound to suffer.

TRENDS IN GLOBAL COMPENSATION. The fact that so many are unhappy with the state of expatriate compensation is certainly not caused by a lack of available methodologies. The problem is that most pay methodologies make universal assumptions about where expatriates come from, their roles, and where they are going. The population of international managers is increasingly diverse. No single system can provide solutions to the multiple demands of expatriation.

Some observers argue that if a firm's expatriate population consists of several categories (for example, senior executives, mid-level professionals, and junior trainees), then compensation packages should be tailored to the specific needs of each group. After all, the motives for expatriation vary from one category to another—agency, problem-solving, and competence development, respectively. This may lead to a unified global compensation plan for the senior executives irrespective of their location, a balance sheet approach for other expatriate managers and professionals, and local pay systems for entry-level and junior assignees. Alternatively, the company may have one system for career expatriates and another for those on short assignments.

Consequently, when it comes to the choice of expatriate compensation strategy, the starting point is to clarify two key questions:

- What categories of expatriates does the company have, or will it have, in the future?
- Shall all categories of expatriates be paid using the same method?

The answers to these questions will depend on the evolution of the internationalization strategy, the HRM philosophy, and the composition of the expatriate population. It is also important to bear in mind that compensation is only one of the factors that determine an employee's desire to accept an international assignment. Nonfinancial rewards such as learning opportunities and expectations of future career gains are also important motivators. When expatriation is a "ticket to nowhere," no amount of effort to fine-tune the compensation package will produce a committed and dedicated expatriate workforce.

Repatriation and Reentry

At least with respect to the expatriates from the home office, most eventually come home. However, coming home is not an easy matter. What may seem to some a routine business may in reality be a complex process of renegotiating one's identity, rebuilding professional networks, and reanchoring one's career in the organization.[101] Many expatriates find it particularly difficult to give up the autonomy and freedom they have enjoyed on their international assignment. Even more frustrating are "make-work" assignments, doled out to the returnees who are stuck in a holding pattern while waiting for a real job opportunity to open up. Empirical research with German and Japanese expatriates suggests that the most troublesome problems in expatriation originate from poor career management systems and impaired relations with headquarters rather than adjustment to the foreign culture.[102]

Combining all this with loss in social status—no more invitations to the Prime Minister's Christmas party—and loss of financial benefits associated with expatriation,[103] it is no surprise that many observers argue that the cultural shock of coming home may be even larger than the shock associated with the initial expatriation,[104] and that available data point to a relatively high turnover of employees after return from international assignments.[105] This can lead to a vicious circle, increasing resistance to expatriation and thereby to the firm's ability to implement a strategy of global integration.

As with data on expatriate "failure" however, there are reasons to be conservative about the scope of the problem. One should compare the turnover of expatriates to the general turnover of managers, also recognizing that any job transition is stressful, even within one's home country.[106] Nevertheless, more can be done at relatively low cost to improve the odds of success. Visibly successful returns can have a positive impact on the willingness of others to accept an international assignment. The starting point is to get high performing international managers recognized and promoted upon their return home.

The best repatriation practices emphasize advance planning in order to provide meaningful opportunities upon return, emotional and logistical support during the transition, and continuous dialogue with the expatriate through formal or informal networking or mentoring programs.[107] At such firms as IBM, Shell, and Lafarge, where international mobility is considered essential, a "career manager" or "advisor" monitors the expatriate's development throughout the assignment, keeps him or her informed, and serves as an advocate for the expatriate during the home country succession planning process.

Some companies fix an end-date to every foreign assignment so as to facilitate succession and repatriation planning. Another frequently applied policy is to require the dispatching unit to take formal responsibility for finding a position for the expatriate comparable to the one he or she left. However, after being away for three to four years, the repatriate may actually experience a demotion, the fate of a surprisingly large number of the returnees.[108] At Coca-Cola the employee is provided with repatriation counseling and a "safety net" of one year to find another position at the parent firm.[109]

An important objective of the career discussions is to enhance the opportunities for utilizing the knowledge and skills acquired during the foreign assignment, and not just those linked to a specific country or job abroad. The valuable acquired learning may reflect a new ability to deal with ambiguity and change, understanding of how to learn quickly about an unfamiliar environment, and skills in leading multicultural teams.

Finally, the authors' experiences with a number of multinational firms suggest two observations on how to increase the odds of a successful repatriation. First, seeing is believing. If most senior executives have international experience, this demonstrates the value of expatriation and eases worry about repatriation. Second, the best predictor of successful repatriation is the performance of the expatriate before his or her international assignment. Successful repatriation starts with careful selection.

Employees with an outstanding track record prior to their expatriate assignment will usually be easier to place in good jobs upon their return.[110]

A Summary of Practices Supporting Effective Expatriation

A number of key themes[111] regarding best practices supporting effective expatriation are summarized in Figure 3–4. Sending personnel abroad is a multifaceted challenge for any firm.

In the area of *staffing and selection,* the thrust of HR activities in leading global firms is making sure that the international track attracts those with the best potential to succeed in the firm. Assessment for international assignments is becoming increasingly rigorous and often involves the candidate's spouse. From the *management development* perspective, international assignments are increasingly viewed as an intrinsic part of career progression, providing opportunities for the transfer of know-how as well as learning new competencies. While leading firms invest heavily in training their international managers, this is not just at the predeparture stage. Expatriates are expected to continue learning about the host culture, improving their international skills during the assignment. Family well-being is now recognized as an important element of expatriate effectiveness.

The first step in building *effective reward systems* is to recognize that "equitable" does not mean "equal." The expatriate role, the duration of the assignment,

---

FIGURE 3–4. Human Resource Practices That Support Effective Expatriation

Staffing and Selection
- Communicate the value of international assignments for the company's global mission.
- Ensure that those with the highest potential move internationally.
- Provide short-term assignments to increase the pool of employees with international experience.
- Recruit employees who have lived or who were educated abroad.

Training and Career Development
- Make international assignment planning a part of the career development process.
- Encourage early international experience.
- Create learning opportunities during the assignment.
- Use international assignments as a leadership development tool.

Performance Appraisal and Compensation
- Differentiate performance management based on expatriate roles.
- Align incentives with expatriation objectives.
- Tailor benefits to the expatriate's needs.
- Focus on equality of opportunities, not cash.
- Emphasize rewarding careers rather than short-term outcomes.

Expatriation and Repatriation Activities
- Involve the family in the orientation program at the beginning and the end of the assignment.
- Establish mentor relationships between expatriates and executives from the home location.
- Provide support for dual careers.
- Secure opportunities for the returning manager to use knowledge and skills learned while on the international assignment.

the long-term implications, the nature of the business—all have a bearing on what kind of compensation approach is the most appropriate. Effective reward systems also look beyond salary and benefits. Access to career development and learning opportunities and even support for the spouse are some of the tools that companies can use to motivate and retain talented expatriates. Finally, *repatriation* is not a routine matter and needs close attention. Visibly successful returns have a positive impact on the willingness of others to accept an international assignment.

BEYOND THE TRADITIONAL EXPATRIATE MODEL

Few firms launch their international expansion without at least a small core of expatriates. However, as companies pursue internationalization, the inevitable tensions of expatriation become apparent. These tensions, together with the changing demographics of the expatriate population—the growing number of women, third country nationals (TCNs), and younger expatriates, and the added need to adjust to dual careers—are changing the way in which companies approach international assignments.

The Tensions in the Expatriate Cycle

Five types of tension are common to most expatriate situations:

Home/host tensions. The presence of expatriates may generate tensions with the local workforce for a number of reasons. Expatriates who are well socialized into the ways of the parent company are often insensitive to local cultural norms. They enjoy a standard of living not available to local employees; they are costly in comparison to the value they are bringing to the local business.[112]

Global/local tensions. When top positions in a subsidiary are continuously occupied by rotating expatriates, many of the capable local managers become discouraged. They either leave or their willingness to make an effort on behalf of the firm slackens. Over time, these disadvantages offset the benefits stemming from an expatriate presence, that is, the simple control structure and the ease of communication with headquarters. In addition, as foreign operations increase in size, an intimate knowledge of local operations becomes as or more important than communication and coordination with the parent head office, and the emphasis then shifts to localization, with expatriates shrinking in number and influence.

Short-term/long-term tensions. Expatriates are often criticized for taking short-term decisions from a perspective limited by the duration of their assignment. Expatriates may shrink from taking necessary actions if the benefits are long term but the cost or risks are immediate. In one such case, a poorly negotiated initial labor contract in the subsidiary of a foreign airline in Japan has for years inflated its labor cost relative to competitors. Renegotiating the contract to align it with the existing practice in the industry so as to generate future savings would be temporarily costly, perhaps even triggering a strike by the union. No one in the long line of expatriate executives has been willing to take the risk "on his watch."

On the other hand, newly appointed expatriates experiencing a heady sense of freedom may take actions to generate change for the sake of change so as to attract the attention of the head office and promote their careers. Not surprisingly, a fast track expatriate was defined on a European website frequented by employees of a U.S. subsidiary as one who "can outrun his mistakes."

Tension between cost and investment. The considerable expense associated with expatriation is often viewed as the cost of market entry, to be reduced if not eliminated in the long run. Indeed, the need to reduce the costs of expatriation is often one of the major drivers of localization. Yet while companies can benefit from smarter management of expatriate costs, the expense of expatriation can be seen as an essential investment in building the linkages necessary for managing a transnational firm and in learning across organizational boundaries.[113] Thus a push to increase short-term profits by reducing expatriate costs may result in the reduction of long-term revenues as a consequence of underinvestment in global learning and coordination. The cost-driven expatriation strategy often leads to "boom-bust" pendulums. The number of expatriates increases in good times, only to be cut when growth slows and recession looms, creating havoc and imbalance in the local organization.

Demand/supply tensions. Some observers have suggested that the demand for experienced and capable expatriate managers is becoming more acute, caused mainly by the accelerating pace of internationalization.[114] However, constraints on international mobility are also increasing, many of them stemming from family considerations and changing career expectations. Employees are increasingly reluctant to move abroad if it will handicap the educational opportunities for their children or mean that one spouse in the family has to put his or her career on hold. Parental care is also a growing concern. In a competitive environment, good people have alternative employment options.

Changing Demographics of the Expatriate Population

Traditionally, policies and practices governing international assignments were built on a number of assumptions about expatriate characteristics:

- Expatriates were selected from the employees in the parent country.
- The expatriate population was homogeneous in ethnicity, gender, and experience—home country, male, technically experienced, possibly married but with an adaptable spouse.
- Expatriate assignments were temporary (3–4 years in duration), often occurring only once during a career.
- The objective of the assignment was to maintain control over the affiliate and to transfer know-how from the sophisticated parent to the underdeveloped subsidiary.
- After completion of the assignment an expatriate was expected to return home, to be replaced by another expatriate.

Today, these assumptions are less and less valid. The expatriate population is increasingly heterogeneous, and what is needed is a contingent approach to expatriation.[115] In a number of multinationals, the prototypical experienced male executive from the parent country is already in a minority. Because of growing use of expatriation as a tool for learning and development, many expatriates are relatively young. And as companies throughout the world are removing obstacles to gender diversity in management, an increasing proportion of expatriates are women.

WOMEN EXPATRIATES. Although international experience is seen as one of the critical foundations for developing future leaders, until the late 1980s only 5 percent of all American expatriates were women. According to some recent surveys, this proportion has increased to about 17 percent, a major advance but still substantially below the participation rate of American women in management. Yet, comparing this number with the rest of the world, America is far ahead in terms of women expatriates.

A number of explanations have been forwarded to account for the small number of women expatriates: cultural prejudices, including the low acceptance of working women abroad; lack of support and access to male-dominated expatriate networks; inflexibility and resentment by male peers; particular difficulties linked to family and dual career issues; and the unwillingness of women to accept foreign assignments.[116] Adler identified "three common myths" regarding women expatriates:[117]

- Women do not want to become international managers.
- Companies refuse to send women overseas.
- Even when women are interested in international assignments, the prejudices of foreigners against women may render them ineffective.

Exploration of these myths stimulated a number of studies of female expatriates, not only in the United States, but also in Europe. The box "Research on Female Expatriates" summarizes key findings in this research domain. Some studies pointed out that women may actually have an advantage in their roles as expatriates. For example, at least until more women take over expatriate roles, the factors of visibility and novelty may enhance access to the local business network.[118] More broadly, Tung argued that women tend to possess attributes that make them more suitable for overseas work than men, such as indirectness in communication, good listening skills, and emphasis on cooperation over competition.[119] Also, because women executives have long experienced being outsiders, they may be better equipped to manage the stress that often accompanies isolation in foreign settings.

DUAL CAREER CONSIDERATIONS. An observation from the research on female expatriates is that they are more likely to be single than their male colleagues. Female managers are more likely to have working partners than men, and so they may be more constrained by dual careers. When an expatriate moves, the spouse may find it difficult to find a comparable job at the new location. Often there are no available jobs, a situation aggravated by the obstacles of visa regulations, professional licensing rules, and language barriers. And even if a job is available locally, it may not contribute to a meaningful career, reducing the likelihood that the couple will be willing to move.

Research on Female Expatriates
Research Box

One stream of research focuses on *the desire of women to become expatriates.* Examining responses from more than 1,000 students from multiple universities, Adler concluded that male and female students displayed no differences in their interest in pursuing international careers.[A] Similar results were observed in a more recent study conducted by Tung.[B] However, contradictory results were obtained in another study that examined willingness to accept assignments for particular destinations.[C] Here, substantial variance among males and females was observed, influenced by differences among countries on indicators of cultural distance and human development.

With respect to *willingness to select female expatriates,* Adler concluded that 70 percent of HR professionals in sixty multinational companies were hesitant to choose women.[D] Among the reasons offered were difficulties in accommodating dual careers and gender prejudice in the countries to which women would be sent. Others have argued that qualified female employees may be getting overlooked because men make most of the decisions about whom to send and many hold traditional stereotypes about women in international jobs.[E]

Several studies have focused on *the adjustment and performance of women expatriates.* American female expatriates were found to be just as successful as their counterparts overseas—even in so-called male dominated cultures such as Japan and Korea.[F] Other results suggest that male and female expatriates can perform equally well in international assignments regardless of the country's predisposition to women in management, but that female expatriates self-rate their adjustment lower in countries with few women in the workforce.[G] Female expatriates were perceived as being effective regardless of the cultural toughness of the host country.[H] Also, female international assignees feel more strongly than their supervisors that prejudice does *not* limit women's ability to be successful abroad,

saying that host country prejudice may be less of a problem than past research has claimed.

However, there is some evidence that it is more difficult for women to reconcile international assignments with the careers of their spouses. Companies with a high number of female expatriates are more likely to report problems resulting from the inability of spouses to continue careers.[I] Not surprisingly, therefore, half to two-thirds of the women on international assignments were reportedly single in contrast to 15 percent of men.[J] In another study, almost 80 percent of men on international assignments were married and accompanied by wives, while this was the case for less than a quarter of women expatriates.[K]

Harzing examined a number of *factors influencing the proportion of women in the expatriate population.*[L] She found that this ratio bore a relationship to the type of industry (some are more male-dominated than others) and to Hofstede's masculinity-femininity dimension—feminine countries such as Holland and the Scandinavian nations have a much larger share of female expatriates than masculine countries such as Japan. At the same time, it seems that where there is a will there is a way. Companies reporting problems in finding home-country staff with sufficient international management skills employ a larger number of female expatriates.

[A]Adler, 1986.
[B]Tung, 1997.
[C]Lowe, Downes, and Kroeck, 1999.
[D]Adler, 1984. However, a more recent study of U.S. and Canadian multinationals (Stroh, Varma, and Valy-Durbin, 2000) seems to contradict these results.
[E]Chusmir and Frontczak, 1990.
[F]Adler, 1987; Taylor and Napier, 1996.
[G]Caligiuri and Tung, 1999.
[H]Stroh, Varma, and Valy-Durbin, 2000.
[I]Harzing, 1999.
[J]Adler, 1987; Westwood and Leung, 1994.
[K]Reynolds and Bennett, 1991.
[L]Harzing, 1999.

In an expatriate survey conducted by Shell, the spouse's career and employment came out as the second most important constraint on international mobility—right after children's educational needs.[120] While half of the spouses accompanying Shell staff on international assignments were employed until the transfer, only 12 percent were able to secure employment while abroad, while another 33 percent wished to be employed—and these numbers do not include those who chose not to go.

What can companies do to make it easier for dual career couples to pursue international careers?[121] There are a number of possibilities for action, from better assignment planning to spouse repatriation:

- Plan the assignment in terms of location, timing, and duration based on professional preferences and personal circumstances of the couple.
- Approach the partner's employer and jointly prepare expatriation plans.
- Provide career counseling and assistance in locating employment opportunities for spouses abroad.
- Subsidize educational programs for a spouse while abroad.
- Support entrepreneurial initiatives by spouses.
- Cooperate with other multinational organizations in finding jobs for spouses.
- Provide reemployment advice to partners after repatriation.

YOUNGER EXPATRIATES. The issue of dual careers is often easier to manage among younger expatriates. Their partners (if any) may be more flexible in terms of available opportunities as they have less at risk from an international career detour. Another factor driving an increase in the number of younger expatriates is the cost of expatriation being sensitive to the presence, age, and number of children. Family expenses such as housing, education, and home leave can easily surpass salary cost at lower professional levels. So placing younger employees who are single or who have small families in international jobs can substantially reduce the total compensation cost.

This point is important because the prime aim of international assignments is shifting from demand-driven to learning-driven objectives, as discussed earlier. Instead of agency or problem-solving aims, assignments are increasingly targeting the competence development of the firm and the career enhancement of the individual.[122] These learning assignments are naturally suited for the younger employees.

As a sidenote, a complementary trend is that there are opportunities for international transfers later in employees' careers, when they may be looking for lateral challenges, free of child-rearing constraints, and open to new challenges. Some emerging countries are more interested in benefiting from the experience of these senior managers rather than in securing young professionals who are more intent on making their own careers than in developing local talent.

THIRD COUNTRY NATIONALS. Expatriates from countries other than the parent country of the multinational are commonly referred to as third country nationals (TCNs). The scarcity of suitable candidates for international assignments and attempts to hold down the cost of expatriation are two factors driving TCN employment. For example, a U.S. multinational may seek to employ expatriots from the U.K., Canadian, and Australia, countries with a common language and relatively comparable compensation and living standards, but no tax on expatriate income. With accelerating globalization, companies are looking for the most suitable candidate irrespective of country of origin, and thus the proportion of TCNs in the expatriate population is bound to increase.

The most frequent HR problems associated with TCN assignments center on how to pay them and how to keep them. While it may seem logical that pay levels should be based on home country levels adjusted for a cost-of-living differential (plus housing and similar allowances), the TCNs do not necessarily identify with their home country. And when the differences in living standards between the home country and country of assignment are large, problems are bound to arise—often compounded by misapplication of the traditional expatriate compensation logic.

Consider the case of a corporation that wanted to move Czech engineers to Switzerland. After finishing a major project in the Czech Republic, an international engineering firm wanted to relocate several of its best Czech engineers (trained at considerable cost) to Switzerland, the site of its next major project. Using its standard expatriate tables, the corporate HR department determined that the expatriate cost-of-living difference between Prague and Basel was about 10 percent. Therefore the offer of a Czech base salary plus 25 percent relocation premium was seen as generous. However, what was important for the Czechs was not the expatriate base but how much they needed to earn so as to maintain their former living standards at Swiss price levels, which would require several multiples of their old salaries. Not surprisingly, none of the Czech engineers accepted the transfer offer, and most resigned. The company lost valuable talent, and rather then earning goodwill by providing local employees with international opportunities, it was widely condemned in the media for what was construed as a ruse to avoid the cost of involuntary separation.

Today, TCN expatriates have become an increasingly heterogeneous group posing new challenges in the management of international transfers. The best among them have many alternative opportunities. As with conventional expatriates, there is no single best formula for TCN expatriate compensation. The purpose of the assignment, its duration, the expected work location after its completion (many TCNs do not return home, continuing to the next international assignment)—all impact on the choice of the compensation scheme. Any compensation formula that relegates TCNs to second-class "cheap labor" status will in the long run cause serious damage to morale inside the organization, notwithstanding its underlying mathematical "rationality."

For the increasing number of expatriates who originate from countries other than the corporate parent, repatriation creates a particularly acute dilemma. Even with the best career planning, there may simply be no comparable position back at home. Finishing an assignment sometimes forces an agonizing choice—to return home and leave the company, or to accept a posting in yet another country, which in turn makes an effective later return even more problematic. For them, this is a difficult choice to make because of the consequences not just on the expatriate's career but on the well-being of the whole family.

The Changing Nature of International Assignments

With these changes in the composition of the expatriate population, the conventional expatriate assignment may become an exception rather than the rule. The impact of changing demographics is accentuated by two other trends—the shorter duration of such assignments and the diminishing security of expatriation.

SHORT-TERM ASSIGNMENTS. We earlier identified short-term learning assignments as an increasingly frequent type of expatriation. Many problem-solving and project assignments also have short spans, so it is not surprising that short-term transfers (less than one year in duration) are the fastest growing type of international assignments among European multinationals, for example.[123] Recent surveys indicate similar trends among U.S. multinationals: Up to 20 percent of all international assignments are short term.[124]

Short-term assignments are popular because they offer flexibility and are simpler to plan and execute. Even more important, they typically cost less—expensive housing and cost-of-living allowances are not necessary. Short-term assignments also facilitate repatriation to the home organization. From the employee point of view, they avoid uprooting the working spouse and family. The partner may stay at home or take a short sabbatical. Many companies limit such assignments to less than six months, while longer transfers are treated as a regular international assignment.

THE INSECURITY OF EXPATRIATION. Not only are international transfers increasingly short term, they are also becoming less secure. Although expectations that international experience will be a career booster may not materialize for many expatriates, as it depends very much on the initial purpose (management development assignments may lead to upward mobility though problem-solving transfers may not), expatriate postings in the past provided at least a temporary haven from the turmoil of home-office reorganizations since the terms for international assignments in most Western companies (and virtually all Japanese or Korean companies) included the guarantee of a return position. Now, however, the pattern in at least some countries is changing.

Perhaps owing to the large-scale restructuring, one survey reported that the number of multinationals giving written or informal guarantees decreased overall from 69 percent in 1995 to 46 percent in 1997.[125] In particular, only a minority of Anglo-Saxon companies in the U.S. and U.K. guaranteed a return position, although a majority of continental European firms still provide an expatriate safety net. But with accelerating restructuring in Europe, this trend may spread to the Continent as well. In part, this reflects general changes in the employment relationship—"If we cannot guarantee jobs for people at home, how can we promise them to people abroad?" But it is also a sign that expatriate positions are not exceptional today, so companies do not see the need for any special treatment beyond simply guaranteeing relocation back to the original place of work.

There are mixed signals here. One message from international corporations is that international experience is an asset. However unintentional, another is that it may be risky for the career.[126] There is a growing gap between the rhetoric and the reality. While the logic of "equal" treatment may have some merits, there is no question that employees temporarily located abroad may have substantially more difficulties in lining up alternative job opportunities at home, or at least that they may perceive this to be the case. And an increased *perception* of insecurity naturally leads to increased resistance to international mobility.

Alternatives to Expatriation

How can companies respond proactively to such tensions? With changes in the nature of expatriate jobs and the conditions of the assignment, is there a future for expatriates?[127] Is expatriation the only answer to the challenges of global integration? There are certainly some emerging alternatives.

Global Integration without Expatriates

The ongoing revolution in communications is dramatically expanding the possibilities of "virtual expatriation"—assignments in which employees have responsibilities abroad but manage them from the home country. Some managers with heavy international coordination responsibilities spend so much time on the road that it does not matter where they live. One of Nokia's top European executives works from home in Switzerland, which is closer to most of the countries he has the responsibility for than is the corporate center in Helsinki. Unilever allows its regional managers to decide whether they will live in the parent country or the region—one way or the other, they will be traveling a lot in the other direction.

A variation on postexpatriate management is the "international commuter." Just as many U.S. executives routinely commute across the American continent to their jobs after every weekend, so the new generation of European managers prefers the weekly commute to relocation, for example, taking the high speed train between Brussels and Paris. For them what is important is to secure a stable environment for the family, while companies benefit because of considerable cost savings and because they can substantially expand the pool of candidates for international jobs when relocation is not required.

However, "virtuality" has limits. No amount of electronic communication can replace human contact. The cost of fewer international postings may be more short-term trips. During business downturns, companies are usually quick to issue edicts against unnecessary travel, but all data indicates that business travel worldwide continues to increase.[128] How many times can one jet across the ocean before fatigue sets in? The wear and tear of international travel is a hidden health threat whose cost is yet to be calculated.

Beyond such solutions afforded by new technologies, globally integrated companies are seeking new strategies for organizing international activities. The Spanish company Zara, a rapidly growing global fashion retailer established in 1975 in a remote and impoverished area of Spain, today has over 1,000 stores in more than thirty countries on three continents.[129] In contrast with the established industry logic, Zara makes two-thirds of all its clothes in the company. Zara has its own factories in Spain. It restocks stores around the world twice a week. The team of core designers in the head office continuously redesigns its products.

In managing its tightly integrated empire, Zara uses expatriates only for temporary assignments in connection with start-up operations. Indeed, Zara learned that using Spanish expatriates to run local operations does not necessarily provide good results because of the diverse cultural idiosyncrasies of the host countries.[130] The company relies instead on hiring and socializing local managers into the corporate culture (many of them with some ties to Spain), and Zara will not operate in countries in which local talent is not available. At the same time, the autonomy of local management is subject to rigorous controls.

Zara's core competencies are in design and production processes, and the capabilities required in the subsidiaries to support these core competencies can easily be transferred through formalized procedures in logistics, inventory control, marketing information systems, and centralized product design and pricing. In addition, the company resolves cross-border issues through extensive use of international management meetings and deployment of auditors from the headquarters who monitor local activities. The corporate auditors, who reside in Spain, perform various coordination roles that are often assumed by expatriates in other firms.

Impatriation: The Next Step in Fostering Global Integration

Zara and many other international companies discussed in this chapter invest substantial resources in the socialization of their local managers. An important tool of this process is often a temporary assignment to the head office or parent country operations. Such foreign nationals on nonpermanent assignments in the parent country of the multinational are frequently called "impatriates."[131]

The number of impatriates is increasing worldwide. For example, a survey of U.S. multinationals showed that over 70 percent expect the number of foreign nationals coming to the United States to increase.[132] Similar trends are at work in Europe, where there are more than forty nationalities represented at the headquarters of some major multinationals such as Nestlé and Shell. Only in Japan and Korea is the number of impatriates small.

Most impatriates are young employees or middle managers who come to corporate headquarters for developmental assignments, to absorb the corporate culture, or to participate in project teams. Some come with the explicit aim of preparing themselves to replace expatriates; others stay and join the home organization on a semipermanent or permanent basis. Several well-known global companies, such as Coca-Cola and Financial Times, are run by CEOs who are impatriates.

What kinds of HR policies are best suited to support impatriation? Are typical expatriate policies suitable for impatriates? Are there differences between impatriates and expatriates that would argue for different HR approaches? The situations facing expatriates and impatriates may be similar, but they are not the same. Most impatriates are assigned for learning reasons; very few are "corporate agents." By national origin, they are more heterogeneous as a group than are expatriates, so defining "one-size-fits-all" policies is fraught with difficulties.

The environment in which expatriates and impatriates work is different. Communication is often a major constraint. Employees in foreign locations are generally used to interacting with expatriates. They chose to work for a foreign-based firm and they expect to see foreigners around. The office language is usually the language of the expatriate and the locals have to adapt. Not so for the impatriates. In the home office, communication problems with impatriates are often unexpected and sensitivity to communication difficulties on both sides is required. Indeed, HR may have to support impatriation through cross-cultural training for the locals.

A British manager relocated to the head office in the American Midwest experienced an initial warm welcome, but then social interactions with co-workers cooled off. He felt frozen out. Sharing his concerns with the HR manager, he learned that the locals were upset with his perceived values—putting his career ahead of the family as demonstrated by his leaving two young children behind at boarding school in England. Of course, this was before Harry Potter!

Many companies simply treat their impatriates as local staff, integrating them into the home office compensation and benefits programs. They do not provide foreign-service premiums, housing support, or related benefits to their impatriates, assuming that the corporate HQ is the center of the universe. If the impatriates are expected to remain permanently in the parent country, this may be the most sensible approach. But for temporary transfers, it may be better to treat impatriates in the same way as home country expatriates on learning assignments are treated, with a degree of support appropriate to the expected length of stay.[133]

As the number of expatriates continues to increase, there is an emerging trend to treat people transferred across borders the same, at least in principle. Some companies are beginning to develop global transfer policies that cover everyone regardless of location of origin. The terms are determined by the purpose of the assignment, its duration, and the career circumstances.

THE LIMITS OF GLOBAL INTEGRATION

The main weakness of global integration strategies is the potentially negative impact on the firm's ability to be responsive to local needs and demands, be it those of customers, host governments, or the local employees. For example, as Nokia continued to grow globally, new organizational challenges emerged—especially in their infrastructure business. In the past, the company was offering universal GSM technology based on global standards. Now, customers demand specific solutions fitting local needs that require extensive customization.

Coordination demands on the organization increased dramatically. As the market expanded beyond the traditional operators, Nokia was expected not only to provide equipment but also to manage the whole project on a turnkey basis. This required a new set of skills that needed to be shared across the whole organization. And where Nokia acted alone before, the rapid evolution of technology now required engagement in multiple partnerships, involving extensive coordination. The old approach of global integration that had proven so successful during the first decade of global expansion began to outlive its usefulness.

The tensions created by global integration also impacted many of the employees. Nokia had been considered as an outstanding employer worldwide, with a nurturing and empowering culture that created excellent opportunities to learn and grow. But more and more local employees perceived the company as providing only limited career opportunities since the majority of "good" jobs were filled by expatriates—most of them from Finland. Retaining the best local talent began to be a problem, requiring the firm to rethink its approach to global HR management.

McDonald's, another famous meganational, has not escaped the consequences of its global success. As customers around the world increasingly demand customization to local preferences, its menus are becoming more heterogeneous. But that is the easy part. The company's biggest challenge, common with many other meganational firms, is the perception of insensitivity to local social issues.[134] McDonald's has a poor image in the European media of being anti-union, with allegations of interfering in worker council elections, and its success in creating a global brand makes it a frequent target of protesters opposed to the impact of globalization.[135]

The charges of imperialism leveled at global firms are not limited to American firms. The recent restructuring of Marks & Spencer, the world famous British retailer, ran into opposition not only from the employees who were losing their jobs, but also from the French government accusing the firm of violating the country's labor laws and social expectations. Most host governments are not great fans of global integration.[136] Governments value foreign investment mainly because it creates jobs, while the integration of manufacturing and logistics operations generally reduces labor content.

Many other companies have experienced the drawbacks of becoming global. After 1980 Coca-Cola transformed itself from an essentially decentralized multidomestic firm into a well-oiled global machine that pursued a tightly orchestrated strategy of global integration. The objective was to centralize control so as to manage global expansion in over 200 countries, ensuring that these businesses worldwide operated cohesively. The first fifteen years of this strategy were an incredible success, and Coca-Cola became the paragon of a global firm. However, the same forces that were making the world more connected and homogeneous and thus enabling the firm to reap the benefits of integration were simultaneously triggering a powerful backlash in the shape of desires for local autonomy and preservation of local cultural identity. The now global Coke was simply not fast, sensitive, and transparent enough to react to these changes.

The lack of speed and sensitivity became apparent in 1999 with the contamination of one of the Coke bottling plants in Belgium. Instead of initiating a quick recall and reassuring the public, the company procrastinated, waiting for decisions from the head office in Atlanta. By the time the company moved to respond to the public relations crisis, it was too late to prevent major damage to the brand image. Soon after, the company CEO resigned. The new CEO, who had spent most of his Coke career outside the HQ, immediately announced a dramatic departure from its past global strategy. The new motto is "think local, act local."[137]

But how far can pendulums swing before the organization becomes unstable? How can companies become more responsive to their customers and employees, while maintaining the benefits of integration? We will come back to this dilemma later in Part III.

TAKEAWAYS

1. Global integration means centralized control over key resources and operations that are strategic in the value chain. Decisions are made from a global perspective—in the extreme, the meganational firm operates as if the world were a single market. Expatriation is a principal tool of global integration.

2. The levers of global integration are centralization, or personal control; standardization, based on control through formalization; contracting, focused on control of outputs; socialization, focused on control of norms and values; and mutual adjustment, or control through informal interaction.

3. There are three complementary ways to implement globally integrated strategies: alignment of decision making to ensure that local decisions reflect a global perspective, particularly through personal control exercised by expatriates and performance management; standardization of work processes using formalized control; and the socialization of key individuals who will occupy key positions both at the center and in subsidiaries.

4. There are two types of international assignments—demand-driven and learning-driven. The former are driven primarily by corporate agency requirements (control and knowledge transfer) or by problem solving needs; the latter focus on organizational competence development and/or personal career enhancement.

5. Making an expatriate assignment into a success for the individual, the family, and the firm requires paying attention to many factors from the time of initial selection until repatriation. A starting point is the recognition that expatriation is a process, not an event.

6. Which personal traits and skills are the most relevant depends on the role the expatriate is expected to assume. For agency-type assignments, clear managerial qualifications together with the relevant professional skills and leadership skills are the essential foundation. In contrast, for learning-oriented assignments, relationship abilities and cultural awareness may be more important.

7. The focus of research has shifted from explaining expatriate failure to understanding intercultural adjustment—adjustment to work, the general environment abroad, and (most difficult of all) to interacting with local people—as well as to other factors such as conflicting allegiances.

8. Family well-being is a critical element in expatriate effectiveness. The inability of the family to adjust to the new country is often the reason for assignment failure. Dual career couples are also more likely to experience stress in international assignments because of the expected negative effects of a career interruption.

9. Tensions embedded in the expatriation process together with the changing demographics of the expatriate population—the growing number of women, third country nationals, and younger expatriates, and the need to adjust to dual careers—are changing the way in which companies approach international assignments.

10. Global integration strategies may have a negative impact on the firm's ability to be responsive to local needs and demands, be it those of customers, host governments, or the local employees. A big challenge facing many meganational firms is a widespread perception that they are insensitive to local social issues.

NOTES

1. "The King of Nokia: Jorma Ollila," reported in The City tourist newspaper, Helsinki, August 2000.

2. We remind the reader that the terms integration, global integration, and coordination are often used in different ways. In this book, we attempt to be consistent in our use of such terms, though our definitions may differ from those of others. Our definition of integration is close to Prahalad and Doz (1987) who define it as "centralized management of geographically dispersed activities on an ongoing basis" (p. 14).

3. Decision makers may or may not be located in the home country. While the former is the usual pattern, what matters is the centralization of management, not the location.

4. J. Fox, "Nokia's Secret Code," Fortune, May 1, 2000.

5. Our "meganational" firm is labeled "the global firm" by Bartlett and Ghoshal (1989), a label that we find to be confusing for nonacademic audiences.

6. V. Griffith, "Inside Track: As Close as a Group Can Get to Global: Interview with Al Zeien, Chief Executive of Gillette," Financial Times, April 7, 1998.

7. Nohria and Ghoshal (1997) do find empirical support for the match between industry and structural fit. Scientific measurement instruments, cement products, industrial chemicals, aircraft engines, and mining machinery are among the industries that are traditionally globally integrated.

8. Pucik, Hanada, and Fifield, 1989; Kopp, 1994; Yoshihara, 1999.

9. Prahalad and Doz , 1987, p. 160.

10. Economists view the market as the prime mechanism of control over transactions since the market price contains all the information that an individual needs to decide whether or not to enter into a transaction. Coase (1937) asked why transactions are not all performed by markets—why do organizations exist? Williamson (1975) developed his influential transaction cost theory to address this question, essentially arguing that since the rationality of human behavior is bounded or limited, organizations have advantages over markets as control mechanisms under conditions of high uncertainty and complexity (and also under conditions of high asset specificity and high transaction frequency).

11. See Galbraith (1977), Lawrence and Lorsch (1967), Mintzberg (1989), Martinez and Jarillo (1989), and Harzing (1999).

12. The classification we use is largely drawn from Harzing (1999), who reviews the literature on control mechanisms. However, she omits the fundamental mechanism of informal mutual adjustment, which we have added as a fifth category.

13. Organizational theorists typically see control and coordination as the same in principle, and there is often some confusion around terminology. Both are means to achieve organizational

goals. Harzing summarizes a review of the literature by saying that "control is a means to achieve an end called coordination, which in turn leads toward the achievement of common organization goals" (Harzing, 1999, p. 9).

14. As Brewster (1991, p. 33) comments: "Only rarely has control been identified as the aim of expatriate postings in the previous research. This requires explanation. Evidence from European MNCs . . . shows it to be the central rationale for a majority of MNCs. . . . For the key managerial postings, at least, it is clear that management in these organizations trust their 'own' people to operate as they are required to do, more than they trust the locals they employ."

15. Standardization is a prerequisite for formal control, as it is nearly impossible to formalize work processes that are not standardized.

16. One study of diversified corporations identified three different approaches to output control (Goold and Campbell, 1987). In "financial control" companies, objectives are set in terms of financial performance. In "strategic control" firms, objectives cover both longer-term strategic objectives as well as annual financial targets. In "strategic planning" firms, there is far more emphasis on the planning process, driven by an intention to develop bold strategies. Objectives blend both short-term financial targets and long-term strategic aims.

17. See Mintzberg's typology of seven organizational configurations, each employing different prime control/coordination mechanisms: the entrepreneurial, machine bureaucracy, professional, diversified, innovative, missionary, and political organizations (Mintzberg, 1984).

18. Studying 287 headquarters of MNCs in nine countries, Harzing found that personal control (centralization) was used more by British and German corporations than their Swiss and Swedish counterparts. The latter made much more use of normative control through socialization and building networks for mutual adjustment (these being used infrequently by French and Japanese firms with respect to their subsidiaries). Formalized control through standardization and output control was most strongly employed by U.K. and German firms, and least by Japanese corporations. See Harzing (1999) also for a review of other research on comparative differences.

19. Cited in Griffith, "Inside Track."

20. Hennart, 1991.

21. In some export-oriented German companies international subsidiaries are run jointly by a managing director of local nationality and an expatriate Kaufmann (broadly trained commercial manager), who reports back to senior management at home. Japanese subsidiaries abroad often have locals heading functions such as marketing and sales, but Japanese nationals are placed in roles demanding close liaison with Tokyo (usually product planning and finance).

22. Egelhoff, 1988; Hennart, 1991.

23. Pucik, 1994.

24. Rudlin (2000), a former manager of a large Japanese trading company, argues that advances in information technology allow Japanese managers to increase the exclusivity of informal communication. In the past, phone conversations in Japanese were at least audible to the local staff. While they may not understand, they get an idea that something is going on and follow up with questions. With one-on-one e-mail, the locals are totally excluded.

25. The importance of aligning performance management with strategic goals is of course not limited to meganational firms. We will revisit in greater detail some of the same issues in Chapter 7 when we examine global performance management process as a key coordination tool in a transnational firm.

26. For detailed discussion of issues related to the measurement of subsidiary performance see Pucik (1985).

27. Schlesinger and Heskett, 1991.

28. The company's legendary founder, Ray Kroc, recognized the power of training. "Hamburger University" (HU) was started in 1961 in Oak Brook, Illinois, only six years after he acquired the business from the McDonald brothers. By 1999, the school had trained more than 65,000 "bachelors of hamburgerology," adding new graduates at the rate of 7,000 per year. Equipped with state-of-the-art technology, it is part business school, part technical workshop, but mostly a teacher training college. Its students are mainly operating managers with at least 2,000 hours of prior local training, and their mission will be to go forth and teach others at home. Thirty resident professors at HU teach courses on store management, team building skills, staffing and retaining crew, sales growth strategies, business planning, but most importantly McDonald's global operation standards ("Face Value: The Burger King," The Economist, October 23, 1999).

29. Cited in Bartlett and Nanda (1990), p. 8.

30. "Shopping All over the World," The Economist, June 19, 1999, pp. 59–61.

31. See Womack, Jones, and Roos (1990), MacDuffie (1995).

32. See Kenney and Florida (1993); Pil and MacDuffie (1999); Shimada and MacDuffie (1999). For the role of Japanese expatriates in this transfer see Peterson, Peng, and Smith (1999).

33. The transfer of the bundled management practices that constitute a capability (such as the manufacturing capability of a Japan auto firm) is discussed further in Chapter 9, where we discuss strategic change—notably how a globally integrated company can transfer such capabilities at home to other countries and markets.

34. O'Reilly and Pffefer, 2000.

35. Fox, "Nokia's Secret Code," pp. 160–74.

36. Ouchi, 1981. See also Evans (1984).

37. Jaeger, 1982.

38. Much of the know-how that the individual acquires will be organization specific (how to get things done around here) rather than job specific so that people have lower value on the external market. This effectively locks people into the firm. When such firms were forced by global competition to downsize and restructure, we have often witnessed the panic of talented managers who have broad experience but no external prospects.

39. Edström and Galbraith (1977) provide a more extended account of how geographic transfers act as a vehicle for socialization.

40. Edström and Galbraith, 1977.

41. Other scholars, such as Hays (1974) and Tung (1981), also examined expatriation with respect to the responsibilities and positions assumed by the expatriates. Integrating these various viewpoints, Derr and Oddou (1991) identified two types of expatriates: those who are assigned abroad to fix a problem, including persons in specialized functional positions; and those who go abroad as "high potentials" to broaden their development before moving up to senior management.

42. Pucik, 1992.

43. When followed up with yet another international transfer, expatriation can become a career, a pattern not uncommon in many international firms. For example, if expatriates at IBM do not return home within four years, they will typically be managed by a special corporate system for career expatriates.

44. During the 1980s, some companies chose to reduce the role of expatriates (particularly in U.S.-based firms). For a discussion of this phenomenon see Kobrin, 1988.

45. Expatriating for development reasons has long been practiced by British "hongs," trading houses such as Swire operating in Asia, as well as the Danish multinational A. P. Møller. Some people may be sent to business schools, a practice common among Japanese multinationals.

46. A survey of U.S. multinationals showed that the proportion of assignees on short-term transfers of less than 12 months increased from 5 to 16 percent between 1992 and 1998 (Solomon, 1998).

47. GE estimates that 25 percent of its managers will need global assignments to gain knowledge and experience necessary to understand the global markets, customers, suppliers and competitors the company will face in future (Black, Gregersen, Mendenhall, and Stroh, 1999).

48. Tung, 1981; Mendenhall and Oddou, 1985; Ronen, 1990; Oddou, 1991; Arthur and Bennett, 1995.

49. Baker and Ivancevich, 1971; Misa and Fabricatore, 1979; Tung, 1981; Black, Gregersen and Mendenhall, 1992.

50. Some researchers suggest that expatriate failure rates in European multinationals may be lower than in the United States due to more effective expatriate policies (Brewster and Scullion, 1997), better selection (Scullion, 1995), and more emphasis on the value of international experience (Björkman and Gersten, 1993). An alternative explanation may be that European multinationals accept lower standards of performance to avoid the loss of face involved in a premature return (Scullion, 1995).

51. For example, see Windham International 1999. Unfortunately there is little systematic data on the causes of the turnover. The data is also open to question since we do not know the turnover rate for employees in comparable domestic positions, or for those completing domestic transfers.

52. Mendenhall et al., 1987; Black, Gregersen, and Mendenhall, 1992; Scullion, 1994.

53. Tung, 1981; Black and Stephens, 1989; Dowling, 1990; Windham International, 1999.

54. Stephens and Black, 1991.

55. For research on time-to-proficiency, see Waxin, Roger, and Chandon (1997).

56. Black and Gregersen, 1999.

57. Suutari and Brewster, 1999.

58. Black, Gregersen, and Mendenhall (1992) criticized what they believed was "the most common American approach" to expatriate selection: a quick screening of candidates on the basis of their technical and managerial ability to put "the foreign fire out." In their view, such an approach is destined to lead to problems for both individual and organization.

59. Tung, 1981, Scullion 1994.

60. For a review of academic research on the characteristics of successful expatriates, see Pucik and Saba (1998).

61. Tung, 1981.

62. Mendenhall and Oddou, 1985.

63. Ronen, 1990.

64. Oddou, 1991.

65. Sparrow, 1999.

66. NEC has formally assessed the interest and aptitude of 20,000 employees for international assignments. The top 25% are placed in a candidate pool for future expatriation. GM maintains a candidate pool of over 5,000 executives on a central database for international assignments.

67. 16% of multinationals surveyed by Aon International in 1997 used family readiness evaluations, 11% utilized psychological profile instruments, and 11% applied cultural proficiency tests ("No Common Thread in Expat Selection," Global Workforce, 1998, p. 9).

68. Black, Gregersen, Mendenhall and Stroh, 1999.

69. Ibid.

70. Brett and Stroh, 1995.

71. See Torbiörn (1982), Black and Stephens (1989), Brewster (1991, ch. 6). Our own work with international companies suggests that self-reported expatriate failure rates due to family issues may be somewhat exaggerated. We have observed several cases where although the cause of the failure was poor performance or adjustment, the explanation for premature return was given as "family"—perhaps to allow the returnee to save face, or perhaps to shift the blame for an expensive selection error outside the HR department.
72. Black and Gregersen, 1991.
73. For example, Marks & Spencer has long had an explicit policy that all managers and high potentials have to be prepared to move home and family once a year, if needed—"if you don't like that policy, don't join us!"
74. For example, Toyota provides one to three years of ongoing training for employees who may be targeted for overseas assignments, in a program called "training for overseas duties." Two types of training are offered: preparation for a U.S.A. assignment and preparation for a non-English speaking country assignment.
75. Mendenhall, Dunbar and Oddou,1987; Harris and Brewster, 1999.
76. Dowling, Welch, and Schuler, 1999.
77. Tung,1981; Mendenhall and Oddou, 1986.
78. Harris and Brewster, 1999.
79. Preparatory training is at best only a foundation for future learning—unless it is properly designed, it can have unintended consequences. In one of the early studies on expatriation to Japan (Black, 1988), the predeparture knowledge was negatively correlated with expatriate work adjustment—most probably because the cultural stereotype of Japanese organizations presented in the standard training package did not correspond to the multifaceted reality.
80. For example, Nestlé offers language training to expatriates assuming leadership roles in local affiliates over the 14 months period between acceptance of assignment and departure. Other companies may offer, or even demand, short-term intensive immersion training.
81. Research on adjustment is mainly focused on experiences of American expatriates. For conceptual background, see Black, Mendenhall, and Oddou (1991). With respect to the three dimensions of adjustment, studies have shown that these three dimensions are independent of each other (Shaffer, Harrison, and Gilley, 1999; Cerdin and Peretti, 2000).
82. Caligiuri, Hyland, Joshi, and Bross, 1998.
83. Black, Gregersen, Mendenhall, and Stroh (1999), p. 108. See also the recent empirical research of Stahl (2000) on the coping problems of German and Japanese expatriates.
84. A concise summary of research on expatriate dual allegiances can be found in Black, Gregersen, Mendenhall and Stroh (1999), pp. 130–55.
85. Ibid., p. 143.
86. Nevertheless, in one of the very few empirical studies on expatriate performance appraisal by Gregersen, Hite, and Black (1996), 79% of the responding U.S.-based firms described themselves as average or above average with respect to its accuracy.
87. While the topic may be highly relevant, data and empirical evidence concerning these issues is still scarce. In contrast to the extensive literature on expatriate selection and development, the research domain of expatriate performance management (e.g. criteria, processes, and outcomes) is substantially unexplored.
88. Tahvanainen, 1998.
89. Borkowski, 1999.
90. Most U.S. firms use standardized "global" appraisal forms (Gregersen, Hite, and Black, 1996).
91. The perception of expatriates as "short-termers" is so common that it may block any effort to drive long-term change. Advice that is often given to expatriates who are assigned to manage a change project is "Never reveal when you are going home!"

92. According to Gregersen, Black, and Hite (1995) only 11% of U.S. HR managers involved in planning expatriate assignments have international experience.
93. Tahvanainen, 1998.
94. Pucik, Hanada, and Fifield, 1989.
95. Stening, Everett, and Longton, 1981.
96. Reynolds, 2001.
97. The idea is that expatriates never receive less than they would be paid at home.
98. For a comprehensive review of expatriate compensation methodologies, see Reynolds (1995) and Reynolds (2001), chs. 23 and 24.
99. For a summary of tax strategies for expatriate compensation see Orchant (2001).
100. Black, Gregersen, Mendenhall, and Stroh, 1999, p. 180.
101. Brewster, 1991; Black, Gregersen, and Mendenhall, 1992; Stroh, 1995; The Conference Board, 1996.
102. Stahl, 2000.
103. Studies referenced in Black, Gregersen, Mendenhall, and Stroh (1999, p. 219) have shown that about three-quarters of expatriates, regardless of nationality, have experienced significant decreases in their standard of living after returning home.
104. Adler, 1981; Black and Gregersen, 1991a.
105. According to research of Black and Gregersen (1999) "one-fourth of those who completed an assignment, left their company . . . within one year after repatriation."
106. Some turnover can always be expected—see Nicholson (1984) for research on work transitions. When expatriates gain new competencies during their assignments, it is quite possible that their market value on the external market may be higher than inside the old organization, so naturally they leave. The return of the spouse to work may result in family relocation that is not compatible with the job offered to the returnee. While many firms undergoing restructuring are loath to terminate employees during an international assignment (partly for legal reasons in some countries), the employees are laid off as soon as they return.
107. Allen and Alvarez, 1998; Black, Gregersen, and Mendenhall, 1992.
108. Research studies quoted in Black, Gregersen, Mendenhall, and Stroh (1999), p. 219.
109. As with the initial expatriation, it is the whole family and not just the employee that is coming back. Support with job-hunting for the spouse (often after an extended absence from the job market), counseling for teenage children, or simply setting up welcome programs often go a long way to eliminate the stress and confusion associated with returning home.
110. Allen and Alvarez, 1998.
111. Pucik and Saba, 1998.
112. For example Western or Japanese expatriates in China may cost the employer $400–500,000 annually, perhaps twenty to thirty times the salary of local Chinese managers.
113. This issue is discussed in detail in Chapter 7.
114. Dowling and Schuler, 1990; Scullion, 1994; Gregersen and Black, 1995; Hsieh, Lavoie, and Samek, 1999.
115. The need for a contingency approach to expatriation was first raised by Mendenhall and Oddou (1985). See also the empirical research of Stahl (2000).
116. Moran, Stahl, and Boyer, 1988.
117. Adler, 1984.
118. Many of the women in a study of Western expatriates in the Pacific Rim reported advantages to being highly visible, benefiting from the curiosity of local business people eager to meet them (Adler, 1993).
119. Tung, 1995.

120. "Special Report on Expatriate Management: Case Study: Shell International," HR Focus, March 1998, p. 10.
121. Hsieh, Lavoie, and Samek (1999), based on a McKinsey survey of five Dutch multinationals.
122. Merck and Exxon send engineers on short-term assignments for technology transfer and personal development. Some European multinationals have long done this (see Note 45 above).
123. "International Assignments: Many, Brutish, and Short," The Economist, December 16, 2000, p. 80.
124. Solomon, 1998.
125. See Price Waterhouse Europe (1997); see also the Conference Board (1996).
126. See Dowling, Welch, and Schuler (1999, pp. 208–10) for further data and discussion.
127. T. Jackson, "Time's Up for the Man from the Head Office," Financial Times, October 8, 1997, p. 10; K. Groh and M. Allen, "Special Report on Expatriate Management Global Staffing: Are Expatriates the Only Answer?", HR Focus, March 1998, pp. 1–2.
128. See Price Waterhouse Coopers' study of 271 companies in 24 European countries cited in "International Assignments: Nasty, Brutish, and Short," p. 80.
129. L. Crawford, "Style with Rapid Response," Financial Times, September 26, 2000.
130. Bonache and Cervino, 1997.
131. Harvey, Speier, and Novicevic (1999b) proposed that impatriate employees who are well integrated into the home organization may provide the international firm with a number of significant advantages such as (1) unique cultural/social knowledge and insights that are difficult to imitate; (2) acting as a critical communication point for host country managers to ensure the clarity of the strategy; (3) a diversity of perspectives when developing international business strategies, policies, and plans; (4) a pool of talent that can replace high cost/high failure expatriates in the host countries.
132. Hewitt Associates survey, cited in Solomon (1995).
133. A major challenge arises if salaries or lifestyle expectations abroad are higher than at the corporate center. And this is not just about money. How much holiday should be granted to a French or German employee assigned to the United States?
134. "McParadox," Newsweek, July 10, 2000, pp. 14–17.
135. See Royle (2000), and "It Is Better to Rob a Bank than Work at McDonald's," Across the Board, Nov.–Dec. 1999.
136. Singapore may be an exception. The country explicitly targets investment in regional and corporate centers.
137. "Back to Classic Coke," Financial Times, March 27, 2000; "Repairing the Coke Machine," Business Week, March 19, 2001, pp. 58–60.

CHAPTER 4

Becoming Locally Responsive

Bertelsmann, Europe's largest media company, is headquartered in Gütersloh, a sleepy community between Dortmund and Hannover. Although it is the largest trade-book publisher in the United States, owner of the Bantam, Doubleday, Dell, and Knopf imprints, the company's name sparks little public recognition outside its native Germany. Bertelsmann's music division, BMG, encompasses the Arista, RCA, and Windham Hill record labels. And its European subsidiaries, such as Gruner & Jahr in Germany, France Loisirs in France, Plaza y Janés in Spain and RTL in European broadcasting, remain better known than the parent company. Before taking over as CEO, Thomas Middelhoff spent time in the United States to acquaint himself with the lead market, and recalls: "When I told [people] Bertelsmann was the third biggest media group in the world, they looked at me as if I was crazy."[1]

The family firm's success is rooted in the concept of book clubs, introduced by Reinhard Mohn after World War II. To manage the spectacular growth generated by these book clubs, Mohn quickly introduced a divisional structure, profit centers, and decentralized responsibility. He firmly believed that managers should be encouraged to behave as if they were running their own companies, taking charge of decisions regarding personnel, capital needs, products, and market. The decentralized structure enabled the divisions and the individual units to take on lives of their own—doing business with external customers, diversifying their activities, making acquisitions, and entering international markets. In the 1960s, the book club concept was exported, first to Switzerland and Austria, then to Spain and France, and later to the United States—but all were run as local operations.

Subsequent acquisitions, such as Gruner & Jahr magazines and Bantam Books, were run along similar lines, with the publishers preserving full editorial freedom. The idea was that products should cater to the requirements of each particular market. For example, some magazine titles, such as *Family Circle* and *McCall's,* are specific to the U.S. market. But even magazine concepts such as *Geo* or *Prima,* which have been rolled out across several European countries, are tailored to local needs. With few exceptions, the content is locally generated not translated.

When central and eastern Europe opened up to foreign companies following the fall of communism, Bertelsmann quickly carved out strong positions in these new markets by entering the daily newspaper business. Many of its offerings are aimed at local populations, such as *Délvilág* and *Délmagyarország,* two regional Hungarian newspapers, or *Sächsische Zeitung,* aimed at the Saxonian province of what was once East Germany.

Similarly in music, Bertelsmann has big name artists with global appeal, such as Whitney Houston, but most of its revenues come from local artists. Thanks to acquisitions, such as *Fun House* (Japan), *Music Impact* (Hong Kong) or *Elite Music* (Taiwan), Bertelsmann has accumulated over 200 record labels in 53 countries, designed not just to market its superstars but also to develop and distribute local music. With over 70 percent of the group's revenues generated outside the home market, Bertelsmann is by far the most international of the big media companies.

Clearly, Bertelsmann is playing the local game. This multidomestic strategic posture is particularly striking in an industry in which success is conventionally associated with heavy branding and leveraging of "content" (in as many ways as possible) for global consumption, as epitomized by Disney and Time-Warner. The fact that the privately held Bertelsmann continues to hold its own against such titans suggests that it must be doing something right. Few established multinationals can match the entrepreneurial drive generated by Bertelsmann's highly independent managers.[2]

CHAPTER OVERVIEW

Bertelsmann provides a good example of a locally responsive firm that uses a multidomestic strategy to adapt to diversity in market demands. We start off by considering the advantages of such a strategy and its implications for people management practices. Many suggest that HRM practices in particular should be managed in the local way because they are subject to the rich diversity of cultural and institutional contexts.

Three different theoretical perspectives provide insights on sources of diversity and why and how HRM practices should be localized. The first school of thought focuses on cultural values, the idea that people and companies are products of their own cultures. The second emphasizes national business systems, which implies understanding the institutional arrangements in the host context. The third centers on the network to which the company belongs, focusing on how managers tend to copy the practices of their peer-group. We use examples of comparative differences in HRM practice as illustrations, also reviewing issues such as whether or not there is increasing global convergence in approaches to the management of people.

The next section of the chapter asks how firms should respond to this diversity as they expand internationally. One argument is that these cultural and institutional differences should guide decisions on the sequence and mode of entry into new countries. How strategic the country may be is another factor. A stronger view is that firms can learn to capitalize on diversity, either by building cultural synergy or by capitalizing on institutional advantages, moving jobs to people rather than trying to fit people to jobs.

However, it is not enough to be locally based—responsiveness means above all localizing management. Just as expatriation is the key lever of an integrative strategy, so localization is the main plank of a responsive strategy. The following section explores why localization is often mishandled and maps out in detail the pitfalls and lessons for a localization strategy. We give special emphasis to the critical role of expatriates in implementing localization and to recruitment, development, and retention of local staff.

We round off the chapter by considering the limitations, inefficiencies, and excesses of a multidomestic strategy. The thorny issue of ethics is singled out for particular discussion—doing things the local way can undermine corporate trust, contributing to the maintenance of practices that undermine the development of a sound local economy. This leads to the conclusion that local managers must have the necessary judgment and breadth of perspective to wrestle with ambiguity and moral dilemmas. It also anticipates our wider discussion in Part III on how transnational companies achieve the balance between local responsiveness and global integration *through HRM.*

THE ROOTS OF RESPONSIVENESS

Local responsiveness was often the route chosen by multinational companies active in the early part of the twentieth century. To start with, national preferences were more compartmentalized in an era when communication and transport were restricted. More important perhaps, logistical barriers meant that the cost and delays in shipping goods internationally offset the economies of global mass production for all but a limited range of products. Moreover, with local competitors quick to spring up, it was often preferable to set up a fully integrated local operation capable of rapid response.

Rising trade barriers in the 1920s and 1930s, forcing even the most ardent pursuers of global economies to set up manufacturing facilities behind high tariff walls, further encouraged local responsiveness. In certain cases, the onset of World War II isolated overseas operations from their parent organizations, especially those located in Europe. For example, the fear of German confiscation led Philips to spin off its companies in Britain and the United States and to restructure them as legally independent companies owned by trusts.

The U.S. companies that internationalized in the 1960s and 1970s faced less pressure to be responsive to national differences and encountered fewer barriers to capitalizing on global-scale economies. But since then, the market leaders in most business sectors have become evenly matched on access to capital, know-how, and technology. So local responsiveness, the capacity to sense and answer varied customer needs, has acquired more value as a source of competitive advantage. Coca-Cola, which during the 1990s constituted the epitome of the globally integrated firm, felt the need to "rediscover" its own multilocal heritage. As the new CEO noted in 2000: "In every community, we must remember we do not do business in markets, we do business in societies . . . [This means making] sure that we stay out of the way of our local people and let them do their jobs."[3]

In the process of "rediscovering" local responsiveness, our understanding of it has also changed. For a long time, the term "local" was generally understood to imply "national." For cultural and institutional reasons, nations remain important drivers of differentiated needs, but they are by no means the only ones. In fact, "local" refers to any market that has distinctive needs. One of the challenges for multinational companies is precisely to differentiate customer needs more finely market by market. Clearly, "local" needs can be aggregated at various levels, with pressures for responsiveness differing significantly, not just between countries, but also across countries and within countries. Ultimately, local responsiveness refers to a market of one consumer, as captured by the oxymoron of "mass customization."

Business Advantages of Responsiveness

Sensitivity to local conditions has important advantages associated with better market acceptance. By providing a local face, behaving like domestic firms, and adjusting products to local tastes, the foreign entrant is likely to have wider customer appeal or to compete more effectively in local labor markets. Local responsiveness helps to overcome the "liability of foreignness" (see the box "The Strategic Drivers of Local Responsiveness").

This was particularly important to Bertelsmann in our lead case. Not wanting to be perceived as some kind of "evil media empire," it has always kept its corporate identity in the background—even when the Bertelsmann name appears, it is subsumed under an acronym (BOL for its online activities or BMG for its umbrella music label). In each of its markets, it is assumed to be a local company. So successful has it been, that when it acquired Random House, an eminent New York University professor felt duty bound to warn an unsuspecting public of the company's reach: "The people that brought you Puff Daddy's records are now in firm control of Knopf and other of the nation's most esteemed imprints."[4]

The multidomestic strategy based on local responsiveness has both internal and external advantages. Externally, a locally responsive company is likely to be more receptive to local trends, emerging needs, and product usage patterns—and therefore less likely to miss subtle market opportunities. For example, Motorola realized that people in China often used their pagers to send entire messages. That was not how the pagers were intended to be used, but the company redesigned its product to have greater appeal in China by displaying more lines of information.[5] It is a good example of increased penetration of the local market through incremental innovation. But to pick up that kind of qualitative information requires first-hand experience of the products in use—and the local discretion or clout to act on that information.

Besides the issue of customer receptiveness, there is also the question of acceptability to the authorities and the business community. If the subsidiary can become a legitimate participant in the local economy, it is more likely to have a say in the shaping of new policies and regulations, and to be invited to play a significant role in industry or trade associations. If a firm can become a local insider, it is more likely to be privy to precious information and to have a chance of participating in local deals. For example, in the regulated world of petroleum exploration and marketing, being close to local authorities is important, as Royal Dutch/Shell recognizes.

The Strategic Drivers of Local Responsiveness
Research Box

The pressures for local responsiveness stem from a mix of market, organizational, and political considerations:[A]

Industry characteristics: In certain business sectors, there is no competitive advantage to be gained from standardizing or coordinating across different subsidiaries. For example, nonbranded foods and small household appliances face weak forces for global integration because of an absence of scale economies. Cement companies such as Lafarge and Cemex engage heavily in local production in every country they have entered. This is largely because the shipping and tariff costs neutralize any cost advantages of centralized sourcing.

Customer needs: Historically, branded packaged goods companies, such as Danone in foods or Unilever in various nondurable goods, have tended to respond to different customer expectations, preferences, or requirements. But even businesses with "global formulae" such as McDonald's or Disney may be forced to modify their offerings in order to cater to local traditions or expectations. For example, European dining habits forced both Disney's Paris theme park and McDonald's European franchises to abandon cherished no-alcohol policies applied in the home market.

Local substitutes: Competition from local products or services with different price/performance characteristics may lead a company to local adaptation. Nestlé varies its infant cereal recipes according to local raw materials—in Europe they are made with wheat, in Latin America with maize and sorghum, and in Asia with soya. Whirlpool, contrary to its worldwide policies, introduced a locally manufactured brand of appliances in eastern Europe to compete against low-priced competition.

Markets and distribution: National differences in market structure and distribution channels can have repercussions on pricing, product positioning or design, promotion, and advertising. For example, the distribution infrastructure, particularly in emerging markets, may require adjustments to product design or packaging in order to cope with the challenges of dust, heat, or bumpy roads.

Host government regulations: Host government concerns—for national development or national security—may force a business to be locally responsive. Petrochemical firms have to build close relationships with national authorities controlling a resource that is critical for economic development. Local content requirements can force a firm into development partnerships with suppliers. Retail practices that are standard in the United States, such as opening 7 days a week, 24 hours a day, or refunding the price difference on any item sold for less elsewhere, are illegal in Germany, forcing Wal-Mart to adapt its approach when it entered the German market.

[A]See Prahalad and Doz (1987) for a more extended analysis; also Prahalad and Lieberthal (1998).

Deutsche Shell is expected to be a German company, and Shell Malaysia is expected to present a Malaysian face to the government and consumers. However, maintaining a delicate balance is critical. Being too close to the authorities can spill over negatively onto public image when the local government comes under public attack, as was the case for Shell with its links to the regime of former General Abacha in Nigeria and to the former Nationalist government in South Africa. Consumers around the world perceived Shell as colluding with a highly corrupt government in Nigeria and with the *apartheid* practices of the South African government, leading to boycotts around the world and a serious compromising of its corporate image.

Internally, being perceived as a local company can enhance credibility vis-à-vis the workforce. Unless local employees are convinced that senior managers understand

and honestly represent local interests to headquarters, so that their concerns are given due consideration, those senior managers may have difficulty eliciting loyalty or commitment—and the efficiency of the local operation may suffer, regardless of strategy. In competitive labor markets, the presence of local executives in the management ranks of the subsidiary provides role models for younger employees and improves recruitment and retention prospects.

Localization of People Management

Alongside the business arguments for local responsiveness, there are equally compelling people management arguments for taking a local orientation.[6] These are based on the simple notion that "where you come from" and "where you are" matter. As Hofstede recently put it: "People in different countries use the same computer programs but the purposes to which they put them vary according to the programming of their minds, not their computers."[7] It is a view echoed by Trompenaars, another Dutch intercultural expert, who wants to "dispel the notion that there is 'one best way' of managing and organizing."[8] HRM practices apply to people—and people across the world are different.

Of all the management domains, HR management is generally considered to be the most sensitive to local context.[9] Cultural programming is not the only explanation. National regulatory pressures are equally if not more important—on forms of workplace representation, employee participation, fiscal incentives for training, what is allowed in hiring and firing, working hours, and so on. Some countries regulate employment practices closely, whereas others leave more discretion to the employer. For example, U.S. firms can negotiate their own overtime policies and tend to be reluctant to pay professionals for overtime, this being illegal in Japan and Germany. Moreover, HRM practices are subject to the scrutiny of labor unions, whose strength and attitudes to management vary by nation and industry.

These characteristics make HR practices more context-specific than marketing and manufacturing practices, or the financial control practices that tend to adhere more closely to parent norms. Because people management practices are so specific, one response is simply to delegate HRM practices entirely to the local subsidiaries—an approach that might be characterized as "When in Rome, do as the Romans." Yet this is too simplistic.

The adjustment of HR practices to local context is often framed as a Hamlet choice: *to adjust or not to adjust, that is the question.* In fact, HRM is not a monolithic domain. Within HRM some practices are more culture-bound than others. The practices that affect the rank-and-file correspond more to local norms than those affecting executives and internal decision making.[10] Research on foreign companies in China shows significant differences in the degree of localization of practices such as recruitment, training, compensation, performance appraisal, and promotion criteria,[11] and we will explore reasons for these differences in this chapter.

Some parts of HRM can be regarded as high context, others as low context, to borrow from the terminology of Hall.[12] Low context practices are the more explicit ones, based on clear frameworks and applied in a similar fashion across cultures—job design criteria, objective setting, and quantitative measures of performance. The high context practices are those with a stronger dependence on local norms and values, such as working hours, conflict resolution, and how appraisals are conducted. The real question concerns *what to respect, what to ignore,* and *what to reinvent* when adapting work practices to another environment. And to answer that question requires an understanding of the sources of diversity.

UNDERSTANDING DIVERSITY

This section presents three theoretical perspectives for understanding diversity. They relate respectively to the cultural differences between the parent company and its local subsidiary (know yourself), to the host environment (know where you are), and to the company's way of networking (know who you talk to).

Know Yourself: The Cultural Perspective

This perspective maintains that cultural values shape collective thought and behavior. Culture is believed to differentiate management practices across nations as well as other groupings such as industries or organizations.

From the cultural perspective, attention typically focuses on the local culture. But the starting point in developing local responsiveness is to recognize that the culture of the mother company has an effect on international strategy and the prevailing view of human resource management practices (the so-called "country-of-origin" effect). Simply put, before one tries to understand other people and their practices, one had better understand oneself.

The culture of the mother company actually represents the intersection of various spheres of cultural influence.[13] It is shaped by the influence of founding figures and turnaround leaders, by its particular company history and stage of development.[14] These are unique experiences that distinguish the firm and increase cultural variety. And the corporate culture is also a product of the industry culture and the home country culture.

The most influential body of literature concerning values relates to cultural differences between countries. The landmark study in this field was conducted by Hofstede in the early 1970s (see box "Cultural Values"), based on the worldwide IBM opinion survey. His research showed that despite IBM's strong integrative culture ("company and country of origin"), national culture continued to play a major role in differentiating work values. This was subsequently confirmed by Laurent's research showing bigger differences in beliefs among people working for the same company in different nations than among people working for different companies within one nation.[15]

More recently, Trompenaars has compiled a large database documenting systematic variances in the relative importance of opposing values, such as achievement versus ascription and universalism versus particularism.[16] This dualistic perspective is of particular relevance to our own approach (again, see box "Cultural Values").

Let us take the duality universalism-particularism as an example since it is of relevance to international HRM. Though one should be wary of cultural stereotypes,

Cultural Values
Research Box

Hofstede's landmark book *Culture's Consequences* provided a vital platform for the field of cross-national comparative research.[A] Grounded in one of the largest databases ever analyzed and emphasizing workplace values—attitude surveys of 116,000 IBM employees in 53 countries—it identified four "universal" dimensions along which cultures could be compared.

- *Individualism/collectivism:* Determines to what extent social ties and group membership are important to the individual.
- *Power distance:* Reflects tolerance for unequal distribution of power in organizations.
- *Uncertainty avoidance:* Indicates the level of risk aversion as reflected in the use of planning, procedures, and contingency arrangements.
- *Masculinity/femininity:* Describes the influence of materialistic and competitive concerns as opposed to the values of caring for others and quality of life.

Hofstede argued that these four dimensions influenced the way in which organizations were structured and managed in different countries. Some years later he added a fifth dimension to reflect East Asian societies:

- *Long- versus short-term orientation:* A focus on the future implies a tendency toward delayed gratification by practicing persistence and thriftiness. A focus on the present encourages spending even if it means borrowing money.

Though criticized concerning the internal validity of the dimensions, Hofstede's work continues to dominate the field, not least because it codifies cultural traits along a numerical index. His quantitative measures of culture gave birth to the notion of "cultural distance" between home and host country and al-lowed the notion of culture to infiltrate other fields of research, including strategy.

This is not the only map of cultural values, however. Hampden-Turner and Trompenaars identify seven tensions along which to differentiate cultures:[B]

- *Universalism versus particularism:* When no code, rule, or law seems to cover an exceptional case, should the most relevant rule be imposed, or should the case be considered on its merits?
- *Analyzing versus integrating:* Are managers more effective when they break up a problem or situation into parts or integrate the parts into a whole?
- *Individualism versus communitarianism:* Approximately equivalent to individualism and collectivism.
- *Inner-directed versus outer-directed:* Should managers be guided by internal standards, or should they be flexible and adjust to signals, demands, and trends?
- *Sequential versus synchronic view of time:* Should managers get things done as quickly as possible, regardless of the negative impact that their actions may have on others, or should they synchronize efforts so that completion is coordinated and the negative impact minimized?
- *Achieved versus ascribed status:* Should individuals be judged primarily or solely by their achievements, or by their status, as reflected in age, length of service, or other ascriptions?
- *Equality versus hierarchy:* Should subordinates be treated as equals and allowed to exercise discretion in decision making, or should relationships be delimited by hierarchy?

[A]Hofstede, 1980a.
[B]Hampden-Turner and Trompenaars (1993, 2000).

universalist cultures believe in guiding rules, procedures, and principles, whereas in particularist cultures everything depends on the nature of the relationship and the specific context.

- The United States may be seen as one of the more universalistic cultures, with a strong belief in contracts, standard operating procedures, and systems. Trompenaars and his colleagues argue that people from such a culture will tend to look for a single way of dealing with cultural differences, a "solution" to the problem. For example, codes of conduct are supposed to solve differences in ethics. Koreans may be different from Americans, but if the firm has a clear set of values, it can select its local staff from among the "5% of Koreans who fit with our value system."

- Mid-range cultures, as those in many European nations, are more cautious about such universalistic principles and global value systems. They tend to be critical about what they label as American "one-best-way" thinking and more open to situational adaptation. International HRM is more likely to be considered as the local implementation of strategy and business objectives, as opposed to selecting people who will conform to particular practices.

- The Japanese and Koreans are seen as highly particularistic. In such high context cultures, everything is subtle, depending on the circumstances and the relationship. On-the-job training is favored over formal training, seen as too black/white to capture the nuances of reality. Whereas the universalist may believe that an experienced person can teach you to manage cultural differences, the particularist believes that you can only cope with cultural differences after years of intensive experience in that culture. Japanese firms want to hire non-Japanese managers who will spend ten years understanding the delicate context of the way in which they operate before they will entrust that person with significant responsibility.

While the dimensions used to map differences may vary considerably,[17] culturalists consistently argue that cultural values are deeply anchored and enduring; that they vary systematically between societies; and that they condition organizational practice.

Consider the case of HRM practices. Hofstede has argued that the motivation theories dominating management thinking reflect American cultural values, especially individualism.[18] They stress achievement and self-actualization as the ultimate human needs. Culturalists suggest that the development of HRM theory is based on a set of assumptions that are deeply embedded in U.S. culture, thus limiting the applicability of this template to other cultures. Performance may even signify different things in different cultures (see the box "'Performance' Doesn't Mean the Same Thing Everywhere").

Schneider has teased out some of the cultural assumptions underpinning standard HR practices, from selection to socialization.[19] For example, in the realm of performance management she highlights a number of underlying assumptions that have particular resonance in the United States: the idea that goals can be set and reached (assuming control over the environment); and that objectives may be given 6- to 18-month time-frames (assuming that time can be managed). Bosses and subordinates are expected to engage in a two-way dialogue to agree on what has to be done, by when, and how. Again, this assumes that power differences are not an issue, that subordinates are free to argue with their bosses, that employees have the right of input in determining their goals and are eager to take responsibility. These assumptions may not hold true in some other cultures.

"Performance" Doesn't Mean the Same Thing Everywhere
Research Box

Do not think that the idea of performance means the same to everyone, or that there is an objectively best approach to performance management! AT&T undertook a study of the cultural meaning of quality and goals.[A] Americans, they found, tend to be turned on by problems, even crises, which provide the opportunity for a short-term breakthrough. The idea of a goal as a long-range target, to be achieved step-by-step by small incremental improvements, is more native to the Japanese, alien to the West. For the Japanese and Koreans, perfection is an end to strive for, whereas for Americans it is associated with "no place else to go," "no more challenge," and "death." Perhaps we learn different notions of performance back in childhood and at school.[B]

The rhetoric of Western performance management is focused on results delivered by the individual, typified by management-by-objectives systems. As Ulrich and his colleagues advise, "Begin with an absolute focus on results."[C] Appraisal is crucial so as to link achieved results to pay, be it individual, team-based, or organization-based. As the specialists from Hay Group say, the bottom line is "if performance can't be accurately measured, if employees don't understand how it is evaluated, or if they can't see the link between their efforts and the desired results, the program won't work or will be less than fully effective."[D]

The Japanese concept of performance is often contrasted with that in the West, particularly the United States. It focuses on *Kaizen* or continuous improvement, steered by more collective action.[E] Kaizen is an umbrella for a variety of processes oriented toward the aim of constant continuous improvement—statistical tools, TQM, suggestion schemes, small group consultation, etc. Japanese management efforts are directed at supporting and stimulating the efforts of subordinates to improve the *processes* that generate results, and the time horizon for improvement is much

longer than in the West. What is appraised are the employee's skills and efforts (discipline, collaboration, involvement) that will lead to continuous improvement, not the results themselves.

But is this cultural difference or management practice? It is hard to separate the two. One interpretation of the birth of modern "Japanese" performance management attributes it more to the Allies after World War II, who removed the authoritarian heads of the great *Zaibatsu* corporations and left middle level production managers in charge of rebuilding Japan. This resulted in a highly egalitarian and operations-focused concept of management that relied heavily on the ideas of two Americans, Deming and Juran, who had initially been rejected in their home country.[F] The stage in economic development matters as well. The Japanese concede that Kaizen works best in a steady growth economy, whereas the focus on innovation and step breakthroughs that characterize the "American" approach may be more suited to a fast changing environment.[G]

[A]Zuckerman, 1989.
[B]Americans are brought up in an educational system in which the "A" grade that defines top performance is achievable. School is a constant series of challenges, graded as A, B, and C. Not so for the French. School in France is one long challenge to make the Baccalaureat exam, graded on a 20-point scale where 20 is unachievable (if you average 16 in your final exam, you may be congratulated by the President of France).
[C]Ulrich, Zenger et al., 1999, p. 171.
[D]Flannery, Hofrichter et al., 1996, p. 249.
[E]See Imai (1986) for an analysis contrasting Japanese management with that of the West.
[F]Deming believed that individualized appraisals (especially on bell curves), pay-for-performance, and bonus systems are unfair and arbitrary, automatically creating more winners than losers and thereby battering morale. They do not take into account natural variation in performance and are consequently inherently unfair, and perceived as such by employees (Gabor, 1990).
[G]Imai, 1986.

The ultimate expression of this culturalist perspective is the memorable description of HRM as "a contemporary manifestation of the American Dream."[20] Not surprisingly, this came from a European HR scholar.

Avoiding the Pathologies of the Extreme

Most culturalists assess differences between national cultures in terms of dualities. Hall talks of monochronic versus polychronic (view of time) and high context versus low context (language);[21] Hofstede speaks of masculine versus feminine and individualist versus collective orientations; Hampden-Turner and Trompenaars identify the particularist versus universalist continuum and one opposing ascription and achievement (status).

The common point among all the leading culturalist scholars is that they emphasize that the polarities have virtues that merit respect. Branding a particular set of cultural values as "bad" or "inferior" is to ignore some feature of life and organization—and one does this at one's peril. Monochronic use of time—doing things systematically, one-at-a-time, sequentially—is associated with efficiency. But polychronic use of time—undertaking five matters at once—allows the person to see interfaces and is likely to be more creative. Respect for the individual and respect for the collective team are equally valuable precepts.

If a particular value system is taken to the extreme, it risks creating dysfunctions, a pathology. As Laurent points out, if one wants to learn about short-term "bottom line" management, then go to the United States. And yet taken to an extreme, this can create organizations in which behavior is so rigidly driven by quarterly reports that the firm is destined to go from crisis to crisis. If one wants to learn how social relationships can lead to opportunities, then visit Italy or China. Yet taken to the extreme, this *Guanxi* can drive out broad-based social trust, viewed by Fukuyama as essential for economic development.[22]

Hofstede argues that the only candidate for a universal value, and a must for organizations aspiring to be global, is the principle of *moderation:* seeking a middle way. He points out that this principle is found in the thinking of Buddha, Confucius, and Socrates—any virtue becomes a sin when extended too far.[23] Reconciliation of cultural dualities can lead to virtuous circles of development, whereas polarization of cultural qualities can lead to vicious circles.[24] From this perspective, it is not surprising and it is healthy that the individualistic Americans are concerned with teamwork,[25] while the collectively oriented Japanese are focusing on the individualization of management systems.

Ultimately, a consciousness of the firm's culture is important in order to maintain a balance. As Hampden-Turner and Trompenaars put it when introducing their dilemma framework: "That one value in a pair [duality] is more extolled than the other is a fact of culture. Our thesis of economic development is, however, that each value in the pair is crucial to economic success . . . [This] will accrue to the cultures which do the best job balancing the scale."[26]

Commentary

Cultural explanations hold considerable intuitive appeal for international managers. They supply multiple plausible interpretations for the many frustrating difficulties of working with people from different countries. That is both their strength and their weakness.

The work of Hofstede, in particular, has heightened sensitivity to the influence of cultural values in shaping organizational practices. A compelling case can be made for the importance of the cultural perspective in understanding different attitudes towards authority, teamwork, and conflict resolution. The problem is that culture too easily becomes a catchall for complexity, both in academic and managerial circles—and may even foreclose the search for alternative drivers of a particular phenomenon.[27]

The cultural perspective tends to overemphasize value differences and sometimes neglects the fact that the cultural traits found in a particular country represent only a central tendency. Even assuming that particular values can be accurately defined and measured, individuals and indeed companies inevitably differ in the extent to which they adhere to those values. For example, Intel and Hewlett-Packard have strikingly different corporate cultures in spite of their shared national and industrial roots.

Cultural knowledge in human resources implies knowledge of differences "within culture" as well as "across cultures." A barrier that hinders effective cross-cultural interaction is not just the distance between national cultural modes or means, but also the lack of comprehension about the diversity within a given culture by outsiders. One study showed that the intracultural variance is as large as the variation of means across cultures.[28] We stopped stereotyping gender and race; perhaps we should tackle culture with the same determination.

The cultural perspective also underestimates the capacity of people from different cultures to adapt to alien practices. As Hofstede himself recently conceded:

> The fact that organizational cultures are shaped by management practices and not by cultural values explains why such cultures can, to some extent, be managed. . . . Multinational organizations are kept together by shared practices, not by shared values. . . . International cooperation consists of doing things together, even if each partner does them for a different reason.[29]

Research that focuses on values or attitudes typically stresses differences, while research on practices tends to uncover similarities.

Among local managers, culture is often used as an alibi for not introducing change, protecting local fiefdoms against head office interference. Because culture is "impenetrable" it is difficult to argue against such explanations. When the local manager in Thailand tells the head office that "confronting poor performers is not possible here for face saving reasons," there is some truth in it, but it is also an exaggeration. It is often a question of adapting the approach, rather than the objective.

For companies trying to adapt their HRM strategies to local needs, focusing exclusively on cultural values would be inadequate. The cultural lens needs to be supplemented by consideration of the institutional, legal, and economic factors.

Know Where You Are: The Institutional Perspective

In 1991 the U.S. firm Lincoln Electric acquired a company in Germany since this country was the major market for arc-welding machinery in Europe.[30] Lincoln expected to apply its fabled incentive management philosophy, built on self-reliance. American workers at Lincoln's U.S. plants made top wages with a working week that could average up to 58 hours. However in Germany all sorts of procedures have to be followed if someone is to work more than 38 hours a week, and working more than 48 hours is downright illegal. Standard appraisal practices in the United States can lead a company into court if they are applied in Germany. Losses quickly mounted at Lincoln's German operations. To stop the hemorrhage, the German subsidiary was closed down and liquidated within three years. Lincoln had not adequately considered the differences between the institutional environments of the United States and Germany. Such institutional arrangements place numerous constraints on the transfer of HRM policies.

The institutional perspective holds that the key to understanding business behavior in different countries lies in the interrelationships between economic, educational, financial, legal, and political systems. For example, differences in institutional frameworks have manifested themselves clearly in national responses to the worldwide pressures to cut costs. Significantly, it was the U.S.—the country with the fewest legal restrictions—that launched the first wave of downsizing and personnel reduction in the mid-1980s. Then came the U.K., where Margaret Thatcher had removed impediments to labor mobility and wage rigidity. France and Germany have followed more slowly—German labor law makes it extremely difficult to implement large-scale redundancies (neighboring Denmark happens to be the European country with the least restrictions on hiring and firing). Bringing up the rear is Japan, where downsizing conflicts with the traditional corporate governance model, with the attachment in big companies to life-time employment.[31]

One school of research describes the interaction of legal and economic context, organizational forms, HR practices, and business strategies as "the societal effect." The interaction, evolving over time, leads to different configurations within the same industry, as shown by the studies of Maurice, Sorge, and their associates.[32] Chemical and food companies in Britain and the Netherlands and microelectronic firms in Germany and Britain show different configurations that are products of this societal effect, with different concepts of HR management. Such comparative European studies reveal distinct national patterns of work organization in terms of hierarchy, promotion avenues, wage differentials, and the worker/management ratio. Organizational issues such as compensation, training, job design, and industrial relations are most heavily influenced by societal factors.

This concept of configuration is at the heart of the institutional school, and institutional configurations have been dubbed "national business systems,"[33] "industrial orders,"[34] and "varieties of capitalism."[35] Whitley and other scholars argue that these specific configurations shape and constrain the structure and processes through which business is conducted. Their systemic character explains their persistence. As Child puts it: "They are likely to be 'sticky' in the face of economic and technological change."[36]

Redding (and Whitley) argue that there are six successful configurations of capitalism (there are others but they have not proved their success).[37] Each is characterized by distinctive differences in ownership, coordination, and employment practices, as well as different approaches to financial, human, and social capital:

1. The main purpose of the *Anglo-Saxon individualist form,* dominant in North America and the U.K., is to provide returns to shareholders (shareholder value), and this colors its employment and HRM practices.
2. The stakeholder perspective characterizes the more communitarian *European large-scale form.* Here social commitments and obligations are more important, taking the form of different social contracts.
3. The *European industrial district form* of networked enterprise, based on family ownership (but also containing skilled employees committed to the firm), is found in Italy (for example in the Bologna and Veneto regions) as well as in Scandinavia.

    Its aim is to optimize the interests and values of the family owners and senior professional managers associated with the firm. An internationally known example would be Benetton.
4. The *Japanese form,* with its emphasis on integration and complex coordination (also via associated *Keiretsu* networks), has as its prime purpose the stable employment of people.
5. The *Korean chaebol* is oriented to fulfilling the national plan for economic development, though this configuration is evolving after the Asian crisis of 1997.
6. The *Chinese capitalist form* is represented by family businesses throughout the Asian *diaspora,* with main bases in Taiwan, Hong Kong, and Singapore, and increasingly in China. It exists primarily to serve the needs and ambitions for wealth of particular families.

Even within the framework of the capitalist system, there are alternative ways of organizing economic activity.

The European Debate on the American Model of HRM

Reacting against perceived American universalism, there was a flood of research during the 1990s on HRM in Europe from this institutional or contextual perspective, spearheaded by the Price Waterhouse/Cranfield project.[38] Let us single out one of the most relevant findings, namely that the concept of human resource management varies significantly from one country to another, even among contiguous Scandinavian countries.[39] Two dimensions of difference are *devolvement* (the extent to which HRM is viewed as a line management responsibility rather than a functional role) and *integration* (the extent to which HR tasks are closely integrated with business/strategic activities). This is shown in the box "Different European Concepts of Human Resource Management."

European researchers tend to view the "American" model of HRM, shaped by the U.S. institutional context, with a certain suspicion, debating the extent to which it applies to Europe with its different and multiple institutional contexts.[40] Whether or not there is a corresponding "European" model is an issue of some contention.

Different European Concepts of Human Resource Management
Research Box

Brewster and Holt Larsen measured differences in the relative size of the HR function, its representation at board level, its involvement in rank-and-file pay determination, and other variables in companies across ten European countries. Their study revealed different degrees of integration of HRM with business strategy and different degrees of devolvement of HR responsibility to line managers. Mapping the scores, they came up with four quadrants (the further the point is from the middle of the grid, the clearer the pattern is in that country).

In the *Professional Mechanic* quadrant, HRM is seen as the responsibility of functional specialists, who are however not linked to the business processes or work of the management team. HR's focus is on ensuring respect for legal imperatives (particularly important in Germany) and on technical matters of employee selection, compensation, training, and the like.

The *Guarded Strategist* or "Policeman" quadrant refers to a human resource function that has real strategic influence, exercising a high degree of centralized control over recruitment and development as well as evaluation and rewards.

In the *Wild West,* line managers view HRM tasks such as recruiting, developing, and rewarding as a vital part of their own role. The HR function itself plays only a technical support role, and there are no long-term strategic links between strategy development and talent development.

The *Pivotal* or "Business Partner" quadrant shows a human resource function that is closely involved in business strategy development. The operational responsibility for HRM lies with line management, sometimes with functional support. The senior HR person is seen as a catalyst and coordinator at the policy level, and the HR team is small.

Country Codes : CH = Switzerland; D = Germany; DK = Denmark; E = Spain; F = France; I = Italy; N = Norway; NL = Holland; S = Sweden; UK = United Kingdom.

Source: Adapted from C. Brewster, and H. Holt Larsen, "Human Resource Management in Europe: Evidence from Ten Countries," The International Journal of Human Resource Management, *3 (1992), 409–34.*

One study identified three broad distinctions between the institutional frameworks of the United States and continental Europe which overrode internal differences within Europe.[41] First, there is the higher level of state regulation in Europe that constrains organizations in their HR practices, particularly with regard to hiring and firing. Second, there is the greater size and influence of unions in many European countries (union recognition can be a legal requirement for the purposes of collective bargaining). Third, there are stronger European traditions of employee representation. This is particularly the case in Germany and the Netherlands, where employee representatives are members of supervisory boards and have recourse to the law to delay managerial decisions in key HR areas such as recruitment and redundancy. But it is also true of several other countries where works councils are legally required once the firm reaches a certain employee threshold or when the employees request it. However, others hotly disagree that there is a "European" model, pointing to the variation across countries; and in domains such as equal opportunity, U.S. firms are arguably more constrained than their transatlantic counterparts.[42]

Projecting One's Own Institutional Context Abroad

As a company internationalizes, it is well advised to reflect on the way in which the institutional structure in its own home country has shaped its approach to human resource management—the so-called "home country effect."

Consider the possible repercussions on HR practices of the approach to capital financing in the parent country. Companies in Japan and Germany have relied heavily on banks for finance. This tends to promote long-term relationships with suppliers, customers, and financiers, and consequently production and commercial functions are often the promising routes to the top. In the U.S. and the U.K. there is greater dependence on capital markets for financing, leading to formalized financial control systems that are reinforced by the focus on shareholder value.[43] Thus it has traditionally been careers in finance that attract many of the best brains. The powerful expatriate in subsidiaries abroad is often the commercial manager in German firms, whereas it will be the controller in U.S. multinationals.[44] In terms of skill development and training, capital market-based systems promote "management by the numbers" and short-term horizons, which may discourage investments in human capital and longer-term organizational learning processes.[45] When there is a profit squeeze, the first budgets to be slashed are those for training and development. Arguably, German and Japanese companies in credit-based systems in which shareholdings are more stable enjoy greater leeway to invest in skill development with a longer payback period.[46]

The institutional tradition of management development in the home country certainly influences the way in which companies create pools of international managers. In the United States, and to a lesser extent the United Kingdom, career paths are less specialized and more generalist in their orientation. This is institutionalized in broad business school education and expectations of rapid movement from job to job. This is in stark contrast to the long-term acquisition of specialist expertise more typical of the German system, in which business schools until recently were alien. There, as in Japan, managers expect to spend a longer period in each job, leading to very different skill profiles. The highly political nature of the promotion process in France may inhibit international mobility because of the need to remain visible to top management. Overall, the heritage at home in management development, anchored in national business systems, will color the way in which the company goes about international management development.

Commentary

The institutional perspective emphasizes that firms are constrained by their local environments, and this is widely held to be true regarding blue collar and unionized labor. It also suggests that national institutional arrangements facilitate certain types of organizational processes—such as incremental innovation in high quality manufacturing in Germany, rapid product development in Japan, and in France the complex engineering in sectors such as nuclear power and defense that require political support. But these arrangements will tend to impede others. As we will discuss later, such distinctive configurations of institutional features may confer what Porter calls "the competitive advantage of nations."

Yet one of the dangers of the institutional perspective may be to exaggerate the persistence of national characteristics. For example, many foreign firms regarded the German market as off limits in terms of takeover activity until the British mobile phone operator Vodafone shattered the perception of impenetrability by acquiring Mannesmann. German firms such as Daimler and E.ON have eagerly embraced "shareholder value," reorienting their accounting systems to Anglo-Saxon standards as they entered the U.S. stock exchange so as to access cheaper sources of capital.

Some regard the influence of national business systems to be declining, pointing to the individualization of practices in Japan, to the changes in the Korean *chaebol,* and to what one British scholar calls the "Anglo-Saxonization" of management.[47] They foresee a gradual shift towards the looser institutional arrangements prevailing in the U.S. business system. American commentators, in particular, often feel strongly about the virtues of the free market open economy, resenting the degree of state intervention and regulation that prevails in many parts of Europe and Asia.[48] Most scholars take a more measured view, and we would side with those who argue that capitalist free market extremism is likely to create degrees of social injustice that can ultimately lead only to a swing of the pendulum. If the U.S. model is widely praised as the winner in the world's economic beauty contest,[49] Singapore embodies the opposite model of pervasive institutional intervention. Going from developing country to an economy with one of the highest projected growth rates, some view it as an interesting model of how to modify the institutional context so as to attract investors, to develop highly skilled people, and to foster growth.[50]

The institutional perspective must be complemented by a third view on cultural diversity. In an increasingly professional-based and knowledge-based world, there is more and more awareness of management practices in other countries. Managers in Europe and Asia are bombarded by press reports on the latest trends in the United States and elsewhere, and the Internet will only accelerate this. The idea of cultural cocoons that are prisoners of their own heritage is less and less true. It all depends on who you talk to—and this leads us to the network perspective on diversity.

Know Who You Talk To: The Network Perspective

Multinational companies are not only influenced by their origins and the norms in countries where they operate. There are also pressures to conform to international peers or competitors that are called "isomorphic" pressures.[51] A growing number of studies document the important role of interorganizational networks in diffusing significant organizational practices.[52]

To better appreciate this idea of networks, consider an unpublished research study by Maria Arias. As a management scholar from Ecuador she was interested in the transfer of modern management technology to developing countries like her own. She chose to study how HR technology spreads from multinational corporations operating in Ecuador to local firms. However, her study found hardly any transfer at all. Managers in local Ecuadorian firms compared themselves to other local firms, and the multinationals compared themselves to other multinationals operating in Ecuador. They constituted two separate networks with virtually no overlap—and no transfer of know-how. This shows that beyond similarities in cultural values or institutional context, organizations define themselves by the company they keep.

One can perhaps understand such compartmentalization in a country such as Ecuador, where local firms are smaller and less sophisticated than the multinational subsidiaries. Why would multinationals cultivate contacts with lower status players? What could they learn from them? Yet a similar phenomenon is also visible in Japan, where one would expect exchange between Japanese multinationals and locally based foreign subsidiaries. In fact, they are two separate worlds. Japanese managers working for foreign subsidiaries even have their own union, the Foreign Affiliated Managers Association (FAMA). These managers hardly ever cross over to Japanese multinationals, or vice versa. To a lesser extent, the same is true of France where networks of graduates from the *grandes écoles* or "great schools" tend to dominate the major French companies, leaving graduates from other institutions to opt either for the foreign company "circuit" or the nonestablishment business sector. In France, as in other countries, this creates separate networks and labor pools with little exchange between them.[53]

On the other hand, particular cross-networks can lead to distinctive national systems. France is again an illustration. The elite grandes écoles produce both the captains of industry and the heads of government. As mentioned earlier, the resulting tight connections help explain France's success in sectors such as nuclear engineering that require close collaboration between state and business.

The network perspective, while ill researched, is particularly relevant to the HR/personnel domain since professional associations have long played an important role in prescribing what is best practice. However, these associations are almost exclusively national networks, with members often coming from a particular circuit within that country. In the case of Europe, one of the authors of this book co-founded the first pan-European HR network of practitioners in the early 1990s. However, even today its 200 corporate members are almost exclusively international firms—local players continue to network with and copy other local players.

Consequently, we found that Danish firms systematically mismanaged expatriate reentry because they compared themselves only to other Danish firms.[54] Foreign companies in Japan pay higher wages than local firms since their salary surveys compare them only with other foreign firms. Most are not even aware that they are paying this "*gaijin* tax" (foreigner tax) because they would never think of networking with an indigenous Japanese corporation.

The problem with such strong ties in an insulated network, as highlighted by network theorists, is that they limit access to information from the wider environment and are less likely to introduce decision-makers to fundamentally new ideas and insights.[55] Interorganizational networks can influence a company's capacity for adaptation.[56] There are good reasons, however, why networks remain tightly focused. The probability of finding relevant know-how decreases as one widens the network. The company ends up devoting inordinate attention to processing confusing information. Put simply, one can waste a tremendous amount of time in networking!

Learning From Friends When Abroad

Managers operating in foreign environments have a particular incentive to build networks with those from other multinationals since the appropriateness of proposed practices is often unknown. Expatriates who are responsible for introducing practices that may be risky, expensive, and irreversible are naturally keen to discuss the benefits or frustrations that peers may have experienced when implementing similar changes. As Burt puts it: "Adopting innovation entails a risk, an uncertain balance of costs and benefits, and people manage that uncertainty by drawing on others to define a socially acceptable interpretation of the risk."[57] And there is research evidence that firms tend to imitate changes previously adopted by network peers.[58]

All this suggests that local adaptation of HR practices may be influenced as much by what other foreign subsidiaries are doing or what regionally based consultants are recommending as by the workings of indigenous operations or the best practices back home. This three-way tension has been highlighted by a study of foreign firms operating in Russia. It showed that the practices of foreign firms "were more similar to their parent firm's HRM practices *and those of other foreign firms operating in Russia* than to HRM practices in local Russian firms" (italics added).[59] Sharing the same clubs, sending their children to the same schools, living in the same areas, expatriates from different multinationals quickly develop strong ties, especially in developing countries. Such relationships provide natural channels for sharing useful information about what works and does not work, and international firms sometimes foster this through regional structures or overlays.[60] A firm's choice of HR practices therefore also reflects the networks to which that company belongs.

Global Fashions and Fads

Of course, organizations can also look outside their immediate networks for ideas about what works. Increasingly, organizations have access to a kind of surrogate network in the shape of cases gleaned from business professors, consultants, management gurus, and journalists. These "fashion setters" serve as carriers of best practice and benchmark information across borders (whether geographical or industry).[61] Each proposes new exemplar companies and organizational innovations. Companies are exposed to the routines and practices of key international competitors. What self-respecting international manager has not heard of GE's Workout or ABB's Abacus? In a broad sense these companies and practices become part of an organization's extended network—legitimate sources of comparison.

Via the business media, these "leading edge" practices reach a broad audience and therefore converge on the company's network from several points at once. This can create intense pressure to follow suit in order to maintain the appearance of a "legitimate," "modern," or "progressive" organization, as defined by the network. This is plain bandwagon imitation.[62]

Moreover, access to this detailed and dispersed body of information has been immensely facilitated by the advent of the Internet. Executives in Europe, Asia, or Africa may be just as familiar with the latest practices as their American counterparts. Already in the early 1990s, one survey noted that many European company directors perceived a narrowing of the gap between American, European, and Japanese management philosophies and practices, "especially in multinational corporations which are in direct contact with the three continents."[63] And that was before the Internet had properly taken off.

Some degree of convergence seems inevitable among the network of sophisticated multinationals that invest aggressively in the same emerging markets, recruit from the same business schools, and send their executives to the same conferences and on the same training courses. These companies are subjected to some generic cross-national pressures—how to do things better, cheaper, and faster. They have to wrestle with similar issues—managing change, transferring knowledge across boundaries, coping with e-opportunities, and fighting the talent war, to name but a few of the current concerns.

On the other hand, the resulting convergence is more nuanced than it often appears. One investigation into the Anglo-Saxon influence on European multinationals reveals important variations.[64] Though French and German multinationals are adopting Anglo-Saxon practices in the fields of executive compensation, job restructuring, and corporate governance, they do so in a local manner. For example, German preoccupations with long-term orientation and with social responsibility have been merged with the new concerns for shareholder value and responsiveness, leading to distinctly German ways of responding to the latter pressures. Layoffs through restructuring are more moderate than in Anglo-Saxon countries, accompanied by an emphasis on "partnership" and "cooperation" with the workforce. Statements about the importance of medium- and long-term profitability mitigate the emphasis on shareholder value.[65]

International networks may rapidly spread new concepts such as value growth or 360° feedback, but successful adoption means that they have to be worked coherently into the cultural fabric of the firm. Indeed a detailed study on the transfer of Japanese TQM practices to five firms in the United States showed that while simplified rhetoric may be necessary to start off the process of transfer, successful implementation requires detailed technical attention and adaptation to the specific circumstances of the enterprise.[66] There may be generic ideas, but there are no generic solutions.

Moreover, those with a longer-term perspective should be wary of endorsing the so-called Anglo-Saxon model as objectively virtuous. Only twenty years ago, Japan was the worldwide model, and who knows what fashions the future will bring. New models for internationalization have recently been upheld, as some Indian and Brazilian firms leapfrog ahead in going global.[67]

Commentary

Traditional models of organizational adaptation tend to portray companies as deciding how to respond to new circumstances in social isolation. The emerging theory and evidence on networks suggest otherwise. Besides home context and host context influences, there is also the influence of the international networks to which organizations belong.

These interfirm ties may be of particular relevance to foreign subsidiaries given the high uncertainty that they face. These are conditions under which one might expect intense communication with peers who have been through it already, or who are facing the same challenges. Network ties multiply the repertoire of potential responses in adapting to an uncertain environment, "making linked organizations more astute collectively than they are individually."[68]

Moreover, if the subsidiary eschews home practices as inappropriate, adopting the practices of an internationally recognized peer may appear more legitimate (vis-à-vis the head office) than those of a successful local company. Local managers who must create the impression that they are conforming to the "norms of rationality" may yield to those pressures. However, this need for social legitimacy can trigger bandwagon effects that highlight the drawbacks of networks.

At a higher level of aggregation, networks serve to promote a dominant economic ideology, currently that of capitalism, fueled by international management education and international business publications. But homogenization of perspectives leads to impoverished choice. In order to remain alert to choices, to preserve healthy cynicism, and to avoid me-too decisions, we need to be aware of how our networks shape our reality.

RESPONDING TO DIVERSITY

Diversity exists, be it cultural or institutional, minimized or maximized by networks. Despite its appeal to some and the horror it evokes in others, we are not sure that globalization will result in homogenization. How does the enterprise that is internationalizing cope with this diversity?

Rather than perceiving diversity as a constraint, one view is to allow the organization to be carefully guided by contextual differences. An even more proactive approach is to try to capitalize on diversity, using it as a lever for competitive advantage. We turn now to discuss how corporations can respond to diversity as they spread their international wings.

Be Guided by Diversity

Taking our own culture as the frame of reference, as we must, some cultures are clearly more distant from us than others. When firms expand beyond their national borders they have to adjust—and the higher the cultural distance the higher may be the risk of failure.[69] Therefore, the basic response to local diversity is to respect it.

Companies that are expanding internationally can let cultural issues guide them on two key decisions: the internationalization sequence and the method of entry.[70] A third way of being guided involves identifying the organizational practices thought to be nontransferable to this particular location. From a managerial perspective, these decisions correspond to the questions: where next, how to go in, and what to adjust? Companies that use diversity as a guide take an incremental approach to internationalization, learning as they go along.

The Internationalization Sequence: Where Next?

Take the example of Cemex, the Mexican cement company. From a standing start in the late 1980s, the company began to internationalize its operations. First, it expanded into Latin America via start-ups and acquisitions. Then it moved into the United States targeting the states in the South and West that have a large Spanish population. When it crossed the Atlantic to Europe, it entered via Spain. Lorenzo Zambrano, the CEO, was determined to expand further, but was also concerned not to undermine a successful formula based on fast but centralized decision-making, agility, and intolerance of bureaucracy. These capabilities were rooted in a common ability of all senior executives to speak Spanish and in shared cultural values pertaining to personal trust and intense social interaction combined with acceptance of authority.

In the mid-1990s, with the most promising opportunities clearly lying in Asia, Cemex needed to establish a foothold in the region. So where did it look first? The Philippines, a former Spanish colony where Spanish is still widely spoken and where it acquired a 30 percent stake in Rizal Cement. From there the company set up a joint venture in nearby Indonesia in 1998. This internationalization strategy has been successful for Cemex. It now ranks number three in the world cement industry and generates over 60 percent of its sales outside its home market. It is one of Mexico's few truly multinational companies.

This is not an isolated example. IKEA, the furniture retail chain, expanded first from its Swedish base to culturally contiguous Scandinavian countries, then to Holland, France, and the U.K., before using Canada as a lead into the American market, later entering Asia via Hong Kong. Indeed, some researchers have found that firms moving to culturally distant countries after establishing a presence in more proximate countries were more successful than those using a random expansion strategy.[71]

Given such findings one might urge managers to pay careful attention not just to market opportunity but also to ease of entry in terms of cultural distance, especially with respect to its impact on human resources. The firm needs to move to cultures that it can manage. This can apply to specific locations as well as countries. Japanese manufacturing firms entering the United States and Europe for the first time during the 1980s tended to place their new plants in rural locations rather than in traditional centers of U.S. manufacturing. Typically they set up in regions where the value system (tight knit communities) and institutional environment (for example, unionization and supplier networks) were both closest to Japan and most flexible—the Midwest in the U.S., Wales in the U.K. From this perspective, internationalization can be seen as a progressive learning process, allowing the firm to take bigger and bigger risks. However, a study of high rates of failure among Canadian retailing companies entering the supposedly proximate U.S. market suggests that assumptions of similarity can prevent executives from learning about critical differences.[72] The risks can be minimized by ensuring that executives with experience in that market are part of the decision-making teams.

Entry Mode: How to Go In?

Cultural distance may also guide the entry mode—greenfield, joint venture, or acquisition. For example, Japanese firms have an unusual appetite for wholly owned greenfield operations. Why? Because "starting from scratch" means that staff can be selected and socialized into nontraditional practices. These firms are sensitive to cultural differences, but prefer to sidestep them where possible.

Research on foreign firms entering the U.S. market has shown significant relationships between entry patterns and both cultural distance and national attitudes toward uncertainty avoidance.[73] In contrast with the penchant for greenfield investments of Japanese firms, their Scandinavian and especially French counterparts leaned toward joint ventures. U.K. firms, meanwhile, went for acquisitions—this being regarded as the riskiest option by virtue of the "double layered acculturation" (adjustment both to a foreign national and to an alien corporate culture). The findings suggested that cultural distance increased the probability of choosing a joint venture over an acquisition, while high uncertainty avoidance also made the acquisition option less attractive. However, as a firm learns how to master a new culture through initial joint ventures, so wholly-owned entry may be favored over a joint venture or acquisition over a greenfield investment.

HR Practices: How Strategic Are They?

To a greater or lesser extent, organizations obviously have to adapt their management practices to the local institutional and cultural context. One of the important challenges is to know what to adapt and what not to adapt. Which HR practices really are "strategic," that is vital to the strategy or capabilities of the firm? And which practices can be freely adjusted or changed to fit local circumstances?

Although most companies consider leadership development to be highly strategic, perhaps the single most strategic domain of international HRM,[74] what is critical may sometimes be taken for granted until the firm goes abroad. It is like the fish that does not know it is a fish—until it is out of the water. Once again, local adaptation starts off with "know yourself."

Some U.S. firms in professional services, for example, have a practice of not paying any employees for overtime. Salaries are generous, objectives are clear, there is a high degree of delegation, and there are generous amenities in the offices so that people can stay on in the evenings if they wish to work. In the United States, all this is taken for granted. It becomes an issue only when the company sets up operations in Japan where not paying people for overtime goes against both practice and the law. Is this practice really strategic? Should the firm conform to local norms or should it invest in finding ways of respecting those norms but maintaining its practice (for example, trying to negotiate an exception with the authorities or finding a way of including overtime in salary)? The firm often has not thought about what is strategic until it is confronted with the dilemma.

What is strategic may have to be undertaken in different ways in different cultures. Consider the case of Bertelsmann. Back in 1974, the company introduced what it called its "January discussion"—an annual opportunity for each boss to receive collective feedback from his or her subordinates. This practice matched well the formalized orientation that characterizes many German firms. While the company has become very attached to this feedback mechanism, it has not imposed it on its U.S. operations. The relationship there between executives and other employees is considered more open and less complicated, with "day-to-day business carried on in a critical and even adversarial spirit."[75]

This is an important example because contention management can be considered highly strategic in many fast-moving industries facing multiple contradictions, as we will see later in this book. Whether or not and how it adapts its performance appraisal system to cultures that value harmony (such as Thailand, Indonesia, and Japan) may not just be important for performance management but also for aligning the culture of the local firm to strategic objectives.

It is essential, however, to recognize that not all foreign subsidiaries are equally strategic. Bartlett and Ghoshal rightly emphasize that national affiliates in a multinational firm have differentiated roles and responsibilities.[76] Some local environments are particularly important to the firm's global strategy because of the size of the market, the presence of key competitors, or its sophistication in terms of technology. A second dimension affecting whether or not a country is strategic is the strength of the local resource base in, for example, technology, marketing, or production. Together these two dimensions provide a map of different types of national organizations, shown in Figure 4–1.

This differentiated conceptualization adds another dimension to what "local" responsiveness implies. Local means not only national and institutional culture but also the position of the affiliate within the firm's strategic priorities. The firm should pay a great deal of attention to the consequences of adaptation (or nonadaptation) of local HRM practices in markets that are *strategic leaders*—the United States for Bertelsmann. The decision as to how to proceed will generally be reserved for the corporate head office. Paying the same attention to an *implementer*, however, would be misguided (for Bertelsmann, its U.K. magazine firm is an implementer, while the British music company is a strategic leader). It would be more rational to allow the local management of an implementer to make the necessary adaptations as they see

FIGURE 4–1. The Four Generic Roles of National Organizations

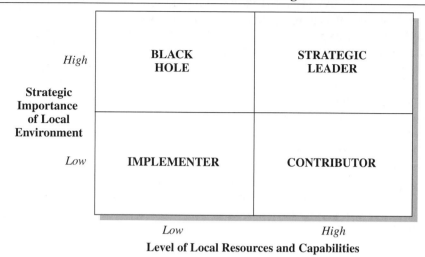

Source: C. A. Bartlett and S. Ghoshal, Managing across Borders: The Transnational Solution *(Boston: Harvard Business School Press, 1998), 122.*

fit. Across the board, integrated norms and practices do not correspond to this differentiated reality.

Capitalize on Diversity

Traditionally, cultural and institutional differences have been viewed as obstacles or threats to business efficiency—driven in part by a personnel logic that everyone should be managed in the same way.[77] With accelerating globalization, there is a strong counterargument that cultural and institutional differences can be a potential source of competitive advantage. One strand of the argument is based on the psychological and culturalist orientation, while the other builds on the institutional perspective.

Building Cultural Synergy

The idea that cultural diversity can be a resource rather than a liability to the organization has strong intuitive appeal. Geoff Unwin, the British chief executive of the French IT consultancy Cap Gemini, notes: "People ask why this very French company put a Brit in charge. My answer is that it was because I was different. I thought differently. Not better, just differently. When people think differently, it puts a different perspective on problems. We exploit that. . . . It is a very, very multi-cultural organisation. This diversity brings a lot to the company."[78]

Adler makes a useful distinction between three forms of local adaptation. The first is *cultural accommodation,* which involves imitating the practices of the host culture (the opposite of cultural imperialism). The second is *cultural compromise,* whereby both sides concede something in order to work more successfully. And the third is *cultural synergy,* which means developing new solutions that respect each of the underlying cultures. Adler's view is: "The synergistic approach minimizes potential problems by managing the impacts of cultural diversity, not by attempting to minimize the diversity itself."[79] For example, in its new sports utility vehicle plant in Alabama, Mercedes-Benz made a deliberate effort to blend practices from its different locations. Its success in fusing German strengths in quality and workmanship with American norms of informality and openness established new speed, innovation, and quality benchmarks for the company.[80]

Cultural diversity, Adler argues, can generate richer perspectives in describing and interpreting situations and in finding creative responses to business issues. Simply put, diversity means fewer blind spots and more insights. Research suggests that, once settled, culturally diverse teams can outperform monocultural teams in "identifying problem perspectives" and "generating alternatives,"[81] although cultural differences also increase the risk of emotional conflicts that can paralyze or blow up such teams.[82] HR has a particular responsibility to legitimize cultural differences and to encourage managers to capitalize on those differences rather than try to suppress or ignore them.

Cultural synergy is not just an individual process—it is a vital step toward transnational organizational learning which some scholars view as the principal source of competitive advantage of the multinational corporation in the future.[83] One study of German multinationals highlights this process.[84] First, some firms deliberately test out new policies and practices in vanguard subsidiaries such as the United States or the U.K. These "strategic leaders" become vehicles for experimentation in management practices that in turn may lead to changes in the mother company. Second, executives with experience in such affiliates are transferred into key positions at headquarters with the responsibility for change, adapting foreign practices to the circumstances at home. This reversal of the flow of knowledge, from foreign subsidiary to home base, is one of the significant steps toward the transnational corporation. Responsiveness to local diversity provides a critical foundation for organizational learning and capability development.

Moving Jobs to People

Institutional structures can provide a nation with sources of competitive advantage, as Lee Kuan Yew in the city-state of Singapore has long been aware. Studies of Japan have stressed the benefits its export industries derive from a highly educated labor force, discerning local consumers, interlocking supplier relationships, and the stimulus of vigorous rivalry between domestic producers.

Porter tested this notion systematically with a wide range of industries in ten countries, reported in his book *The Competitive Advantage of Nations.*[85] Taking world export share as his benchmark, he highlighted successful sectors as diverse as Italian tile-making, U.S. medical equipment, and Japanese robots. His inquiry into why some countries excel in some types of business but not others identified a "diamond" comprising four drivers: (i) factor endowments, such as a supply of skilled labor or infrastructure; (ii) the intensity of the local competition; (iii) the proximity of competent suppliers and adjacent industries; and (iv) the quality of demand from domestic markets. However boldly companies expanded abroad, Porter argued, their dynamism was dependent on their "home base." Hence a nation's prosperity depended on how efficiently its companies exploited the distinctive strengths with which the nation had been endowed by history, circumstance, or aptitude.

Porter's conclusions have implications for strategy and human resource management. If local institutional factors provide competitive advantages in a particular domain of importance to the international firm, then why should the firm not move that domain to the location that provides competitive advantage? HRM used to be a matter of moving people to jobs (expatriation). Increasingly it is also becoming one of moving jobs to people.

The archetypal example is the attraction of Silicon Valley (remember our Business Objects case at the outset of this book). Why does the Valley attract companies from all over the world? Because it has nurtured a constellation of factors that forge a unique labor market, including leading edge educational institutions, risk taking venture capitalists, and favorable local legislation. The reputation of the area attracts even more entrepreneurs and people with exceptional skills, producing a self-reinforcing process—and soon, companies in that line of business cannot afford to miss out on developments there. Many European firms have moved the headquarters and major operations of their microelectronics or software divisions from Europe to Silicon Valley, driven by the lure of tapping into competencies and skills.

Silicon Valley is but one example of this clustering. Locations such as the Caribbean, Ireland, and India are recognized respectively for their sophistication in administrative processing, customer service support, and software development. By distributing to specific areas around the world key activities which had until now been carried out domestically, companies are trying to gain access to sophisticated knowledge and networks. In the automobile industry, many companies including some in Japan have their car design centers in San Diego, while engine environmental conversion is located in Ann Arbor, Michigan, close to the U.S. Environmental Protection Agency. Swatch has placed its design units in Italy and production engineering in Switzerland. This applies equally to product lines. Nestlé, with its global headquarters in Switzerland, put its confectionery business headquarters in the U.K. and its pasta business in Italy. This trend may even be touching head offices. Among conservative German corporations, there is discussion today of relocating the headquarters to London so as to separate global management from that of the domestic market.

Responsiveness to market and resource opportunities is most easily achieved when the local subsidiary is able to become well connected, an insider in the local community. But this is easier said than done. To capture all these advantages, it is not enough to be locally based; companies also need to be localized. And that is another challenge.

THE CHALLENGES OF LOCALIZATION

Localization takes a variety of forms—for example, Hideo Sugiura, the former vice chairman of Honda, distinguishes between localization of products, profit, production, and people.[86] Our focus in this book is on the people aspect, taking localization to mean the systematic investment in the recruitment, development, and retention of local employees who can take over the running of local operations. Unilever provides one of the earliest documented examples of this policy in action. Sensitive to the national aspirations of newly independent countries, the company started to replace expatriates with indigenous managers. Known internally as the "ization" policy, it started in the 1930s and 1940s with "Indianization" and "Africanization" of local subsidiaries.[87]

Since then, localization has become part of the corporate mantra for multinational enterprises around the world. Building strong local management teams is considered a sign of enlightened management and especially of good corporate citizenship. It supplies a lever for attracting local talent worldwide and for improving the firm's international perspective, and represents an integral strand in the globalization strategy of many companies.

Our concept of localization equates this with the degree of local responsibility for decision-making.[88] A subsidiary may have only one expatriate, but if that person takes all decisions of importance, its degree of localization is low, as would be the case in which a local general manager has to check out every decision with the HQ in the mother country. On the other hand, a high degree of localization is not synonymous with complete subsidiary autonomy in the extreme sense of that word. Decisions may be taken by locals after consultation with other subsidiaries and regional or worldwide headquarters, and local managers may have had substantial foreign experience as part of their own development. What a high degree of localization implies is that the subsidiary is responsible for its own decision-making and lives with the consequences of its own actions.

The case for localization is fairly straightforward (see the box "Why Localize?"). Localization seems to offer a cheaper and more culturally appropriate response—establishing better community links, placing greater trust in local staff, building on their experience, expertise, and local knowledge.

There is also some evidence that localization influences long-term profitability. A survey of twenty-eight U.S. companies operating in China revealed that among the best performing firms expatriates made up 18 percent of the staff, compared with 39 percent for the companies overall.[89] Another study found that companies with an active localization policy in China consistently had turnover rates well below the industry average.[90]

Localization of management is not just a challenge in emerging countries where skill availability may be a serious concern. It is also a major issue for meganational firms which historically relied on managing local operations worldwide through expatriates. In 1982, when Matsushita president Yamashita launched "Operation Localization," three Americans were among the six divisional presidents reporting to the Japanese CEO of MECA (Matsushita Corporation of America). But it was not until 1994 that Matsushita finally appointed an American to head up this U.S. company.

While localization may be embraced as an important business objective, progress is often slower than anticipated owing to the complexity of the process. While this is a key challenge for many international firms, there is little systematic

Why Localize?
Practice Box

International firms pursue localization policies for a variety of reasons:[A]

Local authorities and public opinion: Authorities often evaluate foreign firms by their level of localization, while media, politicians, and trade union officials stress the importance of local talent development. Some governments impose quotas, restrict work permits, or impose fiscal controls on expatriate salaries. Therefore a company with expansion plans in the country may look upon localization as a means of developing goodwill or of shedding a colonial or ethnocentric image.

Local network: Localization helps foreign multinationals penetrate the network of personal and business contacts needed to build and consolidate a presence in the country. Local managers know the vernacular, understand how business is done, and have access to critical relationships. Expatriates may be capable of surmounting some of the linguistic and cultural barriers but their expatriate status works against them. Why would key industry players or government officials bother to cultivate relations with someone whose assignment terminates in three years? Expatriates are dismissed as "temporary fixtures" with whom it is not worth doing business.

Local workforce: There is the internal commitment and motivation argument. Opportunities for growth and advancement are important concerns for local employees—and dissatisfaction with those opportunities features among the most frequently cited reasons for turnover. The continued employment of expatriates is seen as blocking promotional avenues and reflecting a lack of trust in local managers. Paradoxi-

cally, local executives may also have less difficulty than expatriates when it comes to implementing difficult strategic decisions, such as layoffs or reorganization. The allegiance of expatriates is more suspect and their decisions tend to be closely scrutinized.[B]

Cost: Localization reduces the high costs of maintaining a large contingent of expatriate managers in far-flung operations. One recent study estimates that for more than 75 percent of companies, the cost of expatriates amounts to more than three times that of local employees.[C] In many ways, the big reward packages for expatriates only add to the strain. First, there may be a source of ill-feeling between expatriate and local staff. One study showed that local employees typically have detailed knowledge of expatriates' salaries and allowances. Second, high salaries encourage head offices to drive expatriate managers hard, which may explain the numerous incidences of early burn-out: "After many months or years of working six- or seven-day weeks under difficult conditions even the most energetic expatriates tend to hit a mental wall."[D]

[A]For some studies on localization, see Lasserre and Ching (1997), Wong and Law (1999), Hailey (1996).
[B]Prahalad and Doz, 1987.
[C]Conference Board, 1996. Another report suggests that for a senior executive in China for example, the total package can reach as much as six times the cost of a local manager. V. Griffith, "As Close as a Group Can Get to Global," *Financial Times*, April 7, 1997; Melvin and Sylvester, 1997. See also Jones and Wright (1992) and Bonache and Barber (2000) for an assessment of the transaction costs associated with expatriation.
[D]Economist Intelligence Unit, 1996; see also Melvin and Sylvester (1997).

research on this topic—it is almost a blindspot in the international HRM field. One explanation for the blind spot is that research has been dominated by a focus on expatriates. In fact, getting localization right requires an appreciation of the difficulties, clear expatriate responsibility, a sustained strategy for the development of local managers, and indeed in the case of some meganational firms such as those from Japan and Germany a fundamental reorientation of their approach to management. Let us examine some of these challenges, with a particular emphasis on localization in emerging markets.

Barriers to Localization—The Catch-22 Dilemma

Two interrelated problems systematically plague corporate efforts to localize. First, competent local managers are often hard to find. Second, once found, they may be hard to retain. The two problems sometimes create a catch-22 dilemma. If good local managers are going to leave us in any case, why bother to invest time and money in developing the locals?[91]

Finding and Developing Local Talent

In emerging markets, there may be a genuine scarcity of talent with specific functional, market, or managerial competencies. In developed markets it is more likely to be a problem of accessing the labor market. For example, as mentioned earlier, the number of Japanese who can be lured from local corporations to foreign firms is small (though growing). Headhunters cannot spot or access high performers in Japanese firms and are forced to limit themselves to executives already in the *gaishikei* (foreign-affiliate) world.

Because of the difficulties of accessing and retaining experienced managers, some companies opt to "grow their own timber." They will take on young recruits, placing more emphasis on their future potential than on their current technical skill. This entails big investments in their development, both through formal training programs and through on-the-job learning and individual coaching. It may even involve building local training institutions, as VW did in China.

But given the time frames involved in developing competent managers, attrition is bound to play a role. In response, some multinational firms hire at least two local trainees for each expatriate position to be localized.[92] Inevitably this drives up the costs. It also creates a corporate surfeit of highly skilled managers, sometimes with international exposure—allowing rival firms to benefit from the company's development efforts. Paradoxically, turnover also increases because the trainees suspect that they may not be the chosen one.

Retaining Local Talent

Over time, certain units that excel in local talent development, such as Honeywell Italy or Procter & Gamble Europe back in the 1980s, may come to be regarded as training grounds for other competitors in the industry—an obligatory first stop for the headhunters. General Motors and the German automakers building U.S. manufacturing sites systematically raided Japanese transplants to capture local talent, weakening the ability of the latter to localize. On the other hand, that is perhaps a price worth paying if it means that the company is still able to attract and retain the very best, as GE believes it does.

A disproportionate number of local managers trained to take over expatriate positions never actually fill those posts or do so only briefly. One study invoked inadequate or biased selection and inappropriate training as part of the explanation, but found that a more significant factor was the post-training terms and conditions.[93] These fell a long way short of what the market was prepared to offer to ambitious and well-trained individuals. Consider the case of Russia. Prior to the fall of the Berlin Wall, it counted only a handful of foreign firms. Today, thousands of foreign firms are based there, which results in significant competition for qualified employees. In addition, private Russian firms are increasingly able to make competitive employment offers and thus join the competition for skilled employees.[94] The local educational and training infrastructures will take a long time to close the gap between demand and supply. Increasing levels of foreign investment and scarcity of managerial talents make staff retention a delicate issue for all multinational companies.

High turnover rates have other consequences. In emerging markets, jealousies between locals and the "pseudo-locals"—returnees with freshly minted MBAs who command salaries well above market rates—reproduce the resentments previously caused by lavish expatriate packages. Turnover also puts pressure on salary costs. For example, the general manager of Fuji Bank in London struggled to retain qualified specialists wooed by European and U.S. institutions in the City, noting that "for us localization is no longer a cheap alternative."[95]

Given these pressures, companies become reluctant to invest in local employees, preferring instead expatriates or third country nationals with a proven commitment to the company. If there is a shortage of local talent, this can turn the catch-22 into a vicious circle. Expatriate-heavy structures restrict career opportunities for local managers, encouraging turnover as well as weakening morale and the talent pool. Over time, this may be reflected in stagnating sales or dwindling market share. This comes to the attention of corporate headquarters who sends in new expatriates to put things right, an action that merely confirms suspicions of a glass ceiling for locals, making it even harder to attract or retain local talent. Local people stop believing the "propaganda."

The lesson is that localization, with all its advantages, is unlikely to be successful if it is the faddish concern of passing expatriate general managers or regional directors. Breaking out of that vicious circle requires long-term corporate commitment right from the top. It requires holistic attention not just to recruitment, motivation, and compensation but also to retention, to the wider package of rewards (challenge, opportunity, and international projects), and especially to career development. This means paying as much attention to the role of expatriates as to locals, for it is the expatriates who ultimately carry out the localization strategy.

Expatriates Are Responsible for Localization

When giving expatriates responsibility for implementing localization, firms must pay close attention to three key areas: their selection, their mandate, and their motivation.

SELECTING THE RIGHT PERSON. Ceding control to local managers is not an overnight effort. It needs to be prepared. The implementation of a localization process starts in the parent country, with the selection and training of suitable candidates for expatriation. In addition to the managerial and technical skills expected of any expatriate, they will need to possess mentoring and coaching experience. As the China-based HR manager of a large U.S. manufacturing company put it: "Expatriates should be able to transfer information even to people who don't know what questions to ask."[96]

There is also the question of the required experience profile. The young high potentials that Shell traditionally sent out to emerging markets were not successful in managing the localization process. They had neither the motivation nor the depth of experience to pass on their skills. This accorded with the reaction of one local manager in East Asia who observed: "Most expatriates learn on the job, and the locals end up teaching them."[97] Under pressure from local governments, Shell switched tack and started sending out experienced end-of-career people to manage localization.

SETTING OBJECTIVES. Prior to the assignment, the localization objectives and timetable must be clearly negotiated with the expatriates, otherwise it risks becoming another of those items on the wish list. Unless these expectations are articulated, expediency and the need to meet business results will dominate, with only token attention given to developing local managers or to identifying their training needs.

Coming on top of the need to meet operational objectives, the tasks associated with training a local replacement—including transfer of technical know-how, business knowledge, and corporate norms, as well as introductions to people back at headquarters—may take longer than the typical two- or three-year expatriate posting. Expanding its brewery operations into China and Vietnam, San Miguel used a "two-plus-two-year" assignment rule for its Philippine expatriates: two years to settle in and identify a local successor, and two years to develop that person. ABB's objective in China is to try to localize higher management positions within five years.[98] An unrealistic schedule ends up being ignored or poorly implemented. Firms that localize in a hurry, without sufficient training for the incoming local manager, can quickly lose financial discipline, quality control, and corporate identity.

MOTIVATING LOCALIZATION. Equally important is the need to encourage expatriates to implement the localization plan. Expatriates will take the localization challenge seriously to the extent that they are measured not just on their business performance but also on their ability to develop local managers. One way of evaluating performance against localization objectives would be to include feedback from multiple sources, both expatriate and local.[99]

The localization objective may seem all the more authentic if the company attaches incentives to its implementation. One study recommended replacing the traditional hardship allowance with a "successful completion bonus" for expatriates who train competent local replacements.[100] On the other hand, it must be clear that "successful completion" means more than just installing a local successor. That person must have the experience, perspectives, and the necessary contacts to be effective. Partial localization can sometimes be more detrimental to the morale of the local workforce than no localization. It reinforces doubts about whether the foreign owners know how to run a local business, so perhaps it is time to head for the door.

A more compelling incentive for effective and timely localization may be the prospect of an attractive follow-up assignment—after all, are most companies not looking for people who can manage the duality of operational performance and longer-term human capital development? If there is high uncertainty about repatriation and the future career, where is the incentive to train local successors who are destined to make the expatriate obsolete? Repatriation arrangements therefore play an important role in successful localization.

Developing Local Staff

When it comes to finding suitable local candidates to take over from expatriates, the effort starts upstream with investments aimed at creating a meaningful presence in the local market. This leads to a professionally managed process spanning recruitment, training and development, and retention.

HR MARKETING AND RECRUITMENT. The development effort starts early with investments to create a visible presence in the local labor market. In emerging countries, well-known and professional Western companies may have no more established image than fly-by-night operators. Consumer products companies may have to invest in advertising to promote their image as an employer as well as their products. But business-to-business firms may have to be still more creative, investing in public relations, sponsoring sport or charitable activities, or forging links with educational institutions by making presentations, through scholarships, or by providing technology.

When talking to prospective recruits, the company should communicate its localization objectives and connect those plans to the career prospects of the local managers. A reputation for thorough training and skill development can enhance recruitment, particularly in emerging countries. Typically recruiters look for people with the right attitude—to teamwork, to learning—even if those people are underqualified. Developing a formal set of criteria is often difficult. For example, when recruiting in Russia, Cadbury's quickly realized that it had to relax its stringent requirements concerning work experience and educational background. As some recruiters see it, selection is often a matter of "gut" feeling.[101] The question is: "How good is your gut outside your home environment?" Not surprisingly, many companies use a probation period to evaluate new employees before entering into a long-term relationship.

TRAINING AND DEVELOPMENT. In some countries, training programs may have to start with the very basics in their curriculum. Even highly educated recruits may have only a basic understanding of the market economy. For example, marketing, customer satisfaction, human resource management, profits, and working environment may be vague concepts for recruits from centrally planned economies such as Russia or China. Trainees need to acquire a basic business awareness and a common vocabulary. They need to develop an understanding of time management, problem solving, and customer service.

There is some evidence that the perception of the quality of training is the single biggest influence of all HR factors on the perceived organizational and market performance of the firm.[102] This is one of the reasons why companies such as Volkswagen and Nokia have invested heavily in local training in China. Russian managers are reported to be willing to forgo a bonus equivalent to one to two months of salary in order to receive one week of training abroad.[103]

The focus of training in emerging markets is not only on employees but often equally importantly on first and second tier suppliers. When Volkswagen built its first Chinese plant in Shanghai, at times more than half its expatriate technicians were busy helping subcontractors develop and manufacture parts so as to meet local content requirements. By 1993, now with 80 percent local content, formerly unwilling Chinese suppliers helped VW become the most profitable joint venture in China.[104]

RETENTION. Inevitably, compensation looms large among the mechanisms to retain local technicians and managers. Paying above market rates is a typical measure, but market rates are less than transparent in emerging countries, which perhaps explains why the vast majority of companies claim to be in the top quartile. Moreover, pay is only one part of the compensation package. Some companies propose more binding facilities such as interest free loans, private health insurance, or housing assistance programs.

Ultimately, an attractive compensation package is necessary but not sufficient as other companies can always offer more. The decisive factors may have more to do with career development and involvement in decision-making. The firm has to be prepared to develop and promote talented people more rapidly than it might like, with necessary training, coaching, and feedback. Mapping the career paths of high potential candidates is an important signal of the company's commitment to them.[105] Social climate may be important. Characteristics such as company atmosphere, friendship ties, social activities, and the promise of a stable future in a firm with high local growth prospects have been observed to be decisive factors in employee retention in Russia.[106]

Paradoxically, an underlying problem in the development of such a strategy is that many firms localize the HR function at an early stage. While a local person may be best at operational matters—knowing the employment legislation and labor market, coping with troubleshooting—that person rarely has either the perspective that is needed to develop a coherent long-term localization strategy or the clout with the headquarters to ensure its implementation. Otis Elevators, which established the second joint venture in China after the Maoist years, learned together with its mother company United Technologies to build a careful balance of local and expatriate HR managers in its Asian operations. Other firms use regional HR managers in Asia or central Europe to ensure the development of a coherent HR strategy for localization, and this is today a corporate priority for Motorola with a worldwide global staffing function within HR.

Making Localization Work

Localization is not a one-time-only effort. The challenge does not end with the appointment of a competent local management team. Once implemented, localization efforts need to be sustained and carefully managed. The main challenges have to do with balancing autonomy and support.

Only One Bullet

It is important for international companies to take localization initiatives seriously right from the start. Companies that get it wrong the first time around can find themselves caught up in a difficult process of "serial localization." The initial implementation is cavalier and the reality does not match up to the rhetoric. Locals cannot cope when the expatriates pull out. Troubleshooters are sent in, followed by a second wave of managers who have a mandate to localize. By this time, however, the indigenous cynicism is such that talented staff have left. The efforts have to start again from scratch. And so it continues through several rounds. Localization becomes a campaign rather than an effort to harness and develop local capabilities.

Beyond the First Generation

Often, the cost of developing and promoting local managerial talent is such that efforts are scaled back as soon as the first generation of local managers takes over. At Guinness in Nigeria, the first generation of local managers received extensive training and support but the next generation of local managers did not benefit from the same policies. Blocked by the career log-jam of senior first generation managers, the best were easily tempted away by international agencies and local businesses. When the seniors retired or moved on, there was no one of high caliber in the succession pipeline. The "return expats" and consultants ("disguised expats") brought in to fill the vacuum were viewed by some as evidence of a headquarters' hidden agenda to discredit the localization process.[107]

At the same time, the Nigerian story illustrates the dangers of excessive localization. Local managers may not have an interest in investing in a new managerial elite that might jeopardize the status quo or threaten their positions. Anything taken to an extreme can create a pathology, and excessive localization can lead to fiefdoms, excessive respect for local culture, and loss of control. Indeed, localization is a step on the journey toward transnational development and not an end in itself. If a corporation is so localized around the world that mobility is limited, then it becomes difficult to turn local managers into international managers. It has been argued that the swing toward localization among U.S. multinationals may be excessive—reducing opportunities for international exposure and putting senior U.S. managers at a disadvantage when facing global competition.[108] Put simply, if everyone is local, who is global?

THE LIMITS OF RESPONSIVENESS

We started this chapter by describing Bertelsmann's success in being locally responsive. However, such a strategy may have its limits. Indeed the experience of Bertelsmann in electronic commerce illustrates the drawbacks of excessive localization.

In 1996, Amazon launched its online book store which quickly spelled trouble for Bertelsmann's book and music clubs. Yet it took Bertelsmann two years to respond to the threat. By that time, Amazon had established itself as a powerhouse in online book retailing. Bertelsmann now had to pay a high price to close the gap, forking out $200 million in 1998 for 50 percent of the website business of Barnes & Noble, one of America's leading bookstores. It was not until February 1999 that Bertelsmann's multimedia division launched its own online book-retailing business, BOL, in European countries, although Amazon was now already firmly settled into the U.K.

Bertelsmann's initially sluggish response was largely attributable to its decentralized structure. The gap between New York and the Gütersloh headquarters was one reason for Bertelsmann's failure to perceive how the Internet would affect its business. The American subsidiary in New York had been warning Gütersloh about the dangers of Amazon for eighteen months before anybody paid attention. Another problem, given Bertelsmann's heavily decentralized structure, was that no one could decide which unit should lead the charge since the response necessarily involved collaboration between entrenched divisions: the publishing houses, the book and music clubs, and the distribution and multimedia divisions. As the CEO himself put it: "For too long we sat in endless coordination sessions and asked: Who should respond? To whom does this business 'belong'?"[109]

This example gives some indications of the limits of a locally responsive strategy. When localization of staff is combined with a decentralized federal structure, it can lead to local fiefdoms and inhibit collaboration. It can generate other inefficiencies as well, such as duplication of effort (reinventing the wheel), needless differentiation, and resistance to external recommendations or ideas—the "handmaidens of decentralization," as Bartlett and Ghoshal dubbed them.[110] For Bertelsmann, the limitations of responsiveness were already becoming evident in 1996 and had even evoked the following in a collection of celebratory essays on the company.

> It's no good having each profit center re-invent the wheel. Also we don't network enough among ourselves. As a minimum we must have an integrated data bank—and we're too decentralized in our management development. That is a competitive disadvantage. (Peter Olson, chairman of Bertelsmann Book Group North America)

Just as the meganational may fail by blindly applying domestic rules and practices to the new environment (underadaptation), so to the multidomestic firm can fail by playing entirely by the local rules (overadaptation). The headquarters may be slow in responding to signals on developments from advanced countries, as with Bertelsmann. In trying to be "more local than the locals," the responsive firm fails to leverage its home-base knowledge, a problem initially encountered by Sony and Matsushita in Hollywood. Purchasing, respectively, MCA Universal and Columbia Pictures and warned in advance that only American managers could understand the movie business, they took a hands-off attitude. The degree of delegation was unusual for multinationals, but for Japanese ones it was unprecedented. Within five years, both had to declare multibillion dollar losses.[111] By giving the studios so much freedom, the two Japanese firms in effect guaranteed they would not be run in the parent's interest. This was responsiveness to the point of abdication.

Regionalization as a bridge between globalization and localization may sometimes be a way of responding. One study examined the role and structure of fifteen regional HQs in Asia of Western firms and fifteen regional HQs in Europe of Japanese firms. These regional headquarters often played an important functional coordination role and provided a strong link between the local subsidiary and the global head office.[112]

The impatriation of local managers to the regional or global headquarters, thereby creating a talent pool in which the qualities of the person count more than the passport, is a big step toward the transnational organization. To ensure international mobility, Unilever has long had a policy of reserving at least one slot on all management teams in both emerging and developed countries for an expatriate—a European in Asia and an Asian or Latin American in Europe. At 3M, they attenuate the risk of local empire building with an informal rule that executives cannot become managing directors in their own country. Promising local managers are appointed as heads of subsidiaries in other countries. This reduces the danger of indigenous managers becoming fixtures for several decades and clogging the career pipeline, and it ensures that local stars gain international exposure.

Localization Doesn't Necessarily Mean Playing by the Local Rules

A final paradox is that local responsiveness does not always mean playing by the local rules, as the story of the Japanese in Hollywood reminds us. Indeed one of the benefits of localization is that indigenous managers have a better sense of which local rules they can break! Local managers have a better sense for *intra-cultural* variation—the tolerance for differences within a nation—as well as for the flexibility of its institutional structure.

The transnational ideal is that of local managers who have had exposure to methods and practices by virtue of both their networks and their sojourns in lead countries, perhaps working with some expatriates who are there to gain international experience. Rather than embracing the local way, they can redefine the boundaries of what is considered to be "local"—showing smart disrespect.

Local responsiveness, as we view it from a human resource perspective, simply means local authority over decision-making, as contrasted with headquarters or expatriate authority. In Part III, we will discuss how the capacity of "local" managers (be they indigenous, from the mother country, or third country nationals) to be *creatively* local can be fostered. Transfer of best practice, cross-boundary project management, international leadership development, and other forms of transnational practice facilitate this.

Responding to Ethical Diversity

An important limit to responsiveness concerns the area of ethics. In this domain, a locally responsive stance can push indigenous managers to adopt practices that would be unacceptable to some stakeholders such as head office managers, customers and suppliers, peers, and influential members of the local and host country public.

We meet the most complex expressions of cultural diversity when it comes to ethics. The issue of ethics in business typically contrasts the "financial returns" with "social costs" such as exploitation of labor, unemployment, environmental damage, crime, corruption. Attitudes toward such ethical dilemmas vary widely from one country or community to another. Such distinctions make sense when the decision is whether to do business with low cost suppliers who deny employees basic human rights. But in reality, it is rarely so clear-cut. As de Bettignies has put it: "Most ethical decisions have mixed outcomes. Social benefits and costs as well as financial revenues and expenses are associated with almost all of the alternatives in ethical choices."[113] And ethical dilemmas are met not just in the developing world, but also in the home back yard of Silicon Valley.[114]

Ethical standards are influenced by a variety of institutional and cultural factors. Governments in some countries impose stricter disclosure laws and more active enforcement, but in uneven ways. For example, in Germany, exacting environmental laws make violation very risky, yet by U.S. standards there are relatively few laws against kickbacks and payoffs in the corporate sector. Other institutional pressures come from the media, which may play a role in publicizing ethical breaches and in investigating them. Shareholder activism and consumer boycotts are additional variable influences on corporate ethical behavior. While many issues are of universal concern—bribery, pollution, harassment, stealing from the company, patent protection, intellectual property rights, creative accounting, misrepresentation of products, and employee safety—the thresholds of tolerance on each vary widely between cultures, as does the cultural propensity of insiders to blow the whistle on particular infringements.

A question for the responsive firm is whether it should conform to local practice. Variations from the norm in local business practices can present a real challenge for international managers, whether locals or expatriates. They have to try to reconcile centrally generated ethical guidelines with local practices. Physical remoteness from the head office may make it particularly tempting to adapt to local practices in order to compete. Indeed, some measure of ethical flexibility is often touted as a condition of entry, "the price of doing business here." For example, a senior U.S. manager in Russia conceded the need to bend the commercial laws in order to survive in the local business context: "If the [Russian] central bank ever wanted to, I'm sure there's a basis for catching every person in this country—resident, nonresident, whatever."[115]

A particularly difficult issue for many multinationals is how far to go in buying business. The dilemma is where to draw the line. Which "fees" are acceptable? What payments are legitimate to win orders? Companies finding themselves obliged to make lavish gifts may justify these in a variety of ways: It may be seen as respecting local tradition, "a norm of reciprocity," or akin to "tipping" for a service. Bribery becomes a simple transaction cost, stripped of its moral overtones. Moreover, if it helps to win contracts, it helps to create jobs at home—so some argue that it can even be morally justified, ignoring the larger question of whether the end justifies the means.

Learning to Cope with Ambiguity

Ethical dilemmas create tension and ambiguity. One may find oneself faced with a paradox which only fine judgment can slice through. There are valid ethical arguments which, if taken to the extreme, become misguided. One common view is that good ethics pay off, and there is surely truth in this. Yet if this argument is taken to the extreme it leads to the "instrumentalization of ethics" (see box "Do Ethics Pay?").

Another guiding principle in responding to the diversity of practice is to adhere to local custom and common sense. For example, Motorola has developed specific

Do Ethics Pay?
Research Box

The line taken by many U.S. academics is that ethics do pay. The basic premise is that the market itself cultivates virtue. This notion can be traced back to the writings of Adam Smith, who observed that commerce invariably brings with it probity and punctuality. More recently, the economist Kenneth Arrow noted: "A great deal of economic life depends for its viability on a certain limited degree of ethical commitment."[A] Clandestine payoffs, for example, distort market mechanisms in terms of the rational allocation of resources, handicapping the process of economic development.

Today's scholars would reinforce those claims by adding that trustworthiness is needed to find reliable partners; that fairness and justice can influence the commitment of both employees and suppliers; that respect for others is important for customers and employees. In short, cultivating virtue enhances reputation, creates a good image, and ultimately attracts both customers and top-flight recruits.

It has been noted: "Integrity significantly increased the overall levels of trust throughout the organization. . . . When crossing cultural, national, functional, and business unit lines, trust is an essential, irreplaceable ingredient for effective execution."[B] As de Bettignies puts it: "If you are not trustworthy, the

sanction is not so much that you might go to court, but that you would just lose business. If people cannot trust you, the cost of writing a contract comprehensive enough, and the means to monitor compliance with the terms of the contract, would [create excessive] transaction costs."[C]

This argument taken to the extreme, however, leads to the "instrumentalization of ethics," as de Bettignies points out. That is, we behave ethically *because* it pays. Others argue that it is unethical to base the case for ethics on economic self-interest: "If corporate social responsibility amounts to nothing more than enlightened self-interest, why would anyone need to devote any special effort to understand it or to persuade others to pursue it?."[D] Decisions to behave in an ethical way are neither trivial nor devoid of virtue, and sometimes, indeed, there can be a monetary price to pay for doing what is right. In many ways, the ethics debate has been hijacked by the line that "ethics pay," shunting aside the moral discussion on self-respect, citizenship, community, and humanity.

[A]Arrow, 1973, p. 313.
[B]Gregersen, Morrison et al., 1998.
[C]de Bettignies, 1999.
[D]Vogel, 1991, p. 115.

guidelines for gift giving in Japan, where elaborate gift giving rituals traditionally governed intercompany relations. The local guidelines differ from the company's guidelines on gift giving in other countries.[116] Taken to an extreme, however, this approach becomes what is known as *cultural relativism.* The position of the relativist is that "it depends"—on the country, the culture, the players, the situation. Relativism asserts that "words such as right, wrong, justice, and injustice derive their meaning and value from the attributes of a given culture."[117] Thus to cultural relativists, ethical standards are culture-specific and not to be evaluated. Except in blatant cases, distinguishing between custom and corruption would amount to cultural imperialism, imposing the standards, values, and ethics of one cultural region upon another. While the cultural relativists may have a valid point, this argument is sometimes taken to the absolute extreme that everything is relative. It may justify petty bribery as "local practice," a contribution to the living standards of underpaid local officials. Yet in the end such bribery, the sum total of many such small actions, nourishes capricious officialdom, undermines market efficiency and predictability, denying people stability and their right to a reasonable standard of living. A sense that everyone will play by the same transparent rules is necessary for the development of a sound economy.

Another sort of ethical dilemma faced Levi-Strauss in Bangladesh. Its suppliers were employing children under the age of fourteen, a practice not prohibited locally. Forcing the suppliers to remove the children would not have ensured that they received an education, and it would have caused hardship for the families depending on the children's wages. The company resolved the dilemma by arranging with the contractors to stop further hiring of underage workers. The children already employed would continue to work but they would also attend school on the factory site. They were promised full-time jobs in the plant on reaching working age. Levi-Strauss in turn agreed to pay the children's tuition and to provide books and uniforms.[118] Instances of this sort, not always resolved so thoughtfully, have appeared frequently in the media in recent years.

The tension of such ethical dilemmas comes when ethics diverge from the law. Business opportunities that are neither legal nor ethical are easily shunned. Ones that are both legal and ethical can be judged on their business merits. The real dilemmas faced by managers often concern policies or actions that are either ethical or legal, but not both. For example, when apartheid law governed South Africa there was a legal requirement for segregated wash rooms for employees—an unethical law contravened by many foreign subsidiaries. Other such gray areas include the arms trade, child labor, birth control, abortion, euthanasia, genetic engineering. Many of these fall outside the law because of wide splits in public sentiment, or because legal codes cannot keep up with advances, particularly in medicine and technology. Compliance with the law, therefore, serves only as a baseline for making ethical judgments. The fact that the law authorizes certain practices or at least does not ban them should not preclude individuals from exercising their own judgment. Indeed, it is only one's own judgment in such cases that one can fall back on.

Sometimes ethics and the law seem to diverge in another way, and there is widespread flouting of the law so much, so that a practice, though not perceived as right, is not really considered quite unethical. To return to our earlier dilemma, petty bribery, the fact that "everyone does it," "it's the local custom" does not render the behavior legitimate in the eyes of the law.

Indeed, the steady migration of responsibility for codes of conduct from boards to legal departments is regarded by some as regrettable: "As soon as you get into compliance, you get into compulsion. Ethics is not that and it sends the wrong signals."[119] Explicit codes of conduct are important (90 percent of the Fortune 500 have such a code), but again they are not a panacea. They may preclude the necessary work in helping managers to develop their capacity to perceive, debate, judge, and respond effectively to ethical issues.

The cultural relativists have a valid point to the extent that it is important to learn to distinguish between practices that are merely different and those that are wrong. For example, in India it is common to promise employees a job for one of their children. This practice reflects a deep moral concern for employees' families, yet it may contravene a Western company's policy against nepotism. Both policies are based on moral values—one based on kinship and community, the other linked to values of minimizing conflict of interest. Here, there is a tension between two valid perspectives. In order to find an appropriate solution, the local managers must grasp the religious, economic, social, political, and historical forces that influence business practices in different locations, while not relinquishing their own roots and any deeper values that are at play.

This leads to a nuanced view of local responsiveness where ethics are concerned. In the context of ethics, responsiveness means sensitivity to the local values, rather than adherence to the local practices. The local manager has to probe below the surface, consider the ethical values that underpin particular practices. Ultimately, then, this is a problem for the judgment of the individual manager. The litmus test remains, "How would it look on the front page of the newspaper?" and "Could I look myself in the mirror?"

In the end, striking the appropriate balance between providing clear direction and leaving room for individual judgment calls is a fine balance. Donaldson puts it well: "Managers living and working abroad who are not prepared to grapple with moral ambiguity and tension should pack their bags and come home."[120]

TAKEAWAYS

1. What local responsiveness means is changing. Traditionally, multidomestic strategies were driven by market access arguments. Increasingly local responsiveness is driven by notions of learning and by access to dispersed know-how or resources. Furthermore, local responsiveness, though once synonymous with country boundaries, now applies to any market with distinctive needs.
2. HRM practices are more sensitive to local context than finance, marketing, or manufacturing practices, because HRM deals with people, and people differ across the world. But within HRM, some practices are more sensitive to context than others.
3. National values and national business systems shape both the culture of the mother company and the need for adjustment in the host environment.
4. Adjusting to local conditions is not just a trade-off between mother company practices and host country practices; it is also driven by the practices of international peers. Be aware of how your networks also help to shape your reality.
5. When expanding internationally, firms can use the concept of cultural distance as a guide to incremental learning in terms of where to head next, how to enter, and what practices to import.
6. Differences in culture can be leveraged to generate more strategic insights and alternatives, while differences in national business systems can be used to locate particular business activities in more stimulating environments. Local responsiveness does not just mean adjusting people to jobs, it also implies moving jobs to people.
7. Localization involves carefully developing a long-term strategy with commitment at all levels to developing locals and retaining them. As much

attention needs to be paid to the expatriates responsible for this task as to the locals themselves. Shortcuts lead to protracted difficulties.

8. Localization does not necessarily imply "playing by the local rules." Ultimately localization means local authority over local decision-making, tapping into the experience of headquarters, expatriates, and other subsidiaries. It is a question of who makes the decision and on what experience base, rather than where the decision is made. Localization is typically only one step toward transnational development, which means knowing which local rules one can break.

9. Excessive local responsiveness tends to inhibit collaboration across boundaries, and this may be just as detrimental to learning as excessive centralization.

10. Adhering to local norms may contravene acceptable ethical standards back home, while imposing centralized standards may remove personal responsibility for distinguishing between practices that are merely different and those that are wrong. The area of ethics is the ultimate test of the ability to cope with the ambiguity of international business.

NOTES

1. F. Studemann, "Publisher with His Eye on Cyberspace," *Financial Times,* December 7, 1998, p. 15.
2. See Barsoux and Galunic (2000) for further details on the Bertelsmann story.
3. D. Daft, "Back to Classic Coke," *Financial Times,* March 27, 2000, p. 16.
4. M. Reilly and G. Steinmetz, "Bertelsmann to Buy Random House," *Wall Street Journal,* March 24, 1998.
5. Prahalad and Lieberthal, 1998.
6. The relationship between these two types of responsiveness, business and people, remains unclear. One might believe that companies with meganational business strategies, exercising a high degree of parent control, would be less locally responsive in their people strategies than firms with multidomestic strategies. However, a lone study on this, focusing on 249 U.S. affiliates of foreign MNCs, found no clear evidence to support this belief (Rosenzweig and Nohria, 1994). Many firms have a view that while strategy may be centralized, strategy implementation through people is a strictly local matter. Other firms take a different stance, as did IBM in the 1980s—tightly controlling HR policy so as to facilitate future integration of separate business units.
7. Hofstede, 1999, p. 38.
8. Trompenaars, 1993, p. 2.
9. O'Hara-Devereaux and Johansen, 1994; Rosenzweig and Nohria, 1994; Gooderham, Nordhaug et al., 1999.
10. Rosenzweig and Nohria, 1994; Goodall and Warner, 1997.
11. Lu and Bjorkman, 1997.
12. Hall and Hall, 1990.
13. Schneider and Barsoux, 1997.
14. Schein, 1985.
15. Laurent, 1983.

16. See Trompenaars (1993), Hampden-Turner and Trompenaars (2000). The work of Trompenaars was strongly influenced by the dilemma (duality) concept of Hampden-Turner.
17. See for example the research of Segalla, Fischer et al. (2000), a European study based on the responses of 900 managers in different countries to HRM scenarios.
18. Hofstede, 1980a,b.
19. Schneider, 1988.
20. Guest, 1990.
21. Hall and Hall, 1990.
22. *Guanxi* refers to a Chinese system of doing business on the basis of personal relationships—see Yang (1994); Lovett, Simmons et al. (1999). Fukuyama's arguments are found in Fukuyama (1995). The source for the observation on taking things to extremes is a personal communication with André Laurent; see also Laurent (1983); A. Laurent, "L'art du management: Réinventer le management au carrefour des cultures," *Les Echos,* April 5, 1997.
23. Hofstede, 1999.
24. Hampden-Turner and Trompenaars, 1993; Trompenaars, 1993.
25. See Katzenbach and Smith (1993) and myriad books in the United States on teamwork.
26. Hampden-Turner and Trompenaars, 1993, p. 10.
27. By way of example, see Moriguchi's structural explanation for the difference between Japanese implicit contracts and American explicit contracts in employment relations, originating in the bifurcation during the Great Depression years (Moriguchi, 2000)(see our Chapter 1, p. 13).
28. Au, 1999.
29. Hofstede, 1999, pp. 39, 43.
30. See Chapter 2 for the story of Lincoln's international expansion.
31. Porter, Takeuchi, and Sakakibara, 2000.
32. See Maurice (1979), and Maurice, Sorge, and Warner (1980) for the formulation of the "societal effect" concept. Findings from this stream of research are summarized in Sorge (1991).
33. Whitley, 1992.
34. Lane, 1989.
35. Orrù, 1997.
36. Child, 2000, p. 20.
37. Redding, 2001, Whitley, 1999. See also Hampden-Turner and Trompenaars (1993).
38. The Price Waterhouse/Cranfield project on international human resource management, led by Brewster, involved successive surveys undertaken in 14 European countries (Brewster and Hegewisch, 1994). For summaries of other European comparative research on HRM, see also Pieper (1990); the encyclopedic work of Sparrow and Hiltrop (1994); and Clark (1996).
39. Brewster and Larsen, 1992.
40. See the following for such critiques of American HRM and reviews of the European literature: Sparrow and Hiltrop (1994); Legge (1995); Clark (1996).
41. Pieper, 1990; see also Brewster (1995).
42. Clark and Mallory, 1996.
43. Pauly and Reich, 1997.
44. Many German firms have a distinctive structure where the foreign subsidiary is run by a collegial team consisting of a German commercial director and a local general manager. Another study of Euro-elites finds such distinctive differences in orientation to be enduring—the signs of convergence are there, but this is slow (Mayer and Whittington, 1999).
45. Lazonick and O'Sullivan, 1996.
46. Organizational learning and continuous improvement have long been a dominant preoccupation in Japan (as evidenced by the influence of Japanese thinking on Western concepts

of learning—see Sullivan and Nonaka (1985); Takeuchi and Nonaka (1986); Nonaka (1988).

47. Ferner and Quintanilla, 1998.

48. Yergin and Stanislaw, 1998. The business press, notably *The Economist, The Wall Street Journal,* and *Fortune* magazine, tend to take this position, though the majority of economists and political scientists on both sides of the Atlantic are far more cautious.

49. However many question the United States as a model. *The Economist* argues that growth in GDP per capita and productivity for the years 1989–1998 was higher in Japan and Germany than in the United States, though the United States outperformed Germany on job creation and employment (*The Economist,* April 10, 1999, p. 89). The Netherlands is often upheld as a better model, where some argue that economic growth, social regulation, and job creation have been effectively combined.

50. See Wilkinson and Leggett, 1985; Schein, 1996.

51. Zucker, 1988; Powell and DiMaggio, 1991.

52. Kraatz, 1998.

53. The network may often be a more interesting unit of analysis than the nation. If France has the networks of establishment and extra-establishment firms, so do other countries. In Germany there is the network of big industrial groups such as Bayer and Daimler, and then there is the very different *Mittelstand* of smaller and often family firms (Simon, 1996). In Japan, the "three pillars" of life-time employment, seniority-based pay and enterprise unions applied to the big corporations who recruited cohorts from the elite universities, but not to the vast majority of the Japanese working in small and medium-sized enterprises (Pucik, 1984). The same is true for Italy, with subcultural networks such as the family enterprises in Bologna and Verona, and for many other countries.

54. Working closely with Danish firms, one of the authors noted that many companies there continued to make the same mistakes concerning expatriate reentry. Line managers in Denmark tend to take the responsibility for persuading people to move abroad. Danes do not believe in HR systems or formalized succession planning, and there were no mechanisms to manage smooth reentry—leading other managers to be increasingly reluctant to go abroad for fear of being lost. Why did they all tend to fall into a similar trap? Because they compared themselves only to other Danish companies who were all adopting the same approach—and using the same benchmarks for acceptable retention/failure rates.

55. Granovetter, 1976.

56. Kraatz, 1998.

57. Burt, 1987.

58. Hauschild, 1993; Westphal, Gulati et al., 1997.

59. Fey, Engstrom et al., 1999. See also Child and Yan (1998), who observed the same in JVs in China.

60. Some companies such as Unilever organize themselves on regional lines in emerging markets, though they may have a product line structure in established and sophisticated markets. Others have a strong regional overlay on their business line organization in developing areas such as Asia (Schütte, 1998). The regional structure facilitates networking across product divisions, as well as the mobility of those scarce people who have expertise in local adaptation.

61. Micklethwait and Woolridge, 1996; Abrahamson and Fairchild, 1999.

62. Abrahamson and Fairchild, 1999.

63. Calori and De Woot, 1994.

64. Ferner and Quintanilla, 1998.

65. Ibid.

66. Zbaracki, 1998.

67. Bartlett and Ghoshal, 2000.
68. Kraatz, 1998.
69. There are ways of empirically mapping cultural distance. In research, the most commonly used map was developed by Kogut and Singh (1988), largely based on Hofstede's data.
70. The importance of sequencing and method of entry were identified in the so-called Uppsala process model of internationalization, see Johanson and Vahlne (1977).
71. Barkema, Bell et al., 1996.
72. O'Grady and Lane, 1996.
73. Kogut and Singh, 1988.
74. Consequently strategic leadership and talent development is the focus in Chapter 8.
75. Von Keller and von Courière, 1996.
76. Ghoshal and Bartlett, 1998, ch. 6.
77. IBM, until its crisis in 1991, embodied this personnel logic, as did Marks & Spencer (Evans and Farquhar, 1986). At IBM personnel/HR policy was tightly regulated around the world, partly to combat unionism but also to facilitate linkages between different units and subsidiaries. When its PC business was spun off to Florida in the early 80s, the one area where this unit was not allowed autonomy was over personnel policy. If it were to grow its own culture, it would be impossible to reintegrate the PC unit into the mainstream of the business. The important underlying issue of cohesion or glue management is explored in Chapters 7 and 8.
78. V. Houlder, "A Language to Unite Our Multicultural Team: My Secret Weapon," *Financial Times,* April 4, 1998, p. 24.
79. Adler, 1997, p. 106.
80. Rosenzweig, 1997.
81. Watson, Kumar et al., 1993.
82. Amason, Thompson et al., 1995.
83. Kogut and Zander, 1993.
84. Ferner and Quintanilla, 1998.
85. Porter, 1990.
86. Sigiura, 1990.
87. Kuin, 1972.
88. As discussed in Chapter 3, p. 112.
89. This survey was undertaken by the U.S.-based National Foreign Trade Council; see K. Heim, *The Wall Street Journal,* "Using Local Staff Is Key to Profitability for Firms in China," December 12, 1997. However, such statistics do not conclusively prove the point since one can argue that reverse causality plays a role—profitable subsidiaries are better able to invest in development and retention of local staff.
90. Lasserre and Ching, 1997.
91. Some firms in Asia, such as San Miguel from the Philippines and the French luxury goods corporation LVMH, look closely for third country nationals (TCNs from Australia, New Zealand, and the localized British or Americans), finding them to be more loyal than Chinese.
92. Wong and Law, 1999.
93. Cohen, 1992.
94. Fey, Engstrom et al., 1999.
95. E. Terzono, "Japanese Banks' Local Feel: Expensive Expatriates Are Being Replaced," *Financial Times,* January 29, 1997.
96. Melvin and Sylvester, 1997.
97. Hailey, 1996.
98. Lasserre and Ching, 1997.

99. Even here, one runs into perversions. Asian staff with one Western multinational company discovered that if they said anything negative about a poorly performing expatriate, the odds were that they would be saddled with the individual for a long time! The norms became ones of being polite and evasive, under the guise of Asian discretion, whenever one was asked to provide feedback on Western expatriates.

100. This study was sponsored by the U.S.-based National Foreign Trade Council of multinational companies operating in China, reported in *The Wall Street Journal,* December 12, 1999.

101. Fey, Engstrom et al., 1999.

102. Harel and Tzagrir, 1999.

103. Fey, Engstrom et al., 1999.

104. Lasserre and Schütte, 1995.

105. Wong and Law, 1999.

106. Fey, Engstrom et al., 1999.

107. Hailey, 1993.

108. Kobrin, 1988.

109. Middelhof, 1998.

110. Bartlett and Ghoshal, 1989. The point was also made when discussing the global-local duality in Chapter 2.

111. M. Gunter, "Alas, Poor Sony," *Fortune,* September 30, 1996, pp. 76–79.

112. See Schütte (1998). This study found that regional HQs (RHQs) were instrumental in integrating the region by supporting and guiding functional activities such as HR, though they rarely were able to create synergies between businesses or divisions. The thirty MNCs operating in Asia and Europe were by and large successful in the region concerned, attributing that success in part to their RHQs. Indeed, the regional dimension of coordination, particularly concerning HR and talent development, merits further attention by researchers.

113. de Bettignies, 1999.

114. J. Useem, "New Ethics or No Ethics? Questionable Behavior Is Silicon Valley's Next Big Thing," *Fortune* March 20, 2000, pp. 82–86.

115. M. Whitehouse, "For Businesses in Today's Dysfunctional Russia, Solutions Are Creative but Not Necessarily Legal," *The Wall Street Journal* June 3, 1999, p. 19.

116. Buller and McEvoy, 1999.

117. Donaldson, 1989, p. 14.

118. Donaldson and Dunfee, 1999.

119. A. Maitland, "The Value of Virtue in a Transparent World," *Financial Times,* August 5, 1999, p. 23.

120. Donaldson, 1996.

CHAPTER 5

Managing Alliances and Joint Ventures

In the late 1960s, the U.S.-based chemical company Chemco (name disguised) decided to enter the booming Japanese market. However, the country's investment policies at that time precluded direct entry. Facing the choice between licensing and a minority joint venture (JV), the company decided to establish a 49/51 percent partnership with a well-known Japanese firm to build a local plant and set up distribution. Chemco would contribute technology in exchange for help in market access. Soon after its launch, the joint venture, led entirely by local managers, became the leader in its industry segment.

After the liberalization of the Japanese economy in the mid-1970s, the U.S. parent decided that obtaining a majority position in the JV would give them more influence on its future direction. In their opinion, the JV was becoming "too independent." Besides, drawing upon the support functions of the head office could lower costs. After protracted negotiations, the Japanese partner agreed to sell 2 percent of equity to the Americans to give them control, and the board composition was changed accordingly. The JV management was instructed to streamline the product portfolio and to cut costs by integrating several support functions into the global organization. While the local managers did not question the need for more efficiency, most of the integration projects never really got off the ground. This was officially justified by the pressing local customer needs that called upon already available resources.

Frustrated by the difficulties in "integrating Japan," the U.S. management determined that additional equity could give it the necessary influence. After another round of long negotiations, the U.S. parent gained control of 65 percent of the shares. The company was renamed in order to put its U.S. partner's name first. A senior vice president of finance (who did not speak Japanese) was dispatched to join the local management team. In spite of these changes, the venture continued to be run pretty much as before, profitably with nearly $1 billion of sales, but with margins well below corporate expectations. As Japanese customers began to migrate to lower cost sites in other areas of Asia, poor coordination with other affiliates was now a serious business problem.

A third generation of U.S. top management decided to address the problem head-on. They retained a consultant to advise them what to do next. Buy even more equity? Send in more expatriates? Or even sell the existing business and start again?

It turned out that the company could not sell the plant in the open market because the surrounding infrastructure belonged to the Japanese parent. In addition, the Japanese partner (located right next door) was the legal employer of the vast majority of employees, including virtually all top managers. Even those recruited well after the JV was established were not employees of the joint venture. Their salaries were determined by their position in the Japanese parent career hierarchy and they were simply dispatched to the JV at the discretion of the Japanese partner. All the training, starting with new employee induction, was conducted jointly with employees of the Japanese parent—and they all belonged to the same company union.

All of this was a "good deal" when the JV had been set up years ago—it had meant that there was no need to invest heavily in staff or to worry about HRM issues in an unknown market. Since the original agreement, each step in the evolution of the relationship had focused on only the financial aspects of control. It was only when the consultant was brought in that a first thorough analysis of HRM and organization was undertaken. Today, will more equity buy more "respect"? Will more expatriates help the integration? What can be done to change the direction of the joint venture?

CHAPTER OVERVIEW

Alliances are a useful tool for internationalization, but they are also difficult to implement. The introductory case illustrates the complexity of alliances and the importance of attending to the management dimensions of such a strategy and especially to the human resource factors. We review the many motives for entering an international alliance and the different organizational forms alliances can take, and we present several perspectives on what constitutes alliance success.

An important dimension of alliances is that they are inherently unstable. We introduce a framework that helps us think strategically about alliances and how they may evolve over time. We identify four types of alliances on the basis of their competitive context and knowledge-creation requirements, each with a different set of management and HRM challenges. We illustrate how HR practices and tools can contribute to the company's competitive advantage.

The middle part of the chapter focuses on the planning and negotiation of alliances, paying particular attention to the human resource factors that must be taken into account and presenting key management roles in the alliance building process, with a focus on the implications for the selection and development of managers for these positions. Once the agreement has been negotiated, we consider its implementation through people and organization, highlighting the HRM agenda in international joint venture management.

The final part of the chapter explores the concept of alliance learning. After introducing theories of interorganizational learning, we analyze the key obstacles to alliance learning to show the importance of linking HRM to alliance learning objectives. Then we describe the human resource processes that can contribute to successful alliance learning and contrast examples of successful and unsuccessful learning. To conclude, the chapter reviews the evolutionary perspective on alliances and raises next-generation challenges facing HRM as alliances become an organic part of the globalization process.

THE WHYS AND WHATS OF ALLIANCES

Why Are Alliances Formed?

Joint ventures and other forms of cross-border alliance are today important and commonly used tools of international growth. Companies engage in alliances for many reasons.[1] Some are created to cut the cost of entry, others to cut the cost of exit. Some are set up with an objective of leveraging opportunities, others with the aim of acquiring knowledge. Some alliances are focused on economies of scale, others on economies of scope. Understanding *why* a company participates in an international alliance is the first step in defining the human resource role.

International alliances, usually in the form of joint ventures, began to multiply during the 1960s and 1970s.[2] Their primary objective was to enable firms expanding internationally to secure access to markets where direct presence was not permitted or where market entry was deemed too costly, too risky, or both. For example, foreign companies targeting the Japanese market, such as the above-mentioned Chemco, were not allowed to invest independently in Japan until its foreign investment regime was deregulated in the mid-1970s. The only way to enter the booming market early was either to license technology to a local partner or to establish a joint venture. The flow of foreign direct investment into China in the 1980s and 1990s followed a similar pattern.

Entering a protected market is only one reason why alliances are formed. Even when direct investment is feasible, there are many arguments in favor of market entry through a partnership with a local firm. This can provide knowledge of the local business conditions, desirable location and infrastructure, access to the distribution system, contacts with government, and a supply of experienced labor and management. The need for rapid entry into emerging markets is another reason. After the collapse of the Berlin Wall, alliances minimized the risk of entry into uncharted territories in eastern and central Europe.[3] As anticipated in the initial agreements, many local partners have since been bought out.

Alliances may support internationalization strategies. For example, while global competition often requires "insider" presence in a number of countries, it is difficult for all but the largest firms to achieve such universal market coverage. In car manufacturing, parts suppliers are expected to follow major car companies as they expand around the world, though it may not be viable to set up independent operations everywhere. "Sharing" the customer with a local partner may be a better idea. Within the European Union, the reduction of market barriers meant that the pattern of competition shifted from within each country to the whole continent. Many firms were left with only two choices: either to be acquired or to negotiate alliances with others in a similar position.

Alliances are not always transitory joint ventures. The Airbus consortium was established more than 20 years ago by leading European aerospace firms to compete against the then dominant U.S. commercial aircraft manufacturers. Risk reduction and economies of scale and scope in R&D and production were and remain the primary drivers behind the push for collaboration.[4] Because the vast majority of Airbus employees are on the payroll of the partner firms (although Airbus is scheduled to become a single firm owned by the consortium partners), the consortium organization creates major challenges with respect to managing mobility and coordinating cross-border projects.

In high technology industries today, international alliances are the norm, not the exception. Most high tech firms throughout the world are engaged in scores of technological, manufacturing, and marketing alliances. Their objective is to leverage their current know-how quickly over the broadest possible market and to foster the creation of tomorrow's know-how. The success of IBM and Toshiba in the laptop computer market is partly a result of their long-term collaboration in designing and manufacturing state-of the-art flat screens. While the two companies never ceased to compete for the final customer, the upstream collaborative efforts allowed them to maximize return on R&D investment and to gain valuable economies of scale in manufacturing. The challenge for both firms was to assure that competencies created inside the alliance could be quickly transferred to the parents while maintaining learning parity. This was accomplished by a carefully balanced flow of personnel between the alliance and the two partners.

In short, there are many good reasons for companies to engage in international alliances. Some firms are heavily involved with alliances; others find them tangential to their global strategy. However, most companies will engage in some form of international alliance as they expand abroad. Consequently it is important to understand the strategic and management issues relating to international alliances and the role of human resources management in alliance success. Indeed the question of what is a successful alliance is often not easy to answer (see box "Defining Alliance Success").

What Kind of Alliance?

Alliances come in multiple configurations, each with specific HRM implications. So choosing the right type of alliance for a given strategy is difficult if the strategy is not clear. What is the business objective of the proposed alliance? What is the value added of engaging in a business relationship that will inevitably consume significant resources before yielding results? What form of alliance should a company choose given its objectives, and what are the HR implications of such a choice?

There are a number of different ways to classify alliances. It is possible to take a functional orientation and identify R&D alliances, manufacturing alliances, marketing and distribution alliances, and so forth. Another way to classify alliances is to look at the number of partners involved, from a two-partner agreement to multiple partner consortia. However, the most common distinction is whether the contractual agreement covering the alliance creates a new jointly owned business unit—

Defining Alliance Success
Practice Box

The Chemco case raises the question, What is a successful alliance? This may seem an obvious question, but it does not have an obvious answer. Does the mere survival of an international alliance indicate success? Is success measured by the return on the funds originally invested? By current profitability and cash/dividend flow? By market share? By transfer of knowledge or creation of new knowledge? The appropriate measure depends on the objective of the alliance, remembering that objectives typically change as the alliance evolves.

Contrary to a popular metaphor, an alliance is *not* like a marriage—longer alliances are not necessarily better. Problematic alliances drain away management energy and resources, but they often limp on since shutting them down would imply "failure." The only viable measure of alliance success is the degree to which an international alliance helps the firm to improve its ability to compete.

For an alliance to be sustainable, it must benefit all partners: respect for the partner's needs and mutual value creation is a prerequisite for a successful relationship. But this does not imply that value creation must be equal or that all alliances should be sustainable for an indefinite period. Most are transitory in nature, reflecting a particular competitive situation at a particular point in time. When the situation changes, so does the need for the alliance. A "win-win" strategy is only a tool to create a healthy alliance; it should not be seen as the goal in itself. The definition of a "win"

may change as the company strategy evolves, as will the role that the alliance is expected to perform.

From this perspective, Chemco's alliance in Japan, although growing and profitable, was not as successful as it could have been. This does not mean that the original entry decision was wrong. In fact, in terms of ROI, the deal was the best the company had ever made. But as the company's internationalization strategy evolved, the alliance in Japan did not follow, largely through inattention to the management and human resource issues involved.

There is considerable evidence that alliances improve corporate performance.[A] But there is also ample data showing that many alliances fail to meet expectations and that the cause of the failure is in many cases poor implementation.[B] It has been estimated that less than 50 percent of joint ventures in Japan met the foreign partner's business objectives,[C] and recent observations from China suggest a similar pattern.[D] The complexity of managing a business with international partners is a challenge that few firms seem equipped to handle. When alliances break up, HRM issues are often cited as one of the key factors contributing to "irreconcilable differences."[E]

[A]Conference Board, 1997.
[B]Kanter, 1994; Morosini, 1998.
[C]Bleeke and Ernst, 1993.
[D]R. Tomlinson, "Why So Many Western Companies Are Coming Down with China Fatigue," *Fortune*, May 25, 1998, pp. 60–64.
[E]Pucik, 1988a; Cascio and Serapio, 1991.

usually described as a joint venture (JV)—or whether the collaboration is essentially non–equity based, such as a licensing agreement.

Yoshino and Rangan present a comprehensive classification of alliances (see Figure 5–1) based on the fundamental nature of the contractual relationships between the partners.[5] There are many other classifications, some focusing specifically on human resource issues.[6]

There is general agreement that as one moves through the spectrum of alliances from "simple" marketing agreements with a foreign distributor or OEM manufacturing agreements to stand-alone joint ventures, so the management challenges increase, as does the necessary attention to human resource management. Much of the discussion in this chapter will therefore focus on the role of HR factors in the most

FIGURE 5–1. Classification of Strategic Alliances

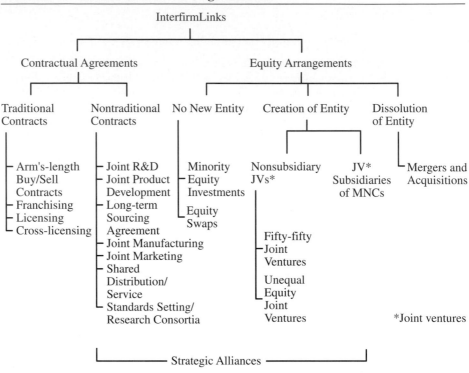

Source: M. Yoshino and U. S. Rangan, *Strategic Alliances: An Entrepreneurial Approach to Globalization* (Cambridge, Mass.: Harvard Business Press, 1995).

complex of international alliances—joint ventures between firms based in different countries. However, even among joint ventures, the differences in strategic logic behind their formation may require differentiation in HRM strategies and the HR tools applied.

Four Types of Strategic Alliances

As the Chemco case illustrates, an alliance is typically a dynamic phenomenon. The alliance nature may change over time with shifts in the relative bargaining power of the partners and in their expectations about the alliance objectives, with corresponding HRM implications.

There are two dimensions of alliances related to HRM that require careful consideration: first, the strategic intent of the partners; and second, the expected contribution of the venture to the creation of new knowledge. With respect to strategic intent, alliances among firms with competitive strategic interests may require different approaches to HRM from those whose interests are complementary. With respect to knowledge creation, while all alliances involve learning, some are actually formed with the main purpose of knowledge creation. This learning/knowledge-creation aspect of alliances has major implications for the organizational arrangements and thus for the HR challenges and roles. Both of these dimensions can change over time.

Figure 5–2 shows the four archetypes of alliance strategies based on their strategic and knowledge-creation contexts: complementary, learning, resource, and competitive alliances. A *complementary alliance* is formed when two (or more) partners with complementary strategic aims join forces to exploit their existing resources or competencies—say, by linking different elements of the value chain—and where knowledge creation is not a prime objective. A typical complementary alliance is the traditional joint venture in which one partner contributes technology and the other facilitates entry into a difficult market. Another example may be when two partners contribute complementary technologies that may lead

FIGURE 5–2. A Strategic Framework for Understanding International Alliances

	RESOURCE ALLIANCE	COMPETITIVE ALLIANCE
Competitive		
Long-term Strategic Context		
Complementary	**COMPLEMENTARY ALLIANCE**	**LEARNING ALLIANCE**
	Low	*High*

Opportunities for Knowledge Creation

Alliances can be evaluated on two dimensions. The first reflects the competitive context of the alliance. The second dimension reflects the need and opportunities for knowledge creation.

Strategic context: competition versus collaboration

The dimension of strategic context positions the alliance with respect to the complementarity of interests between the alliance partners. Is the alliance a link with a partner whose long-term strategic interests are in principle complementary (e.g., Airbus), or are they more likely fundamentally competitive?[A]

Knowledge-creation context: low versus high knowledge creation opportunities

Some alliances rely exclusively on exploitation of existing resources and competencies (partners contribute money, patents, production capacity, distribution networks); others are designed explicitly to generate new knowledge by combining the resources and competencies of the partners.[B]

[A]It is important to bear in mind that the strategic interests can change over time, and that what was once a collaborative relationship may turn into a fierce competition. A common experience of many Western firms with their joint ventures in Japan is an often-cited example in this regard (Reich and Mankin, 1986; Hamel, Doz et al., 1989).

[B]In principle, all alliances have the potential to generate new knowledge—at least partners can learn about each other and how to work together. The difference is in the intensity of the knowledge-creation process.

to a new product stream. In non-equity alliances, this may take the form of a long-term contract, such as between TI and Nokia in the mobile phone chip manufacturing process.

A *complementary alliance* may evolve into a *learning alliance* if both partners share an interest in enhancing their individual competencies. This can happen through the exchange of existing knowledge between the partners, or through the development of new knowledge where the partners jointly participate in the same value chain activities. An example of a learning alliance is the Fuji-Xerox joint venture in Japan. Originally set up to facilitate Xerox's penetration of the Japanese market, it now serves as a critical source of competency development for the Xerox Corporation worldwide.[7] Other alliances such as the Airbus consortium may be designed with learning in mind from the outset. Compared to complementary alliances, learning alliances require much more interaction, shared work, and interface management, creating demand for HR systems and processes that can facilitate effective knowledge creation.

Competitive pressures such as resource constraints, political and business risks, and economies of scale may lead competitors to join forces in a *resource alliance.* Exploration consortia to develop and operate oil and gas fields are increasingly common in the energy industry. One company takes the lead but the others share the risk by contributing resources and often staff. For example, BP explored oil deposits off the coast of Vietnam together with Statoil from Norway and the Vietnamese state-owned oil company. Another example would be the sharing of manufacturing facilities in Australia by Nissan and Ford when the government restricted the number of manufacturing sites in the country. Compared to complementary alliances, resource alliances require particular HR attention to reduce the frictions that might hamper collaboration.

Finally, there are also learning alliances between partners who are competitors in global markets. One of the best-known examples is NUMMI—a 50/50 joint venture between General Motors and Toyota.[8] This venture was nominally designed for the joint production of small cars for the North American market, but at the same time it was intended to serve as a "learning laboratory" for the two competitors. GM gained insights into Toyota's manufacturing system, and Toyota learned how to operate a U.S.-based manufacturing facility. Such partnerships can be described as a *competitive alliance.* Another example is Boeing's long-term collaboration with a consortium of Japanese firms that built segments of Boeing airplanes while at the same time pursuing a strategy of becoming aircraft designers themselves.[9] This type of alliance, with its emphasis on knowledge creation in a competitive context, is the most complex to manage and requires the highest level of attention to human resource management.

None of these types of alliance is "better" than the others. One cannot argue that one strategy should be pursued and another avoided. Alliances in all four quadrants can enhance a firm's competitive advantage. The management challenges associated with each alliance scenario are fundamentally different, however, and the HRM strategies, processes, and tools should reflect those differences. Problems occur when the company does not know what kind of alliance it has entered or, as in the case of Chemco, when it does not read and respond appropriately to early signals that the nature of the alliance is changing.

For example, in a complementary alliance it might be possible to rely on the local partner to recruit and train the alliance workforce since the loyalty factor may not be an issue—at least in the short run. However, in a competitive alliance such an approach could prove costly in the event of subsequent conflict between the partners. In a complementary alliance, it may make sense to set up the venture as a stand-alone entity to promote internal entrepreneurship. In a resource partnership, there are also benefits in creating an entity with clear boundaries so that the competitive strategic context does not inhibit the performance of the alliance.

In learning alliances the boundaries between the venture and the parent should be thin to maximize opportunities for knowledge sharing, and HR practices in a learning alliance will therefore focus on facilitating the interface between the parent and the venture to increase the speed and quality of learning. In contrast, it is not just fast learning that matters in a competitive alliance but also speed and effectiveness relative to the partner—maintaining learning parity is the key to sustaining such a relationship.[10] The HR approach has to reflect this—for example, by integrating measures of the learning outcomes into the performance management process.

In all cases, it is important to remember that alliances do not always fit neatly into conceptual boxes. Some partnerships are complementary in parts of the value chain and competitive in others, and a nuanced approach to HRM may be needed. The character of alliances also may change over time. Some alliances are born competitive, while others migrate into a competitive alliance zone over time, an indication that the original need to collaborate may have vanished, primarily because the partners have learned so much from each other that their respective knowledge gaps may have disappeared.[11]

Precisely when a complementary alliance becomes a learning or a competitive alliance is a matter of interpretation. Alliances are typically defined as complementary in the opening public relations statements, but a shift in partnership orientation has to be expected. The anticipation of such shifts needs to be taken into account in formulating the HR strategy so that the appropriate tools can be used proactively to facilitate such a change. In the Chemco case, the alliance started as complementary, combining the technology of the U.S. partner with the market access capability of the Japanese partner. However, the U.S. partner neglected at an early stage to commit the necessary resources to ensure the future integration of the JV into its global network (training, exchange of staff, and so forth). There were no incentives for the Japanese staff to pay attention to global strategy. They were rewarded solely on local results, and they saw no future for themselves in Chemco's global organization.

One of the few redeeming factors in the Chemco joint venture was that the alliance never migrated into the "competitive" domain, simply because the Japanese partner firm had no wish to enter this particular business segment. Had it chosen to do so, there was not much the U.S. partner could have done to protect its market position as it had little influence over the employees or management in Japan. Because the partner's position was essentially cooperative, however, Chemco's top executives and the human resource managers did get another opportunity to consider long-term actions to remedy the unsatisfactory situation. We will review later what they have done.

What Matters Is the Process, Not the Deal

An alliance is not just a deal between two or more partners; it is a complex process that is full of ambiguities and contradictions that reflect the paradoxes and dualities of international competition. Indeed, as we will see later, companies often learn to manage the contradictions of transnational organization through their alliance experiences. Most alliances either die early or evolve, just as any other business venture. Alliance stability is a contradiction in terms.

There is no best way to structure an alliance. Specific configurations of organizing patterns, equity ratios, and reporting relationships do not seem to differentiate between winning and losing alliances.[12] In the case of joint ventures, some argue that 50/50 arrangements work best since the partners are forced to anticipate each other's interest.[13] Others assert that such arrangements lead to paralysis, for example, with respect to staffing and compensation issues, and that it is better when one partner has the power to make a decision in case of a deadlock.[14] In fact, both types of ventures appear to generate significant but distinct HRM challenges.[15]

It is not the structure of the deal but the quality of the management process that makes a difference. Indeed this is the focus of the rest of this chapter, as we work through the steps in planning, negotiating, and implementing an international business partnership. Even here there are differences. At HP and Motorola—two high tech firms with extensive histories of successful alliances—the alliance management process is well defined, highly structured, and institutionalized. On the other hand, Corning—with most of its income derived from alliances—favors a more intuitive and informal approach that reflects the company's culture and mode of decision-making. Others use a mix of the two. Whether the approach is formalized or embedded in the company culture, successful alliance players have in common a *rigorous and disciplined* approach to alliances that includes an appreciation of the HRM contribution.

PLANNING AND NEGOTIATING ALLIANCES

From the perspective of negotiating the partnership agreement, a number of key issues relating to control and influence are closely tied to expertise, policies, and practices in human resource management. The HR function must therefore be involved early in exploring, planning, and negotiating alliances. This is fundamental, although, alas, it often does not happen.

Another factor driving HR involvement is the fact that ability to create value through superior human resource management can be a source of competitive advantage for the partnership. For example, a partner with proven competence in implementing high performing work systems, in staffing and recruitment, or in managing innovation through people has additional negotiating leverage. This competence should contribute to the success of the venture—provided that it is backed up by know-how on adapting to different cultural circumstances and strategic aims.

Outstanding HR strengthens bargaining power in the negotiations. A reputation for good HR systems and practices is part of the corporate culture "brand equity."[16] Well-managed partners are more in demand than poorly managed ones. A company with poor foundations in its own approach to HRM and without proven know-how in aligning HRM with competitive strategy will find itself disadvantaged when it comes to negotiating and implementing alliances.

HR's Role in Developing the Initial Strategy

Successful alliances start with a strategy, not with a partner. This may seem obvious, but it is not always followed in practice. Companies, or more precisely their chief executives, sometimes "fall in love." Notwithstanding the importance of personal relationships at the top, there is a danger in selecting the partner before the strategic purpose is clarified.

As discussed in the previous section, it is difficult to identify what kind of relationship and what kind of a partner may be appropriate without fully understanding the long-term objectives. Japanese manufacturers of car components entered the United States in the late 1980s since their customers such as Toyota and Honda expected just-in-time support of their newly transplanted assembly plants. These OEMs knew that they did not have the competence to operate in an alien environment. Given the urgency, the alliance route seemed the most feasible entry strategy, although in the long run they intended to establish an independent presence.

Consequently, human resource considerations played a major role in partner selection.[17] The Japanese firms searched for local partners situated in rural environments perceived as having harmonious labor environments conducive to Japanese manufacturing methods. They also preferred partners who were family owned but with no clear succession. This would give them the opportunity to acquire full control with a friendly bid once the U.S. partner decided to retire.

The impact of HR issues in an alliance is always framed by the specific strategic and business context. These considerations are often contradictory, however, requiring careful analysis. For example, when a firm decides to enter an unfamiliar foreign market, the choice of an experienced local partner may seem to be a smart move that overcomes the existing "market competence" handicap. Yet, with a strong local partner, there may be less urgency to develop internal market know-how, and investments in knowledge creation may not be a priority. In a complementary alliance, this may not matter. But if the alliance ever becomes competitive, it may put the foreign partner at a serious disadvantage.

A well-defined alliance management process provides an arena for a full consideration of human resource issues.[18] Early involvement in strategy discussions allows the HR function to understand the business logic of the alliance and to contribute to its clarification, highlighting early the issues that may handicap implementation. In addition, important human resource decisions regarding the alliance may need to be taken early in the implementation process (such as decisions on negotiation training or selection of an alliance manager).

The HR Alliance Strategy Plan
Practice Box

HR issues that may impact partner selection:

- Desired competencies that a partner should possess.
- Need for venture HR support from the partner.
- Assessment of HR skills and reputation of potential partners.
- Assessment of the organizational culture of potential partners.

Venture HR issues that need to be resolved in negotiations:

- Management philosophy, notably concerning HRM.
- Staffing: sourcing and criteria.
- Compensation and performance management.
- Who will provide what HR service support.

Desired negotiation outcomes and possible bargaining trade-offs

Specific HR activities that must be implemented early and resources required:

- Negotiation stage:
  Negotiation team selection.
  Negotiation training.

- Start-up stage:
  Staffing decisions.
  Alliance management training.

Estimated timelines for HR actions, and allocation of responsibility

Measurements to evaluate the quality of HR support:

- Recruitment target.
- Training delivered.
- Skill/knowledge transferred.

HR's involvement in alliance strategy is often guided by a plan that will be fleshed out as implementation proceeds. A sketch of the issues to be considered is shown in the box "The HR Alliance Strategy Plan." Given the typical uncertainty surrounding alliance creation, such a plan is only a rough guide that will become more specific when a partner is selected, paving the way for rigorous implementation when the alliance is launched.

Partner Selection

There are two main HR issues to consider in the process of partner selection: the expected contribution of the partner; and how much the HR systems of the partners will interface within the alliance.

The first issue refers to the degree to which the partner's competencies in human resource management are expected to contribute to the alliance. Will the partner be responsible for staffing the alliance or some of its critical functions? Is the partner expected to provide HR services to the alliance? Does the partner's HR reputation matter? As we will discuss later in this chapter, getting the staffing right is the "make or break" issue for many alliances, and the probability of success can be enhanced by making these questions a part of the selection screen.

The second issue addresses the degree to which the organizational and people processes of the partners will be linked in the course of the alliance which is likely if one of the strategic aims is learning. Will the alliance be clearly separated from the parents, or will the boundaries be ambiguous? Will there be a lot of mobility between the venture units and the parent companies? Who will evaluate performance of venture management and on what criteria? To what extent will cultural differences impact the nature of the HR linkages?

When the expected contribution of the partner to HR management in the venture is high or when the venture is unlikely to be autonomous because of interfaces with the parents, it is vital to include the partner's HR philosophy, policies, practices, and culture as factors in partner selection (see box "Assessing the Culture and HR Practices of the Potential Partner"). The issue here is not to find a perfect match, that is, to find a partner who shares the same view on management selection criteria or the role of incentive compensation in the reward package. Rather, the purpose is to identify the potential differences, to what extent these differences can influence the execution of the alliance strategy, whether any differences can be reconciled, and what the business risks are if the gaps cannot be bridged.

Assessing the Culture and HR Practices of the Potential Partner
Practice Box

HR policies and practices have a major impact on the culture of the organization, and research has shown that differences in organizational culture may influence alliance success.[A] A cultural audit is therefore an essential part of "due diligence" in the audit of a potential partner. A number of factors may impact the cultural compatibility between partners and these should therefore be included in the audit:

- Communication style (degree of formality).
- Hierarchical boundaries (rigid vs. flexible).
- Control mechanism (tight vs. loose).
- Mode of conflict resolution (explicit vs. implicit).
- Compensation philosophy (market position, degree of salary compression).
- Performance management (open vs. hidden).
- Career stratification (gender, race, age, religion, qualifications).

Various maps exist to understand differences in culture. One simple but useful map has been developed by Goffee and Jones, using two dimensions that are well established in sociological and management theory: *sociability* (friendships, emphasis on relationship, networking) and *solidarity* (collective task and goal orientation).[B] They map out four types of cultures: networked (strong on sociability), mercenary (strong on solidarity), fragmented (low on both), and communal (high on both). Each is reflected in different ap-

proaches to management and HRM, and each exists in a positive and negative form (for example, the danger for communal cultures is that they become arrogant and inward looking, while mercenary cultures can become ruthless).

It is particularly important to clarify key operating policies and the actual practices:

- How do employees enter the company and what are the selection criteria?
- What are the promotion requirements and timetables?
- Which behaviors are encouraged and which are scorned?
- What are the performance criteria and how much do they matter?
- What are the determinants of salary and how large are the differentials?
- How open is the communication about individual performance?
- How open and transparent is the whole HR system?

This material may not be easily available, but it can be obtained through consultants, a thorough review of press literature, and local intelligence—and not just by leafing through annual reports. Doing the homework eliminates subsequent surprises.

[A]Parkhe, 1991.
[B]Goffee and Jones, 1998.

A U.K. company decided to set up a joint venture in Malaysia to assemble its product for the local market. Soon after the first year results were in, a row erupted at the JV board meeting when the U.K. managing director proposed a performance bonus plan payout that differed nearly 40 percent between managers at the same level of responsibility. The local partner objected, as this would violate the standards of internal equity among managers and hurt morale. The foreign managing director was puzzled. "You told us that bonuses in your company could be up to 40 percent of the total compensation. That is what I believe our best performers deserve." "Yes," came the answer, "but in our company the bonus percentage is the same for everyone."

Differences in management style and HR practices can actually be a powerful argument in favor of an alliance. In the GE Silicones joint venture in Japan, one of the factors that motivated Toshiba to join forces with General Electric and then transfer management control to GE was to get an "insider" view of GE's renowned management system. Toshiba's top management actually encouraged GE to introduce many of its systems and practices into the joint venture so as to see how such practices might be adapted in Japan and what learning the Japanese parent might gain from the experience.

Selecting Alliance Managers

One of the first HR issues in the alliance formation process is often the selection of an alliance manager. An alliance manager is typically appointed on a corporate level, responsible for planning, negotiating, and implementing alliances. This role should ideally be kept separate from the venture manager role,[19] responsible for managing a specific project, business unit, or joint venture within the alliance (see box "Roles and Responsibilities of Alliance and Venture Managers"), though obviously not all firms have the resources to do so.

The alliance manager may monitor several existing alliances, supporting business units in identifying opportunities where a partnership could create value. When such opportunities are identified, the manager will take the lead in developing the negotiating strategy and framing the partnership contract. After negotiations are completed and a new alliance is formed, the person will oversee the evolution of the alliance and the relationship with the partner. This is like managing a portfolio in which new ventures get negotiated, added, and monitored.

The alliance manager has a determining impact on the quality of the relationship between the partners and on the ability of a firm to execute its alliance strategy. When selecting alliance managers, it is important to recognize that their role will change from visioning/sponsoring to networking/mediating as the alliance evolves from the stage of initial planning through negotiations, start-up, maturity, and on to eventual decline and dissolution.[20]

Typically, the key requirement for the alliance manager's position is a high degree of personal and professional *credibility,* also reflecting business competence. Mutual trust is the glue that cements the alliance relationships, and without credibility it is difficult to establish trust. When Motorola established a strategically key

Roles and Responsibilities of Alliance and Venture Managers
Practice Box

Alliance Manager Roles and Responsibilities[A]

Building trust/setting the tone—unless there is trust and the right chemistry among managers involved in the alliance, it will not go anywhere.

Monitor partner contributions—how well a firm meets its obligation to an alliance is the most tangible evidence of its commitment.

Managing information flow—drawing the line between the flow of information that ensures the vitality of the alliance and unbridled exchange of information that can jeopardize competitiveness.

Assessing strategic viability/evaluating synergy—as strategic needs of the firm change over time, what are the implications for the alliance and the relationship with the partner?

Aligning internal relationships—as an alliance involves many people inside the firm, the alliance manager role is to mobilize the essential support across the organization.

Venture Manager Roles and Responsibilities

Managing the business—the primary task of the venture manager is operational responsibility for the success of the venture.

Representing venture interest—the venture manager has to represent without bias the interest of the venture as a business vis-à-vis its parents.

Aligning outside resources—many resources are located outside of the venture boundaries inside parents' organizations, and tapping effectively into those resources is a venture manager's responsibility.

Building collaborative culture—irrespective of the competitive context of the alliance, trust inside the venture is the essential ingredient of success.

Developing venture strategy—successful alliances evolve as any other ongoing business, and this evolution should be guided by solid strategy.

[A]Yoshino and Rangan, 1995.

---

alliance with Toshiba in the semiconductor business, it appointed as alliance manager a corporate vice president with a stellar business record, who played a central role in developing the overall corporate strategy in this sector.[21] The focus of the alliance was to share Motorola's microprocessor know-how with Toshiba in exchange for access to Toshiba's memory-related technology. The alliance manager's personal credibility and reputation were critical in aligning Motorola's internal resources behind the alliance, convincing Toshiba that Motorola's management was determined to make the alliance work.

The job of an alliance manager also requires a high degree of *flexibility* and *adaptability* to different national and organizational cultures, management styles, and individual behaviors. Alliances are by nature unstable and uncertain. The multiplicity of influential stakeholders in and around an alliance makes it difficult to operate under precise rules or to follow an intended strategy to the letter. Managers who are not comfortable working under conditions of ambiguity will find it difficult to cope. As one experienced alliance manager put it, "high tolerance for frustration is a must."

Much of what alliance managers are expected to do involves mobilizing resources across organizational boundaries, managing laterally in much the same way as an international project leader. The skills are similar to those of an effective general manager with the difference that the alliance manager does not have either large budgets and staff or direct authority over resource allocation.[22] Instead the manager has to rely on networks of people inside and outside the firm that they have to influence. As one senior executive in a Fortune 500 company put it:

> A leader is one who gets people to do what he wants, but who at the same time makes them think that it was all their idea in the first place. An alliance manager also has to work along the same lines. He has no battalions of his own, yet he has to get the job done. He has to get people to buy into his vision of the alliance, make it part of their own job assignment, and actively work to make the alliance a success.[23]

Preparing for Negotiations

The HR function can start contributing operationally to alliance negotiations long before the first encounter between the potential partners. The initial focus is primarily on two areas: selecting the negotiating team and facilitating training in handling negotiations.

Selecting the Negotiation Team

Once the long-term strategy of the alliance is in place, its objectives set, and the potential partners established, it helps if the negotiation team is selected quickly. The strategic context may influence the staffing decisions. Different types of ventures may require different mixes of entrepreneurial, analytical, and political competencies in the team.[24] The context might also influence the choice of the alliance manager, who in most circumstances should be the core member of the team.

There are differences of opinion regarding whether future venture managers should be involved in the negotiations. When venture managers are involved in negotiations they have a vested interest in "getting it right" rather than just "getting the deal" since they will be responsible for implementation. However, when negotiations are protracted (most last longer than anticipated), it is not easy to free up managers who have other responsibilities so as to participate in negotiations that may fail. An alternative is to assign the responsibility for the venture before the negotiation is completed, but to have another position available in case the negotiations fail.

Training for Negotiations

Alliance negotiations resemble other business negotiations, although they tend to be more complex because of the strategic and cross-cultural issues involved. Some team members may be experienced alliance negotiators, while for others this could be their first exposure to complex international negotiations. For the latter, properly structured negotiation training could be a worthwhile investment.

An essential part of such preparation is to help the negotiators become familiar with the business and cultural context of the partner's country. Given the stakes involved, a number of studies suggest that companies underestimate the need to prepare carefully.[25] Without preparation, it is all too easy to fall back on cultural stereotypes. It is also important to sort out the individual roles in a team and to review and practice different negotiation scenarios. HR professionals often have strong process facilitation skills, and they may serve as internal consultants to management teams. Such expertise is valuable in alliance negotiations. Especially in more complex negotiations, the presence of an experienced facilitator may be highly beneficial, observing the flow of interactions, interpreting behaviors, and coaching the key actors.

Addressing Key Negotiation Challenges

Control issues, senior appointments, and approaches to HRM inside the alliance are some of the areas in which HR can contribute most to the success of the negotiations.

Equity Control versus Operational Influence

A difficult issue in joint venture negotiations is often that of control. Generally, both parties seek to be in the position of majority owner, as this is considered the best way to protect one's long-term interests, particularly in the context of a competitive alliance. However, in the absence of other supporting mechanisms, equity control is no guarantee that the venture will evolve in line with the intended strategy.

There is nothing wrong with attempting to gain a majority position, which may provide a tax or financial reporting advantage. However, it is a fallacy to assume that equity control equals management control. A minority equity position, coupled with effective representation on the venture management team and an influence over the flow of know-how, may have more real impact on how the venture operates than a nominal majority exercised from a distance. From an accounting perspective, 51 percent of the shares may entitle the owner to 51 percent of the dividends, but these are often the last piece of the cash pie to be distributed. Internal transfer pricing, purchasing decisions, the cost of services provided by a local partner, payroll determined by compensation levels, all have an impact on cash flow long before any dividends are declared.

Not surprisingly, "the last two percent" (going from 49 percent to a 51 percent share) is the most expensive piece of equity. While intangible contributions may substitute for capital in a minority position (the infusion of technical or market know-how, transfer of depreciated assets, brand equity), a majority position usually requires cash. The important point is that a careful human resource strategy that secures influence can be less costly and more effective than a strategy that focuses on securing equity control.

Acquiring such influence typically starts with the key appointments—the composition of the board, senior management appointments, and the venture manager.

Board Composition

Companies often strive for a majority equity position simply to achieve a majority on the board of directors, thus protecting their voting interests in the event of a dispute between partners. In reality, joint venture boards seldom if ever vote. Pushing through a majority vote, in most circumstances, constitutes the first step in dissolving an alliance. If the partners have a common interest in maintaining the relationship, disputes are resolved in private, and boards act only to approve such agreements. In addition, the protection of strategic interest can be achieved by other means, such as specific clauses in the agreement or articles of incorporation that stipulate which actions require unanimous or qualified majority consent of the shareholders.

There are side advantages to using such a board primarily to oversee rather than to control. Positions on the board can be used for a variety of other purposes. An appointment to the board can be used to recognize the outstanding contribution of an alliance executive. In many countries, "company director" status is considered the pinnacle of a business career, and such opportunities may serve to increase the morale and retention of senior management. Board appointments can be used to expand linkages to outside business circles and the wider community in the local country, broadening learning and business opportunities. A position on the board can also be reserved for an individual who may mediate potential conflicts between the partners.

When setting up the board, there is a natural tendency to appoint alliance champions, people who favored the deal from the outset, who were involved in the negotiations and who know the partner best. It is also useful, however, to appoint at least one "bad cop," who will keep the champions from forgetting that the venture is a business rather than just a relationship—someone a little more skeptical, who sees the potential downfall of various alliance initiatives.[26]

Appointing Senior Management

In most joint ventures, senior managers wield far more strategic and operational influence than do members of the board. Tasks that determine the venture's success—setting business objectives, establishing performance expectations, interfacing with key customers, monitoring the transfer of knowledge, developing the organization's culture—are all operational responsibilities of the senior managers inside the venture, not the board. Moreover, it is always preferable to resolve the inevitable conflicts and differences of opinion at the operational level rather than referring disputes to higher levels of alliance governance. As for the board, it oversees what it can during the half-day meeting every six months that seems to be customary for most JVs.

There is a paradox here. The shortage of international managers who can implement a market-entry strategy in an unfamiliar environment is often a motive for choosing a joint venture over a wholly owned subsidiary; yet without a pool of suitable candidates, bargaining about positions is a meaningless exercise. Having such a pool ready requires attention to HR from the very early stage of alliance planning, since it takes time to select and groom potential candidates. It may be preferable to recruit them on the local market and then provide them with opportunities to learn the organizational ropes before dispatching them to the JV—again a time-consuming effort. If these HR issues are raised only after the agreement is signed, it may be difficult to find the right candidates in time for the launch. The cost of fixing the problems later grows exponentially with time since misaligned cultures, attitudes, and behaviors are difficult to uproot once embedded.

Note however that executive role expectations may vary from one culture to another. In a 50/50 French-Swedish joint venture located in France, the Swedish company agreed to the appointment of a senior French executive as chairman in exchange for de facto control of the operations. But in the French organization the chairman was not the honorary figure that the Swedes expected. He was seen in the venture as the ultimate decision-maker, while the opinions of the Swedish managers were ignored. Although the venture continued to make strategic sense, the operational frictions generated so much ill will on both sides that it had to be dissolved a few years later.

WHO SHOULD "OWN" THE JV MANAGER? The nomination of the venture manager can generate intense debate. One can argue that the venture manager must have the goodwill of both parents in order to operate effectively.[27] Installing somebody as venture managing director who represents only the interest of one partner may be counterproductive. And special care is needed when the joint entity is essentially independent of the parents' operations, as in the case of many complementary or resource alliances.

If the venture activities need to be integrated with those of the parent, however, then an arm's-length relationship may not be appropriate. There is a fine line between representing the best interests of the venture *and* those of the parent company, one of the many dualities that must be faced in alliance management. If an insider from one firm seems the logical choice as venture manager—because of his/her knowledge of the business or geographical area—it is important to minimize incentives that show favoritism. It should be clear that the manager's future career depends on the success of the venture rather than on building the ticket to come back home.

THE ROLE OF VENTURE CHAMPIONS. An alliance succeeds because managers and employees believe in the promise of the concept and are willing to invest personal effort to make it happen. Alliances without champions do not survive for long. The ambiguity and the uncertainty of the relationship impair the capacity to deal with the complex issues embedded in most partnerships. To prosper, alliances require champions, business leaders who believe in the purpose and who work hard to make it succeed.

Identification of venture champions and recognition of their contribution to the implementation of the alliance strategy is a critical driver of venture success. Venture champions, like venture skeptics, can be found on both sides of the partnership. Knowing who the champions are on the "other side" with internal credibility is of great value in the negotiations over managerial appointments.

When Whirlpool Corporation established a manufacturing joint venture with Tatramat, the Slovak washing machine maker, Tatramat's former top executive, Martin Ciran, became managing director of the joint venture.[28] The new company later ran into serious financial difficulties that enabled Whirlpool to gain majority control. Yet Ciran retained his position as he was recognized as the key champion of the alliance. His leadership was deemed essential to making the venture a success. Today, Whirlpool's Slovak factory—now fully owned—ranks among its top performing European subsidiaries, but it has the same management team as when Whirlpool was still the minority partner.

Human Resource Policies within the Alliance Venture

The need to influence the alliance strategy is only one of the arguments for addressing the HRM issues early in the alliance formation process. When the success of the alliance depends heavily on people issues such as competence transfer or reaching new standards in quality and productivity, leaving HR "until later" in order to simplify alliance negotiations may handicap the future odds.

It is particularly important to pay early attention to HR policies and practices when there are likely to be many complex interfaces between the venture and the alliance parents, as discussed earlier.[29] In contrast to licensing or supplier-buyer agreements, up-front agreement on HR philosophy and policies may be vital to success in manufacturing joint ventures or shared projects in new product development.

Some researchers advocate a detailed contract clarifying HR policies inside the alliance in order to reduce the uncertainty and conflict over matters of staffing, transfers, promotion, and compensation.[30] But detailed contracts do not guarantee compliance. Venture synergy comes from shared business interests, not from legal formulations. A clear statement regarding HR principles is in most cases sufficient, without limiting contractually what can or cannot be done.

Sometimes companies take the position "when in Rome, do as the Romans" and delegate all responsibility for human resource matters to the local partner. This makes sense provided the "Roman" organization is a paragon of effectiveness, quality, and customer service. If it does not have solid HR foundations in place, then this attempt to show cultural sensitivity or realize cost savings will only result in replicating the dysfunctional aspects of local practice. It is said of many foreign joint ventures in Japan that they represent "museums of Japanese management." They are repositories of obsolete practices that their Japanese parents ditched a long time ago but which are still presented to the foreign parent as the "Japanese" way of managing people.

IMPLEMENTING ALLIANCES

Once the contract is signed and the partnership becomes operational, a new set of people related issues appears. How to manage the evolution of the partnership? How to ensure that the knowledge developed inside the alliance is properly shared among the partners? How to keep the partnership objectives aligned with those of the parent?

These issues have two major HR implications. The first is managing the interface with the parent, which involves influencing the attitudes and behaviors of staff at home who are in contact with the alliance. The second relates to the management of people inside the venture itself.

Managing the Interfaces with the Parent

An important challenge is to manage the interface between the parent organization and the partnership. The objective is to align the internal processes back home so they support rather than hinder external collaboration. Often the organizational units that provide resources to the alliance are not those receiving its outputs. The asymmetry in the perceived costs and benefits of collaboration with the venture may cause internal tensions that undermine willingness to support the partnership. The value of collaboration is sometimes not visible in the hustle and bustle of daily operations, so explicit reinforcements of the message may be required. When Ford entered into broad cooperative agreements in Japan, the question "What have you done to support Ford's alliance strategy?" featured in the performance evaluations for a large part of the organization.

In the mid-1990s, a rapidly growing U.S. securities firm with global ambitions set up an alliance with a European brokerage to offer their European customers "preferential" access to U.S. financial markets. However, even after the alliance was launched to great fanfare, the operational practices at the New York trading desk did not change. The relatively small orders from Europe did not get the same attention as those from large U.S. institutional clients, reducing profit opportunities for the European partner. The new partner received a similar second-class treatment from other units of the U.S. firm.

Why was this happening? The rigid "meet-the-numbers" reward system in the United States was incompatible with a strategy that did not yield immediate earnings like the European partnership. No amount of presentations on the benefits of globalization could make much difference. In Europe, the initial irritation quickly turned to anger and then to suspicions about the true motives of the American partner. Less than two years later the alliance was dissolved. As noted by one of the American HR managers involved: "If this alliance was important for our future, then perhaps it should have been partly my job to create an environment where phone calls from our partners were returned without delay."

Top Management Role

The company's execution of its alliance strategy places particular demands on top management who must "walk their talk." The box "The Anniversary Speech" illustrates what happens when top management is not involved.

The Anniversary Speech
Practice Box

A 50/50 joint venture between a Japanese and a U.S. firm celebrated its twenty-fifth anniversary. Over time, the JV had evolved from a small marketing start-up to a fully integrated firm with an independent R&D and manufacturing capability that enjoyed a very profitable leadership position in the Japanese market. Given its commercial success, the friction between the two partners in the early days regarding the future direction of the business was replaced by a grudging willingness to continue working together. On the American side, however, executives often voiced concerns that the joint venture operated as if it were a wholly owned affiliate of the Japanese parent, while their influence was being eroded. The loyalty of the workforce was seen as tilted in favor of the local partner.

On the anniversary date, the employees assembled in one of Tokyo's exhibition halls for an afternoon of celebration. The company glee club warmed up with some speeches and songs. Then, the ninety-six-year-old former chairman of the Japanese parent, who signed the original deal, was helped onto the stage in his wheelchair to deliver a message of thanks to all employees for bringing his dream to life. His speech was short, owing to his failing health, but it was emotional and made a big impact on the audience. His speech was followed by a prerecorded video message from the current American CEO who, in three years of tenure, had visited the venture once. He said nothing wrong, but the impersonality of the presentation defeated its purpose. Another skirmish in the loyalty battle was lost.

Capturing the loyalty of the alliance workforce is only one of the human resource tasks that require the support of top management. Internal communication is another; top management plays an indispensable role in ensuring that the reasons for the partnership are well understood inside the firm, especially when it comes to balancing the competitive and collaborative aspects of the alliance. Top management must also work closely with the HR professionals on the selection of alliance managers, on resource allocation for learning activities, and on ensuring that reward systems are well aligned with the partnership strategy.

Human Resource Tasks in Managing the Venture

Just as there are no generic alliance strategies, so there are no blueprints for effective HR policies and practices. Attention to HRM in the alliance depends on the strategic objectives (as discussed earlier) and the position of the alliance in the value chain. The more critical the role of the partnership in creating value, the larger the need for commitment of HR resources and support.

Staffing Alliances

Staffing matters! See the box "A Block Apart, a World Apart." Inappropriate staffing is one of the major causes of alliance failures, and this is typically the most important aspect of HRM in the venture. As mentioned earlier, perhaps the foremost qualification for a potential alliance partner is having sound HR foundations at home. Without that credibility, it may be impossible to establish respect abroad.

A Block Apart, A World Apart
Practice Box

On a steamy Monday morning during a tour around JVs in China, one of the authors visited two ventures between Western firms and Chinese state-owned enterprises in the industrial zone north of Guangzhou.

In the first, two friendly Western executives on their first foreign assignment welcomed us with a litany of complaints: "Modern HRM in China? Impossible, nothing can be done. You have to understand. This is China—the iron rice bowl, where everyone expects to be taken care of. And remember, you must always protect face. Nobody can succeed,. . . We do all we can under the circumstances." The factory was visibly overstaffed and undermanaged. The venture was losing money, partly because of the extraordinary expenses associated with flying in SWOT-teams of experts to solve basic operational problems. We later learned that both executives had been given a choice of either taking an early retirement or accepting a well-rewarded two-year posting to China.

A block away, in another East-West joint venture that was structured just as the previous one, the walls of an older but spotless building were plastered with charts indicating the individual and team performance of all employees. The place was humming with activity. The Chinese general manager, recruited several years earlier from the local market and trained extensively in the Western firm's best-performing operation, seemed confident. He was genuinely puzzled by our questions: "HRM in China? Well, you hire the right people, train them well, evaluate their performance fairly, pay them accordingly, and make sure that they can see how they can grow. Is that different from what you do in America?"

Using partnerships as a dumping ground for unwanted executives may prove to be an expensive staffing strategy. Most staffing errors are not so gross, however; they arise unintentionally because the leadership and behavioral demands on managers in the venture are greater than those in fully owned affiliates. Managers simply do not have the experience to cope with the ambiguity and challenges.

Every strategic plan for an alliance should include a review of staffing requirements. Other HR matters such as training and compensation have an important impact, but problems in those areas can be addressed—with proper determination—in a relatively short time. Difficulties created by poor staffing, correcting the consequences of bad decisions made by people who are not qualified to meet the challenges of managing an alliance, may take years to fix. While the staffing issues will vary from one alliance to another, there are some generic matters to consider:

- What are the number and skill mix of employees required?
- Who is responsible for forecasting manpower demands?
- Who will do the recruiting? Each partner individually? Jointly?
- Which positions are to be filled by each parent?
- Which positions are to be filled by expatriates?
- In joint ventures, for whom do the new employees work—for one of the partners, or for the new entity?
- Who decides on new hires? Must there be an agreement among partners?
- How will staffing conflicts be resolved?

Given the importance of staffing, a case can be made for formally addressing these issues in the alliance contract, although as noted earlier views are divided since contractual arrangements may be too rigid for evolving staffing needs. Mutual agreement on policies may suffice.

"MANAGING" YOUR PARTNER'S STAFFING.   Asymmetry in the quality of the assignees is often an early signal that the venture is heading for trouble since it raises questions about the managerial competence or sincerity of the deficient partner. To the extent that key operational staff may come from the partner organization, it is important to find ways of ensuring that they possess the required competencies and skills. This means developing some sense of who the talented people are in the partner organization, and understanding the basis on which the partner differentiates between high-potentials, solid performers, and low performers.

Cases of inappropriate staffing decisions are not infrequent. The partner's management may not understand the skill level required for jobs in the partnership venture. It may overestimate the capability of its internal candidates, or it may not have the basic HR capabilities. It is essential to intervene *before* any decisions are taken. Forcing a change once the appointment has been made may be difficult.

The right to be consulted on key appointments is a useful stipulation in a partnership agreement. Exercising this right requires familiarity with the "rules of the game" in the partner's organization, understanding the internal score cards, knowing how careers evolve there, as well as gaining access to the levers of influence. Much of this is tacit knowledge, acquired through extensive informal interaction and built on trust and personal credibility.

ONE-WAY VERSUS TEMPORARY TRANSFER. When partnerships are formed to create a new business, it is important to consider the costs and benefits of two alternative staffing strategies. One approach is to assign personnel to the JV, especially the management group, on a temporary transfer from the partner firm. The other is to staff the JV positions on a "permanent" basis. While it is not unusual to combine the two methods, it is important to consider the conflicting priorities and career aspirations of the two groups of employees. Every position filled—usually at higher cost—by a temporary transferee is an opportunity lost for the permanent staff. If the value-for-money of the transferee is not readily apparent, resentment and conflict are not far behind.

There is research evidence, at least in the case of joint ventures, that it is better to staff the venture with dedicated management teams.[31] If employees are transferred from the parent, they should expect to remain in the venture without a guaranteed ticket back to the parent so that their future career opportunities are linked entirely to the growth of the new business. In Japan, a country where few JVs survive, several successful joint ventures have at their helm executives who have spent all or most of their careers in the venture. Fuji–Xerox, headed for many years by Yotaro Kobayashi, is probably the most notable example of what strong and stable leadership can do for JV performance.

On the other hand, temporary transfers do have merits. They are useful when the required management skills change in a rapidly evolving venture, or when skill gaps cannot be covered internally, or as a tool for organizational learning. Transferees are more likely to remember that their task is not to preserve the alliance at all costs. Indeed, temporary transfers are generally the only way in which the foreign partner can insert its employees into the venture. Any assignments should be of a reasonable duration since frequent churning of key venture managers makes it difficult to establish a shared culture.

The foreign partner may experience greater difficulties than the local partner in convincing first class employees from the parent firm to transfer to the JV.[32] In such cases the personal involvement of top management can make a difference. When Procter & Gamble entered the Chinese market in the 1980s, joint venturing with local partners was the only alternative. In order to encourage its best candidates to accept these challenging assignments, P&G's top management including the CEO took a visible role in candidate selection, in mentoring during the assignment, and in repatriation. Because of leadership commitment to staffing, the supply of good managers willing to work in China ceased being a major constraint and P&G was able to grow aggressively.

Either a shortage of qualified candidates or cost considerations may persuade foreign partners to limit their representation to a single executive. One person is expected to play the role of corporate ambassador, shadow CEO, chief learning officer, and business developer—quite a challenge! Notably in competitive alliances, this may not be in the best interest of the business.

In most cases, the best strategy is to recruit and develop local talent. When joint ventures are an important part of a company's strategy in a particular market, it may be worthwhile establishing a wholly owned affiliate that can serve as a holding company for all operations in the country. Local managers can then be hired by the holding company and trained and dispatched to joint ventures so as to represent the interests of the foreign partner, thus lessening the reliance on expensive expatriates with limited local know-how. Many foreign firms investing in China have chosen this route to develop their local management team.

Meeting the Development Needs

The implementation of an alliance often requires developing new knowledge, skills, and competencies. The first set of needs focuses on building understanding of alliance dynamics among the many people in the parent company who will be involved directly or indirectly in the partnership. Second, employees and managers dispatched to the alliance may benefit from specific training, both to enhance their ability to cope with the inevitable complexities and frustration of the alliance environment and to increase their understanding of the social and cultural context of their new jobs. Finally, a third focus is on building open communication and trust inside the partnership and on facilitating integration between the alliance venture and the parent firm.

In companies where alliances are critical to the business strategy, alliance training is often used as an integral part of their implementation process. For example, Hewlett-Packard, which is engaged in scores of international partnerships, organizes workshops on a massive scale for its managers involved in alliances. The HP alliance management framework, constituting an elaborate knowledge management system focused on alliances, is disseminated using case histories, toolkits, and checklists, as well as comparisons of best practice from other firms.[33]

One of the dilemmas in preparing executives for an alliance assignment is that companies may be reluctant to devote resources to alliance management training, or even to select potential venture staff, until the partnership has been agreed upon. This is a double bind since there is seldom time for extensive training once an agreement is reached. Estimates suggest that only one-third of firms involved in alliances offer alliance training.[34] One of the authors has directed alliance management seminars for over fifteen years. It is not unusual to see participants subscribing for the course at the last minute, departing for a foreign location virtually as soon as the course ends.[35]

One of the focal areas for management development within the alliance venture itself is helping the venture team to interact and work effectively with each other and with the parents. Ideally this process starts when the alliance is launched, helping employees get to know each other and learn about each other's company culture and mode of operations. This can have a substantial payoff in speeding up the success of the venture. When Corning creates new alliances, venture staff are briefed on the respective organizational cultures and traditions, corporate values, and venture organization in order to minimize confusion and misunderstanding.[36] Other companies organize team-building workshops, ranging from traditional Organizational Development (OD) interventions to outdoor experiential learning.[37] It also pays to follow up the "honeymoon training" with periodic workshops, jointly working through specific business and cultural challenges facing the partnership.

In the case of the problems facing Chemco, the U.S. partner modified a series of functional training workshops aimed at improving coordination in Asia Pacific. Initially limited to wholly owned subsidiaries, participants complained about the lack of support from the Japanese, but no action could be taken since no Japanese representatives were in the room. In the new format, Japanese JV employees were invited to take part, and the program was redesigned to take language problems into account and to facilitate dialogue. They jointly identified the obstacles to collaboration, suggested actions to remedy the problems, and committed to new joint business initiatives. The bottom line? Profits from joint projects generated by the first three workshops equaled the annual training budget for the whole region.

A good and relatively inexpensive way to foster the alliance integration process is to open up in-house training to the staff in the alliance unit and when appropriate to those from the partner. Aside from skill development, this may lead to the creation of personal networks across the alliance boundaries. Real trust cannot be built through contracts, but only through human relationships.

Influencing Performance

During the planning stage, it is generally not difficult for alliance partners to agree that "performance matters." For the operating managers dispatched to the actual JV, however, it can be much more difficult to agree on what constitutes "performance," how to measure it, and what should be the consequences of high or low performance.

Earlier in this chapter we mentioned an oil exploration joint venture created by British, Norwegian (state-owned), and Vietnamese (government) partners. The parties did not hold the same views about performance management, yet the split did not cut along East-West cultural lines.[38] British expatriates and locally recruited young Vietnamese managers were in favor of individually focused, achievement-oriented performance criteria with substantial financial benefits for top performers. The Norwegians and the senior representatives of the Vietnamese partner, concerned with equity and harmonious work relations, preferred to give more emphasis to team goals and process implementation, with much less internal differentiation. Although the business principles in the agreement contained a commitment to create a performance-oriented culture, the specifics were never spelled out. The net result was confusion, frustration, conflict, and high turnover—the opposite of what the performance management system was supposed to achieve. It is not that one partner was right and the other wrong. The real issue was the lack of a common perspective.

The many dualities involved in performance management can lead to disagreement—short-term versus long-term time horizon, focus on output versus behavior, individual versus group scope, objective versus subjective evaluation, direct versus indirect feedback, parent versus venture orientation. This last issue—whether managers are evaluated on the performance of the venture or the parent—can become particularly contentious. But an even bigger problem is to align strategic aims. In Chemco's case, as long as the objective of the local management team was only to grow profitably in Japan, the wider strategic aims of the U.S. firm to grow in the region remained neglected.

Differences in perceptions about managing performance are frequently attributed to differences in national culture. This may be misleading. Differences within cultures on performance issues are often just as large as differences across cultures, and the initial search for an appropriate partner tries to take this into account. Strategy matters. In a complementary alliance, a hands-off approach to setting the performance objectives may be appropriate, whereas in a competitive alliance this may be a recipe for disaster.

Performance management tensions tend to come from three sources: (1) applying home-grown principles inappropriately to a different context; (2) using different standards for parent company and alliance employees; and (3) attempting to combine incompatible approaches.

In a Japanese controlled JV in the United States, merit increases were linked to performance evaluations, as is the local practice. The performance feedback process, however, was decidedly "Japanese," indirect and informal. Japanese bosses spent most time with the laggards, hoping that with some encouragement their performance would improve. On the other hand, they loaded more responsibility on those considered outstanding so as to signal to them that they were trusted and were on the way to a bright future in the firm. While these signals might have been correctly interpreted in Japan, several of the top American performers quit, complaining that the merit increases did not reflect the additional responsibilities, that the bosses did not care, and that they did not know where they stood. Others complained that the Japanese were not honest since the encouraging words were not matched by what they saw in their paychecks.

Not surprisingly, resistance to "foreign" ways of managing performance is most pronounced in competitive alliances, since managing performance is one of the keys to having an influence inside the venture. The way performance is managed indicates to the alliance staff who is in charge and whose interests have to be taken seriously. Without influence over the performance management process, a partner (especially a distant partner) can expect only nominal control over the direction of the venture; therefore, performance management issues often become a lightning rod in the latent struggle for influence.

The proper measure of influence is not how much alliance performance management resembles the parent's, but how it furthers the parent's strategy. First, this means making sure that the parent's strategic objectives are reflected in the venture performance targets. Second, achievement of these targets has to be measured. Third, attainment or nonattainment of targets should have consequences.

In Chemco's case, the first and second requirements for effective performance management were met once the United States partner attained formal majority control, and regional targets were included in the annual objectives set for the local management team. However, target setting was a mere ritual since the results had no consequences, positive or negative—and this would remain the case as long as Chemco had no influence over salaries, bonuses, or promotions, which leads us to the reward aspects of performance management.

Aligning Rewards

One of the first actions taken by Chemco to increase its influence was to negotiate a gradual transfer of all employees in Japan from the payroll of the Japanese parent to JV employee status. The work conditions offered were more favorable, but they did not increase the cost, as the compensation and benefit system was tailored to the JV workforce. The union and nearly all employees accepted these conditions. As a next step, the management bonus was linked to the achievement of two sets of targets, regional and local. For senior management, regional targets were made the key objectives. In addition, the variable part of total compensation was increased dramatically, and the company is discussing a stock option scheme. Today, the Japanese partner considers its JV a "human laboratory," in which new HR practices—novel to the Japanese market—can be tested before introducing them in the parent company.

Among all compensation issues, those relating to variable pay require the most sensitivity and flexibility. Compensation has a strong impact on strategy implementation. People tend to do what they believe they get rewarded for.[39] But beyond that, people in different countries have very different attitudes to variable pay. This is partly the result of wide differences in accounting standards and tax regimes—for example, regarding stock options.[40] There are also different cultural attitudes to issues such as uncertainty avoidance and salary differentials. Again, the primary consideration is to align rewards with the alliance strategy rather than to import HR practices because they are successful in the parent firm.[41]

No compensation formula or measurement matrix can overcome a disagreement about strategy. If one partner wants to build market share and the other is interested in cash flow, then developing common performance targets is going to be difficult unless the two partners first agree on priorities. Also, in more complex alliances, building a clear linkage between strategic aims and rewards may not be possible—another argument for keeping the alliances simple and focused.

Another important compensation issue to consider is the dualistic tension between external equity with the parent for expatriates and internal equity for venture staff, frequently leading to asymmetry in earnings among different groups of employees within the alliance. For example, it is estimated that total compensation of an expatriate manager in China or Russia could easily be a hundred times more than the income of a typical local JV employee (whose pay in turn may be several times that of a counterpart in a local firm). The differences in compensation levels may also impact the balance of influence in the alliance since loyalties, not surprisingly, tend to shift toward the higher paying partner.[42]

These differences, while unavoidable in ventures involving companies from countries with widely different standards of living, may lead to motivational problems and conflict unless the added value of such expatriates or local staff with superior compensation is visible and appreciated.

Disparity in compensation sometimes makes it difficult to persuade the local partner to accept expatriate staff even when this could be in the best interest of the venture.[43] Or local partners try to use this for their own advantage. For example, the authorities in China often subject the approval for JV projects to the condition that there be equality of compensation between foreign expatriates and local managers. Of course, Chinese managers are paid only a small fraction of what is stipulated in the contract, and their state-owned employer retains the rest. In this case, the foreign partner is disadvantaged as it is forced to bear the full load of the expatriation cost while the Chinese partner earns a corresponding profit.

There is also a need to balance internal equity issues within the parent firm with the supply and demand for high quality venture managers. Alliances, in comparison with wholly owned subsidiaries, are difficult to manage. Rightly or wrongly they may be seen as risky; and the venture may be seen as more removed from the politics of getting ahead in the parent company. High performers, who tend to have options, may elect to stay clear of such assignments unless they are sufficiently compensated. On the other hand, in order to facilitate corporate cohesion, there is also a need for a certain degree of consistency in compensation strategy across all affiliates, irrespective of the organizational form.

This paradox cannot be solved simply by recalibrating compensation. To achieve the necessary balance, other components of the HR system have to be aligned as well. The deliberate positioning of alliance assignments as a key element of long-term career progression is a powerful tool to ensure a supply of requisite talent, as we saw in the case of P&G's staffing strategy for China. Influencing and shaping careers provides stronger leverage over expatriate staffing than short-term financial incentives.[44]

Shaping Alliance Careers

Commitment by the parent to career development for joint venture employees is essential in gaining their allegiance. Shortly after transferring Japanese employees to the JV payroll, Chemco offered some younger staff the possibility of moving to their subsidiaries in Southeast Asia with the assignment of coordinating sales with Japanese customers in the region. The conditions offered were the same as for any other Chemco expatriate. One benefit for Chemco was improved customer service and sales. The other was a dramatic change in the perceptions of regional integration on the part of Japanese staff. The earlier view that this was a power game, us versus them, quickly faded. Expatriate perks such as housing were attractive to the young Japanese since they could not afford this at home. But what made the difference was the feeling that career opportunities were now open to all.

Such career development can promote organizational cohesion, though as with any HRM practice the execution depends on the alliance's strategic context. In competitive alliances, this needs to be carefully considered. The worst outcome is to accept a transferee for the sake of the relationship, and then to cut him or her off from information and influence because of a perception that the particular person should not be trusted. Some transferees will view this as another example of the partner's duplicity and bad intentions.

The form of the alliance also has implications for career development.[45] Employees transferred from the parent to a joint venture can feel isolated especially if they have few colleagues from the parent with whom to share the uncertainties of coping with conflicting interests. The temporary nature of the assignment only reinforces the anxiety about career prospects. Assurances from corporate HR—"Don't worry, we'll take care of you when you come back"—lack credibility in an era of continuous restructuring. As discussed earlier, the difficulties of managing dual allegiance is one of the arguments in favor of "one-way-transfer" staffing strategies. This is often not practical or desirable, however—either from a staffing perspective, or, as we will see in the next section, because of a need to foster knowledge exchange between the venture and the parent.

Visible involvement in career development decisions is one of the most effective ways to build influence. Being an absentee parent may be a cost-efficient strategy in the short term, but it can be costly in the long term. In a stand-alone JV, when the initial growth levels off, career development prospects may diminish and the best and the brightest may leave unless they see the same opportunity to move to increased responsibilities as they would have in a wholly owned subsidiary. If only one of the parents seems to care, then it is likely that commitment and loyalty will shift accordingly. Buying more shares will not make much difference.

Developing Shared Culture

In contrast to acquisitions, one has to live with conflicting loyalties in alliances. Whether or not this becomes dysfunctional depends on the type of alliance and the ability of the partners to deal with the contradictions in most alliance relationships. One way to cope is to foster a distinct and shared culture inside the alliance that could ease tensions between partners, building an atmosphere of responsibility for the results of the partnership. As discussed earlier, however, this depends on the business strategies underlying the venture. Alliance independence is not a goal in itself—the purpose of alliances is to create value for the partners. Instructions to general managers, such as "run this like your own business," when the venture does not have decision-making autonomy, can only create mistrust and cynicism.

The key outcome of a shared culture is trust.[46] Creating a shared culture inside the alliance does not mean ignoring differences between the partners' strategic priorities, but even in a competitive alliance, without trust on an operating level, the partnership will not succeed. The best way to build trust is to get to know each other. HR can support this by promoting personnel exchanges and supporting visible examples of commitment to common goals.

Another source of shared culture may be a common enemy, as illustrated by the experience of three middle-sized manufacturers of electronic components. American, German, and Japanese, respectively, they established a global alliance aimed at combining R&D resources in a market dominated by two giant competitors. Management teams met regularly around the world to coordinate development activities. However, traditional rivalry, parochial departmental interests, and cultural insensitivity slowed down decision-making, causing the alliance to miss several critical deadlines and to jeopardize relationships with key customers. On the initiative of one of the HR managers, the wired logos of the two competitors were installed on the walls in the conference rooms. Pushing one of the buttons hidden under the conference desk would cause the signs to flash, reminding everyone that competition does not go away while participants waste time in unproductive arguments. After only a few meetings, it became embarrassing for anyone to get flashed for allowing a parochial agenda to get in the way of common interest. The speed and decision-making and quality of implementation improved dramatically.

SUPPORTING ALLIANCE LEARNING

All alliances include some learning aspects, not the least of which is how to work effectively with partners.[47] As discussed earlier, however, some alliances are created with knowledge creation and learning as the focal objectives.

In both learning and competitive alliances, effective alliance learning is important not only to prevent the erosion of a firm's market position, but also as a building block for future competitive advantage. An example cited earlier of a successful learning alliance is Fuji-Xerox, a joint venture between Fuji Photo and Xerox Corporation that lasted over thirty years.[48] The venture was started to facilitate Xerox's entry into the Japanese market. In the late 1980s, other Japanese companies such as Canon and Ricoh aggressively attacked Xerox in its home U.S. market with innovative products, competing on price and quality. Initially, Xerox was not able to respond and lost significant market share. Recognizing that Fuji-Xerox competed successfully against the same players in Japan, however, the company launched a massive "learning from Japan" campaign aimed at transferring Fuji-Xerox's capabilities back to the mother firm.[49] Because of this "reverse technology transfer," Xerox was able to stem the market erosion and begin to recapture the lost share.

The success of Fuji-Xerox illustrates that strong strategic alliances focus on mutual learning. The trust between the partners allows them to concentrate on managing the business rather than on monitoring and control, and their mutual learning strengthens their position in the markets worldwide. Healthy alliances are based on mutual strength, while mutual weaknesses lead to paranoia and fear. Indeed, selecting partners who are known to be poor learners so as to guard against competency leaks is shortsighted. Weak learning capability is a sign of poor management, and poorly managed firms make poor partners.

An organization has many tools to manage the process of learning, but in principle, the learning ability of an organization depends on its ability to transfer and integrate tacit knowledge that is difficult to copy, thereby building invisible assets.[50] Since invisible assets are embedded in people, HRM is critical to organization learning. This is especially true in international alliances, in which the learning occurs in a complex context of competition and cultural differences. Many of the difficulties with implementation of long-term alliance strategies can be traced to the quality of the learning process and the underlying human resource policies and practices. The ability to learn is especially important in competitive alliances in which asymmetry in learning can result in an uneven distribution of benefits.[51]

An objective of human resource management in international alliances is therefore to complement business strategy by providing a climate that encourages organizational learning and by installing appropriate tools to guide the process of knowledge creation.[52] We first explore key obstacles to alliance learning in order to highlight the challenges for HRM. (We focus on competitive alliances—most of the points apply to other forms of alliance, though the cost of failure may not be so high.) Then we review the strategies and practices that support and enhance learning.

Obstacles to Alliance Learning

The rapid development of competitive capabilities among leading Japanese firms in the second half of the twentieth century is often attributed to successful alliance learning. Alliances were used as the main vehicle for inward technology transfer and capability improvement. More recently, many other companies in developing countries in Asia and Latin America have pursued the same strategy with success. On the other hand, many of the traditional U.S. and European firms have struggled to kick-start the learning process. Examples of alliance learning, on the Fuji-Xerox model, are rela-

FIGURE 5–3. Obstacles to Organizational Learning in International Strategic Alliances

HR Activities	HR Practices
HR Planning	• Strategic intent not communicated • Short-term and static planning horizon • Low priority of learning activities • Lack of involvement by the HR department
Staffing	• Insufficient lead-time for staffing decisions • Resource-poor staffing strategy • Low quality of staff assigned to the JV • Staffing dependence on the partner
Training and Development	• Lack of cross-cultural competence • Unidirectional training programs • Career structure not conducive to learning • Poor culture for transfer of learning
Appraisal and Rewards	• Appraisal focused on short-term goals • No encouragement of learning • Limited incentives for transfer of know-how • Rewards not tied to global strategy
Organizational Design and Control	• Responsibility for learning not clear • Fragmentation of the learning process • Control over the HR department given away • No insight into partner's HR strategy

Source: Adapted from V. Pucik, "Strategic Alliances, Organizational Learning, and Competitive Advantage: The HRM Agenda," *Human Resource Management* 27(1988): 77–93.

tively rare. So what are the obstacles? Some are consequences of ill-conceived strategies; others stem from poor HRM practices, or a combination of both (see Figure 5–3).

Defensive Strategic Intent

One of the obstacles may be that many alliances are driven by a defensive strategic intent. Firms perceive partnership primarily as a way of reducing risk and conserving valuable resources.[53] This built-in defensive posture may make managers reluctant to undertake the necessary investments in learning, especially if one of the alliance objectives is to minimize the cost of developing new competencies. The hesitation will invariably result in a deterioration of a firm's competitive position, leading to an asymmetry in the relationship and eventually to a conflict with the partner. Dissolution of the relationship is then the logical next step. Successful learning alliances are most often driven by a "top-line" orientation in which investment in the development of new competencies is recovered through the growth of business.

A corollary to defensive intent is the belief that preventing the partner from learning (and thus avoiding asymmetry) may be easier and cheaper than investing in one's own learning. A partner committed to learning will always learn, even if this is made difficult by obstacles put in the way. Meanwhile, the customer feels the obstacles. Secrecy and internal walls lead to suboptimal solutions, excessive costs, and delays. In highly competitive markets, companies that hope to build defensive walls around themselves to prevent "seeping" of knowledge to the partner often end up losing the customer.

Low Priority of Learning Activities

Decisions on alliance learning strategy are often based on the assumption that the existing balance of contributions to the venture will not change over time. Consider the case of a partnership in which one party provides technology and the other secures market access. The executives of the technology firm may believe that the partner will have to rely on their technological leadership for the foreseeable future, so they see few incentives to invest in learning about the market. However, if the other partner gradually closes the technological gap—after all, technology transfer is often a part of the deal—the basis for the alliance becomes problematic. One partner now has both technology and market access, so why share the benefits?

One problem here is that many firms do not recognize the importance of developing soft or invisible competencies as opposed to hard resources. Learning often has to be focused on mastering tacit processes underlying product quality, speed of product development, or linkage to key customers. Firms frequently fail to benefit from alliance learning because they do not recognize the benefits of acquiring the "soft" skills.[54]

Learning through alliances may be faster than learning alone, but it still requires investment. The learning strategy may be compromised by a reluctance to commit the necessary financial resources. In many companies, the traditional focus of the business planning process is return on financial assets, while the accumulation of invisible assets is not evaluated directly since a financial value is hard to assign to these outcomes. Activities that cannot be evaluated in financial terms may be seen as less critical, so learning efforts are given only token support.

When learning investments are made, they may be poorly placed. An example is the countless seminars on "Doing Business in China" that have been fashionable in recent decades. In spite of major learning investments, the performance record of foreign ventures in China is mixed at best. Perhaps spending resources on generic seminars, as well as on travel and photo opportunities with government leaders (building the relationships), created a false assurance that "learning" was taking place, without paying enough attention to what was actually happening on the ground. "Strategic investment" became a euphemism for losing money; "long-term strategic investment" indicated that losses were significant.[55]

Inappropriate Staffing

Expatriate staffing is costly, and firms are tempted to reduce alliance costs by limiting the number of personnel assigned to the foreign venture. As a result, the few expatriates (sometimes only one) are often overwhelmed with routine work, struggling just to get by in the unfamiliar culture. The opportunities for active knowledge acquisition—for example, through relationships with local customers or interactions with the partner—are minimal. However keen the expatriate may be on learning, operational matters drive out all possibilities.

In Chemco's case, the company policy for nearly twenty years was to dispatch only one senior level executive as ambassador to Japan, occasionally augmented with an experienced engineer helping to bring knowledge into Japan. In most cases, the expatriates retired after their assignment in Japan so there was no organizational transfer of learning. When the company decided to refocus its Japan strategy, the total accumulated experience in the Japanese market among the top management team (Japan was at that time the largest overseas market for Chemco), including business trips longer than one week, was less than six months.[56]

The staffing agenda, however, is not just about how many and where, but also about who. If the managers assigned to oversee or manage an alliance are not credible within their own organization and with the partner, learning will be difficult to achieve. Because these are relatively longer-term assignments, they clash with the expectations of fast upward mobility and may not be attractive to high potential managers. The managers who land in this role may not have the influence to cope with the complex give-and-take of a learning relationship. Long-term career planning is often lacking, as is effective repatriation (as in Chemco's case), which may hinder the effective exploitation and dissemination of the acquired know-how.

Poor Climate for Knowledge Exchange

A characteristic of alliance learning is that partner interactions often take place in a context of competitive collaboration.[57] Not surprisingly, competition and learning commonly go hand in hand in high technology industries in which fast learning is an imperative of the business model.

When requests to one's partner for learning support are ignored, it may awaken suspicions of duplicity, inviting retaliation. Very soon, the whole atmosphere of partnership is poisoned, although the executives at the top are still espousing collaboration. How to deal effectively with the two contradictory faces of the partnership is a major managerial challenge.

In a competitive alliance, transfer of knowledge to a competitor will often generate a legitimate concern among staff for what will happen to job and work groups when their unique knowledge is disseminated to others. Principles of equitable exchange at the company level do not necessarily translate to perceptions of equity at the operational level. Initial obstacles of lack of focus and unclear priorities can quickly mushroom into widespread resistance to knowledge exchange.

Moreover, internal barriers to the acquisition of learning are often just as serious as unfriendly actions of the partner. The learning from the outside threatens the status quo. The typical attitude is defensive: "It's a good idea, but it will never work here." Contrast this with the attitude guiding GE's approach to alliances: "Stealing with pride" is a phrase that made it into the company's annual report.

No Accountability and Rewards for Learning

A decade ago, one of the authors conducted a survey among foreign joint ventures in Japan. One of the questions put to the HR managers was "Who in the parent firm organization is responsible for learning from Japan?" Less than 10 percent identified a person or a function (usually the top representative in Japan), about a third mentioned "nobody," and over half considered the question "not applicable." Since learning is taken more seriously today, the answers might be more positive, but the lack of clear responsibility for learning remains a major obstacle to alliance learning.

If there is no accountability for meeting learning targets, they are unlikely to be taken seriously. In complex organizations, perceptions of the potential value of learning from an alliance may vary according to the business unit, function, and territory, and the commitment to provide the necessary support will vary accordingly. This can lead to asymmetry—one unit supplies the people while another unit expects the learning. A European high tech company entered a number of partnerships with dot-com companies in Silicon Valley, also with the aim of exploring ways of leveraging its technology in the Internet world. Several young engineers were dispatched to California to work on specific projects as well as to provide feedback to the technology managers in the mother company. Within a few months, the word came back: "If you want to learn about the Internet, do it yourself. We don't have the time to teach you."

In addition, traditional market-driven reward systems may implicitly encourage the hoarding of critical information, rather than the diffusion of learning. People who have valued knowledge can command higher salaries on the market. Diffusing this knowledge to others (for example, by sharing critical alliance contacts) may diminish one's market value, so why do it? Being indispensable is the ultimate in employability.

Human Resource Foundations for Effective Learning

A major role of HR is to help create an organizational context in which alliance learning can flourish (see the box "Core Principles for Alliance Learning"). However, alliance learning is not about collecting binders of data in the alliance "war

Core Principles for Alliance Learning
Practice Box

1. Build learning into the alliance agreement.
2. Communicate the learning intent inside the parent.
3. Assign responsibility for alliance learning.
4. Secure early HR involvement.
5. Maintain HR influence inside the alliance.

6. Staff to learn.
7. Support learning-driven careers.
8. Stimulate learning through training.
9. Reward learning activities.
10. Monitor your partner's learning.

room." Rather, effective alliance learning is focused on absorbing know-how and developing or broadening capabilities.

In the context of learning and competitive alliances, the need for early HR participation is especially critical. Acquisition of new knowledge and competencies happens only through people, and if the people strategy is not aligned with the learning objectives, the chances of this happening are greatly diminished.

Setting the Learning Strategy

One of the first questions to address in the context of developing alliance strategy is how much this issue should be addressed in the alliance agreement.

When the alliance is set up as a separate organization, for example, as a joint venture, the partnership agreement or operating principles should provide at least broad guidelines on key HR policies and practices that influence learning effectiveness. These may involve issues such as freedom to move people across alliance boundaries as necessary and determination of their learning roles and responsibilities. Clarifying HR issues that impact learning is especially important if the alliance operates abroad since it is often difficult to renegotiate HR policies after the venture is launched.

In a learning alliance, clarifying learning expectations among partners is a more straightforward process. But what if the learning is to take place in the context of a competitive alliance? Does it make sense to be open about one's learning strategy, or should this remain a closely guarded secret?

The best, but probably hardest, way to deal with the paradox of competitive collaboration is to accept and be open about the "race to learn." Hiding the learning agenda increases mistrust and encourages opportunistic behavior. Alliances that create learning asymmetries do not survive long. Both parties should therefore be explicit about their learning objectives, put forward strategies to accomplish such learning together with their HRM implications, monitor mutual progress, and discuss with each other any important reservations. If the learning objectives cannot be openly discussed, the merits of the whole alliance may become questionable.[58]

Once the strategy is set, it has to be clearly and consistently communicated across the organization. What is the purpose of the alliance, what are its boundaries, what needs to be learned, what is the partner expected to gain? Sometimes, companies are reluctant to communicate clearly that the alliance is actually competitive because of the fear of setting a bad tone for the relationship. The lack of communication does not change the reality; competition does not disappear because it is not talked about. The result is confusion and disbelief among the employees. Clear and unequivocal rules of engagement are essential.

While aligning HR processes to the learning strategy is vital, the responsibility for managing learning belongs to the line, not to HR or any other staff function. Who is responsible for learning sends a signal about how important this is. In a product development alliance between an American and Japanese high technology firm, the HR function put itself forward as the champion of alliance learning, one of the explicit objectives for the alliance.[59] Many of the engineers who were expected to participate dismissed the whole activity as another "HR program." As for the Japanese, the role of the American HR "learning manager" remained a mystery throughout.

HR's contribution to alliance learning may cut across all functional activities. However, there are four basic HR areas in which line management and the function can leverage alliance learning: (1) selection and staffing, (2) training and development, (3) career planning, and (4) performance management. We will discuss these four areas in turn.

Staffing to Learn

The focus on learning starts with appropriate staffing since the quantity and quality of people involved in the learning effort are fundamental to its credibility and success.[60] There is no such thing as free alliance learning. Strategic intent is no substitute for resource commitment.[61] Obviously, justifying the necessary staffing investments requires fixing clear and measurable learning outcomes. And when some of the desired knowledge resides with partner's employees, as is usually the case, then the partner's commitment to support the alliance with competent staff is also essential.

The most powerful learning often happens in joint alliance teams in which employees from both partners work together on solving business issues. Here it is important to consider the difference between traditional in-company teams and alliance teams. Common company culture, implicit hierarchy (expatriates versus locals), and above all shared long-term goals facilitate the team process when working in the company. In alliance teams, none of these "glue" factors exist, introducing additional ambiguity and uncertainty into the learning environment. Selection criteria for alliance learning teams need to take into account the ability of employees to cope with this complexity.

Several years ago, a European consumer products company assigned a group of its fast track employees to work on a team with their Chinese partner in developing strategies for expansion in China. All assignees had a record of successful postings to wholly owned subsidiaries in the region. However, the added difficulties of working with a partner's organization required an adjustment in behavior, communication, and leadership style that several of them could not handle. The project team had to be restructured several times, causing delays and disruptions to the new product launch schedule.

Another critical staffing issue concerns the trade-off between staffing for learning and staffing for effective execution. Consider the case of a joint development project between a U.S. and a European telecommunication company. The main idea behind the collaboration was to pool the complementary technical capabilities of the two firms so as to deliver a novel solution to global customers. A second objective was to learn from each other so that both companies could improve their competitive offerings at home. The execution perspective suggests that each partner should field a team in their areas of special expertise, which will foster speed and efficiency in executing the business plan. But if the partner's only focus is on what they are good at, how will they acquire new skills? In order to learn, additional staff would have to be assigned to join the team, which might hinder progress in getting the job done, not to mention the additional cost that the project would have to bear. Getting this balance right requires a very clear understanding of the strategic objectives behind the alliance.

Learning to Learn

Different types of training and development activities can stimulate a climate conducive to effective alliance learning. Some training is best conducted internally, with attendance limited to the parent firm so that sensitive issues can be openly discussed. Internal training can help employees understand the importance of the learning aims of the alliance, as well as how to learn through collaboration, and this type of training should take place early on in the alliance lifecycle. This is especially important if the alliance is or is likely to become competitive, with competition and collaboration in learning evolving simultaneously and alliance learning potentially handicapped by high levels of anxiety.

When a U.S. high tech manufacturer decided to set up a joint new product development project with a Japanese partner, one of the first actions was to conduct a series of alliance management workshops for all key employees who would be directly or indirectly involved. The strategic logic of the project, its scope and boundaries, the learning objectives and opportunities as well as ideas on specific learning processes were presented and discussed in detail. As a result of these discussions, top management decided to redesign the alliance manager role in order to foster clearer accountability for learning and to adjust the resources allocated to specific learning activities.

Since alliance learning is based on relationships with the partner, joint training activities can enhance collaboration by raising both competence and trust. Team building and joint cross-cultural communication training are especially useful to speed up the getting-acquainted process. These can include intensive discussion on organizational values, structures, decision-making patterns, and the like, so that employees understand the context in which they are expected to work together. Communication problems may otherwise be attributed to "cultural differences." People learn through such workshops that the real problems are often more tangible matters, such as different interpretations of performance expectations and rewards.

Career Paths Facilitate Learning

The rotation of employees through alliance positions and back to the parent firm facilitates the transfer of knowledge between the venture and the parent.[62] This requires addressing such issues as the harmonization of salaries/benefits so as to facilitate moving people back and forth. While such issues do not have to be addressed in the text of the partnership agreement, the transfers need to be planned carefully, especially with respect to future career expectations.[63] If the individual knows that the knowledge acquired in the venture will be put to good use on return, this increases the motivation to learn during the assignment.[64]

The need for an explicit strategy to transfer and implement acquired knowledge is well illustrated by the case of NUMMI, the Toyota–General Motors manufacturing joint venture in California.[65] Only a handful of selected GM managers were assigned to the venture in the early years—apparently so as not to "contaminate" its new culture with old GM practices.[66] After two or three years of working with the Japanese, these managers were converted to the virtues of Toyota's lean manufacturing system, with a good grasp of its workings. They moved back to different GM locations with the mission of implementing the learning from NUMMI within the GM organization. All these efforts ended in failure—not because of inadequate personal learning but because there was never a critical mass of ex-NUMMI staff at one location to make a difference.

Asymmetry in personnel transfers is usually a good indication of asymmetry in learning. While GM shuffled isolated individuals, Toyota trained more than 100 of their personnel on how to collaborate with NUMMI's American workforce. They were then assigned to Toyota's new wholly owned plant in Kentucky to replicate the NUMMI experience. In contrast, it took over a decade for General Motors to leverage properly their own acquired knowledge. An alumni team from the ventures at NUMMI and CAMI (GM's JV with Suzuki Motors) took charge of a decrepit East German car plant in Eisenach, and within three years they turned it into the most advanced car manufacturing facility in Europe.[67] The knowledge that specific individuals had gained about Toyota's manufacturing system resulted in action only when there was a coherent organizational strategy for applying that learning.

Reinforcing Learning through Performance Management

While successful learning from alliances requires champions of knowledge creation—people who believe in the value of learning and who support the necessary investments—this may not be enough. The old adage "what gets measured gets done" applies here. To the extent possible, alliance learning objectives should be translated into specific measures, such as quality or productivity improvement, speed of new product development, or customer expansion. An important source of the measurement targets is information on the partner's learning achievements, so that any asymmetry can be addressed quickly and openly.

In Motorola's 12-year alliance with Toshiba to design and manufacture advanced semiconductors (a typical competitive alliance), both companies used explicit learning targets. In Motorola's case, these were translated into individual level objectives linked to rewards. The explicit measurements allowed both firms to mobilize their internal resources to support the learning efforts. Externally, the tangible learning outcomes provided a valuable benchmark to assure learning symmetry during the life of the alliance. It should be noted that the two executive positions considered to be most important in this alliance were split between the partners, but rotated every couple of years. One was the role of venture chief executive, the other the human resource manager.

The climate for learning is best when alliance performance is satisfactory. When the alliance does not meet its expected targets, it may be more difficult to focus attention on the learning agenda, and necessary investments may be cut.[68] But even a failed alliance can be a source of valuable lessons. During its ambitious drive to internationalize in the early 1990s, General Electric organized a workshop in which executives who had been involved in failed alliances presented their experiences at a company forum. No amount of lectures on alliance strategy can match the impact of a high level manager explaining how his assumptions about the foreign partner's business culture were wrong, resulting in a loss to GE of 50 million dollars. Why were these managers willing to share their painful experiences? Because sharing experience, positive or negative, with others was part of their performance objectives.

There are also alliances designed solely for the purpose of learning, in which the business results are secondary, at least in the short term. However, problems quickly surface if the partners have different priorities in terms of business results versus learning, especially if this issue was not addressed during the formation of the partnership. In the words of a German manager in a Chinese JV: "We pay the tuition and they go to school." Conflicting priorities usually translate into ambiguous performance indicators for managers assigned to the venture, generating tension and disagreements among the executive team.

Successful learning alliances exhibit a bias for action. The best way of learning, sometimes the only way, is to do things together. "Don't just talk about learning collaboration. Do it!" Such was the advice of a Japanese executive in charge of a highly successful learning alliance in the electronics industry. In this alliance, the approach to stimulating mutual learning was straightforward: focused joint development teams were assigned to specific tasks and then held responsible for achieving results, with the coleaders being directly accountable to their parents. Those who were unwilling to share their know-how were quickly moved aside; those who were not keen to apply what they had learned did not last much longer. The race-to-learn lasted three years. With the learning mission accomplished, the alliance was dissolved, and the companies renewed their competition, both of them stronger than they would have been if they had operated alone.

THE EVOLVING ROLE OF ALLIANCES

Just as alliances themselves evolve, so the role of alliances as part of corporate strategy is evolving. One increasingly frequent pattern of alliance development is the emergence of alliance networks, in which firms engage in multiple linkages and relationships often across the whole spectrum of the value chain from R&D and manufacturing all the way to distribution and after-sales service.[69] Originally limited to the high technology sector in which multiple alliances were used as a protective device against obsolescence and other technology risks, today networks can be found in a number of sectors[70] (from airlines to fashion to pharmaceuticals), and they pose new challenges for HRM.

Learning to Manage Network Boundaries

In the airline industry, we see the spread of alliances among the carriers, promising the customer a seamless package of air services around the world. Code sharing (when a particular flight is shared by several airlines) is the most visible example. For example, traveling with Star Alliance[71] may involve purchasing a ticket in Asia from Singapore Airlines, flying on a Lufthansa plane serviced by United (and by GE) to South America, and completing the final leg of the trip with Varig. If a service complaint on such a journey met with the response "sorry, but those people were not our employees," then customer loyalty would clearly be compromised. But this does raise the question of whom the employees work for—just their own airline, or also for the Star Alliance?

From the time of reservation until the delivery of luggage at the end of the trip, airlines are a people intensive business. Some observers argue that people and the service experience they provide is the only differentiator.[72] Is it possible to deliver a seamless experience without coordinating or perhaps ultimately integrating HR strategies, starting from the profile of who will be hired, to the kind of training they receive, and how they will get paid? How can the airlines share best practices? If at least some amount of coordination of airline HR standards is essential, what kind of process is needed to make it happen? Who should lead it, and where is the accountability?

These are new challenges for HRM, particularly since the traditional orientation has been strongly domestic. A typical airline today is international only because it flies to foreign locations. Most major airlines outside the United States have been national flag carriers, with close relationships to the government and strong national unions. Even if the respective management teams agree on what behaviors are expected from the employees, the implementation of HR policies influencing these behaviors may be restricted by historical, institutional, and cultural factors.

In the case of Star Alliance, the Lufhansa Business School took a lead, perhaps because it had played an important role in the 90s in the process of transforming a bankrupt national carrier with a civil service mentality into one of the most profitable global leaders in this industry. Participation on its project-oriented programs has been broadened to include partner members with the aim not just of facilitating coordination but of speeding up the internal transfer of learning from one partner to another.[73] Most of the partners bring particular distinctive strengths—Singapore Airlines in customer bonding, United in logistics, Lufthansa itself in maintenance and managing learning. The HRM vision is that the alliance can be used for mutual learning to convert weaknesses of individual partners into collective strengths.

The HR challenge in airline alliances is an indicator of things to come. As one senior HR executive in a European airline put it: "Anybody who delivers value to my customers is my employee." This is a bold statement, not yet backed up by practice, but with broad implications that go well beyond that particular industry. The density of international alliances is increasing in all sectors as companies engage in a broader variety of relationships from the supply to the customer end of the global value chain. It raises issues for later discussion—how the HR role is changing in the "age of networks."[74]

Alliances as Training Grounds for Transnationalism

The ambiguity of boundaries in an alliance and the need to anticipate future shifts are only one cause of the tensions in this domain. Alliances are full of tensions between competition and collaboration, between global and local interests, between the venture and its parents, and between leveraging and developing competencies. Ambiguity and complexity are the norm. Bearing in mind that the principal challenge in the globalization process is learning to manage tension, dilemma, and duality, our observation is that mastering alliance dilemmas and contradictions helps firms to learn to manage transnational pressures.

In conclusion, let us summarize some of the paradoxes and dualities that the multinational firm learns to confront through its experience in managing alliances:

- Learning how to manage differentiation. There is no such generic thing as "an alliance"—each alliance has different aims and strategic objectives, implying different courses of management and HR action. The parallel for the transnational is that it has to differentiate the roles of its units and subsidiaries, managing them in different ways.
- Learning "to manage the future in the present"—the strategic aims of tomorrow may be quite different from those today.
- Learning to balance the fundamental tension between short-term performance and the long-term learning or knowledge creation that comes through collaboration (the exploitation versus exploration duality). As in the Chemco example, being a hands-off parent can be advantageous in the short term, but with a corresponding long-term cost.
- Learning to recognize and deal with trade-offs in which if one extreme is pushed too far, pathology can be created. We see many examples of this in alliances. If either the interests of the venture itself or the interests of the parent are pushed too far, this can irreparably damage achievement of the alliance aims. Similarly, the deal itself is most important, though excessive attention to detail can create rigidities (the Star Alliance deal is one page in length). There is the need for a delicate balance between external equity for expatriates and internal equity for long-term venture staff. There is the need to make the venture itself successful and yet not confuse this with the wider strategic aims of the parent.
- Learning to take important but "soft" aims such as learning and convert them into "hard" objectives through measurement and accountability.

Alliances are a challenge for the individuals who are involved in them. One learns how to manage boundaries, how to deal with ambiguity and conflicting interests, how to mold a culture that balances competing interests, as well as how to manage the tensions between exploitation (operating results, cash flow, and profit) and exploration (learning). One of the best breeding grounds for transnational managers may be venture management.

TAKEAWAYS

1. Initially considered only a means of securing market access, alliances today are an integral part of global strategies in all aspects of the value chain. Using alliances to generate new knowledge is increasingly important.

2. Alliances are mostly transitional entities; therefore, longevity is a poor measure of success. The aim is not to preserve the alliance at all costs but to contribute to the parent's competitive position.

3. Alliances are dynamic, migrating from one strategic orientation to another. Very few alliances remain complementary for long. Alliances among competitors are increasingly frequent, but they are also the most complex.

4. The approach to HRM is largely driven by the strategic objectives of the partnership. This requires a focus both on managing the interfaces with the parent companies and on managing people inside the alliance itself.

5. The firm's HRM skills and reputation are an asset when exploring and negotiating alliances. Do not enter a complex alliance unless you have a good grasp of HRM basics, and avoid picking a partner who does not. The greater the expected value from the alliance, the more HR support is required.

6. The failings of an alliance are too easily attributed to cultural differences, when the real culprit may be the lack of attention to HRM issues such as appropriate staffing, performance measures, compensation equity, and career management.

7. Equity control is a costly and relatively ineffective form of alliance control, compared with investing in a carefully designed and implemented HRM strategy.

8. Conflicting loyalties, complex relationships, boundary management issues, coupled with uncertainty and instability, are characteristic of most alliances. Managers assigned to the alliance need high tolerance for ambiguity.

9. Alliance learning is neither automatic nor free—there must be clear learning targets, sufficient investment in people, and a tight alignment of HRM practices with learning objectives.

10. Alliances are full of tensions between competition and collaboration, between global and local interests, between leveraging and developing competencies. Mastering alliances helps firms learn to manage transnational pressures.

NOTES

1. Contractor and Lorange (1988, p. 9) identify seven overlapping objectives for the formation of various types of alliances: (i) risk reduction; (ii) achievement of economies of scale and/or rationalization; (iii) technology exchanges; (iv) co-opting or blocking competition; (v) overcoming government-mandated trade or investment barriers; (vi) facilitating initial international expansion; (vii) linking the complementary contributions of the partners in a "value chain." See also Kogut (1988).

2. Hergert and Morris, 1988; Gomes-Casseres, 1988.

3. Cyr and Schneider, 1996.

4. J. Rossant, "Birth of a Giant," *Business Week*, July 10, 2000.

5. Yoshino and Rangan (1995) describe alliances as linkages based on nontraditional contracts that reflect the long-term and unique nature of the relationship between the partners, such as long-term product development collaboration, not just routine buy-sell agreements. They point out that not all relationships between businesses should be considered alliances—although the word "alliance" has become quite fashionable. They also note that not all equity-based alliances need to be joint ventures; partners may simply decide to invest in each other in order to cement the relationship, or one partner may make a unilateral investment in the other partner. Joint ventures can be further classified based on dominant (majority) or non-dominant (50/50) partnerships and where they fit in the organizational structure of the firm (integrated or stand-alone).

6. One of these classifications compares different forms of alliances, from licensing arrangements to manufacturing joint ventures, based on the degree of *interaction* between partners and alliance entity employees. This scale is determined by the level and frequency of interaction, and the number of people interacting (Cascio and Serapio, 1991). The intensity of focus on human resource factors and the involvement of the HR function are expected to mirror the intensity of people interaction.

Another framework links the HR role with two dimensions of business strategy: the strategic importance of the cooperative venture for the parent organization and the degree of control over its own resources by each partner (Lorange, 1996). Alliances fall into four groups: project-based cooperative networks, strings of renegotiated cooperative agreements, ventures with permanently complementary roles, and jointly owned business ventures. Each alliance type requires a different approach to staffing, personnel control, and evaluation.

7. Gomes-Casseres and McQuade, 1992.
8. O'Reilly, 1998.
9. Moxon, Roehl et al., 1988.
10. Hamel, Doz et al., 1989.
11. A good example is NUMMI; General Motors and Toyota continue their collaboration even after the original learning objectives of the partners were fulfilled. The business is profitable and provides advantages for both partners in the market as well as in its contribution to creation of new knowledge.
12. Janger, 1980.
13. Beamish, 1985.
14. Killing, 1982.
15. Zeira and Shenkar, 1990.
16. Ulrich, 1997.
17. Cole and Deskins, 1988; Kenney and Florida, 1992.
18. Pucik, 1988b; Schuler, 2000.
19. Yoshino and Rangan, 1995.
20. Spekman, Forbes III et al., 1998.
21. Yoshino and Rangan, 1995.
22. Ibid.
23. Cited by ibid, p. 146.
24. Lorange and Roos, 1990.
25. Weiss, 1994.
26. Killing, 1997.
27. Ibid.
28. Ferencikova and Pucik, 1999.
29. Cascio and Serapio, 1991.
30. Shenkar and Zeira, 1990.

31. Killing, 1982.
32. Tung, 1988.
33. In the HP framework, workshop materials are organized in a 400-page proprietary manual, supported by an electronic library devoted to alliances. This serves as a repository for the know-how accumulated by HP over time. Internal knowledge management is important for learning from alliance experience and disseminating that know-how (discussed further in Chapter 7), complemented by internal training if the company has the resources to develop this.
34. Findings from Booz Allen's 1997 survey as cited in The Conference Board (1997a).
35. This is one of the management development areas in which Web-based distance learning may create opportunities for greater flexibility—providing access to just-in-time relevant information anywhere, including links to in-company alliance knowledge base.
36. The Conference Board, 1997.
37. The context of the relationship will determine the most beneficial development applications. However, off-the-shelf cultural training using the traditional "Doing Business with . . ." approach is probably of limited value—perhaps even dangerous in building stereotypes.
38. See Chapter 4, p. 166, box "Performance Doesn't Mean the Same Thing Everywhere."
39. Kerr, 1995.
40. A common incentive plan (e.g. stock options) could be a logical tool to support synergy among alliance staff. However, among various tax issues that hinder harmonization of compensation across boundaries, incentive plans are probably the area where the differences are the widest. In some countries, such as France, even the initial exercise of stock option rights is a taxable event, which makes awarding options risky and expensive. In addition, even when tax benefits are available, there are differences, for example, which kind of stock options qualifies for tax benefits in the United States and in Germany.
41. Geringer and Frayne, 1990.
42. Shenkar and Zeira, 1990.
43. Sometimes, expatriate cost alone makes a difference between profit and loss. In a dispute between Procter & Gamble and its Vietnamese partner, the local company alleged that the high cost of expatriates, brought in to deal with unanticipated product launch difficulties, caused the JV to incur major losses. The local partner was ultimately faced with the choice of accepting the JV bankruptcy or allowing P&G to gain equity control through a recapitalization that the local partner could not match ("P&G Plays Down Vietnam Venture Problems," Reuters, 1997).
44. Lorange, 1996.
45. Non-equity alliances are generally temporary and from a legal perspective have no "direct" employees. Even those who are assigned to the alliance on a full-time basis are typically paid by and report to their own parent. They expect to return to the parent organization, so that there is no confusion about the focus of their careers. Even if a foreign assignment is involved, a disciplined career development process, which ensures mentoring and a periodic dialogue with the employee, is generally all that is needed to avoid a sense of isolation.
46. Child and Faulkner, 1998; Parkhe, 1993.
47. Barkema, Shenkar et al., 1997; Westney, 1988.
48. Gomes-Casseres and McQuade, 1992.
49. Kennedy, 1989.
50. See Hedberg (1981) for an analysis of organizational learning. See Teece (1987) for a discussion of how learning ability depends on the ability to transfer tacit knowledge. See our Chapter 1, p. 33, for a discussion on invisible assets as a source of competitive advantage. Issues of transfer and creation of knowledge are discussed further in Chapters 7 and 9, respectively.

51. Hamel, 1991.
52. Pucik, 1988b.
53. For example, when both partners perceive the partnership as a complementary or resource alliance, the collaboration can be mutually beneficial for a long time without much need for new knowledge creation. However, as we discussed earlier in the chapter, the focus of the alliance often shifts as the partnership evolves.
54. Doz and Hamel, 1998.
55. R. Tomlinson, "Why So Many Western Companies Are Coming Down with China Fatigue," *Fortune*, May 25, 1998, pp. 60–64.
56. One of Europe's largest banks formed a learning alliance with a major Japanese bank about twenty years ago. The Japanese used this as an opportunity to send hundreds of managers over on two- to six-month learning assignments to Europe, during which time the Europeans only got around to sending two people to learn from the Japanese. By the time the financial services industry started to globalize seriously in the early 90s and the Europeans awakened to the benefits of the deal, the Japanese had reached their learning objectives and lost interest in maintaining the alliance.
57. Hamel, 1991.
58. Open discussion about learning needs may result in explicit limitations on knowledge exchange. A clear definition of what is in and what is out is preferable to the fuzziness of the learning boundaries that only encourages illicit behavior detrimental to trust between the partners.
59. Pucik and van Weering, 2000.
60. Westney, 1988; Schuler, 2000; Cyr, 1995; Cyr and Schneider, 1996.
61. Simonin, 1999.
62. Harrigan, 1988; Pucik, 1988b.
63. Lei, Slocum Jr. et al., 1997.
64. Conversely, if there is a perceived imbalance in career opportunities, employees may either be willing to move to the alliance venture but less willing to return to the parent, or conversely not want to move to the venture in the first place (Inkpen, 1997).
65. For more on NUMMI see also Chapter 3, p. 112.
66. O'Reilly, 1998.
67. Haasen, 1996.
68. As argued by Inkpen (1998), unexploited learning opportunities may in turn lead to perceptions that the performance of the alliance is not satisfactory.
69. Doz and Hamel, 1998.
70. J. Weber and A. Barrett, "Partners," *Business Week*, October 15, 1999, pp. 72–76.
71. Star Alliance links operations of thirteen major international airlines, such as United, Lufthansa, and Singapore. The member airlines coordinate schedules, share codes, match frequent flyer programs, and coordinate activities to benefit from lower costs in such areas as plane maintenance, ground service, and purchasing.
72. Pfeffer, 1998.
73. Project-oriented training is discussed in Chapter 8, including an example from Lufthansa.
74. The issue of the changing role of HR in an age of networks is discussed in Chapter 10.

CHAPTER 6

Forging Cross-Border Mergers and Acquisitions

On May 7, 1998, the CEO of Daimler-Benz AG Jürgen Schrempp and the CEO of Chrysler Robert Eaton announced that they had decided to get together in a "merger of equals." The deal was the largest industrial merger the world had ever seen, resulting in a new global company with over $130 billion in sales and more than 400,000 employees. Although Chrysler shares were priced with a 40 percent premium, the new DaimlerChrysler, with its headquarters in Stuttgart and registered under German commercial law, was 58 percent owned by former Daimler shareholders. The two CEOs became co-chairmen, although Eaton was expected to retire once the integration process was completed.

The merger was driven by what seemed an impeccable logic.[1] The product and geographical fit between a top European luxury-car manufacturer known for its engineering excellence and an efficient American maker of Jeeps and minivans known for innovative marketing seemed ideal. The main task would simply be to reap all the economies of scale in R&D and engineering. The two companies made a public commitment to obtain $1.4 billion in savings during the first year of the merger and to complete the integration process within three years—although the internal goal was to do this in twenty-four months.

The guiding principle behind the first wave of integration was to treat the two companies as equals, respecting differences in national and corporate cultures while taking full advantage of all opportunities for achieving synergy, under the banner of "one company—two cultures." After studying over fifty large-scale mergers to look for possible integration models, the company adopted a blended approach—delegating accountability for integration activities to individual executives, but under a central coordinating structure. The two co-chairmen and six other top executives (two from Chrysler and four from Daimler-Benz) formed the Chairmen's Integration Council. Ten other executives, five from each company, rounded off the management board. Each board member was jointly responsible for at least one of the twelve Issue Resolution Teams focused on functional challenges such as purchasing. Coordinators on these teams from each company formed the Post Merger Integration Team, which oversaw all integration activities—in total over a hundred projects.

While the initial savings were achieved fairly quickly, it became clear that the merger was proceeding with more difficulty than expected. Mercedes feared dilution of their brand image, and this stopped most of the ambitious plans to leverage each other's strengths. With no clear synergy between the two arms, the merger was heading toward a worst-of-both-worlds scenario. Second-guessing the intentions of the head office in Stuttgart led many Chrysler executives and middle managers to leave. Chrysler's president Stallkamp, a fervent believer in the importance of thoroughly integrating the two companies, was forced out in the summer of 1999, and Eaton himself left early in 2000.

With its aging product lineup in the United States and deteriorating market conditions, Chrysler's operational problems grew unheeded. At the time of the merger Chrysler had the highest profit per vehicle of any automotive company in the world, though by the fall of 2000 it was losing hundreds of millions of dollars per quarter. As a consequence, DaimlerChrysler shares lost more than 60 percent of their value over a two-year period, one of the biggest losses in shareholder value in German history. Chrysler's American president, hand-picked by Schrempp less than fifteen months before, was replaced by a duo of German executives who were dispatched to stop the bleeding. The company's autonomy was radically curtailed.

Meanwhile, Schrempp admitted in an interview with the *Financial Times* what everyone had long suspected—the acquisition was a takeover right from the start and was never supposed to be "a merger of equals." "Me being a chess player, I don't normally talk about the second or third move. The structure we have now with Chrysler [as a stand-alone division] was always the structure I wanted," Schrempp told the interviewer.

CHAPTER OVERVIEW

We start this chapter by reviewing the merger and acquisition (M&A) phenomenon—the many reasons why cross-border mergers such as DaimlerChrysler are attractive—and the startling statistics showing that most acquisitions do not meet their original objectives. We explore what contributes to success and failure. Here, the human and cultural factors associated with the acquisition process emerge as critical. We also introduce a framework for how to interpret the strategic logic behind the merger or acquisition, for this will determine the orientation of the integration process and the role of human resources in it.

In the second section of the chapter, we discuss the planning and preparation work that should be undertaken in order to explore targets and continue until the deal is closed. This is known as due diligence. The assessment of the strategic and financial factors needs to be complemented by equal attention to assessing the people and cultural factors ("cultural fit"). We pay special attention to conducting the cultural assessment and the human capital audit.

The third section focuses on the post-merger integration process, in which the formula for success combines speed with careful attention to HRM and people processes. We analyze key issues, starting with the implications of the so-called merger syndrome during the "first hundred days." Retention of key talent is an essential condition for success in most acquisitions, and so we review the steps necessary to make it happen. We also discuss how different aspects of the change process, including communication, need to be managed so as to facilitate the smooth integration of the new subsidiary into the parent firm, with an emphasis on the role of integration managers and transition teams.

Firms that are successful in acquisitions recognize that they must capture their learning so as to enhance their ability to execute acquisitions in the future. In this way M&A competence can become a vital source of competitive advantage in the global economy. This is the central idea in the concluding section, in which we summarize the chapter through the lens of what General Electric has learned over the years about how to conduct the complex process of acquiring and integrating another company.

THE M&A PHENOMENON

Mergers and acquisitions (M&A) are an increasingly popular alternative to greenfield investments and strategic alliances as a vehicle for internationalization. The growth in mergers and acquisitions in the global marketplace during the last decade was exceptional. The number of worldwide deals involving U.S. firms increased during the 1990s from about 3,500 to nearly 10,000, while the value increased more than tenfold from about $140 billion to over $1,700 trillion. Companies in Europe and other parts of the world joined in the game—these non-American deals went from about 6,000 in 1991 to 12,000 in 2000, and from $200 billion to $1,750 trillion in value.[2] Even if M&A fever is subsiding as the global economy cools off, more deals can be expected in the long run.

The fastest growing type of deal is the cross-border acquisition. More than 30 percent of the U.S. deals involved an international transaction in which a non-U.S. firm was either buyer or seller, with a total value of $470 billion. In the same year, nearly 2,500 cross-border deals in Europe had a value of over $500 billion (see Figure 6–1). The single European currency (the Euro) fueled this cross-border consolidation to a degree that few had anticipated even a couple of years before. Worldwide, the value of acquisitions outside the home country reached well over a trillion dollars.[3]

The ultimate driver of international M&A activity is the increase in global competition and the corresponding erosion of national boundaries. Until the 1980s international M&As were relatively rare since the governments in many countries did not look fondly on foreigners acquiring local assets. The liberalization of foreign direct investment resulting from the multilateral and GATT agreements over the last decades greatly accelerated the phenomenon. In industrial sectors such as oil or cement as well as "new economy" sectors such as telecommunication and software, internationalization is increasingly linked to acquisitions. And while the global mega-deals continue to grab the headlines, more and more cross-border acquisitions take place among small and medium-sized firms. Understanding the logic of such internationalization strategies and their human resource implications and mastering their implementation are becoming a required global management competency.

FIGURE 6–1. Trends in International Mergers and Acquisitions

U.S. Acquisitions Overseas
1991 to 2000

Foreign Acquisitions of U.S. Companies
1991 to 2000

*U.S. Dollars

*U.S. Dollars

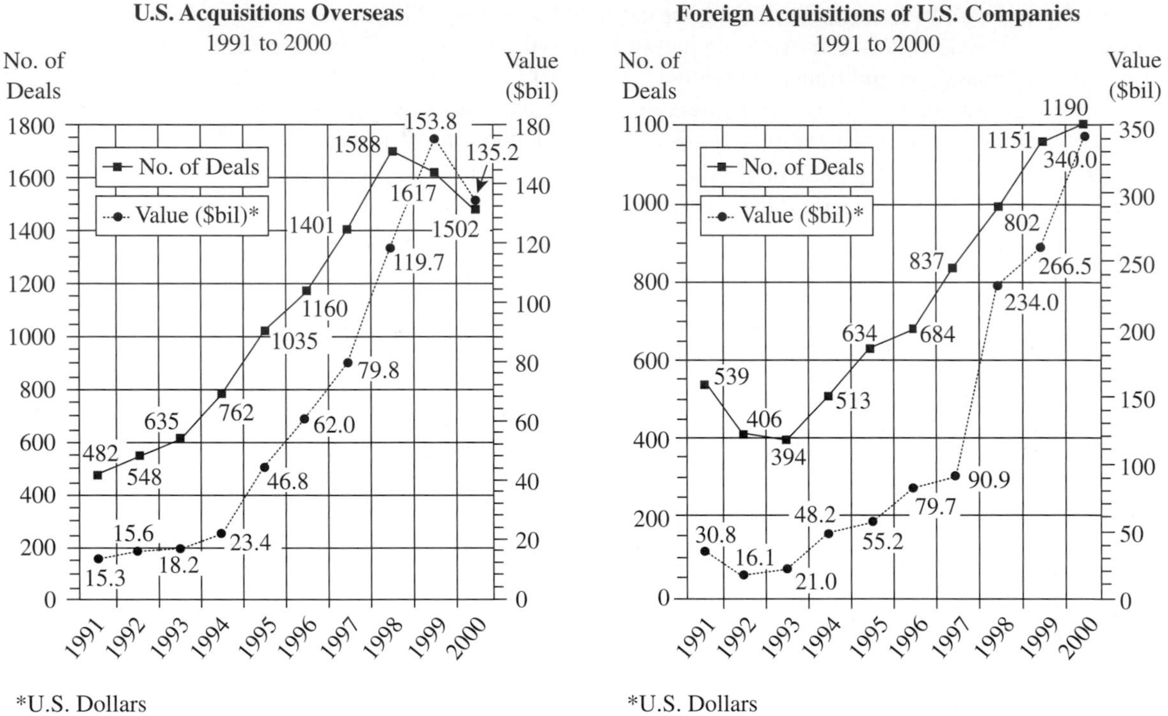

Source: Mergers and Acquisitions Almanac, February 2001, p. 37.

The Business Drivers of Mergers and Acquisitions

What is a merger and what is an acquisition? From a legal point of view, in a *merger* two companies join together and create a new entity. In an *acquisition,* one company acquires sufficient shares to gain control of the other organization. In reality, how the transaction is labeled depends mainly on the accounting and tax implications of the deal and strategies for public relations and communication. Some mergers are structured as acquisitions, while some acquisitions are framed as mergers. There are actually very few "mergers among equals." After the agreement is signed, most mergers look very much like acquisitions. We will focus primarily on acquisitions, which represent the majority of cross-border deals, referring to mergers when appropriate. What matters is the strategic intent, not the label.

Acquisition bids can be classified as "friendly" or "hostile." From the perspective of shareholders or top management most acquisitions are friendly, although the workforce often does not see it that way. There are clear winners and losers since "being acquired" is seen as a symbol of failure. Cross-border hostile acquisitions are still relatively rare. When they occur, they tend to generate strong emotions and a lot of public interest (the acquisition of German Mannesmann by the U.K.'s Vodafone was a landmark event in Europe). Erasing old organizational boundaries is difficult; eliminating barriers of national cultures is an additional challenge.[4]

There are a number of reasons why companies pursue cross-border mergers and acquisitions. These are outlined in the box "The Strategic Drivers of International M&As." Achieving competitive size and increasing market share by adding brands or distribution channels are the main reasons behind the majority of cross-border M&As.[5] Larger firms, emulating Jack Welch's GE mantra of "becoming global number 1 or number 2," aim to gain market power by acquiring companies in territories where they are not yet present. Or they pursue the "merger of equals" strategy to leapfrog their competitors—who then try to catch up through their own mergers. Smaller firms resort to cross-border deals to leverage their niche competencies in new markets more quickly than they would be able to do through organic expansion. Cross-border acquisition also seems to be a relatively fast method of responding to

The Strategic Drivers of International M&As
Practice Box

International mergers and acquisitions happen for multiple reasons. Some are strategic, some are tactical, and some involve corporate egos. Here are some current examples:

Market Dominance

Banks and insurance companies in Scandinavia are merging across the region to create Nordic financial institutions such as Nordea and SEB in order to gain economies of scale and control over distribution channels.

Geographical Expansion

Major global players in the brewing industry (Heineken, Interbrew) are using acquisitions to extend their geographical reach and global market share through new market entry.

Leveraging Competence

Foreign companies (General Electric, Axa) embarked on large-scale acquisitions in the financial industry in Japan, leveraging their competence in new product development, credit risk, and debt management.

Resource Acquisition

In the petroleum industry, acquiring existing companies with proven oil reserves can be a more economi-

cal way to grow than through investment in the exploration of new energy fields and sources (BP, Exxon).

Capability Acquisition

With market shift from voice to data transmission, European wireless manufacturers (Nokia, Ericsson) rushed to the United States to acquire small start-ups with competence in emerging data communication technologies.

Adjusting to Competition

Companies are sometimes forced into acquisitions by the acquisition strategies of their principal competitors. Matsushita launched its ultimately disastrous acquisitions in Hollywood after Sony purchased Columbia Pictures.

Executive Hubris

Most companies launch acquisitions for sound strategic reasons, although good strategy does not guarantee successes. However, there are also cases in which— whatever the press release says—the outside observers see no logic in the move beyond the CEO's desire to run a bigger company.

the twin pressures of globalization and diversification; here, the primary opportunities for value creation are likely to arise from cross-selling existing products or services and from accessing new markets.

HR issues dominate the agenda in some mergers and acquisitions. In high technology industries, an increasing number of acquisitions are motivated by the need to access talented people and their know-how. Often the employees are seen as more valuable than the company's product—price per engineer is what drives the price of such deals. In contrast, the strategic driver in other deals is consolidation and cost cutting. Here the focus is on workforce reduction, which in some countries may be as tricky as the retention of Silicon Valley entrepreneurs.

Alliance or Merger?

An alliance is often a first step toward an acquisition. In countries such as Korea in which emotional resistance to "foreign acquisition" may still be strong, gradual entry through a joint venture alliance with a local partner may be a particularly effective strategy. The alliance may reduce the risk of entry into an unfamiliar territory. And if the partnership is successful, then acquiring the partner's interest or the partner itself may be the next step. The timing and conditions for this evolution are frequently anticipated in the partnership agreement.[6]

On the other hand, settling for an alliance rather than making an acquisition may reduce control over decisions within the venture, including those on human resources. The consensual governance process in international alliances increases the costs and limits the possibilities for rationalization.[7] This was one of the main reasons for the failure of Swissair's strategy to expand into the European Union by acquiring minority stakes in Sabena and two ailing French airlines. Because of EU restrictions on airline ownership, Swissair had to accept a minority position. And this was not enough when difficult decisions regarding staff reductions and changes in work practices were to be made. Instead of turning the ailing airlines around, the loss-making partners dragged Swissair into bankruptcy.

From the HR perspective, the most significant difference between an alliance and an acquisition is that the former limits the degree of leverage over people-related decisions. The freedom to select, promote, and compensate people is such an important management tool that it leads many executives to favor acquisitions. On the other hand, retaining talent may be easier in a partnership, and alliances are often better at preserving entrepreneurship in the individual units. In a cross-border context, they are easier to align with the local environment.

When making a strategic decision about whether to build an alliance or pursue an acquisition, it is important to put the human resource considerations on the list. These may sometimes be difficult to resolve, as a U.S. start-up has discovered in an alliance with a smaller German partner to develop jointly breakthrough technology. In order to pursue an IPO (initial public offering), the company's investment bankers have pushed the two companies to merge so as to clarify ownership over the intellectual property rights. However, for the German company a merger would mean loss of independence, possibly sapping the motivation of its top engineers. In addition, the compensation philosophies in the two firms are radically different, highly leveraged toward stock options in the United States but with more traditional salary structures in Germany, so the employee gains from an IPO would be asymmetrical. As this book goes to print, the two boards are still debating which way to go.

Observing the M&A Experience

Given the rapid increase in M&A transactions in all regions of the world, the obvious question to ask is to what extent all these corporate marriages have worked. What contributes to the successes? And to what extent do HR factors account for the failures?

How Successful Are Mergers and Acquisitions?

There are no large-scale studies focusing on international acquisitions, although the database on acquisitions in general is rather extensive. Research has been mainly conducted by consulting firms and investment banks, and it seems to suggest that only a few of the deals during the 1990s achieved the promised financial results:[8]

- A widely cited 1997 *Business Week*/Mercer study reported that over a ten-year period, two out of three deals have not worked as planned. According to *Fortune* only 23 percent of U.S. acquisitions earned their cost of capital.[9]
- Not surprisingly, financial markets are skeptical. According to a study conducted by the U.S. investment bank Salomon Smith Barney, the shares of acquirers underperformed the S&P index as well as their peer groups.[10]
- A more recent 1999 study conducted by A. T. Kearney asserts that 75 percent of merging firms fall short of meeting the strategic goals that inspired the merger and that 58 percent of them actually destroyed shareholder value. The study concluded that "on balance, mergers hurt shareholders."[11]
- According to a study of cross-border acquisitions sponsored by KPMG, 17 percent of deals increased shareholder value, 30 percent left it unchanged, and 53 percent decreased it.[12]

While the overall success rate appears to be quite unsatisfactory, there is also some unexpected evidence that the success rate of cross-border deals may be higher than for purely domestic transactions.[13] The main reason is that cross-border acquirers buy companies in familiar businesses to which they can add value. They also execute multiple acquisitions, not one-of-a-kind deals, learning from mistakes and accumulating experience, putting in place tools and processes that enable them to execute cross-border deals more and more effectively. Moreover, the cross-cultural issues lead them to pay great attention to the "softer," less tangible but critical HR aspects of M&A management. Some firms such as GE and Cisco view competence in making international acquisitions as one of their core capabilities.[14]

Research on acquisitions is full of interesting paradoxes regarding the motives and behaviors of acquiring companies and their managers (see the box "The Acquisition Paradox"), reflecting the underlying complexity of designing and implementing merger and acquisition strategies. Much of that complexity is related to human factors.

The Acquisition Paradox
Research Box

Research on acquisitions highlighted numerous paradoxes. Here are a few examples.

1. A study of United States banks *showed that merged banks cut costs more slowly than banks that did not merge.*[A] In other words, merged banks were too busy merging to cut costs, while others acted more aggressively to improve their operations.

2. Another survey showed that *increasing revenues by 1 percent has five times greater impact on shareholder value than decreasing operating expenses; yet managers in most acquisitions spend the bulk of their time searching for ways to reduce expenses.*[B] In acquisitions and mergers, companies talk a lot about creating synergies and about the lower costs of the combined operations. But there may be a greater impact on shareholder value if the merged companies focused on increasing revenues rather than reducing cost.

3. According to one management scholar, *nearly half the time top management spends on M&A goes into creating the deal, in contrast to 8 percent of time devoted to implementation.*[C] Far too much management time is spent on the deal itself rather than making it work.

[A] "Making the Mergers Work," *The Economist,* January 9, 1999, p. 25.
[B] Feldman, 1995.
[C] Kanter, 1989.

Why Do Acquisitions Fail?

There is little doubt that acquisitions, particularly those that reach across borders, are complex and difficult to get right. The business press is full of stories of international mergers and acquisitions that failed to meet the original objectives. Even when the merged firm should apparently enjoy great synergy benefits, one of the major reasons for failure is the *difference in the vision* about where the two sides want the combined entity to go. For the sake of the deal, these differences are often glossed over. But if firms do not start with a common and *specific* understanding of where they want to take the new organization and how they want to get there, the process of integration is likely to be fraught with destructive internal politics, as with the case of DaimlerChrysler.

The acquisition can fail because of *attrition of talent and capabilities,* or because of the *loss of intangible assets.* Customers are not asked for their opinions about the merger and they may feel disgruntled about being passed on to another entity. That can lead to a loss of potential value almost overnight. Relationships with vendors, community, and government can also suffer when the new owner is perceived, rightly or wrongly, as insensitive to local interests.

An Egon Zehnder study reported that lack of clarity around systems and processes in the acquiring company is the major problem in at least a quarter of all acquisitions.[15] This also means that firms that are pursuing an internationalization strategy based on local responsiveness will find it more difficult to handle acquisitions than those with tightly integrated approaches.

International mergers can also suffer from underestimating the *high transition and coordination costs* in linking the new entities owing to physical distance, negating some of the advantages of the potential synergies. Related to that is the danger of *synergy gridlock,* a situation when management so desperately searches for ways to deliver the savings promised to the stock market that it loses track of the business and costs begin to spiral up.

Finally, the failure of international mergers and acquisitions may be linked to the *lack of "cultural fit"* between the two organizations. It is often said that companies should not entertain deals for which a significant cultural mismatch might be a problem. Differences in history, environment, and national culture will amplify the difficulties of achieving the merger aims.

In spite of such difficulties, companies will continue to acquire and merge as they seek to accelerate their international growth. Companies which learn how to manage mergers and acquisitions well so as to overcome the obstacles mentioned above can benefit from significant advantages—and not only because of scale. They are more flexible. They can acquire needed competencies more quickly in an era when these are often located in another country. And the know-how to acquire and integrate new competencies boosts their confidence in selling businesses to other companies or sectors which can more easily add value. Most of the opportunities for improving the success in managing mergers and acquisitions are related to people and human resource management.

What Do We Know about Key Success Factors?

In acquisitions, *size and business focus* do matter. Winners in the merger game tend to acquire companies that are smaller and that are either in the same business or a closely related business. French automotive component manufacturer Valeo successfully expanded its international reach by buying smaller companies or those with narrow product lines. In contrast, according to at least some observers, one-third of so-called "mergers of equals" significantly destroy value.[16]

What happens before a deal is signed is important. A well-thought-out strategy and thorough due diligence have a significant impact on the ultimate success. However, even well-negotiated deals have to come to terms with the complexities of merging organizations across boundaries. The highest returns go to organizations that execute the *postmerger integration process* effectively.[17] The ability to add value in the merged company depends mostly on what happens after the deal is done.

Managing integration involves combating the winner-loser syndrome, preparing the employees for the change, setting up a transition organization, and preparing the schedule for the changes; and putting in place the new structure, policies, and practices. Integration is a change process. Not surprisingly, companies that have a good track record in managing change also tend to be good at managing acquisitions.[18]

Companies that have solid foundations in HRM and other domains of management are at an advantage when it comes to mergers and acquisitions. Each side needs to teach the other how it goes about business, and this is difficult unless good foundations are in place. The ideal merger is one in which each company has clear policies and practices in areas such as HRM so that the new company can pick from the best practices on either side and integrate them into a coherent whole, or introduce innovations into the practices of the acquiring firm. A firm such as GE is able to move fast and confidently with its integration strategy when it acquires a company largely because its own systems and practices are well developed and quite explicit (we will discuss the approach of GE Capital later in this chapter).

However, probably the most consistent predictor of success is past experience in acquisitions. The more the company merges, the better it gets at merging and the stronger the talent and experience for the next merger.[19] The ability to learn from past acquisitions, including the mistakes that are inevitably made, is one characteristic that many successful acquirers such as GE, Cisco, and BP have in common.

Frameworks for Thinking about M&A

In successful mergers and acquisitions, partners share the purpose and accept the terms of their relationship. However, the reality is that corporate marriages are often based on unattainable assumptions. Carefully defining and making explicit what is the purpose of the acquisition and what is the desired end-state are the first steps in making the new relationship work. Managers and employees in the new entity are then able to focus on the business and let go of any wishful thinking that may run counter to the reality of the deal. Surely, people may resent and resist change, but they are likely to adapt if they know clearly what the new rules of the game are that will allow them to be successful in the future.

What Is the Intent behind the Deal?

One way to think about the M&A process is to consider the strategic intent behind the acquisition and its implications for the execution of the deal. According to Bower, acquisitions occur mainly for five reasons—to deal with overcapacity through consolidation; to expand geographically; to extend product line or market coverage; to acquire technology; or to foster industry convergence. Each has its own integration logic and HR challenges.[20] For example, in the *overcapacity acquisition*, one has to expect conflict and struggle for control, especially if the acquired company is as large as the acquiring one. In contrast, the *geographic acquisition* offers more opportunities for win-win outcomes. The chances for success of *extension acquisitions* tend to increase with prior acquisition experience, while *technology acquisitions* are dependent on the ability to retain talent.

It may be useful to assess the complexity of the acquisition task by asking whether this is a traditional or a transformational acquisition (see the box "Traditional versus Transformational Acquisitions"). The former uses the traditional skills of exploitation, leveraging existing capabilities through rationalization or transfer. The latter involves more complex exploration skills so as to create new capabilities or to do things differently.

Transformational mergers or acquisitions must be managed in a very different way from traditional acquisitions, with a great deal more focus on human resource issues. They are more risky, and since the emphasis is essentially on reinventing the company, they are much more complex from the organizational and HR perspective.

Traditional versus Transformational Acquisitions
Practice Box

The type of M&A deal can influence many of the factors related to HRM. Most transactions can be categorized into one of two types. The first exploits existing capabilities, and the second explores new ways of doing things.[A]

Traditional M&A

Consolidation M&A: These deals are aimed at rationalization, reduction of overcapacity, and improved competitiveness. There are many international acquisitions of this kind: examples include BP/Amoco in oil and petrochemicals, and Aerospatiale/Matra/Dessault in the aerospace industry.

Resource M&A: In this case, acquisitions are used to secure scarce resources. These may include technology, talented people, or access to the customer. For example, most of Cisco's acquisitions target new know-how, while Wal-Mart bought several German retailers to enter the local market.

Expansion M&A: Companies such as Volkswagen or Nestlé use international acquisitions to rapidly grow their brand portfolio, geographic reach, or both. GE Capital acquires financial companies in new markets in which it can leverage its know-how and access to funding.

Transformational M&A

"New Portfolio" M&A: The purpose is to refocus the portfolio of business that the company is engaged in through a steady stream of acquisitions, usually together with divestments of businesses that the firm is no longer interested in. An example is ICI's shift from generic to speciality chemicals, or Nokia's more radical transition from the paper and pulp sector to telecommunications.

"New Business Model" M&A: The aim here is to create a new business model by capturing scale/scope/asset advantages created by the acquisition. An example is the emergence of a global universal financial company such as Allianz or Citigroup through the merger of a bank and insurance company.

"Global Leap" M&A: In this most complex type of international merger, the objective is a dramatic expansion of geographical reach and/or product range, often together with cultural transformation. Daimler/Chrysler and Vodafone/Airtouch are two recent examples of such acquisitions.

[A.]The basic source for these observations is Steger (1999).

Failure to understand the differences can be costly, even deadly. Kvaerner used acquisitions to jump from being a Norwegian shipbuilder to becoming a global engineering company, successfully managing a series of domestic resource type acquisitions. But when it acquired U.K.-based Trafalgar it moved toward a large-scale *new business model acquisition,* without understanding that this was a different situation, in which the old integration mechanisms might not work. The merger failed since the company neither had the management capacity nor the cash to make the cross-border and multicountry transformation a success.[21]

What Kind of Organization Do You Want?

A typical M&A agreement spells out in detail the financial details of the deal. What happens thereafter depends on the process of combining the two entities. Many factors will influence what kind of organization and culture will emerge from the deal—the motives for the merger, the industry dynamics, complementarity of skills and capabilities, coordination needs, management style, implementation skills.

One simple but powerful framework for approaching acquisitions frames them in terms of two dimensions: the degree of strategic interdependence between the two companies and their needs for organizational autonomy.[22] When the acquisition is motivated by strategic interdependence but the needs for autonomy are equally strong, a careful symbiotic integration of the two units may be the desirable path. But when the degree of strategic interdependence is low, a preservation strategy that leaves the acquired company largely alone may be a better route, unless the autonomy need is also low—in which case absorption of the acquired firm may be the best path.

An alternative way of formulating the acquisition logic, as shown in Figure 6–2, is to focus on the cultural "end-state" and the path to reach this. What kind of culture is desired for the new entity and how much change will be required within both acquiring and acquired companies in order to get there?[23]

When no cultural change in the acquired company is desired, then it can be considered a *preservation acquisition.* When a large amount of change in the acquired company is expected but with relatively little change for the acquirer, then *absorption* is the most likely path. An expectation of major cultural change in both entities results in a *cultural transformation,* while the selective combination of the most appealing features of the two cultures is often described as a *"best of both" acquisition.* In rare cases, the culture of the acquirer is blended into that of the acquired firm in a *reverse merger.*

FIGURE 6–2. Strategies for Post-Merger Outcomes

High	**ABSORPTION** Acquired Company Conforms to Acquirer– Cultural Assimilation		**TRANSFORMATION** Both Companies find New Ways of Operating– Cultural Transformation
Degree of Change in Acquired Company		**BEST OF BOTH** Additive from Both Sides– Cultural Integration	
Low	**PRESERVATION** Acquired Company Retains its Independence– Cultural Autonomy		**REVERSE MERGER** Unusual Case of Acquired Company Dictating Terms– Cultural Assimilation
	Low		*High*
	Degree of Change in Acquiring Company		

Source: P. M. Mirvis and M. L. Marks, *Managing the Merger: Making It Work* (Upper Saddle River, NJ: Prentice Hall, 1994).

PRESERVATION ACQUISITIONS. When such a deal is announced, there is often a reference to the acquired company's preserving its independence and cultural autonomy. One of the rationales behind the merger is to get hold of talented management or other soft skills (such as speed of product development) and retain them. Or conformance to the acquiring company rules and systems could be detrimental to the acquired company's competitive advantage.

The key to success here is to protect the boundary of the new subsidiary from unwarranted and disruptive intrusions from the parent, although this can be hard to ensure. Even with the best of intentions, there can be a form of creeping assimilation as the acquiring company encourages the acquired one to begin to work in the same way and to develop systems and processes which match those of the parent organization.

Because of operational pressures, most stand-alone acquisitions do not last. While the acquired company may appear independent to the outside world, some functions at least are merged with the rest of the organization. Or else "stand-alone" is a temporary phenomenon, until other aspects of the strategy are realized such as further acquisitions.

ABSORPTION ACQUISITIONS. This kind of acquisition is fairly straightforward, and it is probably most common when there are differences in size and sophistication between the two partners in the deal. The acquired company conforms to the acquirer's way of working, with a focus on full cultural assimilation. Such deals are particularly common when the acquired company is performing poorly, or when the market conditions force consolidation.

Most of the synergies may be related to cost cutting, most likely on the side of the acquired company, although some may come from improvements in systems and processes brought in by the acquiring firm. The key to success is to choose the target well, to move fast so as to eliminate uncertainty, and to capture the available synergies.

But absorption does not necessarily mean large-scale firings and layoffs. Cisco, for example, buys companies for their technology and R&D talent and then assimilates them into the Cisco culture, but it attempts to retain most of the employees, including top management. Here, the emphasis is on finding targets that will match Cisco's way of managing the business, increasing the likelihood of cultural compatibility.

REVERSE MERGER. This is a mirror opposite of assimilation, and it does not happen very often. Usually the organization that buys hopes to gain capabilities from the one it bought. The acquired company becomes a business unit that absorbs the parallel unit in the acquiring firm. When Nokia, for instance, bought a high tech firm in California for its R&D knowledge, it gave the new unit global responsibilities, which meant that part of the business in Finland now reports to California.

Sometimes, the reverse merger is unintended. A few years ago, a French metal product company acquired its smaller British competitor. Today, to the surprise of many, the management style and systems of the new company resemble the culture of the acquired firm. What happened? When the two companies merged, it was easier for everyone to adopt the explicit and transparent systems of the British firm, more suitable for cross-border business, than to emulate the more ambiguous and subtle rules embedded in the French organization. If the practices of the company that has been acquired are clearer and more transparent, it is quite possible that they will prevail.

BEST OF BOTH. The intriguing option is the "best of both," often described as a "merger of equals." This holds out the promise of no pain since in theory it takes the best practices from both sides and integrates them. There are, however, very few examples of such mergers that have succeeded since it is very difficult to do. The strength of a culture comes from the internal consistency of the practices, which may not be there when the "best" parts are put together. Another danger in the "best of both" integration process is that it may become too political and time consuming. Who decides what is "best"?

The process of making the decisions can be very complex. If two companies declare that the merger is one of equals, does that mean top management is split 50/50, even if in terms of excellence the real split is 80/20? The controversy surrounding the Daimler/Chrysler merger is a visible example of this frequent dilemma. Without strong mutual respect for the knowledge and skills of each company, this kind of strategy will not work.

The key to success is the fairness of the process. The test of the "best of both" approach may be the ability to keep the people who do not get the top jobs. Having similar cultures helps. The AstraZeneca and Exxon/Mobil mergers have proceeded relatively smoothly because the similarities were more pronounced than the differences. The new groups have been relatively successful at identifying the best practices from each side, as well as having a balance of top management from the two firms.

TRANSFORMATION. In contrast with "best of both" acquisitions that take the existing cultures as they are, both companies in a transformation merger are hoping to use the merger to break sharply with the past. Merger or acquisition can be the catalyst for trying to do things differently, to reinvent oneself. This can involve the way in which the company is run, what business it is in, or both. When Novartis was created by the merger of two Swiss-based pharmaceutical firms, the proposed management style for the new company reflected the desired transformation: "We will listen more than Sandoz, but decide more than Ciba."

Another example of transformation is Nortel, the telecom equipment manufacturer. Several years ago it bought Bay Networks in California to spearhead its shift away from voice to digital and optical networks. It also moved its headquarters to California (though retaining Canada as its legal base) with the aim of benefiting from Bay Networks' culture of speed and entrepreneurship. This was a case of the parent company changing its culture by incorporating learning from the junior partner. It also led to a new name, a new management style, and a new business strategy.

This kind of merger is obviously the most complex and the most difficult to implement. It requires full commitment, with focus and strong leadership at the top so as to avoid getting trapped in endless debates while the ongoing business suffers (Percy Barnevik's transformation of Asea and Brown Boveri is one positive crossborder example).

What Is the Difference between Assimilation and Integration?

The framework above is useful for understanding an important distinction in approaches to implementing cross-border acquisitions: assimilation versus integration. Most companies use the term "integration" to describe the post-merger activities designed to bind the acquiring and acquired companies. But what happens is actually assimilation—a process fundamentally different from that of integration. As when acquisitions are described as mergers, this is another example of how euphemisms are used, sometimes misguidedly, to gloss over the realities.

The logic of assimilation is simple: make the acquired company just like the purchaser, as in absorption acquisitions. However, companies are sensitive to public perceptions of being a foreign bully, and they are often hesitant to proclaim their objective of assimilating the acquired firm, fearing that it may compromise the deal. But this often creates confusion and mistrust. In contrast, GE Capital, the financial services arm of General Electric, offers blunt advice to the management of firms that it acquires around the world: "If you do not want to change, don't put yourself for sale." GE makes it very clear to the acquired company that it now has to play by GE's rules, and it provides a framework in which to do so.

In the case of true integration, the emphasis is on capturing hidden synergies by swapping and leveraging capabilities. At times, the companies may decide to establish a new identity, as with Novartis, which was formed through the merger of Ciba-Geigy and Sandoz in 1996 to create a global life sciences giant. Or the objective may be sharing strengths while maintaining separate identities, as was the publicized strategic intent of DaimlerChysler described in the introductory case study.

Both approaches to M&A implementation have their merits. The choice of either assimilation or integration depends on the strategic intent behind the acquisition and the desired cultural characteristics in the new organization. Choosing an approach that does not match with the strategy or the desired cultural outcome can significantly reduce the value created by the acquisition, if not doom the whole deal. When Deutsche Bank acquired U.K.-based investment bank Morgan Grenfell, the strategic intent was to build a global financial powerhouse. However, heavy-handed attempts to assimilate Morgan's aggressive free-wheeling entrepreneurs into the bureaucratic and centralized culture of Deutsche simply did not work. Within the first two years after the merger, many top ranking Morgan Grenfell contributors left, destroying the value of the very assets that had made the deal attractive in the first place.

Yet too much caution can also be counterproductive. When Japan's Bridgestone purchased U.S.-based Firestone, it refrained from making significant changes in the organization, even though the acquired company was losing money. Bridgestone did not want to be seen as "ugly Japanese" taking over a venerable local institution. In reality, many local middle managers were looking forward to the takeover, expecting that their new owners would tackle both the unions and the entrenched old-style top management—but when nothing happened, they left in droves. Faced with growing losses, Tokyo finally moved in several years later to "clean up the mess." But it was too late. The company was now too thin on talent. Firestone never fully recovered, and today the once powerful brand is on the verge of extinction.

It is also worth noting that companies that are good at assimilation may not be very effective integrators, as we saw in the example of Kvaerner on page 259. Assimilation and integration require very different organizational routines, and mastering both simultaneously is a formidable task. As we will discuss later in greater detail, past experience with acquisitions does not necessarily guarantee success when the company enters unfamiliar territory.

Finally, a complicating factor in international acquisitions is that there will often be parts of the organization in which a particular approach to the merger makes sense and others in which it does not. There are few M&As that fit neatly into the assimilation, integration, or other categories. For some countries or regions, or for some parts of the business, a full assimilation may be the best approach; in other parts of the firm, a reverse merger could be a more appropriate strategy. Time and the degree of competition are also important—one cannot search forever for a perfect partner.

Key Human Resources Issues

There is no shortage of evidence that attention to "soft" factors or people issues is one of the most critical elements in making the acquisition strategy work. In a recent McKinsey study of international M&A, the four top ranked factors identified by responding firms as contributing to acquisition success are all people related:

- Retention of key talent (identified by 76 percent of responding firms).
- Effective communication (71 percent).
- Executive retention (67 percent).
- Cultural integration (51 percent).[24]

A similar conclusion can be drawn from the Conference Board study cited earlier. At the top of the list of HR concerns in mergers and acquisition is the *retention of critical talent* identified as a very important or important factor by 86 percent of the respondents. Second on the list is "blending culture," listed by 83 percent of the respondents, closely followed by retention of key executives (82 percent). Differences in approaches to compensation/benefits were ranked fourth (73 percent). Perhaps surprisingly, impact on the workforce size (37 percent), downsizing (35 percent), and redeployment of employees (25 percent) are at the bottom of the list.

Finally, in another recent survey sponsored by KPMG, the three "keys to success" were selecting the management team, resolving cultural issues, and communication.[25] For example, companies that are in the planning stage prioritized the selection of the management team were 26 percent more likely to execute a successful acquisition. An early focus on identifying and resolving the organizational culture issues had a similar impact on success.

In fact, it is hard to find an acquisition in which people issues do not matter. When the objective is to establish a new geographic presence, then managing cross-cultural, language, and communication issues tops the list of priorities. When the aim is to acquire new technology or to buy market share or competencies, retaining key technical staff or account managers is the principal challenge. When the objective of the deal is consolidation, dealing effectively with redundancies at all levels is the dominant concern.

On the basis of these observations, it may be seen as natural that the HR function should play a significant role in all phases of the acquisition. Yet while this tends to be true during the merger implementation phase, the overall influence that HR has during the whole acquisition process is spotty. In addition, many companies have neither the resources nor the know-how to give this HR area the priority it merits.[26]

WHEN SHOULD HR GET INVOLVED? Although it does not always do so, the human resource function can make a substantial contribution at all stages of the acquisition process. As noted earlier, this depends on the type of acquisition—transformational acquisitions should demand far more attention to HRM than traditional acquisitions. But according to a study of eighty-eight major corporations in the United States and Europe conducted by the Conference Board, HR is involved in the M&A planning in less than a quarter of responding firms. HR involvement is marginally higher during the negotiation stage, but it is only after the deal is signed that 80 percent of the firms see HR as fully engaged. It is obviously not easy for HR to ensure the smooth implementation of the deal when it has had little or no part in shaping it. U.S.-based companies seem to put somewhat more emphasis on getting early HR involvement than their European counterparts.

One reason for "keeping HR out of the room" is the secrecy surrounding most acquisitions before the bid or agreement is announced. In many companies, communication about pending acquisitions is treated, for commercial as well as regulatory reasons, as strictly confidential, disseminated on a need-to-know basis. HR is not seen as having any need to know. A determining factor is whether the top human resource executive is a member of the senior management team and a full participant in the strategy planning process. HR is unlikely to be involved if it is not already perceived as a valuable contributor to strategy development.

FROM PLANNING TO CLOSING

A typical cross-border acquisition starts with the development of the acquisition strategy and the selection of a company to acquire. An integral part of the selection process is the evaluation of the feasibility of the acquisition—known as "due diligence." This examination moves to the center stage when formal negotiations begin with the company to be acquired (or a hostile takeover bid is launched). If the negotiations or takeover are successful, the transaction proceeds to closing as long as the conclusion of the due diligence investigation is positive.

Some companies create a special acquisition unit that is involved in the planning and execution of every transaction.[27] Much of what is done during the planning and negotiation stage requires specialized and often highly technical financial and legal expertise. However, such units should not work in isolation from the managers who will have the responsibility for implementing the strategy and/or managing the acquisition. At GE, the future business leader and the designated HR manager are part of the acquisition team from the very beginning.

Planning Acquisitions: The HRM Perspective

Without doubt the most important contribution that HR can make during acquisition planning is to assure that the due diligence process covers all the important HRM considerations, including culture assessment and a human capital audit. Research has shown that cultural compatibility or incompatibility is relevant in many domestic acquisitions, and it is probably the most talked about factor when acquisitions take place across borders. We will come back to this issue in the next section.

Another important component of the acquisition planning is making sure that the company has in place the appropriate leadership team. When Renault considered acquiring a 37 percent stake in Nissan, a big factor in the decision-making process was its confidence that it had a team of seasoned managers who could be dispatched to Japan to guide the restructuring efforts. In the words of Renault's chairman Louis Schweitzer: "If I didn't have Mr. Ghon [who was sent by Renault to Tokyo to become president of Nissan], I would not have done the deal with Nissan. That means I sent him in because I had absolute confidence in his ability."[28] Contrast this with the Daimler "merger" with Chrysler that saw three teams of top executives during the first two years after the acquisition.

In international acquisitions, human resource strategy cannot be separated from its cultural and social context. Often the company may not have any expertise in the particular country or geographical area, so it is important to plan early how to mobilize the necessary resources to guide the firm through unfamiliar territory. At this early stage it is also important to provide the necessary orientation to the members of the due diligence team, who are likely to be selected for their analytical and technical skills, not because of their familiarity with the culture and the environment of the target firm.

Some HRM issues that may have a direct bearing on selection of the acquisition candidates are: What is possible and what is out of bounds? How to get a quick reading on the quality of human assets before committing resources to full-scale due diligence? Here HR can serve as a valuable resource and a sounding board, providing it has the capacity to obtain and analyze the information. No one can expect HR to have all the information readily available, but in the words of a GE HR manager who participated in planning a number of acquisitions: "Even if you know the industry, each acquisition is different: different culture, legal framework, management team in place. We are at the table not because we have all the answers, but we certainly know the questions that we have to ask."

Finally, even at the planning stage it is important to figure out broadly how success will be measured and how to learn from the pending acquisition experience. As the saying goes: "Success has many fathers, but failure is an orphan." It is not easy to discover what went wrong after the fact, and valuable insights are often lost if they are not recorded in "real time." Facilitating the process of knowledge retention is a contribution that HR should be well equipped to handle, starting at the planning stage.

The Due Diligence Process

Getting the strategy right depends very much on doing the homework. Good planning is not possible without good data. Due diligence in an acquisition has two aspects. One is, of course, to clarify the legal, financial, and business picture. The infrastructure to get this kind of information is well developed, as are the analytic methodologies. The other aspect, equally important but often neglected, is learning about the "soft" factors influencing the fit between the two organizations, such as the culture and the people practices in the target organization. Since the soft issues are among the most critical factors determining acquisition success, as discussed above, it is important to understand this side of the deal before proceeding.

The Art of Being Truly Diligent

In cross-border acquisitions, the due diligence team must be sensitive to the fact that attitudes toward acquisition due diligence vary from country to country.[29] Under Anglo-Saxon practice, lawyers and their clients expect comprehensive due diligence before the acquisition is completed. In other countries, due diligence may be interpreted as intrusive at best, or as so many signs of mistrust or bad intentions on the buyer's part. Getting information about the people side of the business, such as the quality of the management team, requires particular care.

A due diligence team from a U.S. company and their consultant visited a senior Japanese banker in his office to solicit opinions about an internal candidate to be installed soon as the CEO of their new acquisition. Since the banker did not express any reservations, the team felt confident about their selection. At the conclusion of the cordial meeting, the banker invited the team members to dinner that evening. This was politely declined, as it conflicted with the time reserved for a videoconference with HQ, but the consultant (always eager for a good sushi) decided to accept the invitation. During the dinner, the banker presented a list of reasons why the choice was wrong. Why didn't he tell the visitors directly? "But I did," replied the banker. "Why would I otherwise invite them to dinner?"

The typical list of topics on the HR due diligence can easily run to several pages, especially if the acquirer comes from North America (see the box "A Human Resource Due Diligence Checklist" for the broad categories of issues to investigate). As time is short, it is important to start with key priorities rather than getting lost in technical details. Some items are checked to protect the company against potential financial exposure, such as pension plan liabilities, employee grievances, and litigation. Others reflect the strategic intent of the acquisition, such as talent identification, employee rights to technology, trade secrets, and confidentiality.

Where does this information come from? In the first stage, HR due diligence is a part of building the overall acquisition roadmap. Former employees, industry experts, consultants, executive search firms, and customers who know the company are usually the best source. Cultivating some of these sources on a longer-term basis helps to mediate the constraints of confidentiality. Some of this data may be in the public domain, and Web-based search engines can speed up the process of finding the information. Once the agreement to acquire or merge is reached, HR records and interviews with managers in the target company can be used to supplement and verify the assessment.

Transparency and accessibility of this information vary from country to country. Companies often bemoan lack of information when in fact the real issue is lack

A Human Resource Due Diligence Checklist
Practice Box

Organization and Management

Organization Charts
   Job Title Hierarchy
Management Committees
Succession Plans
Employment Contracts
Employment Agreements

HR Policies

Hiring Procedures
Employment Documents
Job Descriptions
Work Rules
   Vacation Policy
   Discipline
Performance Management
Early Retirement
Termination/Severance

Compensation/Benefits

Executive Compensation
General Compensation
Incentive Compensation
   Bonus Eligibility
   Stock Plans
Pension Plan
   Coverage
   Assets and Liabilities
Nonmonetary Rewards

Labor Relations

Litigations and Claims

HRIS (Human Resource Information Systems)

   Employee Records

of familiarity with the local sources for this information. Often information about HR policies is relatively easy to obtain, although the problem is the amount. For example, acquiring a firm in the U.S. may involve reviewing over twenty categories of benefit plans and policies, going back six years to understand all the potential tax liabilities.[30] However HR due diligence is not just about collecting reams of data in order to avoid potential financial landmines or to be ready to harmonize the policies and practices quickly after the deal, important though these tasks may be. The fundamental purpose is to understand how the HR system impacts on the values, norms, and behaviors of the company to be acquired.

To do this well is not easy, even in domestic acquisitions. Less than a third of United States HR professionals consider that HR was effective in the due diligence phase of acquisitions.[31] The process of collecting "soft" due diligence data typically assumes friendly relations between the parties. Often companies believe that this kind of information is not available abroad, especially during the initial planning stage when secrecy and confidentiality are important. Of course, access to information is especially constrained in the case of a hostile acquisition.

What is often lacking is not information, but discipline and rigor in collecting and analyzing the data. Two methodologies can be especially useful here: culture assessment and the human capital audit.

Cultural Due Diligence

We have already introduced the issue of cultural assessment in the context of selecting alliance partners.[32] This is even more critical with respect to mergers and acquisitions, because organizational culture issues come out close to the top of the list of factors influencing M&A success. Despite this, culture assessment is generally not given priority *before* the deal is done. In a survey of European executives actively involved in mergers and acquisitions the assessment of cultural fit came close to the bottom in terms of importance.[33] It is therefore not surprising that culture clashes are so often a source of difficulties after the deal is done.

Much of the research on organizational culture focuses either on assessing beliefs and values or on observing behaviors, with less emphasis on surfacing underlying assumptions. Evaluating culture in due diligence is not as simple as comparing numerical scores and looking for a perfect fit. Indeed, Marks and Mirvis argue that if the cultures of the merging companies are identical, a combined organization will not necessarily be better than the sum of its parts.[34] As depicted in Figure 6–3, a moderate degree of cultural distinctiveness may be beneficial. The best acquisitions occur when a fair amount of culture clash prompts positive debate about what is most appropriate for the new organization. Ideally, this debate includes consideration of cultural norms that may be present in one of the two firms but that are desired in the combined organization.

FIGURE 6–3. Cultural Differences and M&A Outcomes

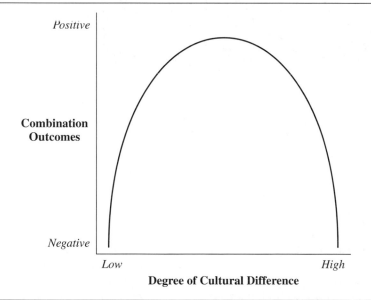

Source: Adapted from M. L. Marks and P. H. Mirvis, *Joining Forces: Making One Plus One Equal Three in Mergers, Acquisitions, and Alliances* (San Francisco: Jossey-Bass, 1998), 67.

HOW TO ASSESS THE CULTURE OF THE TARGET FIRM. The purpose of cultural assessment is to evaluate factors that may influence the organizational fit, to understand the future cultural dynamics as the two organizations merge, and to prepare a plan of how the cultural issues should be addressed if the deal goes forward. Depending on the stage of the negotiations and the resources available, cultural assessment can be formal or informal, based on a variety of potential sources such as market intelligence, external data, surveys, and interviews. What is important is to have at least a rudimentary framework that helps to organize the issues and draw the proper conclusions.[35]

Some assessment questions should look at the leadership of the target company and its view of the business environment, as well as its attitude towards competition, customers, and change:

- What are their core beliefs about what it takes to win?
- What drives business strategy? Tradition, or innovation and change?
- Is the company long or short-term oriented?
- How much risk is the company used to accepting?
- What is its approach to external partners? Competition or collaboration?
- Who are the important stakeholders in the organization?

Other questions may examine broader leadership attitudes and how the company manages internal systems:

- Is the company result oriented or process oriented?
- Where is the power? Concentrated at the top, in certain functions, or diffused?
- How are decisions made? By consensus, consultation, or authority?
- How does the company manage information? Is the flow of information wide or narrow?
- What counts in being a valuable employee? Values, skills, and competencies, or getting results?
- Is the culture oriented to teamwork or to individual performance or both?

Some companies use cultural assessment as an input into a stop/go decision concerning the acquisition. For example, Cisco avoids buying companies with cultures that are substantially different from its own, recognizing that it would be difficult to achieve its aim of retaining key staff if there are substantial differences in views on how a business should be run. On the other hand, GE Capital is less concerned with retention, and they are more aggressive in their approach. Cultural assessment is also a must, but mainly as a tool to plan integration. One cannot say that one approach is better than the other, but both companies are clear about what is important and how they want to get there.

Cultural assessment is not just a question of assessing the other company's culture; it is also a matter both of having a clear culture oneself and understanding it. The "know thyself" adage applies equally well to companies as it does to people. The criteria used in cultural assessment of the acquisition target will to a great extent reflect the cultural attributes of one's own organization.

An example is the story of the second largest bank in Denmark. Unibank was constituted by a classic "merger of three equals" in 1989. The compromise decisions proved to be disastrous, leading to a financial crisis when economic conditions turned tough in 1991. A new CEO, Thorleif Krarup, was appointed. He restructured the organization and restored profitability. But Krarup realized that the future would bring a further consolidation of financial services not only in Denmark but also in Scandinavia. Unibank would not be in a strong position to take advantage of such opportunities unless it had a clear and unified identity, in the shape of coherent control systems, banking policies and practices, management attitudes, and leadership development. Building this strong identity was his priority during the mid-1990s, and he turned down several opportunities for mergers or acquisitions because Unibank was not ready. Today Unibank is part of the Nordea Group, a merger of leading Scandinavian banks in 1999, and Krarup is the group CEO.

The challenge in conducting a cultural assessment is to approach the subject with an appropriate perspective. After all, most difficulties in cross-border acquisitions can ultimately be traced back to culture. Even disagreement over the price of the deal can be attributed to cultural differences. Where some see cultural obstacles, others may simply observe poor management. "It was like two drunks trying to hold each other up," commented *The Wall Street Journal* on one case of a spectacular cross-border merger fiasco attributed to cultural misunderstandings. At the same time, there may be a limit to how many cultural boundaries one can cross. Every time a large Japanese "old-economy" company has tried to buy a Silicon Valley start-up, the result has been a failure.

Conventional wisdom suggests that companies should avoid any deal in which cultural differences might prove to be a problem. This posture is rooted in the assumption that cultural differences are largely unmanageable and that they will undermine the success of a deal. However, in today's global business environment, in which strategic imperatives drive many potential M&A deals forward, companies no longer have the luxury of avoiding potential deals on account of cultural issues.

A recent empirical study demonstrated that, contrary to popular perceptions, cross-border acquisitions do not necessarily create more employee resistance than domestic acquisitions.[36] This does not mean that cultural differences and other soft factors can now be ignored. Quite the contrary, because they are so critical they have to be well assessed and well managed. The proper response is not to avoid deals in which there is a risk of cultural clash but to manage and mitigate the risks. This requires disaggregating imprecisely defined "cultural issues" into discrete, manageable issues. Most of these are connected to the management of people.

The Human Capital Audit

There are two dimensions to the human capital audit. One dimension is preventive, focused on liabilities such as pension plan obligations, outstanding grievances, and employee litigation, or other employment-related constraints that may impact the acquisition—for example cost of anticipated restructuring. It also includes comparing the compensation policies, benefits, and labor contracts of both firms.

The other dimension is focused on talent identification, and in the long run it is probably more critical to the success of the acquisition. A number of facets of this are important—ensuring that the target company has the talent necessary to execute the acquisition strategy, identifying which individuals are key to sustaining the value of the deal, and assessing any potential weaknesses in the management cadre. It is also important to understand the motivation and incentive structure and to highlight any differences that may impact retention. Finally, understanding the structure of the organization means not just reporting lines but also clarifying who is who.

Here are some examples of questions to consider:

- What unique skills do the employees have?
- How does the target's talent compare to the quality of our own?
- What is the background of the management team?
- What will happen if some of the management team leave?
- What is the compensation philosophy?
- How much pay is at risk at various levels of the firm?
- What are the reporting relationships?
- How are decisions made?

Getting access to talent data may take some effort, and many companies ignore the talent question in the early stages of the M&A process. They do not take the time to define the types of skills embedded in people that are critical to the success of the deal, relying instead on financial performance data as a proxy. However, without early assessment, companies may acquire targets with weaker than expected skills or talent that has a high likelihood of departure. Early assessment helps to pinpoint the potential risk factors so that the acquiring company can develop strategies to address anticipated problems as early as possible. Moreover, this will speed up the eventual decision-making about who should stay and who should leave.

An important component of the human capital audit is the development of action plans necessary to retain key talent since these measures must typically be implemented immediately after the deal is concluded. For example, the employee stock option plan may provide for option grants to be fully vested when there is a "change of control," as after an acquisition.[37] Many valuable contributors thus have no incentives to stay. In such cases, key employee retention must be considered a "deal breaker" to be incorporated in the acquisition agreement.[38]

At the same time, the audit may also uncover significant weaknesses that may call for replacement candidates (external local hires or expatriates) to be ready to step in immediately after closing. Without advance planning, this may not be possible. And with each replacement there is a potential termination, which again has to be carefully prepared, based on local rules and practice.

Closing the Deal

Until the agreement to acquire is signed (or a hostile tender offer is announced), much of the vital HR involvement in the acquisition process will go on behind the scenes. Immediately after the deal is signed, however, (and well before it actually is put into effect), the scope of the HR agenda expands rapidly. Companies often wait until closing before considering HR issues because the period between the signature of the agreement and implementation can be anywhere between several months and a full year, depending on the need to obtain shareholder and regulatory approval. This time should not be wasted.[39]

Pre-Closing Action Plans

The first priority is to complete the due diligence, now with full access to data. How much direct access to managers and employees there is and under what conditions is often a part of the M&A agreement. This is a sensitive period, and the first impressions of the new "foreign" owners may last for a long time. For example, when interviewing, opinions should be solicited from all, not only from those competent in the language of new owners. In many countries, union consent is desirable, if not essential, for the transaction to go ahead. As in any other labor relations situation, honest and open communication with the union representatives is typically most effective.

All this highlights one of the challenges for HR, namely, rapidly acquiring and internalizing new cross-cultural competence, including familiarity with the legal and social context. HR managers involved in cross-border acquisitions have to be capable of learning fast! Of course, if the company is already present in the country, the task is much easier. For most companies, however, cross-border acquisitions are one of a kind, and they require at least some reliance on outside resources such as local consultants. Assessing and contracting with outside resources will require time, so planning ahead is essential. Indeed who you hire to work on your behalf may tell the local employees a lot about your intentions and capabilities.

As the Japanese market opened up for acquisitions, a European pharmaceutical firm made a "friendly" offer to buy one of their large but struggling distributors. To facilitate the transaction, the company retained an HR consulting group that, unknown to the Europeans, had a local reputation for a confrontational approach to post-merger restructuring. Those Japanese who could headed for the door; the rest set up a union with the aim of blocking the acquisition. Faced with unexpected resistance, the offer was withdrawn.

As discussed before, the acquiring company needs to have in place the key components of the HR implementation blueprint by the time the acquisition is ready to close—elements such as the organizational structure and reporting relationships, the composition of the new team, the timeline for action on specific HR issues, and the like. This exercise is fairly straightforward in the case of single country acquisitions. But international acquisitions are sometimes offshoots of domestic acquisitions since the firm has subsidiaries or units in other countries. Here it is important to determine key priorities, resources, and timing and to avoid the "one-size-fits-all" approach. For example, while absorption may be the best approach at home, a "reverse merger" may be more appropriate in a particular foreign location. The local context influences which acquisition strategy may be most feasible, as well as the desired state of the new organization.

The final element of pre-closing activity is the selection of the integration manager and the transition team, who will be charged with combining the two organizations. If the team includes expatriates, which is often the case, they may need to have at least rudimentary cross-cultural orientation and coaching since most of them are selected for technical and functional expertise.

THE POST-MERGER INTEGRATION PROCESS

Signing the acquisition contract and the change in ownership triggers changes in organization and leadership. Now is the time to put in place a new organization, appoint new leadership, and make sure that key talent is retained—and to manage what is called the merger syndrome. Some changes happen quickly in the months after the closing; others, such as the development of a new culture, need more time to coalesce. A final stage in the acquisition process is the codification and dissemination of learning—what did we learn so next time it can be done faster and better. These are some of the critical challenges for HRM that we will discuss in this section.

During the early stages of the acquisition, it is the responsibility of human resources to ensure a sharp focus on people and leadership issues, making sure that transitional organization and teams are in place on day one, fully prepared to deal with the complexities of a cross-cultural deal. The next step is staffing—who will stay and who will go? Here, the ability to evaluate the talent rapidly within the newly acquired organization is essential. It is not easy to assess people quickly in a different culture; most HR professionals find it difficult to trust their experience outside their own cultural milieu.[40] And finally, what kind of policies and practices should be introduced in the acquired organization? Human resource management provides a subtle control mechanism by which a parent company can influence its acquisition, so the choice of HR approach is intrinsically linked with the overall strategy for integration.

Recognizing and Managing the Merger Syndrome

Announcing mergers may be fun—for top management. It attracts lots of publicity and senior management can enjoy their time in the spotlight. But lower down in the ranks the reactions are different to this bolt that often comes out of the blue. However well the merger has been planned and prepared, there is always the merger syndrome. At a basic level this simply reflects the fact that any process of change is stressful.

However the merger is presented in the press, for those who are taken over there is invariably a sense of being losers. Reactions follow the pattern of the shock syndrome experienced by people following the death of a loved one. Initial disbelief and denial are followed by shock, colored by overreaction ("we are going to lose our jobs"), or underreaction ("oh, it won't change anything"). This leads in turn to anger, then attempts to bargain or dig in heels so as to take care of oneself, followed ultimately by acceptance. Acceptance itself may take different forms that characterize the mood of the firm for long after—fatalism, bitterness, wistful regret, or, ideally, proactivity. To some degree or another, this syndrome is unavoidable because it reflects the process of human adaptation, and it is only aggravated when the "victor" comes from another country. This means that it must be managed carefully.

There is typically a parallel cycle in the acquiring company, in which the initial reaction is one of victory ("We've won!" "We'll show those people how to manage customers!"). Attitudes toward the "losers" become condescending, which can only worsen the post-merger integration problems. Managers in functional departments and out in the subsidiaries of the acquiring firm may have fantasies about expanding their power and scope of responsibility. A sense of rush and urgency takes over, leading to confusion and growing doubt about whether this really is a victory. Senior managers start taking over; there is increasing command-and-control and a growing war-room mentality, which also creates an unhealthy climate for the serious tasks of the post-merger integration teams.

People often talk about "the first hundred days" of a merger, and how this sets the tone positively or, more frequently, negatively for the longer task of integration. In a merger, as in any change process, there will typically be some negative costs of the transition process, for there is indeed a cost to any change. This is measured in lost productivity because of distractions (less focus on today because of worries or fantasies about the future), lost people and the upheavals this creates (some talented people will almost always jump ship and some will be asked to leave), and employee satisfaction. Whether these negative consequences of change are moderate and quite transitory or whether they are debilitating for the integration process depends on how one manages these first hundred days. The stress that accompanies change can be made constructive, or it can be allowed to become dysfunctional.

How can this be managed? Let us take Cisco's practice as an example. Immediately after the acquisition, literally the next day, one or more of their acquisition team (typically the HR officer) meets with the new employees:

> Mimi Gigoux [corporate acquisitions director responsible for the HR side of due diligence] welcomes new employees with an acknowledgement that change is painful and that—like taking off a Band-Aid—Cisco will do it fast. Her goal is complete honesty. She pulls no punches, informing people that this was an acquisition, not a merger of equals. She also offers a first lesson, noting to the new employees that "The more flexible and positive you are, the better it will be for you." But she also points out the plentiful good news, such as retention plans, compensation, benefits, increased vacation days, tuition reimbursement, and career opportunities.[41]

Integration teams in MIS, product fields, and logistics act immediately to see that new employees are up on the Cisco intranet, have free soft drinks (one of Cisco's symbolic benefits), and get immediate training in the Cisco way. Typically engineering, marketing, and sales units will be reorganized within the acquired company, while HR, service, manufacturing, and distribution will be folded into the Cisco infrastructure.

Managing Stress and Uncertainty

What lies behind the Cisco example is what Marks and Mirvis call the "four I's" that are necessary to manage the stress and uncertainty of the first hundred days—Insight, Information, Inspiration, and Involvement.[42]

Insight means helping employees to acknowledge that change will be stressful and to cope effectively with their emotional reactions, with the knowledge that this is a part of healthy adaptation. Pretending that nothing will be different or that there will be no stress only increases the tension, undermining the credibility of the acquirer. Some companies organize workshops for the employees so that they have an arena for voicing their anxieties and concerns and also learning about how the integration process will unfold. The benefit is that staff feel more able to tackle the integration challenges in a constructive way, reassured that their own feelings have been taken into account. With hindsight, most executives say that they should have paid more attention to immediate employee concerns in the period immediately after the merger announcement.

Regarding *information,* one cannot do enough to satisfy the thirst of employees in the weeks after the merger—and in the case of a major acquisition, this includes staff in the company that has made the purchase. What often happens is that the management team in the acquiring firm is misguidedly reluctant to provide any information until the fine details on the integration plan have been settled. The rumor mill takes over, amplifying and distorting events, aggravating the stress, and distracting people from the day-by-day work that must carry on.

To manage the merger syndrome, a multimedia ongoing communications campaign must be set up. If the firm has little prior experience in acquisitions, it may not be able to provide information on the specifics of restructuring or integration plans, but it *can* say what is being done to develop such plans. And that will have a positive effect in reducing the stress, minimizing the risk of perverse or unmanageable reactions. The guiding principle here is to communicate what is known, and to be clear about what is unknown. Road shows and videos, e-mail bulletins, telephone hotlines, and careful press announcements need to be orchestrated to manage the ongoing communication process, which needs to be targeted not just at senior management who are overloaded with tasks but at the first line supervisors who receive the majority of questions from their concerned staff.

Inspiration means starting at the earliest stage to build positive expectations for the future. The business plan for the future of the two companies may take time to elaborate, but inspiring statements can pave the way and uplift morale as long as they are genuinely realistic: "This is not just a consolidation of two firms so as to cut costs. It is building the best organization so as to ensure industry leadership in the twenty-first century." One of Cisco's principles is to make sure that there are visible and quick wins to counteract the despair and anger. These range from the immediate installation of symbolic free beverage machines, to the benefits of their sophisticated intranet system, to increased sales as the acquired firm's products get the advantage of access to broader distribution.

Finally, *involvement* implies the face-to-face contact that is most effective in breaking down the stereotypes of "them and us," "the winners and the losers." As in any change process, the more people are involved in the combination in direct and personal ways, the more they will understand its rationale and feel committed to successful implementation. Integration teams, discussed later, are obviously a major tool. Joint orientation sessions and the opportunity to exchange with functional counterparts assist the process as well.

With the players separated by language and distance, the merger syndrome is more difficult to combat in a cross-border acquisition—yet equally important. Cisco trained its local HR managers (and other members of local acquisition teams) in countries such as China and Korea in their approach to managing the four I's, having them participate in the integration process of acquisitions back in the United States. The result is that they felt quite comfortable in managing the "one hundred days" integration process when acquiring companies back home in China, making necessary adaptations in the process.

Approaches to Post-Merger Integration

All acquisitions require some degree of integration (even the preservation deals generally require the integration of financial reporting systems). It is important to tailor what is integrated and how this is to be undertaken to the purpose of the acquisition and the characteristics of the companies involved. The critical part of the process is focusing on the areas in which the acquisition can create new value while maintaining the ongoing business.

The pressure of ongoing everyday work multiplied by the need to manage integration well in the unsettled conditions can be formidable. If you add to this the possibility of intercultural misunderstanding, the tendency of people to resist change, and the likely shortage of qualified management talent, you have a recipe for an overstressed, underperforming workforce. When acquisition performance falls short of the target, it is not surprising that the difficulties of the integration process are likely to be identified as the cause of failure.

Moving with Speed

When companies are asked what they learned from their past M&A experiences, they *always* say: "We should have moved faster, we should have done in nine months what it took us a year to do." GE Capital, for example, has cut down the hundred-day process to sixty to seventy-five days because it learned how to move faster and because it developed the tools to do so. Speed is essential because if a company is taking two to three years to integrate, not enough attention is being spent where it really counts—with the customers. According to GE:

> Decisions about management structure, key roles, reporting relationships, layoffs, restructuring, and other career-affecting aspects of the integration should be made, announced, and implemented as soon as possible after the deal is signed, within days if possible. Creeping changes, uncertainty, and anxiety that last for months are debilitating and immediately start to drain value from an acquisition.[43]

The desire to move fast may come from the firm that has been acquired. A survey of European acquisitions of U.S. high technology firms in Silicon Valley reported that speed in integration was one of the key drivers of successful post-merger integration—but also one of the most problematic.[44] The understanding of what was "fast" by most of the European acquirers (usually large, established companies with entrenched routines and procedures) was very different from the norms of the Valley. This created confusion, frustration, and ultimately the loss of market opportunities.

Often, restructuring is an essential step to get to the necessary synergies. Restructuring should not be confused with integrating, but here the rule is similar: it should be done *early, fast, and once,* ideally part of the first hundred days. A problem jeopardizing the success of many acquisitions has been a tendency to restructure slowly, motivated by the best of intentions. While time and resources are being spent on giving people time to adjust and not upsetting the old culture, competitors come along and take away the business.

The other dimension of speed is the focus on delivering *quick, visible wins* such as new sales generated through a joint effort or profit improvements based on shared practices. It is important to take time to celebrate each success and to communicate the accomplishments to the whole organization. For the acquired employees, a quick win can be motivating because it offers tangible proof that the merger or acquisition was a step in the right direction, showing that their efforts are appreciated. The identification of such opportunities should be part of the due diligence process so that implementation can start immediately after the deal closes.

Yet speed can have unintended consequences. Under time pressure, bad decisions are made that could have been avoided through a more judicious review of the issues. Or good decisions meet resistance because there was no time to explain the new business logic. What is the optimal speed depends on the strategic intent behind the acquisition and the desired end-state for the culture of the new organization. Absorption or transformation strategies generally require more urgency than those oriented to preservation. When the objective of the acquisition is to acquire knowledge and intellectual capital, the pace of change must be especially carefully calibrated so as to minimize the risk of alienating talent, as we discuss later.

Research also shows differences in the speed of the integration process according to the national origins of the acquiring firm. Japanese and northern European acquirers tend to move cautiously, conscious of the potential cultural conflicts.[45] This works well if the approach is one of preservation, but it may exacerbate the stress of the hundred days when expected decisions are not forthcoming. Analysis and consultation should not cause decisions to be put off. There are few occasions when the answer is unanimous—there is always another way to do things. If a company waits until there is consensus, it risks finding that it has lost the window of opportunity.

How to Organize the Integration Process[46]

Most integration efforts that involve the merger of companies across borders are organized along one of the three models outlined below, each with its advantages and disadvantages.

The Centralized Leadership Approach. The centralized approach to post-merger integration starts with designing the blueprint for the new organization. When ABB was created by the merger of Sweden's Asea with the Swiss Brown Boveri, Percy Barnevik, the new company's first CEO, kicked off the integration by announcing the structure for the new organization at the outset. He then hand-picked 500 executives from both companies to lead it.

With this approach, it is clear from the start how the new company will be organized, guiding the integration effort in a rigid but unambiguous way. The newly appointed executives will take the responsibility for "rolling out" this new organizational design. They will address the relevant integration issues through a series of appointed task forces. A support team acts in an advisory role to the CEO as overall leader.

The advantage of the centralized approach is that it provides clarity about structure and leadership from the outset. The emphasis is on urgency and speed, and there is no agonizing over roles and responsibilities. This approach, however, requires a high caliber of available leadership. The leaders must be able to inspire people with the new vision. They must excel in face-to-face communication across organizational and national boundaries, instilling the new common values by walking their own talk. They must be capable of setting up the new policies and practices. Otherwise the organization ends up by centralizing all decisions at the top, which slows down the process and undermines the credibility of the new organization.

The Decentralized Leadership Approach. This second approach structures the new organization around the key integration areas. Task forces are appointed to address the major integration challenges in each area, usually co-led by executives from each company. The task force leaders will normally take over the formal responsibility for those areas following the completion of their work. In contrast with the previous model, there is no overall blueprint. Each task force leader is expected to come up with his or her own design for the area.

A number of mergers in the global financial and pharmaceutical industries were tackled in this manner. The key advantage behind the decentralized approach to integration is its bottom-up orientation to problem solving, involving a larger number of managers from the merging companies. When endowed with strict accountability, these task forces can be utilized effectively to resolve the many complex implementation issues.

However, the lack of an overarching organizational structure for the new entity may lead to problems of coordination between the integration task forces, as well as leaving two parallel organizations running in tandem for too long. A decentralized approach makes it more difficult to create shared values for employees in the new company. Since executives are focused on their own domains, there may be less trust and teamwork at the top that shows up in stronger conflict at the operational levels lower down.

The Distributed Leadership Approach. A hybrid approach to integration is sometimes used when the company expects each unit of the newly merged firm to retain a high degree of autonomy while looking for shared benefits (as opposed to a full integration like ABB). This was the approach adopted by DaimlerChrysler. The members of the top management board or executive committee each have decentralized responsibility for overseeing a series of joint integration task forces focused on functional topics. The top board with the leaders of these task forces coordinates, supports, and monitors the overall integration process, with its aim of identifying and realizing the synergies between the merging firms.

The advantage of this approach is that it tries to combine decentralized responsibility for daily operations with central coordination of the integration work. Each entity preserves autonomy where it makes business sense, but the core team, which focuses on overall coordination, makes sure that areas that should be common and standard are tackled from a common perspective (finance, IT, and some elements of HR). An example is the successful acquisition of Italian white goods manufacturer Zanussi by Swedish-based Electrolux.[47]

The downside of the hybrid model is the complexity of balancing autonomy and synergy during the integration process, which may drain away a great deal of emotional energy. Given their functional orientation, the teams may have a tendency to focus on technical issues, neglecting the soft aspects of organization and culture. When business conditions get tough and quick decisions are required, the committee-based decision-making may get in the way.

Managing the Transition Period

Regardless of the approach, the integration of the acquired company with the new parent is a delicate and complicated process. Who should be responsible for making it happen? After closing, the due diligence team with its deep knowledge of the acquired company disbands or goes on to another deal. Meanwhile, the new management team is not yet fully in place. To avoid a vacuum, companies are increasingly turning to dedicated integration managers supported by transition teams to guide the process immediately after the deal is concluded.

THE ROLE OF THE INTEGRATION MANAGER. The integration manager is a specialist in dealing with transitions. His or her role is to make sure that timelines are followed and that key decisions are taken according to the agreed upon schedule, while removing the bottlenecks and making sure that speed of integration is maintained. Integration managers help to engineer the short-term successes that are essential to creating positive energy in the merger. They should champion norms and behaviors consistent with new standards, communicate key messages across the new organization, and identify new value adding opportunities.[48]

An important aspect of the job is helping the acquired company understand how the new owner operates and what it can offer in terms of capabilities. Acquired companies typically do not know how things work in the corporation which now owns them. The integration manager can help the new company take advantage of the owner's existing capabilities and resources, forge social connections, and help with essential but intangible aspects such as interpreting a new language and way of doing things. The integration manager can also help the parent to understand the acquired business and what it can bring. This is important because outside the acquisition team few people in the parent organization are familiar with the capabilities of the acquired unit.

Equally important is the integration manager's role as information "gatekeeper" between the two sides, protecting the acquired business from the eager embrace of an owner who unintentionally could undermine what makes the business work. A major source of frustration in many of the deals is not so much what the parent wants the newly acquired unit to do, but what it wants to know. New information requirements must be submitted in a very specific format, and reports are full of incomprehensible jargon—indeed corporate HR is often the guilty party. When Nokia acquires small high tech venture companies, one of the rules is that all requests for information from the parent go to the integration manager. He or she will decide if and how the unit should comply with the request.

What combination of skills is required in the integration manager? First of all, that person must have a deep knowledge of the parent company—where to get information, who to talk to, how the informal system works. The integration manager should have a flexible leadership style, since he or she must be tough about deadlines and yet be a good listener and be able to relate to people at all levels in the organization. Other traits that go with this role are comfort with ambiguity, emotional and cultural intelligence, and the willingness to take risks.[49] An integration manager is not the leader of the business, though this job is often a stepping stone into business leadership roles.

THE RESPONSIBILITIES OF THE TRANSITION TEAM. In most acquisitions, integration teams and task forces support the integration manager. These should have a clear mandate, with targets and accountability for a specific area in which integration is required. Since many of these teams are expected to start work on the first day after the acquisition is closed, the identification of potential members should ideally be one outcome of the due diligence process. HR professionals are often key members of the teams because many of the teams' activities will have implications for human resource policies and practices.

The specific charter of the transition teams depends on the integration approach discussed above (centralized, decentralized, distributed). Overall their role is to take the high level vision, objectives, and synergies and translate these into concrete action. The key priorities, such as business synergies with which results can be achieved quickly, should be identified early in the integration planning process so that these specific integration projects can be launched immediately after the deal is closed.

Prioritization is critical. Too many task forces and teams slow things down, creating coordination problems, conflict, and confusion. The complexity of Daimler-Chrysler's transition structure was one of the reasons why its integration process came quickly to a standstill. The integration should focus on those projects with high potential savings at low risk, leaving those with greater risk or lower benefits until later. As stated by one experienced M&A manager: "We only attack things that will bring benefits to the business. We do not integrate just for the sake of integrating."

Another task of the transition team is to spell out the logic of the new business model and translate this into operational targets. This is important in international acquisitions where "big picture" statements from the corporate center may not mean much in a different national and business context far away. The transition team should also serve as a role model for how the new organization should act. It should disseminate the shared vision and make sure that practices are appropriately aligned with this. And by facilitating personnel exchange the transition team can help to develop a better understanding between the two sides of each other's capabilities.

Who should be appointed to the transition team? The idea of working in what we have called a "split egg" way may be attractive, but here the mixing of line responsibility with transition taskforce roles often means that neither is done well. Customers do not like to wait until the transition team reaches consensus. On the other hand, integration teams should not be staffed by second tier managers or by "losers" in the race for line business jobs—they would not have the credibility to get the job done. So probably the best staffing approach is to appoint up-and-coming managers, leaving the daily business under the original leadership until the new organization can be put in place.

Transition teams are most effective when members come from both the acquired and acquiring companies. People who are suited for a transition team usually have a mix of functional and interpersonal competencies (including cross-cultural skills), backed up by strong analytical skills. Having an ability to accept responsibility without full authority and being effective in mobilizing resources across organizational boundaries are two competencies that are especially important, and consequently such roles are good development opportunities for those with high potential.

Focusing on the People Challenges

Merger integration is a change process. Companies that are unskilled in managing the people side of change processes within their own firms should be particularly wary about tackling complex acquisitions. As indicated earlier, the single factor that correlates most strongly with the ultimate success of the acquisition is the skill of the acquiring firm in managing change. Time and time again, top management falls into the classic change trap of focusing on the content of change (the financials, the restructuring plans for the functions), and not on the process of change. All of the lessons of change management apply to merger integration—the need for communication, the necessity to establish a vision for the future, the need to restructure so as to remove resistance and to empower champions, the management of the learning process by measuring progress against milestones.[50]

There are some people challenges involved in the integration change process that merit particular attention: communication; retaining talent; managing the process of culture change; and ensuring learning from the process. We discuss these, and then consider how the approach varies from one national culture to another.

Communication

Communication is always a vital part of any process of change, but it is critical in cross-border acquisitions because misunderstandings owing to cultural differences and distance may intensify tensions. In the design of the communication process there should be two objectives that are particularly important in mergers. One, an aim of communication should be to alleviate the anxiety and stress that accompany every acquisition; two, communication should provide feedback to top management about the progress of the integration process and any potential roadblocks.

The need for flawless communication starts on the day the deal is announced. Top management has to clearly express the rationale for the acquisition, the synergies sought, and the degree of integration required.[51] They should also clarify their expectations regarding the organizational architecture. Although the transition teams can work out the details, the message to the shareholders and the public has to be consistent with the message to employees in both the acquired and acquiring companies.

This is far from being the case. In a survey of European acquisitions in Silicon Valley cited earlier, every single target firm reported a lack of clarity as to its role in the combined organization![52] The issues that most employees are anxious about do not get addressed. What is the intended end-state or vision guiding the new organization? Will one side dominate, will it be the "best of both," or will a transformation be attempted? Consistent and coherent communication helps to build morale and reassure those unsettled by the changes.

Lack of clarity and consistency in what top management is saying can have disastrous consequences. In the failed Deutsche-Dresdner banking merger, mixed signals from the leadership about the future of the combined organization's investment banking operations created opposition in both camps, ultimately forcing the cancellation of a deal that looked promising on paper.[53] The collapse of the deal hit share prices and the Dresdner CEO was forced to resign. And because of the high rate of defections from Dresdner during the confused weeks after the initial merger announcement, Dresdner Bank was left substantially weakened, forcing it to accept a less favorable offer from another financial institution several years later.

It is imperative, as discussed earlier in this chapter, to communicate a *clear vision* of how the acquisition or merger will *create value*. A company can talk as much as it wants about synergy, but unless the employees understand the logic behind this there is a danger that that they will see the deal only as a manifestation of the CEO's ego. A well-articulated communication campaign conveys to the workforce a sense that the leadership has a clear sense of where to take the acquisition.[54] It also gives people something constructive to talk about, rather than rumors and worst-case scenarios. Additionally, a clear message can help deal with any potential political and/or competitive issues which arise once the deal is announced, an increasingly important concern in cross-border acquisitions.

Straightforwardness is a guiding principle. In the case of a hostile takeover or when a poorly performing company is put up for sale, it is better to say that the aim is to take over the other firm and assimilate it than to pretend otherwise. Hard truth may not go down well, but the consequences are easier to handle than the alienation and mistrust stemming from lack of integrity. DaimlerChrysler's Jürgen Schrempp paid this price when he conceded that his intention had always been to take over Chrysler.

BP-Amoco is an example of playing it straight. BP took over Amoco with the clear aim of accessing the oil reserves owned by Amoco. Since BP felt that these fields could be more productively exploited under its management, the model for the new company's organization and culture was unambiguous. In the words of a BP executive, "It is nonnegotiable for us. We have developed a structure and systems that have worked for us, and we are anxious to apply them to a larger company." If you were a manager at Amoco with twenty-five years' experience, you might not be happy about this. But at least you would know how things stand. You either go along with the BP way of working, or you leave.

Effective communication during the integration is a two-way process, from the company to the employees and from the employees back to top management. Irrespective of the chosen road to integration, it is important to monitor progress in order to surface hidden issues and concerns that may create conflict in the new organization. In cross-border deals misinterpretations of the language can poison the atmosphere and create confusion. Alertness and attention to this possible problem are essential. So is the ability to react quickly when false rumors spread. Today it is possible to use the company's intranet to receive feedback on how people in the acquired company feel about the integration process so that something can be done before unhappy staff walk away.

Retaining Talent

Many acquired businesses lose key employees soon after the acquisition, and this is a major contributing factor to the failure of acquisitions. Research evidence from U.S. acquisitions indicates that the probability of executives leaving increases significantly when their firm is acquired by a foreign multinational. About 75 percent of the firms' top management leaves by the fifth year, with a majority departing during the first two years.[55]

When insufficient attention is paid to retaining talent, and especially if staff cuts are expected, employees will leave—and the best will exit first since they have other choices. After a deal is announced and well before the actual closing, headhunters inevitably move in to pick off any promising managers who are unsure about their career opportunities with the new and distant owner. For employees confronted with the uncertainties of a new organization, a firm job offer from another company looks attractive.

Retention of the key employees is therefore crucial to achieving acquisition goals in both short-term integration tasks and long-term business performance. This means knowing exactly who the talented people are and why they are essential to the new organization, including those lower down in the acquired firm. Getting this information is not a simple task. Vague discussions are not helpful. The typical top-down cascading talent identification process often yields flawed results since local managers may be protective of their people and unable to be objective about what they offer to the new organization. One of the biggest obstacles in international acquisitions is the difference in performance measures and standards.[56] Even if standards are comparable, many companies are not aware of where their talent is; in McKinsey's "War for Talent" study only 16 percent of surveyed executives believed that their employers knew who their high performers were.

The starting point for talent identification is the talent map developed during the due diligence stage, and this map needs to be refined quickly using feedback from direct superiors, peers, and subordinates, past performance reviews, personal interviews, formal skill assessments, and direct evaluation of performance during the integration period. However, while multiple sources of assessment are desirable, the quest for precision should not be allowed to get in the way, slowing things down and increasing the uncertainty and risk of defection. Since the pace of the integration may not allow a comprehensive assessment of all individuals, the focus should be on those most critical for the success of the acquisition.[57]

Fast and open communication is crucial to retaining talent. As mentioned earlier, Cisco's integration team holds small group sessions with all acquired employees on day one to discuss expectations and answer questions. Often, members of the integration team were themselves brought into Cisco by acquisition. They understand well what the newly joined employees are going through, so their messages are received with additional credibility. GE Capital uses GE's Change Acceleration Process (CAP) methodology to clarify expectations and quickly unearth possible concerns and anxieties so they can be addressed.[58]

The second building block for talent retention is financial motivation. Companies often offer stock options, retention bonuses, or other incentives to employees who stay through the integration or until a specific merger-related project is completed.[59] An important consideration is highlighting the differences between short-term business needs (retention incentives for employees who are not expected to be employed after the completion of the integration process) and long-term talent requirements.

For the latter, long-term group, even the most elaborate retention incentives cannot substitute for a one-on-one relationship with executives of the acquiring firm. Senior management involvement is critical to successful retention. High potential employees in most companies are used to senior level attention. Without the same treatment from the acquiring company, they question their future and will be more likely to depart. Distance may be an obstacle to be overcome, but it cannot be an excuse. Meetings and informal sessions in the early days of the acquisition, if not before the closing, can go a long way to building the foundations for long-term relationships. When BP-Amoco acquired Arco, another international oil major, it quickly organized Key Talent Workshops—two-day events to network senior BP executives with Arco's high potential employees.[60]

Talent retention efforts should not stop with the completion of the first hundred days of integration. Junior employees may find the initial impact of the acquisition quite positive, offering them opportunities for responsibility and higher pay (especially if their seniors leave en masse). But many of them depart later because they are not integrated into the leadership development of the new parent company.[61] This may have negative consequences for the company's ability to execute future deals since its track record in retaining talent affects its reputation and credibility in managing mergers. In contrast, Cisco's ability to retain acquired talent long after the integration facilitates Cisco's undertaking new acquisitions, reinforcing a key strategic capability.

While the link between talent retention and acquisition success is widely recognized, this does not necessarily translate into support for specific HR initiatives. For example, in a recent survey of top executives in the United States, Asia, and South America, 76 percent of the respondents indicated that talent retention was the most critical element of integration success. But only 8 percent named human resource management as their top priority during integration.[62] Part of the problem is the lack of clear measures of talent retention so as to monitor progress; HR activities that cannot be measured are not likely to get top management attention. Without retention data, companies have no way of measuring the success of their talent management efforts, no way of holding managers accountable for success in retention, and they find it difficult to improve their practices with future acquisitions in mind.

Finally, the retention of talent is obviously important for firms in which the value of the deal lies in the acquisition of intangible assets—the knowledge and skills of the people inside the acquired firm (see the box "Integrating Knowledge-Intensive Acquisitions"). Many deals in the high technology sector are of this type, when companies use acquisitions to plug holes in their R&D portfolio or to rapidly build up new capabilities. Retention issues are important in all acquisitions in which the main assets are intangible, such as in professional service firms or where intimate knowledge of the customer may be the key market leverage.

Building the New Culture

The new organization will have a culture, whether it is by default or by design—a culture that may be marked by conflict or a culture that may be strongly accepted. The process of building the new culture goes on long after the combination phase (it is sometimes part of what is called postcombination). Sometimes hankering after the

---

Integrating Knowledge-Intensive Acquisitions
Practice Box

Knowledge-intensive acquisitions require more focus on people during the due diligence phase and during integration than do other types of acquisitions.[A]

Due Diligence Phase

- The first step to knowledge-intensive acquisitions is to understand who has the knowledge. Look beyond current products or services toward deeper competence and intellectual capital.
- Seek out commonality in vision, strategy, and goals. Check if key people would be comfortable at the acquiring company. Cultural match is especially important when acquiring larger companies with established ways of doing things.
- Check whether employees at the target company have material incentives to stay. Most high tech companies worldwide give out stock options. If these are largely vested, many may take their money from the acquisition and leave.

The Integration Phase

- Give new people mental security by presenting a high level product roadmap and a market vision that shows how the purchased company—and they—fit in. Show visible respect to the talents that have been acquired.
- Companies brought in to work on breakthrough technologies should generally be treated as separate entities. The greater the innovation, the less need for rapid integration.
- Build the new organization as much as possible on the strength of the acquired unit. Tolerate some duplication of activities; the best way forward is to invest in work-related interactions between the acquiring and acquired units.

[A] Birkinshaw, 1999; Chaudhuri and Tabrizi, 1999.

old ways can drag on for a decade, as it did after the merger between Ciba and Geigy back in the late 1970s (now merged with Sandoz into Novartis).

Companies with strong and successful cultures such as GE and BP impose their culture onto the company they acquire, as BP did when it bought Amoco. Indeed they see their success as originating from their culture and the practices built on it. Therefore GE will bring to the acquired company its meaning of a performance commitment, anchored in stretch goals, the underlying business planning process, and the way it goes about appraisal.[63]

Acquiring a "culture" may even be part of the reason behind an acquisition, such as in one pending takeover of an Anglo-Saxon competitor by a French multinational that is the global leader in its industry. Top management in the French corporation had known for some time that their own culture had to change, but it was not able to do so organically. The most attractive feature of the acquisition of its competitor was not the expanded market share but the opportunity to accelerate change in the mother company, bringing in more transparent Anglo-Saxon performance management and related practices. Its senior management recognized that the whole integration process would have to be managed with this aim in mind. One of the vehicles to be launched after the acquisition is approved will be a series of seminars and workshops for managers from both firms, at which the agenda will be as much focused on global leadership and management as on merger integration.

Culture change is difficult to manage unless there is some explicit management philosophy with values and norms that guide practice and behavior. To build the new culture of ABB after the merger of Asea and Brown Boveri in the late 1980s, Percy Barnevik spent three months with the new senior management team defining a policy bible to guide the intended new organization. This was a manual of "soft" principles such as for speed in decision-making ("better to be quick and roughly right than slow and completely right") and for conflict management ("you can only kick a conflict upstairs once for arbitration"); as well as of "hard" practices such as the Abacus measurement system that would apply across all units of the newly merged enterprise. Lafarge, today the world's largest company in the cement and construction materials business, did the same in the early 1970s. Its French president at the time, Olivier LeCerf, felt that there was an absence of cultural glue in the many new businesses and companies that had been acquired across the world in a wave of acquisitions. The top fifty executives in the corporation spent six months developing the Lafarge "Principles of Action," a set of strategic principles, values, and management practices that still today, thirty years later, are used to guide the process of cultural assimilation in companies that they continue to acquire.

Above all, the values and norms have to be translated into actions guiding the process of culture building or cultural assimilation after an acquisition. Barnevik notes that unless top management walks the talk, such values will not be credible. Again we can draw on the theory of change to guide the implementation of these new values. One model of change implementation argues that it is a four-step process.[64] It starts with the *new roles and responsibilities* after the restructuring, ensuring that skilled champions of the desired culture are in place to drive the culture change process. The second step is *coaching and training,* helping people to develop the desired competencies and behaviors. Meanwhile, the third step is being prepared, focusing on *recruitment, succession planning, and rewards.* People who are not responding well to the coaching will be replaced, and those who are responding very well will be given broader responsibilities. The fourth and last step in the implementation and culture change process is the *fine-tuning and formalization of the new system* into a coherent, consistent, and transparent whole. Change implementation is an HRM process that in our experience takes two to three years to accomplish.

The quality of coaching is particularly important for the effectiveness of culture change. Take AXA as an example, another French company that in the space of a decade has grown via acquisitions from being a local player in the French insurance industry to becoming a top global financial services institution. It makes no pretence that its acquisitions are mergers, acting quickly to AXA-ize the cultures of the firms it acquires. Managers from companies brought into AXA commented that one of the most helpful tools for them to assimilate quickly into the company was the 360° feedback process. The AXA values are encoded in this instrument, and to accelerate the process of cultural integration all managers and professionals in the acquired company go through 360° workshops. For most of the managers, this is the first time that they will have been exposed to such a multifaceted assessment, and they find that the rigor of the approach reinforces the credibility of AXA as a highly professional organization. It makes the desired culture and values concrete, identifying personal needs for improvement and leading to follow-up coaching in the AXA way.

Learning from Acquisitions

There is a broad consensus from research that acquisition success tends to increase with experience, while sometimes past experience may not be relevant to a current acquisition. Firms that made multiple acquisitions within the same industry benefited most from past acquisition experience. But for a dissimilar acquisition, the acquisition experience often had a negative influence on acquisition performance. Also, the effect of experience is not linear. The best performers appeared to be either those without experience, who were unlikely to make inappropriate generalizations, or those who had a significant amount of experience and who had learned how to apply their knowledge.[65]

One issue to consider is whether it is better to have many individuals involved in acquisitions in order to gain and share wide experience or to rely on a team of experts. Some companies create a special acquisition unit that is involved in every transaction. Obviously, this creates a desirable pool of expertise. On the other hand, acquisition competence is increasingly seen as an indispensable "generalist" skill—having experience with an acquisition is a ticket that should be punched by all high potential employees. This latter approach is adopted by GE, and because HR is one of the functions with a guaranteed seat at any GE acquisitions, smart young employees seek out HR jobs to get a shot at joining the acquisition team.

In either case, managers who have developed extensive experience in international acquisition should be viewed as a valuable resource for the organization. Part of HR's responsibility is to ensure that it knows who and where they are, so they can be mobilized quickly when required. From the employee point of view, participation in a cross-border acquisition team is a good way to put to use skills accumulated during past international assignments. There is a significant overlap in the behavioral competencies required by expatriates and integration team members—indeed the integration team is in a quasi or literal expatriate role. Both roles demand emotional maturity, cultural empathy, tolerance for ambiguity, and skills in interpersonal communication.

In order to learn from experience it is important to build the appropriate organizational memory. This requires that learning is documented to capture lessons learned, and for that to happen someone must have the responsibility for facilitating the collection of information and making it available—a role that in many successful acquirers is performed by the HR manager assigned to the transition team. But to get on the team requires doing the homework—being proactive is a prerequisite if HR professionals are to be involved.[66]

Perhaps even more important is development of tools to facilitate and speed up the cross-border acquisition process—from due diligence to integration. There is a qualitative difference in the approach to learning here. Acquisition "best practice" books present scenarios and suggest roadmaps for managers to follow. In contrast, acquisition tool kits provide managers with lists of issues and questions to be addressed at each stage in the acquisition, broad guidelines on what to consider, simple and concise instruments, and sources of advice inside and outside the firm. In repetitive acquisitions, the best practice approach may be sufficient, although most international acquisitions are one of a kind. In all cases, a feedback loop recording what worked, what did not, and what can be added is essential.

It is useful to keep in mind that effective learning and a solid track record in implementing acquisitions can sometimes have unintended consequences. Confident that missing skills can always be brought in, the acquiring managers may see outsourcing organizational skills as more attractive than retaining people so as to build those skills internally. This, however, may stifle in-house innovation and experimentation. For example, it has been reported that acquisitions have a negative effect on both R&D intensity (a measure of R&D inputs) and patent intensity (a measure of R&D outputs). Other evidence shows that firms making acquisitions introduce fewer new products into the marketplace.[67] A similar logic may apply to entering new markets via cross-border acquisitions. Firms with successful M&A experience may choose to enter quickly through an acquisition, although the slower greenfield investment path may give the company more leverage over people-related issues such as organizational culture and workforce composition.

MEASURING M&A SUCCESS. A critical component of the learning process is feedback on the progress achieved by the organization in reaching the integration goals. The foundation of feedback is measurement. And there is no shortage of measures that can be used to assess the progress on the HRM side of the integration process. Some of these measures focus on key organizational priorities, while others reflect the functional agenda of the HR department:

- *Integration goals*: Reorganization and restructuring targets in terms of schedule and cost, including breakdowns for specific business units or geographical areas.

- *Integration of key HR systems*: Tracking integration objectives in combining systems for HRIS, compensation, talent development, and performance management according to established time frame and budgets.
- *Retention of talent*: Retention of acquired talent, success rates for different retention tools, retention rates for specific business units and functions, and cost-effectiveness indicators such as retention/replacement expenses.
- *Best practices* shared and adopted compared across organizational units, including estimation of the impact on revenues, cost, and other performance indicators such as customer satisfaction.
- *Employee feedback data* includes attitude surveys and data from exit interviews.

In complex international acquisitions there are usually too many balls in the air to be able to rely on anecdotes and impressions. Costly mistakes can be avoided by instituting rigorous measurements and having real-time HRM data on the progress of the integration process. These measures stimulate management to take early corrective action, and they establish benchmarks for future acquisitions. Most important, they establish accountability for the people dimension of the acquisition. And without accountability, learning may not get the priority required.

In the long term, the only valid measure of acquisition success is the satisfied customer. Does the acquisition create customer value? From a customer's point of view, has it made sense? If it hasn't, then there is not much chance for long-term growth. When short-term synergies are exhausted, deals that do not create customer value have not much chance to be sustained. Strong focus on the customer can also help generate the energy to push through the necessary changes, cutting down on internal politics that divert management attention away from the business. And bear in mind that creating customer value occurs only *after* the deal is done, which makes post-merger integration such as critical success factor.

Do National Cultures Vary in their Approach to Acquisitions?

There is some evidence that firms of different nationalities differ in their approach to HRM in their acquisitions.[68] U.S. firms are seen as very results oriented, quick to "hire and fire." They also use HR practices as a conscious integration tool, a way of teaching the new subsidiary the "way to do things around here." In contrast, the Japanese prefer to stay more local and subtle, using HR practices to convey their business philosophy—their long-term approach to business, their concern for people, and their relatively slow but careful approach to decision-making. French acquirers plan for career development more than those of other nationalities, and they attach importance to formal qualifications, with a preference for managers of French origin, while the Germans look for technical expertise. Among the nationalities studied, the Germans approached HRM policies in the least clear and purposive way. They also generally were the least effective in their integration efforts, reinforcing our earlier observation concerning the need for transparency.[69]

At the same time, the available evidence indicates that international acquisitions promote some convergence in HRM policies and practices toward accepted best practice. This includes output or result-oriented performance appraisal (although applied with varying degrees of explicitness), individual performance-related pay, and team-based work organization, even if such practices are not widely used in the parent organization. It is likely that international acquisitions provide a convenient breeding ground for new directions of HRM that may not always be easy to transfer back to the parent country.

M&A AS ORGANIZATIONAL CAPABILITY

For many companies, implementing mergers and acquisitions is still a formidable challenge. The complexity of cross-border deals caused by cultural and physical distance makes the implementation even more difficult. Yet there is little doubt that companies that master the art of international acquisitions will gain significant market advantage, despite caveats regarding some long-term advantages of organic growth. When there is a sound strategy behind the merger and when the acquisition process is well managed, acquisitions become an important tool for international growth. For some companies, such as GE and Cisco, expanding through acquisitions is already a well-proven part of their business strategies. They understand well that the capability to execute acquisitions is one of the core competitive capabilities for the future, and that the intangible human aspects of an acquisition are just as important as its financial dimensions.

We would like to summarize this chapter by outlining GE Capital's approach to acquisitions (see Figure 6–4), which well illustrates the importance of human resource management in implementing acquisitions. Figure 6–4 captures the key elements of GE's proprietary acquisition process that, although developed originally in the United States, has been applied successfully in scores of international transactions. This detailed process provides guidance on what needs to be done, and it highlights the key organizational issues and decision points, providing the methodology and resources. It is documented on paper and online, and as the company accumulates more experience, it is continuously updated and fine-tuned. Perhaps the most critical feature, moreover, is that it lets the people involved in the process find the right answers for themselves. All deals are different, so flexibility in arriving at solutions is important.

The merger implementation process starts setting the framework for integration well before the deal is in the open. It begins with an assessment of the culture of the organization to be acquired in order to identify any potential cultural barriers. As a part of due diligence, the strengths and weaknesses of the business leaders are assessed so that who will stay and who may need to be replaced is clear before the deal closes. The integration manager is selected; he or she proceeds to assemble the transition team. When the deal is signed, the communication strategy is ready to go into action on day one.

The integration manager and the transition teams, now expanded to include employees from the acquired firm, together formulate a specific integration plan. Key processes, including HR, are aligned. Through workshops and other communication tools, the new employees are oriented to the acquiring firm's way of doing business.

FIGURE 6–4. The Wheel of Fortune at General Electric

Source: R. N. Ashkenas, L. J. DeMonaco, and S. C. Francis, "Making the Deal Real: How GE Capital Integrates Acquisitions," *Harvard Business Review,* January–February 1998, p. 167.

The involvement and visibility of senior management is critical. So is accountability for specific integration tasks. This is the stage when, if necessary, painful decisions concerning terminations are made quickly and fairly, so that the new organization can move forward.

As integration proceeds, various process tools and techniques are used to accelerate the integration and deal with any resistance to change. The transition team helps to identify opportunities for demonstrating success, and these projects are given high priority. Short-term international exchanges so as to get acquainted provide motivation at this stage. While the integration is tightly managed, there are regular learning reviews to allow for adjustment and take into account the feedback from employees.

The process of integration does not finish in "a hundred days." In order to assimilate the new employees into the parent firm, the development of common tools, practices, and processes continues. Corporate education and long-term management exchanges are two sets of tools that help in diffusing the shared culture. In acquisitions, learning never stops. Auditing the whole integration process and incorporating any learning into the core blueprint completes the cycle—so that the next acquisition can be done even faster and better.

TAKEAWAYS

1. Most merger or acquisition failures are linked to problems in post-merger integration. Cultural and people issues consistently rank among the main difficulties in executing acquisitions. Do not underestimate the importance of cross-cultural differences, but on the other hand do not confuse culture with poor management.
2. Probably the most consistent predictor of M&A success is past experience in acquisitions. The more the company merges, the better it gets at merging and the stronger the talent and experience for the next merger. Companies that have solid foundations in HRM and a good track record in managing change also tend to be good at managing acquisitions.
3. There are various strategic logics behind mergers—stand-alone, absorption, reverse merger, "best of both," and transformation. Each has different implications for the nature of the post-merger integration process. Think about the end-state before you start.
4. HR should be involved early in the acquisition planning since the "soft" aspects of the due diligence process, such as the assessment of culture and people practices in the organization to be acquired, are just as important as the financial analysis.
5. The integration process starts with the creation of a vision and strategy for the combined organization. Clear communication of the vision and strategy is an essential foundation for success. The guideline for effective communication is "play it straight."
6. However well the acquisition has been prepared, one cannot avoid the merger syndrome—the shock/stress cycle experienced by the "losers" and the victory cycle experienced by the "winners." The "first hundred days" need to be carefully managed, providing insight, information, involvement, and inspiration.
7. Many acquisitions fail because of the loss of key talent, so retention is a key priority, an effort that should begin during due diligence so that retention plans can be put in place from the first day of the acquisition. In the long term, retention requires commitment from senior management to building personal relationships with the acquired talent.
8. It is important to move with speed. Key decisions about management structure, senior appointments, and people's careers should be made as soon as possible.

Uncertainty and anxiety after the acquisition drain energy from the business, increasing the risk of loss of customers.

9. Several steps in the post-merger integration are known to foster success: appoint an integration manager to speed up the process; measure M&A outcomes; assign accountability; secure and celebrate quick wins.

10. Some firms see their competence in making international acquisitions as one of their core capabilities. They are distinguished by their ability to learn from past acquisitions, including the mistakes.

NOTES

1. "The DaimlerChrysler Emulsion," *The Economist,* July 29, 2000.

2. *Mergers and Acquisitions Almanac,* February 2001, pp. 37–39.

3. This is a conservative estimate. In many domestic M&A deals, a significant part of the transaction may involve affiliates in different parts of the world.

4. A survey of top managers in large European acquirers indicated that 61 percent of them believed that cross-border acquisitions are riskier than domestic ones (Angwin and Savill, 1997).

5. According to a Conference Board study, the major reasons for M&A were to achieve competitive size (61 percent of responding firms) and to gain market share (57 percent) (Conference Board, 1997, p. 5).

6. For example, the Whirlpool alliance agreement with Tatramat (discussed in Chapter 5) stipulated terms under which Whirlpool can acquire full control of the venture (Ferencikova and Pucik, 1999).

7. Garette and Dussauge, 2000.

8. Most of these and similar studies looked at the financial outcomes of the M&A transactions. There are other stakeholders in the acquisition process, including the employees, local communities, and customers.

9. "The Case against Mergers," *Business Week,* October 30, 1995, p. 122.

10. P. Krass, "Why Do We Do It," *Across the Board,* May/June, 2001, pp. 22–27.

11. A. T. Kearney, 1999.

12. KPMG, 1999.

13. The authors of the KPMG report described this as "a quirky result." However, an earlier study of Bleeke, Ernst, Isono, and Weinberg (1993) came to a similar conclusion, namely, that "cross-border M&A for the largest companies has a relatively high success rate compared with other forms of corporate expansion" (p. 79).

14. Hitt, Harrison, and Ireland, 2001.

15. This Egon Zehnder study is outlined by Marks and Mirvis (1998).

16. A. T. Kearney, 1999.

17. Ibid.

18. While this book does not discuss in depth how to manage change processes, some of the lessons are reviewed briefly in Chapters 2 and 9. GE is a good example, as discussed in Chapter 9. Their Change Acceleration methodology (CAP) is applied by GE integration teams to manage different facets of the acquisition integration process.

19. Hitt, Harrison, and Ireland, 2001, pp. 105–109.

20. Bower, 2001.

21. Steger, 1999.

22. Haspeslagh and Jemison, 1991.

23. Marks and Mirvis, 1998.

24. Kay and Shelton, 2000.
25. KPMG, 1999.
26. Ibid., p. 15.
27. Hitt, Harrison, and Ireland, 2001, p. 111.
28. "Renault Steers Forward," *The Wall Street Journal Europe,* February 15, 2001, p. 31.
29. Chu, 1996.
30. Johnson and Rich, 2000.
31. SHRM, 2000.
32. See Chapter 5, p. 215.
33. Angwin, 2001.
34. Marks and Mirvis, 1998, pp. 66–67.
35. One frequently used assessment tool is the Denison Culture Survey (Denison, Cho, and Young, 2000). For an example of an internally developed instrument, see the Merging Cultures Evaluation Index (MCEI) described in Marks and Mirvis (1998), pp. 65–66.
36. Larsson and Finkelstein, 1999.
37. Some plans allow for employees to cash out immediately after an acquisition is approved by shareholders, but before the closing. In such cases, the closing should be made contingent on retention of key staff.
38. In knowledge-intensive acquisitions, it is particularly important to protect the value of the deal from the competitive implications of employee defection. We will discuss later the specific post-merger retention strategies, but during due diligence it is essential to clarify who has rights to technology and the know-how, the acquired company or individual employees, and who are the key contributors who should be contractually obliged to remain. When trade secrets and confidential information are important assets of the acquired companies, then it is wise to tie the closing to no-competition, no-disclosure agreements with key employees.
39. Not all acquisition agreements go through. Some collapse because of drastic change in market conditions between announcement and closing; for others regulatory hurdles may prove to be insurmountable; and there are those where parties simply change their mind and find a way to get out of the deal. Meanwhile, of course, people at all levels of the organization speculate about their future in the new organization, some with great expectations, others with fear. It is important that such contingencies are considered in the HR plan, in particular since this affects retention of talent.
40. To assure the fairness and objectivity of this process, many companies are turning to outside vendors.
41. O'Reilly and Pfeffer, 2000, pp. 63–64. Some of the other elements of this description are also taken from O'Reilly and Pfeffer.
42. Marks and Mirvis, 1998.
43. Ashkenas, DeMonaco, and Francis, 1998.
44. Inkpen, Sundaram, and Rockwood, 2000.
45. Child, Faulkner, and Pitkethly, 2001; PA Consulting, 2001.
46. This section is adapted from Morosini (1998). "Mega-mergers: The 'Real' Challenges Start after the Deal Is Signed," *Perspectives for Managers,* IMD, September 1999.
47. Morosini, 1998.
48. Ashkenas, DeMonaco, and Francis (1998); Ashkenas and Francis, 2000.
49. Ashkenas and Francis, 2000.
50. Some of these principles of change management are reviewed briefly in Chapters 2 and 9. GE applies its change acceleration process (CAP) methodology (described in Chapter 9) to the merger integration process.

51. According to research conducted by Krug and Hegerty (2001), the decision of top managers in an acquired firm to stay rather than leave is correlated with their positive perceptions of the merger announcement.
52. Inkpen, Sundaram, and Rockwood, 2000.
53. "Torch That Sent a Deal Down in Flames," *Financial Times,* April 12, 2000, p. 22.
54. Marks and Mirvis, 1998, p. 74.
55. Krug and Hegerty, 1997.
56. On differences in performance standards across cultures, see p. 166.
57. Corporate Leadership Council, 2000, p. 37.
58. GE's CAP methodology is discussed in Chapter 9.
59. Retention bonus guidelines provide desirable consistency, specifying eligibility, amount, performance criteria, etc. Their effect depends, however, on employees' expectations as well as on labor and tax legislation in the countries involved.
60. Corporate Leadership Council, 2000.
61. Krug and Hegerty, 2001.
62. Watson Wyatt, 1999.
63. GE's approach to performance management is described in Chapter 7, p. 331.
64. See Beer, Eisenstat, and Spector (1990).
65. Haleblian and Finkelstein, 1999.
66. When Citibank top management announced its intention to grow in Europe through acquisitions, senior HR leaders in the region quickly organized an intensive M&A workshop to prepare their key staff for challenges ahead. Several weeks after the workshop the bank announced a major deal in Poland—and the local HR manager was there ready to fully participate in the acquisition team.
67. Hitt, Hoskisson, Ireland, and Harrison, 1991.
68. This section is based on a study of HR practices in forty acquisitions of U.K. firms by U.S. French, German, and Japanese acquirers as reported in Child, Faulkner, and Pitkethly (2001), pp. 166–80.
69. See p. 257.

PART 3

The HRM Agenda in the Transnational Firm

Our focus turns now to the transnational enterprise, introduced earlier in Part I, which is characterized by contradictions that are experienced as tensions. One of the roles of human resource management is to assist the organization in steering through underlying dualities. A certain sophistication in HRM is required by the transnational to confront these tensions for it is impossible to separate the human resource issues from the broader strategic and management context.

In Chapter 7 we explore the role that human resource management plays in building network coordination and "organizational glue," vital to the functioning of the transnational firm. Coordination mechanisms such as cross-border project groups and steering boards are built on a fundamental vehicle—relationships between people. These mechanisms rely on some degree of what is called "normative integration"—shared language and concepts, norms and assumptions, and deeper values, leading us to discuss an important duality in the transnational firm—maintaining the necessary cohesion but avoiding the weakness of excessively strong cultures.

How does the transnational go about talent and leadership development? This is the focus of Chapter 8, where we review the guiding ideas behind the development of talent, the particular issue of international leadership development, and finally the wider need for developing a global mindset. In the course of this review, we discuss how competencies can help the transnational firm to steer talent development by providing common, firm-specific frameworks across its worldwide operations. We discuss why a rigorous process for the identification and development of potential is necessary, how firms in different cultures have tackled this, and why global mindset is an essential tool for managing the contradictions embedded in the international management process.

In Chapter 9 we explore the "tortuous path" of change as corporations face up to transnational pressures. Building on a conceptual review of complex change management, we discuss three paths of strategic change: how a multidomestic firm deals with the pressure to become more integrated; how a globally integrated firm fosters local initiative and distributes capabilities around the world; and how professional service firms, built exclusively on human assets, tackle the difficulties of managing knowledge as they internationalize. We conclude this part of the book by asking how the transnational firm can manage the creation and transfer of knowledge. Many view this as the major challenge for the future. We discuss recent concepts associated with innovation and knowledge management, as well as their practical implications, going from theories of social capital to research on the management of innovation in international firms.

CHAPTER 7

Mastering Network Coordination

If there is a prototype of an organization that has pioneered the route to becoming a transnational, an archetype of the global network corporation, it must be ABB (see the box "Coordination and Connectivity at ABB").

The result of a merger in 1987 between the Swedish Asea and the Swiss Brown Boveri, ABB grew in ten years to the position of a leading global power engineering company. Headquartered in Switzerland, ABB employs 220,000 people in more than fifty countries around the globe, with over $30 billion in sales. Aside from power engineering, its products range from industrial robotics to five-dollar mass produced electrical components sold to wholesalers. Under the leadership of Percy Barnevik, Asea and then ABB outperformed even GE in return on shareholder investment between 1980 and 1996 (30 percent ROI, compared to GE's 21 percent, and a mere 9 percent for ABB's other archcompetitor Siemens).[1]

There are many ways of structuring and operating on a global scale, but all of them require difficult choices between centralized integration and local autonomy. ABB was built on the management challenge of combining worldwide reach with the flexibility and speed of a local competitor. As Barnevik put it, "We want to be global and local, big and small, radically decentralized with central reporting and control. If we can resolve those contradictions we can create real organizational advantage." ABB achieved this by creating what some observers called "a globally connected corporation," a network of processes, a spider's web of relationships between committed people, held together by a rigorous financial measurement system called *Abacus* (an acronym for the ABB Accounting and Communication—not control!—System), as well as strongly held principles of management.[2] In this chapter we will be considering the role of HRM in building that type of connectivity.

As Percy Barnevik put it, "The common denominators in these efforts are communication, understanding and patience. There is no question that the price to pay for a high degree of 'multinationality' is a major investment in two-way communication and consensus building across borders. Even after making full use of technical means of communication, a significant amount of time must still be invested throughout the

Coordination and Connectivity at ABB
Practice Box

ABB is highly local in its extreme degree of decentralization. Barnevik believed passionately in decentralization to maintain flexibility and customer contact, to motivate good people, to be close to local authorities. Until 1998, ABB was structured around 5,000 business units, each with profit and loss responsibility, averaging 50 people—from a small sales unit in Finland to a large manufacturing plant in the Midwest of the United States.

Over 30 percent of ABB's revenues came from the collaboration of these business units. The first source of coordination was the structure. ABB was held together by a matrix of business segment managers and country managers, grouped into three business areas and three major geographic regions. But within this structure, the roles and skills of the managers were more significant than the hierarchic reporting lines. Business and country managers were coordinators and coaches more than controllers. All had wide international experience, and most of them had worked previously in both country and business positions. A third project dimension was added later to the matrix, with central managers heading up large-scale projects that might involve 100 business units cutting across business areas and countries.

However, matrix at ABB did not mean that all important decisions needed the approval of both business and country managers. Matrix reflected differentiation, the fact that the importance of consulting with business and country bosses varies according to the market. While ABB simplified this complex organization in 1998, giving business areas the dominant responsibility, the matrix culture still prevails.

Behind the structure lie a vast array of coordinating mechanisms that supply the connectivity, the "soft" glue—and the "hard" glue, such as *Abacus*, the rapid and transparent measurement system that makes accountability very real. "Abacus is a unifying factor,"

says a profit center manager. "It allows you to enter results and comments/criteria which is all fed back to Zurich . . . . You can see what is happening by business area, by company, by profit center. If you are failing to perform, you will get a call. They will come back to you with comments and suggestions. It is a very good way to run a global business." Clarity on strategy is another source of glue. The top 100 managers meet four times a year to reach a clear understanding on strategy, with the senior 500 people meeting every two years. Investment in common IT platforms is a source of connectivity that will continue to grow in importance.

The hard glue is complemented by soft glue. Norms concerning performance in people development are vital—financial performance is not enough. "Some managers get good results, but they are always taking people," says Barnevik. "Others get good results and they also give good people to other parts of the firm. We are looking for givers and not takers." The soft glue is embodied in the ABB policy bible that was mapped out at one of its first management conferences.

There are principles for managing creative tension. Conflicts are frequent in such a matrix, and the motto is that the customer must come first, the Group second (including the business area and/or country), and the profit center third. There are innumerable forums for exchange, both formal and informal, and the widespread use of multinational teams. With a Swedish CEO and ABB headquarters in Zurich, the language for all exchange and documents is English. There is a carefully managed rotation of managers to ensure that their experience provides them with the perspective to understand both local and global interests. And then there are the vital face-to-face relationships through which conflicts get worked out. Travel, travel, travel . . . . Barnevik himself reckoned that he met with 4,000–5,000 people each year.

organization in face-to-face meetings and teamwork. In the final analysis, openness, trust and respect are the key words in all this."[3]

But there is a flip side to the use of this coordination technology. It can create an extremely complex organization—it is difficult to imagine the degree of coordination that is required to hold an organization of 5,000 business units together, as at ABB! Excessive coordination may slow down strategic decision-making on alliances and buying or selling businesses. Indeed, under Barnevik's successor, Goran Lindahl, ABB simplified its organization along business lines. In 2000, ABB paved the way in moving to a front-back organization to try to combine customer orientation with global-scale advantages. If they are successful, it will be because of the lessons of their experience in managing connectivity through people.

CHAPTER OVERVIEW

The purpose of this chapter is to understand how to build the connectivity and coordination that characterize the transnational enterprise and the role of human resource management in facilitating it. It is a vital role—indeed we think of HRM as "glue" technology.

The vertical or hierarchic model of integration that has characterized management thought since the industrial revolution has reached the limits of its usefulness. For the last thirty years, we have witnessed attempts to develop a new horizontal or lateral technology of coordination. ABB is one of the numerous pioneers in this respect. Hierarchic integration and control do not disappear—their use is transformed and becomes an element in the technology of coordination.

This chapter has three parts. The first part discusses the logic of the transition from hierarchic integration to lateral coordination. We discuss this from three different angles: the nature of competition facing a transnational firm, people management implications of a knowledge-based society, and what organizational theory tells us about managing in a complex environment.

The second and the main part of the chapter considers how to build horizontal coordination. Starting with the understanding that coordination takes place essentially through relationships, we focus in particular on four coordinating mechanisms:

- Cross-boundary teams.
- Cross-boundary steering groups.
- Know-how sharing, leading toward knowledge management.
- Regional or global process management.

These mechanisms rely on some degree of what is called "normative integration"— shared language and concepts, norms and assumptions, and deeper values. We explore what this implies in the third part of the chapter, leading us to discuss an important duality in the transnational firm—maintaining necessary cohesion but avoiding the weakness of excessively strong culture.

We return to the matrixed reality of the transnational firm in conclusion and summarize by standing conventional thinking on its head—matrix everything *except* the structure! Finally, we look ahead to the next chapter, where we will focus on the implications of network coordination for talent and leadership development.

FROM HIERARCHIC TO HORIZONTAL COORDINATION

The traditional model of corporate governance and integration is hierarchic, employing rules, standard operating procedures, and central policy guidelines; central planning backed up by staff experts at headquarters; central decision-making; and expatriates as agents of headquarter control. Clearly, it is a model that is breaking down—indeed it has already broken down in industries facing strong transnational pressures to operate both locally and globally.

The hierarchic or structural concept of integration and control led firms down two routes as the complexity of international coordination increased—the paths of matrix structure and of headquarters staff. Both these routes largely failed, leading to the search for new ways of managing coordination. Since then, the focus has increasingly been on horizontal processes of coordination, side-by-side relationships between partners (be they internal or external, individual or organizational). This is captured by the metaphor of the organization as a *network*.

Horizontal coordination does not replace vertical integration—it transforms it. The leader becomes a strategic coach rather than a controller. General management becomes a responsibility of all middle and senior managers—the only clear-cut general management jobs are in entrepreneurial business units quite low down in the structure. The focus of planning shifts from content to process, with an emphasis on working through conflicts and building commitment to strategies.[4] As for corporate staff, their roles change from functional experts to network facilitators. Global or regional processes for connecting different activities together replace policies. Measurement becomes an instrument for enhanced self-management rather than control.

How can we best understand the logic of this transformation?

The Competitive Perspective

Today's transnational organization faces a situation different from the past. The American, European, and Japanese companies that spearheaded the process of internationalization in the post-1945 era had most of their know-how located at the center. Those firms could exploit scale economies through their facilities at home. That is less so today and will be far less true in the future.

Consider the new realities:

- Subsidiaries in other countries may be of paramount importance to the multinational, sometimes representing larger markets than at home. This has long been the case for MNCs from smaller countries such as Switzerland and Sweden. The technical and managerial sophistication of some lead subsidiaries may outstrip that in the parent country so that information has to flow from the subsidiary to the headquarters. Businesses may be centered in these other countries, and these multiple centers must be linked together.

- Subsidiaries vary in their strategic importance and in their competencies and resources.[5] The transnational organization is highly differentiated, and traditional notions of structure, policy, and planning cannot cope with this—there is a need for "variable geometry." For subsidiaries that are strategic leaders, planning may involve intensive interaction with the headquarters, whereas distant "contributors" may be left alone as long as they deliver the targets. In the former unit, staff development and compensation policies may be negotiated so as to balance corporate and local interests, whereas the contributor adjusts more to local practices. As the box "Coordination and Connectivity at ABB" indicates, ABB's matrix was no more than a reflection of this differentiation in reporting and consultation.

- If one could afford to be slow in the past, this is no longer true. The pace of competition, the need to be "better, cheaper, faster," has increased. Instead of competing with local companies that were often relatively weak on technical and management expertise, companies like ABB compete today with sophisticated multinationals such as GE in its many different battlefields around the world. With the current wave of acquisition consolidation, this is likely to increase.

- In many industries, competitive advantage for the future cannot be secured through further economies of scale, downsizing and delayering so as to improve operational effectiveness. Companies such as Texas Instruments and Xerox, having pushed the limits of operational improvement, realize that competitive advantage in the future can come only through leveraging know-how across manufacturing and sales functions in their affiliates. Innovation is increasing local-to-center, local-to-regional, local-to-local, and regional-to-regional.

Collectively all these trends mean that the traditional focus on headquarters-subsidiary relationships and on ways of structuring the multinational corporation are giving way to the question of how to coordinate relationships, how to build and maintain ties and how to manage complex webs of connections. The focus on center-to-subsidiary relations remains, but to this one adds the focus on subsidiary-to-center(s), and subsidiary-to-subsidiary ties.

The People Perspective

As societies began the transition to the now visible postindustrial society based on cerebral knowledge skills rather than manual ability, so the top-down, hierarchic control mode of organization came under increasing attack from the perspective of how to manage people. The wave of bestsellers in the 80s launched the assault.[6] But the origins lay in Douglas McGregor's elegant formulation of two assumptions about the nature of management. He contrasted the pathologies of the traditional control-oriented Theory X underlying the hierarchic model with his Theory Y, which assumes that people can be trusted to perform well if they are given appropriately challenging work and feedback.[7]

The top-down control model of management could not cope with the global pressures to be better, cheaper, and faster. The cost of multiple layers of supervision and control weighed heavily, and the people undertaking the work were adding little if any value. It became more rational to invest in self-control (complemented by automation) rather than boss-control—essentially via HRM, through emphasis on selection, skill development, objective setting, feedback, and performance- and skill-based rewards—in "empowerment," as the Americans started to call it.[8] And as innovation began to matter, traditional hierarchical firms found that they could neither attract nor retain the new generation of skilled knowledge professionals. Controllers had to become coaches.

The Organizational Theory Perspective

Organization theory has shown that as the environment becomes more complex, as the information processing demands increase, so the organization has to complement its reliance on hierarchic modes of information processing and decision-making with attention to lateral modes. Galbraith showed that the best way of coordinating in simple and stable environments is to use hierarchic mechanisms such as rules and standard operating procedures, hierarchic referral (ask the boss), and planning systems that lead to goal setting (explicit performance contracts).[9] But as complexity and turbulence increase, these hierarchic mechanisms can no longer cope. On the one hand, the organization will try to reduce the need for information processing by creating self-contained units, such as accountable business units—even going to the extent of creating separate companies, as AT&T/Lucent, Hewlett-Packard, Shell, ICI, and others have done recently. On the other hand, it will increase the coordination capacity by creating lateral or horizontal relationships, complemented by investments in vertical information systems. Research shows this shift from structure to horizontal coordination over the last thirty years.[10]

Consequently, it has become increasingly common to think of organizations as networks of internal and external relationships. Research is beginning to catch up to the metaphor (see the box "Network Analysis and Theory"), although the analytic tools for studying organizations as networks are ahead of the theory. We will be meeting this perspective frequently in Part III.

In terms of network theory, bureaucratic or mechanistic structures have a low degree of connectivity. Relationships are asymmetric (top-down with little upward feedback) and centralized (focused on a few key actors in hierarchical positions). In contrast, organic or adaptive organizations are characterized by dense, strongly interconnected networks, with many lateral and reciprocal relationships. The overall degree of integration is much higher.[11] The principle of requisite complexity is satisfied—that the internal complexity of the firm must mirror the complexity of its external environment.

In summary, the three perspectives on the transnational firm introduced here all lead in the same direction, emphasizing the importance of horizontal network coordination. In the rest of this chapter, we discuss how to build this through HRM, not omitting to mention some of the pitfalls.

Network Analysis and Theory
Research Box

The focus of network analysis is on *relational data*—contacts, ties, and connections—rather than on *attributes* such as income or attitudes as in traditional research or on *patterns* as in ethnographic research. Network theory points out that all economic action is embedded in networks of social relationships.[A]

Until the late 80s, the focus was on developing analytic techniques rather than theory development. A sophisticated range of methodologies and analytic concepts began to emerge.[B] Organization and management theory got interested in network analysis with work on interlocking directorships of companies. In recent years network analysis has been increasingly adopted by researchers on the multinational organization seeking to understand how networks shape the knowledge-based firm.[C]

The network perspective influences organization theory in important ways. Rather than viewing a firm's environment in terms of abstract concepts of uncertainty and complexity, it sees environment as a network of other organizations. It captures the actual configuration of relationships that underlie concepts such as centralization and decentralization, rather than simply measuring these in terms of perceived asymmetric rights over decision-making. In contrast to the idea that "big is beautiful," the network perspective emphasizes that small is not trivial if many small organizations link themselves together to form a network.

Since practitioners are often bewildered by the jungle of unfamiliar and often mathematical terminology, there is a risk that the idea of a network may be-

come no more than a powerful but loose metaphor, rather like that of "organizational culture" in the 80s.[D]

[A]See Scott (1991) for an account of the history of social network analysis, as well as for an outline of its analytic techniques. See also Krackhardt and Hanson (1993) for an account of network analysis applied to organizations.

The origins of network theory go back to anthropological studies in the 1930s of cliques and social structures in communities, as well as psychological studies of small groups leading to sociometry. Social network analysis moved ahead in the 60s and 70s as specialist sociologists and anthropologists studied the mathematical basis for social structures.

[B]Among these methodologies and analytic methods of network analysis are the following: (i) matrix mapping techniques known as block modeling that are used to discover structural relationships; (ii) ways of mapping ties in terms of the content of connections (friendship, information exchange, advice, trust); (iii) structural concepts such as *density* (the degree of linkage within a matrix of relationships, or more formally the ratio of actual to potential ties), *centrality* of actors within a network, *connectivity* (the degree to which actors are linked together through direct and indirect ties)(see Nohria and Eccles, 1992, for a brief explanation of these concepts); (iv) many other concepts of which the most important are *cohesion* (high density in a group reflecting strong mutual relationships), *equivalence* (groups that are structurally similar in relation to third parties), and *brokerage* (linkage to otherwise disconnected groups); (v) concepts distinguishing the strength or intensity of ties (weak versus strong ties).

[C]Network analysis is currently being employed to explore many questions. Why do some people move faster ahead in their careers than others? What explains the strategic decisions of firms, notably over alliances? How to explain knowledge creation and transfer in organizations? For example, there will be a high degree of transfer of know-how in dense and highly interconnected networks, though there may be less creation since few individuals have high structural autonomy.

[D]An interesting source book on networks and organizations, written so as to prevent the network concept becoming a tired metaphor, is Nohria and Eccles (1992).

COORDINATING MECHANISMS: USING THE TECHNOLOGY OF ORGANIZATIONAL GLUE

Coordination technology has a content and a process side. The content side of coordination has received a lot of attention, assessing the aims, benefits, and risks of "synergy." This has been called "sizing the prize"[12]—breaking down the general objectives of coordination into more specific deliverables. For example, the general aim of leveraging international products in a consumer products company has to be broken down into more concrete objectives so as to be doable—transferring know-how on positioning and segmentation from successful countries; decreasing duplicated costs while increasing brand recognition through careful redesign of packaging in selected countries. A general map of coordination benefits is shown in Figure 7–1.

Because network coordination is applied with a purpose in mind, we often use the term "organizational glue" to describe the underlying process technology rather than more general terms such as cohesion or coordination. Glue is something that can be used to stick two parts of an organization together with a specific purpose in mind. Indeed the term that we started using fifteen years ago seems to strike a responsive chord and to be catching on. *Glue technology* is to a great extent the application of human resource management.

Our framework of the coordination tools, or glue technology, is shown in Figure 7–2. The vertical pillars are the actual tools of coordination, while the horizontal bars are enabling mechanisms without which the application of the tools will be handicapped. Let us give an overview by working up from the bottom of this framework.

The foundation of most mechanisms of coordination is *relationships between people.* Put simply, lateral coordination means communication between people, increasingly facilitated by electronic technology. Relationships are the means through which coordination takes place, not the ends. We have seen many companies bringing their senior managers together for an annual meeting so as to build relationships between them. Yet, while this may provide a break from daily routine, all too often they go back to their individual units and nothing happens.

The first of the tools that builds on relationships so as to make things happen is *cross-boundary teamwork.* Team or project work has become a basic and accepted building block of coordination, so as to tackle boundary problems or to deliver products or services across borders to a customer.

FIGURE 7–1. The Potential Benefits of Coordination or Linkage Management

1. **Improved Internal Trading**

2. **Coordinating Strategies**
   • Avoid unhelpful competition.
   • Avoid unintentional damage.
   • Help outmaneuver competitors.

3. **Pooling Power Regarding Outside Groups**
   • Suppliers (purchasing).
   • Customers (common service, account management).
   • Employees (recruitment, retention, career development).
   • Bankers.
   • Government; pressure groups.

4. **Better Utilization and Development of Tangible Assets** (example: overhead cost sharing)
   • Plant, machinery, buildings.
   • Logistics and distribution.
   • Sales forces.
   • Functions; experts.

5. **Better Use of Intangible Assets**
   • Know-how (e.g. transfer of best practice, share-and-compare).
   • Ideas, opportunities, and innovation (e.g. new product/market development).
   • Skills and competencies.
   • Connections.
   • Reputation and brands.

Source: Adapted from M. Goold, A. Campbell, and M. Alexander, *Corporate-Level Strategy: Creating Value in the Multibusiness Company* (New York:Wiley, 1994).

FIGURE 7–2. Coordination Mechanisms

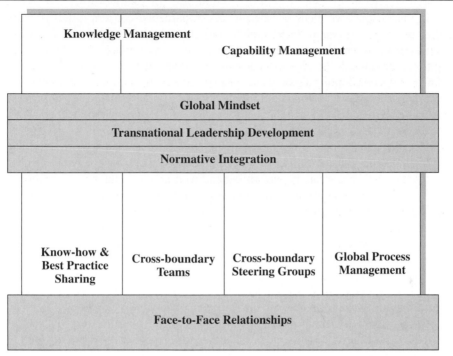

The second tool is *cross-boundary steering groups,* which take the shape of internal boards and councils, as well as the steering groups that guide and supervise cross-boundary teams. Transnationals use these steering groups to complement the basic structure, broadening the perspectives that can be brought to bear on strategic decisions. Their membership is flexible; they can be formed and disbanded as circumstances require.

The third element of glue technology is *know-how sharing.* Know-how is becoming vitally important for the transnational firm, but it is scattered around the world. It needs to be transferred or collected. Whereas teamwork typically focuses on problem solving and customer delivery, know-how sharing concerns learning and improvement.

The fourth tool is *regional or global process management.* Since formalization and standardization are ways of achieving coordination, organizations have traditionally tried to standardize behavior through rules, policies, and operating procedures. While these can no longer cope with the differentiated complexity of the transnational, formalized and standardized *processes* can avoid reinventing the wheel. Process management represents a "horizontalization" of these traditional vertical tools, capturing the advantages of global integration while respecting the local differences. A worldwide recruitment process, for example, does not specify who should be hired for business X in country Y. But it does spell out the steps, considerations, consultations, tools to be used, and the like that will lead to an appropriate decision, guided by explicit assumptions that allow for the exception.

In this chapter, we focus on one process of particular concern to HRM, namely, *global performance management,* which goes from the "upstream" aligning of units around appropriate goals and strategies through measurement metrics, to "downstream" appraisal and rewards. In its process design, how does the transnational firm strike the balance between adopting a global and uniform approach facilitating coordination and the need to take into account local differences? Performance management provides a basic discipline to the organization. Coordination across poorly performing and badly managed units is of questionable benefit. The costs will outweigh the benefits, and the energies of managers will be split dysfunctionally between cross-border coordination and the nuts-and-bolts of getting their own units in shape. Conversely, the benefit of coordination between strongly performing and well-managed units is tremendous.[13]

The four coordination mechanisms discussed above, the pillars shown in Figure 7–2, go hand in hand. For example, the ability to manage teams across borders requires steering group competence and it is facilitated by the discipline of performance management. We speak of pillars since competence in each of these areas of coordination is built up step by step.

The three horizontal bars in the middle of Figure 7–2 represent important enabling mechanisms. The first is *normative integration*—the shared language, norms, attitudes, assumptions, and values that are a result of careful socialization of organizational members. There is not much likelihood of payoff from investment in know-how sharing or performance management unless there is some degree of cohesion in the way people think, the norms for tackling conflict, and the interpretation of terms such as "high quality" or "poor performance."

Leadership development, the second horizontal bar, has long been recognized as a critical enabler of coordination. Socialization efforts to build normative integration will initially be focused on future leaders, the "critical few." The transnational firm will run into problems, however, if the myriad conflicts are constantly being referred upward to those leaders for arbitration. This leads to the third and final bar, what we call *global mindset*. The ability to cope with conflict and contradiction may have to be built into the mindset of these managers and professionals. Global mindset is a set of attitudes that predispose individuals to cope constructively with competing priorities (for example global versus local priorities) rather than advocating one dimension at the expense of others. We will discuss leadership development and global mindset separately in the next chapter.

One can argue about what are "pillars" and what are "bars" in the schematic framework. The important point, however, is that these mechanisms go hand in hand and reinforce each the other. At the very top of Figure 7–2, we see knowledge management and the management of organizational capabilities. The point is that sophisticated coordination abilities such as these are unlikely to work well unless there are solid foundations in all of the other areas of glue technology.

After this overview of the mechanisms of coordination, let us now go back to the basic foundation, the starting point—the recognition (underlying network theory) that all economic activity is embedded in relationships.

Building Face-to-Face Relationships

Things get done through relationships—and notably coordination.[14] Relationships (or *ties* as they are called in network theory) are the *social capital* of the enterprise. Ties are the basic unit of coordination. Network coordination simply implies broadening the structure of relationships, where they add value, beyond the hierarchic reporting line.

It is not that everyone has to know everyone else, quite to the contrary. A small number of relationships can greatly increase the coordination capability of the firm. Those ties provide potential access when necessary to other people ("someone who knows someone who knows someone").[15] To build up their social capital, individuals build ties that span boundaries.[16]

Organizations in the past were driven by relationships that were often formed early in life—the old boys' network, the clan formed at a university, the team of people who built up and internationalized the company. These clans and clubs drove alliances, projects, and innovations. Rather than allowing yesterday's networks to steer business development, relationships in the transnational organization are built with today's and tomorrow's needs for coordination in mind. This means bringing people together where there are current or future linkages, where coordination needs are felt to exist. Typical tools are company conferences, annual jamborees, regional or worldwide functional meetings, exchange seminars, workshops between two companies after a merger, or central training programs.

While there may be some informational or educational input at these meetings, the main objective is to build necessary relationships. There is considerable art to the design of such functions—managing process is if anything more important than managing content. The expensive failures are those at which people feel they have listened only to inputs they could have read on the company intranet and have socialized only with regular colleagues. The successes are when participants build useful relations with new people, learn new perspectives, and modify stereotypes of others. Appropriately designed, these occasions develop the interpersonal networking skills that are fundamental to the functioning of the transnational enterprise.

Consequently international firms have long viewed interpersonal and communication skills as a basic competency for professional people especially in leadership roles. Companies recruiting from international business schools such as INSEAD and IMD say that the most essential attribute they look for in potential recruits is skill in dealing with people who are different from themselves. The majority of company seminars organized by business schools around the world are designed in part to build the network of relationships between key people.

Managers sometimes ask us how the conflicts in transnational management can be minimized. It is the wrong question. Given the contradictions and tensions that define the transnational, as ABB recognizes, conflict is inevitable in such an organization. What is important is to provide constructive mechanisms to work through matters of contention. At the heart of contention management is the insight that all conflicts get worked out through relationships. This is an observation to which we will return. The following is one illustrative example.

About fifteen years ago there was a merger between a large French company and its British competitor to form the largest packaging group in Europe. On paper, the merger made a great deal of sense, but the business analysts discounted the potential advantages because they felt that two such arch competitors would continue to fight with each other. The president of the newly formed group decided to invest seriously in building relationships. The top twenty-five executives, half French and half British, were told to clear their desks for ten days. They were flown to Saudi Arabia, then on by helicopter into the middle of the desert. Landing on a sand dune, they got out and found two caterpillar trucks with camping equipment, food, and water—and, as the helicopter took off, a letter from the president saying that he looked forward to seeing them in four days' time for their first management meeting at a hotel in Riyadh! This unexpected "outward bound" experience in the desert heat was a dramatic but successful way of breaking the ice and building relationships! It was a real "team" that arrived at the hotel, spending the next four days hammering out the strategy for the new group. The team building paid off in open and constructive surfacing and resolution of conflicts. The strategy was highly successful, and the share price soared.

In this instance, the relationship building effort had a clear objective, namely, developing a strategy for the merged corporation. We return to a point mentioned earlier. Unless there is a well-thought-out purpose, backed up by careful preparation, the cost of relationship building may exceed the benefits. In the case of a Belgian corporation formed by the merger of a dozen companies ten years before, each year the senior executives had met for an annual three-day conference, and for the first three years the effort had seemed useful. But after another seven years, there were complaints about the time-wasting "annual mass" (as they called it, referring to the Catholic ritual), where all they would do was discuss the annual results and exchange viewpoints. Although this had been useful on the first few occasions, there had never been any follow-up in terms of specific collaboration between the merged companies.

Relationships that have no ongoing specific purpose, that exist as a consequence of shared experiences in the past, can be thought of as "weak ties." A recent study of 120 new product development projects in a large electronics company shows that weak ties are effective in searching for and transferring information that is relatively simple and codified.[17] If you want some straightforward technical information, send out an e-mail to twenty acquaintances to ask them if they know anyone who has it. However, when the know-how to be transferred is more complex (tacit and interdependent with other elements of knowledge), then stronger glue technology involving joint working parties, project groups, and the transfer of personnel is needed.

Cross-Boundary Teams

Heineken needs to wrestle with the issue of how many breweries of different types and sizes they will need in Europe as they move into the new century; Kodak has to decide how to launch global marketing of a new type of digital camera; BP-Amoco wants to beef up performance management in its subsidiaries while respecting local constraints.[18] The common element in these challenges in very different industries is that attacking them will involve cross-boundary or project teams. Such teams in different shapes and forms are a fundamental coordination mechanism in the transnational enterprise. Indeed one might argue that teamwork of this sort is the basic unit of the global economy. Strategic decisions in global organizations are complex, and the best way to achieve sound decisions is often through a transnational team of managers and specialists whose talents have been carefully blended.

The resolution of complex challenges depends not only on working through conflicting priorities but also on building commitment to the implementation of what is decided. Appropriately managed, cross-boundary teams achieve both. While some important projects may involve full-time work, most are undertaken by managers and professionals in addition to their operational responsibilities, requiring them to work in matrixed or "split egg" ways.

Cross-boundary teamwork takes different forms. The Heineken strategy team that will be set up to decide on its European brewery locations is a focused *problem solving team.* Temporary or permanent *steering teams* (overlay teams), such as boards and councils that will be discussed in the next section, sometimes guide their work. *Delivery teams* are a third type, in which expertise scattered across the organization is brought together to deliver some service to a customer. These teams typically work full time on a project, and the members move from one project to another. Such projects may be directly satisfying a customer need, as with construction engineering projects and engagement teams in consulting firms, or they may be part of a relay process in different stages ultimately intended to satisfy a market need, as with product development teams in which the lead role moves from R&D to marketing to operations. Cross-border teams may be contrasted with two other types of teams, namely, *work teams* and *management teams*, which are part of the structure of the organization.

Instead of an army of HQ staff who study opportunities and solve problems, a few central network leaders are needed to form cross-border teams for specific purposes, with appropriate members from the decentralized units. This teamwork in turn fosters the development of the network. So the role of senior management becomes that of sponsoring teamwork on the one hand, and enabling teamwork on the other.

Enabling teamwork is a big challenge for international human resource management. As discussed earlier, it requires that people are used to working in "split egg" ways.[19] This means that managers (and indeed many professionals) have two roles. The bottom of the egg is the operational job in the local business, with its targets and objectives. If this job is not achieved well, then in the extreme he or she can get fired. But promotion and rewards come from activities in the "top of the egg" project role, requiring initiatives that are guided by the strategic priorities of the overall global business. The operational role is local but the project role is often global, involving teamwork with people in other units.

Organizations that are still at the initial stage of "building HRM foundations" will find it difficult to do this. Good operational basics have to be solidly in place to allow "top of the egg" project initiatives that cut across boundaries. Teamworking within a unit is difficult enough, and the obstacles multiply with international and indeed virtual teams. Using in our discussion some of the existing research, we turn now to consideration of enabling factors and obstacles to cross-boundary teamwork.

Teamwork Builds on Relationships

The initial point to recognize is that effective team management builds on face-to-face relationships. Teams are chosen to confront complex problems and conflicting pressures, and there is widespread agreement from both research and observation that this requires personal relationships. We illustrate this with the experience of an alliance in the European financial services sector.

An alliance involving three main corporations, French, German, and Danish, was formed to address a clearly identified new market that cut across national borders. A high level working party was set up, meeting periodically to work out the strategy and thereby implement the intent behind the partnership. The meetings every three weeks were task-oriented, and there was little time to build relationships. The busy executives spent the luncheon breaks on the phone dealing with issues back home, and flew off at the end of each session. It took them a year to recognize that the French had a different conception of a working party from the Germans and Danes.

For the Germans and Danes, the objective was to negotiate decisions that would then be implemented. Consequently, they prepared meetings seriously, checking out their positions with their CEOs. They met with an agenda for negotiation, and they made sure that decisions were carefully worded in the minutes. Working parties were viewed in the traditional French company, however, as a consultative mechanism in the spirit of what the French call *concertation* to help the president reach his or her final decision. Only the CEO could take such final decisions, after having been appropriately briefed on the results of the discussions. Consequently, the French prepared for the meetings on the plane journey, alternating between surprise and amusement at the earnestness of the Germans and Danes. The French considered the minutes as a document to prepare the later briefing session with the president.

While frustrations surfaced early, they were never openly discussed. Relationships between the working party members were superficial, which did not permit confrontation on such sensitive issues. The frustration created a self-fulfilling prophecy. Within a few months, all the busy executives sensed that the work was getting nowhere and so even the Germans and Danes spent less energy on preparation. The alliance was eventually disbanded because it had yielded no results. Yet we are convinced that this would not have happened if the team had spent some evenings together at an early stage in the project, building relationships. The conflicts would have surfaced in informal discussions and been worked through. There will *always* be cultural differences of one type or another, even between people of the same nationality. Without relationships these will invariably handicap the task.

One of the intriguing questions is how electronic communication opens up the possibility for teamwork without meetings, known as *virtual teams*. A virtual team is defined as co-workers who attempt to achieve an organizational task while linked geographically and organizationally through telecommunications and information technologies.[20] This practice has attracted some research, and the evidence suggests that personal relationships and interpersonal skills remain important at particular stages in virtual teamwork (see box "Building Virtual Global Teams"). We are beginning to develop a situational understanding of when to use e-media and when to meet face-to-face. One of the first edicts of Goran Lindahl, the new CEO of ABB replacing Percy Barnevik, was to ban criticism by e-mail. If you have a problem with someone's actions or decisions, call them in person. E-mails tend to depersonalize the relationships, appearing curt, arrogant, and lacking emotion. And as many have learned to their dismay, they cannot be recalled.

Lessons on Team Management

Research on international project teams suggests that the general principles of project management apply to such teams.[21] But owing to the greater complexity and diversity of transnational projects, the failure to apply these lessons rigorously amplifies the risk of team failure.

Failure is sometimes attributed to the difficulties of communication and conflict arising from cultural differences. But this is a difference in degree, not in kind. Even a local project team faces complexity and conflict because of the diversity of its members, with a consequent risk of misunderstanding and personality clashes. In transnational teams, that diversity is greater, with correspondingly greater risks of failure.

Indeed, there is some evidence that the effectiveness of the transnational team is likely to be bipolar—either disastrous or superb—whereas that of national teams is more likely to be simply satisfactory.[22] On the one hand, there is a higher probability of affective or emotional conflict in the multinational team, associated with hostility, distrust, cynicism, and apathy. The differences cannot be managed, leading the team to blow up, compromise, or fizzle out. Yet on the other hand, multicultural teams are more likely to be outstandingly effective because of higher levels of cognitive conflict—a consequence of complementary differences in knowledge, perspectives, and assumptions.[23] There is experimental evidence that cross-national teams take significantly longer time to reach decisions but that they consider a wider range of options than do homogeneous teams.[24]

Given the importance of teams, a great deal has been researched and written during the last fifteen years.[25] From these, we can single out a few lessons that are particularly relevant for international human resource management.

CLARITY ON GOALS AND DELIVERABLES. Perhaps the most ubiquitous finding about project management is that success depends on the clarity of the task and the goals.[26] What distinguishes a team or a project group from a committee is clear goals and deliverables. As long as the mandate is fuzzy, as is often the case initially, then the project group risks developing into a time-wasting talk shop no matter how important its mission. Since most team members will typically have their own operational jobs to undertake, lack of clarity undermines commitment to the project and creates a self-fulfilling prophecy. Shell, an organization with substantial experience in project management, encourages clarifying goals by insisting that all such groups should prepare their "brief" and get the buy-in of appropriate sponsors to this.

Overambition is a related trap—setting up too many project groups that overstretch the organization. The speciality chemicals division of a European firm illustrated this. The division grew organically, complemented by a number of acquisitions. In the words of its human resource director, "There was a clear need for consolidation, which initially took the shape of a series of conferences, internal seminars, and workshops. These started to break down some of the barriers, and then we set up a series of project groups to work through challenges that had been identified by senior management. With hindsight, we were too ambitious—there were about

Building Virtual Global Teams
Research Box

A topical issue concerns the extent to which electronic technology can facilitate teamwork across boundaries, permitting virtual teams. Such technologies are categorized as *synchronous methods,* which allow people in different places to interact at the same time (desktop, audio and video conferencing, electronic meeting systems); and *asynchronous methods,* which facilitate delayed interaction (e-mail, group calendars and schedules, e-bulletin boards, web pages, non–real time database sharing and conferencing—all facilitated by intranets). While there is no doubt that the convergence of communication and computer technologies is changing the shape of work, including global work, there is relatively little research that shows clearly how this is happening.

Research and experience suggest that communication technology such as intranets and e-mail can greatly facilitate the exchange of structured and codified information, be it engineering diagrams, access to computerized libraries, or computerized "yellow pages" indicating who has what expertise. However, the culture of the organization must support this.[A] E-mail is effective in solving routine problems for which answers already exist and in generating ideas and plans.[B] It facilitates the exchange of information between people who would not normally interact.[C] Information technology clearly opens flexible work in the shape of telework or telecommuting.[D] One report suggests that 90 percent of larger firms with more than 5,000 employees in the United States today allow

telecommunicating, and 52 percent use some form of virtual teamworking, though smaller firms are much less on board.[E]

But what about the work of international project teams? Some studies suggest that electronic mail increases the quantity of communication, but decreases its quality. There is substantial evidence that electronic communication is less effective with ambiguous or complex tasks for which there is not a neat technical outcome, and in negotiating interpersonal or complex technical conflicts.[F] Those with experience emphasize that the more complex the project, the more important are face-to-face relationships. In a study of global R&D management in fourteen multinational enterprises, the senior product development manager of the company with the most sophisticated electronic communication system said the following:

Videoconferencing, integrated CAD/CAM databases, electronic mail, and intensive jet travel all contribute to lowering the communication barriers. All things considered, however, the most effective communication, especially in the beginning of a project, is a handshake across a table to build mutual trust and confidence. Then and only then can electronics be really effective.[G]

The author of this study estimated that the "half life" of a personal meeting in R&D networks—the time it takes before trust falls below a dangerous threshold—is less than three months. In an experimental study of virtual teams using MBA students in Europe, the United States, and Mexico, the difficulties

twenty project groups and this overloaded the organization. Five or six were successful, but many developed into time-consuming discussions that led nowhere. A certain cynicism started to prevail because the many failures drowned out the successes. We face this problem today because no one really believes in collaboration."

What is important is to ensure that the first projects that are set up are visibly successful and that they clearly add value to the corporation.

IMPORTANCE OF STAFFING. Cross-boundary teams are staffed for diversity. Selecting people involves balancing multiple criteria such as technical or functional skills, representation of different parts of the firm, and the interests of global integration as well as local responsiveness. This becomes difficult because of limits on

Building Virtual Global Teams
Research Box *(Continued)*

were found to spiral as problems interacted: problems of communication (minimized where teams used multiple media to communicate), cultural differences (in the meaning of concepts, terms and norms), technological problems with media, and project leadership.[H]

A review study of the issues distinguished between the successive phases in an international project:[I]

The Creating Stages in the Project
1. Orientation: "Why are we here?"
2. Trust building: "Who are you?"
3. Goal/role clarification: "What are we doing?"
4. Commitment building: "How do we do it?"

The Sustaining Stages in the Project
5. Implementation: "Who does what, when, and where?"
6. Execution
7. Review and renewal

If the first four stages are undertaken effectively in a face-to-face way, then communications technology will facilitate the later steps of implementation and execution, which after all constitute 80 percent of the work. A study of seventy-five international virtual teams provided supporting empirical evidence.[J] Although these teams never met, exercises were conducted over the web to build trust, having a positive effect on perceptions of the ability and integrity of other team members. The high trust teams had better informal leadership and used e-mail much more frequently to achieve their task of building a collective website than the low trust teams.

A study of the use of Lotus Notes showed that it did not change patterns of communication. People who communicate regularly and frequently used Lotus Notes to facilitate this, whereas people who did not interact before did not communicate after its introduction.[K]

The complementarity between electronic and face-to-face communications is well summarized in this quote from a book on network organization:

What the electronic network can do is accelerate as well as amplify the communication flow, but its viability and effectiveness will depend critically on the robustness of the underlying social structure. This implies that one has to be careful in [replacing] face-to-face ties with electronic ones. It is vital to maintain a critical ratio of face-to-face to electronic interactions. It may be even more critical to maintain face-to-face relationships with those individuals who can serve as bridging ties, gatekeepers, champions and so on. These are the relationships that provide the foundation on which the rest of the network depends.[L]

[A]Constant, Sproull et al., 1996.
[B]Duarte and Snyder, 1999.
[C]Sproul and Kiesler, 1991.
[D]Kurland and Bailey, 1999.
[E]Hansen, 1999.
[F]Duarte and Snyder, 1999.
[G]De Meyer, 1991, p. 56.
[H]Kayworth and Leidner, 1999.
[I]O'Hara-Devereaux and Johansen, 1994.
[J]Jarvenpaa and Leidner, 1999; Leidner, Kayworth et al., 1999.
[K]Vandenbosch and Ginzberg, 1996.
[L]Nohria and Eccles, 1992, pp. 304–5.

the size of the team. The internal difficulties of team management as well as cost and scheduling problems appear to grow almost exponentially with the size of the international team. Psychologists suggest that the optimal number of people in a team is typically 5 to 9, and never more than 10 to 15. Where technical constraints argue for larger teams, the task has to be structured so that it can be broken down into work for subgroups.[27]

Another paradox of staffing is that available people for projects are rarely ever the right people—indeed, that is precisely why they are available! In this sense, the formation of a project team is a political process. When individuals see a lineup forming that will be successful, they are eager to join the bandwagon—and vice versa. The director of the speciality chemical company mentioned above noted that the most successful project had been in coordinating management information systems. "There we were lucky," he said. "The director of information systems should have headed up the project, but he was too busy. This allowed us to give the responsibility to a general manager who had been arguing for some time about the benefits of coordinating MIS. He roped in some of his colleagues, and you could see from the lineup that it was going to lead to something. The information systems director saw the way things were heading and quickly maneuvered himself on board—as a team member and not as the leader, which was the right role for him. It worked out very well indeed."

In the case of a problem solving team, the team members have the responsibility for testing and probing with their own parts of the organization to ensure effective buy-in—teams need to balance external probing with their own internal focus.[28] This means that their personal credibility with their own units in the firm must be high. Members have to command the time and attention of key external people over whom they may have no direct authority.

Leadership is clearly the most essential decision in staffing. Given the diversity of cross-boundary teams, the leader has to be highly skilled in coaching behind the scenes, in conflict resolution, and in team building. The leadership skills may vary at different stages of the project. Advocacy skills are needed in the early stages to build legitimacy, to obtain resources and to break through bureaucratic barriers. At the intermediate stage, catalytic skills in building commitment and negotiating with external stakeholders are required. Integrative skills in coordinating and measuring progress are necessary as the project matures.[29] An experimental study of virtual teams in which the members came from different countries showed that effective leaders demonstrated the capacity to deal with paradox by performing contrasting leadership roles simultaneously. For example, they were able to act as mentors who showed empathy while asserting authority in influencing the responsibilities of members.[30] The dualistic demands of project work is one of the reasons why such assignments are a cornerstone in the process of developing leadership competencies and global mindset.

SEQUENCING COMPLEX PROJECTS. Larger international delivery projects go through different sequenced stages, and research has shown that one of the major problems is the failure to anticipate and manage the transitions between phases. People who get involved only in later stages and who have not been consulted before want to have earlier work redone. These problems were apparent to Shell in large ten-year projects involving many different functions, such as designing and building a refinery. Such projects may go through a dozen different stages from the initial feasibility study to the handover to the refinery operating team. Shell calculated that the costs and delays in transition management were such that it was theoretically more effective to load all staff onto the project at the beginning, including the operating team, and to phase people out—rather than phasing them in as is conventional practice.

This applies particularly to large international projects, in which the problems of linkage between phases lead to loss of direction or momentum.[31] The theory of project sequencing is that the next phase should be clearly anticipated, with the future leader functioning as a team member earlier. The striking reality in Western firms is that when product development projects are passed from R&D to manufacturing and then from manufacturing to marketing, there is virtually no overlap. Manufacturing views the project as "finished" when the prototype has been passed on to marketing. Since marketing has not been previously involved, there is no internal pull. There are conflicts and delays as they request redesign from R&D, which no longer has ownership. When the passage from one phase to another works well, it is often because of the intervention of experienced business area managers who ensure that the sequencing problems are anticipated and dealt with through staffing and coordination meetings.

There appears to be an interesting asymmetry between Western and Japanese strengths in project management. Western firms tend to master the international aspects of project management quite well, having learned to deal with the problems of communication and culture that plague Japanese companies. They invest considerable effort in choosing project members from lead countries, in probing to test out reactions in different geographic regions, and in ensuring that cultural differences do not act as a blockage. What creates problems for Western firms is lack of cooperation between functions. Each project phase tends to be led by a particular function (R&D, operations, marketing) with little involvement from other functions, creating transition difficulties. On the other hand, Japanese firms are more talented at interfunctional coordination, while they experience converse difficulties in handling the international aspects of the project. The project goes smoothly through the different stages in Tokyo, with a high degree of interfunctional teamwork, but the foreign people are involved at too late a stage to prevent misunderstandings.[32]

MANAGING CONFLICT. As we argued earlier, given the diversity of crossboundary teams, contention and conflict are inherent in such teams. From a theoretical perspective, it is not conflict that is the problem—difficulties come from either *too much* conflict (typically emotional in nature) so that the team blows up, or *too little* conflict (particularly of the cognitive type) so that the team dissolves through apathy.[33] Conflict is dualistic—it is the extremes that create difficulties. Typically, it is not the conflict itself but its avoidance that disrupts the team. So among the most important skills are those in surfacing conflicts, cognitive and emotional, and then working through them.

Managing conflict requires open dialogue. ABB's Percy Barnevik reflected on the dangers of suppressing debate when our colleague Manfred Kets de Vries interviewed him, asking him about his personal strengths and weaknesses:

> My strengths?—I think that others can talk about them. Regarding my weaknesses, I sometimes tend to be too impatient. One can be too impatient, especially when dealing with other cultures where people think more slowly or express themselves more slowly. I sometimes make the mistake of demanding things too quickly and so I lose out in my dialogue with people. Since I think pretty fast, I can scare people. I know more than they do, and so I dominate and subdue the discussion . . . if I react too quickly, that person will never tell me what he or she believes to be the truth.[34]

APPRAISING AND REWARDING TEAMWORK. While the appraisal and reward system of the organization does not drive cross-border teamwork, it can act as an obstacle. A first observation is that a major source of appraisal difficulties is the tension between job accountability and lateral teamwork (the operational and project roles in the "split egg"). This is seen in dilemmas in which individuals are asked to work on cross-border projects and then reprimanded because of poor performance in their own jobs. What this implies is that reward problems are likely to be most acute if the performance of individual business units and the people within them is less than satisfactory, so that they are under pressure to improve their own individual performance *and* to work on lateral coordination teams. Unless there are sound HRM foundations that ensure basic job competence and performance, cross-border teamwork overstretches the organization.

A second observation is that the conflicts in priorities have to be explicitly recognized. At ABB, the priorities are formulated in the "policy bible." Conflicts are inevitable, and the guiding principle is that the customer must come first, the corporation second (including the business area and/or country), and the profit center third.

A third observation is that important problem solving teams and project teams have to be linked closely to the hierarchy structure of the firm so as to ensure alignment with organizational priorities and to provide teams with needed resources. Indeed cross-border authority and sponsorship (in the shape of steering groups discussed below) are typically needed to set up such teams, ensuring that they are appropriately staffed, have clear objectives, get rewarded, and avoid other traps mentioned above. There is evidence that larger and more critical projects in relationship to the size of the business are more likely to succeed than smaller projects because they get more attention and sponsorship from senior management.[35] The latter are forgotten in the allocation of resources necessary to see them through.

Beyond this, the specifics of appraisal and rewards need to be carefully considered, also since the problems vary with the nature of the cross-boundary task. Full-time delivery projects should be rewarded on the basis of overall performance, not on the performance of the individual members. Problem solving teams may be rewarded on a bonus basis, though if the extent of cross-border linkage is moderate, then the best way of appraising and rewarding individuals is through the career development review process—indeed cross-boundary projects are an integral tool of leadership development. Problem solving projects provide intrinsic rewards in terms of learning challenges, increased visibility, and opportunities to build personal social capital. But when the linkages are important and regular, there may be grounds for a fundamental overhaul of the appraisal system.

Appraisal and reward systems that take cross-boundary performance into account are commonplace in organizations that are project oriented, such as professional service firms. At Accenture (formerly Andersen Consulting), senior partners spend up to a quarter of their time on this, collecting the views of clients, research and back office departments, managers and subordinates about the contribution of partners and managers—"You are not going to be receiving a top bonus this year because although the client is happy, the research department did not get the collaboration it needed."[36] In industrial firms, there has been a parallel spread of multirater (360°) appraisal systems, in which the appraisal and reward decisions are undertaken by the N+1 or N+2 managers who collect the views of project peers as well as the boss and subordinates.[37]

PROMOTING FEEDBACK AND LEARNING. Our final observation on cross-boundary teams is that this is a domain that must involve both organizational and individual learning. Transnational industrial and commercial firms are well advised to follow the route of professional service firms in deliberately trying to develop know-how in cross-border teamwork—and to follow IBM's discipline of ensuring that every project ends with a learning review that contributes to individual know-how.

We recall urging the human resource function in a major information technology firm to get involved in four key global projects that the firm was setting up. Project expertise was clearly a critical future capability in this industry, and there was no internal know-how concerning the management of such complex global projects (such as on how to speed up the slow process of successive adoption by countries). To our regret, the HR function turned down the opportunity—"Sorry, but that is not part of our job." No one undertook the role, mistakes were made, but more importantly there was no learning from those mistakes.

Cross-Boundary Steering Groups

Cross-boundary steering groups are part of the internal governance of the firm. While the structure of the firm may be quite simple, the creation of cross-boundary groups to steer strategic or operational projects/problems gives a great deal of flexibility to the governance of the transnational firm. Consequently this mechanism is fundamental to the way in which such firms function.

There is a dangerous popular belief that networks and hierarchy are opposites, that networks are replacing hierarchy. Not at all. Networks need hierarchic authority mechanisms—what we call steering mechanisms. Without strong leadership that establishes clear goals to which people are committed, networks can become social clubs, and the extreme of chaos can potentially replace the other extreme of excessive order.[38] Networks transform the form of hierarchy, however. Enabling or coaching management replaces the traditional command-and-control approach.

The Shapes and Forms of Cross-Boundary Steering Groups

Cross-boundary steering groups take many different shapes and forms as internal boards, formal or informal steering groups, functional councils, product development committees, strategic development councils, regional boards, and the like. Alternatively, the steering "group" may be a single person, for example, someone who has not only vertical functional responsibility with a business unit but also horizontal responsibility across businesses in a region for that functional area.

Steering groups can allow an organization to coordinate regionally, to manage the introduction of a new technology, and to tackle other complex problems—all without introducing the complexities of a matrix structure. Such groups can manage emerging boundaries or new strategic activities so as to nurture them into formal existence. As pointed out above, steering groups facilitate cross-boundary teamwork and increase commitment to action. Given the complexity of decision-making in the transnational, it is often quite inappropriate that go/no-go, resourcing, and other decisions should be taken without different perspectives being brought to bear.

The key benefits are flexibility and avoidance of formal bureaucracy. While it is difficult and slow to change the basic structure of a multinational organization, such steering groups can be set up and then disbanded more or less from one day to the next as the priorities emerge and change. The composition of steering groups can shift with the priorities. For example, a Scandinavian firm that is organized on worldwide product lines decided that its operations in Asia were of strategic importance, needing greater coordination across businesses as well as careful resourcing. Within a few weeks it set up an Asian Board consisting of the COO, the heads of two divisions active in Asia, and three key individuals from its Asian operations. Projects that were floundering now came under the supervision of this board, and new projects were set up. As the projects moved to the stage of implementation, the internal board membership changed to bring in more operational executives.

The trade-off between size and necessary perspectives, discussed in the previous subsection, applies equally to steering groups. Effective transnational leadership development allows steering groups to resolve the paradox of bringing multiple perspectives to bear on decision-making while remaining small enough to be effective.

Many companies manage transnational projects through a structure of permanent steering groups, such as the project management group at the headquarters of ABB in Zurich (see earlier box "Coordination and Connectivity at ABB"), complementing the matrix of business areas and geographic regions. This project organization has the responsibility for overseeing the collaboration between hundreds of business units on large-scale strategic or engineering projects.

Best Foods, currently being acquired by Unilever, is widely regarded as one of the most professional firms in the consumer products industry. Global teamwork between hitherto local firms was their motto for the last decade. This was embodied at the highest level by the global steering role of the number two executive in the firm. Meeting regularly with regional councils that were set up in parallel, his role was to identify challenges that cut across country lines and to set up projects to deal with them. Such projects went from the consolidation of manufacturing facilities to tactics on how to defend themselves against focused attacks by a competitor on successive countries.

Such coordination can in time replace the traditional centralized head office functions. For example, while GE is one of the largest companies in Europe today with over $22 billion in revenues, it does not have a European head office. All necessary coordination is implemented through horizontal councils and task forces that have limited budgets and no formal resources. Not surprisingly, to be nominated to any of these coordinating bodies is a badge of honor for any up-and-coming GE executive.

Avoiding the Traps in Cross-Boundary Steering

Steering groups are not representational committees—those who have tried to run complex companies by committee have usually failed. The roles and responsibilities of steering boards and councils have to be clearly defined and well communicated throughout the company to ensure that decisions can be taken quickly when necessary. Sony's first attempt to create a pan-European organization in the mid-90s failed in spite of top management support and the evident business logic behind the plan because operational roles and responsibilities were not properly clarified.

To steer functional areas such as corporate HR, corporations like ABB make use of functional councils. Keeping them small to prevent "committee disease," an HR council might consist of a couple of key generalists from lead countries, a few line and HR executives in emerging businesses or markets, and a few people heading expertise areas, all coordinated by the head of corporate HR. Global initiatives are prioritized, set up, and then report to the council.

It is vital that the members of steering groups have an integrative leadership orientation.[39] When we see firms with a big gap between desired and actual levels of coordination, part of the explanation is typically that mechanisms for cross-border teamwork and know-how sharing are missing. But the other part is that senior management is not encouraging and rewarding horizontal collaboration. If senior management intervenes on details and always plays the role of arbiter (many like to play this role), there is no end to the upward escalation of conflicts.

One of the guiding principles at ABB is that disagreements among horizontally aligned units (for example, on internal transfer prices or product specifications) should be resolved by the managers themselves—not delegated upward for solution by top management. As the company folklore has it, one can ask twice for help, but the third time top management will put someone else in the job who can get problems resolved without involving superiors. The ability to resolve issues horizontally with one's peers is a leadership behavior that is monitored and rewarded.

Sharing Best Practice and Know-How

Increasing the sharing of know-how and best practice is another dimension of coordination, again of critical importance. With increasing competition and the importance of speed in responsiveness, reinventing-the-wheel can be ill afforded. Some scholars have argued that the main competitive advantage of the global corporation is its ability to learn from its experience throughout the world: "What firms do better than markets is the sharing and transfer of the knowledge of individuals and groups within an organization."[40] Know-how sharing is also a necessary step toward global process management since processes are typically built in part on successful practice. And the experience in sharing know-how lays the foundation for more sophisticated systems of knowledge management that are emerging in both industrial and professional service firms.

In the past, know-how and best practice would get disseminated through corporate policies and standard operating procedures. Headquarters staff, often chosen for their experience and expertise, would consolidate state-of-the-art knowledge, issuing policy guidelines. For the fast moving transnational organization, this vertical process no longer works. It takes too much time for know-how to be gathered by the center and then redisseminated. Moreover, the context of know-how is typically removed in this process, leaving sterile generalizations that are void of flesh and blood. Tacit know-how (which typically is the most important for competitive advantage) is highly context specific, and the process of transfer involves understanding the origin context, unpackaging the know-how from that context, and then reassembling it in a different context. This can be done in a faster and more effective way by being able to tap directly into the relevant expertise and experience. So the medium of knowledge transfer is increasingly horizontal—site visits, best practice workshops, personal exchanges, transfers of staff, and the like.

Research suggests that the major obstacles to the transfer of know-how across a company are sheer ignorance and lack of relationships.[41] Those who have the expertise and experience do not realize that others may find it useful. Even if there is encouragement of sharing, there is no way of advertising one's knowledge. And even if one knows where relevant expertise lies, it is unlikely that anything except the most simple information will be transferred unless there is a personal tie. The strength of the relationship between source and recipient has been found to be the strongest predictor of best practice transfer.[42] Indeed all studies emphasize the vital importance of relationships.

Lack of "absorptive capacity" has been shown to be another obstacle.[43] Even when managers know of best internal practice, they lack the budget, time, or management support to pursue and study it so that it can be made useful. Know-how transfer requires the adaptation of what may be successful in one environment to the cultural, institutional, and contextual constraints of a different environment. One study examined in detail the transfer and assimilation of TQM practices from Japan to the United States in four companies, with mixed degrees of success.[44] The overall observation was that successful transfer required a combination of "rhetoric and reality." Rhetoric in the shape of simplified representations of TQM as a "solution" was needed to get the attention and commitment of key sponsors. But without detailed attention to technical and contextual adaptation, the assimilation of the practices into the firm was disappointing.

Getting Know-How Sharing Under Way

Know-how management typically involves getting those who need expertise in contact with those who have it, particularly if we are talking about "core know-how" that is tacit, valuable, and firm specific. Let us consider some examples of how this is done.

Building social networks is one starting point. An ancillary aim of corporate management training may be that of building social capital—"to make sure that you always have a friend in Uruguay." Intranets are useful in getting information around the world quickly and at low cost, but they cannot transfer complex tacit know-how. Starting a major logistic redesign project, you see news on the intranet of a successful project in Uruguay. But unless you have a local friend, such as someone you met on a corporate training program, who can give you the inside information and put you in contact with the right people, the odds are that you will have forgotten about this in five minutes.

Training programs are also used to share specific best practice cases, though one-way presentations are rarely the appropriate format except to provide basic information. Since know-how always exists in a specific context, its transfer to another context requires active two-way interaction. GE has long organized best practice seminars. They send a wad of advanced information to participants—after all, if your business unit is paying for the travel costs, the participants should be motivated to be well prepared. At the seminar the presentation time is brief, simply a warm-up to introduce the key people. And then attendees are told that the manufacturing director will be in room 1, the finance manager in room 2, and so forth. Participants are interested in learning how to adapt the experience of others to their own realities, not in a lengthy presentation of someone else's reality.

Know-how sharing may initially take the shape of ad hoc dissemination of best practice. When ABB acquires a company and is planning how to restructure the plant, it calls in those with experience as advisors. Many firms use internal referrals. A subsidiary is considering the introduction of variable compensation. Its general manager asks the regional head of HR: "Who's got good experience of this in a culture like mine?" With their broad overview of operations, business area and regional managers can spur business improvement by marrying opportunities and exemplars.

Measurement can facilitate transfer. The growth of Banc One during the 80s in the United States can in part be attributed to their "share-and-compare" approach. New banks were acquired in friendly acquisitions with the promise of helping them to help themselves. The performance of all affiliates would be measured monthly with a uniquely detailed and transparent reporting system on more than forty different product and market parameters. The ranking of all affiliates on these measures was made available to everyone so that they could learn from each other to improve their performance. The treasurer explained, "They don't necessarily go to the affiliate with the best performance. That might be too threatening. But they will identify one with a similar profile that is a little better than them in some key areas and set up an exchange of ideas and experience."[45] At the international level, ABB uses its equally sophisticated Abacus monthly reporting system in a similar way, to foster learning, best practice transfer, and improvement, rather than to reward and punish managers.

A paradox in the knowledge transfer area is that munificence in resources acts as an obstacle, whereas reasonably constrained resources act as a spur. If resources are freely available, then managers will often go ahead and reinvent their own wheel. Sharing across the HR function at Ericsson, the Swedish telecom equipment firm, was catalyzed by a global cost reduction drive in the early 90s. The HR function was given the role of facilitating a major worldwide reorganization, but like everyone else without any increase in staff. However, there were no constraints on travel budgets that would restrict networking. Britt Reigo, the Ericsson VP for Human Resources, decided to build a network of product and country personnel managers, using two worldwide HR workshops as the initial vehicle.

The program design involved a couple of two-week modules six months apart, using inside and outside speakers. But two days into the first program, a process began of surfacing specific problems and frustrations and of matching these with the expertise and assistance that others could provide. This was formalized in an open market for exchange on problems and resources, and the invited speakers were roped in as resource providers rather than lecturers. "We need help in designing a performance-oriented reward," one group would say. Others would respond, "We've got a lot of experience there—let's get together." Within a year, the workshops had stimulated many best practice visits and a total of sixteen projects in areas such as management planning, reward systems, professional recruitment, and international leadership development.

Know-how sharing may start with a group of people who take a focused initiative. The human resource function at Colgate Palmolive consolidated know-how on rapid market entry, a mix of guidebook and map of internal resources, based on the experiences of scores of people in the worldwide organization. Professional service firms go further in terms of know-how management. New associates at consulting companies such as A. T. Kearney and Booz-Allen can tap into corporate yellow pages that supply references, presentations, reports, and contacts on practice areas.[46] Or they can e-mail a request for information to a research department, which will provide answers or contacts within a short period of time.

A number of French companies organize a periodic innovation fair to facilitate best practice transfer. Sodexho is an example, being a $6 billion concern that is the world leader in the catering industry. The group is structured into no less than 18,700 operating units, each undertaking, for example, the catering for a hospital or a business. The highly successful annual fair parades internal examples of innovation and best practice. Benchmarking tours are also organized by the product line managers and project groups to study leading restaurants and competitors in search of new ideas, and one focus of internal training is on the transfer of know-how.

Business analysts in the past were skeptical about the value of conglomerates such as GE, where ideas of synergy rarely paid off. Jack Welch was determined to prove the value of what he first called "integrated diversity" and later "learning organization." GE adapted new product introduction techniques from Toyota and GM and Six Sigma quality initiatives from Motorola and Ford. Part of GE's current success comes from the "boundaryless" culture that was progressively molded, a culture of shamelessly grabbing and copying ideas and innovations.

Structuring Knowledge Management

More systematic management of know-how requires a structure. There are several components including *technology, culture,* and *leadership infrastructure.*[47] But the initial element is *focus.* What type of know-how will add value to the firm? Unless the firm can provide an answer to that question, know-how sharing will never go beyond its informal or ad hoc stages.

One recent book on know-how sharing argues that focus should be guided by a value proposition.[48] Such value propositions tend to fall into one of three categories—customer knowledge (customer needs and segments, and how to market and sell more effectively), product-to-market excellence (accelerating time to market), and operational excellence in plant and back-office operations.

Defining focus or value propositions to guide know-how management leads the firm to confront deeper questions about how it adds value. What indeed are our core competencies? Professional service firms such as consultancies, in which knowledge management is particularly important since it constitutes their livelihood, wrestle with the question of defining their practice areas and competence domains. GE has identified an array of critical competencies in nine domains, in consultation with other firms such as Motorola and Xerox, specifying key areas of management that cut across businesses and countries (though certain competencies may be more important in some businesses than others):

- Quality leadership.
- Supplier management.
- Process control in operations and improvement.
- Quality information management.
- Problem solving techniques.
- People commitment.
- Customer satisfaction.
- The introduction of new products, services, or technology.
- Change capability.

HRM is part of all of these competencies, and some such as "people commitment" and "change capability" center on HRM.

Focus facilitates the use of *technology.* By technology, we mean intranet, e-mail, databases, and other computer-assisted software systems. Such electronic systems open up tremendous potential for sharing of information and accessing expertise in other parts of the organization (see the earlier box "Building Virtual Teams"). It is quite feasible, and indeed powerful, to create computerized "yellow pages" on staff and their areas of expertise, as long as one has carefully constructed the index of added-value competence.[49]

Cultural barriers to know-how sharing are perhaps the most difficult to manage, as surveys suggest.[50] This was demonstrated in one study of information exchange in a major international computer firm, at which access to technical information was successfully facilitated by electronic information networks.[51] The study showed, however, that unless the culture actively supports and promotes information sharing, the cost of such networks and their infrastructure are likely to outweigh the benefits. Norms of generalized reciprocity, as academics call them, lead people who can provide useful help to do so. They are sustained by values of corporate citizenship—a sense that it is part of one's job to assist others and to help out with problems that are important to the company.

Cultural barriers cannot be "fixed" or removed by simple tools and interventions—the issue at stake here is the basic culture of the firm. If there is no communal sense of identity, if there are no shared norms and values, people will act in mercenary, opportunistic, and self-interested ways.[52] We will be discussing this issue of normative integration later in this chapter since it cuts across all aspects of glue technology. Changing the culture of a firm is a process that can take years if not decades since it involves changing the socialization practices of the firm.

Traditional reward systems typically emphasize individual performance, encouraging the hoarding of know-how. GE has persisted in trying to build a culture that overcomes hoarding. People naturally promote themselves by talking of their own breakthroughs and achievements. However, the question that is thrown back to them is "Who else is using your breakthrough?" Keeping know-how to oneself is compared to stealing, while sharing information leads to greater personal visibility that is likely to be beneficial for career prospects. But this in turn creates the danger of unjustified boasting, and one of the roles of the leadership development function at GE's Crotonville training center is to certify the extent to which know-how at particular sites exemplifies best practice in the nine domains that were mentioned earlier.

Professional service firms have typically changed the reward system so as to include knowledge sharing among professional staff as an important criterion. At McKinsey and Kearney, the number and frequency of use of a consultant's publications and reports are an important input to promotional decisions.

A *leadership infrastructure* is the last enabling element. Without facilitators, internal change agents, knowledge champions, or process managers (different firms use different titles), knowledge is unlikely to be well structured and accessible. These are typically not full-time roles but matrixed roles that complement another activity. At GE, the responsibility for knowledge transfer lies with the department for Leadership Development within the corporate HR function. At Coca-Cola, the facilitators around the world report to a person who in turn reports to both HR and the CEO. In other companies, the infrastructure is housed within the Corporate Quality department. At Ernst & Young, knowledge sharing is led by a Global Knowledge Steering Committee of key people from the major countries and by particular functional councils in each focused knowledge domain.

The scope and complexity of the enabling infrastructure naturally varies from one firm to another.[53] This may go from a simple self-directed structure built around a database (yellow pages or intranet) and maintained by a few people, to a more elaborate knowledge service with practice networks, discussion databases, a help desk, and information services. At this level, the systematic management of know-how starts to become part of the management of the firm's capabilities, and we will discuss this further in Chapter 9.

Global Process Management

A last pillar of coordination in the transnational firm is global or regional process management. This builds on and complements all the other facets of organizational glue technology. What is a process? It is fundamentally a methodology that links together a series of activities so as to add value. In the case of global process management, we are talking about connecting activities across a variety of organizational boundaries—businesses, functions, and most importantly, countries and regions.

The concern with process management was boosted by Michael Porter's concept of the value chain, raising the awareness of the need for what he called "horizontal strategies and organization." It was reinforced by the influence of process reengineering that started in the early 90s with the objective of reducing costs and time-to-market and by the spread of cross-functional quality management efforts (such as TQM or Six Sigma).

While a process implies standardization and simplification, this is different from a top-down policy or guideline. Processes are a *horizontal standardization* of sets of activities that are regularly repeated and that focus on clearly identified deliverables. Companies are beginning to recognize that change, acquisitions, and alliances are not occasional incidents but recurrent events for which one has to build process know-how. Such processes build on successful experience in different parts of the firm, and they represent agreements on frameworks and principles to guide a specific chain of activities so as to capture economies of scale, scope, and knowledge. A well-designed process leaves sufficient room for adaptation and differentiation at the local operating level.[54]

How do global processes emerge? They may be developed by project groups, by task forces, and through the coordinating devices described above. They may also result from know-how sharing, as the accumulated know-how is codified in the form of a process methodology—as with project management processes in consulting and engineering firms, quality management processes in manufacturing, Cisco's acquisition integration process, even change acceleration methodologies.

Global process management is of critical importance to HR. How does the central HR function add value to the organization? Central policies, rules, and guidelines are increasingly impotent in the face of the complexity of the transnational enterprise. An alternative that fits better with its differentiated reality is HR process development, building on the experience of leading subsidiaries as well as experts inside and outside the firm.[55]

Take as a simple example the aim of meeting employee needs for skill training, a task which often consumes a great deal of time and resources. Intranets and other IT innovations allow staff to find appropriate training opportunities that match employee needs and schedules. But the consequence is sometimes a proliferation of such software-based packages. Under the leadership of new CEO Carly Fiorina, Hewlett-Packard is tackling the consequences of its culture of decentralization that has led to excessive duplication and inefficiency. "We have a lot of soloists in the company and what we need is an orchestra," she says. Her favorite example: more than 750 internal websites for employee training.[56] Global process management offers the prospect of effectively linking demand and supply of training, capturing economies of scale (also in the use of IT), while leaving openness to experimentation and local variation.

A global HR management process usually shares six different characteristics:

1. *Linking together line and HR:* General managers tend to think naturally in process terms since their focus is on targets and deliverables, while functional staff tend to focus on specific activities. Line managers know the importance of HR activities such as appraisal and rewards, but their concern is with these activities as steps toward fulfilling business objectives. Process thinking and methodology facilitate line ownership.

2. *Linking multiple activities together:* Activities such as business planning, HR planning, objective setting, appraisal, and rewards tend to become ends in themselves, each with its own focus. While this may have some benefits when the company is at the basic foundation stage of HRM, ongoing improvement can best come from improving the fit between the individual elements and aligning them with business strategy. The focus on process is a way of managing the fit between the different elements, perhaps the only effective way. How many organizations have tried to increase performance by introducing performance-based compensation, finding to their dismay that they only escalate payroll costs? Without a process focus, there was no upstream link to business planning so as to define performance standards and no clear metrics for measurement.

3. *Focus on deliverables and measurement:* Process management forces a focus on deliverables and the issue of how to measure effectiveness, which is important for the alignment of HRM and business objectives. The emphasis on desired outcomes facilitates the linking of activities, and it clarifies what should be generic and what should be differentiated. This encourages explicit recognition of the trade-offs rather than pushing these under the table.

4. *Led by a process owner:* As with knowledge management processes, a leadership infrastructure is needed to provide the steering. But there is a subtle change from the traditional functional expertise orientation. The process owner will sometimes be an individual, as with IBM where one executive (a former sales manager rather than an HR specialist) has the responsibility for IT-based learning systems (combining intranet technology with distance learning and workshops to deliver competency training). He works closely with the HR function and line managers throughout the world. More typically, the process owner will be a team of people, line managers concerned with the deliverables and functional people who have the expertise.[57]

5. *Global responsibility for the process, but local responsibility for execution:* The concept behind global process management is that while the process methodology is global, applying across the board, the responsibility for execution and re-

sults lies locally with the individual business unit. If adjustment in some elements of the process is needed to ensure its specific deliverables, then it is up to the local unit to take such decisions.

6. *Oriented toward continual updating and improvement:* Processes are dynamic, not static, steered by their focus on deliverables. Local adjustment may lead to innovations that improve the process. If, for example, a recruitment process is not delivering on its aim of securing the supply of skilled professionals, then the process needs to be redesigned, building perhaps on the experience of successful experiments in certain countries. The new know-how needs to be quickly circulated around the world so that units can adapt accordingly.

Although there is virtually no systematic research on HR processes, we will focus on the two that are of the greatest potential added value to the transnational organization.[58] The first is the operational process of *performance management* that we will discuss here. The second is the strategic process of *leadership development*, to be discussed in the next chapter.

Global Performance Management

Performance management is the crucial process behind the challenge of organizational alignment. Leading edge companies sometimes view this performance management process as a genuine source of competitive advantage and are consequently secretive about their approach.[59]

Attention to performance management is a vital step in building network coordination in the transnational. As noted earlier, it is of questionable utility to attempt to build organizational linkages and tight coordination between underperforming units or units that have a different understanding of what performance means. Eisenhardt and Galunic capture this well in a recent analysis of what it takes to make synergies work in global businesses.[60] It is the *combination* of constructive competition, guided by clear goals, metrics, and the other elements of performance management, together with collaborative teamwork, that stimulates valued added development (what is called coevolution). Without clarity on objectives and measurement, collaboration is often ineffective—divisions source themselves from inside when there are better deals outside; they protect themselves from internal competition only to lose out to competitors. Without collaborative lateral teamwork, companies fall back into costly reinventing-the-wheel and the slow vertical decision-making processes. Competition fostered by measurement goes hand in hand with teamwork.

Today's general concept of performance management is associated with the practices of some leading Anglo-Saxon firms.[61] It is a process that links firm-level business objectives and strategies to individual goals, actions, appraisal, and rewards. The principles of performance management are well known, involving three successive elements—(i) a planning phase leading to objective setting or specification of desired performance; (ii) performance evaluation, feedback, and corrective action; and (iii) the linkage of rewards and development to evaluation. However, these elements are all too often disconnected—indeed HRM attention is regrettably often focused only on the latter downstream elements.

It is the tight link across the three phases that differentiates the performance management process from other methods for improving performance such as critical path analysis, job evaluation, and quality management.

This is simple in principle but potentially very complex in practice. There are infinite variations in the approaches, varying by corporate and national culture as well as by industry. Probably the most important question for the transnational is whether it should adopt one single global process, organize the process by business line or region, or allow each local company to develop its own particular process.

The answer will be influenced by the basic structure of the company. But to the extent that one can generalize on this question, we would argue that the response depends on the phase in the process. Let us break the process of performance management down into some of its elements, starting upstream with the planning cycle and then moving downstream toward appraisal and rewards.

The Upstream Side of Performance Management

In the transnational, the upstream phase of the performance process should certainly be tightly coordinated from a global perspective, at least by business area and probably by the whole firm if there are many linkages between businesses.[62] This is the stage that leads to the determination of the strategic and business objectives that are the fundamental drivers of performance management. The strategic, business, and budgetary planning cycle acts as a basic "hard" coordination device for the firm, leading to clarity of purpose (objectives and goals).

Obviously, there are many types of planning approaches, and strategic management studies have analyzed the tensions involved in the choice of approach (long-term strategic focus versus short-term financial focus, detailed planning versus entrepreneurial decision-making, and other dualities).[63] Aside from the content issue of how the HR function is involved in the business planning cycle that was discussed earlier,[64] there are some important HRM-related issues at this upstream level. Let us focus on a couple of them.

The first process challenge comes from recognizing that the planning cycle is essentially a commitment building process. As Mintzberg has pointed out, strategic planning processes used by many firms in the past were organized by a small group of senior executives and planners working on the numbers, leading to strategic objectives that were understood by only a handful of people.[65] Since there was no commitment lower down, their implementation was often ineffective. Shell took a different view of the planning process, arguing that planning should be considered as a process of *learning*—of understanding how a competitive situation may be changing, of mobilizing action, and of building commitment to action down in the organization.[66] After all, it is these units that must come up with the necessary actions.

The only way of working information into understanding reasonably fast, and then into commitment, is two-way dialogue. A critical task in the planning cycle is therefore the design of interlocking conferences, workshops, and reviews, together with process facilitation to ensure appropriate preparation and constructive two-way dialogue, as well as the interface with training. We are currently seeing a lot of process innovation here, aimed at working through the content issues and trade-offs, leading to commitment to the new strategy.[67] The deliverables here can be measured by the degree of understanding and commitment to action at the end of the line. For example, a Scandinavian multinational firm decided recently to confront the problem of traditionally slow implementation of a worldwide reorganization. The HR group prepared advice on how subsidiaries should communicate this to their staff. The executive committee also announced that a special bonus would be paid in six months, based on the results of random interviews with subsidiary staff about their understanding of the purpose behind the reorganization.

Let us consider another challenge. The ultimate output of the upstream process is agreement on goals and targets, quantitative and qualitative in nature. These goals are the link between the upstream business planning and the downstream process of implementation. However, a great deal of confusion is created by different interpretations of a goal and different readings on the consequences of not achieving the goal. This confusion is aggravated by differences in cultural heritage, both organizational and national.[68] One HRM-related priority is ensuring that the concept of "a goal" has a common meaning. Let us take two contrasting examples as illustrations.

At A.P. Møller, the Danish firm in the Fortune 100 league that is built around container transport and shipping, the meaning of a goal or target is very clear throughout its worldwide operations. A goal, once agreed upon and accepted, is a promise to deliver. This means exercising what the owner of the company calls "constant care"—debating and reviewing thoroughly with all parties any commitment that one will make since it is definitely that—a commitment. As the owner says, "Your word is your bond"—and everyone knows that he means it. An executive we know experienced this recently. An innovative and able general manager, his firm was acquired by the Møller Group. During the next six months, changing circumstances led him twice to revise targets for his unit—for him, they were just that, targets. This was reluctantly accepted the first time since he was a newcomer. At the second change, he was fired.

Contrast this with GE, another company known for its approach to performance management. GE views goals as stretch targets, which means that they may sometimes not be reached. The concept of a goal is differently but equally clearly defined, as the Annual Report indicates:

> GE business leaders do not walk around all year regretting the albatross of an impossible number they hung around their necks. At the end of the year, the business is measured not on whether it hit the stretch target, but on how well it did against the prior year, given the circumstances. Performance is measured against the world as it turned out to be: how well a business anticipated change and dealt with it, rather than against some "plan" or internal number negotiated a year earlier.[69]

All this implies different approaches to performance management, to planning goals, and to their review and consequences. It is not that one conception of a goal is right and the other is wrong—there are trade-offs. It is more a question of whether the business units and countries across the world are playing the same game with the same ground rules. Playing by different rules creates intense frustration that spills over negatively into many other areas of coordination.[70]

We might briefly mention a related process challenge, though it is generic rather than international in nature. This is the tension between short- and long-term planning, which in most Western firms are tackled sequentially. Strategic planning is an initial step that leads to operational and budgetary planning. From then onward, the strategic goals exist only in the distant background. It is these operational goals that are translated into individual objectives, and the connection with strategic objectives is typically vague at best. Corporate development targets that are inherently long term such as talent development get easily pushed out in the process. There may be a need for a long-term breakthrough process to complement the traditional short-term focus of goals, as adopted by firms such as Intel, GE, Procter & Gamble, and Hewlett-Packard.[71]

MEASUREMENT SCORECARDS. What gets measured gets attention. This old idea is no less valid when it comes to implementing processes of global coordination. The common mistake of many firms striving to move down the path to becoming transnational is to equate an understanding of the need to coordinate with actually coordinating practices. However, in our research with managers operating in global businesses, we have consistently seen high gaps between the desired and actual level of coordination. Why was the level of coordination low? Partly because mechanisms such as teamwork and know-how sharing were missing, but even more fundamentally because the performance management measures did not encourage managers to do what they personally believed should be done. When measurements change, so do behaviors.

There are strong arguments that the scorecard for measurement should be global in order to make the different mechanisms of horizontal coordination work in a synchronized manner (we refer to but leave aside the important debate on the respective merits of value-based management and the stakeholder or balanced scorecard approach).[72] The measurement scorecard is different from the goals. The specific goals vary from one business to another, from one subsidiary to another, and different units of the organization will have different strategic priorities—thus different performance indicators will be given different weight. However, having common performance metrics facilitates the resolution of conflicts across boundaries—when we discuss global mindset in the next chapter we will meet an example of different measures leading to conflicts between sales/service units and global product groups that overloaded top management with the need to arbitrate.

Measurement and control systems are often seen as the opposite of decentralized responsibility. But the primary role of ABB's well-known Abacus system is to communicate useful operating level information to managers who need it as quickly as possible. It is designed to allow decentralization to work responsibly, providing prompt, timely measurements on all aspects of operational performance. In so doing, its primary aim is first to help local managers identify and diagnose problems and second to allow top management to monitor performance. Their aim is to help rather than interfere: "What's the problem? What are you doing to fix it? And how can we help?" One of the ways of helping is to suggest to local managers that they go talk with higher performing units, as discussed earlier. Help means helping people to help themselves. It is only if they cannot help themselves that the control system leads to intervention.

Advances in information technology allow real-time measurement worldwide. State-of-the-art global companies such as Cisco are able to close the books on a daily basis. In some companies this may create a fear of "big brother," but if properly used, fast measurement can be a liberating tool that enables self-monitoring and autonomous corrective action at the front line. Cisco itself is a good example. Given the importance of cross-boundary project groups, tapping into know-how, and rapid problem solving, there is no budgetary approval procedure for travel expenses. Managers and professionals are free to take the plane and travel as they wish. This is counterbalanced by a practice of total transparency, however. Any Cisco employee can find out what any other employee is spending on travel at any point in time via their intranet. Total freedom steered by total transparency is a duality that creates a powerful virtuous circle.

Aside from the general issue of measurement, specific measures linked to the appraisal process can be powerful in ensuring coordination. In the early 1980s, Motorola faced a great challenge to crack the Japanese market for its semiconductor and telecommunication products. Several previous initiatives had failed to meet the objectives; the company was too often too late with too little. This time, the company not only changed its product offering and marketing strategy, it also modified the performance appraisal criteria for scores of its managers worldwide. One open-ended question was added to the list of criteria—"What have you done to support Motorola's Japan strategy?" Within weeks, phones started ringing in Motorola's Tokyo office, with colleagues worldwide inquiring how they could help—with information, knowledge, technical resources, even people on short-term assignments.

The Downstream Side of Performance Management

Objective setting, appraisal, feedback, and rewards are often viewed as the heart of performance management, especially from the HRM angle. Here, a big part of the challenge of "getting it right" is again due to the global/local duality. While researchers argue whether there is convergence or divergence in performance appraisal practices, they miss the point that dual forces are at work.[73] We would argue that the transnational firm needs a global template for its objective setting and appraisal, while allowing local companies to adapt that template according to their circumstances, then monitoring the ways in which they do this.

Given its decentralization of accountability to local units, the transnational needs to emphasize global objective setting and appraisal, but with the buy-in of senior management in the subsidiaries as to how it should be executed in practice. This reflects two observations: First, the idea of performance management is now widely accepted by MNCs across the world, while second, its implementation invariably runs into local problems unless there is commitment on the part of the subsidiary management team (typically part of a corporate evaluation system).

There is ample evidence that appraisal is difficult, rife with conundrums, as experienced practitioners know and as HRM texts show, and may have dysfunctional consequences.[74] Appraisal serves multiple functions—communication of organizational objectives, working out tensions in boss-subordinate relationships, providing information for self-improvement, guiding training and career development, providing the basis for pay decisions, leaving paper trails to justify firing—many of which are in conflict with each other. What is appropriate for one situation is often inappropriate for another. There is an ever-expanding range of appraisal practices—some reflecting the latest managerial fad, some leaving a lasting impact on how companies worldwide approach this complex process.[75]

As pointed out earlier, the concept of performance appraisal as practiced today in many multinationals was developed in the Anglo-Saxon context and may not always fit other cultures. There are myriad cultural obstacles to Anglo-Saxon style performance appraisal, many of them well described in management literature.[76] Let us review some of them. For a start, the manager-subordinate relationship is conceived differently in many cultures in which the idea of a two-way dialogue with the subordinate free to challenge the perception of the boss goes strongly against the heritage of what Hofstede calls power distance. In collectively oriented cultures, behaviors that demonstrate loyalty, cooperative spirit, and integrity are likely to be as important as the ability to achieve sales targets, contrary to the belief in the Western mother firm. The legal and social environment may restrict the freedom of the manager to evaluate and reward performance, as in Germany. No German academic reviews of HRM practice make any mention of appraisal practices or performance management.[77] In China, the legacy of the Maoist years, reinforced by the strong authority of the boss, is that Chinese employees sometimes avoid initiative for fear of being punished. Some cultures do not share the sense of internal control of the Anglo-Saxons—how do you react when someone from India puts off a decision inexplicably (the reason being that the horoscope indicates this to be an unfortunate time)?

The whole area of giving feedback is a potential minefield given various cultures' ways of confronting conflict. Discomfort with critical feedback, more or less universal and leading to many of the problems with appraisal, is particularly acute in certain cultures. A comparative study of performance appraisal practices in the three Chinese cultures of Hong Kong, Singapore, and Taiwan showed a common preference for group-oriented appraisal rather than individual assessment (though otherwise there were significant differences on most other dimensions of appraisal).[78] Asian cultures tend to deal with conflict issues in subtle and indirect ways—the idea of constructive confrontation is an alien concept (though one cannot generalize this across all of Asia).

Yet it is vital to train people in how to provide feedback through appraisal on an ongoing basis, for appraisal is a feature of virtually all firms that have successful performance management processes. The design of such appraisal and the training for it will vary from one culture to another, however. So will the aims of appraisal. For example, a study of Chinese employee reactions to Western objective setting and appraisal systems showed that whereas negotiating performance expectations and receiving performance feedback were typically key for Western staff, it was the link between performance and career development that was most appreciated by the Chinese.[79]

We have no doubt that scholars arguing for cultural divergence are correct that many firms will remain local in their approach. Yet despite the many cultural differences, there is ample evidence that Anglo-Saxon style appraisal is gaining ground across the world, at least among multinational firms and those facing strong global competition. There were frequent predictions in the 70s that management-by-objectives (MBO) would never take root in France because of the concept of authority, the avoidance of face-to-face conflict, and the negative connotations of control in that culture.[80] Yet one survey of 220 large French companies reported that by the late 80s over 85 percent had a policy of fixing objectives for managers and conducting annual performance appraisal reviews.[81] Similarly, leading firms in Italy and Germany have been rushing in the last ten years to introduce performance management approaches built around objectives and appraisal working hand in hand with greater decentralization of accountability. In Japan, where appraisal was traditionally frequent but conducted in secret without formal feedback to the employee,[82] the ability to conduct face-to-face performance interviews is now a standard part of managerial practice.

Leading global firms, in particular the U.S.-based multinationals, are redefining the standards, getting tough in the process and opening up new controversy. Their aim is not only to reward the best but also to systematically weed out those who are underperforming relative to their peers. Meeting objectives is not enough—Microsoft annually screens out about 5 percent of its workforce. The appraisal cycle at Cisco takes place every six months. Intel, EDS, and TI have all instituted similar policies. A visible champion of tough performance standards is GE's Jack Welch. GE's worldwide review of performance and potential focuses primarily on rewarding, retaining, and developing the top 10 percent of "A-players" and quickly removing the "C-players" in the bottom 10 percent. In a recent speech to Japanese industrialists, Welch's remarks on leadership were frequently interrupted with applause. His advice on how to deal with C-players, however, was met with stony silence.

What conclusions does this lead us to? Important as it may be, most managers, irrespective of culture, find appraisal difficult, time consuming, and uncomfortable. Performance appraisal is a contentious issue and it is likely to remain so. One size definitely does not fit all. Real commitment to implementing a rigorous appraisal process is more important than the sophistication of the methodology. Such a process starts with a global template, developed with input from around the world and ideally modeled on best practice in leading subsidiaries. Subsidiaries then must face up to their distinctive cultural problems and undertake adaptation of the template where necessary. Finally, the overall process needs to be monitored, with a view to learning and improvement. We discuss this further in the next chapter.

LINKING APPRAISAL TO REWARDS. The final component of the performance management cycle is the link between appraisal and rewards. Here we focus on compensation policy and criteria in the face of global versus local dilemmas (rather than rewards in the form of career advancement).

Historically, compensation policy was typically the most local area of performance management, often within a broad framework such as some version of the Hay-system of job evaluation. In fact, multinational firms exploited local differences by moving manufacturing and other functions from the high cost mother country to low cost countries. During the 90s, for instance, they moved software development and clerical administration to India and the Caribbean. The one problematic and highly complex area was expatriate compensation since it was only expatriates who moved from country to country. Today, this is changing.

Consider the current debate at GIC in Singapore, the government-affiliated fund management firm charged with investing the country's financial reserves on world markets, which in the past recruited local professionals to fill fund management and analyst jobs, paying them according to local civil service standards. As GIC expanded overseas, it hired talented non-Singaporean staff—again paid locally, but often more than their counterparts at the head office. Today the top foreign staff are being transferred to Singapore on a permanent basis—and how should they be paid? The salaries of their peers in foreign-owned financial institutions in Singapore reflect global market conditions. Paying less would violate external market equity, making it impossible to retain the best. But if foreign hires are paid at global rates, this will create internal inequity with their Singaporean colleagues. So why not treat all professionals as "globals"? That is possible, but it would then create external inequity with respect to other government employees.

Similarly, top managers at Norsk Hydro, Norway's largest international corporation, did not worry if a few Americans earned more than they because the Norwegian state would take most of any increment to them in taxes. But when a large number of middle level professionals around the world are earning significantly more than the head of a global business at home, it creates a disturbing sense of inequity, leading them to advocate a worldwide review of compensation practices. While the members of management teams of subsidiaries are today typically part of a common corporate system of performance-based reward management, many companies ask whether variable compensation, skill-based reward practices, and risk-based compensation such as stock options should not be generalized across local operations.

In an American software company that operates development centers in California and Bangalore, India, where the programmers are paid in line with local market rates, a critical project that involved extensive coordination between the two locations required a radical redesign, with a deadline that could be met only through extraordinary effort. The company decided to offer a significant bonus to all the programmers involved as long as the redesign was undertaken in time. The question arose as to how this bonus should be distributed. In proportion to base pay, taking into account the income gap between the U.S. and India? Or in proportion to the individual contribution to the success of the project, irrespective of work location?

What then is the "proper" allocation of global versus local rewards? There are arguments that compensation should be linked only to outcomes that the employee can influence. This would limit linking pay to global results (directly or via stock options) to only a select few in the organization. Pointing to evidence that firm performance improves when the individual rewards deep in the organization are at least partially tied to broader objectives, others may assert the opposite.[83] And of course, in some country or industry environments it is accepted that employees may share some of the firm level risk, whereas elsewhere such choices may be constrained by custom or regulation.

These are just a few of the emerging challenges facing transnational firms when considering global compensation. What guidelines can we get from research? One recent academic review by Bloom and Milkovich points out that the evidence suggests that the design and functioning of reward systems—from pay-for-performance to team-based pay, from stock options to executive compensation—are highly dependent on context.[84] There are national institutional limits (for example, it is legally difficult to pay on a piece rate basis in Germany or not to pay for overtime in Japan), and differences in taxation systems often argue for local differentiation. And national culture is only one element of context. Variations in norms and values within cultures are just as important as variations across cultures.[85] Consequently, there is tremendous variance in compensation practices across firms, industries, and sectors within most nations.

To the extent that reward practices are an integral element of a firm's processes, it may choose rewards to create a unique, value adding organizational culture thereby creating its own context, within limits.[86] An American firm operating in China can pay attention to selecting and socializing people who fit with its approach to reward management (and the other elements of the performance process in which this is embedded)—just as Southwest Airlines with its distinctive culture pays great attention to selecting people who will thrive there rather than in a more "traditional" U.S. airline company. The approach to reward management at Lincoln Electric (combining pure piece rate compensation with norms of total transparency to create a strong culture of self-reliance) is fundamental to the success of that firm. Such an enterprise might be obliged to consider extremely carefully the location of its operations. It might avoid countries where institutional barriers render the reward system nonviable, paying meticulous attention to the selection of people (as Japanese firms have done when establishing operations in the United States) as well as to any modifications in reward and related practices. In other firms, compensation practices might be less strategic—sometimes downplayed in favor of rewards through career development[87]—and consequently more strictly an issue for local management.

The Lincoln example leads us to emphasize that it is the internal consistency of practices and norms that is powerful. One cannot consider rewards separately from the other elements of performance management or from the wider context of recruitment and socialization. By the same token, unless compensation is aligned to reward broader dimensions of performance beyond one's job or immediate business unit, it is unlikely that we will see strong collaborative behavior (see our earlier discussion on rewarding teamwork) or support for wider corporate initiatives.

All in all, appraisal and rewards is one domain of transnational performance management in which we currently face more questions than answers, and we suspect that the implications of those questions will challenge conventional assumptions about how we reward valued professionals and managers in the global economy.

NORMATIVE INTEGRATION: COHESION MANAGEMENT

"Normative integration" is a term organizational theorists use to describe the socialization that leads to shared attitudes, values, and assumptions—the shared culture. Some degree of normative integration is essential to facilitate the methods and mechanisms of organizational "glue." The starting point is a common language, both in the linguistic sense that the corporate language may be English and in the deeper semantic sense of concepts that have sharing meanings. Remember our earlier example of how the meaning of "goal" or "commitment" might be quite different between cultures.

Without normative integration, communication across borders would be time consuming since people would have to figure out what terms and concepts meant to others and repeatedly establish new norms for social exchange (leadership expectations, how to surface and deal with conflict, the nature of reciprocity, and myriad other such norms). When groups got together across boundaries, disruptive emotional conflict would be the rule rather than the exception. The time demand and frustration would put an effective barrier up to cross-boundary teams and exchange.

Organizational theorists such as Kogut who argue that knowledge transfer is the basis for multinational competitive advantage emphasize the importance of this communal sense of identity.[88] Individuals will freely participate in knowledge exchange only if they share some common identity. Indeed the idea of the firm as a social community with a commonality of values and beliefs is deeply rooted in sociology (Durkheim, Etzioni, Selznick, and more recently Ouchi). This precludes the risk of opportunistic and self-interested behavior. If there is no commonality of norms, attitudes, and values across the firm, glue technology simply will not work.[89]

Normative integration results from the socialization in which an individual learns the ropes and internalizes the culture of an organization. Socialization is effected through selection, induction, training and apprenticeship, transfers, and the selective promotion of individuals who have internalized the core values of the organization. The measurable outcomes of socialization are loyalty and commitment to the organization—and conformity. Conformity is the downside of normative integration. If the socialization is excessive, the ability to challenge the status quo or to think in innovative ways will be dampened if not suppressed.

Balancing socialization and innovation is thus another duality. As they enter the organization and then each new job, individuals have to learn the ropes. But with time in the organization and in the job, they then have to be able to challenge, query, and experiment with new behaviors if the firm is to maintain its adaptive ability.[90] It is this point that underlies the delicate dilemma in the transnational of ensuring cohesion but avoiding cloning.

Broadening the Use of Socialization in the Transnational

The careful use of socialization to develop leaders is as old as antiquity. It was widely practiced at the time of the Roman Empire. Potential governors and legates were strongly socialized and then those who had the Roman Empire "in their minds" were sent out to administer the distant provinces.

All organizations except temporary groups are particularly concerned with the socialization of "corporate property," "high potentials," and people with the talent for key leadership roles. Corporate entrepreneurs focus on their sons and daughters. In other organizations, the socialization starts off with a shared *weltanschauung* that comes from a demanding and common education—that of U.K. Oxbridge elites or the French "Grandes Ecoles," the high tech institutes and Ivy League universities of the United States, the administrative training system that has produced the Mandarins of China for thousands of years. We remember the son of the British *tai pan* of a Hong Kong conglomerate fifteen years ago saying "no one except a male graduate from Oxford or Cambridge will ever get ahead in this firm" as they recruited thousands of Asian men and women with high career aspirations. The socialization of the technicans, workers, and the lower level employees was a matter left to local management.

The complexity of the transnational, the limits of structural and central control, and above all the shift to a highly qualified workforce of knowledge-based professionals spread out across the world have changed all this. Broadening the scope of socialization from "the critical few" to "the critical many," from those hired in the mother country to all professional staff regardless of passport, becomes imperative to facilitate cross-border teams, the transfer of know-how, and other forms of coordination. The transnational has to find, bring on board, and develop the "right" people in all its subsidiaries around the world, not just those from the parent country. This is one of the reasons why companies have become so concerned with developing competency frameworks to guide local selection and development.[91]

Shell presents an example of this broadening scope. The process of socialization there has long been known as "cohesion management," allowing Shell to function as a well-integrated group yet with a high degree of decentralization. Indeed it was the study of Shell's practices that alerted management theorists to the power of socialization in multinational firms.[92]

The principle of decentralization and autonomy to local operating companies has been Shell's basic organizational philosophy for the last forty years. Thus Shell Oil is an independent U.S. company, while Deutsche Shell in Germany is expected to function as a German firm. But as Lo Van Wachem, a former chairman of the Group, said: "There are three things that hold this group of autonomous companies together. The first is the common logo, the Shell pecten, and the values that this represents. The second is common financial systems [its performance management process]—the rationale behind the performance evaluations is the same for all operating companies. And the third and most important source of cohesion is management development—close attention to common training principles and particularly to career management."[93]

Hewlett-Packard is another well-known example, where people are selected not just for their technical skill and potential but for their fit with the culture. Such companies exploit the variation that exists within cultural differences. When HP is recruiting engineers for its facilities in Büblingen Germany, they are looking for "deviant" German engineers who would not be attracted by a more typical German enterprise such as Siemens. Career progress depends on learning and adjusting to the code of values, behaviors, and beliefs that is called "The HP Way." As Hewlett-Packard people say, the outcome of that process is that when a salesman is faced with a dilemma in some distant place, without any means of contacting the boss for instructions, he or she knows what Bill Hewlett or Dave Packard would have done in that situation.

On one side of the Atlantic, Unilever, Marks & Spencer, Péchiney in France, A.P. Møller and EAC in Denmark all exemplified this approach. For decades, both Marks & Spencer and EAC even went to the extreme of recruiting individuals from high schools rather than universities because these youngsters were malleable, less likely to be contaminated by the individualistic ideas that a university education can bring. On the other side of the Atlantic, IBM and Procter & Gamble also practiced strong socialization, like Hewlett-Packard. These were all outstandingly successful companies at the time, leading to a common belief in the 80s that strong cultures are successful cultures. It was a belief fostered at that time by the success of the Japanese, who excelled in the practice of normative integration of their own Japanese staff.

The Weakness of Strong Cultures

If the logic of normative integration is taken to the extreme, however, it creates a pathology, as the theory of duality predicts regarding any attribute. Despite the belief in the 80s that strong cultures are effective cultures, there is no evidence for this. Empirical research shows that there is no significant relationship between the strength of corporate culture and the long-term performance of the firm.[94] Some degree of diversity is necessary in order to adapt if the environment changes. When the environment changes, as it did for Japanese firms forced to move from a meganational export orientation to transnationalism, what was previously the strength of normative integration becomes brittle rigidity.

Excessively strong cultures may lose their strategic flexibility. Cohesion can be taken to the extreme of conformity, indeed uniformity. Hewlett-Packard is a good illustration. The HP Way reflected the company's heritage in the instruments business. But instruments started to be computerized and HP was led into the computer sector where different values are required to be successful. HP faced a choice in the mid-80s—whether to differentiate its values (and the underlying management practices) so as to permit diversification, or to stick to its values and limit its mission to instruments. We predicted that cultural values would win out and that HP would abandon its venture into computers.[95] It was not as simple as that. The short term proved us wrong, but recent events have shown we were correct. Initially, Hewlett-Packard committed itself to strategic diversification with the acquisition of Apollo Computers and other companies, and then it engaged in a difficult process of trying to create a culture with more tolerance for diversity.[96] Some values such as avoidance of debt were abandoned, other values such as "promote from within" were modified, and a distinction emerged between values that are core and those that are peripheral. That was not enough. In 1998, Hewlett-Packard decided to bite the bullet and split itself up into two different companies, one based on the instruments culture and the other based on the computer culture.

Stickiness was also a problem for Royal Dutch/Shell. The organizational logic of strong autonomy for the operating company made sense in the downstream oil exploration business, in which it is vital to be close to local partners and government, but it created problems in the chemicals business in which executives had long argued for stronger global integration. In 1997, Shell also decided to break itself up into four companies, one in Exploration & Production (a sector requiring a more local orientation), one in Chemicals (dominant orientation toward global integration), one in Oil Products (dominant regional orientation), and one in Supply & Trading (again global in orientation).

As we said earlier, the focus on building network coordination does not replace structure—it complements it. There is a danger that the pendulum may swing too far in favor of network glue with corresponding underutilization of classic structural technology. Remember that organizational theory suggests that firms in complex and turbulent environments can increase their capacity for information processing either through lateral relationship and vertical information processing *or* by reducing their need for information processing by creating self-contained structural units.[97] Hewlett-Packard and Shell are not alone in finding that there are limits to cohesion management, leading them to create structurally more autonomous companies or divisions.[98]

Glue such as normative integration has to be administered in moderate doses and with care, without forgetting the importance of structure. A Shell executive expressed this with an analogy:

> One of my son's hobbies is building model aircraft. The key to building an aircraft that will fly is dosing the glue at the right places. Too little glue at the key spots, and the plane falls apart when you try to fly it. But sometimes he falls into the opposite trap. He and the plane get covered with glue, and the plane is so heavy with glue that it won't fly. It's the same for organizations—some are so sticky that they can't fly.

MATRIX EVERYTHING . . . EXCEPT THE STRUCTURE

One way of summarizing the challenges of coordination in the transnational firm is to stand conventional thinking on its head.

Go back to the law of requisite complexity. Transnational firms face the highest degree of environmental complexity, and this law says that the internal complexity of the firm must mirror that external complexity. That complexity is captured by the image of matrix. The environment is highly matrixed—product markets, geographic markets, customer segments, basic technologies, management technologies. Consequently, as Jorma Ollila, Nokia's architect and CEO, correctly says, organizations cannot avoid matrix. But matrix does not have to mean structure as it was implied in the past. Structure is a powerful tool that is difficult to change.

A good guideline for the transnational organization might be—matrix everything . . . except the structure! To manage that complexity, matrix through project groups, steering committees, internal boards, management processes, business planning, and measurement. Matrix roles and responsibilities, so that people have vertical and horizontal accountabilities. Matrix minds and mindsets—we will discuss how to do that in the next chapter. A project group can be set up quickly, an internal board can be formed, reconstituted or disbanded in a few days, roles and responsibilities can be rapidly revised—but structures take years to adjust.

Like every guideline, please do not take this to the extreme! There is a role for matrix structures of dual reporting relationships in most organizations, as at ABB in the early 90s, reflecting differentiated consultative arrangements. However, the forces toward alliances and acquisitions currently push in the direction of structures that are clearly aligned on product lines. But who knows? If social and legislative forces swing against megaglobal consolidation, as they may, that too is a pendulum that might swing again.

TAKEAWAYS

1. Vertical and hierarchic means of coordination cannot cope with the complexity of demands facing the transnational firm. They must be complemented by worldwide horizontal coordination mechanisms—glue technology.

2. The important tools of glue technology are largely the application of HRM: cross-boundary teamwork, cross-boundary steering groups, know-how transfer leading to global knowledge management, and global process management.

3. Horizontal coordination takes place fundamentally through relationships and social ties. Electronic technologies leverage relationships but do not replace them, except for the transfer of simple codified knowledge.

4. Unless there are sound HRM foundations that ensure basic job competence and performance, cross-border teamwork overstretches the organization.

5. The generic lessons of project management apply to cross-boundary teams—on issues such as goal clarity, the importance of staffing, sequencing complex projects, managing conflict, paying careful attention to evaluation and to feedback/learning—though the risks of failure if they are not applied rigorously are greater.

6. Cross-boundary steering groups in the shape of internal boards, functional councils, network leaders, and the like provide flexible and potent means of maintaining control while promoting empowerment and accountability at the lowest level possible.

7. The ability of the transnational firm to transfer knowledge is a major source of competitive advantage. This can start by informal dissemination, creating social networks, focused initiatives, and innovation forums. But building systematic knowledge management capabilities involves focus, technology, a leadership infrastructure, and above all removing cultural barriers.

8. Global processes in the transnational firm can be viewed as horizontal standardization that links together critical activities with clear deliverables in mind. Two basic processes of concern to HRM are global performance management and leadership development, though there are many other candidates.

9. While global performance management is conceptually simple, the different stages in the process—going from upstream strategic/business planning to

downstream appraisal and rewards—involve difficult decisions as to whether these subprocesses should be applied worldwide or be subject to local adaptation. Some commonality in the process of global performance management is needed, though the local context will always influence the actual implementation.

10. Network coordination always requires a certain degree of normative integration (shared concepts, norms, attitudes, and values) induced by socialization. But excessive socialization can lead to dangerous organizational rigidities.

NOTES

1. Barham and Heimer, 1998. ABB's business portfolio has changed since 1997—for example high speed trains were sold to Daimler and the turbines business to Ahlstrom. The organization has recently changed from a matrix to a front/back template, going beyond the "transnational" model.

2. Ibid.

3. Ibid., p. 274.

4. Planning becomes learning, to use the image of a former Shell corporate planner (De Geus, 1988). See also Mintzberg, 1994.

5. See Chapter 4, Figure 4–1 on the generic roles of national organizations.

6. Peters and Waterman, 1982; Ouchi, 1981; Kanter, 1985; O'Toole, 1985.

7. McGregor, 1960. The European work on socio-technical systems, participative management, and organic (as opposed to mechanistic) working systems also spurred the change, adopted In the United States under the umbrella of the Organizational Development movement. Myriad articles and volumes have been written on this, and the history and arguments are well summarized from an HRM perspective in the publications of Lawler, who contrasts hierarchic or bureaucratic management with what he calls "high involvement management" (Lawler, 1992).

8. The concept of "empowerment," with its emotive connotations, has created a great deal of misunderstanding. The best formulation of what this implies is to be found in Mills (1994), who provides the following formula: Empowerment = Goals × Delegated "Respons-ability" × Measurement and Feedback. The term "respons-ability" (our word) means having the necessary skills to respond. This formula emphasizes both the hard and soft elements of empowerment. If any element is zero, then anything multiplied by zero nets out to nothing. In other words, attempts to delegate will not lead to significant results unless there are clear goals, measurement criteria, feedback that allows learning, and appropriate skill development.

9. Galbraith, 1977.

10. To cite but three examples of this shift in research focus, Porter argued in his value chain analysis for the importance of "horizontal strategies," viewing this as the most important contribution of HRM to the way in which a firm adds value (Porter, 1986). Martinez and Jarillo (1989) reviewed the stream of research on coordination in multinational firms, clearly noting this shift in focus from concern with hierarchic and structural mechanisms to informal and lateral means of coordination.

    More recently, St. John, Young et al. (1999) studied how 48 international firms managed linkages between marketing and manufacturing. They found that firms with relatively simple multidomestic strategies used traditional planning and scheduling methods, while firms with more complex global strategies used a wider variety of coordination tools, including lateral teams and relationships. Firms with even more complex transnational strategies used the widest range of coordination mechanisms.

11. Ibarra, 1992; Baker, 1994.
12. Goold, Campbell et al., 1994; Goold and Campbell, 1998.
13. This is an issue that has implications for strategic change in the transnational firm, as we will discuss in Chapter 9.
14. Daft and Lengel, 1986.
15. Granovetter, 1976.
16. Burt, 1992.
17. Hansen, 1999.
18. These examples are taken from our own experience as well as Snow, Snell et al. (1996), who report on one of the focused studies of international teams.
19. The matrixed role or "split egg" concept is explained in Chapter 2.
20. This definition of a virtual team is provided by Townsend, deMarie et al. (1998).
21. Hedlund and Ridderstraale, 1995.
22. Adler, 1991.
23. Amason and colleagues argue that handling these two faces of conflict is critical for team performance (Amason, Thompson et al., 1995). Affective conflict is associated with team failure, while cognitive conflict is associated with team success. Their empirical research supports this argument (Amason, 1996), leading them to suggest that knowing how to steer a group toward constructive conflict is the key to successful team management.
24. Punnett and Clemens, 1999.
25. Davidson Frame, 1987; Katzenbach and Smith, 1993; Johansen, Sibbet et al., 1991; Bettenhausen, 1991.
26. Davidson Frame, 1987.
27. One of the paradoxes of staffing project teams is that the most energized and committed groups are those in which the members complain most about being overworked and understaffed. This has been called "optimal undermanning" or "n-minus one" staffing, keeping it lean and mean rather than representational, large, and consequently bureaucratic (Snow Miles, and Coleman, 1992). Yet the extreme of the duality, that is understaffing so that it does not have the needed perspectives, would be dangerous.
28. Although it was not international in focus, the study of Ancona and Caldwell (1992) on new product team managers showed that effective teams follow cycles of external activities (aimed at molding the views of senior management, getting feedback, and general scanning) and internal processes that were associated with long-term success.
29. Snow, Snell et al., 1996. Behavioral complexity theories of leadership seem appropriate to understand these demands. These theories argue that leadership effectiveness depends on the ability of managers to display multiple, dualistic leadership styles, supported by a high degree of cognitive complexity (Hart and Quinn, 1993; Denison, Hooijberg et al., 1995). Situational leadership ideas, widely used on training programs, embody the same notion.
30. For the research on leadership in virtual teams, see Leidner, Kayworth et al. (1999).
31. Hedlund and Ridderstraale, 1995.
32. These differences almost certainly reflect different patterns of career socialization, as discussed further in Chapter 8. Western professionals tend to move up in their functions, and so are often exposed to their international functional colleagues through training, conferences, and projects. In contrast, the Japanese work on interfunctional projects early in their careers and are frequently moved to a different function as part of their initial training. Yet they rarely

have contact with their peers outside Japan, language barriers aggravating this. Consequently these differences in project staffing and cultures show up in different sequencing challenges.

33. Tjosvold, 1991; Brown, 1983; Amason, Thompson et al., 1995.
34. M. F. R. Kets de Vries, "Percy Barnevik and ABB," INSEAD video, 1994.
35. Hedlund and Ridderstraale, 1995.
36. Ghoshal, 1991.
37. For a review of 360° multiple appraisal systems, see Tornow, 1998.
38. Gittell (2000) illustrates the importance of hierarchy for coordination. This study contrasts American Airlines with its flat organization with broad spans of control and rigorous performance management with the smaller spans of control at the phenomenally successful Southwest Airlines. The price that American pays is poor coordination. In contrast, supervisors at Southwest play cross-functional coordination roles—diffusing blame, providing coaching and feedback.
39. Integrative leadership orientation and how it can be developed is discussed in Chapter 8.
40. Kogut and Zander, 1992, p. 383. Their ideas build on the concept of a firm as a "social community" with a commonality of values and beliefs, precluding the risk of opportunistic and self-interested behavior, an idea that is deeply rooted in sociology (Durkheim, Etzioni, Selznick, and more recently Ouchi). Individuals will freely participate in knowledge exchange only if they share this communal sense of identity. See also Kogut and Zander (1996) and Nahapiet and Ghoshal (1998).
41. Szulanski, 1994; Szulanski, 1996; O'Dell and Grayson, 1998.
42. Szulanski, 1996.
43. Szulanski, 1994.
44. Zbaracki, 1998.
45. Banc One's linkage and learning practices are described by Myers and Kanter (1989). The quote from their treasurer is cited in Goold, Campbell et al. (1994, p. 149).
46. For example the case on managing knowledge at Booz-Allen & Hamilton; see Galunic and Weeks (1999).
47. O'Dell and Grayson, 1998.
48. Ibid.
49. For example, TI's best practice knowledge base in manufacturing is organized using Lotus Notes around sixteen processes, and then 130 keywords that apply to these processes. The database contains more than 500 practices, each documented with a short narrative and contact information.
50. Alavi and Leidner, 1997; Special issue on Knowledge Management, *Management Review,* April 1999.
51. Constant, Sproull et al., 1996.
52. The concept of organizational culture as formulated by Goffee and Jones (1998) explicitly recognizes this. They view culture as having two dimensions that they call *sociability* and *solidarity.* Without some measure of sociability, people in organizations tend to become mercenary.
53. O'Dell and Grayson, 1998.
54. See for example Ostroff (1999) for a practice-oriented analysis of process thinking in what he calls "the horizontal organization."
55. One of the main findings in recent Global State-of-the-Art (SOTA) surveys undertaken by the Human Resource Planning Society in North America has indeed been the emphasis in companies on horizontal sharing of HR expertise and experience, reducing the occurrence of reinventing-the-wheel. These SOTA surveys are reported annually in their journal *Human Resource Planning.*

56. *Financial Times,* December 7, 1999.

57. See Ostroff (1999, ch. 11), for a more detailed outline of process ownership.

58. There are other areas for potential application of global HR process management. We will discuss recruitment and socialization later in this chapter, balancing the deliverables of immediate job needs, normative integration, and long-term development. Alliance management and acquisition integration were discussed in earlier chapters. As mentioned earlier in this chapter, GE regards "people commitment" and "change management" as processes. When GE acquires companies in, for example, Europe, they estimate that the toolkit of processes allows them to add eight percentage points of margin within a couple of years (T. Stewart, "See Jack. See Jack Run," *Fortune,* September 27, 1999, p. 69).

59. As reported by Grote (2000), a recent survey of best practice in performance management ran into problems when many clearly model companies declined to take part. As one HR VP said, "We would no more show our performance-appraisal form to a bunch of outsiders than the Coca-Cola Co. would let you come in and look over the secret formula for Coke."

60. Eisenhardt and Galunic, 2000.

61. Note that one should avoid associating performance management with "Anglo-Saxon cultures," as in some popular characterizations. We know of many well-established Anglo-Saxon firms for whom the performance management ideas discussed here are as alien as for the Chinese state-owned enterprises in the era before the period of economic reforms.

62. The importance of tight coordination in this upstream planning process may not be obvious to corporations with a successful multidomestic heritage of local responsiveness, now moving toward transnationalism. We are currently working with one successful European corporation which has long been organized on multidomestic lines. Country business managers focus on delivering their operating results, while top management's attitude is, "We don't want them worrying about strategy since it will just distract them from focusing on their own local targets." But now their industry is moving rapidly in a transnational direction. Customers are buying across borders in certain product areas, and some want global service. Investment decisions are becoming more complex, involving global-local trade-offs. All of this is made more difficult by the fact that the transnational trend is differentiated—a lot of their business is still strictly local-for-local as in the past. Top management is beginning to recognize that local heads of business have to be more closely involved in the whole strategic and business planning process.

63. See the study of Goold and Campbell (1987). This study recognizes that corporate strategies and styles reflect choices on dualities and the necessity to cope with the limitations of any choice.

64. See Chapter 2, the section on Alignment, and also Chapter 10.

65. Mintzberg, 1994.

66. De Geus, 1988.

67. At BP, Unilever, GE, and other firms, there is much process innovation in this domain of strategic and business planning, often under the umbrella of change management and guided by experienced process consultants (internal and external). Examples are "conferences" that bring together hundreds of key executives, with intensive preparation to ensure two-way dialogue; training programs to introduce a common language for discussing strategic marketing; workshops that bring together heads of businesses for a week of intensive confrontation on issues that have been suppressed; "Workout"-type processes; and fishbowl meetings at which local management teams present their plans to top management while other teams sit in on the review.

68. One of the frequent critiques of MBO-type processes is that they place too much emphasis on determining individual objectives (often to facilitate the functioning of individualized re-

wards), at the expense of collective ownership of business strategy. This may not be appropriate in some cultural contexts.

69. Quoted from the GE 1994 Annual Report.

70. See Chapter 4, page 166, for cultural differences in the meaning of performance.

71. People have criticized this since the process of performance management tends to focus on incremental rather than breakthrough change (Goss, Pascale et al., 1993). Some firms have moved to parallel processes where operational goals are run through the individualized MBO-type process, whereas the long-term stretch targets are managed collectively through review processes and knowledge management. GE is an example, where four-year corporate stretch targets were set in 1991 to increase operating margins and inventory turnover. New targets were later set on Six-Sigma quality and leadership development. Other corporations such as Hewlett-Packard have similarly broadened the conception of performance management so as to complement the MBO cycle of operational planning with a *Hoshin Kanri* process oriented toward long-term breakthroughs.

72. It is not surprising that a metrics war is currently raging between the advocates of Value-Based Management (VBM) and those taking a multiple stakeholder approach to measurement and control. This important debate goes beyond the scope of this book but it illustrates the need for clear metrics, be it economic profit or some form of balanced scorecard. In general, Anglo-Saxon firms tend to favor shareholder logic while continental Europeans favor stakeholder logic. But Redding (2001) and Whitley (1999) remind us that different forms of capitalism have different aims and metrics.

73. Paik and Stage, 1996; Clark, 1996. We refer back to Chapter 4 for a discussion of these issues, notably concerning the network perspective. Transnational firms increasingly compare themselves with other such MNCs (witness the way in which GE's practices became a global benchmark during the 90s), whereas local firms typically model themselves on the practices of their neighbours.

74. See for example Chapter 10 in Baron and Kreps (1999) for a good analysis.

75. The complexities and trade-offs are such that it is legitimate to raise the question as to whether it is worth evaluating individuals at all. Deming argued forcefully that appraisal is so dysfunctional that performance improvement efforts should be focused on system improvement, getting at the root problems rather than the symptoms (see Gabor, 1990).

76. See Schneider and Barsoux (1997). To give one specific empirical study as an example, Vance, McClaine et al. (1992) found significant differences in managerial style across the United States, Indonesia, Malaysia, and Thailand that hamper the transferability of appraisal practices across borders. See also Hofstede (1999).

77. Sparrow and Hiltrop, 1994, p. 557.

78. Paik and Stage, 1996. For example, Hong Kong managers disliked participative appraisal practices, whereas the Taiwanese accepted close supervision more than those in Singapore or Hong Kong.

79. Lindholm, 1998.

80. A frequently cited study is that of Trepo (1973), which Hofstede, Trompenaars, and other culturalists frequently use as an example.

81. Reported by Sparrow and Hiltrop, 1994.

82. Pucik, 1984.

83. Milkovich and Newman, 1996.

84. Bloom and Milkovich, 1999.

85. Pucik, 1997.

86. Bloom and Milkovich, 1999.

87. Pucik, 1992.

88. Kogut and Zander, 1992; Kogut and Zander, 1996; and Nahapiet and Ghoshal, 1998.

89. This view challenges the transaction cost theory of the firm, based on assumptions of human opportunism and the resulting conditions of market failure.

90. This balance between socialization and innovation is discussed by Schein (1968). A study of the characteristics of enduring organizations singles out this, among other dualities, as an essential feature of firms that appear to be "built to last" (Collins and Porras, 1994). The appointment of Jack Welch as CEO of GE is an example, an individual who was strongly steeped in the GE values and yet who argued forcibly that GE's culture should evolve.

91. This topic is discussed at length in Chapter 8.

92. We refer to the classic study by Edström and Galbraith (1977).

93. In Chapter 8, we will discuss how Shell developed and implemented a competency management framework during the 80s so as to broaden the scope of socialization to all professional employees throughout the world, just as firms such as Motorola and Ford are doing today.

94. This empirical study is reported by Kotter and Heskett (1992). They found that balanced attention to stakeholders correlated most strongly with business analyst perceptions of long-term performance.

95. Evans and Lorange, 1989.

96. Rogers and Beer, 1995.

97. As argued by Galbraith (1977); also see page 304.

98. Other examples are the split-up of AT&T into a telecom and an equipment business (Lucent), Arthur Andersen's divorce creating separate audit and systems consulting companies, and ABB's decision in 1998 to abandon the matrix and organize on clear business lines—allowing it for example to sell off its operations in high speed trains to Daimler.

CHAPTER 8

Developing Talent for the Transnational Enterprise

The concept of a leader as a steward of human capital, whose primary job is leaving a legacy of talent that can carry the company forward, may not be accepted by all senior executives. This is, however, what GE's Jack Welch believes, and GE's "leadership engine," as it has been called, has become a worldwide exemplar for talent development.[1] Executive search agencies around the world target GE as the most talent-rich firm. When we meet former GE managers in Germany and China as well as in the United States, they invariably speak with praise about their GE training, and former executives today head up international firms such as Italy's Fiat. The fact that a lot of companies cast their nets for GE-trained managers is a source of little concern to Welch given the underlying strength of the bench.

"We have made leadership development the most important element in our work," says Welch. "We focus on some aspect of it every day. It is in our blood. We put people in the right job and let them develop a strategy, in that order. You can't start with strategy and then appoint someone to execute it. So my most important job is to choose and develop business leaders who are bright enough to grasp the elements of their game, creative enough to develop a simple vision, and self-confident enough to liberate and inspire people."[2]

There is a slate of candidates for the top 500 positions at GE worldwide, and since he took over the company in 1981, Welch has made a practice of carefully reviewing every slate of two to four candidates for a key job. He takes names off the slate and adds new names to it—the hiring manager is then free to select someone from that slate. It is a process backed up every spring by a field review, with Welch in attendance, with each of GE's twelve businesses around the world. They work through the performance and development plans for the top 3,000 managers, together with the results of a survey on what employees are thinking, with a follow-up in the fall. Over the years, as the leadership bench at GE has strengthened, Welch has become increasingly intolerant of managers who get good financial results but who do not stretch and develop their own people. The heads of GE's European businesses reckon that they spend 30 to 50 percent of their time on explicit HR matters.[3]

Most people, even outside GE, have heard of Crotonville, even though they may not know much about the little town north of New York City on the Hudson River. GE's training center was created there in the 50s when the company went through a process of decentralization. Top management at the time felt that such a center would be needed to help managers adapt to their new responsibilities, as well as to provide what we call the "corporate glue" that must accompany autonomy. Under Welch, Crotonville became a prime driver of change. Attended by nearly 10,000 people every year (now with regional "Crotonvilles" in Brussels, Singapore, and Tokyo), the center became a platform for massive corporate change projects, from Workout to Six-Sigma quality to change acceleration. But Crotonville plays many other roles connected with development. Leaders at various levels are socialized into their jobs through participation on key programs. Globalization permeates the agenda, such as the landmark three-week Manager Development Course whose aim is to "develop executive skills in relation to key business issues such as developing business strategy, competing globally, diversity and globalization, leading teams and change, and advancing customer satisfaction."

The style of exchange at Crotonville, informal and confrontative, models the type of corporate culture that Welch believes is needed—as the annual report notes, "GE is the best place to work in the world for people who like to compete." The center sets the example for best practice exchange, and the Crotonville staff play the lead role worldwide in fostering knowledge sharing across borders. Many of the programs are for global customers. GE managers will be paired up with Russian managers from Aeroflot on a program intended to facilitate GE's entry into the Russian aircraft engine industry; or with influential Chinese leaders who are interested in learning from GE. A few years ago there was even a workshop headlined "the failures of globalization at GE," at which executives openly reviewed the lessons of costly mistakes.

CHAPTER OVERVIEW

While GE may be one of the few corporations to set it as a top corporate priority, talent development is one of the most important processes in the transnational enterprise. We focus in this chapter first on guiding ideas behind the development of talent, then on the particular issue of transnational leadership development, and finally on the wider need for developing a global mindset.

Given the complexity of developing people, we start by taking the reader back to the basic principles of talent development, identifying three elements that must be borne in mind: challenging assignments, risk management, and hardship testing. We move on to discuss how competencies can help the transnational firm to steer talent development by providing common, firm-specific frameworks across its worldwide operations. There is a lot of confusion in this domain since there are at least four different organizational logics, each with strengths and weaknesses.

Talent development is understandably focused in transnational enterprises on leadership, which we discuss in the next section. Again, we start by going back to the basics of what leadership is and how to develop it, as well as discussing the implications of increasing discontinuities in career paths (what is known as intransitivity). We discuss why a rigorous process of leadership management (the identification and development of potential) is necessary, mapping out four different models for how this is undertaken. Three of these models, anchored in the heritage of Japanese, Latin, and German firms, respectively, have different strengths. All however are incompatible with transnational development, and this leads us to explore a fourth process that has developed in multinational firms, along with key issues that must be the focus of attention.

More recently, attention in talent development has broadened from leadership to the wider population of managers in the transnational firm. If they do not have what is called a global mindset, they are likely to push the conflicts upstairs for arbitration, overwhelming the leaders of the global firm. In the last section, we discuss two conceptions of global mindset, one psychological and the other strategic, and we explore the tools for measuring and developing that mindset, including the role of action learning in education and training.

INVESTING IN TALENT

Investment in management and leadership development is one type of human capital investment. The transition to a postindustrial service economy in the latter part of the twentieth century has led to a growing concern for human capital investment, as opposed to investment in areas of wealth creation such as natural resources and capital equipment.

If an organization makes an investment in people, it wants to get a return. Gary Becker, the economist who is the father of human capital theory, distinguishes between investments in *general-purpose* and *firm-specific* human capital. Firms should be reluctant to invest in general skill development in a competitive market for talent since this simply increases the market value of their employees.[4] What is to prevent that person from taking a newly trained general skill in say process control to another employer in return for an increase in salary? There is, however, some empirical evidence that investment in general skills does increase the commitment of the workforce to the firm.[5]

We will discuss both generalized skill development and firm-specific development of managers and leaders in this chapter, though with more emphasis on the latter. Let us start, however, by addressing some of the generic issues.

Generic Issues Regarding Talent Development

Talent development is naturally a major preoccupation of top management. Indeed, Edith Penrose's seminal study in economics *The Theory of the Growth of the Firm* points out that lack of firm-specific talent is the major constraint on the economic growth of an enterprise.[6] Yet the lack of basic knowledge regarding talent development is conspicuous. Even HR specialists get lost in the myriad tools and techniques, failing to see the wood for the trees. Assessment centers, needs analysis, training programs, transfer systems can easily become ends in themselves.

How Does One Develop People?

Developing people is indeed a complex task. But there is virtue in the old idea that when things get complex, take them back to basic principles. We often take managers back to basics by simply asking them the question, "How do you develop people?" They quickly come back with responses: coaching, feedback, assessment of their qualities, providing goals, responsibility, allowing them to make reasonable mistakes, training, mentorship, and so forth.

What should be at the head of the list? Our research and experience suggest that it should be *challenge.* People develop through challenge. The one common denominator that we found in our early research among leaders who make a difference, be it in technical or managerial positions, is that they respond more than others to challenge.[7] As others have noted, at the heart of development lies the simple principle that people learn most by doing things they have not done before.[8]

Test this out with your own experience! Simply ask people to tell you about their most developmental experiences. Surprisingly enough, training and education are hardly ever mentioned. A few responses concern a relationship with a significant mentor or role model. All the others are descriptions of some stretching challenge that people worked through, often succeeding but sometimes failing, often in professional life but sometimes in private life, sometimes planned but equally often by chance.

What is the general implication of this for development? The implication is that people develop through *challenging assignments.* The planning of such assignments is one of the three basic elements of development management—in the transnational enterprise as well.

Having stated that people develop through challenges, however, we see a major hitch in the argument. The bigger the challenge, the greater the risk of making mistakes. And whatever may be said about allowing people to learn from their mistakes, most organizations want to minimize that risk. Mistakes can be a great tool for development, but at the expense of operational performance.

The ideal is to get long-term development AND short-term performance. This leads us to the second element of development, what we call *risk management.* Coaching, mentoring, feedback, training, assessment, and expectation setting are all part of risk management. Take training as an example. When a person moves into a new job, the aim of training is to avoid the risk of making mistakes and perhaps also to boost the confidence of the individual to take the necessary actions. Or consider assessment—what might be a positive challenge for one person could be an experience with which another cannot cope.

Taking the second element to an extreme, however, can be a real danger if the coaching and risk management effectively minimize any risk of failure so that people never learn to stand on their own feet and face up to tough situations. This leads us to the third element of development, dealing with *hardship experiences,* business failures and mistakes, learning how to bounce back from emotional traumas, building emotional resilience to deal with situations that are outside the comfort zone. While the risks of challenge must be managed, the real risk of failure must remain—another delicate duality.

The problem with some approaches to talent development is that being identified as "high potential" is virtually sufficient to guarantee someone's meteoric rise to a position of leadership responsibility. Such high potentials move so rapidly from one challenging assignment to another that they have to master only one part of the job—starting off new initiatives. There may be so much coaching and training that the risk of any failure is minimized. Those individuals ultimately move into the leadership post for which they have been groomed. For the first time, they have to live with the consequences of the initiatives that they start off—they are now accountable for whatever happens during implementation. They are alone, with no surrounding infrastructure of coaching. And sometimes they experience a sense of failure for the first time in their lives. Their training has never anticipated this, never equipped them to cope with failure. They react differently. Some fall apart in humiliating ways. The dark side of others' personalities comes to the fore—the decisive leader who has learned to consult with others becomes a tyrannical autocrat, the cautious individual becomes compulsive on detail.[9] Or arrogance fostered by past success leads them into undue risk. The trouble is that the lives of dozens, even thousands, of other people are affected. Morgan McCall and his colleagues call this the phenomenon of "derailment."[10]

Challenging assignments accompanied by risk management, together with the experience of coping with hardship experiences, are the three basic elements of talent development (Figure 8–1 provides a summary of these elements).

Four Organizational Logics Guiding Talent Development

A surprising number of firms have no systematic global approach to talent development—the "cream" is simply left to rise to the top by natural or political processes, or attention to talent development is focused on the mother company alone. One survey of U.S.-based Fortune 500 enterprises suggests that three-quarters of them are only just beginning to think about leadership development in a systematic way.[11]

If there is no global framework then it is natural that top management will tackle this task in the easiest practical way—by focusing on key people from the mother country. A self-perpetuating model counteracting localization and transnationalism is created. Only individuals who are visible to senior management will get the challenging assignments and coaching, these being invariably people from the parent country and the mainstream product divisions. Capable locals in the subsidiaries quickly get the message that their future opportunities are limited.

A necessary starting point is to define what "talent" and "leadership" mean for the firm. This leads to a firm-specific map of sets of desired skills, know-how, and personality characteristics to guide selection and development processes, rather than leaving these to the personal preferences of individuals in positions of authority. These valued skills and abilities are typically known as *competencies* (see box *"What Is a 'Competence'?"*). Translating organizational needs into competence implications has been an important focus of HR attention during the last decade.[12] As they decentralize responsibility to local business units, companies try to maintain

---

FIGURE 8–1. Developing Talent: A Summary

People develop through **CHALLENGING assignments** . . .

. . . this requires **RISK MANAGEMENT (coaching)** so as to avoid failure that the enterprise naturally wishes to avoid . . .

. . . but not so much that success is guaranteed and that people will never learn **to deal with HARDSHIP.**

Assignments:

- Scope: Increase in numbers of people, dollars, and functions to manage (traditional vertical development in responsibility).
- Project/task force assignments (integrative skills): Working with other experts, negotiating and defining objectives, and working collectively so as to deliver a result that meets the often unclear needs of sponsors.
- Cross-functional assignments (integrative skills): Moving to a job where one has no expertise, and learning how to lead in the sense of getting results through people who have more expertise than oneself.
- International assignments (integrative skills).
- Starting from scratch: Building something from nothing.
- Change projects: Fixing or stabilizing a failing operation.
- Entrepreneurial projects: Being given the go-ahead and resources to test out a project initiative that the person has been fighting for.

Risk Management:

- Assessment of the skills, motives and attitudes of the individual.
- Clarification of the goals and targets in the new assignment.
- Coaching (supervision or informal).
- Mentoring.
- Exposure to role models.
- Training.
- Access to people with experience.
- Feedback.

Hardship Testing:

- Business failure and mistakes: Ideas that fail, deals that fall apart.
- Demotions, missed promotions, poor jobs.
- Subordinate performance problems: Confronting a subordinate with a serious performance problem.
- Breaking out of a rut: Taking on a new career in response to discontent with the current job.
- Personal trauma: Crisis such as being fired, divorce, illness, or death.

Source: Adapted from M. W. McCall, *High Fliers: Developing the Next Generation of Leaders* (Boston: Harvard Business School Press, 1998).

---

cohesion (normative integration) by centralizing the frameworks and processes guiding local selection and development. Unilever, to cite one of numerous examples, made firm-specific competence development its major corporate HR priority (driven by the executive committee) during the 90s.

A competence map thus provides a *common language* for line managers and HR professionals across the matrix of operations so as to steer talent selection, performance management, development, and advancement decisions.[13] But while the idea of providing such a global platform for talent development is appealing, the journey is typically fraught with frustration and disillusionment. ABB is currently involved in discussions as to whether it needs to broaden global competence management beyond the

What Is a "Competence"?
Practice Box

The language of skills, attitudes, values, and personality traits has always guided talent identification and development. Since the early 80s, these have often been referred to as "competencies." Is there something special about this term?

The modern usage of the term "competence" owes much to the studies of Richard Boyatzis.[A] He argued for a performance-based approach to skill development based on the observation of effective individuals (the research-based logic). His research on Anglo-Saxon organizations identified 15 competencies that were causally linked to excellent performance, grouped into five clusters: goal and action management, leadership, human resource management, directing subordinates, and a miscellaneous cluster. He also distinguished between "threshold competencies" that are essential for a job but not causally linked to superior performance and "superior competencies," usually defined as characterizing the top 10 percent of performers.

The concept and methodology took off since it met the new need for strategically oriented HR practices to link desired "organizational competencies" to their talent development implications. It provided a basis for linking organizational demands to appraisal and training needs, and the multilayer (360°) feedback movement in the 90s further fueled use of competence maps and frameworks.

Many debates broke out among practitioners. Boyatzis saw a competence as including knowledge, skills, attitudes, values, traits, motives, self-image, and social role. But distinctions were made by others between deeply rooted "qualities" or traits/motives that might guide selection decisions on the one hand, and behavioral know-how and skill that might guide development decisions on the other.[B]

To give one successful example of competence management at work, Hewlett-Packard faced a problem in Russia with a lack of qualified salespersons to meet their needs. Based on their research on the competencies of high performing salespeople in emerging markets, they developed clear criteria for both selecting and training a Russian salesforce, quite different from the skills needed, say, in the United States. Training workshops were organized to develop these competencies, reinforced by regular assessments. Skill-based compensation was used to focus the learning and development process.

[A]Boyatzis, 1982.

[B]For a review of some of the debates around the concept, see "Management Competence: The Debate in Management Learning," *Personnel Review* 22:6 (special issue, 1993); Boam and Sparrow, 1992; Spencer and Spencer, 1993; Antonacopoulou and FitzGerald, 1996. See Sparrow and Hiltrop, 1994, ch. 10, for a discussion of the concept in a comparative management context.

corporate high potentials, and many executives are not convinced. Competence frameworks are often too generic to be useful, the means become ends, and company task forces spend large amounts of time and money generating sterile wish lists of desirable qualities. Why is this competence journey so difficult?

A study of thirty-one North American firms finds that the major reason for this confusion in linking organizational needs to individual competencies is that there is not one single guiding logic, but at least three.[14] Twelve of the firms took a *research-based approach,* nine adopted a *strategy-based approach,* four used a *values-based approach,* while others had adopted hybrid approaches. The researchers, Briscoe and Hall, added an important fourth *learning-based approach.* Each logic has its merits and its disadvantages, so that there are trade-offs rather than a single correct approach. Our experience is that the source of confusion stems from people using the concept of competence in different ways, without realizing that they are applying different logics and dealing with trade-offs. Let us map out these four logics and their implications (see Figure 8–2), returning to the issue of implementation in the transnational at the end.

The Research-Based Logic

The research-based approach stems from the methodology underlying the modern concept of competence (see again the box "What Is a 'Competence'?"). This logic says that what we should do is focus on the characteristics of individuals who are high performers so as to reproduce more of this profile. These individuals are studied in order to find out their distinguishing characteristics.[15] If the study is rigorous,

FIGURE 8–2. Profile of Four Organizational Logics Guiding Developing Talent

	Description	Advantages	Disadvantages
Research-based approach	Competencies based on behavioral research on high performing individuals	Grounded in actual behavior Air of legitimacy Involves people, which fosters acceptance	Based on the past, not the future May omit tangible and unmeasurable competencies Requires extensive resources
Strategy-based approach	Competencies forecasted to be strategically important, based on an anticipated future	Competencies based on the future, not the past Focuses on learning new skills Can support organizational transformation	The scenario for the future may be incorrect or distant Difficult to implement unless top management walks the talk
Values-based approach	Competencies based on a holistic view of norms and values	Can have strong motivating power Can provide strategic stability for long periods of time, especially in fast growing environments	Top management must be prepared to develop a holistic philosophy Competence development process may lack rigor Can be difficult to translate into actual behavior
Learning-based approach	Consists of two metalearning competencies: the willingness to expose oneself to new challenges, and the ability to learn from experience	Well suited to a fast changing, unpredictable environment High degree of legitimacy Non–firm specific	Complements other approaches, but not sufficient as a stand-alone mechanism Can foster an excessive focus on learning rather than exploitation

Source: Adapted from J. P. Briscoe and D. T. Hall, "Grooming and Picking Leaders Using Competency Frameworks," *Organizational Dynamics,* Autumn 1999, pp. 37–51.

those high performers will be compared to more modest contributors so as to identify clearly these distinguishing behaviors.

One of the authors of this book assisted the Shell Group in developing such
a framework in the mid-80s. Shell had earlier pioneered an influential general
management–based competence framework, backed up by research. General
management potential had been correlated with the so-called "helicopter quality." This quality explicitly recognized that such leaders should have a mastery of
duality, combining a strong sense of imagination that allows the leader to build a
vision with a pragmatic sense of reality. The ability to link these comes from two
other qualities, analytic ability and the "helicopter" perspective (being able to
look at facts and problems from an overall viewpoint).[16]

With the broadening of general management and with accelerating globalization, there was a need at Shell to renew the framework. The aim behind our project
was to decentralize the responsibility for management training and development to
local operating companies around the world, but within the discipline of a common
framework. The research-based approach made sense—since it was rooted in actual
data, it was more likely to be accepted by local companies. The methodology involved selecting seven diverse countries (Singapore, the Netherlands, the U.K.,
Nigeria, etc.) and surveying outstanding individuals at different hierarchical levels
in these subsidiaries. The pilot stage of the project identified eighty behavioral characteristics that were used to guide the surveys.

The research results fell into a pattern that became the framework guiding management and functional development at Shell for the next decade, recently modified
so as to allow more room for self-management. This framework is shown and explained in Figure 8–3.

A research-based approach requires some model of the professional or career
structure in the enterprise, with transition points. Otherwise it will be so generic as
to be useless.[17] In the Shell case, the framework is built on the model of traditional
hierarchic career progression. An important issue in the international firm is cross-
cultural validation and adaptation. At Shell the validation surveys and focus groups
showed that the framework was valid across the world. However, it was clear that
each business and country had to develop its own behavioral descriptors for what
goes into each box, and that these would vary. For example, one specific skill in
"managing others" in level II supervisory roles (see Figure 8–3) would be feedback
skills. In an individualistic Western culture, the behavioral indicator might be "confronts people constructively on their failings," whereas in a collective culture such
as Thailand this might read as "ensures that subordinates know how they stand while
maintaining team harmony." In defining "external relations," the downstream exploration business might emphasize community relations, while customer relations
would be highlighted in the upstream marketing business.[18]

The research-based approach has some clear advantages.[19] Depending on how
the methodology is applied, it is potentially rigorous. This gives the "soft" domain
of talent management an air of scientific legitimacy. The fact that real managers are
studied facilitates its acceptability and implementation. It is above all pragmatic,
and with appropriate cultural adjustment the results can easily be incorporated in

FIGURE 8–3. Linking Competence to Career Progression: A Research-Based Framework Developed by Royal Dutch/Shell

Anticipating Future Technology Impact/ Options	Personal Imprint on Organization	Represent–ational Leadership	Mediating Stakeholder Demands	Creating a Culture for Change	Policy to Strategy	Corporate Vision and Direction
Balancing Sectorial Demands	Taking New Perspectives, New Mental Maps	Transform–ational Corporate Leadership	Renewing the Business	Supporting Organiza–tional Learning and Adaptation	Strategic Management	Contributing to Reshaping and Redirection
Orchestrating Interfunct–ional Relationships	Promoting Growth in Self and Others	Developing Broader Relationships	Developing Business Creativity	Managing Major Change	Responsive–ness to the Environment	Sharing and Carrying out Vision
Specialism in Wider Commercial Context	Human Resource Management Skills	Developing People and Organizations	Managing a Business Unit	Skills for Change	Strategic Business Planning	Matching own Business Direction with Strategy
Deepening Expertise of Self and Others	Motivating, Negotiating and Influencing	Managing Others	Integrating Business Skills and Intrapre–neurship	Participating in Change	Monitoring Performance	Impact of Mission on Job
Developing Functional Technical Skills	Managing Self and Use of Expertise	Teamworking and Networking	Commercial Awareness	Under–standing Organizat–ional Change	Awareness of Strategy	Awareness of Mission
PROFESSIONAL	PERSONAL	PEOPLE	BUSINESS	CHANGE	STRATEGY	VISION

EXPLANATION:

The horizontal axis indicates seven areas of skill or competence, while the vertical axis indicates hierarchic career progression from individual contributor positions (I) through supervisory management posts to business unit management (II and III), up to positions as a member of the management team of an operating company and as managing director of such a subsidiary (IV and V), to Group top management (VI).

The concept behind this matrix is that the added value in development lies by sticking close to the diagonal boxes. For example, development attention should focus above all on developing skills in "managing others" in level II supervisory positions. The groundwork will have been laid earlier through demonstrated ability in teamworking and networking. Good skills in managing others will allow people to develop broader competence in developing people and in network relations as they move up in their careers. The further one moves from the diagonal, the lower the added value.

Source: The Shell competence matrix was developed by Rei Torres and colleagues from the Shell/Royal Dutch Group Training Department.

performance appraisal guides, selection criteria, and training schemes around the world. It can be used to tackle focused challenges, such as how to develop a sales-force from scratch in an emerging market (see the example in the box "What Is a 'Competence'?").

However, there are some equally clear disadvantages. It is fundamentally a rear-window methodology, oriented toward the past and the status quo rather than to the future. While there may be merit to using such logic in a slow moving industry, the approach is poorly suited to the discontinuities of a fast moving hypercompetitive environment or to the complexities of a multidimensional professional service firm. Since it is based on historic data, it may perpetuate an outdated structure of career paths.

All too often the analysis skimps on the research, leading to a generalized rather than firm-specific approach. Generic frameworks are sold by consultants or disseminated at HR conferences, modified after a few superficial interviews and then labeled as "Company X competence guidelines." Vital firm-specific behaviors get missed or drowned out by generic skills. Or a single framework is used to cover people in different disciplines, pushing it up to a level of abstraction that leads people to question its usefulness.

The Strategy-Based Logic

The original theory behind "strategic human resource management" emphasized this second logic—translating strategy for the future into its current implications for talent selection and development, thereby implementing strategy faster.[20] While the strategy-based logic lacks the rigor and legitimacy of the research-based approach, its big advantage is that it is oriented to the future. It is often appealing to the senior management of firms that are undergoing substantial transformational change and to those in fast moving competitive environments. For example, BP used such an approach, undertaken with considerable rigor, to drive transformation change during the 1990s.[21]

Strategic logic influenced talent development at ABB, especially at senior levels. Neither of the merging Swedish and Swiss companies constituted a model for the rapidly globalizing power engineering industry, and Percy Barnevik anchored a new strategic logic in a bible of principles. One concerned the global-local competence that could be developed only from international experience. This implied working in a local subsidiary and in the next job in a global business role. Another principle concerned appraisal criteria, to be based on both financial performance and people development. A third concerned speed of decision making—"It's better to take decisions fast that are roughly right rather than to take decisions slowly that are totally right." The latter was a dramatic change in an engineering firm where a strong but slow moving consensus culture had ensured that critical decisions were correctly taken.

European researchers have strongly critiqued this "American" strategic logic, describing it as "normative rhetoric" (which in the research world is a polite way of saying unscientific), lacking in solid descriptive evidence.[22] This is obviously true, since strategic logic is based on a vision of future needs. Even human resource professionals at senior levels may fail to comprehend the strategic logic if they are not part of the strategy and business development process. BP invested eighteen months in cascading their OPEN competency framework down the organization to build the understanding of their new strategic values such as "Open thinking" and "Networking." Consistency of behavior at senior levels is important. ABB's Percy Barnevik argued that the implementation of the strategic approach depends first and foremost on "walking the talk": "If we talk about the need for fast decision making and then top management procrastinates on important decisions, then it just isn't credible."[23]

Despite the enthusiasm in the early days of Strategic HRM, this is more difficult as a steering mechanism than the research-based logic, except at times of impending crisis. Procter & Gamble came to the conclusion that skills in innovation would be more important in the future than traditional operational marketing competencies. While this may be obvious to top management, it was far from clear to lower level managers in far-flung companies where the basic decisions on recruitment and promotions were taken. The new competencies are seen as the whim of the current CEO or as headquarters politics. There may be a need for more innovation in the distant future, but today has to be taken care of first.

The quickest way to implement the strategic approach is to bring in the new strategic skills from the outside, as happens at the top in times of crisis. Extraordinary promotions are also effective in communicating strategic signals in complex multinationals—a particular individual, widely regarded as a maverick, is promoted to a position of major responsibility. This was the case at the media giant Bertelsmann, where a person who risked his career on a controversial decision to invest in AOL was then leapfrogged over more established candidates into the CEO position. Within a short time, the whole organization veered hard toward e-commerce.

The Values-Based Logic

While the values-based logic behind talent development may be linked to a competency framework, it is much wider than that. Hewlett-Packard is a good example, where values-driven logic led to strong normative integration.[24] Dave Packard describes in his autobiography how he and Hewlett wrestled for decades to articulate their emerging management philosophy, and to communicate this to their expanding staff.[25] If they could do this, they could allow the staff far greater autonomy than in a conventional hierarchy. The resulting list of values (or competencies) was called "The HP Way." The elements—such as long-term perspective, listening to customers, trust in people, and management by objectives—are only the surface of a deeper philosophy. In fact, we are tempted to call this approach "the philosophy-based logic" since the competencies cannot be understood without comprehending the underlying philosophy of management and organization, which recruits learn slowly as they are socialized into the firm.

Jim Collins and Gerry Porras find this to be one of the main features of enduring organizations in their study *Built to Last*.[26] Firms that have survived successive changes in technology and leadership such as CitiCorp, IBM, Sony, 3M and Hewlett-Packard were all built by leaders who wrestled with the question of how to build an institution rather than simply make money out of an opportunity. A distinguishing feature was that they are all guided by a clear philosophy of management and organization, manifested in a strong set of values.

A number of reputable firms that have previously employed analytic competency approaches are moving to values-based systems, though it is premature to talk of a trend.[27] One successful high technology enterprise which had previously used a research-based approach got the top management involved in deep thinking on what leadership in the firm was all about. The executives were energized by the process, leading them to define cultural and leadership values so as to identify future talent. But to be effective, this has to be communicated to staff in richer ways than simply a recruitment checklist or criteria on a performance appraisal form. It needs to be anchored in a more holistic understanding.

The values-based logic may be particularly relevant to the fast growing "instant transnational," such as our first case study in chapter 1, Business Objects.[28] Within say three years, this start-up must work through all of the challenges of becoming a transnational enterprise—balancing local responsiveness with global integration, rapidly leveraging products across the world while investing in future generations of products.

Experienced MBA students working on ambitious start-up projects come to the authors and say: "Recruiting people and bringing them on board is going to be the single biggest challenge. How can we go about it? In particular, how do you know if someone is going to be right for you?" They are not looking for testing methods or recruitment techniques. The challenge is defining what "right for us" really means. The start-up team has to wrestle, like Hewlett and Packard, with the question of what their management philosophy is. Only then will the techniques and HR marketing be useful.

The values-based logic may initially be implicit, as was the case in the early days of Apple Computers. Until the mid-80s, Apple was widely seen as a firm with exciting technology but a highly uncertain future. The people attracted to Apple tended to be self-selecting entrepreneurs, and the company attempted to formalize the philosophy so as to provide coherence across the expanding subsidiaries.[29] However, as Apple became an established enterprise in the mid-80s, it began to attract people who did not share this entrepreneurial orientation. Apple did not have HP's rigorous induction and socialization based on a semicodified values logic, and internal conflicts and political struggles started to characterize the firm.

The Learning-Based Logic

This fourth logic to guide competency development is a deduction from academic research, although many illustrations can be found in corporate practice. It may be particularly relevant to the transnational environment, in which promotions represent qualitative changes rather than mere increases in responsibility (we will discuss the issue of increasing intransitivity later).

The learning-based logic reflects our earlier point that people develop essentially through new challenges (assignments). Challenges are opportunities for learning. If this is so, then two qualities are important for development: first, the willingness to expose oneself to new challenges; and second, the ability to learn fast and well from both positive and negative experiences.

A study in the early 1980s of ninety prominent leaders in fields from the arts to business singled out personal learning ability as the quality most required for leadership.[30] Another more recent study of 838 managers working for six international corporations on three continents suggests that the ability to learn may be particularly important for international managers.[31] Eleven competencies distinguished high potentials from solid performers, and on examination one sees that three of them suggest the willingness to expose oneself to challenge: "seeks opportunities to learn," "has the courage to take risks," and "adapts to cultural differences." Four others concern the ability to learn from experience: "insightful, sees things from new angles," "seeks and uses feedback," "learns from mistakes," "is open to criticism." Overall, two-thirds of the eleven competencies distinguishing talented international managers related to the two sides of the learning logic. Let us discuss these two facets.

WILLINGNESS TO EXPOSE ONESELF TO NEW CHALLENGES. Many people are understandably unwilling to expose themselves to new challenges. They prefer to exploit their existing skills, and they want reasonable challenge at a measured pace with liberal coaching, allowing room for private life. Challenge involves priority or sacrifice, depending on one's perspective. A new challenge in a multinational firm often involves transfer to another country, with disruption for the individual and the family, or extensive travel that has a similar effect. The more significant the challenge, the more stressful it will be—stress, indeed, is part of the mobilization to learn and master the challenge. As we found in our extensive research into the relationship between professional and private life among 14,600 managers in most major countries of the world, stress inevitably spills over into private life.[32] This can be expressed bluntly but accurately with the principle that "for the first six to nine months in a new assignment, forget about quality time with the family and leisure life."

ABB's Percy Barnevik once commented that people have a right to lead a balanced life—except for the top 400 people out of the 200,000 at ABB. Those very few people in leadership roles, with the responsibilities for the welfare of the other 99.8 percent, were expected to give clear priority to ABB.

Before we go on, a serious caution must be added (see box "The Consequences of Taking Learning to the Extreme"). The learning-based logic is far from new in the sense that talented individuals have sometimes pursued it in a one-sided way, seeking development opportunities at the expense of performance. They and their organizations can pay a serious price for this.

THE ABILITY TO LEARN FROM EXPERIENCE. The other side of the learning coin is the ability to learn from experience. While some people confidently attack new challenges, they do not have the ability to learn from their experiences. Fast track cycles of zigzag mobility reinforce this. Recent research suggests that incompetent people are excessively confident, blind to their inabilities, and therefore unable to learn from their successes and mistakes, particularly susceptible to derailing.[33]

The ability to learn is singularly difficult and important in the international environment. As studied by management psychologists, it involves a cycle of learning abilities—the ability to read the signals and sense that something needs attention, collecting data and feedback, thinking and analysis, leading to decisions that are experiments.[34] Reading the signals is difficult since the cues people give to indicate a problem vary from one culture to another, as does the way in which they provide feedback (often in highly indirect and subtle ways). It is much more important when working abroad to consider decisions as experiments, so that one learns from

The Consequences of Taking Learning to the Extreme
Practice Box

In some corporations, the emphasis on learning and mobility is taken to a pathological extreme. The career game is to take on new project initiatives that will be visible in the eyes of senior management, at the expense of operational performance in the job itself. As long as this leads to rapid promotion or transfer, it works out fine for the individual—because when the performance problems show up, he or she has moved on to another position.

Rapidity of movement becomes the best indicator of talent or potential. This creates a zigzag management pattern in which a new leader of a foreign subsidiary seeks out initiatives that respond to the strategic logic of current senior management. But just when the initiatives in quality management or value-based management or whatever are beginning to take hold, the individual is promoted. The successor is left with the responsibility for implementation. Obviously if the successor is of the same breed, that person will take the unit off on a different initiative since there are no rewards for implementing changes started by someone else.[A]

People are products of their own experiences. The consequence of this cycle is that if and when these individuals find themselves in top management, they are superbly skilled at learning—starting off new corporate initiatives (acquisitions, strategic reorientations) and building relationships with external stakeholders. But they are largely untrained at implementation and the in-depth management of change. Consequently they excessively delegate the responsibility for implementation and change, often with disastrous consequences.[B] The risk of derailing is effectively maximized.

[A]All this is aggravated, as we discovered, by the deferent appraisals of the local staff. They learn that if they say negative things about the performance of the manager, then they will be saddled with an individual who from their perspective is incompetent. So the only way of getting rid of the individual quickly is to provide positive performance evaluations!

[B]As mentioned later in the chapter, Japanese firms manage this exploitation-exploration dilemma in a different way. The typical norm in a position of managerial responsibility is that it takes four years to do a good job. High potential individuals can be expected to move soon after the fourth year.

failures. People who are poor learners in their own home environments may be unable to cope abroad—there is little point in challenging assignments if people do not have the ability to learn from them.

Overall, the learning logic is well in tune with the complexity of the transnational world as well as the rapid pace of competitive change. We live in an age of discontinuities. People who experience change as challenge and who have strong abilities to learn from experience are clearly well equipped. That is why the learning logic has been described as a metacompetence, one that overarches the other three.[35]

What Does This Imply?

Competency management is not a fad that will disappear—the basic idea of identifying needed skills is as old as antiquity and common sense. Some of the modern lessons of using competencies to steer talent development in transnational firms can be summarized as follows:

- Remember that the fundamental aim is to provide a common language so as to boost the rigor of recruitment and talent development around the world, thereby ensuring that the mother country does not have a monopoly on talent.
- Be clear about which approach or approaches you are using—lack of clarity around the underlying logic creates confusion.

- The learning logic is powerful given the complexity of the transnational environment and increasingly discontinuities, although it can create pathologies if it is not complemented by attention to performance driven logic.
- The need to steer toward the future as well as to anchor the lessons of operational excellence means that most firms will adopt hybrid approaches.
- Don't undervalue the values approach.

A final lesson might be to focus on process as much as framework—competency-based steering logics are only a guide. In the global firm, such processes typically focus on those with leadership potential, and we now turn to consider this.

THE PROCESS OF LEADERSHIP DEVELOPMENT

David Whitlam is CEO of Whirlpool, facing tough competition in the appliance industry, in which it is important to respond to local habits in the use of appliances while harnessing all possible global economies. During the 90s, his challenge was to build a global firm, as Whirlpool went from being a domestic U.S. player to a global firm with the acquisition of Philips' appliance division. He comments: "I've often said that there's only one thing that wakes me up in the middle of the night. It's not our financial performance or economic issues in general. It's worrying about whether or not we have the right skills and capabilities to pull the strategy off . . . It is a simple and inescapable fact that the skills and capabilities required to manage a global company are different from those required for a domestic company."[36]

Whitlam is not atypical. Surveys show that global leadership development is the number one human resource priority of chief executives in multinational firms. Without the right skills global strategies cannot be implemented. And leadership development is one of the vital facilitating elements of coordination glue in the multinational enterprise. We begin by reviewing some of the generics, albeit with the international context in mind, before turning to the specifics of the process of leadership development in the transnational enterprise.

Generic Issues Regarding Leadership Development

What Is Leadership?

Concepts of leadership and management are culturally bound (see box "Cultural Differences in Concepts of Management"), as well as subject to fashions. Since leadership moved to the center stage in the 80s, many different types of leadership have been projected as the norm—transformational, empowering, visionary, charismatic—often reflecting the problematic focus of attention at a particular point in time. Peter Drucker notes from his lifetime of working with leaders that "'leadership personality,' 'leadership style,' and 'leadership traits' do not exist."[37] Are there any common denominators to leadership across cultures?

While there are differences across space and time in leadership ideas, the common denominator is summarized well by a recent Hay-McBer study of leadership competencies in various countries, from the United States to Japan, from France to Korea. *Leadership is about setting direction and aligning people.* The art of leadership is how

Cultural Differences in Concepts of Management
Research Box

In the research of André Laurent into cultural differences in concepts of management, the question with the biggest range of views across cultures (even within the same company) is the question below on attitudes toward answering the questions of subordinates.[A] If one stops to think about it, this is a fundamental question about managerial and leadership behavior:

"Is it important for a manager to have at hand precise answers to most of the questions that subordinates may raise about their work?"

Percentage agreement rates

Key:

S	Sweden
NL	Netherlands Holland
DK	Denmark
UK	United Kingdom
CH	Switzerland
B	Belgium
D	Germany
F	France
I	Italy
INDO	Indonesia

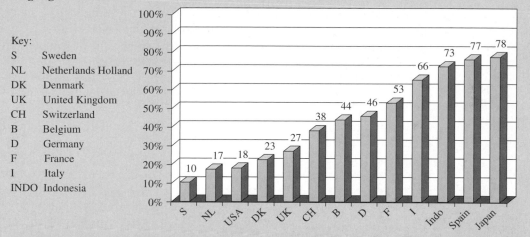

One interpretation is that the data above reflects differences in concepts of authority. Managers in Latin and some Asian countries to the right of the distribution tend to agree that it is important to have answers. These are countries where *hierarchic authority* is strongly rooted, where the boss is expected to command and control. The Germanic countries in the middle (including Switzerland) have a heritage in *expertise-based authority* in highly functional structures. There is a strong obligation to provide answers since the boss is expected to be a superior expert. However, in Sweden, Holland, and the Anglo-Saxon countries, the boss is not expected to be an expert or an authority figure. Authority is based on skill in *managerial leadership*. The manager is expected to spend time on leading the business, forging new directions and improvements, while subordinates should be encouraged to find answers themselves. As some American managers put it,

"I wouldn't necessarily provide the answer even if I had it because otherwise subordinates would keep coming back to ask me questions—and I wouldn't have time for my job of leadership."

Some people are surprised at seeing that the Japanese have the highest agreement rate with this proposition. Although Japan is changing, there is a deep respect for authority in the Japanese culture. Japanese comment that they would never ask their boss a question directly unless they were sure in advance that the boss had the answer! The attachment to traditional authority is combined with a strong expertise orientation built up prior to World War II, and a strong leadership culture developed after World War II as described later in this chapter.[B]

[A]Laurent, 1983.
[B]See Pucik (1984).

one goes about setting the agenda, and how one brings people on board. The only other quality found in the Hay-McBer study was self-confidence: If the leader does not believe in the agenda, how can one expect others to do so?[38]

Leaders have clear goals and are determined to reach them. Reviewing 100 years of leadership research, Peter Drucker describes this as the only thing we know about leadership across all situations (Harvard's John Kotter calls this "setting direction," while others call it "management of attention," or "setting and implementing agendas").[39] There are myriad ways of doing this—leadership personality and style do not exist out of a particular context. While there was earlier a belief in a generalized "professional leader" independent of context, research has shown that leaders have to know their business environments well.[40]

Different leadership orientations will be nurtured by different assignments and challenges (as was shown earlier in Figure 8–1). Taking responsibility for start-ups and new ventures will foster *entrepreneurial* leadership skills. Moving up vertically in terms of responsibility will develop *functional* leadership skills. *International* leadership orientation will be nurtured by foreign assignments, while taking responsibility for change projects develops *change* leadership skills. People are products of their experiences. Moreover, a particular leader does not have to possess all the qualities required by a given situation, since leadership involves teamwork between different people with complementary qualities.[41]

If there is an essential core to leader development in the transnational enterprise with its coordination demands, it would be the *integrative ability* that is associated with being able to set direction and align people. In the past, this was often equated with a role, that of the "general manager"—leadership and general management were once synonymous. However, one of the implications of the pervasive coordination needs of the transnational organization is that there may be few, if any, autonomous general management roles. An old image capturing the requirements well is that of the "T-shaped manager" (similar to our split egg concept; see Chapter 2). The stem of the T is the specific skills needed for a particular job whereas the bar of the T represents the integrative or generalist know-how that is increasingly necessary in many if not most managerial roles.

We think of this integrative core as the ability to set direction and deliver results through other people who ideally have *more* technical expertise than the leader him- or herself. The integrative leadership mindset is demonstrated in attitudes toward delegation. Our research shows that managers who lack this integrative orientation, whose authority is based on their technical or functional expertise, tend to underdelegate or overdelegate.[42] They underdelegate anything within their expertise domain. Since their authority is based on their expertise, it would be foolish to give challenges to subordinates who would then develop the expertise of the boss—the boss is no longer needed! And they tend to overdelegate anything lying outside their area of expertise since this does not overly interest them.

In contrast, we find that leaders who have this integrative orientation very much want to delegate operational matters (even if they have the expertise to do it themselves). They want to free up as much time as possible to focus on the task of integrative leadership: figuring how to build the business, how to tackle competition, how to shorten product lifecycles, all in coordination with other units or departments.[43] Strategy and business development are 5 percent ideas and concepts that can be taught at business schools and on executive programs and 95 percent hard work—if one is busy doing other people's operational work for them, there will be little time for strategy and business development!

Developing Transnational Leaders

If people develop through learning things that they have not done before, leaders learn the ropes by being put in situations in which they have to learn how to deliver results through people with more expertise than themselves. This forces potential leaders to learn the integrative task of setting direction and aligning people.

In practical terms, this means that the step-by-step process of leadership development starts by successfully making the transition from a functional role as individual contributor to that of functional manager.[44] *Project management* is an important next stage, thereby also contributing to the coordination of the firm. Project management obliges people to learn how to work with others who have different expertise, as well as teaching them how to define cross-boundary goals. The ultimate step in leadership development is cross-functional, cross-discipline or international *mobility.* Being transferred to a different role in which one does not have the expertise consolidates the learning on the art of leadership. The point is illustrated with the story of a leader we met fifteen years ago, who is today the chairman of one of the world's most well-known corporations (see box "The Route to the Top").

The Route to the Top
Practice Box

The tool that is most important for leadership development is not self-assessment techniques or MBA programs or any other form of training. It is *managed mobility*—having to learn how to deliver results through people with more expertise than oneself. In other words, having to learn how to lead!

The example of a senior executive in a major multinational corporation makes the point. At the time when we interviewed him in the mid-80s, he was president of an important subsidiary in Asia, an individual with an excellent record of leadership success, and someone with deep skills in the management of human resources:

Why have I been successful? It is quite simple. I was trained as a geologist and spent the first seven years of my career trying to discover oil. One day when I was heading an exploration assignment, they called me to the headquarters and told me that they wanted me to take over the responsibility for a troubled department of forty maintenance engineers on the other side of the world. Geology is the noble elite, and main-

tenance engineering is somewhere between here-and-hell in the value system. I didn't want the job—in fact my first thought was that they were punishing me for some mistake I had made—and I told them that I knew nothing about maintenance engineering. "We're not sending you there to learn about engineering," they said. "We are sending you there to learn about leadership."

With a lot of doubts, I took the job, and I was there for just over four years. And I learned practically everything I know about management and leadership in that job—all I've done since is refine what I picked up there. Mind you, it was the most stressful job I've ever had—it nearly cost me my marriage! Fortunately, they sent me on a management training program during the first six months, and that helped me to understand what was happening and how I should adjust—otherwise I might not have survived.

Afterwards I returned into a more senior position in geology, but I'd completely changed as a result of that experience with the maintenance engineers.

This person is today the Chief Executive Officer of one of the largest corporations in the world.

The Best Player Does Not Necessarily Make the Best Coach

The fact that the best player often does not make the best coach is known as *intransitivity.* This means that the skills and attitudes of the next position "up" are qualitatively different from those in the previous job. The famous "Peter Principle" captures the idea that the best engineer does not necessarily make the best engineering manager—people get promoted to one level above their competence.

Companies have long tried to manage the problem of intransitivity through career paths (for example, for individual contributors, functional and general managers), paying particular attention to the forks or transition points. Transnational development is increasing the degree of intransitivity, as Bartlett and Ghoshal emphasize. The old model of organization in the multinational firm, they argue, was a top-down structure that was largely transitive, management tasks at each level of the hierarchy being similar but bigger than the tasks a level below (see the top diagram in Figure 8–4). Top

---

FIGURE 8–4. The Traditional and Transnational Models of Managerial Roles

A. The Traditional Model

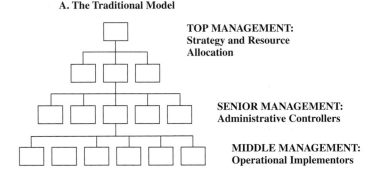

TOP MANAGEMENT:
Strategy and Resource Allocation

SENIOR MANAGEMENT:
Administrative Controllers

MIDDLE MANAGEMENT:
Operational Implementors

B. The Transnational Model

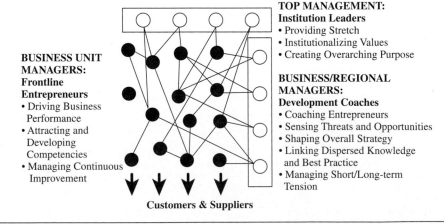

BUSINESS UNIT MANAGERS:
Frontline Entrepreneurs
• Driving Business Performance
• Attracting and Developing Competencies
• Managing Continuous Improvement

Customers & Suppliers

TOP MANAGEMENT:
Institution Leaders
• Providing Stretch
• Institutionalizing Values
• Creating Overarching Purpose

BUSINESS/REGIONAL MANAGERS:
Development Coaches
• Coaching Entrepreneurs
• Sensing Threats and Opportunities
• Shaping Overall Strategy
• Linking Dispersed Knowledge and Best Practice
• Managing Short/Long-term Tension

Source: Adapted from S. Ghoshal and C. Bartlett, *The Individualized Corporation* (New York: HarperBusiness, 1997).

managers were the strategic architects, senior managers were the administrative controllers of these strategic plans, while operating level managers were the front line implementers of strategies that were conceived "up there" by top managers and their staffs. It was like a "Russian doll"—inside the big doll lies an identical smaller doll, with yet another identical doll inside that one. Bartlett and Ghoshal argue that this transitive model is particularly damaging for transnational development.[45]

Their model of the transnational organization is much more intransitive, implying qualitatively different roles at different levels (see the bottom diagram in Figure 8–4). In a fast moving competitive environment, strategic initiatives come from the operating level managers, not from top management. These operating managers heading up business units and subsidiaries need to be aggressive *entrepreneurs,* creating and pursuing new business opportunities, attracting and developing resources including people. They identify new opportunities, and strategies are born out of their initiatives rather than on the drawing boards of corporate planners far removed from the action of the marketplace.

The senior managers heading up businesses and countries/regions, to whom these entrepreneurs report, need to be *integrative coaches,* stretching and supporting the local units, linking their dispersed know-how, and building strategy out of entrepreneurial initiatives. Top managers need to be *institutional leaders* with a longer time horizon, nurturing strategic development opportunities, managing organizational cohesion through global processes and normative integration, and creating an overarching sense of purpose and ambition.

Examples of this structure are Percy Barnevik's ABB and other firms such as 3M and the Danish cleaning corporation ISS.[46] Despite careful selection of people for the top 300 positions at the time of the merger creating ABB in 1988, over 40 percent of these managers were no longer with the company six years later. Many were unable to cope with the very different demands of senior management roles in an organization built around the middle-up initiatives of local business unit leaders.

This intransitive structure has important implications for leadership development. Many people who perform well in entrepreneurial leadership roles will not be able to adjust to the more ambiguous roles as integrative coaches in business area or regional roles. Appropriate developmental experiences need to be planned so as to test out and develop those integrative coaching skills. Bartlett and Ghoshal's framework of the roles and required competencies at these three levels is shown in Figure 8–5.

Although this model of transnational talent development may not be an appropriate guide for all enterprises, the intransitivity of knowledge-based careers is likely to increase in the future with accelerating technological, social, and competitive change. Change is increasingly discontinuous. Consequently, the ability to cope with transitions will become an important metacompetence for leaders, as many scholars of leadership development believe (hence the importance of the learning logic discussed earlier). It is not so much the ability to make a particular known transition that is important. It is more the ability to manage transitions in general, when the nature of future transitions cannot be clearly anticipated today.

FIGURE 8–5. A Model of Management Competencies for Roles in the Transnational Organization

Role/Task	Attitude/Traits	Knowledge/Experience	Skills/Abilities
Operating Level Entrepreneurs • Creating and pursuing opportunities	*Results-Oriented Competitor* • Creative intuitive	*Detailed Operating Knowledge* • Knowledge of the business's technical competitive and customer characteristics	*Focuses Energy on Opportunities* • Ability to recognize potential and make commitments
• Attracting and utilizing scarce skills and resources	• Persuasive engaging	• Knowledge of internal and external resources	• Ability to motivate and drive people
• Managing continuous performance improvement	• Competitive persistent	• Detailed understanding of the business operations	• Ability to sustain organizational energy around demanding objectives
Senior Management Developers • Reviewing developing supporting individuals and their initiates	*People-Oriented Integrator* • Supportive, patient	*Broad Organizational Experience* • Knowledge of people as individuals and understanding how to influence them	*Develops People and Relationships* • Ability to delegate, develop, empower
• Linking dispersed knowledge, skills, and practices	• Integrative, flexible	• Understanding of the interpersonal dynamics among diverse groups	• Ability to develop relationships and build teams
• Managing the short-term and long-term pressures	• Perceptive, demanding	• Understanding the means-ends relationships linking short-term priorities and long-term goals	• Ability to reconcile differences while maintaining tension
Top Level Leaders • Challenging embedded assumptions while setting stretching opportunity horizons and performance standards	*Institution-Minded Visionary* • Challenging, stretching	*Understanding Company in Its Context* • Grounded understanding of the company: its businesses and operations	*Balances Alignment and Challenge* • Ability to create an exciting, demanding work environment
• Building a context of cooperation and trust	• Open-minded, fair	• Understanding of the organization a system of structures, processes, and cultures	• Ability to inspire confidence and belief in the institution and its management
• Creating an overarching sense of corporate purpose and ambition	• Insightful, inspiring	• Broad knowledge of different companies, industries and societies	• Ability to combine conceptual insight with motivational challenges

Source: C. Bartlett and S. Ghoshal, "The Myth of the Generic Manager: New Personal Competencies for New Management Roles," *California Management Review* 40:1, (1997).

Why Leadership Development Must Be a Rigorous Process

Leadership development has to be viewed as a global and long-term *process* that goes side by side with the operational process of performance management. The best way of understanding this is to imagine what happens if such a process does *not* exist. Positions will be filled according to the well-studied logic of vacancy chains. When someone leaves a senior middle management position, there is a scrambling around to find the best available person, which creates new vacancies . . . and the process cascades down the unit. All ideas of systematically developing people through challenge and managing the risks in a new job become distant ideals, overridden by the necessity to find the best available people to fill immediate job needs. Any investment in competency-driven logic is subordinated to the realities of a limited supply of available people. Personal biases override wider but abstract considerations of organizational development. In short, if there is no leadership development process, then the immediate performance imperatives will override long-term considerations of development.

Indeed the conflict between short-term business performance and long-term development is at the heart of the leadership development process. This is simply another manifestation of the exploitation versus exploration duality. Without some rigorous guiding leadership development process, people who can *do* the job will win over people who can best *learn* and develop from the job.

When managers challenge Jack Welch at GE seminars, a typical gripe they voice is that they cannot develop people for the long term when they are under so much pressure to produce short-term results. Welch challenges back: "You can't manage long term if you can't eat short term." He states flatly, "Anybody can manage short. Anybody can manage long. Balancing those two things is what management is."[47]

Moreover, without a rigorous leadership development process the search for candidates will be limited to the immediate network. There will be little if any transfer between countries and divisions. Even if the perfect candidate exists in another division, there is no way of finding this out or of negotiating the transfer. The concepts of building normative integration and "the matrix in the mind" will remain just that—concepts.

Identifying and Developing Potential

A rigorous process of leadership development involves three subprocesses:

- A process for identifying talent (typically referred to as "potential").
- A process for planning the development of that potential through appropriate assignments, complemented by risk management (coaching and training).
- The process of decision-making on who gets which job, ensuring follow-through on development plans, but also to be balanced with career self-management.

There are many different ways of identifying potential, and the heritages differ from company to company and from nation to nation. On the other hand, there is more convergence on the principles for developing that potential—through exposure to challenging assignments complemented by risk management—though there is considerable variation in practice. With respect to the process of decision-making that determines the ultimate outcomes, there is also much variation.

To get an overview of this, we undertook research on different ways of managing these processes in leading corporations from different regions of the world.[48] We identified three very different models, which are shown in Figure 8–6 together with a fourth model that we call the Multinational Approach.

The Elite Cohort Approach

Many Japanese corporations in the latter half of the twentieth century adopted the Elite Cohort approach, though it also characterizes some Western firms.[49] The identification of potential occurs at the time of recruitment, when cohorts of carefully screened people are recruited from top universities. These recruits are trained and developed in different jobs for a seven-to-eight-year trial period. The trial period is characterized by "equal opportunity" in the sense that there are no immediate sanctions for poor performance, recognizing that this may reflect a difficult boss or a misfit job or the mistakes that accompany learning. Performance and behavior are carefully monitored during this period, however. Appraisals by superiors are collected by the central personnel department—at Toyota, for example, this happened at least three or four times a year.

By the time the cohort is in their early thirties, moving into positions of leadership responsibility, the company has a clear idea from the trial as to who are the sheep and who are the goats. The rules change and career progression becomes a tournament, with "winners" and "losers."[50] Those who are deemed outstanding are given challenging responsibilities, while those who score lower are assigned to less important roles with virtually no chance to get back into the game. In many Japanese firms there is a belief that it takes about four years to perform well in a position of responsibility. A person who is strongly placed in the tournament should be promoted into a new challenge, often involving a cross-functional or cross-divisional move, soon after the fourth year. If an individual remains in the same job after six years, this indicates a career plateau. Eventually, such an employee may be counseled out of the firm to join a subsidiary company or a foreign multinational. The whole process used to be elitist in the sense that it was difficult for anyone to enter the race who was not part of the initial recruitment cohort, although this has began to change during the last decade.

Many leading Japanese corporations have followed this Elite Cohort approach, which has some strong merits.[51] It rigorously assures the development of a highly socialized leadership elite whose loyalty is unquestioned, whose skills have been meticulously honed, and which has a strong grasp on the subtle problems of coordination. In Japan, some distinctive cultural characteristics add to the strengths—for example, the *nemawashi* (negotiation) process of decision-making. Important problems are not solved at the top but delegated to junior members of the cohort, also for developmental reasons. They have to consult upward with key individuals, negotiating their way through to consensus.

FIGURE 8–6. Four Models for Leadership Identification and Development

ELITE COHORT APPROACH
The "Japanese" Model

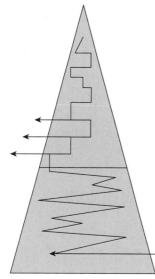

Potential Development:
Time-Scheduled Tournament
- Unequal opportunity, good jobs to the best
- 4-5 years in a job, 7-8 year up-or-out
- Comparison with cohort peers
- Multi-functional mobility, technical-functional track for minority

Potential Identification:
Managed Elite Trial
- Elite pool or cohort recruitment
- Recruitment for long-term careers
- Job rotation, intensive training
- Regular performance monitoring
- Equal opportunity

ELITE POLITICAL APPROACH
The "Latin" Model

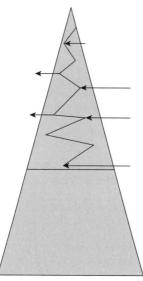

Potential Development:
Political Tournament
- High fliers
- Competition and collaboration with peers
- Typically multi-functional mobility
- Political process (visible achievements, get sponsors, coalitions, read signals)
- If stuck, move out and on
- The 'Gamesman'

Potential Identification:
Elite Entry, No Trial
- At entry
- Elite pool recruitment (non-cohort)
- Predictive qualities
- From schools specialized in selecting and preparing future top managers
    - "Grande Ecoles"
    - MBAs
    - Scientific PhDs

(continued)

FIGURE 8–6. Four Models for Leadership Identification and Development *(continued)*

FUNCTIONAL APPROACH
The "Germanic" Model

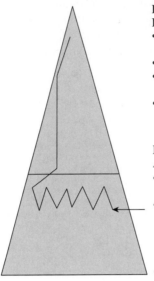

Potential Development:
Functional Ladders
- Functional careers, relationships, and communication
- Expertise-based competition
- Multi-functional mobility limited to few elitist recruits, or non-existent
- Little multi-functional contact below level of division heads and "vorstand" (executive committee)

Potential Identification:
Apprenticeship
- Annual recruitment from universities and technical schools
- 2-year "apprenticeship" trial
  - Job rotation through most functions
  - Intensive training
  - Identification of person's functional potential and talents
- Some elitist recruitment, mostly of PhD's

MANAGED DEVELOPMENT APPROACH
The "Multinational Corporation" Model

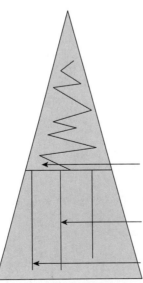

Potential Development:
Managed Potential Development
- Careful monitoring of high potentials by management review committees
- Review to match up performance and potential with short and long term job and development requirements
- Importance of management development staff (often reporting to GM/CEO)

Potential Identification:
Locally-managed Functional Trial
- Little elite recruitment
- Decentralized recruitment for technical or functional jobs
- 5-7 years trial
- No corporate monitoring
- Problem of internal potential identification via assessments, assessment centers, indicators
- Possible complementary recruitment of high potentials

But the approach has a major weakness—it is quite incompatible with localization. Since potential is identified at the time of recruitment, all the people entering the cohort pipeline are Japanese. Consequently the output is Japanese. Career development of talented non-Japanese working for subsidiaries abroad is generally not part of this process. Foreigners get frustrated when they realize that future prospects may be limited. Even when Japanese firms attempt to include foreign employees, the practice of cautiously appraising potential over a number of years discourages the very best who want quick signals that they have a future. As a consequence, while the Japanese work practices at the factory level are widely admired, Japanese firms abroad have a poor reputation for manager development, particularly in service industries such as banking and entertainment. Since the approach has been successful, it is not easily modified. Indeed at a time of globalization, it has been described as the Achilles' heel of Japanese management practices.[52]

The Elite Political Approach

A second heritage in leadership development is similarly elitist but more political (less managed) in its process. While it characterizes some U.S. firms, it is historically the typical pattern in establishment companies in Latin Europe, and we can take France as an example.

As in the cohort approach, leadership potential is identified at entry. Owing to the institutional structure in France, however, these individuals are recruited from schools that specialize in grooming an elite for positions of future leadership responsibility. The whole French educational system leading to the high school *Baccalauréat* is a funnel that progressively selects people for their intellect, ambition, and ability to conform to establishment values.[53] After high school, the top of this elite spends two years preparing for a competition to get into the so-called *Grandes Ecoles* (great schools); the choice of college depends strictly on one's national ranking in this competition. At the top colleges, the education focuses on preparing people for future leadership responsibility. The graduates of the top "great schools" are virtually guaranteed a position as a top leader.

The establishment corporations recruit exclusively from these "great schools," and the individual will immediately enter into a position of managerial responsibility, without any trial period. The equivalent in the United States is those firms that recruit people who have graduated from an Ivy League university following this with a top MBA degree. The promotional tournament starts immediately. However, the tournament is political in nature rather than managed. Put simply, the name of the game is to get visibility with senior executives (if they come from the same school, that helps) and to play a subtle game of collaborating with peers while ensuring that one is always on top. While everyone else in the firm (graduates of lesser schools and universities) moves up in functional paths (what the French call "les métiers"), this elite will move on a path of cross-functional challenge that develops their leadership skill further. The indicator of one's potential is speed of reassignment and promotion from one job to another, a sign that senior people are impressed and want him or her as a collaborator. There are no norms regarding minimum tenure in a job as in Japan. If other people are moving faster, then the person is well advised to use his or her connections to stay on a fast track in a smaller or less prestigious enterprise.[54]

As in Japan, these firms have difficulty in internationalizing their leadership as localization takes hold, though the difficulties are less acute since the political model is more widespread across Western (and indeed Asian) enterprises. Leadership development remains quite ethnocentric in orientation, though a French or Italian firm may admit some U.S. or European MBAs to the tournament game. Since potential is synonymous with speed of reassignment, the risks of derailing and of developing learning skills at the expense of those in execution are maximized. Moreover, the approach tends to create a two-class system—the functional managerial culture and the elite leadership culture.

The Functional Approach

Germanic firms exemplify the third model, though variants can again be found throughout the world. It is less elitist in nature, and the distinctive feature is that leadership is associated with functional expertise rather than the generalist orientation that comes from mobility.

Future leaders in German firms are recruited from universities and engineering schools. As in the elite cohort approach, there is an initial trial period, but of a very different nature: Following the apprenticeship tradition that is deeply rooted in German heritage, these persons are rotated from department to department for a two-year period (a practice also found in some American and other European firms).[55] The objective is twofold—first, to provide the recruits with a broad exposure to the business and organization; and second, to find out where their talents really lie. At the end of this trial period they are assigned to the function that appears to suit them best. And then they will climb up that functional ladder to higher and higher levels of expertise. With the exception of a very few deviants (likely to be elite PhDs with a brilliant technical background or people recruited into headquarters staff roles), cross-functional mobility has in the past been quite alien to such firms.

The approach to decision-making that evolved in such enterprises reflected their strongly functional cultures. At middle levels, managers would rarely venture out of their zones of expertise when coordination problems arose—these would be passed up the hierarchy. The responsibility for coordination was assumed at a high level of the firm by management committees, guided by the strongly consensual norms that are characteristic of large German enterprises.

The advantage of the functional approach is the in-depth expertise that it develops, the meticulous attention to detail that is associated with the renowned quality of German engineering. The disadvantage is the slowness of decision-making, especially when it comes to strategy in a fast moving world of global competition. As the complexity of coordination has increased, corporate staff in these firms has expanded to facilitate the consensual process. It is difficult to bring the desired new skills of outsiders into line management roles, so these outsiders are brought into staff advisory positions. The pressures to downsize headquarters bureaucracy and to decentralize strategic decision-making were long resisted in Germany since they were quite incompatible with the development culture associated with consensual processes of decision-making among functional leaders. Again, internationalization has proved to be difficult since foreign managers get frustrated with the slow centralized consensual decision-making, arguing for more autonomy over their operations.[56]

The Emergence of the Multinational Approach

While each of the three models has distinctive strengths, all have come under pressure from progressive globalization. One of their dysfunctions is that talent and potential, particularly in the elitist models, are identified so early. While there are clear advantages to this since talented persons can then be exposed to developmental challenges over a longer period of time,[57] it inevitably leads to a parent country bias since the elite comes from the home country.

One European multinational corporation struggled for decades with the challenge of how to internationalize senior management. Despite persistent efforts, this had not happened. They finally realized that the main blockage was the highly professional central recruitment department in the parent country, which devoted a great deal of skilled resources to the recruitment of talent, bringing on board excellent people who were given privileged challenges. Out in the subsidiaries, local people were recruited for specific jobs rather than for their potential, and any talented locals were likely to leave when they saw the interesting positions going to parent country expatriates. Twenty years later, the best candidates coming out of the pipeline into executive positions were those from the mother country.

Consequently a fourth model has emerged that is more in tune with the needs of the multinational enterprise, particularly those facing transnational challenges. The distinctive features of this model are that it is not elitist in identifying potential at entry, and it decentralizes the responsibility for functional development to its local subsidiaries while tightly managing leadership development at a corporate level.

IDENTIFYING POTENTIAL FROM THE LOCAL RANKS. The pattern that has developed in multinational corporations, from Exxon to Unilever, from Motorola to international banks such as ABN-AMRO or Citibank, is to decentralize the responsibility for recruitment to local units. The parent country itself becomes just another local unit, and the corporate recruitment or staffing unit is separated from the mother country, as when Motorola recently set up a global staffing function.[58] The role of such a corporate function is not to recruit in the parent country—it is to beef up the rigor with which local companies undertake recruitment and staffing (typically aided by a guiding competency-based logic). Local subsidiaries recruit not just for jobs but also for potential.[59]

Local recruits pursue their careers within the local company, typically moving upward within functions for the first five to eight years of their careers. This is what we describe as a "locally managed functional trial" in the multinational corporation model shown in Figure 8–6. The corporate task then becomes that of identifying those with wider potential from the ranks of local talent, after they have five to eight years of functional experience in the local companies around the world.

Since potential is not identified at the time of entry, a wide variety of techniques are used to identify those with potential. Local general managers may be asked annually to submit the names of their high potential individuals, who will then be scrutinized or even sent through an assessment center. Often this is an integral part of an annual audit or review of the strategy, performance, and development of the local subsidiary. Expatriates working in local firms may be given the role of identifying potential there. If there is a regional structure, identifying potential is a particular responsibility of the regional HR manager while working with the local subsidiaries on projects. In some firms, potential is identified in a more subtle way through local nominations for a landmark corporate "young managers" educational program, in which the training staff observe closely the behavior of the participants. Local personnel who are given exceptional salary raises may come under particular scrutiny, as will those individuals who are assigned by local subsidiaries to work on cross-boundary projects. Exxon used to use a peer ranking methodology,[60] and multiple appraisal remains a reliable method of making such judgements—getting a group of managers who are familiar with the local people around a table for a frank discussion of their qualities. While the choice of a competency-based logic(s) in no way resolves the problem of identifying potential, it provides a common language and concept of potential to guide these methods.

There is often a big gap, however, between the intention and the reality. A major challenge plaguing multinational corporations, especially for those coming from a heritage of local responsiveness, is how to get the local company to pay attention to talent development. Senior management in some cultures may be reluctant to recruit people who question their commands. They may argue with some justification that their cultural circumstances are different so that the corporate competency logic does not apply to them. More particularly, in a small and tightly run, cost-conscious local operation, there is no room at entry level for people who have fancy degrees, high potential and expectations, but no hands-on experience. Furthermore, operationally oriented local HR managers may be ill equipped to cope with the challenges of recruiting, developing, and retaining such individuals.

Such problems may contribute to the creation of a regional support structure. Or an experienced local HR manager may be given the additional responsibility of working with subsidiaries in the region. Some companies bypass the problem, as does Schlumberger. In those countries where the local management is operationally focused and strongly technical in their orientation, the corporate or regional HR function will recruit high potential individuals in local markets. They are then placed in entry level functional jobs in a third country that has a reputation as a talent incubator. When these recruits have learned the operational ropes, they are reassigned as engineering or service managers in their home country subsidiary.

Furthermore, there is a natural tendency for the subsidiary to hide its best people—the more one praises an individual who is indispensable, the more likely it is that the person will be moved elsewhere under the umbrella of corporate leadership development. Consequently CEOs such as GE's Jack Welch and ABB's Percy Barnevik get firm, indeed passionate, about the issue. Talent development is a priority in the corporate values, close to or on a par with financial performance. Welch became quite strong on this issue during his tenure as CEO:

"There's no future here for people who get good financial results but who don't respect our values." Talent belongs to the corporation (many companies describe high potentials as "corporate property"), and hiding talent is an act of corporate disloyalty.

Some companies have practices that foster both international mobility and the development of corporate talent. 3M has a general principle that the country managing director should not be a local person so as to avoid clogging the pipeline. Unilever has a long-standing practice of ensuring that there should be one or more foreigners on all local management teams—and not necessarily from the mother countries of the U.K. and Holland.

Development Planning and Reviews

In the multinational approach, development planning is also carefully managed. As discussed earlier, leadership qualities are ultimately the product of the challenging experiences to which people have been exposed. Thus at the heart of leadership development lies the process of decision-making about "who gets what assignment." If the decision-making is left until the vacancy arises, the logic of performance will invariably override the logic of development—people management will be demand-driven rather than learning-driven. So most processes traditionally involve some form of anticipation or planning.

Some processes highlight *people planning* while others focus on *position planning.* Local operating companies typically use succession planning, which is driven more by position or job logic, resulting in a plan indicating potential successors, the extent to which they are ready for the position, and appropriate developmental actions to increase readiness.[61] Although many multinational corporations use succession planning as a vehicle for steering leadership development, it is typically too position-driven to be satisfactory. It easily becomes a ritual of filling in names and boxes on a chart with few developmental initiatives taken. Such plans are often ignored when it comes to the decision on who fills the vacancy. It is backward looking in its focus on the organization chart, unable to keep pace with the real world where position requirements change so fast that the idea of a "job" loses its meaning. Consequently, succession planning systems have come under increasing attack.[62]

In multinational corporations, the corporate process tends to be focused on people planning, especially in fast moving industries, steered by some structure of management development committees or review boards. At Shell the group executive committee meets weekly. However once a month they meet as the "group management development committee," joined by the two people responsible for management development. Guided by the legwork undertaken by the management development department, they work through the development decisions for the people in key positions and those with the potential to occupy such positions. Decisions on key appointments are taken, and policy matters are discussed. This structure exists at cascading levels lower down in the organization, and the management development department is responsible for following up on the plans as well as incorporating intended moves in the succession plan. At GE development planning takes the form of an offsite spring seasonal review of key people and a follow-up meeting in the fall, with parallel meetings taking place in the regions. This people-focused review process leads not to a succession plan, but to a slate of candidates including people outside the local chain of command that the management resourcing staff present to the local boss when a vacancy opens up.

Some companies have developed systematic review procedures that bridge between the people and position orientation, though initiated more from the people perspective. Companies in the United Technologies group are an example. Each year and at each unit of the firm, there is a review of all professional and managerial employees, undertaken by the regional HR manager with the local team. Each person is assessed in terms of performance and potential, using a 3 by 3 matrix (variants are used by different firms). On the performance dimension, staff are evaluated as unsatisfactory, satisfactory, or outstanding, with the majority of people expected to be in the middle category. Suitability for promotion is the potential indicator, the highest category being 2-step suitability (meaning that the person is expected to occupy a job at least two levels above the present position within say five years), the middle category being 1-step suitability, and the lowest category being nonpromotable.

This leads in turn to intensive discussion on what actions to take, focusing in particular on the people in the corner boxes (having a common competency framework facilitates constructive discussion). Those who are low on both potential and performance may need to be counseled out of the firm, while those who are high on potential but low on performance may need either training or transfer to another function that suits their talents better. Strategies for retention and renewal may be discussed for high performing persons who have low potential, since these persons constitute the bedrock of the organization. The corporate office has a particular interest in the individuals who are high on both performance and potential. To broaden their leadership potential, they may be given special training, assigned to work on cross-boundary projects, or made candidates for rotation to another function or subsidiary. The final results of the review process are incorporated in some form of position- or function-oriented succession plan. Strengths and weaknesses in terms of the professional and management bench appear clearly through this review.[63]

In some multinational firms, such a review is either the backdrop to or an integral part of an annual or periodic "organization and management review." A two-day review with the local management team is common practice, at which the first day is devoted to reviewing financials and the strategy, with the organization/management review on the second day.[64]

Intranets in companies and new software are facilitating such review processes, and will undoubtedly continue to do so more in the future. Through job posting, the intranet is also facilitating the way in which the firm can balance bottom-up personal responsibility for career management with top-down development planning and reviews (see the box "You Are Responsible for Your Own Career!"). Companies such as Dell, Cisco, and IBM use the intranet widely for the management of professional careers.

ENSURING THE QUALITY OF REVIEWS. The mere existence of a rigorous process of planning and review in no sense guarantees a satisfactory outcome. All too often the management review process becomes a ritualistic discussion in which few changes are made to the prepared proposals. How can this process be structured so as to add value?

Whether the review process takes place in corridors or at offsite meetings, what is important is that it engenders constructive debate on the underlying trade-offs in leadership development. The added value of the process is directly proportionate to the degree of constructive debate. Indeed one authority on talent development goes so far as to describe the process as "guerilla warfare."[65]

The trade-offs involved in leadership and talent development are real, to be surfaced and worked through rather than pushed under the table. They reflect real dualities:

- Performance versus development (exploitation of existing skills versus development of new skills).
- Job-based logic (ensuring replacement and succession) versus people-based logic (ensuring long-term development).
- Focus on high potential corporate property versus a wider focus on all talent.
- Top-down steering logics (research and strategy-based) versus more bottom-up logics (learning and self-management).
- The priorities of the organization versus the often conflicting priorities of the individual.

Healthy processes of management development bring out the conflicts rather than suppress them. L'Oréal openly recognizes that the role of the HR function is to act as a guardian of the long-term strategic interests of the firm. The role of HR is to challenge any decision, particularly concerning staffing, in which they see short-term and local interests prevailing unduly over long-term and global development. Other companies foster this culture of contention management by appointing a tough business manager as head of management development and by reorganizing management review panels so that they are small groups of heavyweight executives rather than large committees.

Managing the "Deep Structure" of the Corporation

When we talk of the structure of a firm, we think of the reporting lines and boxes on the organizational chart. Yet this surface structure is quite ephemeral and transitory. The "deep structure" that has a stronger influence on the lives of people, as well as on long-term organizational performance, is the structure of development, which touches on most aspects of life in an organization—the orientation and skills of those in leadership positions; the balance between strategic development and functional execution; how long people spend in jobs; the succession of challenges and assignments that they face; the way in which the firm responds to co-ordination needs; and many other issues that fall under the umbrella of "organizational culture."

While it is natural that firms pay particular attention to developing the capacities of their future leaders to cope with the complexity of the global environment, that capacity increasingly has to be built into the mindset of local managers as well. We turn to these broader aspects of talent development in the transnational enterprise.

You Are Responsible for Your Own Career!
Research Box

The systematic study of careers in organizations is quite recent, having taken off in the early 70s.[A] However, by the mid-90s some scholars were suggesting that the pace of change was such that the "career" is best seen as a social invention that thrived and died with the twentieth century.[B] The verdict is still out, and the debate will continue. Certainly the median employment tenure for U.S. managers and professionals in the early 90s was four and a half years. Even in Japan, that supposed bastion of lifetime employment, the median for male workers is only eight years.[C]

If the boundaries within and between organizations are becoming more fluid, the same is true of careers—they are also becoming boundaryless.[D] Careers still exist in the sense of a sequence of steps, but they are not limited to a single organization or function or conventional path. *Boundaryless careers* are individualized—in fact it is often persons with a distinctive career path who have a unique set of skills that is highly valued by the market.

Facilitating Self-Management

Since few organizations today feel that they can guarantee employment for people, the "employability" argument has taken hold. "While we cannot guarantee you a job for the indefinite future, we can try to help you develop your skills so that you remain employable—perhaps with another organization." This also legit-

imizes the external recruitment of talent, even into senior positions. It facilitates *intransitive* development, allowing people to make zigzag transitions that may build their portfolio of competencies.

From a practical perspective, this means that processes facilitating self-management must be put in place. Job posting, aided by intranets, has gained ground.[E] The intranet also allows the firm to provide a catalog of certified training programs that correspond to specific needs. Helping people help themselves becomes important—through coaching, appraisal, development discussions, and self-assessment workshops, including multi-rater (360°) feedback. But self-management requires a higher degree of transparency about strategic and business information, as well as about the competency steering framework—that is, it requires equipping people with the necessary information to make sound choices for themselves. Otherwise the decisions that they take regarding their own development are unlikely to match the needs of the organization. This is a condition that is far from satisfied in the majority of organizations.

The Dangers of Excessive Self-Management

Self-management complements traditional career management, it does not replace it. Apple Computers was an example of the danger of going to the extreme. In the mid-80s, Apple decided to spurn the traditional

DEVELOPING GLOBAL MINDSET

Several years ago, Nokia Networks, a leading provider of the infrastructure of mobile telecommunications, participated in a benchmark study on how managers perceive a company's global strategy. The survey showed that some parts of the organization such as product lines had a highly global orientation. Other parts were strongly local, such as local sales companies in emerging markets. The reaction of most executives was initially positive—"This is exactly the type of differentiation we need—strongly integrated product lines worrying about global economies of scale and locally oriented sales units worrying about local opportunities."

On reflection, their view changed. They realized that the consequence of this differentiation was that the conflicts were being pushed up to senior management

You Are Responsible for Your Own Career!
Research Box

top-down approach to talent development; it was one of the first companies to state openly: "You manage your own career."[F] There were no competency criteria, succession planning, review boards, or obligatory training. As a consequence, new recruits were not systematically socialized into common values, leading to outbreaks of conflict between different value systems. Personal logic rather than organizational logic motivated the few moves that took place between countries. There was little mobility between disciplines such as sales, manufacturing, and development, leading to an increasing silo mentality at senior levels. The exposure to leadership challenge outside one's comfort zone, sometimes leading to a testing hardship experience, will rarely occur if self-management is taken to such an extreme.

New Individual Dilemmas

DeFillippi and Arthur suggest that these boundaryless careers require three sets of personal competencies—knowing-how, knowing-whom, and knowing-why.[G] *Knowing-how* is the set of skills that people build up, often by moving from one firm to another. *Knowing-whom* is the network of relationships that allow a person to transition into new opportunities. A person may have invaluable skills, but if he or she does not have the appropriate contacts, then they may be unable to find new work environments that value these

skills or that provide further opportunities for building new skills. But *knowing-why* is perhaps the most interesting implication of the boundaryless career. Whereas the career structure in the past provided people with a clear sense of social identity ("I am a manager with IBM," "I am an accountant," "I am a general manager"), the personal challenge for many people today is forging a sense of professional identity out of their portfolio of experiences and skills. How do you respond when your young daughter asks you, "Mummy, what do you *do* when you are away from home?"

[A]The research identified three stages in career development: *exploration* (where people develop their own skills and explore the world of opportunities), *establishment* (when they settle down and pursue advancement), followed by a mid-late period of *growth or maintenance or stagnation* (Hall, 1976). See also Schein (1978).
[B]Cappelli, 1999.
[C]Cheng, 1991. See Arthur and Rousseau (1996) for further data and discussion.
[D]For a full account of the concept of the *boundaryless career* and its implications, see Arthur and Rousseau (1996). The parallel concept of the *protean career* is outlined in Hall (1996).
[E]For example, at Dell Computers almost all internal and external recruitment in lower and middle level positions occurs via Internet and intranet, so that the company is considering eliminating its formal recruitment function.
[F]Evans and Wittenberg, 1986.
[G]DeFillippi and Arthur, 1996.

for arbitration, overloading their own agendas, causing delays in decision-making and leaving little time to focus on institutional leadership. While the product managers indeed needed to be global, they also had to understand the need to work the conflicts through with local sales units—and vice versa. As ABB's Percy Barnevik put it, you can only push the conflict up once! Consequently Nokia Networks launched a number of initiatives to develop a more balanced perspective, the necessary global mindset. These ranged from management education to changes in profit and loss accountability.

The demands in the transnational vary from one subsidiary to another and from function to function, and one of the challenges is to respond to the necessity for differentiation. Headquarters rules and policies cannot cope with this differentiated reality, and yet needs for cohesion and fairness must be respected. This requires a particular intellectual orientation to business problems. We call the attitudes that underlie such thinking a *global mindset*. What is this, and how does one develop it? We discuss these questions in this section.

The need for differentiation may sound abstract, but it has an impact on the lives of people right down to the bottom of the organization, as well as on organizational performance. There are many examples in the practice of international human resource management. Let us take two by way of illustration, the first concerning selection practices and the second relating to management development.

Microsoft has a much-vaunted policy of recruiting the "best" people, measured by IQ and other tests, and this policy is applied across the world. That sounds like good practice . . . but examine the consequences. What works well at the global hub in Seattle may often lead to expensive waste abroad. In many of their sales and development subsidiaries around the world, there are insufficient challenges for "the best." Consequently many bright people who are lured by the Microsoft appeal quickly get bored and leave. However, a policy of recruiting only solid implementers for such subsidiaries would be equally simplistic. Guided perhaps by some thoughtful principles, local general managers and HR professionals need to be able to make their own differentiated judgements about when to act global and when to act local.

The practice of international transfers is another example. As mentioned earlier, norms develop in some firms that people are no longer considered to be high potential if they remain in a job for more than two years. Extending the norms to three years would be equally naïve. The needs of jobs vary. Sometimes six months in a posting is quite sufficient, whereas in other cases seven years may be required to ensure that the manager takes responsibility not just for starting things off but also for finishing them. Once again, a global mindset is needed to cope with the differentiated reality.

In the rapidly changing global competitive arena, sustainable competitive advantage depends on the ability of employees across all regions of the world to implement increasingly complex competitive strategies. What matters is not so much the blueprint of a strategy, but *the organization's capacity to execute that blueprint*. It is not just the leaders who have to cope with the contradictions of transnational enterprise—leadership is vital but insufficient. The key lies in the minds of people inside the transnational enterprise.

What Is Global Mindset?

The organizational challenges of globalization require new skills to manage diversity as well as changes in how managers frame business problems. This is not a new argument. It was proposed more than thirty years ago when Perlmutter developed the first formal outline of the orientations or mindsets of managers in multinational firms, and it parallels other research on managerial cognition.[66] Perlmutter's now-classic typology of ethnocentric, polycentric, and geocentric orientations formed a framework for subsequent theoretical and empirical work. The future need was clearly for more "geocentric" managers, "the best men, regardless of nationality, to solve the company's problems anywhere in the world."[67] Since then many authors have argued that the orientation of managers has become a critical issue facing the multinationals.

The concept of global mindset helps to differentiate between expatriate and global managers.[68] Expatriates are defined by *location,* as managers who are working in a different country from their own. In contrast, global managers are defined by their *state of mind.* They are people who can work effectively across organizational, functional, and cross-cultural boundaries. Some global managers may be expatriates; most have been expatriates at some point in their careers; but not all expatriates are global managers. The international management literature is full of examples of expatriates with an ethnocentric orientation.[69] At the same time, local managers in lead countries may not be expatriates, but they invariably need to have a global mindset.

There are two different and complementary perspectives on global mindset, one rooted in a psychological focus on the development of managers in multinational firms and the other coming from scholars and practitioners with a strategic viewpoint on the transnational enterprise. Let us briefly review these two perspectives.

The Psychological Perspective

One concept of global mindset views it as *the ability to accept and work with cultural diversity,* leading to research that tries to map out the skill or competency sets associated with this. In contrast to an ethnocentric mindset, a firm with a global mindset "accepts diversity and heterogeneity as a source of opportunity."[70] Adler and Bartholomew use the term "transnational manager," viewed as a cultural "citizen of the world," defined by his or her knowledge and appreciation of many cultures and the ability to tread smoothly and expertly within cultures and countries on a daily basis throughout their career.[71]

Rhinesmith observes that people with global mindsets tend to approach the world in six ways that differentiate them from domestic managers, as is shown in Figure 8–7.[72] They have broader perspectives, they try to understand the context for decisions, and they are suspicious of "one-best-way" solutions. They accept life as

---

FIGURE 8–7 Global Mindset Compared to Traditional "Domestic" Mindset

Traditional Domestic Mindset	Global Mindset	Personal Characteristics
Functional expertise	Broad and multiple perspectives	Knowledge
Prioritization	Duality—balance between contradictions	Conceptual ability
Structure	Process	Flexibility
Individual responsibility	Teamwork and diversity	Sensitivity
Predictability	Change as opportunity	Judgment
Trained against surprises	Open to what is new	Learning

Source: Adapted from S. H. Rhinesmith, *A Manager's Guide to Globalization* (Burr Ridge, IL: Business One Irwin, 1993).

a balance of contradictory forces, thereby facilitating their ability to handle the tensions of conflict. Anticipating the unexpected, they trust process rather than structure, understanding that processes are necessary to deal with the ambiguities and needs for adaptation in the transnational firm. They value diversity, to be channeled through teamwork. They view change as an opportunity rather than as a threat. People with global mindsets have the curiosity that leads them to be open to surprise, to the constant necessity to redefine boundaries, meanings, and indeed themselves.

There are many observers of the international scene who advocate the need for this type of global mindset, but relatively little empirical research.[73] One of the rare empirical studies that maps out the skill set associated with global effectiveness was undertaken by researchers at Ashridge in the U.K.[74] They studied the competencies of sixty-one managers with track records of international success in firms such as ABB, Cathay Pacific, SKF, and Nokia. The competencies that distinguished successful international managers from those who did not have international experience are shown in Figure 8–8. Some examples are the championing of international strategy (visioning the future), acting as a cross-border coach (giving and receiving feedback from international teams), cognitive complexity (the ability to step back and see new patterns), and emotional maturity (being able to handle emotional crises).

This map of competencies is a concise statement of what it takes to be a leader in a global corporation today, even a leader in one's own home country—a generic map of global mindset. It provides some empirical backing for the policy of firms such as Unilever, Dupont, and ABB, who believe that all senior managers must have successful international experience, even for positions in their own countries (as discussed earlier). However, it is a generic map that does not take into account the specific strategic focus of the firm. The strategic perspective on global mindset is more concerned with mirroring the dilemmas of the organization.[75]

The Strategic Perspective

This alternative perspective on global mindset focuses on a way of thinking that reflects conflicting strategic orientations. Since most multinational firms face contradictions (the determining feature of the transnational enterprise), scholars have emphasized the need for "balanced perspectives," arguing that a critical determinant of success in such firms lies in the cognitive orientations of senior managers:[76]

> Diverse roles and dispersed operations must be held together by a management mindset that understands the need for multiple strategic capabilities, views problems and opportunities from both local and global perspectives, and is willing to interact with others openly and flexibly. The task is not to build a sophisticated structure, but to create a matrix in the mind of managers.[77]

This idea of "the matrix in the mind" captures well the notion of global mindset and the idea that the contradictions cannot be resolved by structure but need to be built into the way of thinking of leaders and managers in the transnational firm.

The main concepts behind the transnational enterprise are global integration, local responsiveness, and worldwide coordination.[78] Thus the strategic perspective of global mindset refers to *a set of attitudes that predispose individuals to balance*

FIGURE 8–8. The Competencies That Distinguish Managers with Successful International Experience from Those Who Do Not Have International Experience

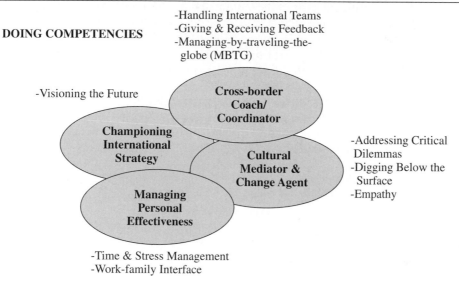

DOING COMPETENCIES

-Handling International Teams
-Giving & Receiving Feedback
-Managing-by-traveling-the-
   globe (MBTG)

-Visioning the Future

Cross-border
Coach/
Coordinator

Championing
International
Strategy

Cultural
Mediator &
Change Agent

-Addressing Critical
   Dilemmas
-Digging Below the
   Surface
-Empathy

Managing
Personal
Effectiveness

-Time & Stress Management
-Work-family Interface

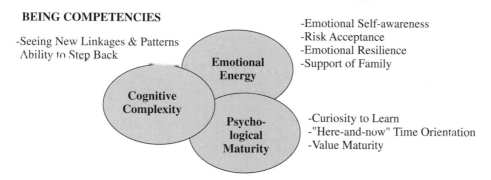

BEING COMPETENCIES

-Seeing New Linkages & Patterns
 Ability to Step Back

Emotional
Energy

-Emotional Self-awareness
-Risk Acceptance
-Emotional Resilience
-Support of Family

Cognitive
Complexity

Psycho-
logical
Maturity

-Curiosity to Learn
-"Here-and-now" Time Orientation
-Value Maturity

Source: Adapted from K. Barham, *"Developing International Management Competencies,"* paper presented at the Third Conference on International Personnel and Human Resource Management, Ashridge College, England, 1992.

competing business, country, and functional priorities which emerge in international management processes rather than to advocate any of these dimensions at the expense of the others. It recognizes that organizational resources are deployed across all subunits and places high value on sharing information, knowledge, and experience across boundaries.[79]

Whether or not managers need to hold a global mindset depends on the competitive position of the firm. Not all companies need to become transnational in order to do business across borders. Multidomestic mindset or meganational mindset may sometimes be just as appropriate, and a polarized mindset may serve a positive purpose at a particular stage of globalization. What matters is alignment and consistency.

Measuring Global Mindset

It is possible to measure this strategic view of global mindset so as to identify the orientations of different parts of the multinational, also as one important step toward developing it. An example of how this can be done and some illustrative survey findings are shown in the box "Measuring Global Mindset."

Measurement is a powerful tool for development. Using repeat surveys to evaluate global mindset provides top management with an objective indicator of

Measuring Global Mindset
Practice Box

Scales for measuring individual and organizational progress towards a global mindset have been developed and validated by Murtha and his colleagues.[A] The aim is to assess a key ingredient for the successful implementation of a global competitive strategy, namely, the capacity of individuals to consider complex interactions and differences in global strategy.

What Can Be Measured with the Global Mindset Scales?

Three core sets of scales representing global integration, local responsiveness, and worldwide coordination have been used in a survey of more than 30 businesses:

Integration refers to the centralized management of dispersed assets and activities to achieve scale economies.

Responsiveness refers to resource commitment decisions taken autonomously by a subsidiary in response to primarily local competitive or customer demands.

Coordination refers to the level of lateral interactions within and among the network of affiliates with respect to business, function, and value chain activities.

These scales are used to evaluate differences in the way in which areas, functions, and business units understand corporate global objectives. For example, do managers in global product divisions conceptualize the importance of integration and responsiveness in the same way as managers in the country units? What about managers with international experience versus those who pursued local careers?

Mapping Out Global Mindset

We have undertaken a study with three firms that operate internationally, all successful but with different ways of thinking about how to compete globally, and the results for major units in these firms are shown in the figure below.

- Company A, a major U.S.-based financial institution, takes a laissez-faire approach to globalization. Each division pursues its own strategy—some are transnational, one of them (selling financial IT systems worldwide) is meganational to the extreme, another (European brokerage house) places more emphasis on responsiveness.
- In contrast, company B is a diversified manufacturing firm, also based in the United States. Its foreign-born CEO has for a long time aspired to operate as a transnational. The data indeed showed that he had achieved this with all the units sharing a balanced view of the needs for both responsiveness and integration.
- The third company C was Nokia Networks, introduced at the beginning of this section. In general, the data showed that integration was valued more than responsiveness and illustrated a polarity between the global orientation of the business units that were part of worldwide product lines and the local orientation of downstream units responsible for regional sales and customer services. Corporate staff held balanced views, but with a relatively low orientation toward both integration and responsiveness, reflecting the difficulties in reaching consensus.

the effectiveness of globalization activities. Before-and-after scores assist in evaluating the effectiveness of international management training or communications programs that are intended to promote global values and priorities within an organization. Individual and group scores can help to assess the effect of HR policies and tools affecting globalization (e.g., international assignments and rotation, global compensation practices, performance management, specific training programs).

Measuring Global Mindset
Practice Box

Previously, this rapidly growing company handled the tensions of conflicting polarities through informal dialogue among the close-knit network of leaders who shared common experiences and values. However, as the business expanded, the ability of a small network of leaders to address all the issues was increasingly strained. This global mindset needed to be shared by a much larger managerial population.

What did the company do? They actively communicated the need to increase local responsiveness,

and they rotated the leadership team so as to give more visibility to executives with local experience. Profit and loss accountability was decentralized. Two hundred and fifty managers were involved in action learning programs to find ways of increasing lateral coordination, replacing the vertical integration. The next round of the survey eighteen months later showed a significant shift to the desired balanced direction.

[A]Murtha, Lenway, and Bagozzi (1998).

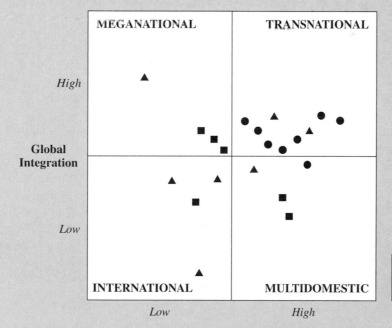

Who Needs Global Mindset?

While it may seem obvious that multinational firms will need more managers with global mindset, translating this attractive vision into an operational reality is not simple. Does every manager need to be "global"? Who really needs global perspective and to what extent? Managers are not born "global"—they acquire this mindset through a series of experiences, many of them at a substantial cost to the organization. Where is the limit of the return on investment in developing people with global mindset?

Just setting the target is not sufficient, however. Other questions regarding development strategies need to be addressed. Should the future global managers be developed internally, or is it better to recruit them from the outside labor pool when the actual need arises? Insiders benefit from the knowledge of the business and the organization; outsiders often bring in ready-made global skills. Also, if global skills are critical for future managers, to what degree should the entry-level selection process focus on an employee's potential to acquire these skills?

How to Develop Global Mindset

How does one go about developing this global mindset, as when the senior management of Nokia Networks decided to move in this direction? How can the tools of human resource management help achieve this?

Equal Opportunity for All—Regardless of Passport

Perhaps the biggest barrier to the development of global mindset is the impression of local staff around the world that one's passport counts more than one's talent. If developmental opportunities are restricted to people from the parent country or those from a few lead countries (even if this is not intentional), then local employees will inevitably tend to adopt local perspectives—that is the only direction for their own future. Thus a key task for those responsible for international human resource development is to ensure equitable access for talented employees worldwide to take advantage of available opportunities.

From a long-term perspective, a transnational enterprise must satisfy a simple but demanding test: "It does not matter where one enters." Today, there are probably only a few companies that can meet this ambitious target, especially if global really means outside of the Northern hemisphere. Among established multinational firms, only a handful, such as Citicorp, ABB, and McKinsey, have developed a cadre of senior executives representing all continents. It took decades of effort to ensure that selection criteria were not biased toward one cultural group and that early identification of talent works as well in Karachi as in New York. But things are speeding up. The new transnationals of the dot-com variety are totally focused on meritocracy. They are increasingly seen as the new beacons of opportunities for the best and the brightest worldwide.

International Transfers and Assignments

As indicated repeatedly in this book, the strongest mechanism for developing global mindset is that of international assignments (see the box "Learning How to Matrix the Mind").[80] International transfers develop many different aspects of global mindset:

- Such transfers foster the development of integrative leadership skills, as discussed earlier in the chapter.
- Transfers develop the portfolio of "doing" and "being" skills associated with global mindset (championing global strategy, facing up to cross-border conflicts, handling complexity), as the study mentioned in this section showed.
- Transfers develop skills in handling cultural diversity. The person learns, to put it simply, that "there is more than one way of skinning a cat . . . and this different way has some merits after all!" More important, this counteracts against the cognitive tendency to think in terms of stereotypes.
- The person working abroad is very likely to be put on international project groups and councils, as well as to be appointed to cross-border steering groups

---

Learning How to Matrix the Mind
Practice Box

Until the mid-80s Kodak had a geographic structure where countries were responsible for marketing photographic film. However by this time the industry was becoming more complex. There were now big differences in markets and technology in the various film segments such as the motion picture industry, graphics, professional photography, and instant photography. While digital reproduction and other technologies would clearly revolutionize the industry, this would happen fast in some segments and slow in others. Kodak understandably decided to reorganize its operations on worldwide business lines so as to manage these new realities. Naturally they put their very best people into the new roles as heads of product divisions. There was only one problem—with two exceptions, none of these people had working experience outside the United States. And many of them had never ventured far from Rochester, NY, the Kodak headquarters—their experience had not equipped them with balanced perspectives.

Dan Carp, who today is CEO of Kodak, noted at the time: "What that effectively did was to neuter the strength in country operations that we had painstakingly built up for thirty years." Determined to do their best, the product line managers from Rochester drove decisions through the organization. The more capable the local manager in Germany or Japan, the more likely he or she was to leave in frustration at the unbalanced blindness of decisions emanating from Rochester.

A few years later, Carp was appointed regional vice president for Europe to repair the damage (having had earlier responsibilities in Latin America, he was one of the few former product managers with prior international experience). He told us at the time that his number one priority was to find and develop a European successor, the first non-American who would occupy that role:

I'll be in this job for four years—none of my predecessors has ever stayed for more than two. I have one year to find the potential candidates. And then I have to use my influence to secure product line jobs for them in Rochester. They have to hone their skills, develop their connections, and prove their credibility over there.

When Carp returned to the United States after his assignment, a Frenchmen took over his position, having credibly shown that a European could successfully run a product group at the headquarters—a Frenchman, like Carp, with a global mindset.

and to be a link in best practice transfer, all of which reinforce the development of global mindset.

- Transfers develop the network of weak ties that come to constitute the nervous system of the firm. Much of the communication in the transnational is informal, based on this cross-border personal network of relationships that came about through international assignments, as well as project teams and the like. These informal global networks provide managers with rapid access to necessary information, and even more importantly, to resources.

- To the extent that performance management and appraisal processes are rigorous, a powerful additional pressure for developing global mindset comes from what is called *anticipatory socialization.*[81] As managers move from a local subsidiary role to a regional or global coordination role, they know that they may inherit any problems of excessive localism in their next job. The career prospects of the foreign assignee hang on being able to satisfy the performance requirements of the subsidiary *and* the demands of headquarters staff *and* perhaps those of the person's mother country. This is an excellent training in global mindset!

FROM DEMAND-DRIVEN TO LEARNING-DRIVEN EXPATRIATION. In the past, and still today, international assignments were *demand-driven,* filling positions where there was insufficient know-how locally or where the authority of the center needed to be maintained. In other words, international managers were *teachers,* transferring capabilities and maintaining order. Given the expense, the emphasis on limiting the number of "teaching" expatriates is only natural.

In the future, however, the role of cross-border mobility will change dramatically, becoming more *learning-driven.* With localization and increasing sophistication of labor markets across the world, there is less need for knowledge transfer from the center. Many expatriates will be *learners,* not teachers. They will learn through experience about market and cultural differences, while developing long-lasting networks of relationships. They are also likely to come from many parts of the organization, not just from the parent country. Learning-driven international assignments are likely to occur relatively early in the professional career, when the learning impact is greatest, becoming an integrated part of the career and development process. This is also spurred by trends across the world that increase the barriers to mobility— dual career families, the constraints of children's education, fewer economic incentives to move later in the career. Travel, short-term assignments, advisory visits, best practice and study tours will obviously greatly increase.

Cross-Border Project Teams and Task Forces

While international transfers, increasingly learning driven, are likely to remain a critical building block for developing global mindset, they remain expensive, reserved for the critical few with clear technical or leadership potential. An equally important building block, and one that is explosively increasing, is that of cross-border project work. We are finding that managers and professionals at all levels are getting used to working in what we have called "split egg" matrix roles.[82]

Since cross-border projects are tools to work through local-global and related problems or opportunities, they are an excellent way of developing global mindset —perhaps the most important instrument for the future. The very purpose of the project group (or cross-border steering group or an internal board) is to bring different perspectives to bear.

Through project work, people learn a set of skills that underlie global mindset— the ability to work with people who have very different perspectives and over whom one has no authority, setting goals on important but ambiguous tasks, working through conflicts, and the like. We would argue that no one, repeat *no one* should move into any position of technical or managerial responsibility in a multinational organization without proven experience in cross-boundary project work. Proven experience means demonstrated results since the tendency for projects to become time-wasting committees must be avoided.

Training for Global Mindset

Training that enhances global mindset can be targeted at a broader cross-section of employees. Conceptually, any training designed to engage participants in exchanging ideas and solutions to business problems can be helpful in developing cognitive foundations for thinking globally. This is one of the appeals of business schools with internationally heterogeneous student populations, such as IMD or INSEAD, for corporate recruiters. Emphasis on classroom discussion, team approaches to case studies, international consulting projects, all are designed to maximize the give-and-take of multiple opinions and orientations, giving the students a better understanding of the richness of various perspectives and the value of tapping into other people's knowledge.

Training has many different objectives—transferring standards and best practice, facilitating recruitment, increasing commitment, implementing organizational change, building network relationships, providing common frameworks, acting as a vehicle for strategic initiatives. But projects, experiential methodologies, and action learning are at the heart of the training in global mindset. It is the exchange and confrontation of different perspectives that develop the understanding of the dilemmas of global management. Indeed there is evidence that action learning, typically focused on projects, is holistic. It develops second-order learning skills, the ability to frame problems in their context, and it satisfies the principle of requisite variety (the complexity of the learning process should reflect the complexity of the outside environment, in this case the global-local environment of the firm).[83]

Many companies today use in-house training as a vehicle to speed up the dissemination of global mindset, J&J, Unilever, and GE being among the examples. GE's management development staff in Crotonville designed short, intensive, and experiential action learning programs with the aim of fostering the globalization of GE.[84] As part of these programs, for example, multicultural action learning teams of GE managers were sent to China, the former Soviet Union, and India to work on specific GE problems in these regions as well as to collect information on GE's best and worst practices around the world. The teams immersed themselves in the issues relevant to each region and reported on their findings, outlining business opportunities for GE to the company top management. Even today, ten to fifteen years after they have taken part, many of the former participants reflect on their "global leadership" training as one of the most influential events of their careers.

Can people change their way of thinking in such a short period? A typical program lasted only about four weeks, but the stakes and tensions within teams were high—the unspoken perception was that credibility (and future career prospects) of team members depended greatly on the quality of the final output. It was clear to everyone that reporting to Jack Welch how the team could not arrive at a common solution was not an option. Pie-in-the-sky planning was also not advisable, as the hottest business prospects were usually assigned to the team members to implement. Why was the training successful? Careful selection of participants, real work, stretch goals, and personal commitment of top management to mentor and coach made it so.

Most of the company-specific programs that we undertake with multinational firms have the development of global mindset as one of their objectives. A typical scenario was a two-week seminar for thirty-six select executives, commissioned by the chairman of a group of companies headquartered in Southeast Asia. The chairman explained his objectives:

> I'm going to be in this position for about six more years, and during that time I'll probably have to face up to about four really strategic decisions, like our strategy toward China. Whether I am remembered as a good or a bad chairman probably depends on getting three out of four of those decisions right. The trouble at present is that I have so many important operational problems on my desk that I can't do my own job—I can't see the wood for the trees. I wouldn't know one of those big strategic decisions until it hit me too late. Why? The reason why I'm snowed under is that Mr. Goh in Singapore isn't collaborating with Mr. Williams in London, and Dr. Muller from business area X doesn't see eye to eye with Mr. Ismail in business area Y. And I'm equally worried about important operational matters that aren't coming up on my desk because they are just getting swept under the rug.

The concept behind this and other such programs was simple: lock up thirty-six executives off-site, get them to understand each other's problems and their interdependencies through project work and discussion of appropriate cases (guided by the conceptual understanding and prodding of outside faculty), and facilitate the face-to-face relationships that will allow them to work through the conflicts. In short, build global mindset.

A decade later, Nokia Networks faced a similar leadership challenge. Because of the rapid growth, the company had a shortage of experienced leaders at operating levels—product business units and area/country management. Many in those positions were young engineers without experience in countries where they now held critical managerial responsibilities. Others who were locally recruited knew the customers and the territory well but were not familiar with how Nokia operated. To address this issue, Nokia Networker, the core training course for high potential managers, was redesigned to include Global Leadership as one of the anchors for the three-module program. On this module, the participants of the program meet in one of the international locations relevant to Nokia's business (e.g. Beijing or Silicon Valley). The red thread during the intensive four days, which also includes visits to local firms, is the survey data on global mindset.[85] Most participants leave the program with specific individual and team commitments to creative, low budget/high impact projects that promote global mindset, reporting to top management.[86] Again, the energy to learn comes from concrete targets and top management commitment to follow through on team learning agendas.

Creating an Environment in Which Global Mindsets Flourish

In the same way as skill training that is not closely connected to the challenges in a job is unlikely to be transferred, so the development of global mindset through assignments, projects, and training is unlikely to be effective unless it is reinforced by other organizational processes. We had a clear illustration of this when working with Nokia Networks.

This division relies heavily on international transfers to implement mobile telecom projects around the world. Our research showed that the expatriates were far more "balanced" in their perspectives than their domestic counterparts, showing a high degree of understanding for the interplay between global and local forces and of the need for coordination. However, in the past, after they had returned to Finland for more than six months, there were no significant differences in mindset between returned expatriates and those who had never left home. At the headquarters, the roles, responsibilities, and corresponding performance criteria were heavily skewed to the global at the expense of the local. Repolarization of the mindset appears to quickly follow. Adjusting performance management metrics was therefore one of the key steps taken by top management as they pushed for more balanced perspectives.

As the examples of successful global leadership training suggest, global mindset starts at the top. The first step is its articulation and reinforcement by top management, in clear and consistent language, across all levels and units. During his tenure as ABB's CEO, Percy Barnevik spent over 200 days per year visiting the operating companies around the world, personally presenting his vision of a global enterprise to thousands of managers and employees worldwide. Even today, down in the organization, "Barnevik's slides" serve as a common source of reference. For Barnevik, communicating the business vision, organizational values, and management philosophy was not something that can be delegated. The same is true for GE's Jack Welch.

Global mindset is not just a part of a vision statement, it is a way the company makes strategic decisions and goes about their implementation. While top management provides the context for the way to think about global strategy, it is up to the senior managers (business unit, function, and country leaders) to make global mindset inside an organization a reality. Their respective roles may be different, but they ultimately share the responsibility for the synergy of responsiveness and integration. Accepting this responsibility is not easy or natural. Acceptance of global mindset requires an environment that creates *consistency* across the elements of organization—the underlying communication network and the coordination mechanisms discussed in the previous chapter, the necessarily clarity of responsibilities and the empowerment linked to responsibility that is necessary for performance management, the attention to leadership development, and the underlying culture and values (see Figure 8–9).

FIGURE 8–9. Best Practices Supporting Global Mindset

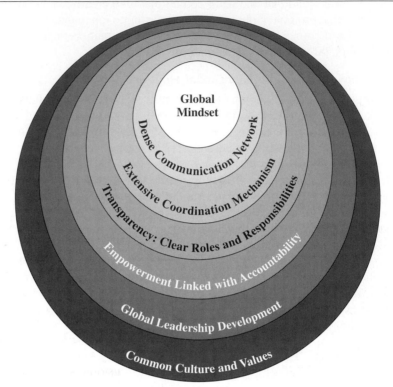

The Dark Side of Global Mindset?

Acceptance of diversity should include tolerance for people who are not "global," perhaps because of lack of opportunities, or perhaps because of personal choice or circumstances. Anything taken to an extreme risks becoming pathological—global mindset is no exception. This is true for companies as well as for individuals.

International management textbooks are full of examples of "dumb" multinationals that are not sensitive enough to cultural differences—which the savvy "globals" navigate with ease. But years of successful navigation sometimes makes one forget about the rocks below the water line. The debacle of Coca-Cola—the ultimate global firm—in dealing with product contamination in Belgium, is only one recent example, contributing to the swinging of the pendulum as that firm tries to rediscover its local roots.

At this point, it may be useful to remind ourselves again that global mindset is about balancing perspectives that at first glance may be contradictory. In their passion to promote global mindset, academics and others writing from a normative perspective sometimes have the tendency to see global or cosmopolitan as superior to local, calling for a "universal way that transcends the particulars of places."[87] What is "local" is seen as parochial and narrow-minded. However, in our view, global mindset requires an approach that may be seen as the opposite to such one-dimensional universalism—it calls for a dualistic perspective, an immersion in the local "particulars" while at the same time retaining a wider cross-border orientation.

Changing the Globalization Paradigm

Since the early 1990s, this duality was popularized in a catchy aphorism, exhorting managers to "think globally, act locally."[88] The phrase reflects the concept of a progressive transnational corporation as an enterprise which considers the whole world as its market, but which at the same time carefully adapts to local priorities. While it is tempting to endorse such an intuitive vision, its implementation has been more difficult than most companies imagined.

What is the key problem? In a multinational firm that incorporated this popular slogan on the first page in its Annual Report, one local subsidiary manager commented on its application in practice: "Our firm is organized on a simple premise. When operating under stress, and that is most of the time, *they* do the thinking, and *we* do the acting." In other words the thinking and acting are two separate roles, performed by two separate groups. The headquarters takes the strategic initiatives which the locals are left to implement. While such a paradoxical outcome may not be what was intended, it may be unavoidable when tensions embedded in managing an international business are dealt with by separation of responsibilities rather than through the development of a shared way of thinking on what globalization implies.

Perhaps the way out of this dilemma starts by returning to the logic of the globalization process. Today, leveraging technologies and service platforms increasingly require a world-scale approach. At the same time, the customers' needs are increasingly individualized, and customers worldwide exhibit a strong preference to be treated as individuals—the "secret" of Dell's business model. What is then the competitive advantage of a global firm? In simple terms, it is the ability to tap global knowledge and skills so as to satisfy the local customer needs.

The highly specific needs of the customer have to be carefully assessed—thus the requirement of being able to understand the local context, the "local" immersion advocated above. The ability to satisfy those needs is however dependent on the "global" mobilization of corporate resources—this is the orientation of the front-back organization that ABB and HP are today attempting to develop.

It may be useful, therefore, to rephrase the original paradigm. Creating a global mindset inside an organization is really about developing leaders who *think locally, but act globally.* Phrased in this way, it is not so easy to separate the corporate mind and the body spread out over the globe.

TAKEAWAYS

1. A generic principle behind talent development is that people develop primarily through challenge. However, this implies careful risk management (coaching, training, and the like), otherwise development can be at the expense of operational effectiveness.

2. While competencies frameworks are particularly necessary in international firms so as to provide a common language for steering talent development, there are significant trade-offs between underlying organizational logics.
3. With rapid change and increasing discontinuities, careers in international firms are becoming more and more intransitive. This means that openness to challenges and ability to learn from experience become more important in talent development.
4. Without a rigorous process of leadership development, short-term and local interests will inevitably drive out long-term and global concerns.
5. There are very different heritages in leadership development, from one firm to another, with different trade-offs. Most have the disadvantage of handicapping transnational development.
6. In multinational leadership development, local companies have the responsibility for recruiting top talent, and then leadership potential is identified from the local ranks of those with technical experience. In steering the decisions on potential development, people-based planning approaches are more effective than traditional position-based succession planning systems—and they also allow more room for people to manage their own careers.
7. It is not just the leaders who have to cope with the contradictions of transnational enterprise—leadership is vital but insufficient. The key lies in the minds of people inside the transnational enterprise.
8. The psychological concept of global mindset emphasizes the ability to accept and work with diversity, while the strategic concept stresses balanced attitudes toward competing business, country, and functional perspectives.
9. A fundamental condition for developing global mindset is equal opportunity for all—it does not matter where you enter the firm. The tools are international transfers, cross-border project assignments, and training/education (where action and project learning are the critical elements).
10. Global mindset complements the use of coordination technology, although it is unlikely to take hold unless there is a high degree of consistency across all transnational management processes.

NOTES

1. Tichy and Cohen, 1997.
2. "Follow the Leader," *Industry Week,* November 18, 1996, p. 16.
3. T. Stewart, "See Jack. See Jack Run," *Fortune,* September 27, 1999, pp. 66–75.
4. Amit and Schoemaker, 1993.
5. A study of the insurance industry by Galunic and Andersen (2000) shows that investment in general purpose skills may have a beneficial firm-specific effect by reinforcing employee commitment to the firm.
6. Penrose, 1959.
7. Evans, 1974; Evans, 1992. In another series of studies into the relationship between professional and private life of 14,600 executives, we found that some people got so caught in a cycle of ego-boosting work challenge that they neglected their private lives, leading to the "prisoner of success" syndrome (Evans and Bartolomé, 1979).

8. McCall, 1998.

9. Our colleague Manfred Kets de Vries has examined the ways in which senior executives derail, calling this "the dark side of leadership" (Kets de Vries, 1989; Kets de Vries, 1995).

10. McCall and Lombardo, 1990; McCall, 1998.

11. Gregersen, Morrison, and Black, 1998.

12. A recent study of the competency frameworks used by thirty-one well known North American firms with good heritages in talent development (from American Express to Eli Lilly, from Hewlett-Packard to Lucent) showed that only 22 percent had been using competency frameworks for more than five years (Briscoe and Hall, 1999). Our experience is that a similar proportion applies across Europe's leading international enterprises.

13. Briscoe and Hall, 1999.

14. Ibid.

15. Interviewing is the traditional method of study. But there are many biases in interviewing methods. Situational interviews, including behavioral event methods, were developed in the mid-80s to overcome some of these biases. This involves choosing concrete incidents or critical events, interviewing people to find out how they would respond.

16. Muller, 1970; "Sure Signs of Success," *International Management,* January 1979, pp. 36–39. This research-based concept was also adopted by other organizations such as Singapore Airlines and the Dutch and Singapore civil services.

17. Many firms use the research-based approach exclusively to specify the competencies needed in senior leadership positions.

18. BP took a similar approach and came to similar conclusions about variation in behavioral indicators when validating the OPEN competency framework that was one of the motors of culture change in its Project 1990 transformation. OPEN is the acronym for the four sets of competencies associated with success in enabling change (the performance criterion behind the BP framework)—Open thinking, Personal impact, Empowering, and Networking. However, the logic underlying the BP framework was strategic rather than research-based, leading to a different implementation process. To internalize these competencies, BP designed an 18-month cascade process. At each level of the cascade, there was the possibility to influence and change the framework, which actually got simplified under way. See Sparrow and Hiltrop (1994) for details.

19. See Briscoe and Hall (1999) for a more extended discussion of the strengths and weaknesses of the four approaches.

20. See Fombrun, Tichy, and Devanna (1984).

21. See Note 18 above.

22. See for example the pointed study of Legge (1995).

23. The quote is from Kets de Vries (1994). See Kerr's famous article on the folly of rewarding A, while hoping for B (Kerr, 1995).

24. For a discussion of normative integration (also using HP as an example of its strengths and dangers), see Chapter 7.

25. Packard, 1995.

26. Collins and Porras, 1994.

27. This was the observation of Briscoe and Hall (1999) in their study of thirty-one U.S. corporations, and it concords with our own experience.

28. Business Objects developed six values that they believe are the foundation of their success: *leadership* (striving for excellence and to be number one); *customer focus; innovation; integrity* (being straightforward, equitable, and financially conservative, as well as treating everyone with respect); *passion* (energy, enthusiasm, and relentless dedication); and *transnational identity* (global approach, drawing on talent and ideas from everywhere, leveraging the best of every culture).

29. Apple's philosophy embodied principles of growing and changing one's job, being able to earn more than one's boss, "activities reviews" to resolve conflicts, and also many principles of self-management. See Evans and Wittenberg (1986) for a description of this at the time nontraditional approach to HRM.

30. Bennis and Nanus, 1985.

31. Spreitzer, McCall and Mahoney,1997; McCall, 1998.

32. Evans and Bartolomé, 1979.

33. Kruger and Dunning, 1999.

34. For research on the learning cycle, see Kolb (1984). The cycle starts off with sensitivity to experience and reactions, to what is working well and what is not *(intuitive, feeling-based concrete experience)*. This leads to *reflective observation,* the ability to listen to others, to search for and accept feedback, and to reflect on the lessons of this experience. This in turn leads to *analytic conceptualization,* the ability to piece together the lessons of this reflection into abstract conclusions on why things went right or wrong. And then these abstract conclusions have to be translated into action implications, leading to a new course of action that constitutes an experiment so as to test out one's learning *(active experimentation)*. Research shows that the learning of many people is handicapped because of their incapacity in one or another of the steps in this learning cycle.

35. Briscoe and Hall, 1999.

36. Maruca, 1994, p. 142.

37. Drucker, 1996, pp. xi–xii.

38. The main advisor on this Hay-McBer study was Harvard's David McClelland (presentation at the *Linkage International Conference on Competency-based Tools for Organizational Performance,* Brussels, October 1996). We arrived at the same conclusions using a research-oriented exercise, undertaken with thousands of managers around the world. We asked participants on seminars to identify an outstanding leader in performance terms whom they knew well, and then to meet to identify behavioral common denominators. The only common feature was that these leaders all had a clear agenda that they were determined to achieve.

39. The term "setting direction" is used by Kotter (1988), while Bennis and Nanus, (1985) call it "management of attention," and McCall, Lombardo, and Morrison (1988) use the phrase "setting and implementing agendas."

40. Kotter, 1982.

41. We have been struck by the fact that if one looks at the leadership structure of many successful companies, one finds "two-in-the-box," to use an Intel expression. This means that the leadership roles are assumed by two or more people with complementary skills, where one is for example a creative commercial strategist while the other is an analytic financial person (see also Bennis and Heenan, 1999). Examples are Hewlett and Packard, Honda and Fujisawa, Warburg and Grünefeld, Lords Hanson and White. The British research of Meredith Belbin on the chemistry of high performing teams and the complementary roles of team members emphasizes the same underlying principle, providing empirical evidence for the idea that leadership is an attribute of teams rather than individuals (Belbin, 1981).

42. Evans, 1992. The transition between technical or functional roles and integrative roles is also the subject of a best-selling video by one of the authors ("Managing People," distributed by Video Management, Brussels and Financial Times/Knowledge, London and New York).

43. The matrix or "split egg" role concept described in Chapter 2 captures this.

44. See Hill (1992) for an analysis of the transition from individual contributor to manager.

45. Bartlett and Ghoshal, 1997; Ghoshal and Bartlett, 1998.

46. Bartlett and Ghoshal, 1997.

47. Stewart, "See Jack. See Jack Run," p. 90.

48. Evans, Lank, and Farquhar, 1989.
49. The Elite Cohort approach is not confined to Japan. For example, the Danish group A. P. Møller, a Fortune 100 multinational in containers and shipping, has long used such an approach to management development, though with some features that are different from the Japanese.
50. Pucik, 1985.
51. See Pucik and Hatvany (1981) and Pucik (1984) for a more detailed examination of this approach to management development in Japan.
52. Bartlett and Yoshihara, 1988.
53. At junior high and high school in France, students are progressively screened out into discipline streams. Since the educational reforms in the 1950s, those who are gifted in analytic subjects such as mathematics, physics, Latin, Greek, and ideally also philosophy (an important subject in French high schools that demonstrates one's ability to structure complex ideas) become the elite. Students following scientific tracks are lower in ranking, while the lowest ranking goes to those studying in the humanity streams.
54. The French system is well described by Sainsaulieu (1977). Research by Laurent (1983) on the perceived determinants of career success in a multinational American firm clearly highlights the elitist feature of the French model. In the U.S. parent company, behaviors such as getting results, skills in leading people, managerial skill, and interpersonal skills were seen as being the important determinants of career success. The perceptions of the British were similar, with the singular absence of "getting results." In contrast, the managers in the French subsidiary agreed only on a single determinant of success: "being labeled as high potential." In Germany, the technical/functional quality of "creativity" was high on the list—managers in other countries did not attribute any importance to this behavioral attribute.

    As was noted in Chapter 4, the virtue of the French system is that leaders in establishment business corporations have close relationships with senior government ministers and officials—often they were close friends at the "grande école." Consequently, French enterprises have been successful in sectors where government business cooperation is important—defense, atomic energy, utilities such as energy and water, telecommunications.
55. As documented by Bray, Campbell, and Grant (1974), AT&T had a practice of bringing in high potential graduates in the pre-breakup days on one of two entry paths. The first was a Germanic type path of departmental rotation for two years, while the second path involved simply giving people a first job assignment. In this long-term study, the researchers found that individuals on the second path rose more quickly into senior managerial positions. Some of them responded well to the early challenge, were promoted more quickly to bigger challenges, and proceeded quickly up the ranks.
56. German firms such as Henkel in fast moving consumer goods were compelled early to adopt alien "American" methods of leadership development such as cross-border mobility. BASF accepted McKinsey's recommendation in the early 80s to decentralize, breaking up the powerful *Zentralebereiche* (central staff). This led to a painful process of implementation since about 90% of the candidates for general management positions had experience in only one functional area, with little exposure to the leadership mentality described earlier in this chapter. Even today, their business unit teams complain of constant interference from headquarters staff and the slowness of decision-making in a consensual culture that still lives on.
57. Elitist approaches are characterized by early identification of potential. This means that the elite can be exposed to developmental challenges over a longer period of time, which should result in higher quality leadership. A natural experiment illustrating this occurred at Exxon. Many Exxon executives started their careers at one of the two refinery breeding grounds in the United States. However senior management consistently came more from one of them,

Baton Rouge. Why? Investigations eliminated obvious explanations, such as differences in working practices, training, or management development policies. Ultimately, they found only one difference—at Baton Rouge, management potential was being identified at age 27–28, while at the other refinery it was identified in the early thirties. The implications were clear. Imagine that there are two talented candidates for a senior management position, both in their early forties. However, one of them has fourteen years of international and multi-functional experience, while the other has only eight or nine years. Everything else being equal, whom does one naturally choose?

58. This often happens in tandem with a corporate restructuring, where the global headquarters is separated from the mother country, since the problem of confounding global management and mother country management is not unique to the HR area. Thus BP kept its worldwide HQ in London, transferring the European HQ (to whom the U.K. reports) to Brussels. Tetra-Pak had earlier moved its HQ (and whole legal structure) from Sweden first to Switzerland and ultimately to London. The examples today are legion, and a majority of companies facing transnational pressures are at least talking about relocating their global headquarters so as to achieve this separation in focus.

59. See the earlier discussion on localization in Chapter 4.

60. Exxon, an early pioneer in international management development, used for many years an annual procedure whereby each manager across the world was given a list of names of people in the immediate working environment. He or she had to rank these names in order of perceived potential. The rankings were summarized, and the final ranking was the basis for a more intensive qualitative review. However, the procedure was eventually abandoned because the judgments reflected performance more than potential, leading the firm to fall into the trap of transitivity.

61. The typical approach to succession planning involves taking each position in the organization and identifying possible successors to the current incumbent, as well as the likely date of promotion or transfer. Formal succession planning is widely used by multinational corporations in Switzerland, Germany, Norway, Sweden and the U.K. though much less by French, Danish, and Dutch organizations who rely on more informal processes (Sparrow and Hiltrop, 1994, p. 461). A U.S. survey of Fortune 500 companies in the mid-90s showed that 8% of them have a comprehensive approach to leadership development involving succession planning and some form of people planning, 16% have an established program of succession planning, while 32% are just beginning the development of a process, and 44% have an ad hoc approach (Gregersen, Morrison, and Black, 1998).

62. Walker, 1998; Mayo, 1991, pp. 239–243; Byham, 2000.

63. At the end of such a performance/potential review, a scenario for the future can be drawn up for each unit, function by function, assigning weights to each person in terms of performance and potential. Adding up the numbers for each function provides an indication of the bench strength in these functional areas. Where that bench strength is low, this is an indication of the necessity for external recruitment action (either from the outside or from other subsidiaries). If the bench strength in a function is particularly high, then that function is a potential incubator of talent for other units within the group.

64. See Mayo (1991) for examples of such reviews and their agenda.

65. McCall, 1998.

66. Perlmutter, 1969 (see ch. 1). In terms of managerial cognition, the principle of *requisite complexity* says that the internal complexity and variety within the organization must reflect the external complexity. For early arguments on the mindset implications of international decision-making, see Aharoni (1966) and Kindleberg (1969). See also March and Simon (1958), Axelrod (1968), Prahalad and Bettis (1986).

67. Perlmutter, 1969, p. 13.
68. Pucik and Saba, 1998.
69. See Black, Gregersen, et al (1999), and the discussion and references on this issue in Chapter 3.
70. "Success is All in the Mindset," *Financial Times,* V. Govindarajan and A. Gupta, February 27, 1998, pp. 2–3. Similarly, Kanter (1995) sees this as a difference between new "cosmopolitans" and "locals," to employ terms that had earlier been developed by the sociologist Gouldner to describe the difference between people who identified with the wider profession as opposed to those who identified with the "local" interests of the firm.
71. Adler and Bartolomew, 1992.
72. Rhinesmith, 1993. Similar distinctions are made by Tichy, Brimm et al. (1992) and Ashkenas, Ulrich et al. (1995).
73. Note studies by Kanter (1991); Calori, Johnson, and Sarnin (1994); Yeung and Ready (1995), though none of these involved empirical research.
74. K. Barham, "Developing International Management Competencies," paper presented at the 3rd Conference on International Personnel and Human Resource Management, Ashridge College, England, July 1992. See also Barham and Oates (1991).
75. While no one can disagree with the general desirability of such qualities and their relevance for managers in multinational firms, such all-encompassing use of the global mindset concept has stripped it of any distinct cognitive meaning (Levy, Beechler, and Boyacigiller, 1999).
76. This point was introduced in Chapter 1 (see pp. 27–30). The importance of balanced cognitive orientation was emphasized by Prahalad and Doz (1987), Hedlund (1986), as well by Bartlett and Ghoshal (1989).
77. Bartlett and Ghoshal, 1989, p. 212.
78. We might remind the reader that *responsiveness* refers to decisions on resource commitments taken autonomously by a subsidiary in response to primarily local competitive, political or customer demands. *Integration* refers to the centralized management of dispersed assets and activities to achieve scale economies. *Coordination* refers to the level of lateral interactions within and among the network of affiliates with respect to business, function, and value chain activities.
79. See Murtha, Lenway, and Bagozzi (1998) for further elaboration, also on the distinction between this strategic perspective and the psychological viewpoint.
80. We discussed in Chapter 1 the classic study by Galbraith and Edström that showed how transfers socialize people into the dilemmas and challenges facing the firm, thereby powerfully building the matrix into the mind (Edström and Galbraith, 1977).
81. Honda uses anticipatory socialization well to facilitate coordination in subtle ways. Mr. Honda felt that R&D should be the powerhouse of the corporation, though not at the expense of collaboration with Engineering and Manufacturing. How to achieve this subtle balance? The norm is that the future CEO will typically be the former head of R&D. This ensures that R&D will be seen as the powerhouse, but at the same time the head of R&D will pick up any problems of poor collaboration in his next job!

    Anticipatory socialization is used today in China to resolve conflicts between the priorities of the Communist Party and those of business improvement and development. In the state-owned airline industry, for example, the conflicts are quite acute as the airlines seek to modernize while the Party wishes to maintain ideological control and minimize social unrest. Recent practice has been to rotate the positions of the airline CEO and the Party Secretary (responsible for ideology and leadership development, and equivalent in status to that of the CEO). The possibility that this may happen fosters creative contention management and collaboration between the two.

82. The reasons for the use of project groups are discussed at length in Chapter 7—in different shapes and forms, project work has become the prime tool for coordination.

83. Morgan and Ramirez, 1983; Ramirez, 1983; see also the theory of experiential learning developed by David Kolb and his colleagues (Kolb, 1984). See Revens (1980) for a full description of action learning; and Raelin (1999) for a recent review. It should be noted that in a high context society such as Japan, all learning processes are project-oriented or experiential—there is little emphasis beyond school and university on Western style didactic learning (Nonaka and Takeuchi, 1995).

84. Tichy, Brimm et al., 1992.

85. The survey data on global mindset (see the box "Measuring Global Mindset") is used in the Nokia program to design an ideal "mindset map" reflecting the firm's global vision, to explore the gaps and differences between functions and units, and to set priorities for action, drawing on "best practice" from Nokia and other global corporations.

86. Typical projects may involve sponsoring learning assignments for employees from other units, sharing best practices across boundaries, or creating communication forums on topics of mutual interest.

87. Kanter, 1995, p. 60.

88. It was the Japanese firm Sony that first coined this now well-known aphorism, later adopted by ABB and other firms as their corporate slogan.

CHAPTER 9

Steering Through the Tensions of Change and Innovation

McKinsey today enjoys an enviable reputation among its peers in consulting. In the quality of its HRM foundations, the firm is an exemplar. Few enterprises pay more attention to recruitment. With what some would call their typical arrogance, McKinsey's advertising compares the professionalism of its recruitment and training to the rigor with which NASA selects its astronauts. And at Goldman Sachs, the elite investment banker, employee evaluation is carried out with equal rigor. A former managing director commented that the real competition is not for clients, it is for people. McKinsey pulls off a much admired balancing act—combining up-or-out promotion (one in ten will make it to directorship) with the renowned loyalty of its former staff, now clients as CEOs and CFOs. In its committee structure, among the most prestigious are the personnel committees that rank partners so as to determine compensation and promotions, while senior partners may spend six weeks flying around the globe to evaluate others. All this is the evolving legacy of the vision and values of Marvin Bower, who took over in the late 1930s to lead an obscure firm of accounting and engineering advisors to become the world's leading consulting firm.[1]

With its offices in sixty-nine countries, McKinsey is one of the most global if not transnational players in the growing professional service sector, at a time when others hotly debate whether or how they should internationalize. Its approach is to look for the same type of person in Frankfurt and Tokyo as it does in Chicago—bright, edgy, achievement oriented, and highly competitive. This reflects its "one-firm" culture—its consciousness that one weak office could lose a worldwide client—its emphasis on common standards. But McKinsey's growth and development have not been without tension.

McKinsey expanded through North America and Europe in the 1950s and 1960s, driven by a conviction that smart, well-trained generalists could solve top management business problems. But the 1970s were years of soul searching as this multidomestic growth petered out. Growth had been too fast, at the expense of in-depth expertise. Clients now needed deeper industry knowledge, looking to the specialized expertise of competitors such as BCG, with highly concentrated thought leadership from its Boston office. After successive changes in leadership, one of McKinsey's top partners reoriented training toward the development of specialized expertise, and a matrix of industry groups and functional areas of expertise was introduced. By the early 1980s, fifteen centers of competence in areas such as marketing, change management, and systems had been developed. These were virtual centers, even before that term had been coined, led by practice leaders who built relationships among appropriate groups of partners. But despite the visible success of some projects, notably the best-sellers by Peters and Waterman and by Kenichi Ohmae,[2] it was an uphill battle to introduce this expertise orientation into the dominant client-oriented generalist culture. Strongly socialized into the same norms, people believed in networking, not in manuals produced by specialists.

The changes accelerated in 1987 when a full-scale global knowledge management project was launched, aimed at building common databases in the practice areas and introducing specialist career paths. But what took hold were the elements that fitted with the network culture. A Yellow Page Directory for contacting key people with expertise was quickly adopted, while attempts to document practice and to build connected libraries of databases failed to win much support. Gradually two decades of tension and change began to pay off in knowledge-building capability, and McKinsey's elite reputation had been restored by the early 1990s. In its own way, McKinsey had found a route to reconciling the tension between its historic strength in generalist client orientation with the need to nurture expertise, a route that we will label "personalization" later in this chapter.

CHAPTER OVERVIEW

Perlmutter rightly described the path to geocentrism or transnational orientation as one of "tortuous evolution."[3] After a long period of letting subsidiaries do things their way, some firms regress to ethnocentric centralization. Other enterprises, such as Coca-Cola in recent years, swing the pendulum from centralized control to local entrepreneurship.[4] In this chapter, we discuss what we know about managing change so as to make that route less tortuous and what the implications are for human resource management. We explore the people challenges of building a global learning organization in the knowledge-based era we have entered.

We start off in the first section with some general observations on complex processes of change, recognizing that we are at the frontiers of our HRM know-how on this and other issues in this chapter. We have long known that tension is at the heart of change—for example, the tensions between planned and emergent change, incremental and discontinuous change, and short-term and long-term change. We develop the idea of sequencing, which means keeping the future in mind in the present, as well as summarizing some of the HR technologies for managing change.

In the "tortuous" route to transnational development, the multidomestic firm, the globally integrated meganational enterprise, and the knowledge-based professional firm have different starting points. The sequenced paths that they take, so as to respond to transnational pressures, raise different challenges of managing change, respectively (i) global rationalization, (ii) local entrepreneurship and the sequenced transfer of complex capabilities from the parent to the subsidiaries, and (iii) the development of capabilities in global knowledge management. The middle section of this chapter focuses on what we know about these three different change paths.

We emphasize in particular the tensions of management, organization, and change within professional service firms (PSFs). This sector experiences particular difficulties in handling globalization. Coordination in the professional service firm is largely synonymous with knowledge management. While limited knowledge transfer occurs in the traditional route to internationalization, namely, in the federation of independent firms, other PSFs have pioneered the two routes *personalization* and *codification.*

In the third section, we steer the reader through the emerging territory of global knowledge and innovation management. While electronic communications may have eliminated distance in information transfer, knowledge transfer remains very much a face-to-face social process—and a vital process since this is the key to innovation and long-term profitability. Whereas knowledge used to reside with the parent company, it is now scattered around the world. Moreover, innovation cannot be dictated or "managed." All that can be done is to create a context in which innovation and knowledge transfer is more likely to occur.

We discuss how to create that context—picking winners (building on evolutionary theory); the need for variable management geometry to meet the different needs of initiation, development, and commercialization stages in innovation; how to build relational and entrepreneurial social capital; and what it means for HRM to focus on value added knowledge. This leads us to explore the intraorganizational and extraorganizational mechanisms to facilitate innovation and knowledge transfer.

Throughout the discussions in this chapter, we meet tensions and paradoxes. We find out in the concluding section that these are indeed at the heart of innovation journey. We discuss how "social architecture" can help keep these tensions constructive, illustrating this with research on the role of procedural justice in the multinational firm.

In this chapter we address some of the frontiers of international human resource management. These frontiers are genuinely international. Whereas in the past, HRM was a backstage domain of concern to specialists, today research on and practice in multinational firms are spearheading our understanding of how to cope with complex change and knowledge management in a global environment.

MANAGING COMPLEX CHANGE PROCESSES

We argued earlier that one of the challenges for HRM is realignment, which involves a complex reconfiguration of the different elements of organization.[5] Sometimes the HR function is a major obstacle to that realignment since it may have a vested interest in maintaining the existing configuration, as was the case with IBM during the late 1980s. Today, the cliché that HR is a "change agent" has replaced the former focus on "strategic human resource management"—though the ideal is far from reality (see the box "The Role of HR in Change Processes").[6] Shell's human resource leaders decided in the mid-90s to respond to the need for change in its HR practices, introducing open job postings. To their surprise, these

The Role of HR in Change Processes
Practice Box

There are relatively few firms in which the HR function lives up to the ideal of being a "change agent." The OD (Organizational Development) movement was born within Exxon in the 1960s, leading to research and practice that established some of the ground principles for adaptive management and planned organizational change. Some firms such as Shell institutionalized this role in an OD or OE (Organizational Effectiveness) subfunction within HR, acting as internal consultants. GE has a particularly interesting approach. Jack Welch came to the conclusion in the early 1990s that the future was unpredictable. The implication, as he saw it, was that GE had to be capable of responding fast to whatever strategic changes it confronted. He commissioned the HR function and outside experts to develop what became its Change Acceleration Process (CAP), one of the eight corporate capabilities cutting across its businesses.[A] GE has trained more than 15,000 coaches (most of them line managers) in the CAP methodology. Other firms train all managers in change management methods as they move into leadership roles.

The potential contribution of HR to the change process has so many facets that we can provide only a few examples:

1. *Promoting champions of change:* GE's fundamental belief is that change does not happen without committed leadership. So its succession management process (known as Session C) is partly oriented to having a slate of people for key positions who have strong change leadership track records. Research indeed suggests that some radical organizational change simply happens because a strong leader takes over a unit, being next in line in the succession process.[B] Remember that the only way of changing fast is to change the key people!

2. *Creating dissatisfaction with the status quo:* As Figure 9–1 shows, change is difficult to manage unless there is an acknowledged need to change. Amplifying the dissatisfaction with the status quo via training, two-way meetings, and project groups is an important role for HR.

3. *Developing the confidence of top management sponsors to communicate directly with employees:* Creating understanding of the need to change and its implications is best undertaken through two-way dialogue, with careful attention to procedural justice. Yet it takes courage for senior managers, the sponsors of change, to communicate directly with the workforce. At firms such as BP and Norsk Hydro, one of the roles of HR change agents is to coach these senior sponsors, building their confidence to act.

4. *Designing processes to build commitment fast through face-to-face confrontation of views:* How does one accelerate the understanding of the need for change in an organization of 100,000 people? One of the important contributions of HR is the design of such commitment processes—the cascade process at BP (described in the next box in this chapter "Transformational Change at BP") being one example.

5. *Vision building/agenda setting:* Change is facilitated if the direction, vision, or agenda is clear in the minds of the change leaders and staff. All too frequently, there is a change solution but no direction, and consequently it is difficult to monitor progress. But building a vision for the future requires facilitation. Often simple tools such as backward visioning (write the story seen from the future) and jotting down key phrases in a potential vision can serve to start off the process.[C]

6. *The people aspects of implementation:* The ability of people to change depends on their willingness (motivation) and capability (skill). Some people are both willing to change and capable and they should be moved into positions

The Role of HR in Change Processes
Practice Box

as champions, often requiring some restructuring of roles and responsibilities. Training and coaching must be provided for those who are willing but lack the capabilities, while those who are neither capable nor willing may be outplaced. But what about those who are highly capable, indispensable for today's operating results, but who just do not believe in the need to change? Here there are no easy solutions—the role of HR is to assist in working through tailored strategies. Indeed, GE's Jack Welch concluded that these are the people who slow down the process of change if they occupy key positions. Part of the motivation to develop his "leadership engine" was to accelerate change by always having a slate of willing and able successors for such people.

7. *Attention to succession management:* One of the problems in organizational change is making it last. In one study, McKinsey concluded that the major reason why change efforts fail is lack of long-term followthrough. Paradoxically, there is too much change in many firms and not enough continuity! Attention to succession management is one aspect—successors who will continue the process of implementation rather than taking the unit off in new directions are often needed. Changing the culture of the firm is another aspect of making change last.[D]

8. *Ensuring the balance between short- and long-term pressures:* One of the important dualistic roles of HR is to fight to ensure that short-term crisis measures do not compromise long-term loyalty when, for example, downsizing. At l'Oréal, the HR function is expected to argue for the long-term view since this risks being compromised by short-term imperatives.[E]

9. *Ensuring consistency between words and action:* One of the biggest factors blocking change is failure to walk the talk. This is rarely deliberate, and

a role of HR is to try to build consistency. One international bank had invested millions in empowerment, but there could be dire consequences if an executive committee member asked a senior vice president a question and she or he did not have the answer readily available. Until this was pointed out, the executive committee was unaware that the bank's staff were mobilized to keep their VPs informed of anything and everything just in case they were asked a question—totally inconsistent with empowerment! It is the classic trap, the folly of hoping for A while rewarding B.[F]

Overall, we conclude this necessarily incomplete list by noting that Ulrich sees four roles for HR in the change arena. These roles are the *champion* who promotes the need for change, the *designer* who assists in mapping out an effective change process, the *facilitator* who acts as a coach and catalyst, and the *demonstrator* who is a role model through consistent behavior.[G]

[A]As noted earlier in Chapter 7, p. 325, change management is one of the eight organizational competencies that GE nurtures. There are seven principles behind GE's CAP. Two general principles are *leading change* (no change happens unless someone puts their neck on the line), and being prepared to *change systems and structures*. The others are stages: *creating a shared need; developing and sharing a vision; mobilizing commitment; monitoring progress;* and *making change last.* The CAP methodology is applied to particular change projects, typically involving the key stakeholders in a 2–3 day workshop with the aim of working through the tensions and accelerating the process of change.

[B]Doz and Prahalad, 1988.

[C]See Gratton (2000) for ideas and analysis on how HR can facilitate the development of the vision.

[D]See Goffee and Jones (1998) for a good analysis of how to assess organizational culture and manage culture change.

[E]See the discussion of l'Oréal's management philosophy in Chapter 2, p. 86.

[F]Kerr, 1995.

[G]Ulrich, 1997.

created immense confusion and disarray in the operating companies around the world. Even in a leading firm, the executives had not understood the implications of the basic principle of consistency—if you change one significant element, you have to be prepared to reconfigure all the other elements such as leadership development, reward systems, decision-making practices, and the like.

Before discussing change processes in multinational firms, let us review what we know about complex change processes. Despite the voluminous popular management literature on organizational change,[7] we have to say up front that such sweeping change processes are ill researched.

What Do We Know about Complex Organizational Change?

There are three guiding ideas about such complex change processes. First, they involve identifiable tensions. Second, they involve a sequence of steps. And third, change is path dependent (the process will vary depending on the starting point).

The Tensions of Change

Change is complex because it involves tensions. One of the classic laws of change, with its roots in the psychology of adaptation, is the inverted U-shaped relationship between change and tension (see Figure 9–1). If the tension is low (in other words, if people are happy, contented, apathetic, or complacent because they feel successful), then change is unlikely to occur. On the other hand, if the degree of tension is too high, then people will react in perverse and unpredictable ways so as to take care of their own interests (as after an acquisition when the most capable people may leave). Change is best managed when the degree of tension is constructive.

Researchers at Harvard recently gathered together some of the leading scholars and consultants on the theory and practice of organizational change.[8] A premise for discussion was that nearly two-thirds of all change initiatives fail (at least in North America), and nearly all the themes of debate reflected tensions between dualities. One of those discussed was the tension between Q and A, referring to the well-known formula that is at the heart of GE's Change Acceleration Process (described in the box "The Role of HR in Change Processes"):

$$E = Q \times A$$

The "E" stands for the Effectiveness of change. "Q" means the Quality of the analysis, the economic or analytic reasoning leading to a proposed action plan or solution. The "A" signifies Acceptance of the change, signifying attention to process, participation, and the people side of change. We are typically well trained at school and on the job in the Q, but less versed in the A. And yet this simple formula recognizes that a superb Q-solution will abort if no attention is given to the A-side (the focus of much of HRM)—anything multiplied by zero nets out to zero.[9]

Change involves many other dualities. Should it be led in a *top-down or bottom-up* manner? In the now widely heralded transformation process of BP, the British petrochemical corporation, insiders observed that the change would not have been initiated without the brash and top-down leadership of Robert Horton. But the trans-

---

FIGURE 9–1. The Relationship between Change and Tension

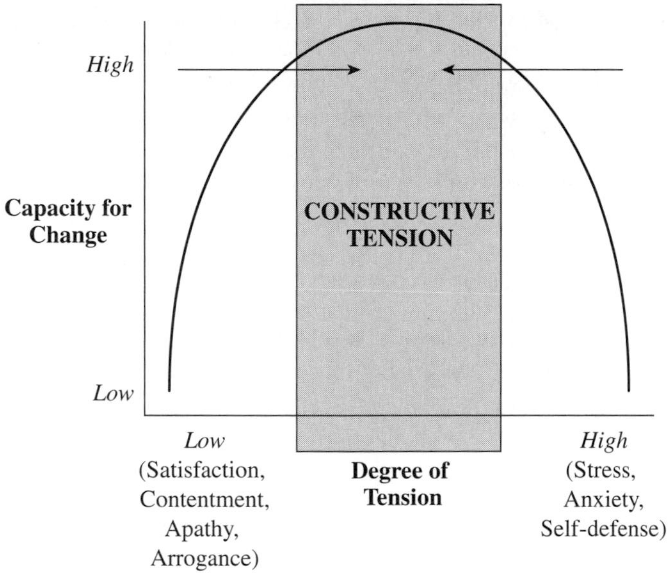

How can one "heat things up," increase the tension so that it becomes constructive? The ways of doing this fall into various categories:

1. Through *sharing information top-down,* information that increases the worry level so that it is easier to mobilize change. This may focus on external information (benchmarking, customer contacts, measurement, competitive analysis) or on internal information (opinion surveys, management-by-wandering-around, 360° appraisal). To create constructive tension, it is important that the information is worked through into understanding.
2. Through sharing *information laterally* (cross-functional or cross-border teamwork, quality circles, e-mail).
3. Through *mobility* (bringing in new people who see problems with new eyes).
4. Through *goal setting,* accompanied by performance management (appraisal, incentives, and rewards).

---

formation would not have been successful if it had not been for the more involving style of his successor, David Simon (see later box on the BP story).

Should change be *planned or is it emergent?* While the focus of the change literature is on planned change, change can also successfully occur by allowing variety, tracking natural experiments, and then selecting and building on potential winners—in fact this is one of the building block ideas in global knowledge management, as we will see later. Many other tensions were identified at the Harvard conference and by other scholars.[10]

One of the biggest tensions in change is the conflict between *the short and long term.* A basic law of change is that there is always a cost to change—when you engage in organizational change, performance will go down before it goes up. Or to put it in another way, you are always better off in the short term by not changing, by simply doing better what you did yesterday. And one can see where this path leads— to the "failure of success,"[11] to a situation in which change will occur only through crisis.

This handicaps research on complex change processes. It means that it is difficult to evaluate the success or failure of a change process, since a perceived failure at one time may be regarded later as a success. The remarkably successful transformation of BP between 1990 and 1996 was evaluated as a dismal failure two years into the process (see the box "Transformational Change at BP"). Similarly, "Neutron Jack" came under heavy fire from the press and commentators in the 1980s for the havoc that he was wreaking on GE. At the time of writing, ABB's management team and HP's Carly Fiorina are under heavy public fire for attempting to take their firms beyond the transnational model.[12]

Transformational Change at BP
Practice Box

BP's transformation during the 1990s is less well known than the GE story under Welch, but it is perhaps the European equivalent. It was initiated by Robert Horton, a tough-nosed and independently wealthy British career manager at BP who had sorted out the mess in the U.S. affiliate after BP had acquired control over SOHIO. Horton was appointed chairman in 1990, at a time when BP was profitable, though in the second league of the petrochemical firms—half the return on capital and efficiency of Exxon and Shell. Horton was convinced that BP would not exist as an independent firm in the year 2000 unless it underwent dramatic change. With hindsight he proved to be correct, but few people in the middle and senior ranks of BP agreed. Frustrated by the culture of decision-making by committee, Horton bypassed these conservatives, asking a group of young tigers to prepare a blueprint for BP in the future. It was a vision of a firm that could liberate the talent and enthusiasm of its people, responding positively to change rather than resisting it. It was presented to the executive group, who approved it at a weekend retreat. Project 1990, the transformation process, was launched.

The reactions of the top hundred people varied from open hostility to enthusiasm, from entrenched resistance to confusion. The drama was written up publicly in a series of articles in the *Financial Times*[A]— Horton had laid BP naked by inviting a sympathetic journalist in as "a fly on the wall" for three months. Our sources at BP told us that this was the chairman's personal decision. He knew that such a transformation would temporarily reduce profits and dividends. If the press reaction was not managed well, then shareholders would panic, dump their shares, and the board would have no alternative except to throw him out.

Horton, working closely with his HR people, who acted as change advisors, was convinced by the theory of change. Transformational change would not happen unless people at BP bought into Project 1990. How could commitment be built among 80,000 employees scattered around the world? They devised a two-year cascade process, in which the vision, template for change, and required competencies would spread down the organization. They recognized that it is difficult to build commitment without two-way dialogue, so the vision and values had to be allowed to change with each level in the cascade. At the fourth level in the cascade, people reacted by saying, "This is too complex . . . what you really mean is Teamwork, Openness, and Initiative, don't you?" Thus the vision

Longitudinal studies are required. One of the few such studies, a survey of nearly 500 of the largest enterprises in Europe, classified the types of change in terms of structure, processes, or boundaries.[13] The results support our arguments earlier that change must involve systemic realignment if it is to have positive outcomes.[14] Econometric analysis showed that only firms that changed structures, processes, and boundaries (less than 5 percent of the sample) enjoyed significant performance benefits (a performance premium of 60 percent). Enterprises that changed structures and boundaries without changing processes in fact paid a price for change, experiencing a decline in their performance.

The Future in the Present: Sequencing

The notion of sequencing helps us understand complex change processes. One of the rare studies of change processes in multinational organizations found four

Transformational Change at BP
Practice Box

was simplified and under way. It was a process that worked best in the tightly networked part of BP close to the U.K., including Europe and the former British colonies—out in Asia, this was felt to be very distant.

As anticipated, profits and dividends did decline, and in 1992 Robert Horton was forced out in a boardroom coup. But the major reason was antipathy to the aggressive and arrogant style of "Horton the hatchet." He was replaced by his COO, David Simon, equally committed to the vision but with a smoother, more diplomatic style.

Two years into the transformation, it was now labeled as a failure. BP was under attack—an icon of British management was being ruined. Even an authoritative source such as *The Economist* noted: "Since ousting its boss . . ., BP has insisted it will not change course. This could be a big mistake, for almost every aspect of the company's strategy has gone awry."[B]

However, BP did not waver in its transformational course. Simon was convinced that Horton was correct. He sold off more than $6 billion of peripheral businesses, downsizing the workforce by almost 50 percent (especially middle management) and narrowing BP's interest to its petrochemical core. By 1996,

results were better than those of their arch rival Shell. Share prices soared, and Simon's communication skills paid off in rebuilding BP internal morale. With its acquisition of Amoco in 1998, Horton's vision of becoming an admired "super major" rather than a candidate for takeover had been realized. A journalist specializing in knowledge management noted that bottom-line savings within two years of the merger of $700 million—just by reusing good ideas, sharing best practice, and accelerating learning—had earned BP a global reputation as the top moneymaker in knowledge management.[C]

Looking back on events, insiders within BP commented on the attack on Horton and his change strategy: "Without Horton it would never have happened. Without Simon, it would never have succeeded. As it turned out, we were lucky in the sequencing of leadership personalities."

[A]C. Lorenz, "A Drama behind Closed Doors That Paved the Way for a Corporate Metamorphosis," *Financial Times*, March 21, 1990; as well as subsequent feature articles.
[B]"BP after Horton," *The Economist*, July 4, 1992.
[C]T. Stewart, "Knowledge Management at Work: Telling Tales at BP Amoco," *Fortune*, June 7, 1999.

stages: *incubation* (questioning the status quo), *variety generation* (middle-up experimentation) leading to *power shifts* (change in the leadership structure), and then the more visible process of *refocusing*.[15] Doz observed the following:

> In the [16] cases we observed, strategic redirection was managed as a sequence of changes over time—changes being broken down in a series of relatively minor steps. Our observation runs contrary to the textbook view of redirection being achieved through rapid comprehensive restructuring. Restructuring—when it takes place (and it does not always do so)—is the consequence rather than the cause of redirection; it is imprinting an already achieved redirection into the permanent administrative infrastructure of the company.[16]

The idea of sequencing leads to the notion of stages. Most of the popular American models of change are linear. Kotter's eight-step framework is the most well-known example.[17] The starting point for another framework was the observation that corporate HR initiatives are rarely if ever successful in initiating change, leading to a six step "critical path."[18] However, most researchers are not convinced that successful change necessarily proceeds through such an invariable sequence of steps.[19] As at BP, some sequencing happens more by luck and circumstance than through deliberate planning. Often a long incubation period of experimentation precedes the visible sense of urgency, and one can argue that change will be excessively risky unless it builds on such experimentation and the confidence of sizeable coalitions of people who have been "fighting against the status quo" for many years.[20]

We have argued elsewhere that from a leadership perspective, sequencing in the management of change takes two different forms.[21] The first is *strategic layering,* a step-by-step process of building capabilities, rather like a staircase. The growth of Japanese firms in the 1970s is a well-known example, first exploiting cost advantages, then developing capabilities in quality, and then turning to invest in global brand image and distribution—all while maintaining earlier capabilities. This is most relevant to the development of transnational capabilities, since the locally responsive firm does not throw away the advantages of local orientation—it tries to build on these so as to develop the transnational capabilities of being *both* responsive and globally integrated.

Indeed, many change processes throw the proverbial baby out with the bath water. Instead of correcting the dangers of excessive focus at an early stage, the pendulum is allowed to swing to the extreme—leaders carry on doing what led them to be successful in the past, reinforcing their efforts when there are signs of problems.[22] The crisis brings in new leaders who then swing the pendulum to the other extreme, as is occurring at Coca-Cola at present.[23] Ejvind Myklebust, CEO of Norway's largest firm Norsk Hydro, told us how he avoids overreacting in the cyclical ups and downs of its natural resource–based industries (fertilizers, oil, and metals). "Over the years, I've learned how to cut off the bottoms of the cycles—and the tops—in my own mind."

Layering leads to a *spiral process* of change and development. To take an example, the management team recognizes the importance of developing functional excellence. But in the back of their minds they recognize that functional excellence can lead to pathologies if taken to the extreme—rivalry over resources and slow decision-making. At the first sign of such symptoms, attention turns to building integrated teamwork . . . but with the awareness that this can lead to group think, compromise, and lowered functional excellence if taken too far. The priorities shift back . . . and forth, gradually developing layers of complex dualistic competence that are difficult to imitate.

Indeed, many authorities on change believe that the spiral, in its virtuous or vicious forms, is a better image of change processes than those of transition or transformation or "changing A into B."[24]

A second and related facet of sequencing was discussed in earlier chapters, and we call this "building the future into the present" or *anticipatory sequencing.*[25] The management processes of today are designed not only with the needs of this year's operating plan in mind, but also with an eye to the inevitability of a future transition. One example is the capacity of successful turnaround managers initially to "take charge" in order to resolve the crisis, but with the next stage of "letting go" (reempowerment of the managers) in the back of their minds.[26] One also has to anticipate the downturn when still on the upturn. A negative example was Cisco's failure to anticipate the March 2000 crisis in the Internet industry. For such a sophisticated firm, the writing was on the wall by late December 1999, but because Cisco had never experienced a crisis there was a denial syndrome. The net result was being stuck with unnecessarily high inventories when the crisis hit three months later, deepening the necessity for severe layoffs and drastic action.

We have met numerous examples of anticipatory sequencing in this book. In terms of centralization-decentralization, the idea of "organizing-one-way-but-managing-the-other-way" is an example—when one is centralizing, the necessity of maintaining local entrepreneurship should constantly be borne in mind. In this way pendulum processes are more smoothly managed through steering. Expatriates are sent abroad because they have skills that are not available locally; but these expatriates are asked to pay attention to localization, to make their expatriate jobs unnecessary in the future. The initial staffing of projects must anticipate later stages to ensure that future project leaders are incorporated in the initial team, thereby minimizing the risk of expensive transition problems.

Anticipatory sequencing is essential to the art of steering, the third face of HRM.[27] The metaphor of the navigator builds on this, anticipating changes in current and wind, steering toward the goal in controlled curves rather than the disastrous straight line. There is emerging empirical evidence that as the pace of competitive change speeds up, anticipatory orientation to change becomes more essential. This is one of the major observations of Eisenhardt and Brown in their studies of high velocity business environments in which survival means operating "on the edge of chaos."[28] In such environments, such as microcomputers and internet development, "semi-structures" are needed (clear priorities, deadlines, defined responsibilities), but they should never be so rigid or orderly that they stifle the capacity for improvisation (informal communication, some flexibility in the use of budgets). Building a successful company in this type of fast changing environment involves developing the capacity to steer between order and chaos, just as the transnational enterprise has to steer between local and global.

Different Starting Points: Path Dependency

The last general observation is that complex change processes depend on the starting point. In organizational theory, this is known as *path dependency*—one cannot ignore the history of a firm in assessing the change route it should take. For example, faced with the necessity to respond to a change in basic technology, an enterprise that is thriving on the previous technology is likely to respond in a different way from an enterprise that is already in a state of crisis.[29] Indeed, change is an area where content, context, and process intermingle, as Pettigrew and other contextualists have pointed out.[30] To give another example, there are good reasons why processes of change are slower and more cautious in the consensus-oriented culture of the cement industry than in telecommunications. In the cement industry, the company lives for the next twenty years with the consequences of a poor investment decision; in fast moving telecoms, on the other hand, if decisions are not taken quickly then the company may miss the three-month window of strategic opportunity.

The context and orientation of change for corporations with a heritage of local responsiveness is quite different from those whose starting point is global integration, while the global professional service firm confronts other change dilemmas. Consequently, we will discuss these change paths and dilemmas in "going transnational" separately in this chapter.

THE PATHS TO TRANSNATIONAL DEVELOPMENT

In the tortuous route to transnational development, the multidomestic firm, the globally integrated enterprise, and the knowledge-based professional firm take different sequenced paths. The focus of these paths is respectively on global rationalization, stimulating local entrepreneurship and the transfer of capabilities, and the development of capabilities in global knowledge management.

The Multidomestic Organization: Focus on Global Rationalization

Let us start with the change path of the organization that has successfully grown through a multidomestic strategy of local responsiveness. Typically it now finds that competitive forces demand a greater degree of global integration for further growth, indeed survival. The multidomestic firm risks duplicating projects and initiatives. Cost-conscious local affiliates do not invest adequate resources in new projects. Its slowness in leveraging knowledge means that the firm is becoming unresponsive, and greater standardization of processes is needed. Consolidation across boundaries of multiple small-scale manufacturing facilities or engineering facilities around the world is required to lower costs and speed up technology change. Time-based competition pushes strategic integration of development and marketing processes so as to speed up time to market across the world.

This is the situation for many firms in industries such as consumer products[31]—Johnson Wax, Johnson & Johnson, Best Foods (now acquired by Unilever), and Pfizer Pharmaceuticals would be among the myriad examples. This is also the case for firms in other industries that successfully grew through a market-oriented approach, now finding that their technologies are changing (Kodak and Philips in the 1980s; or the book and music industries today with the revolutionary impact of Internet distribution). In the case of the "instant transnational," clear anticipatory sequencing may be necessary. Otherwise it may fall into Oracle's trap when in the early 1990s its initially successful individualistic and entrepreneurial culture went into a crisis because of duplication and lack of teamwork. Oracle survived . . . but that may not be the case for other high tech firms in today's competitive global environment.

If a senior executive or the top human resource officer of a corporation in this situation were asked for advice on an appropriate change strategy, how should she or he respond? To our knowledge, there is no empirical research on the issue, though Ghoshal and Bartlett suggest plausibly that there are successful and less successful sequences of steps.[32] Their model of the change process is shown in Figure 9–2.

In their analysis of the transnational organization, Ghoshal and Bartlett return to the simple observation that the performance of a complex corporation depends on two basic capabilities: the quality of performance of the individual units (subsidiaries, businesses, countries) and the quality of integration or coordination across those units. These are the two axes in Figure 9–2. Most multidomestic companies face a portfolio of subsidiaries at different starting points, located in different quadrants of the Figure, though mostly somewhere in quadrant 1 in a state of satisfactory underperformance. There may be a few strongly performing units that may jealously guard the independence that their results provide (quadrant 2). In the multidomestic firm, there is also clearly a lack of linkage, leverage, and coordination across these units.

FIGURE 9–2. Change Paths in Moving from Multidomestic Organization to Transnational

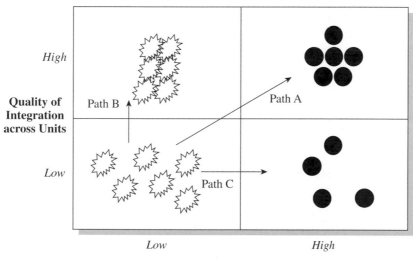

Source: S. Ghoshal and C. A. Bartlett, *Managing across Borders: The Transnational Solution,* 2d ed. (London: Random House, 1998).

The direct transformational route to quadrant 4 in Figure 9–2—high unit performance and high integration—may be appealing. But the researchers suggest that this is misleading, drawing on cases such as GM and IBM, which unsuccessfully attempted to follow this path in the 1980s. The contradictions are too complex, resulting in confusion. Managers join project groups and share know-how, and then they are punished because the performance of their units is not adequate. Ghoshal and Bartlett argue that a sequenced process of change is more effective.

The sequenced path in which the firm initially pursues synergies/integration, assuming that this will improve the performance of subsidiaries, is one such focused path. Companies such as Philips and Daimler-Benz have pursued this route, to their detriment. It is difficult to integrate operations that are struggling with their own individual performance problems. Ghoshal and Bartlett note that Philips managers concluded skeptically that "four drunks do not make an effective team."[33] Others have argued cogently that the attempt to pursue synergies typically does not succeed under these circumstances—in fact, this is one of the reasons why "synergy" has become a concept full of disappointment.[34]

The change path that is likely to be most successful is to focus first on the "sour" and then on the "sweet."[35] Global *rationalization* is the initial step. GE is an example, as was ABB in the period after the merger between Asea and Brown Boveri. Welch's initial change strategy focused on improving the performance of each business so that it would be "number one or number two" in its industry, with clear accountability for results and common performance processes.[36] The phase of rationalization was then followed by *revitalization* (as Ghoshal and Bartlett call it). Now the theme was integration—breaking down the boundaries between these units, fostering know-how sharing and best practice management. Ghoshal and Bartlett argue that this leads to a third stage that they call *regeneration*. For example, GE employees are challenged to enter the e-business world via an initiative that Welch calls *destroyyourbusiness.com*. In so doing, "Welch is trying to develop an organization with the ability to balance the tensions and management paradoxes implicit in each unit's drive to achieve superior individual performance while simultaneously collaborating with other units to leverage the organizationwide benefits of integration."[37] As discussed before, firms such as ABB, HP, and Citibank are going beyond the transnational by introducing front-end/back-end organizations that test the limits of the coordination capabilities that they have developed.[38]

Broader Implications for HRM: Managing the Sweet and Sour

The HRM movement was born in the 1960s and 70s out of a need to umbrella exciting and positive methods—planned organizational change, workforce involvement and QWL (the quality of working life movement), team building, quality management, and the like.[39] HRM focused on the "sweet." When HR managers had to focus on the "sour," assuming responsibility for downsizing and restructuring in the 1980s and 1990s, it was with a sense of taking a step backward.

A different orientation is required and to some extent has taken shape. In managing human resources, the sour has to be anticipated during the sweet times. And the sweet has to be anticipated during the sour times. Apple Computers painfully learned the first of these two lessons. After heady years of growth in the early 1980s, scrambling to bring new bodies on board to fuel 60 percent annual growth rates, Apple was hit by IBM which entered this emerging personal computer market. The pain of laying off people taught Apple the lesson. Its approach to financial management and HRM became conservative. Apple learned to depreciate investments within a year in the good times so as to build a cash pool that would save them in the bad times ahead. Recruitment became more selective, guided by a new value system that emphasized that the downturn might be just around the corner.[40] This is a lesson that Asian HR managers are only now learning painfully. In our work in Asia in the early and mid-1990s, we found that local HR managers ignored our pleas to pay more rigorous attention to selection and to the many low performing managers who had been relegated to what the Japanese call "window watcher" positions. These problems caught up with the firms when the Asian crisis hit with a vengeance. Rigor in performance management is essential.

The opposite reasoning also applies—keeping in mind the future "sweet times" at the moment of tough downsizing decisions. Undertaken poorly, layoffs can undermine (sometimes irrevocably) commitment and loyalty of the survivors for the long-term future. Careful attention has to be paid to communication so as to avoid the risk of what is called "the dirty dozen"—loss of trust, resistance to change, lack of teamwork, etc.[41] Returning to the example of Apple Computers, a plant manager in Ireland learned about the closure of his plant through the press, at the same time as the workforce. Seven years on, the story was still being told around European affiliates to show that you can never trust management.

The Globally Integrated Meganational: Focus on Transferring Capabilities

Let us turn now to the different change path of the organization that has successfully grown through a meganational strategy of global integration. The mother culture dominates the company. The capabilities are located in the parent country. Competitive forces mean that a higher degree of local responsiveness is necessary for further growth, however, as is the case for many Japanese and German corporations for which localization has become a survival issue. Former emerging markets to which goods were exported are now sophisticated markets with innovative local competitors. R&D, with its complex interdependencies between disciplines and functions, can no longer be located solely in the headquarters country. Lead countries need their own R&D centers, and the relevant countries may vary from one business area to another.

How should the firm respond? We focus on two aspects of the change process—encouraging entrepreneurship in subsidiaries and transferring complex capabilities from the center to local units. Both of these have to do with fostering the capacity for innovation that the meganational needs.

Encouraging Subsidiary Initiative

Firms are increasingly dependent on local entrepreneurship. They become aware that strategic innovations originate less and less frequently at the center and more often in some lead market elsewhere. Localization is one basic precondition.[42] A solid track record in fulfilling the parent mandate (good HR foundations and performance management) may be another precondition for entrepreneurial initiative.

A recent study of twenty-eight subsidiaries of multinational corporations in Ireland attempted to map out the stages whereby subsidiaries gradually take initiative so as to become fully-fledged strategic centers within that multinational.[43] Foreign affiliates are seen as going through eight stages from start-up. Their challenge at the early stages focuses on fulfilling the subsidiary mandate in a superior way. This allows the subsidiary to take initiatives—a product development opportunity, or an opportunity to take responsibility for expanding into a third market of marginal concern to the parent. If these initiatives are successful, the subsidiary gradually assumes greater strategic importance in the eyes of the parent. In time it may become a strategic center, and ultimately the worldwide apex for a business. What is critical in this path is the ability of the subsidiary to take developmental initiative at the same time as it defends its credibility through solid performance on its core mandate.

What has also changed during the last decade is that subsidiary initiatives, previously discouraged, are now encouraged. As we move from the era of international expansion to one of international liberalism and knowledge management, there is more recognition that creative and innovative ideas are as likely to be developed at the edge of the corporation as at its center.[44]

There are a number of implications for HRM:

Valuing diversity: One of the broadest implications is that we have to learn to value diversity rather than suppress it.[45] To a great extent, diversity is the mother of invention. As Hewlett-Packard's CEO Carly Fiorina puts it: "We need to recognize the value in diversity. Not everyone must be the same. To build great teams, we need to encourage differences. As a nation, industry, and company, we must start valuing differences. . . . This isn't just the business issue *du jour*—it's a strategic business imperative. . . . Diversity drives creativity, and creativity is at the heart of invention."[46]

Competencies: The criteria for local recruitment need to favor initiative. This has historically been a major concern in some regions of the world such as China, Japan, and Russia, where the political regime or the culture has discouraged initiative. Japanese enterprises are particularly handicapped since their leadership development practices do not foster individual initiative—entrepreneurial locals are unlikely to tolerate the rigorous but slow process of socialization in Japanese firms.[47]

Localization of staff and impatriation of locals are important steps on this route. Bartlett and Ghoshal argue that senior managers in local subsidiaries need to be especially selected and groomed for their qualities of entrepreneurship.[48] Their roles should focus on creating and pursuing opportunities, attracting scarce skills and resources, and managing continuous improvement. This requires the selection and development of appropriate experience and skills. (Return to chapter 8 to Figure 8–5 for a description of this.)

Networking: Local entrepreneurs need a high degree of social capital (networks of relationships) within their organizations, as discussed later in this chapter. There are at least three reasons for this: first, to defend their initiatives against interference; second, to be able to draw on corporate resources and support; and third, to ensure that successful initiatives are leveraged by the corporation rather than leading to local fiefdoms.[49]

International mobility: A delicate balance needs to be maintained with respect to international mobility. International experience develops networks and necessary global mindset; but excessive mobility among senior local managers may be detrimental to entrepreneurship. Delany found that a key factor in raising the ambition of the subsidiary was the tenure of the general manager. Identifying with the subsidiary for their personal fulfillment, general managers had been there for an average of twelve years, with an average of over six years as general manager—a long time in comparison to typical multinational assignments.[50] On the other hand, this creates new tensions. The development pipeline up through subsidiaries gets blocked; and after too many years in a post, the career and renewal prospects for local general managers may be limited.

Competencies of business area and regional managers: While entrepreneurship is required on the part of local managers, a different set of skills is required by more senior business area and country or regional managers, as shown in Figure 9–3.[51] They become strategic coaches. One of their important roles is to exercise judgement in balancing the priority for short-term operational results with sufficient budgetary and resource freedom to pursue new ideas and opportunities. Regional and business managers need to support entrepreneurial initiatives, exercising a delicate balance between control and freedom. Sometimes incubator subsidiaries need to be allowed a free rein. In the transnational firm, progression up the hierarchy becomes less predicable (more intransitive)—the best local entrepreneur will probably not be the best business area coach.[52]

Managing the Transfer of Capabilities across Boundaries

For product- or technology-driven companies, a big challenge is transferring capabilities that were once located in the parent country to appropriate lead countries in different regions of the world and then building the necessary coordination between these multiple centers. Transfer is not a simple technical matter, however, since it involves learning and adapting to a new context.[53] Such capabilities are difficult to transfer because of their complexity—a capability is a firm-specific, interwoven configuration of skills, in which it is impossible to separate the HR elements from the technical or managerial elements (see box "What Is an Organizational Capability?").

The capabilities of the globally integrated meganational firm will be located in the parent country, where they can be carefully nurtured. Toyota's production capabilities were all located in Japan; Hewlett-Packard's product development capabilities were centered in the Silicon Valley. With transnational pressures, localization means localization of capabilities, not just people, roles, or technology—transferring

What Is an Organizational Capability?
Research Box

We have used the term "organizational capability" in passing throughout the book, a term that is used widely in different ways. Entire books have been written on the topic without ever providing any definition.[A] The term usually refers to (i) a whole configuration of skills (technical, physical, human, and managerial) that (ii) is firm specific and therefore difficult to imitate, which (iii) is a source of competitive advantage for the firm, and that (iv) is typically built up slowly over the years through iterative experimentation and performance feedback.

With the acceleration of change, the term and related concepts came into widespread usage in the late 80s as it became clear, for example, that it was not products, more and more ephemeral, that provide competitive advantage but underlying capabilities—in, say, product development. In the shape of "core competencies," Hamel and Prahalad's work

accelerated popular usage of the term.[B] Examples of capabilities would be Toyota's capability in production technology, American Express's capability in mass processing of data, and IBM's capabilities in marketing.

What is particularly important from the HR standpoint is that the capability is a complex bundling or configuration of various elements, developed over time through a continual process of problem solving, experimentation, importation of new knowledge from the outside, all carefully integrated. This step-by-step process is well described in the story of the development of Toyota's production technology during a fifty-year period after World War II, driven by the idea of developing a technology for making small series of automobiles at low cost and high quality (in contrast to the prevailing Ford assembly line technology favoring big series).[C]

a *holistic infrastructure of skills* to a country or region where significant future growth prospects are expected.

Given the holistic nature of a capability, the devil is in the details. As a former director of research for IBM put it, "It is hard to transfer the full complexity of a technology. . . . If the receptor knows very little, he can do very little with even a simple idea, because he cannot generate the mass of detail that is required to put it into execution. On the other hand, if he knows a great deal and is capable of generating the necessary details, then from just a few sentences or pieces of technology he will fill in all the rest. That is why it is hard to transfer technology to the Third World and very hard not to transfer it to Japan."[54]

Let us take the example of a hitherto globally integrated company with its capabilities in production development rooted in Silicon Valley. It foresees that Asian markets will be important in the future and wishes to transfer its capabilities to Shanghai or to Singapore. This process of transferring that production development capability will be a sequenced process of change, which can be facilitated by bearing in mind the future sequences at each preceding stage. In so doing, the effectiveness of the process can be greatly increased. The time that it takes to build a local center of capability that is globally integrated can perhaps be halved or quartered through anticipatory sequencing.

This can be illustrated with the sequenced stages in the transfer of Hewlett-Packard's printing business from California to Singapore, a process that took

What Is an Organizational Capability?
Research Box

One cannot separate the physical system from the approach to compensation, or the managerial philosophy from the training methodologies. A capability is holistic, which means that a narrow functional attitude toward HR basics is quite inappropriate. HR factors cannot be separated from other factors. Leonard breaks down these interdependent elements into physical systems, managerial systems, skills and knowledge, and values, all linked together by an experimental, learning, problem-solving culture of continuous improvement.[D] Except at the level of HR foundations, the idea of an "HR capability" is a misnomer since it implies that HR can be divorced from the wider context.

There is one other important point to mention concerning organizational capabilities. All is not rosy! Having such a capability does not guarantee the success of the firm for the indefinite future. As Leonard has pointed out, the paradox of capabilities is that they bring rigidity to the organization.[E] When technology or market changes threaten a firm with strong capabilities, it is likely to be slow to adjust since its whole identity is called into question. As Hewlett-Packard's former CEO Lew Platt noted, "We have to be willing to cannibalize what we're doing today in order to ensure our leadership in the future. It's counter to human nature but you have to kill your business while it is still working."

[A]The concept of *organizational capability* has its origins in the work of the sociologist Philip Selznick, who assessed the "distinctive competence" of the Tennessee Valley Authority (Selznick, 1957). It was later refined in the notion of interdependent organizational routines (Nelson and Winter, 1982).
[B]Hamel and Prahalad, 1994.
[C]Womack and Jones, 1991.
[D]Leonard, 1995.
[E]Leonard, 1992.

---

nearly thirty years (see the box "How Singapore Became HP's Global Center of Competence for Printers").[55] Other empirical research confirms that the breadth, depth, and speed of technological transfer across international borders are significantly enhanced by the coordination mechanisms discussed earlier—the use of cross-border teams, the formal analysis of successful and failed projects, and the like.[56]

WILL DOMESTIC EXPERIENCE BECOME A HANDICAP? With heightened anticipation and an understanding of the step-by-step sequencing process, Hewlett-Packard might today shorten the thirty years it took to transfer these capabilities from the parent to Singapore to five or ten years. But what about the "instant transnational," created with global operations in mind and free of the legacy of parenthood in the mother country?

Firms that are newly created are not prisoners of their own heritage, and there may be a learning advantage to newness.[57] Enterprises such as Business Objects have the potential advantage of internationalizing from birth and anticipating the tensions.[58] Indeed, a recent study of fifty-seven electronics firms in Finland shows empirically that firms which internationalize early are likely to grow faster overall and in foreign markets.[59] This was particularly true for firms dependent on technological knowledge. On the other hand, enterprises with a long domestic history face considerable difficulty in confronting the tensions of international growth.

How Singapore Became HP's Global Center of Competence for Printers
Practice Box

What started as an assembly outpost in Singapore in the early 1970s ultimately took over global responsibility for HP's computer printers. The story illustrates the gradual transfer of organizational capabilities from the mother company HQ to the subsidiary.[A] Let us outline the HRM challenges at each of these stages:

Stage 1: With HP-Singapore, this was the start-up phase of *assembly operations,* when there was maximum dependence on the mother country. The HRM challenges at this stage are those of the first facet, "basic foundations"[B]—skill training and retention management; managerial and supervisory development; inculcation of basic values such as maintenance ethics, integrity, and safety.

Stage 2: Here the Singapore subsidiary earned an extension of its mandate to *cover adaptation of the product to local markets,* leading to full-scale manufacturing. Now the HRM challenges shift to the development of competencies in local suppliers. A greater degree of discipline must be instilled (also in supplier firms) in areas such as quality management, responsibility, cooperation, and weeding out poor performers.

Stage 3: The subsidiary now begins to seek the right to redesign systems (in this case printers) for local markets such as Japan. This is a critical step in the development of subsidiary competence when there are maximum pressures for local autonomy, which may in some cases be refused. Successful passage through this stage depends on the local development of complex managerial-technical capacities through advanced education of locals (at universities in the parent country), projects, best practice

sharing, and personnel transfers. Unless a strong sense of local initiative has been inculcated, together with a high degree of normative integration (selection and development based on shared values), it is not certain that this stage will be successful. Indeed, HP-Singapore experienced various setbacks at this stage that led the parent to question their competencies, though one can argue that failure is a necessary element of such learning.[C]

Stage 4: Now the subsidiary assumes full responsibility for product design, becoming a global center of competence with peer relationships between the parent and subsidiary. In the transition to this stage, HR attention should be focused on global projects that build reverse transfer competencies (from the subsidiary to the HQ), on developing matrix roles and responsibilities, on associated relationship building, and on transfers (the coordination technology discussed in Chapters 7 and 8). Leonard notes that firms currently tend to be much more skilled in transferring capabilities OUT from the center, and the challenge is one of transferring them back from the affiliates INTO the center. This fourth stage also involves the redesign of project architecture (HP moved from a functional/component project structure to one in which the parent R&D was responsible for the outside design while Singapore took the full responsibility for the inside of the printer).

[A]The HP Singapore story is used by Leonard to illustrate the process of transfer of capabilities from the home country abroad (Leonard, 1995; Leonard-Barton and Conner, 1996).
[B]This first of the three faces of HRM is described in Chapter 2.
[C]Leonard-Barton and Conner, 1996.

The International Professional Service Firm: Focus on Global Knowledge Management

As professional service firms (PSFs) internationalize they experience a great deal of tension. Consider recent upheavals among the "Big Five" global players. There has been the messy divorce within Arthur Andersen, KPMG recently sold a fifth of its consulting arm to Cisco Systems, Ernst & Young sold its consulting business to

France's Cap Gemini, and PWC is considering splitting up into two or three different companies. Earlier HRM research questioned whether there was sufficient "glue" to hold such firms together—and events seem to be justifying this view.[60] Indeed, partly because of their complex matrices, PSFs are an excellent arena for studying the tensions of international organizational development (see box "Tensions in the Professional Service Firm").

Professional service firms (PSFs) are different from capital-intensive or labor-intensive organizations in that they are based on knowledge management.[61] The PSF sells something intangible—not a product, but a promise or expectation. Professions have long been defined in terms of vocations founded on bodies of knowledge and the application of that knowledge.[62] Earlier the focus was on self-regulating liberal professions such as doctors and lawyers, with their codes of ethics policed by a peer review system. But with the transition to a more knowledge-based society, we have witnessed a phenomenal growth in commercial professional service firms in the developed world. This covers management, engineering, and technology consultancies, accounting firms (some of which cut across many professional sectors), investment banks, advertising agencies, marketing and PR services, personnel and HR services, suppliers of software, systems design, industrial design, graphics . . . and the list continues to broaden.

To Internationalize or Not?

The path to transnational development in a professional service firm seems to take a different trajectory from capital- or labor-intensive firms, although there has been little research on this. The question of whether to internationalize or not and how fast to grow globally is the subject of hot debate within such firms, from consultants to legal firms to advertising agencies. The pros and cons are typically complex.[63] On the one hand, there may be pressures in certain sectors such as auditing, insurance, and advertising to globalize so as to service global clients. There may also be significant economies of scale in back office costs and expertise that grow more important with the development of IT. Yet on the other hand, clients are often indifferent as to whether or not the PSF is global—what counts is the reputation and quality of the local partner. In the former Big Eight and now Big Five, there may be distinctive advantages to internationalization in audit that are less obvious in the consulting branch, leading to divisive splits within the firm on strategy. Among law firms, internationalization is the hot issue. Should they expand abroad, following their clients, or should they stay at home?[64]

Indeed the complexities of global organization in a knowledge-based firm may outweigh the advantages. Unless the firm has a solid grasp on the management/organizational dilemmas mentioned in the box "Tensions in the Professional Service Firm," the distractions of "organizational politics" may take away attention from client work and intellectual investment, handicapping the recruitment and retention of outstanding professionals. There is probably no other sector in which it is more vital to have solid foundations in HR before tackling the challenges of internationalization.

One experienced observer of the PSF, David Maister, reinforces the importance of rigor, notably in HRM. He asks, What is the common element among the

Tensions in the Professional Service Firm
Research Box

The dilemmas that PSFs experience may be manageable while the firm is small and focused. But they become overt in large international firms. One such dilemma is how standards and procedures can be applied to an organization focused on customized problem solving (typically PSFs use socialization mechanisms to ensure internalization of standards). A widespread dilemma is how to organize the tasks of management and leadership in a culture which values knowledge and expertise, where management is often a part-time task undertaken in evenings and over weekends, akin to "herding cats." In such an expertise-based culture, the problem of systemic underdelegation is rife.[A]

The latter dilemma leads to a paradox—while the quality of HRM is vital to the PSF since it has no other assets than its people, this tends to get neglected. HRM practices—be it in recruitment, staffing, performance management, development, or compensation—are far more critical to the firm than in capital- or labor-intensive organizations. While there may be a professional HR support function in larger firms, these decisions are so important that they are always the responsibility of managers and partners themselves. Yet these managers are often torn between their professional roles and their managerial roles.

To some degree or another, all PSFs have to figure out how to exploit and explore at the same time. They have to create new knowledge from the ongoing services that they provide to clients. This in turn leads to further dilemmas. For example, how can one persuade the best professionals to make their learning available to be leveraged by others? How can one persuade clients to pay handsome fees for the learning of the consultants, to be applied elsewhere—often to their competitors?

Matrix Tensions

All but the simplest professional service firms are heavily matrixed—with practice areas of skill or know-how, functional distinctions between client/delivery

most admired and profitable professional service firms, which all happen to be global in their reach—Goldman Sachs in investment banking, McKinsey in consulting, Arthur Andersen in accounting, Hewitt Associates in compensation and benefits, and the lawyers Latham & Watkins? He sees the common denominator as a rigorous and internally consistent approach to management, and above all to human resource management, that has been fine-tuned over the years. Clients and engagements may vary from one country to another, but what Maister calls "a one-firm firm philosophy" applies across the world:

> All of its practices, from recruitment through compensation, performance appraisal, approaches to market, governance, control systems, and above all, culture and human resource strategy, make for a consistent whole.[65]

The phrase "one-firm firm" may seem strange to those who are not acquainted with the professional service sector, though its significance is obvious to most people in PSFs. The natural route to internationalization is the federation of otherwise independent firms. Analogous to a limited form of multidomestic organization, it captures some advantages (client referrals and perhaps some exchange of best practice). The PSF that constitutes a single global firm, especially in terms of its management practices, has been the exception rather than the rule.

Tensions in the Professional Service Firm
Research Box

roles and development/research roles, and the front and back office support dimension. Geographic diversification multiplies the complexity—local offices, countries, regions. Even management work versus client/know-how work can be regarded as a matrix distinction in a PSF. Clearly it is utopian to manage all these boundaries well.[B] PSFs live with inevitable tensions within such matrices.

The strategy formulation-implementation dichotomy makes no sense in such firms. Local professionals simply ignore expounded strategy if they do not agree, as long as their own local projects are doing well. Strategy in the PSF is not so much grand vision or strategic intent—it is more about building consensus on the need to shift priorities within the matrix, as well as finding new ways of creatively managing across boundaries. The important strategic steering mechanism in a PSF is consensus on the priorities. *It is priorities and not plans that steer the professional service firm.*[C] And building such con-

sensus takes time. Most senior professionals and managers in PSFs live with an uneasy tension between client or practice demands on their time and incessant internal meetings, taskforces, and corridor discussions.

[A]Maister, 1993. Our own research shows that underdelegation is a major problem in expertise-based organizations (Evans, 1992). If your authority is based on your expertise, then you should never delegate anything important—otherwise subordinates will develop expertise that you do not have, and you will feel more and more uncomfortable!

[B]A federal international structure may be attractive since it tries to manage only one boundary globally, namely the client boundary through referrals. It may try to leverage on an ad hoc basis other boundaries, for example setting up an international development think tank to develop common know-how in a specific domain.

[C]The point is well made by Loewendahl (1997) in her international study of PSFs.

Alternative Paths to Global Knowledge Management

We use the PSF to introduce the theme of global knowledge management. This is particularly important to the PSF since it has no other assets than its people and their individual and collective know-how. Indeed, PSFs have pioneered many of the developments in this emerging domain.

There appear to be three different approaches to knowledge management in order to manage the transfer of know-how across the complex matrix boundaries of the firm (the complexity of the matrix in the PSF is described in the box "Tensions in the Professional Service Firm"). These approaches reflect different configurations of strategic focus and management orientation, and they are called *client-driven, creative problem-solving,* and *solution adaptation,* respectively.[66] Each is characterized by a different orientation to human resource management practices (see the box "Configurations in the Professional Service Firm and Their HR Implications").

AD HOC KNOWLEDGE MANAGEMENT IN THE CLIENT-DRIVEN PSF. In the first and most traditional configuration the strategy is *client-driven.*[67] What the firm sells is its ability to help particular client groups in specific service areas such as legal

Configurations in the Professional Service Firm and Their HR Implications
Research Box

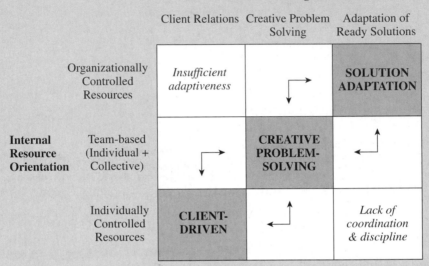

Source: Adapted from B. Lowendahl, *Strategic Management of Professional Service Firms* (Copenhagen: Copenhagen Business School Press, 1997).

The figure above suggests that there are three stable configurations of professional service firms (PSFs), based on the fit between external strategic orientation and internal resource orientation. The off-diagonal forms are inherently unstable.

The Client-Driven Configuration

This is the prototypical PSF. The expertise and power in the client-driven firm rests with the individual partner, who may even recommend other firms to the client so as to maintain credibility. The governance of

the firm is individualized—no decisions can be taken without the buy-in of client partners. Management and administration are primarily seen as overhead, and the coordination capability of the firm is limited.

The recruitment target in the client-driven firm is the mature professional with deep experience within a particular industry and strong generalist skills. The approach to human resource management is highly variable, depending on the client partner. How you get treated depends on whom you work for. This is the opposite of Maister's "one-firm firm." Training is also

advice, insurance brokerage, or compensation/benefits consulting. This ability is typically anchored in experienced client partners, what Maister calls "grey hair" as opposed to "brains" or "procedures." These individual partners who act as counsel to their clients have the power. Coordination, when required, is most likely to be managed by price mechanisms. If international expansion is necessary for client reasons, then this is likely to take the federation route.

In the international federation of partners, the approach to knowledge management is informal and ad hoc. Knowledge management takes place only when there

Configurations in the Professional Service Firm and Their HR Implications
Research Box

individualized (some might say erratic), through mentorship with senior client managers, varying with the skill of these partners. In appraisal, the performance criteria focus on client satisfaction, retention, chargeable hours, and the number of follow-on contracts with a given client.

The Creative Problem-Solving Configuration

What this firm sells is a credible promise to help a client solve a specific problem by means of the creative inputs of a team of professionals. The orientation of HRM will be a careful blend of individualism and teamwork. The creative problem solving firm will devote priority resources to recruiting talented people and then to socializing them into teamwork. After intensive HR marketing and screening of candidates, the chosen few are interviewed by five or more senior professionals and partners before any offer is made: one blackball and you do not get the job! MBA graduates are a perfect target since they like problem-solving, can tolerate ambiguity, are selected for their achievement and leadership talent, and yet must demonstrate team skills. Much of the training will be through personalized mentoring. A promotional system that is up-or-out, accompanied by generous salary raises for those who move ahead, is quite compatible with this orientation—as long as it is rigorously competency-based, and backed up by thorough and fair feedback/appraisal processes. At McKinsey the fairness of the counseling-out system means that former McKinsey staff later become their most loyal supporters as captains in their client firms. The attention that partners pay to appraisal at Goldman Sachs is legendary in that industry, collecting 360° views, data, and opinions, feeding it back and working it through, carefully balancing judgements on individual achievement and teamwork. Tremendous care has to be given to the design and administration of the compensation system, which must balance rewards for individual achievement with teamplaying.

The Solution-Adaptation Configuration

Here the firm sells a proven solution, where it has built up in-depth expertise. The growth of the firm comes from codifying and adding to that expertise in the solution area, as well as by expanding its portfolio of solutions.

The approach to HRM is correspondingly different. The recruitment target is the undergraduate student, often with an appropriate technical background. Training programs are highly structured and ongoing throughout the first part of the career. A prime example would be Andersen's training, starting for six months at their center near Chicago, where some weeding out of recruits will take place. Distance learning facilitates the training. Appraisal processes are more structured around global criteria, taking place every three months at Andersen; career paths and steps are similarly more structured. Overall, there is a higher degree of organizational control through the design of systems and procedures, including in the HR domain.

One cannot talk about a "best way" of managing human resources in a PSF. The approach which will be best is the one that is most consistent with the strategy.

are clearly visible synergies or benefits to client-oriented partners, using the basic coordination mechanisms of face-to-face relations, project groups, limited know-how transfer, and occasional internal boards.[68] Internal seminars may be used to share know-how on key clients and developments. Projects may be set up to ensure cooperation in service delivery if this is necessary. Strategies for attracting and retaining professionals may be developed, with mechanisms for some transfers and cross-assignments. The quality and quantity of knowledge transfer across borders is quite limited.

PERSONALIZATION IN THE CREATIVE PROBLEM SOLVING PSF. In the second consistent configuration, exemplified by McKinsey in consulting or Morgan in investment banking, the strategy focuses on *creative problem-solving*. The firm helps the client solve a specific problem by means of creative professional inputs, be this the challenge of designing an appropriate global structure (McKinsey) or negotiating an acquisition opportunity (Morgan or Goldman Sachs).

In order to manage boundaries, the approach to knowledge management is called "personalization."[69] Most of the knowledge in this firm is tacit rather than codified, anchored in people's brains. The knowledge management strategy focuses on developing networks to link people together so that this can be shared. Thus personalization means facilitating *connections*. The underlying IT infrastructure supports this through internal "Yellow Pages" directories.[70] Through this facilitated network, the manager of a potential engagement in Australia is able to draw on the experience of a specialist in Germany, obtain the part-time collaboration of someone from San Francisco, and draw on presentation material from New York. The incentive systems must reward sharing knowledge directly with other people. At Bain, partners are evaluated on a variety of dimensions, including how much help they have provided to colleagues, and this dimension alone can account for up to a quarter of the annual compensation.[71]

CODIFICATION IN THE SOLUTION ADAPTATION PSF. A different but equally consistent configuration is that of *solution adaptation,* as at Accenture (formerly Andersen Consulting) or in the audit/tax areas of the Big Five. Here what the company sells is a proven solution in a business system, an audit process, or a reengineering project, one that can be adapted to the particular circumstances of the client. The offering is more like a product than the open promise of the creative problem-solving firm, while still remaining knowledge/expertise based.

The growth of the firm comes in part from codifying and adding to its systematic expertise in that solution area, as well as by expanding its portfolio of solutions. Knowledge management is based on *codification* rather than personalized networks, leading to *collections* rather than connections.[72] There is a big investment in the IT infrastructure, focusing on an electronic document system that codifies, stores, and disseminates knowledge and experience. Creative problem solving projects may be set up to tackle new opportunities, formalizing the resulting know-how for reuse on other projects. Revenues for the firm are generated primarily from the economics of reuse rather than the economics of expertise.[73]

Tensions in the Growth of the International Professional Service Firm

These three configurations in PSFs are ideal types.[74] All professional service firms experience tensions between two or all three of these dimensions of client orientation, creative problem solving, and solution-oriented expertise. In the creative problem solving firm professionals will see advantages from global standardization and codification. They often seize such opportunities, splitting off so as to found their own solution-oriented firms. In the solution-oriented firm, "rainmakers" with strong client relationships may argue for more power, including discretion over their human resources. Again they may leave the firm so as to create their own client-oriented practices, taking disaffected professionals with them.[75]

It is difficult for any PSF to grow and deliver superior performance based on multiple strategies simultaneously. The Big Five have tried this, and one can see the tensions as they split up. The management and organizational challenges, especially if the growth is international, excessively tax the capacities of the firm.[76]

In the development of its worldwide knowledge management strategy, McKinsey itself experienced the tension between the pulls of codification and personalization, as mentioned in our opening case in this chapter. In the late 1980s they invested heavily in a computer-based documentation system, backed up by a new career path of specialist managers. But this never took hold, running counter to the strong mainstream culture. Come promotion time, no one reviewed what documents a person had submitted for incorporation in the database. The focus of attention remained on connections—how people had used their internal networks to develop ideas that make an impact on the client. As a senior McKinsey professional commented:

> By the early 1990s, too many people were seeing practice development as the creation of experts and the generation of documents in order to build our reputation. But knowledge is only valuable when it is between the ears of consultants and applied to clients' problems. Because it is less effectively developed through the disciplined work of a few than through the spontaneous interaction of many, we had to change the more structured "discover-codify-disseminate" model to a looser and more inclusive "engage-explore-apply-share" approach. In other words, we shifted our focus from developing knowledge to building individual and team capability.[77]

The challenge for the internationalizing PSF is thus to maintain consistency as it expands across borders, notably in its approach to the management of human resources. The more rapid the expansion, the more difficult this will be. For example, there may be a strong temptation in the creative problem solving firm to hire local client-oriented partners who are inexperienced in its complex appraisal practices, who regard these as alien to the customs of the local country, and who do not believe that this merits the attention of a senior professional. Local business schools may not supply the required talent, people who combine strong creative individualism with teamwork, and local partners may not see the justification for investing in socialization and training to make up for what the market does not supply. The pressure to expand may also lead to ill-advised acquisitions, especially if the technology of integration is not well understood.

WHAT ABOUT THE FUTURE? The internationalization of the professional service firm is a recent phenomena that will accelerate in the new century. We know enough from the past to be sure that one cannot extrapolate it into the future! In industrial firms, the "either/or" logic of consistency dominated thirty years ago. Successful industrial firms at that time had an administrative heritage that was typically either local or global, depending on the industry. The pressure to confront transnational contradiction was a product of global competition, accelerating in the 1980s and 1990s.[78]

We believe that the international service firm, currently best expanding internationally through a consistent strategy, will in the future face transnational pressures BOTH to be creative in its problem solving approach AND to accumulate, codify, and leverage its knowledge base. Global competition in professional services is at an early stage at present, although in some sectors such as advertising it is rapidly accelerating.

Thus the creative problem solving firm such as McKinsey may have to develop capabilities in codifying and levering knowledge. In sequencing, what is important is anticipation and timing. Consider McKinsey's failure to leverage existing know-how through codified practice development. This initiative in the 1980s was perhaps not so much wrong as *ill timed*. It distracted attention from the priority challenge of building personalized networks that were consistent with the orientation of the firm. In the future, with personalized networks in place and with increasing competition, such an initiative may well be appropriate so as to reinforce the global capabilities of the firm, leading to sequenced layering of capabilities.

For the time being, our understanding of global knowledge management is insufficient to handle this degree of complexity. This takes us to the next section of this chapter, where we explore these frontiers.

FRONTIERS FOR INTERNATIONAL HRM: INNOVATION AND KNOWLEDGE MANAGEMENT

Federico Castellanos, regional HR vice president for IBM in Europe, observes that in this new economy where all the profit on a laptop computer must be made within a month, where today's winners are often tomorrow's losers, where one has to rapidly acquire new skills as one converts or disbands those of yesterday, 70 percent of the challenges are people management—leadership, talent and knowledge management, and managing continuous change.

As we move into the twenty-first century, the emerging new territory for HRM is the stewardship of knowledge management and innovation, with an underlying concern for organizational learning.[79] There is an emerging concern, and not just in professional service firms, for creating an environment of flexibility, innovation, knowledge creation and transfer, and learning.[80]

Innovation and knowledge management are two sides of the same coin, and we shall discuss them together in this section. There are zillions of creative ideas that exist in the minds of people, but any revenue-generating innovation (be it an incremental improvement or a new technology)[81] is the result of the transfer of knowledge. Innovation is a social process. Indeed, studies of creative people show that they see their interactions with others as an essential part of creativity.[82] The steps to commercially viable innovation always involve the integration of different forms of knowledge (different technical or scientific strands, commercial and management know-how). In academic theory, this is known as "combinative ability."[83]

It is this integrative ability in recombination that underlies competitive advantage. Most theories of knowledge management, consequently, focus on knowledge transfer and integrative ability rather than on knowledge generation itself (see the box "The Theory of Knowledge Transfer"). It is the collaborative, integrative process of recombination and transfer that generates new know-how. This is particularly important with respect to complex tacit knowledge—the type of knowledge that is most valuable.[84]

Why Are Innovation and Knowledge Management So Important?

What was important in the past was the ability of firms in developed countries to exploit their knowledge abroad in less developed markets. Complex tacit knowledge

The Theory of Knowledge Transfer
Research Box

The theory of knowledge transfer holds that the flows of knowledge into or out of a subsidiary depend on five factors, which can act as facilitators or impediments:[A]

1. *The potential value of the source unit's knowledge.* Unique knowledge that is not duplicated elsewhere is of high value if it can find potential applications elsewhere, and if it is not causally ambiguous or unproven. But it is often difficult to define value, especially with respect to tacit knowledge. Some firms have identified specific capabilities that they wish to nurture, thereby identifying the knowledge that has potential value.[B] At GE, the Corporate Learning function plays a certification role, evaluating the value of practices or know-how. However, in most companies it is subsidiary managers who assess (albeit filtered through many cultural and judgmental biases) the value of knowledge in other parts of the firm via their own networks of relationships.[C]

2. *The motivation of the source.* Since valuable knowledge can be a source of power, there is a tendency for hoarding of knowledge which firms such as GE and consulting enterprises struggle to overcome. Alternatively, the source may lack credibility, making its knowledge suspect.

3. *The motivation of the recipient or target.* The "not-invented-here" syndrome may minimize incentives to acquire knowledge from others, either because of ego defense (blocking information that might suggest that others are more competent) or because of power struggles that lead managers to downplay the worth of the know-how of other units.

4. *The absorptive capacity of the recipient.* Individuals and units such as subsidiaries differ greatly in their "absorptive capacity"—the ability to recognize the value of new information, to assimilate it into their own different context, and to apply it to commercial ends. Absorptive capacity also includes the capacity to unlearn, to challenge existing ways of doing things. Lack of absorptive capacity is consistently found to be one of the most important factors that impedes the transfer of knowledge, making knowledge very "sticky".

5. *The existence and richness of transmission channels.* In order for knowledge to flow, there have to be communication or transmission channels—relationships, meetings, project groups, best practice seminars, the mobility of personnel.[D] Some channels are "narrow band," such as intranet systems or electronic communication, allowing only the transfer of information or codified knowledge. Others such as personnel transfers are "broadband," allowing the potential transfer of complex tacit know-how.

There is empirical evidence from recent studies in MNCs that all of these factors are important in knowledge transfer.[E]

[A]Szulanski, 1996; Gupta and Govindarajan, 2000.
[B]See Chapter 7, p. 325.
[C]Arvidsson has studied the phenomenon of how local managers judge the value of knowledge in other subsidiaries, focusing on marketing capability transfer between subsidiaries of multinational firms (Arvidsson, 1999). He finds that the credibility of HQ managers is low—local managers make judgments on the value of knowledge through their own networks of contacts.
[D]These are discussed in Chapter 7.
[E]See Gupta and Govindarajan (2000).

was transferred abroad in the shape of expatriates. In today's world of multiple sophisticated markets—from Singapore to San Francisco, from Shanghai to Berlin, from Sydney to Sao Paulo—it is increasingly the ability to generate and transfer knowledge from the local affiliate to the region or the parent, as well as between subsidiaries, that is the basis for competitive advantage. One study of innovation in multinational firms found that 66 percent of the innovations did not come from the parent company.[85]

The primary reason why MNCs exist is because of their ability to transfer and exploit knowledge more effectively and efficiently than market mechanisms. Among scholars, this is now generally accepted,[86] and studies suggest that the argument is becoming increasingly obvious to financial markets as well as to managers. One of the five "timeless principles" driving GE is the belief that "the ultimate sustainable competitive advantage lies in the ability to learn, to transfer that learning across components, and to act on it quickly." This drove GE to create a boundaryless company by delayering, destroying silos, purging "not-invented-here," and attempting to create an organization that sees change as an opportunity rather than as a threat.[87]

DISTANCE IS NOT DEAD. Just as the advent of the steamship and the telephone more than a hundred years ago heralded a new era of internationalization, so the e-revolution has contributed to globalization. E-mail, video-conferencing, computerized databases, and electronic forums have eliminated distance.

Or have they? Microsoft insists that its software and systems must work anywhere, anyplace, anytime. But why is Bill Gates equally insistent that all key employees at Microsoft be located not just in the United States but at Microsoft's sprawling "campus" at Redmond outside Seattle? Why does Cisco locate more than 15,000 people in similar buildings in crowded and expensive San Jose in the heart of the Silicon Valley? Why do these leading advocates of virtuality insist on co-location if distance is dead?

The answer is that while the e-revolution may have reduced the obstacle of distance with respect to *information* transfer, it has not changed things with respect to *knowledge.* Microsoft, Cisco, and other firms know full well that it is knowledge that is the source of their competitive strength, not information.[88]

Information and knowledge are two quite different concepts. There has been a fashionable but confusing relabeling of everything as "knowledge management" ("management information systems" become "knowledge management systems"). But it is vital to distinguish between the two. Knowledge is tacit and embedded in a context. Information is converted into knowledge through two-way dialogue, facilitated by shared language and norms. In this section, we will discuss *knowledge* management, which is a people or HRM technology—not information management, which is much more the domain of the IT specialists.

There are other reasons why knowledge management is important for HRM. The so-called talent war has reinforced its importance. Retaining people who do not believe in loyalty or careers becomes more and more difficult, excessively expensive. Instead of focusing exclusively on the retention of *people,* the focus is shifting to the retention of their *knowledge* (through connections or collections) and the transfer of that know-how to others.

Innovation is a closely related reason for being concerned with global knowledge management. According to William Coyne, SVP for Research and Development at 3M, "Most companies now recognize that the best way to increase corporate earnings is through top-line growth, and the best route to top-line growth is through innovation."[89] Many others agree. After two decades of restructuring and downsizing, with more prevailing rigor in performance management practices, the current and future challenge is value growth through innovation.

One 1999 survey claims that of the 1,000 largest enterprises in the world, only forty-one managed to grow profitably during the previous three years.[90] Kim and Mauborge's arguments are well known, advocating a focus on innovation. Studying more than 100 new business launches, they found that 86 percent were "me-too" launches or incremental improvements—these generated only 39 percent of profits. By contrast, the remaining 14 percent of launches that were genuinely innovative generated 38 percent of launch revenues and 61 percent of profits.[91]

Creating the Context for Global Innovation

Innovation is a journey, as Van de Van and other scholars have emphasized. It does not have a dependent variable like financial performance that can be tracked—it involves ideas, people, relations, and context, all of which change and reconfigure during the journey.[92] One cannot decree or control innovation and learning. All one can do is create a context where they are more likely to happen. As Louis Pasteur once said, "Chance favors a prepared mind." Innovation cannot be ordained, but it can be facilitated.

How does one create that context? A number of guiding principles emerge from research and practice.

Picking Winners—Encourage Diversity and Focus on Selection

As mentioned earlier when discussing subsidiary initiative, firms need to foster diversity and value entrepreneurship (which means not punishing legitimate mistakes and allowing some degree of slack). At 3M, a firm renowned for its track record on innovation, virtually all senior line managers have pioneered successful innovations, often having experienced dead ends along the way.

The firm should gear itself to recognizing the *promising* innovations, backing and supporting them with resources and attention. This basic idea is rooted in Weick's model of change with its parallel to Darwinian evolution. Weick argues that a firm should allow for a maximum of variation—natural, unplanned experimentation in its units.[93] Then the enterprise should focus on spotting and selecting viable innovations from these, nurturing them, and retaining those that are successful so as to build on them. This school of thought suggests that firms should focus on *selecting* prospective innovations rather than trying in a centralized manner to adapt to changes in their environment.

Consequently, firms should create an environment for divergent processes that induce a healthy proliferation of ideas *and* for convergent processes in which options are narrowed, resources are channeled, and implementation is undertaken.[94] Thus a combination of entrepreneurial and administrative capabilities is needed. As Weick notes:

> Organizing and learning are essentially antithetical processes, which means the phrase "organizational learning" qualifies as an oxymoron. To learn is to disorganize and increase variety. To organize is to forget and reduce variety. In the rush to embrace learning, organizational theorists often overlook this tension, which explains why they are never sure whether learning is something new or simply warmed-over organizational change.[95]

Variable Management Geometry

A parallel implication is that there are stages in the innovation journey—*initiation, development,* and *implementation* or *commercialization*—and these have different organizational and leadership requirements. Often these stages reiterate in cycles—thus an innovation may go through a cycle of initiation, development, and implementation at the departmental level, then a cycle at the subsidiary level, and in turn at the global level. The product or process will change in each of these cycles.

The factors that increase the probability of success vary according to the stage.[96] During initiation, success is favored by rich personal contacts and exchange forums, by open and transparent information, by the existence of clear conflict resolution mechanisms, by shared language, and by reward systems that encourage initiative and going out of the box (working in the top of the "split egg"). A combination of leadership roles is required—sponsorship, constructive critic, and institutional leadership. In the development stage, more focus and direction are required. The sponsor role becomes more important, while institutional leadership and critique become less important. At the implementation stage, networking once again broadens out, while a combination of sponsorship and institutional leadership is vital. Many firms have a series of product review committees at the boundaries of these stages, which signal a change in mode.

One frequently sees hyperbole these days to the effect that "hierarchy is the antithesis of innovation and knowledge management." It is not as simple as that. Hierarchic processes are necessary at particular stages in the process of innovation, notably during development. An early study comparing innovative and less innovative firms in the instruments industry showed that the innovative enterprises were loosely structured at the stage of initiation, with open communication, collaborative networks, and a certain degree of slack. But when projects reached the stage of development, they ran a tight ship with clear goals and deadlines.[97] What is needed is *variable management geometry*—the ability of people and organizations to appropriately adjust their management style.

Ongoing Swedish research is helping us understand how processes of divergence and convergence, loose and tight management, global orientation and local orientation work over time in international firms. Lindqvist, Söllvell, and Zander have studied the interplay of such processes in three innovative and highly international firms in Sweden.[98] They have found that the process of innovation over time is like an hourglass—initially divergent and global, then convergent and local, finally returning to divergence and globalism. In the exploratory sensing stage, there was a great deal of room for local initiative, tapping into collaborative external networks (universities, conferences), while patterns of communication were a blend of distant media (electronic exchange of scientific information and use of reports) with occasional face-to-face meetings. This changed at the development stage. Work became more internally focused and local, with clear responsibilities attached to particular units. Communication was now more intense and face-to-face, facilitating the sharing of deeper tacit knowledge. As the project reached the commercialization stage, the orientation broadened once again—local trials were undertaken, people were encouraged to participate in appropriate conferences. There was now much wider circulation of information via phone calls, e-mail, and personal visits.

Building a Culture of Trust and Reciprocity

Excellent people do not necessarily make excellent organizations. Indeed, if it were automatically the case that they did, it is questionable whether we would have any need for organizations. Ultimately it is the practice of linking people in subtle, constructive ways that adds value.

We will discuss mechanisms of linking people in the next section. These mechanisms will not work well unless they are rooted in an appropriate culture. As Miles and Snow put it, "The ability to innovate comes from a skill that is underdeveloped in many firms: collaboration."[99] This is the domain of a new theory of "social capital" (see the box "Social Capital Theory").

How can collaboration and trust be fostered? High involvement HRM practices and values have a strong influence on building this social capital:[100] first, long-term employment relationships; second, shared vision and goals, a clear understanding among managers and employees of the firm's direction and major objectives; third, norms of reciprocity (as at GE's boundaryless organization), including principles and systems for equitable sharing of rewards; fourth, socialization leading to shared norms, language, and values builds which social capital. This is a delicate balance since excessive socialization can kill diversity.[101] Lastly, hierarchic roles should facilitate relationships, through feedback, coaching, and trust building.[102] (Such practices create norms of *generalized reciprocity*—one does not just collaborate with other people, one collaborates with the "system." If one does not cooperate with others then the system will respond by making sure that one does not get rewarded or advance far in responsibility.)

Developing Entrepreneurial Social Capital

Trust and collaboration are one type of social capital underlying innovation and knowledge management. But if people are too tightly linked, they become constrained. Another type of social capital is entrepreneurship that comes from spanning "structural holes" in networks (see the box "Social Capital Theory").

Innovation, change, creativity happen at interfaces, and people who have rich interfaces through their networks of connections are more likely to identify opportunities to add value. They will get higher returns on their human capital. To express this the

Social Capital Theory
Research Box

Social capital means networks and relationships, both within and outside the organization. The social capital of a person or an organization can be measured by the structure, breadth, and quality of their relationships. In the past, these informal networks were often viewed negatively as personal politics getting in the way.[A] That has changed. Since knowledge is generated and transferred through face-to-face relationships, it is the way of linking people in informal ways that adds value.

For example, in situations in which technology is changing, the ability to draw on a wide array of trusted contacts, even among competitors, allows a person to investigate potential new developments, rope in experts to work on projects, and explore potential alliances and partnerships. Richness of skills and ideas will amount to nothing without a network of contacts and relationships.

There are two different schools of social capital theory. The first addresses the value of trusting relationships, *relational social capital*. The second focuses on the position of the person or organization within the structure of the social network: *structural social capital*.[B]

Relational Social Capital: Collaboration and Cohesion

This is the traditional view of social capital, with its origins in anthropological studies of cliques and communities in the 1930s, as well as in psychological studies of small groups leading to sociometry.[C] Closely knit social ties facilitate the development of trust and collaboration, allowing a community or organization to pursue collective goals. Fukuyama, who has closely studied relational capital, views the ability to collaborate as a social asset of nations or communities.[D]

This type of social capital can be seen as having various components. First, there is the richness or cohesiveness of network relationships. Second, there is the willingness and ability of participants in an organizational network to subordinate individual goals to collective goals and actions (called *associability*—see the discussion of procedural justice later in the chapter). And third, there is the trust that is an antecedent to and a consequence of collective action.[E]

Structural Social Capital: Brokering Holes in Networks

The second perspective on social capital, pioneered by Burt in particular, focuses on structure, with an eye to the leverage of the position of a person (or organization) in a network. This view emphasizes the entrepreneurial returns for individuals who broker what Burt calls "structural holes."[F] Since this is less obvious, let us elaborate.

Building on Granovetter's classic insight into the strength of weak ties,[G] hole theory points out that actors who are strongly linked to others who are in turn interconnected are in fact constrained. Other people have the same knowledge as they, and they can easily be replaced. They have a high degree of "redundancy," as network analysts put it. Individuals who are in a po-

other way around, people who focus on their own specialized activities in tight cohesive networks where everyone knows everyone else may develop a high degree of competence in what they are doing today. But if technology or circumstances require them to change what they are doing, they will have a rough time adjusting.

How does HRM practice facilitate the development of structural social capital? Mobility is one of the most useful tools—both helping people to make regular transitions and recruiting outsiders into the firm. But since research suggests that deep tacit skill takes at least a decade to develop, there is an important dualistic tension here that underlies the management of mobility.[103] Furthermore, internal and particularly external management development is an important tool. Attendance at confer-

sition to span or who can broker "holes" in a social structure, however, linking otherwise unconnected networks, have unique knowledge, access to special information and opportunities, and higher control. They have an advantage over those who are part of cohesive groups.

Indeed studies have shown that people with wide networks that are rich in structural holes are more likely to get promoted earlier.[H] Replicating these findings, Burt found that whereas human capital investment such as education and experience was important for promotion at lower levels, social capital as measured by nonredundant contacts was more important at executive ranks, reflected in higher levels of bonus and compensation.[I] Resources flow disproportionately to people who connect otherwise disconnected groups. They pick up the signals for change early. Because they know others, they move faster via direct negotiation with people rather than via memos and formal channels. In short, they are able through their network spanning to coordinate and innovate faster.

All this may fit with one's image of the individualistic Silicon Valley American culture—but does it apply in other parts of the world? The functioning of structural social capital was explored in the more bureaucratic culture of the French enterprise, with stronger attachment to internal labor markets and less interfirm mobility.[J] The more successful French managers, like their American counterparts, had networks that were rich in structural holes. However, social capital was found to develop in a different way. The net-works of French managers were based on long-standing personal relationships, mostly within the firm. Their social capital outside the firm was built in particular by contacts in executive education, showing the role that education plays in building networks. In contrast, the networks of more mobile American managers reflected work relationships with people from a wider variety of different firms.

[A]Note that this can be true unless there is rigorous attention to skill development and performance management, as well as clear vision and goals guiding network behavior (alignment).

[B]See Nahapiet and Ghoshal (1998) for a review of these types of social capital and their relationship to intellectual capital or knowledge. They argue that there is a third cognitive dimension to social capital—shared languages, codes, and narratives that facilitate communication. See also Gargiulo and Benassi (2000) for an empirically based comparison of the trade-offs between the relational and structural views on social capital.

[C]See Coleman (1990) for a full discussion of this perspective. See also Granovetter (1976) for a different version of this theory, highlighting the importance of "weak ties" rather than closely knit linkages (outlined in Note G).

[D]Fukuyama, 1995.

[E]Leana and Van Buren III, 1999.

[F]Burt, 1992.

[G]Granovetter found that people who were trying to change jobs were more likely to find interesting opportunities through their "weak ties" (acquaintanceships and friends of friends) than through their "strong ties" (close friends). Close friends would typically be part of their current networks, and they would provide few leads that had not been thought of, whereas acquaintances often had leads into totally new networks and opportunities (Granovetter, 1976).

[H]See Snell (1999) for a listing of these findings on returns to individuals in job prospects and promotion.

[I]These are discussed in Chapter 7.

[J]Burt, Hogarth, and Michaud, 2000.

---

ences and forums encourages the development of networks, as do sabbaticals, leaves of absence, and short-term exchange assignments either within or between firms.

Where Is the Value-Added?

From the HRM standpoint, different types of knowledge should be managed in different ways. The value-added of knowledge varies. Some knowledge is firm specific, unique to the enterprise,[104] and this should be managed differently from knowledge that is more generic. Knowledge also varies according to its strategic importance to the enterprise. This leads to a framework developed by Snell, Lepak, and Youndt that is shown in Figure 9–3.[105]

FIGURE 9–3. Different Forms of Knowledge

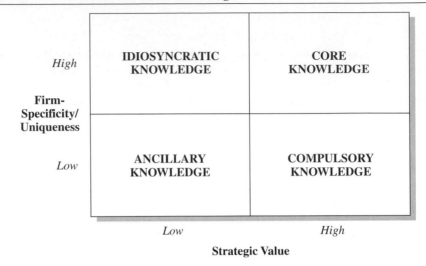

Source: Adapted from S. A. Snell, D. P. Lepak, et al. "Managing the Architecture of Intellectual Capital: Implications for Strategic Human Resource Management," *Research in Personnel and Human Resources Management: Strategic Human Resource Management in the 21st Century*, P. Wright, L. D. Dyer, J. W. Boudreau, and G. Milkovich, eds. (Greenwich, CT.: JAI Press, 1999).

Core knowledge (as shown in Figure 9–3) is both unique to the firm and high in strategic value, such as Wal-Mart's expertise in logistics and inventory control or Toyota's capabilities in manufacturing. This constitutes the firm's current source of competitive advantage, and therefore it must be carefully nurtured by high commitment HR practices. Firms should invest liberally in developing social capital around their core knowledge—through cross-functional teams; the rotation of people through critical functions, carefully balanced with the need to maintain continuity; limiting status and hierarchical barriers that inhibit the sharing of know-how; and investment in sharing and transferring all knowledge that relates to such core competencies. The employment mode here is oriented to internal development.

Compulsory knowledge may be quite generic across the industry, though it is of high strategic importance. It is akin to the notion of "table stakes" in card games, required simply to have a chance of competing, though offering no distinctive competitive advantage. For example, TQM know-how might have been core for Motorola and Xerox in the 1980s, but it has become compulsory knowledge at the present time. Maintenance of the basics is important in such domains since a strike, for example of UPS delivery drivers, may be very costly to the firm. But the approach to HRM is likely to be much more market-based since people with such generic skills can be more easily acquired. Where there is an investment in social capital, it is likely to be around projects that will move compulsory knowledge in a more firm-specific direction—equipping UPS courrier-service drivers with electronic communication devices so that they can avoid bottlenecks. Compulsory knowledge can also be obtained through acquisitions.

Idiosyncratic knowledge refers to know-how that is unique to the firm though not necessarily of clear strategic value today. The likelihood that this may be the core knowledge of tomorrow drives the HRM approach. General R&D and investment in slack resources are ways of generating idiosyncratic knowledge. The approach that makes most sense is to develop entrepreneurial social capital through team-building, lateral relations, mobility, cross-functional projects, and cross-border networks and alliances. The employment mode is oriented toward alliances.

Ancillary knowledge which is low on both strategic value and uniqueness is increasingly likely to be outsourced or automated—administrative activities such as payroll and accounting being examples. There is no value to investment in building either human or social capital. The employment relationship here is one of contracting.

Overall, this emphasizes the need for a differentiated approach to HRM. The same approach applied to all groups of employees is unlikely to be rational.

Knowing When to Stop and Exit

Since effective knowledge management means influencing the odds of successful innovation, it is important to be prepared to exit a business if others can do it better. Paradoxically, an important aspect of knowledge and innovation management is knowing when to stop, when to divest a business or activity. An example is IBM's computer networking business that was core in the 1980s and early 1990s, indeed part of the IBM identity. But by the late 1990s it was apparent that any telecommunication company could add more value through linkages than IBM could—so IBM sold this networking business to AT&T. Anticipation becomes vital so as to sell the business early at a good price, investing the cash in new core and idiosyncratic activities. Incidentally, this is a major reason why previously integrated organizations such as ABB have changed to structures built around product lines—so as to retain this strategic flexibility.

This means being alert to the signals of underperformance. It is questionable whether GE could have built its boundaryless organization if Welch had not established firm principles for performance management ("Being number one or number two in every business"), allowing GE to recognize early signals of poor performance.

In a knowledge-based world, performance management and teamwork go hand in hand. This is one of the principles behind a new area of organizational theory called *coevolution*. Coevolution builds on the joint operation of collaboration and competition between the changing web of units in a multinational firm. Units are encouraged to compete, guided by rigorous performance standards. On the other hand, they are encouraged to collaborate in their own vested interests—working on common projects. As Eisenhardt and Galunic see it, the new rules are counterintuitive:

> Coevolving is a subtle strategic process. In fact, it's a bit counterintuitive—build collaborative teams and yet reward self-interest, let competition flourish, . . . collaborate less to gain more . . . it is precisely this oblique thinking that gives coevolving companies a competitive edge.[106]

Mechanisms to Link People so as to Foster Innovation

Building on these contextual principles, what are some of the mechanisms for linking people so as to foster innovation in the multinational enterprise? These fall under two headings: first, the mechanisms that can be employed within the organization; and second, those that build relationships between organizations.

Internally Oriented Mechanisms

The intraorganizational mechanisms for linking people were discussed earlier in this book.[107] Personal contacts are the basic building block. Much innovation comes from random interpersonal encounters. The weekend meeting in Honolulu is a legitimate way to bring people together in the expectation that an exchange over a coffee break or a dinner discussion will spark an innovative collective project. Kummerle's research on the R&D activities of thirty-two multinational companies shows that the most successful R&D managers are those who meet face-to-face with their geographically dispersed people at least twice a year.[108]

Cross-boundary teams and steering mechanisms as well as know-how sharing are important. Normative integration provides shared language and values that facilitate interaction.[109] Working in "split egg" or T-shaped roles where managers and professionals have vertical and horizontal responsibilities is also vital. This is at the heart of BP's exemplary focus on global knowledge management at BPX, its oil exploration and production business.[110] With the aim of making BPX more valuable than the sum of its parts, "peer groups" of business units heads met regularly together and were then given responsibility for capital allocation and setting unit performance goals, complemented by a host of cross-unit networks on shared areas of interest. Such "top of the egg" knowledge sharing activities take up to 20 percent of the manager's time. "The model here is an open market of ideas," says one business unit head. "People develop a sense of where the real expertise lies. Rather than having to deal with the bureaucracy of going through the center, you can just cut across to somebody in Stavanger or Aberdeen or Houston and say, 'I need some help. Can you give me a couple of hours?' And that is expected and encouraged."[111]

Santos summarizes the different types of cross-border innovation teams, as shown in Figure 9–4.[112] These teams vary in the extent to which the members share the same context. Some teams are high on *confluence or shared context*—people speak the same language, they have shared systems of meaning and common stocks of basic knowledge. Other teams are more diverse, and there is a higher probability of misunderstanding when people work together. *Location* is the other dimension that distinguishes innovation teams. Some teams are located in the same area or building, and there is a high probability of corridor exchanges, spontaneous interaction, and instant feedback. Other teams are separated physically, and the chance of such outcomes is lower.

This leads to the four types of innovation teams that are shown in Figure 9–4. In the *classic team* people with a similar background are all co-located, as at Microsoft's Redmond facilities where people dress in similar ways, talk the same in-house lingo, and share a common socialization regardless of their national or functional background. Microsoft and Cisco believe that the probability of innovation is

FIGURE 9–4. Four Types of Cross-border Innovation Teams

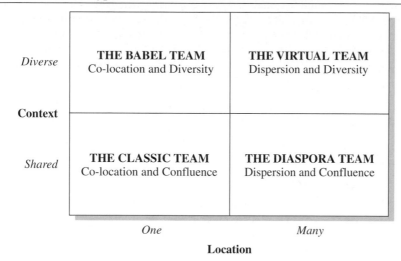

Source: Joe Santos, INSEAD.

highest under such circumstances, though this may not always be possible or desirable. In contrast, the *diaspora team* is exemplified by the strongly socialized expatriates from the parent company who are sent abroad and yet who may function as a tightly knit global innovation network. Although they work in multiple locations, they share a common context by virtue of their socialization by the parent. These expatriates staff the global development projects, working in "split egg" ways—they have dual roles as local agents and as guardians of the global enterprise. The converse is the *Babel team,* in which representatives of different cultures are impatriated to the regional or parent headquarters. Being physically together mitigates against the obstacle of lack of shared socialization. Finally, there are the truly *virtual teams* which share neither context nor location. They may work as teams and look like teams, but despite the fashionable attention devoted to them, their probability of success in innovation is lowest unless there is rigorous attention to project management, facilitated by some degree of shared socialization.[113]

Let us mention a few complementary mechanisms for fostering global innovation within the multinational firm.

Positioning of people: A thesis behind global innovation is that a firm should place the right people where the uncertainties are, where the needs for information collection and processing are the greatest.[114] If a company is in an industry where consumer tastes change frequently and are difficult to assess, then key people in marketing should be located locally, close to the customer. If the firm is in an industry dominated by technological changes that are driven by a "Silicon Valley," then the marketing function should be located in that valley.

Networked manufacturing: Innovation is not just the domain of high technology firms. GKN is a multinational, heavy engineering firm with its headquarters in Britain. Along with GE and Caterpillar, it has been an exponent of networked manufacturing among its 47 plants scattered around the world.[115] It makes components such as $25 constant velocity joints (CVJs) for the automobile industry—an assembly of forged and machined parts with bearings. But driving an average of 6 percent productivity improvement per year are the team-based practices discussed earlier in Chapter 7. Every year, about a thousand people from the CVJ division gather for workshop sessions at a host plant to discuss new ideas. This led to a breakthrough at a German plant, at which machine time was cut from 36 hours to 6 hours. One of the U.S. plants picked this up, and succeeded in further reducing machining time to 4 hours. Such exchange, which leads to visits and e-mail interactions, is complemented by frequent secondments from one plant to another.

Centers of excellence: These are a small group of individuals recognized for their leading-edge, strategically valuable knowledge. As a center of excellence, they are mandated to make that knowledge available throughout the global firm, and to enhance it so as to remain on the cutting edge.[116] In contrast to parent-driven knowledge development, such centers rely on informal networks, often acting as a hub. Three types of centers have been identified in global service firms—*charismatic* (an individual), *focused* (a small group of experts in a single location, as with the McKinsey competence units), and *virtual* (a larger group of specialists in multiple locations, linked together by a database and proprietary tools).[117] The charismatic and focused centers can handle tacit knowledge, while the focused and virtual centers can process more firm-specific knowledge than the single individual.

Communities of practice: The idea of community implies some form of collaboration, and communities of practice are formal, informal, or virtual communities, built around a shared job (for example Xerox technical representatives) or task (e.g. software developers). One of their roles is not just to link together people within the firm, but also to broker relations with external experts. Such communities may exist within a country or may span across geographic borders.[118] These communities of practice also need to be supported with electronic bulletin boards, and reinforced with workshops, training, exchange of staff, and the reward structure.

Externally Oriented Mechanisms

There has been some research on how venture units can be created within the firm so as to provide them with a greater degree of autonomy to foster innovation, or even spun off into separate companies.[119] Increasingly the challenge for knowledge-driven firms in turbulent environments is that their networks and brokering relationships must focus outside the firm.

Federations: As discussed earlier in this chapter, these allow for a closer knowledge exchange between companies that retain their own identities.

Alliances: Knowledge-based learning alliances are now typical in fast moving and highly competitive industries, such as pharmaceuticals, biotech, and electronics.

The knowledge base in these industries is dispersed, and consequently the locus of learning is found in networks rather than in individual firms.[120] We refer the reader to our earlier discussion in Chapter 5 of learning alliances, including the daunting challenge of capturing the individual learning of key people who are involved in such partnerships, and translating it into organizational learning that will lead to commercially viable products. Once again we meet the two-edged sword in mechanisms for knowledge dissemination—informal mechanisms may preclude wide dissemination, while formal procedures can inhibit learning.

Communities of creation: Alliances are typically dyadic, while the community of creation is broader in its membership. This more open form of alliance bridges the advantages and disadvantages of closed R&D systems and of open source governance systems such as that behind the Linux operating system.[121] Corporate R&D structures may result in close alignment between strategy and development, but they do not allow the firm to benefit from the creativity, diversity, and agility of partners. On the other hand, open source systems lack strong coordination mechanisms, making them too unstable. The community of creation strikes the needed balance between order and chaos, and an example is provided by Sun Microsystems' Jini project, a gated community of individuals and organizations, closed outside but open inside. There is an emphasis on self-organization around a common project, though guided by an internal protocol and rules for managing the intellectual property rights, allowing members to capitalize on the intellectual property that they helped to create. These are called *generative webs* in another study.[122]

Knowledge brokers: Building on structural social capital theory, another interorganizational mechanism for generating knowledge that has been studied is the role of knowledge brokers. These are individuals, consultants, university labs, or organizations who span different industries or technologies (for example, computers, communications, medical and measurement industries in the case of an HP venture group).[123] Such knowledge brokers capitalize on the diversity across these industries, bringing together different strands of know-how. These gatekeepers generate new innovations that their client firms can then develop and commercialize.

Overall, we can expect to see a tremendous development in the variety of mechanisms used to transfer knowledge and to stimulate innovation both within and between organizations.

GUIDING INNOVATION AND CHANGE IN THE INTERNATIONAL FIRM

To conclude this chapter, we return to the tensions that characterize the transnational firm, and indeed most organizations since the onset of globalization. Tensions cannot be eliminated. But they can become constructive sources of development—with appropriate social architecture—a new challenge for HRM. We provide one example here, namely, the importance of procedural justice. We return to the theme of social architecture in the next and final chapter of this book.

Tension and Paradox

The fact is that big, complex organizations have difficulty with innovation. As Kanter notes, it is like teaching elephants how to dance. It is not that we do not know how to be innovative—it is that the properties needed to be innovative are the opposite of those needed to be successful.

This is just one of the many paradoxes in the domain of change, innovation, and knowledge management. We have met many dualities in this section—managing cycles of exploration and exploitation, balancing network modes of operating with hierarchic modes (variable geometry), collaboration versus competition, inside versus outside orientation.

Let us take two other paradoxes that we have not explicitly mentioned—the transfer paradox and the evaluation paradox. The *transfer paradox* argues that the most valuable knowledge—tacit knowledge that is complex and contextual—is also the most sticky. It is expensive and difficult to transfer, requiring linkage mechanisms that build on face-to-face relationships. The *evaluation paradox* holds that the most valuable knowledge, this same tacit know-how, is also the most difficult and expensive to evaluate and assess.[124]

There are many other paradoxes. For example, it is clear that external contacts in communities of practice can facilitate new knowledge (the structural holes argument in social capital theory). On the other hand, research also shows that too strong an orientation to external knowledge sources leads people to miss deadlines. Their performance suffers—yet another example of the exploration-exploitation duality.[125]

Organizing for innovation means managing the tensions that underlie such paradoxes. This is the theme running through this chapter, and one of the most universal findings of all recent in-depth studies and reviews of innovation. As Van de Ven et al. note, ". . . contradiction and nonlinearity may be inherent in most innovative undertakings. As a consequence, the central problem in leading the innovation journey may be the management of paradox."[126]

The innovation process involves alternating cycles of divergent and convergent behaviors—exploring new directions alternating with focused pursuit of a given direction; building new relationships alternating with executing through established networks; leadership that encourages diversity alternating with focused leadership guided by goals and consensus. Innovation is a type of exploration, and we discussed one of the dilemmas in the exploration journey earlier in this book—there is a trade-off between a focus on exploration and on exploitation, between tomorrow's profits and today's profits.[127]

Many studies have described the overall quality needed for innovation as being the ability to operate "on the edge"—on the edge between order and chaos. Eisenhardt and Brown found that successful firms in highly competitive computer markets emphasize "semi-structures" as well as improvisation, combining limited structures (priorities, accountability) with extensive interaction and the freedom to improvise.[128] And these firms constantly link time frames, focusing on both present and future. They do not rely on a single plan or scenario, nor are they merely reactive—they constantly use low cost probes such as experimental products, alliances, consultation with futurists and incessant feedback to test out how the future is emerging.

Strong, cohesive ties may promote a climate of trust and cooperation, acting as a defense against opportunism and self-interest. But if the ties become too strong, then the group risks becoming inward looking and rigid.

Galunic and Eisenhardt put it well when they observe from their own empirical study the tensions that highly adaptive organizations balance: "modularity and relatedness, competitiveness and cooperation, and order and disorder . . . the simultaneous presence of competing tensions is an important motor of adaptation within organizations in rapidly changing markets."[129]

Corporate culture plays an important role in making these tensions constructive. Their analysis of Omni (the disguised name for a well-known American high technology firm) illustrates how the value system of the enterprise, a legacy of the founders, supports internal competition—taking personal initiative, rewards for building projects into divisions, the legitimacy of aggressive targets for new product markets in competition with other divisions. However, employees also hold cooperative values that prevent competitive conduct from degenerating into chaos and hostility. Top management goes to great lengths to assist losing divisions; appeals for corporate unity typically override excessive competition; there is careful emphasis on the procedural justice in decision making.[130]

We call this *social architecture,* and we will explore what this concept implies for HRM in the final chapter of this book, where we assess the challenges facing human resource management in this era of globalization. Let us conclude this chapter with one aspect of social architecture that appears to be particularly important in order to thrive in the global knowledge economy—what is called procedural justice.

Procedural Justice: Managing in the Global Knowledge Economy

The ideal of the multinational enterprise as a smooth harmonious entity, a utopian United Nations, is misguided. Tension is at the heart of the concept of the transnational firm. The key is to ensure that the tensions are constructive, positive rather than negative, generating virtuous spirals of development rather than vicious spirals of decline. Paying attention to procedural justice plays an important role.

In multinational firms, there will *always* be decisions and outcomes that go against the vested interests of specific parties—managers, specialists, subsidiaries and businesses. There will *always* be tensions between the interests of exploration and exploitation. Change or realignment will *always* create tensions. How can one be sure that such tensions do not damage human and social capital, leading people to become less satisfied, less committed, less loyal—or even to quit the firm? How can one be sure that these tensions do not undermine the delicate webs of collaborative relationships that are the stuff of the knowledge economy?

The field of HRM has long paid close attention to what is called *distributive justice*—equity and fairness in compensation and incentive systems, the fair distribution of rewards linked to outcomes. But distributive justice is focused on specific goals and outcomes, and outcomes will always favor one person at the expense of another. This is the problem with distributive systems like evaluating people on a forced distribution "A-to-E" scale in performance appraisal, or ranking people in a potential management system—there will always be outcomes that upset some people. Paying attention to *procedural justice* means something different—it is paying attention to the perceived fairness of the process by which decisions are reached. People may be dissatisfied with an outcome that goes against their interests. But if they are satisfied with the process that led to the decision, then they are more likely to respect or buy in to that decision because they know they will get their just deserts in the long run. The integrity of the organization is preserved. Conversely, people may be satisfied with an outcome that favors their interests, though they learn to distrust the organization since the process of decision-making was not fair.

In labor relations and personnel management, there is a long history of study of procedural justice in contexts that go from labor negotiations to layoffs, from appraisal to compensation. Similarly, there is a rich heritage of research on organizational justice and its relationship to commitment and citizenship behaviors.[131] The research of Kim and Mauborgne extends this to multinational enterprises and to the functioning of the knowledge economy. They have undertaken extended studies on procedural justice, capitalizing on a research database of more than 400 subsidiaries of multinational corporations.[132]

What are the elements of procedural justice? Kim and Mauborgne's studies lead them to identify three components: engagement, explanation, and expectation clarity. *Engagement* is two-way communication—asking for inputs from people who will be affected by a decision, and giving them a chance to refute arguments they do not accept. Asking people for their views means showing respect for them, increasing the probability that the outcome will be seen as fair. *Explanation* is comprehensive one-way communication of the decision so that people will trust the intentions of the decision-makers even if they disagree with the decision. *Expectation clarity* involves knowing the rules of the new game after the decision—understanding the targets and intentions so that each person can adjust to the new circumstances. For example, in the delayering and multiskilling of one of the world's largest paper companies, many supervisors were initially upset since the hierarchic career paths that they were climbing were suddenly dismantled. It was a restructuring that went against their personal interests. But they adjusted to the new organization as they understood the reasons for the change. They had been given the opportunity to advocate alternatives and had seen that these were not viable, and they had clearly understood how to get ahead in the newly restructured system.

The studies of Kim and Mauborgne show that careful attention to these elements of procedural justice is closely associated with higher levels of organizational commitment, trust, and social harmony.[133] This is not a radically new insight—it was the basis of many of the concerns with planned organizational change in the Organizational Development movement back in the 1960s (see the earlier box "The Role of HR in Change Processes"). But it does extend those insights to the arena of behavior in multinational organizations, which must pay particular attention to nurturing commitment and trust so as to ensure that tensions remain constructive.

Ultimately, every insight into human and organizational processes in multinational organization generates in turn its own tensions—such is the law of duality. In some firms, including many leading German and Japanese enterprises, careful attention to process and fairness in decision-making leads to painfully slow decision-making. These consensus cultures with an underlying heritage of life employment are incompatible with today's need for speed in both decision-making and implementation. How can fair process be reconciled with speed in decision-making? This leads us to the research on contention management, how conflict can be managed more closely. This is one of the challenges for human resource management and social architecture that we will explore in the final chapter of this book.

TAKEAWAYS

1. The future is increasingly unpredictable. This makes the capacity to change fast particularly important (in contrast to planning), posing new challenges for human resource and organizational management.

2. Complex organizational change involves many tensions—between short-term and long-term success, between planning and experimentation, between bottom-up processes and top-down processes. Indeed, tension and paradox are at the heart of change, innovation, and knowledge management in transnational firms.

3. Change can be seen as a spiral process in which one has to "anticipate the future in the present," guided by an understanding of dualities.

4. When the multidomestic firm experiences pressures to become transnational, the most effective sequence of stages appears to be global rationalization first and then building collaborative integration afterwards. The "sour" is tackled initially, then the "sweet."

5. Subsidiary initiatives and entrepreneurship must be encouraged when the integrated meganational firm experiences pressures for more local responsiveness. This changes the role and competencies of subsidiary general managers and business area managers.

6. Transferring capabilities from the parent to the subsidiary is a complex, stepwise process that can take many years, not simply one of "technology transfer." "Instant transnational" firms that are not handicapped by long domestic experience in the parent country may be able to shorten the process considerably.

7. Professional service firms, with their many internal tensions and complex matrices, face unusual tensions as they internationalize. There appear to be three organizational configurations in such firms, with corresponding implications for their approach to global knowledge management—client-oriented, creative problem-solving, and solution-adaptation configurations.

8. It is impossible to dictate or control innovation (which is the other side of the coin of knowledge management). But one can facilitate it, by encouraging variation/entrepreneurship and then selecting likely winners, by building trust and entrepreneurial social capital, through variable management geometry, by focusing on added value knowledge . . . and by being prepared to exit businesses when this is not possible.

9. The mechanisms for fostering innovation all involve linking people, which is easiest when they are co-located and share a common context through socialization. We can expect to see an increasing variety of internal mechanisms (such as centers of excellence) and external mechanisms (learning alliances and communities of creation).

10. The striking characteristic of global innovation and knowledge management is that it involves managing paradoxes and tensions. Reconciling these tensions, such as between convergence and divergence, means paying attention to procedural justice and other aspects of social architecture.

NOTES

1. The sources for our observations on McKinsey are Bartlett (1997); "How McKinsey Does It," *Fortune,* November 1, 1993; Ghoshal and Bartlett, 1997.
2. Peters and Waterman, 1982; Ohmae, 1992.
3. Perlmutter, 1969, p. 17.
4. The Coca-Cola story was discussed earlier in Chapter 3, p. 148.
5. Realignment is the essence of the second face of HRM—see Chapter 2.
6. See the discussion in Chapters 1 and 2 on how the dream of "strategic human resource management" proved to be illusory.
7. Among the many books on organizational change, some useful references are the following: Beer, Eisenstat, and Spector, 1990; Schein, 1985; Kanter, 1985; Kanter, Stein, and Jick, 1992; Conner, 1998; Kotter, 1996; Goffee and Jones, 1998; Hambrick, Nadler, and Tushman, 1998; Beer and Nohria, 2000. Obviously there is an enormous literature on specific types of change (downsizing, re-engineering, mergers and acquisitions, etc.).
8. The results of this conference on change are reported in Beer and Nohria (2000).
9. Beer and Nohria (2000) use different terminology. They call the Q-side "Theory E" (standing for Economic reasoning), and the A-side "Theory O," meaning Organizational reasoning.
10. Is change best driven by simple aims (maximizing economic value-added) or by the more complex aim of increasing organizational capability and learning? Does change happen by changing the formal structure or by reshaping culture? Are rewards a lead factor or a lag factor in the process of change? See Beer and Nohria (2000).

    In an ongoing study to map out the consequences of change in eighteen international firms in Europe, Pettigrew (2000) was struck by how change involves dualities. Firms were investing in both hierarchies and networks, in vertical performance accountability along with horizontal integration sideways, in centralizing and standardizing while encouraging decentralization and customization. Similarly, the recent issue of a leading journal in management theory was entitled: "Paradox, Spirals, Ambivalence: The New Language of Change and Pluralism" (Eisenhardt, 2000).
11. The "failure of success" sydrome is discussed at some length in Chapter 2, p. 84.
12. "Carly Fiorina's Bold Management Experiment at HP," *Business Week,* February 19, 2001. See the discussion in Galbraith (2000) of the front-end/back-end organization that HP, ABB, and HP are attempting to implement.
13. Whittington, Pettigrew et al., 1998.
14. See Chapter 2 concerning the second face of HRM focusing on realignment.
15. Doz and Prahalad, 1988.
16. Ibid., p. 75.

17. Kotter, 1996. The eight steps are establishing a sense of urgency, creating the guiding coalition, developing a vision and strategy, communicating the change vision, empowering employees for broad-based action, generating short-term wins, consolidating gains and producing more change, and anchoring new approaches in the culture.

18. Beer, Eisenstat, and Spector, 1990.

19. Pettigrew, 2000.

20. Pettigrew emphasizes the long incubation period, the less visible side of change, in his longitudinal study of change processes at ICI (Pettigrew, 1985). The visible change at ICI involved a highly publicized crisis in 1980, the appointment of a new CEO (Harvey-Jones), and a turnaround strategy. But the study showed that change was a much longer process, evolutionary and cyclical in nature. The process started off twenty years before with the mobilization of small coalitions who were discontent with the status quo (informal leadership change). These coalitions engaged in a great deal of experimentation at local levels for nearly two decades, providing confidence and experience (experimentation and localized culture change). The crisis triggered a change in top leadership, with the appointment of the new CEO who had been the focal point of the experimental change (formal leadership change). This led first to a restructuring of top management (structure change), then to formalization of the new strategy (strategic change), and then to implementation (structure change followed by formal culture change).

21. Evans and Doz, 1989.

22. This is described well with detailed case studies of firms such as IBM, Digital Equipment and ITT by Miller (1990). See the discussion on the "failure of success" syndrome in Chapter 2.

23. For the Coca-Cola story, see Chapter 3, p. 148.

24. Among those who argue for the "spiral" image of change are Mintzberg and Westley (1992); Hampden-Turner (1990); Brown and Eisenhardt (1998); Lewis, (2000).

25. Evans and Doz, 1989.

26. Spector, 1995.

27. See Chapter 2 for a discussion of this third "steering" face of HRM.

28. Brown and Eisenhardt, 1997; Brown and Eisenhardt, 1998.

29. Specifically, there is a probability that the latter firm may respond more promptly to the change since it is already, in Lewinian terms, "unfrozen" and in a learning mode.

30. Pettigrew, 2000; Hinings and Greenwood, 1989; Stace and Dunphy, 1991.

31. Ghoshal and Bartlett, 1998.

32. See ibid., ch. 12; Ghoshal and Bartlett, 2000.

33. Ghoshal and Bartlett, 2000.

34. Campbell and Goold, 1998; Goold and Campbell, 1998.

35. BP would be another example, where its Project 90 transformation process was initiated with the hard, driving leadership of Robert Horton, followed by the more participative strategy of David Simon, his successor (see the box in the text "Transformational Change at BP").

36. The need for common processes in performance management is discussed at length in Chapter 7.

37. Ghoshal and Bartlett, 2000, p. 200

38. As discussed in Chapter 1—see Galbraith, 2000.

39. See Chapter 1, page 16, for an account of the origins of HRM.

40. The Apple story is told in Evans and Wittenberg, 1986.

41. See Cameron (1994) and indeed the whole of that journal issue for research on downsizing (notably how to avoid the negative long-term consequences of restructuring). See also the discussion on handling restructuring as part of M&A integration (Chapter 6).

42. The issue of localization is discussed at length in Chapter 4, pp. 183–191.

43. Delany, 2000.
44. Birkinshaw and Hood, 2001.
45. However, it is not quite as simple as that—the paradox is that diversity has to be "constructive," otherwise it can generate adversity! The important issue of contention management is discussed further in Chapter 10.
46. Extracts from a speech by C. Fiorina, reported in *Executive Excellence,* January 4, 2001.
47. The management development practices of Japanese firms are discussed in Chapter 8, p. 372, along with this challenge, seen as the Achilles heel of Japanese management practices in this era of globalization.
48. Bartlett and Ghoshal, 1997.
49. Birkinshaw and Hood, 2001.
50. Delany, 2000.
51. Bartlett and Ghoshal, 1997.
52. The issue of increasing intransitivity in leadership development is discussed in Chapter 8, p. 368.
53. See the discussion on know-how transfer in Chapter 7. For empirical evidence on the difficulty in transferring technology, see Zahra, Ireland, and Hitt, 2000.
54. Cited by Leonard-Barton (1992), p. 215.
55. The source for this story is Thill and Lonard-Barton (1993); Leonard, 1995.
56. Zahra, Ireland, and Hitt, 2000. See Chapter 7 for a discussion of these mechanisms.
57. This contrasts with Stinchcombe's concept of the liability of newness Stinchcombe (1965).
58. Business Objects was introduced in the introduction to Chapter 1.
59. Autio, Sapienza et al., 2000. See also a study on the international expansion of 25 Dutch firms, which similarly find that learning on internationalization is handicapped by the prior domestic success of the enterprise (Barkema and Vermeulen, 1999).
60. Ferner, Edwards, and Sisson, 1995.
61. With respect to knowledge management in professional service firms, see Loewendahl (1997) for a fine analysis; also Eccles and Crane (1987); Maister, 1993.
62. Volmer and Mills, 1966
63. Loewendahl, 1997.
64. See "Lawyers Go Global," *The Economist,* February 26, 2000. European law practices have been hotly engaged in acquiring and merging so as to capture the lucrative market for cross-border deals—particularly mergers between German, British, and some American firms. Lawyers are painfully having to become businessmen.
65. Maister, 1993, p. 319.
66. These configurations were apparent from the research of Loewendhahl (1997), as well as that of Maister (1993). See also Doorewaard and Meihuizen (2000) for empirical support in a study of Dutch and German PSFs.
67. Loewendahl, 1997.
68. These basic coordination mechanisms are described in Chapter 7.
69. Hansen, Nohria, and Tierney, 1999.
70. For a good case example, see Galunic and Weeks (1999).
71. Hansen, Nohria and Tierney, 1999
72. Ibid.
73. Ibid.
74. See Doorewaard and Meihuizen (2000) for a more extended discussion on this point.
75. See Loewendahl (1997) for a discussion of these tensions.
76. Earlier the Big Eight (now Big Five) responded to these pressures by moving away from the PSF governance system and more toward a corporate governance model. There are many ex-

amples of the failure to respect the consistency between strategy, HRM orientation, and the correspondingly appropriate approaches to knowledge management among PSFs.

77. Bartlett, 1997, p. 7.
78. Bartlett and Ghoshal, 1989. See the discussion in Chapter 1.
79. Scullion and Starkey, 2000.
80. Stroh and Caligiuri, 1998.
81. Van de Ven notes that the difference between incremental innovation and radical innovation is one of degree rather than quality (Van de Ven, Polley et al., 1999).
82. Creativity is a social process—see Czikszentmihalyi and Sawyer (1995) for these studies.
83. Kogut and Zander, 1992; Galunic and Rodan, 1998;
84. For some of the basics of Knowledge Management, see the box "Collections and Connections" in Chapter 1 (p. 35).
85. Nohria and Ghoshal, 1997.
86. Gupta and Govindarajan, 2000.
87. J. F. Welch, "Timeless Principles," *Executive Excellence,* Feburary 2001, p. 3.
88. Thanks to Joe Santos for this observation on Microsoft and Cisco—see his book on global knowledge management (Doz, Santos, and Williamson, 2001).
89. Cited by Miles, Snow, and Miles (2000).
90. "Sustaining Profitable Growth," report by the Economist Intelligence Unit and Gemini Consulting, London: The Economist Intelligence Unit, 1999.
91. "Pioneers Show the Way to Wealth," *Financial Times,* August 11, 1998.
92. Van de Ven, Polley et al., 1999.
93. Weick, 1979. For a review of evolutionary theory, see Barnett and Burgelman, (1996).
94. Leonard and Sensiper, 1998.
95. Weick and Westley, 1996.
96. See Van de Ven, Polley et al. (1999) for research on the requirements at different stages in the innovation journey.
97. Johne, 1984. In this study, innovation was measured by the percentage of revenues coming from products introduced within the last five years.
98. Lindqvist, Sölvell et al., 2000.
99. Miles, Snow et al., 2000
100. Leana and Van Buren III, 1999. See also Miles, Snow, and Miles (2000).
101. Socialization is discussed in Chapter 3 and particularly Chapter 7, where the dangers of excessive socialization are emphasized.
102. The importance of tuning hierarchic roles to collaboration is well made in the study of Gittell (2000).
103. The research on skill development was undertaken by Simon (1981). The duality in mobility practices is discussed in Chapter 8, p. 363. Mobility may facilitate the development of structural social capital. But if it is excessive, this may be at the expense of execution and exploitation.
104. The concept of firm specificity is discussed in Chapter 8, p. 351.
105. Snell, Lepak et al., 1999; see also Lepak and Snell (1999).
106. Eisenhardt and Galunic, 2000.
107. See Chapter 7.
108. Kummerle's research is reported in "Winning in a World without Boundaries," *Industry Week,* October 20, 1997.
109. Normative integration and socialization are discussed in Chapter 7.
110. See Hansen and von Oetinger (2001).
111. Ibid., p. 111.

112. Santos, 2001.

113. See Chapter 7 for a discussion of virtual teams.

114. Afuah, 1998.

115. For an assessment of network manufacturing, see the report by De Meyer and Vereecke (2000). They suggest that international plants can be classified into categories—isolated plants, blueprint plants that receive innovations, and network players that generate innovations.

116. See Moore and Birkinshaw (1998) for an account of centers of excellence in international service firms.

117. Moore and Birkinshaw, 1998.

118. See Teigland (2000) for an account of communities of practice, as well as empirical research in one high technology firm.

119. Burgelman, 1984; Burgelman and Grove, 1992.

120. See Powell (1998) for a study in the biotech and pharmaceutical industries. See Chapter 5 for a discussion of learning alliances.

121. Sawhney and Prandelli, 2000. This concept draws heavily on Nonaka's idea of *ba* as a shared space for emerging relationships, acting as a foundation for knowledge generation (Nonaka and Konno, 1998).

122. Eneroth and Malm, 2001

123. Hargadon, 1998.

124. Arvidsson, 1999; Arvidsson, 2000.

125. Empirical research by Teigland (2000).

126. Van de Ven, Polley et al., 1999, p. 12. See also Argote (1999) and Dougherty (1996).

127. The exploitation-exploration trade-off is discussed in Chapter 2, p. 85.

128. Brown and Eisenhardt, 1997; Brown and Eisenhardt, 1998.

129. Galunic and Eisenhardt, 2002.

130. Ibid.

131. See Baron and Kreps (1999) for a review of the procedural justice literature in the Personnel/HR field, and Konovsky (2000) for a wider review. See Cropanzano (1997) for a review of the research on organizational justice and citizenship.

132. Kim and Mauborgne, 1991; Kim and Mauborgne, 1997; Kim and Mauborgne, 1998.

133. Kim and Mauborgne, 1997.

PART 4

Organizing International Human Resource Management

Our last chapter focuses on the paradox that while human resource management is unquestionably important for international firms, the human resource function itself has often come under criticism for its failure to respond to these new realities. We review the international challenges for organizations and individuals from the perspective of the three human resource management roles that were introduced in Chapter 2: the builder, the change partner, and the navigator. We examine the way international firms have been reconfiguring the organization of human resource management so as to face up to the transnational pressures, freeing up energies to focus on social architecture, the most important element of the new human resource role.

Finally, we explore how international human resource management should respond to broader social challenges that are emerging. The market economy is driving global competition throughout the world, but this also may lead to excesses, as witnessed by the controversy around globalization. The new century is bringing new tensions, including the social implications of the widening gap between rich and poor, both within and between countries. This raises immense social challenges that will certainly shape the domain of international human resource management in the future.

CHAPTER 10

Transforming the Global Human Resource Role

Let us introduce this chapter with a number of vignettes that capture the way in which the global role of human resources is changing.

- At one of our seminars, John Hofmeister was engaged in a question-and-answer discussion with HR executives. John is an ex-GE HR professional who now heads up the human resource function for Royal Dutch/Shell. One of the participants asked him, "What will be the task of the HR leader in the future?" Without hesitation, he responded "Managing tension and contradiction." There was a thoughtful silence in the seminar room.

- The chief executive of a well-known corporation that has recently undertaken a major international acquisition presented six core platforms on which the group could compete in this era of intense global competition. The last of these competitive platforms specifically focused on people processes: "We need to be a global benchmark for HR." In many ways, the HR executives in the audience could not have hoped for more—a chief executive publicly endorsing the role of HR and willing to invest in it. But this raises a difficult question—how to respond?

- Many of the GE divisions provide HR services to their external customers. For example, GE Power Systems "sells" organizational change technology together with turbines to state-owned utilities, directly involving the client CEO. Is this the way of the future for leading corporations? What does this mean for HR roles and responsibilities?

- Canon Europe is one of the many companies that are using management development as a tool for strategic intervention, led by HR. To drive a major reorganization of the European businesses, the process helps senior managers to shape and build ownership of the new strategy and to design the steps in its implementation.

- International HR remains a sensitive area in which there is potential for clashes between the HR function and line management. One leading European transnational has introduced global processes in every area . . . except for HR. The corporate HR vice president ceded to the pressures from all over the world—"It's just too political. Despite the strong rationale, it takes away much of the discretionary power of regional, country and business area bosses."

• Globalization is changing the labor market. One of the myriad examples is the "expert" sites for computer support. A Bangladeshi computer student working free-lance can provide online support for a fee charged to a credit card to an American who is stuck with a computer problem—without leaving Dhaka.

CHAPTER OVERVIEW

This chapter focuses on the way globalization is changing HRM roles, notably those of the HR function and its professionals. Building on the vignettes above, we set the stage by reviewing the critiques of and challenges for HR, using our three faces of HRM—the builder (who sometimes becomes a custodian), the change partner, and the navigator. An important message here is that HR should focus clearly on competitive performance.

HR has become a complex, multifaceted domain. This is particularly true of the transnational firm, with its global and local pressures. In the next section, we discuss what this means for the organization of HR activities, providing a framework to assess the appropriateness of different HR delivery mechanisms such as centralized functions, service centers, and the use of global project teams. The role of headquarters staff is discussed, leading us to advocate a quality that we call network leadership. And we also discuss some of the more personal implications for HR managers.

The third section takes us back into the wider challenge for HR, going beyond that of the change agent—that of assisting in social architecture (or shaping the context which guides individual behaviors). Here we single out three particular challenges for discussion: How to build a competitive culture, how to create constructive tension between dualities, and how to create a culture of healthy contention.

In the final sections of this chapter we return to the emerging new role for HR and HRM: tension management. Given the contradictions that the transnational enterprise faces, this is the theme that has run through the whole of this book. We argue first that HR has to be a proactive function, fighting for the long-term perspective as well as managing the delivery of valued added services. We provide various examples of what this long-term perspective implies, emphasizing that it implies the capacity to *anticipate,* and we discuss a vital societal, indeed global, example of the need for anticipation. Although market competition and globalization have brought immense advantages to the world, there are worrying signals that there may be a backlash if more attention is not paid to the legions of the poor and to rising inequality. We discuss the implications of such wider social challenges for HR. Finally, the chapter concludes by asking where the HR function is heading in this era of tension and contradiction.

REINVENTING HR?

HRM is only thirty years old. It had its origins in the early 1970s in the burgeoning social initiatives such as participative management, Organizational Development, and equal opportunity that needed an umbrella that was wider than personnel management. The HRM movement got off to some false starts, such as the rise and fall of "strategic human resource planning." The idea of planning strategy and then working backward to its implications for HRM did not make sense given the increasingly obvious discontinuities created by global competition and technological change. The emphasis on planning was replaced with a growing focus on facilitating change and responsiveness.

Today we face a paradoxical situation. While the strategic importance of HRM to management, and particularly to international management, is now generally acknowledged, the attacks on the HR function have become at times vociferous. The paragons of the past, such as Japanese enterprises, are the pariahs of the present, though many firms such as IBM have undergone a successful transformation in their approach to professional HR management.

In 1996 a leading *Fortune* journalist wrote a commentary titled "Taking on the Last Bureaucracy," in which in an ironic way he questioned the necessity for an HR function.[1] To his surprise, he commented later, few pieces he had written attracted more comment—or were taken more seriously. Many volumes have been written by academics and practitioners who ask whether HR will become just one more outsourced function or emerge as an even more critical factor in developing and maintaining a company's competitive edge.[2] There have been many studies that try to map out the new competencies needed by HR. One of them estimated that only 10–35 percent of American HR professionals possess these new skills such as influencing others and facilitating change.[3] Given this debate, what should be the role of HR in the multinational enterprise?

What Is HRM's Contribution to the Multinational Enterprise?

To answer this question, building on the issues and perspectives that we have covered in this book, let us return to our three-face framework for understanding the contribution of HRM to organizational performance in the multinational enterprise. In this framework, HR plays three successive roles, those of the builder, the change partner and the navigator.[4]

The Builder

It has become fashionable to critique the custodial role of the HR function, and there is a lot of justification for this. However, when pendulums have swung too far to one extreme, there is a dangerous tendency to overcorrect by swinging too far to the other extreme. A study on HR competencies mentioned above showed that senior HR generalists agreed on the necessity for the "new" skills of facilitating and implementing change, influence, and showing a solid knowledge of the business. However only 30 percent of them saw traditional technical HR expertise as required. This can lead to the neglect of the basic HR foundations that, like any foundations, are so vital to the infrastructure that is built on them.

Even admirable leading organizations can fall into this trap. Apple Computers Europe in the 1980s was an example, where the regional HR function was so focused on contributing to business strategy that they were blind to the signals that some staff were so discontent as to unionize. Shell is another example; its HR generalists introduced open job posting without considering the basic principle of consistency that underlies such foundations. The open job posting was not aligned with other elements of the corporation's approach to HRM, creating a lot of confusion.[5]

HR foundations need to be focused on competitive performance, not just on satisfying internal requirements. For the multinational firm, fully exposed to global threats as well as opportunities, competition is a reality and its intensity is relentless. One can argue that if the function wants to be taken seriously, it has only one option—to accept that the key responsibility of HR is to enhance the competitive position of the firm. No ifs or buts. The relevance of HR comes from its focus on performance, for without this, simple administration is quite enough. Of course this is not the only role HR has to perform, although maintaining performance focus amidst different and often conflicting roles is a question of priorities as well as creative balance.

CREATING VALUE FOR EXTERNAL CUSTOMERS. A pertinent demand for HR professionals is the following: "Justify your existence in terms of your added value, not to your *internal* customers, but to your *external* customers!" GE managers have a response to that demand. As mentioned earlier, they use GE's mastery of HR foundations as a way of building relationships with their external customers—"if the customers are so impressed by our internal processes that they can learn from them, they'll stick with us as loyal purchasers of our products." United Technologies is another corporation with benchmark HR practices. We helped Pratt & Whitney, a company within the UT Group, to organize a conference on HRM for their potential clients in China, the regional airlines and the Chinese civil aviation authority. It achieved what technical partnerships and marketing strategy had not been able to pull off, attracting the participation of most of the airline presidents and party secretaries, who then spent the evenings networking with the Pratt & Whitney top executives.

Even a conventional approach to HRM can create value for external customers, as long as it is tightly consistent. The SAS Institute based in North Carolina is an example. They are the largest privately owned software company in the world, with billion dollar revenues from their software packages (used for example to analyze the results of the U.S. census). While their business strategy is built on close customer relationships, their approach to HR in all countries they operate in is like that from a 1980s textbook. In the United States there are offices for everyone; a superbly landscaped campus environment with no parking privileges; average salaries but no stock options or fancy bonuses, though very generous benefits, including workout rooms and medical counseling; a flat organization with a lot of cross-functional mobility so that people are likely to have three or four careers while working for SAS.[6] All of this generates an immense amount of an unfashionable commodity: loyalty.

Turnover rates average 4 percent per annum in an industry where these typically exceed 20 percent. What is the value-added to the customer? On the project team of a competitor, a third of the team are learning the ropes, a third are looking for their next job, and only a third have enough experience and motivation to be effective. At the SAS Institute, almost everyone is focused on the customer project, and many have had years of relationship with that customer. The payoff to the company from this "very traditional" approach to HRM? Better projects, better customer relationships, and better profits for the company.

If HR professionals cannot answer the question of how they add value to the external customer, they may be gambling with their own futures. A focus solely on satisfying internal customers leads easily to a bits-and-pieces approach to HRM, rather than one that is internally consistent and externally coherent. The bits and the pieces can easily be outsourced since there is typically someone who can do these separate activities cheaper and better.

The Change Partner

Focusing HR basics on returns to the external customer and on competitive performance is a transition to the second face of HRM, that of the change partner. This facilitates organizational change, the need for which is invariably sparked off by external changes—changing customer demands, competitive shifts, and technological developments.

Bear in mind that attention to change does not eliminate the focus on the basic foundations. HR foundations have to be reworked constantly and rebuilt periodically—the current impact of e-HR is an example (see the box "Responding to the Challenges of e-HR"). Managers, including HR managers, have to learn to work in "split egg" or matrix ways, where the bottom of the egg is the focus on operational activities, while the top of the egg is the focus on the project role as change agent.[7] The delicate but all important tension between continuity and change, between the short-term imperatives of exploitation and the long-term necessity for exploration, is built into the jobs of everyone at the interface between these two roles. This makes change more manageable since it is no longer the responsibility of top management alone. Some argue that this way of working characterizes the emerging generation of knowledge-based firms[8]—and we fully agree!

We are in the early stages of a period of profound transformation, akin to the Industrial Revolution that started more than 150 years ago. The exploitation of the "virtual" potential of information and communication technology, the trends toward alliances and networks, the need for greater labor flexibility, and above all the challenges of managing knowledge and intellectual capital on a global basis—these issues, discussed earlier in this book, will gradually transform organizations. All such revolutions take time to work through because the consistent patterns of the old must be replaced step-by-step with new configurations. Many thought that the Internet-driven new economy revolution would transform the world within a decade. The hype ended in March 2000 with the collapse of the dot-coms—but this just means that the real transformation is beginning.

Responding to the Challenges of e-HR
Practice Box

The digital revolution will reshape HR practices in ways that still cannot be anticipated. But responses to e-HR appear to follow the path of our three faces of HRM, characterized by three generations:

First Generation e-HR

Initial attempts to exploit e-HR are predominantly transactional, using intranet or electronic means to speed up service delivery (often by allowing self-service) or to reduce costs. Rudimentary examples are payroll processing; more sophisticated instances are providing training information so that people can satisfy their skill development needs on a real time basis.

Second Generation e-HR

The confidence in the use of these new technologies leads to a second generation, involving qualitative changes and improvements. For example, when 360° feedback can be undertaken online, it opens up new possibilities for multiple appraisal, which in turn can have a significant impact on the culture and performance of the firm. Another example would be e-recruitment and the potential for intranet-assisted open job markets.[A] Such tools allow one to undertake things that were not feasible previously, such as benchmarking the functional competencies of the firm.

Third Generation e-HR

Third generation e-HR means using technology to do things that could not be done before. For example, would it not be great to be able to measure on a regular basis the energy that people put into their work? Assisted by technology, it is possible to do what survey methodologists have dreamed of in the past. On a weekly or bi-weekly basis, an eePulse system allows a company to send an e-mail message to its staff around the world with a "Pulse" survey that takes two minutes to complete, linked to the Company's website.[B] Immediately after the close of a Pulse, eePulse can provide managers with summary reports and data to help them understand and address key issues within their organization. The process also allows the company to respond to anonymous participant comments for further information or to provide guidance. The results can guide decisions affecting sales, profitability, turnover and absenteeism, productivity, and ultimately improved firm performance.

[A]E-recruitment is discussed in Chapter 2, p. 70).
[B]eePulse is the trademark name of a service offered by eePulse.com to a variety of firms such as Amazon, Cap Gemini, and GE Medical.

Leaving aside HR's role in facilitating change processes,[9] we focus here on two aspects of the change partner role: enabling business strategy and contributing to competitive advantage through differentiation.

ENABLING BUSINESS STRATEGY. One of the major roles of HRM is to enable strategy to happen, more though facilitating change and building capabilities than through generally outdated ideas of human resource planning. For example, HRM has been critical to Cisco's phenomenal growth in many ways. In an industry in which hardware is obsolete in eighteen months and software in six, Cisco's growth has come in part through acquisitions, first in the United States and now across the globe. These mergers are specifically designed to acquire technology and know-how embodied in people, including the founders of acquired companies. Consequently, Cisco developed a methodology to implement this—to assess the cultural compatibility of a target firm and to integrate acquired firms so as to retain both key people such as founders as well as the rank and file.[10] At home, Cisco had (at least until its recent layoffs) a reputation as one of the best companies to work for, the result of carefully designed recruitment, training, and development policies—contributing to an 8 percent attrition rate, which is phenomenal by Silicon Valley standards.

Linking HR to business strategy remains an ongoing challenge for the HR function. Although the rhetoric has long emphasized the potential contribution of HRM to strategic development, reinforced by the resource-based view of the firm, few would disagree with the view of Hunt and Boxall: "While there is some divergence of opinion, the dominant view in the international literature is that HR specialists, senior or otherwise, are not typically key players in the *development* of corporate strategy."[11]

CONTRIBUTING TO COMPETITIVE ADVANTAGE THROUGH DIFFERENTIATION. As change facilitators, HR professionals should bear in mind that competitive advantage never comes from copying others or being the same as them. It invariably comes from being *different.*

There are divided views on this issue. Indeed, a deep tension divides scholars on either side of the Atlantic, subscribing respectively to an American universalist and a European contextualist paradigm of strategic HRM. In the universalist paradigm, widespread in the United States, research focuses on testing abstract generalizations (e.g., "if you involve people, company performance will be better"). The contextualist paradigm, stronger in Europe, argues that "research is about drawing understanding from complex data; that explanation of difference is more important than firm performance; that there are different views and perspectives on HRM depending on the nature of what is being studied."[12]

There is truth in both paradigms, as Brewster (the author of the above quote) suggests. But as European researchers who were trained in the United States, we beg to disagree with the observation that explanation of difference is more important than firm performance. The understanding of difference is *one of the keys* to understanding firm performance. And by focusing on performance, one learns that being different is what ultimately counts. Let us explain this with a simple image.

Take Formula 1 car racing. From the outside, F-1 racing cars look more and more similar. It is hard to distinguish them as they speed around the track. But if you are an F-1 driver or sponsor, this does not mean that you are indifferent as to which car you drive! The differences lie in the details, and the details are constantly changing. It is the details in the exhaust panel design and in the fuel injection system, indiscernible to the race track spectator, that make for the difference between number one and number four.[13]

The public seldom scold leading-edge companies for being different from their competitors. Rather their idiosyncratic cultures and values are celebrated and often sought out to be emulated. At the same time as we experience pressures to copy others, we are learning to value diversity (see the box "Diversity Management").

Many HR professionals consider being different in a foreign culture somewhat rude and arrogant, if not fundamentally wrong and improper. The hallmark of cultural understanding, however, is being able to go beyond the rudimentary stage of stereotypes, knowing where one has to conform and where one has to be different. In the process of balancing the global business needs with multiple cultures, the role

Diversity Management
Research Box

Until recently, diversity management tended to focus mainly on numbers—knowing how many women, people from ethnic minorities, and people with disabilities there were, and where they were in the organization. Today, the concern with diversity has broadened from this focus on representation. Diversity is about creating a working culture that seeks, respects, values, and harnesses differences.[A]

Does diversity have an impact on organizational performance? The results of empirical studies have been mixed. Sometimes diversity enhances performance, sometimes it has no effect, and sometimes it decreases performance. This is leading researchers to explore the conditions under which diversity does help performance. The evidence suggests this is true when the diversity is well managed, when the task requires creativity, and when the group has had time to jell together so as to form its own identity.[B]

For the multinational firm, cultural diversity is obviously of most importance. A global mindset implies recognizing the benefits that can flow to the whole organization from encouraging and valuing cultural diversity in people. Does cultural diversity enhance or handicap performance? One recent study argues that in the short term, teams that are homogeneous on nationality will outperform culturally mixed teams because the differences in frames of reference in mixed groups

handicap effectiveness.[C] But in the long run, both highly heterogeneous teams and homogeneous teams outperformed moderately mixed teams (an example of the latter would be Dutch and Belgians or Americans and Brits working together). The reason for this nonlinear U-shaped relationship is that in moderately heterogeneous teams, people tend to identify with subgroups and there is no team identity, whereas people in highly mixed teams are obliged to invest in building a special team identity.

Valuing cultural diversity must go beyond the traditional emphasis on passport and stereotypical national characteristics. Deep cultural knowledge about people means knowledge of differences within the culture as well as between cultures. A lack of understanding of the diversity within a given national culture by outsiders who do not understand the historical, political, and social sources of "within culture" differences acts as a barrier to cross-cultural interactions. We stopped stereotyping about gender and race—perhaps we should tackle culture with the same determination.

[A]For a managerial perspective on diversity, see Kossek and Lobel (1996); Gilbert and Ivancevich (2000); R. Schneider, "Managing Diversity: Variety Performance," *People Management*, May 3, 2001.
[B]See Williams and O'Reilly (1998) for a review of forty years of diversity research. See also Pelled, Eisenhardt, and Xin (1999).
[C]Earley and Mosakowski, 2000.

of HR should not be just to defend cultural traditions in the name of cultural diversity, but to implement the necessary organizational strategies with sensitivity to specific cultural influences. Sometimes being fair requires uniformity; sometimes it requires differentiation. Unfortunately, understanding where and how to "push" and where to "give in" to cultural differences is the kind of specific international knowledge that not many HR leaders today have had the opportunity to develop, as we will discuss shortly.

The Navigator

The navigator's perspective is duality. The navigator is always sensitive to the fact that while the weather may be fair today, the storm may be just over the horizon.

There is a real danger at present that first and second generation HRM (the builder and the change agent) become so obsessively focused on the challenges of performance improvement and competitive capability development that they neglect to focus on traditional individual outcomes such as employee satisfaction and motivation.

Critical theorists and postmodernists remind us in healthy ways of this point, as does Ulrich with his HRM role of the "employee champion."[14] Guest undertook a review of these perspectives. For the critical theorists, HRM constitutes at worst a subjugation of employee interests to those of organizational performance, while at best the manipulation of staff, imprinting the core values of the firm on its carefully selected employees.[15] Arguing that one should leave the employees to judge, Guest used the 1997 annual survey of employment relations in the U.K., a carefully stratified random sample, to evaluate whether employees feel subjugated, manipulated or unfairly treated. From the management perspective, the results were reassuring. High commitment working practices were unexpectedly prevalent in the U.K. and they were clearly associated with employee satisfaction, motivation, and positive worker perceptions. However, another academic survey of employee attitudes, also in the U.K., focused on reactions to the way in which change was managed. This showed that although change was accepted as necessary and important, there was considerable cynicism, a sense of overload and initiative fatigue, and widespread concern at the absence of support for the accompanying stress.[16]

The danger of excessive focus on performance at the expense of the employee perspective is to be taken particularly seriously in the international HRM arena because the agenda is so focused on the challenges of global competition and creating value for external customers. Multinational firms sometimes tend to listen only to their staff back in the parent country, while people abroad are anonymous costs to be "rationalized" and shuffled around when needed. Witness the fury of the French, including the French Government, when Marks & Spencer recently announced the closure of stores on continental Europe without having followed legally obligatory procedures for consultation with staff. Treating people abroad as "resources" rather than as *people* risks fueling a possible backlash against globalization that is discussed later in this chapter.

This third face of HRM also involves working through complex changes that have a deep and yet unpredictable impact on the firm, its practices, and its culture, changes that involve close attention to social architecture. In the international arena, let us take the accelerating development of "virtuality" as an example. Using information and e-communication technology, virtual processes aim at delivering services through structures and processes that are fast, flat, and flexible, with responsive and temporary networks of semiautonomous and cross-border teams, project groups, and steering boards. But this requires new skills—self-management, "split egg" skills, faster decision-making combined with careful self-management decision processes, collaboration, virtual team building. In the same way as GE's Jack Welch noted that change management skills must become as much a part of the manager's skill base as using a PC, so virtuality leads to a new set of basic skills.[17] Virtuality means that contractual relationships will be less permanent and more outcome-focused. The management of employee contracts—a traditional core role of the HR function—will become the responsibility of team or contract managers. As with most changes associated with this third face, virtuality will change the nature of basic HR foundations as well as the HR role itself.

Organizing Global Human Resources

Paradoxically, in spite of the opportunities for HR to contribute to globalization in added-value ways, the HR function is not perceived in many companies as a full partner in the globalization process. Sometimes it is viewed as an obstacle, slowing down the process through bureaucratic central procedures. The ethnocentric and parochial HR systems and policies inherited from the past, focused on the parent company and projected onto the rest of the world, are all too often a barrier to the implementation of effective global organizational processes.

In this section, we discuss four of the obstacles. First, there is a need to clearly differentiate the apples and oranges of HR tasks, distinguishing between those that are local and those that are global in scope, those that are neither, and those that are both. Second, this differentiation leads to reorganization of the HR function in the international firm. Third, parenting roles at the headquarters need to change toward what we call "network leadership." And fourth, particular skills are needed in global process management roles. We discuss the more personal implications for career and self-management in the following section.

Differentiating the HR Activities

In the past, the organization of HR activities, roles, and responsibilities was undertaken on a simple binary scale—what should be centralized (global), and what should be decentralized (local)? This started to get more complex as a middle ground came into the picture—what should be coordinated? Today we recognize that there are a variety of delivery mechanisms for HR activities—outsourced activities that are brokered, integrated activities that are either centralized or tightly coordinated, tasks that are best undertaken by local businesses or countries, activities that should be managed by global or regional service centers and those that could best be run by regional centers of excellence, and complex activities that merit the attention of international project groups.

This is shown in a diagram developed by Ulrich (see Figure 10–1), where the two dimensions that guide the organization of HR activities are the assessed requirements of integration and differentiation respectively.[18] Let us discuss the different HR delivery mechanisms within this framework.

HOW CAN HR DOMAINS THAT ARE LOW ON INTEGRATION AND DIFFERENTIATION BE MANAGED? There are many HR activities that are not strategic and are relatively standardized across a region or indeed the world. In the past, before IT opened up new ways of managing them, large administrative departments undertook this work. Examples of such matters are payroll processing, responding to standard employee questions about benefits, pensions and employment rules, basic generic training, and occupational health. Some matters are slightly higher up on integration or differentiation but still relatively standardized, such as rank-and-file recruitment.

Outsourcing may be one way of organizing these HR operations, applied to payroll processing, generic training, or pension fund management. Through contracting with third parties, high quality at low cost can be achieved and maintained. *Regional call centers* are used to provide staff with basic information on employment terms as

---

FIGURE 10–1. Using Different Delivery Mechanisms for Different HR Activities in the International Firm

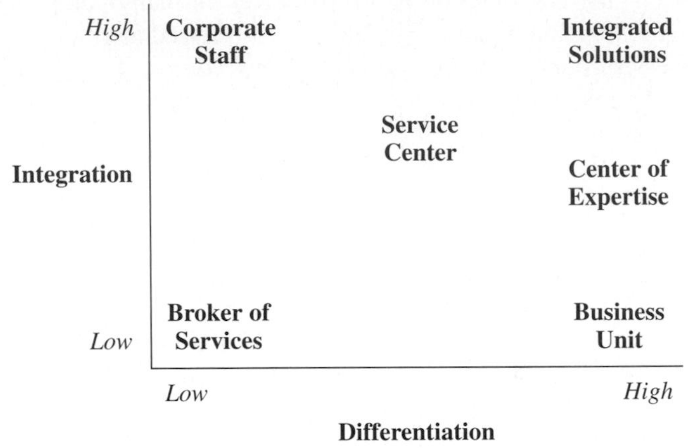

High	**Corporate Staff**		**Integrated Solutions**
		Service Center	
Integration			**Center of Expertise**
Low	**Broker of Services**		**Business Unit**
	Low		*High*
	Differentiation		

Source: Adapted from D. Ulrich, *Human Resource Champions* (Boston: Harvard Business School Press, 1997).

well as rules, pensions, and procedures. *Information technology* provides a growing number of options for streamlining service delivery. If you want training in a basic domain such as negotiation skills or quality management, then you access a corporate website which provides information on certified external courses as well as the names and evaluations of recent attendees. Even the process of learning and training can be standardized using information technology. For example, IBM has invested heavily in *e-learning technology* on generic issues such as the development of basic managerial skills so that staff throughout the world can learn on an anywhere-anytime basis instead of requesting authorization to attend a training seminar. This is guided by a five-step learning model, beginning with basic reading and information, proceeding upward to e-courses, then followed by computer-assisted dialogue sessions and ultimately a face-to-face workshop and certification that is organized locally.

WHAT SHOULD BE TIGHTLY INTEGRATED? We have argued that the most strategic function of HRM in all firms, and notably in the multinational corporation, is management development of key position holders and those with the potential to occupy such roles.[19] Indeed, empirical evidence suggests that this is the case. One recent study showed that firms that do not exercise tight central control over strategic talent face acute shortages of international managers, which handicaps the implementation of their global strategies.[20]

Honda in Japan and the French international retailing group Carrefour are two well-known corporations who resisted functionalizing the responsibility for human resources. In both companies people management is considered to be so important that it firmly remains a line responsibility at all levels. Yet with increasing internationalization, both of them were obliged to create a corporate HR department to bring professional rigor to the process of cross-boundary leadership development.

Aside from this, what should be globally integrated through corporate HR roles depends on the strategy of the firm. If the strategy for growth is repetitive international acquisitions, then the acquisition methodology will be an integrated corporate responsibility involving HR, as at Cisco. A few year's ago, AT&T moved their top HR officer into a position heading up corporate acquisitions and ventures for this reason. Whatever is deemed to be a corporate capability should be reflected in the structure of corporate responsibilities. Recently Norsk Hydro, Norway's largest firm and a world leader in natural resource exploitation (oil and gas, light metals, and fertilizers), set out to develop capabilities in change acceleration. Corporate HR took the initiative, and a methodology was developed in partnership with selected line and HR managers from its businesses. Currently hundreds of HR and line managers are being trained in this methodology that is also backed up by a web-based knowledge management system.

There are strong arguments in many industries for integrating global knowledge management and learning, sometimes in tight partnership with other corporate functions such as IT and planning.[21] GE is a good example, whose boundaryless organization concept is steered by the chief learning officer, who also heads up its Crotonville management development center. The CLO is responsible for steering the process of collecting, certifying, and transferring best practice know-how across the complex matrix of GE businesses.[22]

WHAT SHOULD BE THE RESPONSIBILITY OF LOCAL SUBSIDIARIES OR BUSINESS UNITS? Many HR matters require a high degree of differentiation according to the country or business. Here the locus of decision-making and action should lie with the local unit. In most companies, the recruitment and technical training of the operational workforce falls into this category. Owing to the country specificity of union relations, this is also true of collective bargaining—although that matter can come into question when there are regional trends such as EU social regulation or union pressure for cross-border negotiation of collective agreements. In decentralized, locally responsive companies, the norm is that all HR matters fall into this category—unless there are clear grounds for arguing otherwise. In globally integrated firms, the situation is the reverse—local subsidiaries must adapt to central policies and guidelines, facilitated by parent company expatriates in key positions. However, local responsibility does not necessarily mean an abdication of coordination. There may be an overlay of coordination through best practice sharing or centers of expertise.

HOW TO MANAGE HR ACTIVITIES REQUIRING MODERATE INTEGRATION AND DIFFERENTIATION? How to handle activities that are at the extremes—high on either integration or on differentiation but not on the other dimension—may be clear. But what about the many activities in the middle zone—when some measure of both global integration and differentiated control by countries or business units is needed? Expertise in managing expatriation might be a good example. Here regional structures, service centers (internal and external), and centers of expertise might be useful delivery mechanisms.

Some multinational companies introduce *regional structures* to cope with activities requiring moderate integration and regional differentiation.[23] For example,

Unilever is structured around its product lines, but it has a regional structure in emerging markets such as Southeast Asia. While the businesses have all the necessary HR experience and expertise in developed European markets, this is not the case for business unit managers in China and Indonesia. Here an overlay of regional HR managers (and also in other functions) provides guidance and expertise to local management teams on recruitment, resourcing, development, expatriation, and the like.

Service centers are often used in this middle ground, organized on a regional or a worldwide basis. A service center brings together in one physical or virtual location the expertise to provide tailored solutions to problems, expertise that local units do not possess. Expatriation, management training, and the development of performance management systems are among the services that such centers may provide, and some firms sell more transactional services such as benefits management and employment verification. Typically such service centers have to pay their own way. The norms for the use of their services vary. Ideally, business units are free to buy these services outside if they can find better quality and lower price; and the center may be free to sell its services outside so as to fund its development costs.

Sun Microsystems organizes most of its corporate HR activities through such centers, as does Holderbank in the cement industry. Sometimes this can go too far, and there are dangers in the use of such centers.[24] After its crisis in 1991, IBM put all of its HR activities into such a service center and told it to pay its own way. But it discovered that it thereby lost control over some strategically important HR activities and had to backtrack to a more differentiated approach.

We are also seeing the development of *external service centers*. An example is Microsoft's alliance with a service company specializing in recruitment of software engineers and other knowledge workers. This agency has expertise in leading edge e-technology for recruitment on the web, and it invests heavily in the improvement of that technology. The process is seamless in the sense that when line managers are presented with three external candidates for a job, they do not know that a third party has undertaken the work.

Centers of expertise are another delivery mechanism to provide tighter integration of decentralized activities. A center of expertise differs from a service center in that it builds on "split egg roles" rather than full-time jobs. For example, we may have an outstanding expert in recruitment processes located in our German subsidiary. Germany is no longer growing as rapidly as in the past. Rather than losing that expertise, why don't we leverage it across western and central Europe by appointing the person to head up our European center for recruitment expertise? The individual builds a virtual team of inside and outside resource persons, has a budget for this top-of-the-egg activity, while still continuing with the bottom-of-egg responsibilities for recruitment in Germany.

There are many domains that can be organized in a "split egg" fashion, going from diversity management to employee attitude surveys, from organizational change advice to communications design, from work safety to communities of practice associated with global knowledge management. These are all areas where local commitment and adaptation are needed, where coordination has benefits, but where it is questionable whether there are advantages to having a structure of experts at the corporate center.

WHAT ABOUT HR DOMAINS THAT REQUIRE BOTH INTEGRATION AND DIF-FERENTIATION? These are the most complex matters of global organization, the design of a global process for recruitment or performance management being an example that we will discuss later. Local units see such matters as their own prerogative, arguing justifiably that practices should be differentiated. On the other hand, corporate managers rightly view these matters as strategic for the global interests of the firm.

The basic mechanism for managing these HR challenges (and indeed those in other domains such as IT and planning) is the *cross-boundary project group.*[25] The role of corporate leaders is to form a project group that will define and work the issues. This team should include appropriate people from the businesses and countries, and perhaps line as well as HR people. To the extent that these individuals have a true global mindset, experience that leads to a "matrixed mind," the project group can be kept small and manageable, avoiding the danger of becoming a representational committee. The project group formulates the appropriate policy or response.

Reengineering the HR Roles

Many multinational organizations have been through a process of reorganizing and "reengineering" the worldwide HR function, driven by the principles described above. A large and unresponsive corporate HR function at Norsk Hydro was reorganized over a six-year period. Many HR roles were decentralized to the businesses in oil, fertilizers, and light metals (training, performance management, and the implementation of strategy through HRM). This meant that the skills of decentralized HR managers had to be upgraded so that they could function as business partners on management teams. Regional HR roles were created to coordinate HR activities across businesses in emerging markets such as Southeast Asia.

The corporate function had to assume a new parenting role (described below) in its remaining activities, notably in leadership development. As the divisions grew stronger, the corporate center no longer had the authority to dictate policy and practice, so influence and process skills became important. There was a lot of confusion at the corporate level until vital but operational HR activities were spun off into a service center called Hydro Partner—offering services in compensation system design, expatriation management, and technical training. This service center is expected to pay its own way, selling its services to divisions, though rules still have to be defined on whether such services can also be sold to noncompetitive outside customers. The creation of the service center freed up the streamlined corporate HR center to focus on genuinely strategic activities, including an initiative led by the CEO to develop organizational capabilities in change acceleration.

The pattern is both similar and different in other organizations. Take the Ford Motor Company as another example. Responding to the globalization of the firm, HR created a global Human Resources Council to oversee all HR activities, including corporate. Aside from HR operations that are part of the businesses and a new structure of shared services, Ford decided to exploit information and communications technology through customer centers accessed by phone and the web, and through self-help HR tools that are typically online. At IBM and other firms, emergent areas such as accelerated computer-assisted learning and global knowledge management involve new partnerships between HR, IT, and planning functions—although in firms with strong functional traditions this can lead to political infighting rather than partnership. Modeled on professional service firms, such industrial corporations have also created a Global Professional Service activity, which offers internal consulting services in areas such as organizational effectiveness (OD), change management, and individual development, the costs being charged to the businesses.

Parenting: Network Leadership

The new challenges of global HR require strong leadership from headquarters—or parenting as it is sometimes called (see the box "Parenting: How the Corporation Adds Value"). Parenting is a good metaphor—parents occasionally have to give orders and instructions, though they have to pay careful attention to how these orders are formulated because they also have to help their children (here the subsidiaries or divisions) to grow and stand on their own feet.

Parents at worldwide or regional headquarters cannot undertake the responsibility for solving problems around the world. This might have been true in the early

Parenting: How the Corporation Adds Value
Research Box

Researchers at Ashridge in the U.K. developed the concept of "parenting" to describe the role of the headquarters. Goold, Campbell, and Alexander address the interesting question of how parents add value to their businesses.[A]

In the early days of internationalization, this question did not arise. The parent *was* the business. But in today's more developed and competitive world where each business unit, be it a product unit or a country subsidiary, is expected to add value, the question of how the parent adds value to its individual units becomes relevant. From a shareholder perspective, why is a multinational corporation better off than the sum of its parts?

The Ashridge studies argue that corporate parents add value to their units in one of four different ways: stand-alone influence; linkage influence; through central functions and services; and through corporate development. Each way of adding value has two possible faces. If practiced appropriately, the parent can add value, but if practiced inappropriately, then value can

be destroyed. Goold and his colleagues present each of these vehicles for adding value through the lens of a paradox.

1. *Standalone influence*

    Here the challenge is called the 10 versus 100 percent paradox: How can parents who spend 10 percent of their time on the affairs of a local business improve on decisions being made by competent local managers who are giving 100 percent of their efforts to that business? The clinical case studies of the researchers suggest that the parent can add value through the quality of the appointments to key positions in the affiliates; and through rigorous strategic and performance management (strategic and business reviews, stretch goals, performance metrics and budgetary controls).

2. *Linkage influence*

    Parents can build linkages between affiliates so as to reap coordination benefits, resulting in better utilization of tangible assets, knowledge shar-

stages of internationalization when the necessary expertise was located at the center. That expertise is now located around the world in different centers and subsidiaries.

But this does not mean that there is no need for central expertise. Some firms have gone too far in eliminating headquarters staff, especially in HR, for there are dangers to excessive devolvement.[26] However, the coordination needs of the transnational change the nature of parent roles. A different set of skills is needed at the center, which we call *network leadership.*

Network leadership involves the following abilities:

- *An awareness of leading edge trends and developments.* The network leader, typically either a functional staff manager or a headquarters coordinator, has the advantage of having his or her head out of the sand of operational work, providing the opportunity to be at the cutting edge of leading developments and problem areas. In practice, what this means is that the staff manager must be well networked, both internally and externally, so as to be aware of relevant trends.
- *The ability to mobilize the appropriate resources.* When the network leader senses that a development area is timely, he or she needs to be able to bring together the appropriate people in the form of a project group—those with skills

Parenting: How the Corporation Adds Value
Research Box

ing, and greater negotiation power with outside groups. However, a lot of money and energy has been wasted in the past in the pursuit of such internal synergies. One can encourage local managers to pursue such linkage benefits out of enlightened self-interest—why should corporate managers be better at realizing these synergies? This is the enlightened self-interest paradox. When undertaken effectively, linkage involves applying what we call glue technology to real opportunities for linkage benefits.[B] The glue mechanisms are project groups, cross-border steering groups and know-how sharing, as well as common norms that facilitate the workings of self-interest.

3. *Functional and service influence*

The parent may possess functional expertise at the center that affiliates can draw upon, which they otherwise would not be able to afford or access. But the "beating the specialist" paradox to bear in mind is the following: Can internal staff

or functional units do this better than the outside specialist or consultant? The researchers argue that this question has to be constantly borne in mind to ensure that central staff do add value. Service centers are a way of institutionalizing attention to this paradox.

4. *Corporate development*

This last potential parenting advantage focuses on portfolio management, the creation of new businesses, amalgamating units, buying and selling businesses. Here the paradox is that of the odds: Why should corporate development activities such as M&A beat the odds that appear to be stacked so heavily against them?[C]

[A]Goold, Campbell, and Alexander (1994). See also Campbell and Goold (1998); Goold and Campbell (1998).
[B]This issue is discussed at great length in Chapter 7.
[C]This paradox and its implications for HRM is the topic of Chapter 6.

and experience together with key managers from lead application units. This means that the parent leader needs to have a fair degree of clout and credibility with units around the world, based on that person's track record. Some staff leaders do not command this respect and do not have that clout. The only people from affiliates they can secure are the "available people" who are rarely the right people—that is why they are available! When needed, this also means bringing in outside resources such as consultants and experts, funded by corporate budgets.

- *A sense of timing and context.* Lastly, the network leader needs an acute sense of timing, and this is perhaps the quality that is most often lacking. If subsidiaries are besieged by short-term operational imperatives, nothing undermines the credibility of the parent more than having the focus of key people in the sub-sidiary distracted by a long-term corporate or regional initiative, however important it may be. Over the years, we have witnessed many well-reasoned initiatives by senior steering groups or corporate staff that have backfired because of a poor sense of timing. Sensitivity to whether businesses are in an exploitation or exploration mode is strongly needed in order to exercise parenting skills.

Championing: Process Ownership

HR needs to think in terms of processes, not in terms of activities. Processes link together different activities with an orientation toward targets and deliverables. Staff professionals tend to focus on activities, whereas line managers think in terms of processes. Processes thereby link functional HR staff to line management concern with deliverables.[27]

The development of global processes, as discussed earlier, is a potentially important but complex aspect of the international HR role. Processes need owners who act as champions. Often this ownership is jointly shared (staff and line, or different functions such as HR, planning, and IT), though the responsibility for execution lies with the local units. When HR is the co-owner and champion of a process such as performance management, leadership development, acquisitions, or change acceleration, what are the roles that must be played?

A first role is building the commitment of top management and key executives to utilize a process such as performance management as a key tool in achieving business objectives. The development work needs to be undertaken with senior line managers so as to define a global process that is appropriate to the strategic vision, values, and culture of the firm.

Another important role in process championing is to provide the necessary training and coaching of managers so as to ensure that it works effectively and consistently across the whole firm. For example, the process owner for GE's Change Acceleration Process (CAP) is the Crotonville corporate leadership development function. GE has trained over 15,000 coaches in the use of CAP, coaches who are mostly line managers spread out across the globe.[28]

Few companies invest adequate time in training their staff in the elements of performance management such as goal setting and appraisal, even though we know that the added value of such a process is proportional to the degree of training and coaching.

Monitoring the process is a third set of roles, requiring annual or periodic organizational audits. The monitoring is linked to the necessary learning, updating, and renewal. In fact, processes are best seen as learning vehicles, constantly incorporating changes and improvements.

Career and Personal Implications

The obstacles to globalization of the HR function are also individual in nature—reorganization demands changes in roles and career structures. One of the paradoxes we confront is that while HR has a vital role to play in globalization, which is often openly espoused by those in central HR roles, the reality is that many HR managers and professionals at the headquarters have little if any international experience. Worse still, because they take a plane from time to time to visit the subsidiaries abroad they may *think* that they have a truly international perspective. We joke that there is only one thing more dangerous than the executive who has never been to Japan—the executive who spent two weeks in Japan and who is now a Japan expert! Sometimes the corporate HR executive who takes an occasional plane trip around the world suffers from a delusion that he or she has the answer to all the subsidiary problems.

Multinational companies make sure that their future line executives have international experience, but rarely their high potential HR managers. Schlumberger and United Technologies are exceptions. UT, with businesses such as Otis Elevators and Pratt & Whitney, recognizes that local HR managers often have highly operational roles focused on recruitment and training, without the skills to play strategic roles in long-term development. So matters such as strategic talent development are the responsibility of high potential HR staff recruited by the parent company, working in regional HR roles and thereby developing deep international experience.

Mobility is an important concern, and justifiably so. If one accepts that mobility (both cross-functional and international) is the most important tool for leadership development,[29] then HR has to be central on the map of functions through which high potential individuals will be moved. Many companies accept this in principle— "It would be great to give our high potentials experience in an HR staff role." But companies where this is common practice like Singapore Airlines are the exception rather than the rule.

Our experience is that companies are tackling the wrong end of the problem. Rather than trying to attract talented line managers who have a gift for people management *into* the HR function, they should instead tackle the problem of exit routes *out of* the HR function. In many firms, HR has a reputation for being a one-way path—once you are in it, you will never get out of the function. This has unfortunately been reinforced by former practices of using senior HR positions as parking grounds for loyal executives whose careers in general management did not work out for one reason or another.

Shell felt that it had to prepare one of its highest potential HR professionals for a possible future role as the head of HR. They assigned him to the Philippines for his first job outside HR—as managing director (CEO). He did such an outstanding job that his next role was as regional coordinator for eastern Europe, a strategic position of great importance. While it was uncertain that he would ever come back into an HR role, this gives a positive signal to the organization—people who get ahead can come out of the HR function.

One will never attract good people into HR unless there are clear routes out of that domain. The issue is of considerable importance to the multinational firm. HR does not control price, costs, quality or flexibility, the parameters that for an economist have a direct impact on profitable growth.[30] In that sense, it does not have a *de jure* right to a place at the executive committee table in the same sense as marketing or operations. That right has to be earned. Competent HR leaders can have a tremendously positive influence on profitable growth, but only if they are superbly competent. This is unlikely to be the situation unless the function can attract the very best talent—by allowing this talent also to move out of HR into top line management roles.

There are delicate dualities to be recognized here. We have seen leading multinationals trying to develop a business-orientation in the HR function by bringing in proven business managers to all key HR roles. The evils of one extreme—excessive professionalism where the means become the ends—are replaced by equal evils of another extreme—reinventing the wheel, trying to score quick wins, failing to understand the powerful principles of coherence and consistency—ultimately undermining of the credibility of the HR function itself. Rotation of line managers through HR needs to be balanced with the need for deep HR professionalism.

A subtle but powerful tool, *mentoring relationships,* is increasingly complementing developmental vehicles such as mobility.[31] Indeed mentoring in different shapes and forms may be one of the most significant developmental tools in this new century (see the box "Mentoring: A Vehicle for the Future?"). Many firms pair up HR and line people, headquarters and field people, HR and IT people. At Cisco, HR staff have a business mentor—they prepare their personal development plans with this partner, typically someone in sales (the same applies to sales and engineering, establishing key linkages). *Shadowing* is a related developmental mechanism used by some firms, where junior HR staff are assigned as "shadows" to line managers working on important international projects. This allows them to get involved in international business activities (perhaps contributing by playing secretarial and process roles), to learn the ropes, and to figure out how HR can add value to such projects.

Mentoring in different shapes and forms will be more and more important in the new postindustrial service economy. Take the implications of one social trend. People today are quite likely to have two or three different professional careers during their lives, in contrast to the "career for life" or even "job for life" situation fifty years ago. But it is very difficult to make such transitions. Many people desperately want to make such a career transition, to get out of a job where they are stuck, bored and miserable (with all of the stress of their state of mind spilling over into their private lives). Ongoing research suggests that mentoring relationships with people in alternative occupations facilitate "taking the jump" and making a successful career/life transition.[32]

HRM AS SOCIAL ARCHITECTURE

Companies and organizations have a different feel to them—what Ghoshal and Bartlett call "the smell of the place."[33] You walk into one organization. You are ushered through the corridors to your meeting room. The office doors are closed, it feels like a mausoleum with locked cupboards lining the walls. There is a group of staff huddled in intense discussion, but they break off as you get close, look guilty and then take it up again as you pass by. It is quite clear that they were complaining about something or discussing the latest in office politics. You ask your host, the local HR manager, about whether customers are responding well to their new product, and she tells you that you'll have ask top management for that information. Even though you've only just set foot in the firm, you can predict various behaviors. At five o'clock in the afternoon the offices will be empty—unless the boss happens to still be there, in which case there will be a few ambitious lieutenants present vying for his or her attention.

You walk into another organization. As long as you show the visible security badge, you are left to find your own way to the meeting room on the fifth floor. Groups of employees are hanging in doorways, some laughing, others in earnest discussion. They ignore you as you wander by. Some doors are closed, many are open. There are computer screens everywhere and no secretaries. You bump into your host, the HR manager, who is busy discussing a problem of logistics with some salespeople. There is a very different feel to the place.

A young engineer at a transformed Philips plant in Scotland commented to Ghoshal and Bartlett, "What matters most is that the smell of the place has changed. I now enjoy coming to work. It's not one thing, but overall, it has become a very different company."[34]

Indeed the smell of a place, or the context that guides behaviors that in turn lead to performance outcomes, is not the product of one single facet. It is the product of the way in which everything hangs together—promotion systems, codified or unspoken values, and whether there is "walk the talk," reward and sanction patterns, work practices, whether customer information is shared, and myriad other details. Context is largely the result of HR practices. Context shapes behavior, and so HRM can rightly be seen as social architecture that shapes context.

It is the critical European theorists coming from a post-Marxist tradition (Marx being a practical philosopher who realized the power of social architecture) who have been most vocal in pointing this out.[35] Indeed they regard HRM as social engineering which in the extreme can lead to an Orwellian "1984." Training is manipulation in disguise, teamworking legitimizes taking away an individual's freedom, empowerment means making someone else take the risk and responsibility.[36]

When does social architecture end and manipulation that deprives freedom begin? A realistic view might be to argue that this can be tested empirically by asking people for their own views.[37] One can argue that the limits of Orwellian manipulation are set by the fact that if freedom and diversity are suppressed, this will kill the lifeblood of innovation and flexibility.

Mentoring: A Vehicle for the Future?
Practice Box

The idea of mentoring (or reciprocal coaching) in an organization sounds simple, but in fact it may be one of the important mechanisms for development and learning in the new century.

Mentoring typically means an informal relationship between a senior, experienced person and a junior colleague. It involves some form of reciprocity. The senior person provides informal advice to the junior colleague and may play many potential roles—opening doors and projects for younger colleagues, coaching, providing exposure by taking the junior to important meetings that will enhance visibility, role modeling, boosting the self-confidence to take on a new challenge, and acting as a sounding board. On the other hand, the junior person may perform some formal or informal duties for the senior person, as well as keeping the mentor in touch with what is happening down in the ranks.

Mentoring came into fashion in the 1970s when research showed that successful people often attributed their success in part to a close mentoring relationship at an earlier stage in their careers.[A]

Different shapes and forms of mentoring in companies

When they became aware of its potency, companies started to implement formal mentoring schemes.

There are many examples:

- When *young professionals or graduates* join a firm, they are assigned to a mentor who is not their direct boss—someone who will help them learn the ropes (including how to manage your own boss!).
- Firms trying to build *cross-functional teamwork* may team people up in mentoring relationships. In some multinationals, a local sales director in a subsidiary is paired up with an R&D manager who acts as host when the sales director visits the parent firm. Such informal exchanges can be useful in linking central research and international sales opportunities.
- *Reverse mentoring* is used at GE, Hewlett-Packard, and other firms. Computer-shy senior executives are paired up with young high potential recruits who are at the cutting edge of Internet developments. If the relationship works, it may obviously be a mutually beneficial deal.
- *Expatriate mentoring* has long been a practice at Royal Dutch/Shell, where about 6 percent of the total workforce are on expatriate assignments. All expatriates have a personnel advisor who acts as a mentor. This is an individual who comes from your own function of work so that you share a common way of viewing things, someone who is located at the headquarters, and who will also host you whenever you come back on a trip. He or she is respon-

Leaving aside these important ethical debates, we single out three aspects of HRM as social architecture for specific discussion. The first is the creation of a competitive culture. The second is the design of a behavioral context of opposing dualities. The third is creating a context for the management of contention.

Building Competitive Culture

HR and other management practices alone do not lead to performance—it is an underlying attitude rather that keeps HR foundations dynamic, preventing decline into custodial maintenance. A focus on competitive performance makes all the difference (see the box "An Eastern European Commentary on the Rise and Fall of HR in Japan").

Mentoring: A Vehicle for the Future?
Practice Box

sible for planning your next assignment or your successful reentry back home.

- *International mentoring* is focused on making sure that high potential managers in local subsidiaries are linked with executives in the corporate center. The role of the mentor is to help their young charges to understand the parent company culture, to navigate the intricacies of decision-making across boundaries, and to assist in mapping their future careers in the context of the global organization.

- Mentoring is particularly important in *professional service firms* to get around the catch-22 dilemma of how to become a partner—in order to become a partner, you have to demonstrate all the attitudes and skills of a partner before you are nominated! Research shows that professionals get around this by learning partner behaviors through a mentor relationship with a partner.[B]

- *Life long interfunctional mentoring* has long been practiced by Honda, which has a practice in which research and engineering managers swap jobs for one month every year from the beginning of their careers to the end.

In fact, as we move to a more networked organizational world and away from hierarchy, these types of relationships will certainly grow. However, the only trouble with formally engineered mentoring schemes is that they often do not work—it depends on mutual trust, even friendship. It is difficult to get the chemistry right unless it happens naturally. People often have to take initiative to build mentoring relationships themselves, but in multinational firms cross-cultural differences are often a hindrance. And in male-dominated organizations, there may be particular obstacles for talented women. In fact, a lot of attention has been paid to the gender problem in mentoring relationships, and in the United States it helped give rise to supportive networks of women professionals.

[A]Studies also showed that a lot of senior people like the mentoring role—it is a bit like being a professional father or mother. And research in high technology firms suggested that unless individual contributors become either formal leaders or informal mentors, then the firm's evaluation of their contribution will go down over time. However, other research suggests that spending too long in a comfortable mentoring relationship can damage career prospects. People will start saying that the person being mentored lacks drive and ambition. Like everything else in life, too much of a good thing may be bad!

[B]See Ibarra (1999); Ibarra (2000).

No One Remembers Number Two

One Japanese company that has maintained its competitiveness is Honda. Honda had to fight for its existence from its early days. The Japanese government, which felt that there were too many auto producers, did not support Honda's entry into the car business. One factor that helped Honda to survive and prosper was its highly competitive culture.

During the early 1990s, the company was not doing well in its home market. One of the hot debates inside the firm was over whether they should continue Formula 1 racing. This was not a technical issue but one about their approach to management development. Honda had always used Formula 1 racing to mold the attitudes of future executives, putting their fast trackers on the team supporting the racing specialists.

One thing you learn in Formula 1 racing is that the only thing that counts is to be number one. Nobody cares who is number two. You do not come to the race saying

An Eastern European Commentary on the Rise and Fall of HR in Japan[A]
Practice Box

The atmosphere among the commuters on the somewhat refurbished subway lines and air-conditioned trains in Tokyo was gloomy. The headlines in the morning papers screamed that yet another prestigious Japanese company had declared a record loss. Who would be next and what would be the consequences?

The national mood had changed dramatically since I visited Japan for the first time three decades ago. Then, Japan was booming, having doubled her wealth in less than ten years, completing her emergence from the ruins of the war. Impressed, I asked my Japanese hosts about the secret of Japan's success. Well, this was easy to explain, they responded. In Japan, everyone has a job—so employees are loyal and motivated, people work in teams, which further increases their commitment, and the government makes sure that all teams march in the right direction. Result: years of unprecedented growth.

However, for me, this explanation did not make any sense. In my country, Czechoslovakia, we all had jobs, so nobody worked. We were required to fit into teams since kindergarten, so we resented anything collective. And our government was obsessed with planning and control, so we all tried to beat the system whenever we could. The dismal results are a well-known story. So why was Japan different?

Of course, it's the culture, others would say. No doubt, the legendary punctuality of Japanese trains has something to do with the cultural reverence for order and precision. However, I also noticed that profitable private companies in Japan run the trains on time with fares one-third cheaper than the national railroad, which manages to accumulate trillion yen losses year after year.

The difference between them was not the national culture but the existence of competition. The profitable firms faced competition, the bankrupt national railroad did not. The "Japanese system" works great, as long as there is competition. It motivates and energizes the workforce to win. The reason is rather simple: in a competitive context, "lifetime" employment can exist only as long as the firm survives.

However, as many large Japanese companies grew rich and prosperous, they were able to isolate themselves from the impact of competition. Without competition, the habits of a more "socialist" enterprise gradually sapped the energy and initiative of previously fast growing excellent firms. They even developed their own protected "party *nomenklatura*": the legions of "salarymen," with not much to do, with no incentive to learn the skills necessary to compete in today's economy. Not surprisingly, business performance declined.

At the same time, with less emphasis on competition, the role of the HR function in Japanese firms declined dramatically. In the past, HR was seen as a key strategic function; today it is mostly ignored. Without a focus on performance, why bother with HR? The more HR in Japan is perceived as the chief advocate of the status quo (under the banner of social harmony), the more irrelevant it becomes. The intentions may be noble, but the results are devastating—for the firm and for the employees stuck in jobs with no future whose interests the HR function is supposedly trying to protect. In a global economy there is no escape.

[A]Vlado Pucik, coauthor, was born and raised in Czechoslovakia (now the Czech Republic and Slovakia) and subsequently spent many years working in Japan.

that my strategic objective is to be a strong number two. You might end up number two or number four, but there will be another race. You must figure out what went wrong and try again. So you learn.

The second thing with Formula 1 is teamwork. You can have a brilliant driver, a superb mechanic, and a great engineer, but the only way to win is if you put the whole thing together right. It is a powerful message. What counts is not just you as an individual but also how you work as a team.

Third, you learn that you had better be on time. If your car is late on the starting line, then you have no chance of winning. There are no excuses. And the same is true for quality. If on the twenty-third lap the transmission catches fire, you cannot say that it is the fault of the supplier. You end up as a footnote, a car that dropped out of the race.

Honda saw Formula 1 racing as teaching an even more fundamental principle. Once the race starts, there is nothing that a manager can do to influence the result. Once the race has started, giving instructions over the walkie-talkie will only mess things up. The only thing that you can do is go to the grandstand, observe what happens, and go back after the race to tell people what went well and what went not so well—and help them to win next time round.

The debate at Honda over whether to keep Formula 1 was heated. Some Honda executives felt that the messages conveyed were too one-sided, getting managers to pay less attention to auto manufacturing basics such as energy efficiency and emission standards. The debate was not so much over costs but over the signals that one gives through this social architecture. Honda eventually decided to get out of Formula 1 (though it has since returned), but it pays strong attention to managing context.

Guiding Values and Philosophy

The fact that there was hot debate over whether Honda's Formula 1 racing was giving the right signals is not an indication of unhealthy corporate politics—quite to the contrary. When circumstances change, there must be such debate over what are the norms and values that should guide behavior. Senior executives and high potential managers in particular must internalize the new values.

Highly competitive cultures typically have explicit values, indeed often an explicit philosophy like the Hewlett-Packard Way or the Lincoln Electric value system. The reason why this is desirable, perhaps vital, is once again that it is not work practices that create a competitive culture but the coherence and consistency between these practices. Many firms try to increase competitive culture by introducing more open transparency of measurement and performance-based rewards. But they find that this has only a token effect on the underlying culture. A coherent set of practices, down to the little details such as how the janitor is treated and whether free beverage machines are installed, needs to be guided by a well-thought-out and clearly understood management philosophy. The intense discussion at Honda and the decade-long reconsideration of the tenets of the HP Way reflect a process of internalizing modified guiding values that will pay off in a new but consistent configuration of practices.[38] A firm that decrees new practices or new values at a single weekend conference for key staff is unlikely to enjoy any competitive benefits.

Moreover, the translation of value systems into competitive cultures typically will involve working through conflicts and dualistic tensions, just as Honda's Formula 1 training captures tensions over when managers should be hands-on and when they should be hands-off. Another tension to be anchored in the culture through the careful design of HR practices is that between competition (in the shape of individual accountability and comparison) and teamwork.[39]

Stretch and Support, Discipline and Trust

Tensions guide social architecture in the framework of Ghoshal and Bartlett for creating a dynamic behavioral context in the international firm.[40] They argue that the behavioral context in traditional firms was provided by a configuration of values that may have been internally consistent but which is out of line with the new competitive realities. This is shown in Figure 10–2. Constraints in the shape of boundaries and rule books were part of the culture of compliance that kept people suitably focused on a straight and narrow path rather than wasting time on irrelevant opportunities. This was reinforced by control systems, guided by centralized planning, leading to explicit quasi-contractual obligations, anchored in incentive-oriented compensation systems.

FIGURE 10–2. Frameworks to Guide the Context for Behavior

A. The Traditional Configuration to Guide Behavioral Context

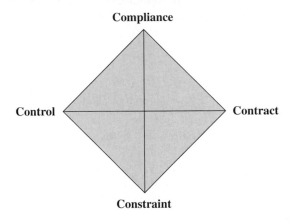

B. Today's Dualistic Configuration to Guide Behavioral Context

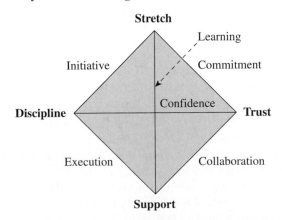

Source: Adapted from S. Ghoshal and C. A. Bartlett, *The Individualized Corporation* (New York: HarperBusiness, 1997).

Critical as one may be today of this configuration, it was one that served many firms well in the early decades of international expansion, particularly U.S. firms.[41]

If the underlying theme behind this book is correct, namely, that we have moved into a global world that is characterized by the tensions between opposites, then the concepts guiding social architecture should reflect these tensions. This is seen in the framework that Ghoshal and Bartlett advocate to guide the building of behavioral context in the transnational firm, shown in the bottom half of Figure 10–2. All of the elements of this dualistic frame have been discussed earlier in this book.

The basic vitality and energy in the firm comes from purpose and shared ambition, an unwavering desire to *stretch* the capacities of the firm rather than fall into complacency. At one level this is seen in the way in which the firm goes about strategic planning and in the performance management system of the firm (the cover and first part of GE's 1994 Annual Report were devoted to clarifying what this implies). But at another level this fuels the deeply competitive culture of the enterprise that we discussed above.

Stretch objectives have become fashionable. However they can easily lead to a debilitating treadmill where last year's achievements are discounted after the bonus has been paid—and we start again with new stretch goals. After a few years of this, capable people who have other alternatives will soon opt out. Stretch has to be counterbalanced with *support*. Support is embodied in the coaching roles of senior business managers, who provide resources, remove obstacles, and build the necessary teamwork to achieve those targets.

If the transnational organization is to maintain control without the pathologies of centralized rulebooks, then an internal sense of *discipline* needs to be fostered through the tools of normative integration.[42] The meaning of a commitment or a deadline needs to be internalized through the socialization of key staff. This includes clear and consistent sanctions in the case of unreasonable underperformance. However, excessive discipline can create pathologies, killing the vital lifeblood of innovation and risk taking. Discipline has to be balanced with the *trust* that comes from involvement in decision-making, having the right to refute arguments with which one disagrees, and other aspects of fairness and procedural justice.

Contention Management

The third aspect of social architecture that we wish to single out for particular attention is conflict or contention management. Conflict is the "stuff" of the multinational corporation—in the shape of contradiction, in the shape of tensions between dualities, in the shape of matrix, in the shape of contending ideas that are the lifeblood of innovation. Dentsu in Japan is one of the largest advertising agencies in the world, and the last of the ten guiding rules of its first chairman, Hideo Yoshida, is the following: "When confrontation is necessary, don't shy away from it. Confrontation is the mother of progress and the fertilizer of an aggressive enterprise. If you fear conflict it will make you timid and irresolute."[43]

Many people do not share this value. For them conflict is something bad, something to be avoided. Prevailing practice in international companies in the past was to try to resolve the conflicts at the top during the business planning process so that middle managers and lower level people would not have their attention distracted by trade-offs, dilemmas, and confrontation. They should focus on execution. In many companies, the practice still today is to refer conflict upward for arbitration—such companies are not likely to survive for long since top management becomes so overwhelmed by operational matters that they will not have time for the big strategic picture. The history of the organizational structure in multinational firms, as they developed ever more complex matrices, can be interpreted as a struggle to find a structural resolution to conflict—leading ultimately to the conclusion that the capacity to cope with conflict must be built into the culture of the firm.

The research says that conflict is not bad.[44] Too much conflict is bad, but too little conflict may be equally bad since it leads to apathy and complacency. The cognitive element of conflict—divergence of perspectives, diversity in factual inputs, differences in assumptions—is productive. As Dentsu's Yoshida said, this is the mother of progress. It is the interpersonal element of conflict that creates problems. As the old adage says, "attack the ideas, not the person." In fact, creating a culture of constructive conflict or constructive debate may be one of the most important challenges for HRM in multinational companies.

Creating a Culture of Constructive Debate

One data point that supports the argument for constructive debate is Kakabadse's studies of management teams in different countries. In over a third of 3,000 European management teams there were serious differences of view about strategic goals that were not discussed, hidden under the table.[45] While differences in view are the basis for sound decision-making, what is striking is that they are so often not confronted and worked through, even though everyone in the organization may know that the management team is divided. If the senior teams shy away from conflict, how can one expect those lower down not to do so?

Contrast this with the research of Eisenhardt and her collaborators at Stanford who have spent twenty years studying why a few companies thrive in Silicon Valley–type environments while the majority go under. In this world of hypercompetition, dot-coms and microcomputer firms must be prepared for strategic windows to suddenly open up. A new technology comes into fruition that changes the ballgame. There is an opportunity for an alliance. The market shifts. This means that a strategic decision has to be taken in three weeks. If the decision is wrong, then the firm will be out of business. If the decision is right but people are not committed to implement it fast, then the firm will be out of business. What characterizes firms that thrive in such demanding environments? Some of Eisenhardt's findings are neatly summarized by the title of one of her articles: "How Management Teams Can Have a Good Fight."[46]

Eisenhardt and her associates find that winning companies anticipate such strategic decisions, closely scanning the environment and reviewing options on a permanent basis. As Intel's Andy Grove notes, you have to be paranoid to survive. This is as transparent a process as it can be. When the strategic decision opens up, the people go into overdrive for several weeks—a hotbed of contention, argument, fact finding. The role of top management is to try to get consensus, though this may not always be possible. In that case, its role is to stop the debate with the final decision. Some firms find it very difficult to stop the debate. In fact, the real debate only begins once the decision has been reached—not a very constructive way of handling conflict.

GE's Jack Welch is a master of constructive debate, modeling this with his own behavior. He used to spend up to 20 percent of his time at GE's Crotonville management training center, where he presented his views on the challenges and goals to the GE managers. But he expected them to argue back:

> Welch's decision-making methods have not changed much since his days at (GE) Plastics. He would corral everyone he could find who knew something relevant about the subject at hand—whether chemists, production engineers, or finance types—and thoroughly debrief them. He wanted on-the-spot answers, not formal, written reports. Then

What Would You Put on Your "ABB-Brazil" Card?
Practice Box

ABB's move into the service management area is being spearheaded by their fast moving Brazilian subsidiary. Brazil is headed by a charismatic leader who looks Brazilian but who turns out to be the stereotype of the matrixed manager—Indian born, educated in the U.K., holding a Danish passport after his training there as an ABB engineer, having then worked in different roles throughout the world.

Discussing contention management, he pulls out of his wallet a plastic card that looks like a credit card. On one side are fifteen guidelines for constructive debate such as "Make sure that you have understood the other person's view before you disagree." These reflect the behavioral norms that the Brazilian management team has worked through. On the other side of the card are the signatures of the top 25 executives from ABB Brazil. The practice is that if one feels that someone is violating the norms for constructive contention management, then you just pull out your card and tap it gently on the table. If three other members of your team are playing with their cards, this is a subtle but powerful signal that you are violating the norms![A]

What are some of the norms that might be put on such a card? In addition to paying attention to procedural justice, research suggests that in Western cultures some of these might be the following:[B]

- *Ensure that there is agreement on goals.* Absence of agreement around goals (or vision or strategic criteria) will lead to political infighting and nonconstructive debate.

- *Actively listen before you disagree.* Showing the other person that you have understood their views increases the probability that they will listen constructively to your different views.
- *Focus on the issues, not the personalities.*
- *Data, data, data . . . measurement, measurement . . .* A focus on facts keeps contention constructive. Consequently companies that have cultures of constructive debate tend to believe in measuring everything.
- *Ensure balanced power structures.* If certain functions or units are left out of the debate in order to simplify the decision-making process, then the probability of debate happening only after the decision is reached is maximized.
- *Inject humor into the decision-making process.* Studies all show that humor assists in keeping the tension constructive.
- *Explore multiple alternatives to enrich the debate.* Sometimes leaders try to simplify the process of debate and decision-making by focusing on their most preferred option or by sequentially exploring alternatives. This slows down the process of exploration and increases the probability of conflict.

[A]Other firms use the football (soccer) metaphor. When a person is violating their internal rules of conduct (typically some rules for constructive debate), people flash a yellow card or even a red card. Obviously this isn't done in practice, but it creates a language—"Watch out! You're getting into the yellow zone!"

[B]Based on the studies of Eisenhardt. See Eisenhardt and Zbaracki (1992); Eisenhardt and Bourgeois (1997); Eisenhardt, Kahwajy, and Bourgeois (1997). The principles of procedural justice (such as having the right to refute) are discussed in Chapter 9.

he would join his subordinates in fierce, no-holds-barred debates about which decision to make. Welch calls this "constructive conflict." His theory is that if an idea can't survive a spirited argument, the marketplace surely will kill it.[47]

To guide constructive debate, some of the general guidelines that stem from research and practice are shown in the box "What Would You Put on Your 'ABB-Brazil' Card?" Take one of the obvious ones—never personalize the conflict. A leading Scandinavian enterprise formed an Operations Council six years ago, sensing that there was a need for a forum for frank, open dialogue among the thirty top executives. At the third meeting one of the executives was talking candidly about the firm's difficulties in China, and this evidently hit a raw nerve in the mind of the chief operating officer. The COO exploded. With a verbal howitzer he attacked and massacred the unfortunate executive who had dared to be so impertinent. There was a stony and embarrassed silence. That was the last meeting when anything useful was said. The council became an arena for ritualistic exchange of information that is already on the intranet sites of the executives.

The norms for constructive debate, such as those shown in the accompanying " 'ABB-Brazil' Card" box, need to be translated into cultural reality through HRM practices. Egg, the British Internet bank, is such an example, recently voted as the most visionary and admired company in the U.K. Since British banks were slow in getting into Internet banking, Prudential Insurance decided to set up this venture unit to steal a march on the banks. The management team quickly came to the conclusion that the entire culture of the unit needed to be built on principles of what we call constructive debate. Whether successful or unsuccessful, they would come under intense pressure—from the banks and not least from their own mother company. So the recruitment criteria, the induction messages, the internal processes, the reward system were all constructed so as to foster the desired culture. Social architecture in action!

We Are Socialized to Handle Conflict in Different Ways

One of the underresearched areas of international management is the way in which different cultures handle conflict, contention, and debate, and what this implies for multinational management practices. Laurent's research shows that some national cultures are more likely to see conflict as bad, whereas others embrace conflict as a source of progress. Across Western nations, few Swedes and Americans saw conflict as something to be eliminated from organizations, whereas 41 percent of the Italians saw it as desirable to eliminate conflict forever.[48]

Different national attitudes to conflict and different ways of resolving conflict create big challenges for the social architecture of the transnational organization. The stakes are immense for firms such as Citibank, Hewlett-Packard, and ABB, who are pioneering front-back organizations, in which the success of the corporation depends on its ability to work through the conflicts between the customer-oriented front organization and the product/function oriented back organization. L'Oréal, the world's most successful cosmetics firm, is a warning here. For a hundred years, l'Oréal's cultural values were built around contention management, embodied in a dualistic value system (to be a creative poet and a financially conservative peasant at the same time) and in practices such as the use of confrontation rooms for taking key decisions.[49] This contributed to l'Oréal's success and functioned well as long as all key managers were French and were well socialized into such practices. But as the firm expanded internationally, it was obliged in the early 90s to localize, to develop non-French leaders, and to give a greater measure of autonomy to its subsidiaries. Its culture began to weaken, and conflicts between different parts of the global firm were either avoided or confronted in less than constructive ways. One of the challenges for l'Oréal and many other firms is to develop norms for contention management that allow people of very different backgrounds to collaborate effectively together. In newly created "instant transnational" firms such as Business Objects, our case study at the start of this book, this probably has to be one of the elements of the founding management philosophy that guides the selection, induction, development, and promotion of individuals around the world.

To illustrate the way in which different cultural norms regarding contention management influence corporate development, let us take the contrasting cultures of Japan and Israel. Most Japanese would probably not identify with Jack Welch's values. The culture embraces *wa,* or harmony, and the social pressures against the open expression of conflict are strong.[50] This does not mean that the Japanese avoid conflict. They tend to deal with conflict in implicit and indirect ways rather than in the explicit and direct manner of an American Jack Welch. Disagreement is expressed indirectly by tone of voice and nuance—in the West there is one word for "no," whereas in Japan there are many different ways of expressing this negative. Many Japanese firms have a strong sense of hierarchy, and it is difficult for subordinates to openly express their views to the boss.

Some Japanese firms developed a process called *nemawashi* (meaning negotiation) to handle the contention necessary for key decisions. Whereas Western firms assign the responsibility for decision-making to the most senior person, the practice in these Japanese enterprises is to attribute the responsibility to a junior high potential individual as a developmental challenge. This person has the task of consulting upwards until agreement is reached, and managers can be quite open in expressing their views to such a low-level subordinate. Senior management verifies that all key people have signed off on the proposed decision, which is then implemented. The advantage of the *nemawashi* is that it pays off in terms of the motivation behind that implementation. The disadvantage is that the process of decision-making is painfully slow, incompatible with a world in which speed is important. In contrast, Sony built a very different culture for contention management, selecting and socializing more combative people—one of its early recruitment advertisements in Japan was headlined, "We want salesmen who can fight like the Americans."[51]

Contrast the case of Israel. Israeli technology labs are hotbeds of innovation, and their universities train superb scientists and engineers. Moreover, the Israelis have a major advantage over other small countries with a similar population, such as Denmark, Belgium, or Finland—the positive side of the Jewish diaspora is that there is an active community of loyal representatives spread out through the world. One would expect Israel to have produced more than its fair share of multinational corporations. So name one Israeli multinational!

You will be hard pushed to do so. Scitex failed in its ambition to become a global player in high technology, there are some growing computer companies, but there are only two or three Israeli firms in the billion-dollar multinational league such as Teva in generic pharmaceuticals.

One can speculate that part of the reason is the way in which Israelis are brought up to deal with contention. Children are typically socialized into behaviors that are diametrically opposite to those in Japan—conflict is quite open. The only way that one can discover truth is to speak one's mind openly and then argue it through. The trouble is that people from other cultures, socialized into more subtle and indirect ways of dealing with conflict, find discussion with a stereotypical Israeli to be threatening. If one accepts that contention is a basic challenge for the transnational enterprise, then Israelis are handicapped because they find it difficult to handle the coordination challenges with people who are different. Teva, one of the only multinationals, grew through a strategy of local responsiveness, and its highly skilled chairman personally mediated the conflicts with daily phone discussions to local executives.

TWO GLOBAL CHALLENGES WORTH FIGHTING FOR

Our discussion of contention management leads us back to the role of HR. The HR function has often been considered as an implementor, focusing on the operational role in the bottom of our "split egg" concept. But what are the projects or issues that HR should fight for? Building on our discussion of contention, we would point out that the HR function will never be considered a vital business partner unless it constructively fights for perspectives that safeguard the interests of the enterprise. Here we would like to single out one general challenge that is worth fighting for, and one that is more specific in nature.

Fighting for the Long-Term Perspective

While everyone acknowledges the importance of long-term perspective, all the pressures today foster a short-term orientation. Quarterly reports driven by accountability to shareholders are becoming the norm, even in Japan and Germany with their traditionally longer-term horizons. Ideas of life-long employment and careers are increasingly incompatible with the more immediate pressures to be flexible and responsive. Bottom-line pressures influence behaviors much more than say twenty years ago. Not least of all, the future has become quite unpredictable, leading to the demise of long-term planning.

Yet HRM has always stood for the long-term perspective. Investments in human and social capital take time to yield rewards. Those rewards are rich in providing competitive advantage precisely because it will take others a long time to catch up. We confess to being worried when we see HR executives ceding to the pressures of our times, saying that the bottom line is the only thing that counts. Sure, HR managers must demonstrate a high quality of operational professionalism . . . but the top line counts as well. What about the top of the split egg role? At a time when the long-term perspective is often compromised, HR wins its credibility both by being highly professional in its day-by-day role *and* by acting as the guardian of the long term.

Acting as the guardian of the long-term does not mean cumbersome planning systems or dated concepts of "strategic human resource management" in which future strategies are translated into present implications on the drawing boards of planners. It means catalyzing and persuading senior managers to think through their values and formalize these. Yes, a business can survive well in the short term without values. But it is questionable whether the powerful coherence of all the elements of organization that provide sustainable competitive advantage can be achieved without the red thread that is provided by a value system. If layoffs are necessary for the survival of the firm, then acting as a guardian of the long term means fighting to ensure that these layoffs will be undertaken in a humane and socially responsible manner. Certainly, a firm will survive in the short term if pink slips are sent one day by e-mail terminating the employment of people who have dedicated their lives to the firm. But it is questionable whether such a firm can thrive in the future if it has undermined all vestiges of loyalty and trust. Acting as a guardian means fighting to ensure that the person who gets a key job in a local subsidiary is not always the best available local person but sometimes an individual from another subsidiary who will benefit from international experience. A subsidiary may do quite well in the short term by focusing on its own people, but it is questionable whether the multinational will do well unless its future leaders have developed the global mindset that can only be fostered by international experience.

This does not mean functional or expertise power—headquarters with large staffs of experts and centralized power cannot cope with the transnational challenges. What it means is that the HRM role, whether it is exercised by the line manager or the HR professional, is to put the long-term consequences on the table for debate. HR has little decision power, but it has an obligation to get dilemmas, dualities, and tensions out on the table for discussion. Sometimes the outcome will favor the short term, sometimes the long term. This is not simply acting as the social conscience of the firm, it is a proactive fighting role—*constructive fighting.*

From Planning to Anticipation

The problem with the long term is that it is unpredictable. Even in the past when there were fewer discontinuities, companies that took a long-term planning perspective often got into trouble. The HR department at Exxon forecasted back in the 1960s that Exxon alone would need more chemical engineers than could be supplied by all the universities in the United States. There were serious discussions with top management about investing massively in the university business. Fortunately caution prevailed, and a few years later, the first of the oil shocks occurred and that scenario proved to be quite unrealistic. Had they acted on it, they would have had thousands of unemployable chemical engineers on their hands.

The future may be unpredictable, and this rules out conventional long-term planning. But if one accepts that there is a pattern that leads from the present to the future, then *anticipation* is the quality that is needed—desperately needed. There appears to be such a pattern or rhythm to life and to organizations. This rhythm is defined by the tension between dualities, and it is the underlying theme behind this book. It is seen in the phenomena of paradox, in pendulum swings, and in the pathologies when people or organizations take something positive to an extreme.

Successful people are aware of this rhythm, and they anticipate. As adults who are more aware of the rhythm than our children, we try to build emotional competence in our offspring by teaching them to delay gratification. We learn through other people's lives (and through research) to anticipate. Men develop the masculine side of their natures, and then those who are likely to be more fulfilled recognize the need to harness the more nurturing feminine side of their selves, what Carl Jung called the "shadow" side of our personalities. We learn step-by-step about what turns us on in the occupational world. But those who do not get sucked in, those who avoid becoming what we called "prisoners of their own success," learn to swing their attention to developing the quality of their private lives.[52] What determines who gets to the top in a firm is often the ability to anticipate. When the firm is focused on decentralization, the person who ultimately gets ahead is frequently the one who anticipates that the pendulum will one day swing to integration and teamwork. When the pendulum does begin to swing, the board will say, "There's an individual who was foresighted."

The same applies to international organizations in the twenty-first century. Leaders must learn to anticipate the need for greater integration and teamwork when they have structures that are built around local entrepreneurship, or vice versa, anticipate the need for local entrepreneurship when their structures focus on global integration. They must learn to organize one way but manage the other way. If they aspire to build "instant transnationals," they must learn to anticipate the key tensions that such organizations experience and build these tensions into the management philosophy that will guide their selection and development practices. They must learn to build the future into the present.

The Social Implications of Extreme Capitalism

When we wrote earlier that HRM has to focus on competitive performance, suggesting that this differentiates Japan from eastern Europe, many of our postmodernist colleagues will have had strong reactions at this overt indication of our slavery to the capitalist system. They are in part correct, and we would like to take their side with a warning to those who are excessively enamored of free market competition.

One of the coauthors was invited recently by the ILO (the International Labor Office in Geneva that is part of the UN family) to chair a panel of distinguished business leaders discussing the theme of "human resource–based competitive strategies." The panel discussed the talent war that was then raging, the importance of localization, and the challenges of leadership and innovation that Japanese and other companies face in the struggle to be globally competitive. When these observations were reported back to the plenary session, there was a strong reaction from the representatives of the Third World who constituted a good part of the audience. "What incredibly elitist ideas! In your discussions of talent, in your attempts to localize management in China and Indonesia, you are focusing on 2 percent, maybe

5 percent of the world's population. The other 95 percent aren't worried about talent. They are just worried about jobs and having enough to keep home and family surviving."

There is a great deal of truth to the argument. After a couple of decades of unchallenged acceleration of globalization, any reader of the press is aware that the pendulum is swinging—the protests at Seattle, Davos, and Gothenberg remind us visibly of this. Are the protesters just an extremist fringe? Or are they the visible tip of a deeper iceberg that stands in the way of a global economy?

Globalization and the triumph of capitalism since 1989 have brought immense advantages in absolute terms to the world's population, including the poor. Some countries in Asia such as Singapore and Korea have in forty years gone from third-world to first-world status. The purchasing power of the average citizen in China nearly doubled during the 1990s. Thriving middle classes have emerged in poor countries such as India. Yes, the majority of the world's population still falls into the category of being far below what is regarded in the developed world as a subsistence level of existence. Regions such as Africa and Indonesia suffer from deeper and seemingly intractable ills, partly since the otherwise successful market framework runs against cultural traditions. Nevertheless continued globalization will undoubtedly benefit the vast majority of the world's population, rich and poor alike.

However, economic progress is a relative matter. The radical protesters could be safely dismissed if one could show that the world's income distribution has also become more equal in the past few decades. Combined with the increase in absolute standards of living, this would be powerful proof for the all-round virtues of globalization. Unfortunately the evidence does not support this view—quite to the contrary.[53]

No one disputes that the industrial revolution last century led to increased inequality between rich and poor, both within nations and between nations. And the gap appears to be widening. While there are big statistical problems in measuring global inequality and the trends,[54] studies show that inequality, however it is measured, has worsened during the last quarter century, and notably during the 1990s. The gap is widening both between countries and within countries (notably between rural and urban China and India) as technological change and financial liberalization have led to a disproportionately rapid increase in income at the extreme rich end of the populations while the income of the extreme poor has changed little. In the United States, the gap between the richest 20 percent and the poorest 20 percent widened between 1979 and 1997 from a multiplier of nine to one of fifteen.

So the rich are getting richer—globalization allows a top performer to capitalize on his or her talents throughout the entire globe rather than just in a single region or country. The gap is widening. Why should we be concerned? On the one hand, there is widespread concern about the extent of poverty, though one can argue that if globalization were extended to the truly poor in rural India and Africa some of the problem might be alleviated. The deeper concern is that the dynamics of duality and contradiction lead to backlashes that undermine what is virtuous, as history shows. The historian Arnold Toynbee argued that this was the basic pattern underlying the rise and fall of civilizations.[55] Societies would take their success formula to the extreme, leading to an unraveling of civilizations such as the Roman Empire or the Spanish Empire of the middle ages. Too much of a good thing is bad, as another concerned commentor, Charles Handy, emphasizes.[56] Backlashes against inequality and injustice last century brought with them trade protectionism, job-guarantee schemes, extension of welfare benefits to middle classes who did not need it, and draconian taxation of the wealthy. Excesses and backlashes have historically undermined the virtues of what led to civilization or growth or success in the first place, leading to historic dark ages of confusion and social floundering.

Globalization and free markets have brought with them immense benefits. Few leading sociologists, developmental economists, psychologists, and social commentators are detractors of either globalization or free market competition. On the contrary, they are aware of the benefits that these have brought to the human race and to them in particular. But many are consciously or unconsciously aware of the dynamics of duality. The global age that we have created is precarious. The poor peasants in rural China can watch the well-off middle class in Shanghai on their collective television screens. Some concerned observers emphasize the need to be conscientious about helping the poor regardless of inequality; others feel that inequality is the principal challenge.[57] In either case, if more is not done to eliminate poverty and if the benefits of global capitalism are not shared more equally, we risk undermining what we have won.

Mickelthwait and Woolridge provide a good analysis of how the enemies of globalization are gathering.[58] But the real enemies are the more subtle enemies within. There are real risks that the powerful beneficiaries of global inequalities will act to preserve their benefits, leading them to argue for national protectionism and even increasing authoritarianism that will undermine the market and global trends that have brought such benefits.

After decades of indifference to such matters, economists and political scientists are increasingly vocal in their parallel concerns. The president of the American Sociological Association recently mapped out what he sees as the agenda for sociologists facing the daunting challenges of the twenty-first century.[59] Feagin assesses "the downsides of a capitalistic world" in terms of the lack of active concern for widespread misery, the exploitation and marginalization of working families, and the huge environmental costs of capitalism. He sees the agenda for the new century as a return to the sociology of social justice that must be brought back to the center of our concerns. Sociology must nurture the countersystem approach (recognizing the dualistic pendulums), and it must teach people about society, not just about techniques.

Handy's major critique is that capitalism and globalization lack a human face. Shareholder value makes no one feel proud, spiraling expectations lead to disenchantment, the pursuit of another dollar provides no meaning to life once the basics of maintenance are assured. He points out that even Keynes noted that capitalism was such a soulless philosophy that it was unlikely to be attractive unless it was remarkably successful. Handy's concerns are shared by a constituency of leading figures ranging from the Pope to George Soros, from Nelson Mandela to Bill Gates. The cover story of the *Economist* at the time of writing is "Does Inequality Matter?"[60]

Why should such matters be of importance to HRM and the HR function? After all, the HR function cannot do anything about such complex issues. If HR takes this stance, it condemns itself at best to pedestrian irrelevancy, at worst to be sanctioned by history as a guardian of the status quo, rather as the arrogant HR function at IBM was blamed for the woes of its massive crisis in 1991. At a minimum, HR needs to be cognizant of these vital social debates that will shape the course of history in the future.

Better still, international HR needs to be a proactive partner in this debate. Ideally, HR needs to be a vital catalyst in building *socially responsible competitive cultures*—what some may view as an oxymoron is a deliberate duality. For HR holds some of the tangible keys to this social challenge. HRM cannot solve this issue, but it can influence it in powerful ways.

The potential backlash against globalization is most likely to be unleashed on the multinational enterprises that are both the principal agents and beneficiaries of this process—the elephants that mate with other elephants, as Handy calls them.[61] These elephants are so necessary to us since they transfer technology, they take ideas from throughout the world and develop them, they provide jobs and livelihoods to billions of people. "How can I be confident that these elephants will continue to do good in the world?" asks Handy. His answer is that this depends entirely on the moral values of the people—the *mahouts*—who are riding the elephants.

Faced with the delicate questions of balance in maintaining and exploiting a global economy, these *mahouts* need to combine global vision with business pragmatism, social conscience with economic realism, an awareness of the imperatives of the present with an awareness of how the future must be shaped. It is not the task of HR to resolve the world's dilemmas. But HR practices such as leadership development shape, consciously or unconsciously, the orientations and value systems of the leaders who must grapple with these issues, molding the world in which their children will live. The press and world opinion will increasingly hold them accountable for the actions of their corporations. They must grapple on the one hand with the pressures of shareholder value—pressures that we as well-off citizens expect them to respond well to since we have invested our funds and pensions in their shares. But they must also be equally concerned with the widespread misery in the world, the potential consequences of inequality, the unpredictable but likely backlash against rampant market capitalism, and the rising call of people even in the wealthy West for a reason for living that goes beyond making money.[62]

In short, once again, our leaders must be able to grapple effectively with duality and the tensions that it creates.

HRM AS TENSION MANAGEMENT

Contradiction is the defining characteristic of the transnational enterprise. As we have moved into this global era, an era that may be lasting or short lived, so we have moved into a world of visible paradox, contradiction, and duality—and the tensions that these create. These tensions can lead us to frustration, vicious circle, and decline, or they can inspire us with vitality and purpose. It is not profit or human fulfillment or innovation that are the dependent variables that we search to understand, but the tensions that are created by the interplay between these parameters of life.

The global era that we live in is fragile, of very recent origin. It is imbued by tensions that we must learn to recognize and work through. Remember that it is for the second time in a hundred years now that we are on the threshold of a global world. The first time was a hundred years ago in the "golden age" of early twentieth-century that ended with the destructive tensions leading to World War I and the thirty years of turmoil that followed.

Some of the tensions relating to HRM that we have met in this book underlie the principles that are shown in the box "Guidelines for Global Leadership in the Twenty-First Century." A duality is embedded in each of these guidelines, with the tension between its opposite poles. For example, the duality between exploration and exploitation is embedded in the idea that "to innovate you need slack, diversity, flexible budgets, and lots of experimentation . . . and to make profits from your innovations you need discipline, targets, and deadlines." The global-local duality is embedded in others, and the reader will find the short-term/long-term, change-continuity, accountability-teamwork, and other dualities. One can clearly see that if anything positive is taken to an extreme, then it risks creating a pathology. Armed with surveys and statistical tools, researchers in the future will undoubtedly unravel the dimensions of these dualities and the tensions they create.[63]

If we accept that we live in a world of dynamic tensions, then this brings deeper challenges to our ways of thinking. As managers, people of action, we are trained to think in terms of coming up with solutions. But there are no "solutions" to tensions. The dualities that underlie them cannot be resolved once and for all. Early researchers on duality and tension rightly used the metaphor of the seesaw.[64] The manager, and particularly the leader, stands with two feet on either side of the fulcrum of the seesaw. The seesaw can never be balanced—the notion of balance or stable equilibrium is a poor image. The seesaw is in constant motion, moving from one side to the other, and the role of the leader is to anticipate and counteract with movement in the other direction. The result of good leadership can be a harmonious and enjoyable game of fluid movement that is enjoyed by all—or it can be a bitter struggle that leads all participants to opt out of the game. We have used the related image of the sailor, the navigator, whose task it is to anticipate the winds ahead.

Because there is no solution that the leader can provide, the nature of the game is different from in the past. It is a game that cannot be played unless all of the key participants understand the nature of seesaw processes. This is what we mean by "global mindset"—understanding the nature of this global seesaw. And one of challenges for human resource management is fostering widespread global mindset. That is the ultimate purpose of this book.

Where is human resource management heading in this era of globalization? The notion of people as resources was born in the minds of scholars and social observers earlier last century as a result of these seesaw dynamics. Attention at the time was focused on natural and financial resources. People were treated by economists as

Guidelines for Global Leadership in the Twenty-First Century
Research Box

Understand cultural stereotypes	. . .	but don't use them in practice.
Be sensitive to local culture and context	. . .	but make sure that a person's passport is of no importance.
Make sure that subsidiaries and people are clearly accountable	. . .	and then focus on building teamwork where it will add value.
Organize one way (for example a globally integrated structure)	. . .	but manage the other way (to encourage local entrepreneurship).
Benchmark against others, copy practices, network externally to learn	. . .	but never forget that superior performance comes only from being different.
Foster constructive debate about your options and alternatives	. . .	so that you will have no debate when it comes to action.
To innovate you need slack, diversity, flexible budgets, and lots of experimentation	. . .	and to make profits from your innovations you need discipline, targets, and deadlines.
The more valuable the know-how that you have in one part of the firm	. . .	the more you are going to have to invest to transfer and exploit it to other parts of the firm.
Tackle "sour" processes like global rationalization and layoffs today	. . .	with the awareness that you will need teamwork, commitment and loyalty tomorrow.
Be prepared to cannibalize what makes you a leader today	. . .	in order to have a chance of being a leader tomorrow.
Nurture your capabilities by fine-tuning the coherence that lies behind them	. . .	but don't forget that these strengths can be your biggest liabilities.
Develop your people by giving them more challenge than they think they can handle	. . .	and train them, coach them, guide them so they won't make big mistakes.
Organizational values and management philosophy provide the consistency underlying great organizational cultures	. . .	and they can lead to cloning, kill the lifeblood of innovation, and lead to the weakness of strong cultures.
Build face-to-face relationships well	. . .	so that you can use e-technology to bridge the distance.
Make sure that your future leaders have business line experience	. . .	in order to function effectively in key country or regional leadership roles.
Work hard as a professional in your operational job	. . .	in order to find a maximum of time for your project role.
Matrix everything	. . .	except the structure.
Embrace market competition	. . .	but with human values in mind.
Think locally	. . .	and act globally.

"labor," a "factor" of production. There was a seesaw reaction against this—surely people should be treated as a resource on a par with other factors generating wealth? What about "human" resources? And then this was adopted by the world of practice to umbrella a host of developments and initiatives that were wider than the technical concerns of personnel management. The HR function was born in the early 1970s.

Today, thirty years later, the phrase *human resource management* is on everyone's lips. No one can deny its fundamental importance, and a vast literature on HRM has been produced. But this brings with it new challenges. Is HRM a line responsibility, ultimately of top general management, or a functional role? Should the HR function focus on the vital but ever-changing foundations or basics, or should it also be concerned with the bigger challenges, such as those discussed above—coping with the tensions of a global society?

It is not just practicing managers that have different views. Academic scholars are divided. We recently organized a workshop on the shape of International Human Resource Management as we enter the new century, convening the top scholars from both sides of the Atlantic. They were split in their views. One-half argued forcefully that research should focus on the challenging basics of HRM while the other half suggested equally forcefully that the field of HRM should be a central player in the big strategic and social debates that will determine the future of our world.

Our own stance in this debate is quite predictable for those who have read this book. It is not a question of either/or—HR's role is to face up to both of these challenges. One cannot be met without the other, just as the top part of our split egg matrix managerial role (the project role) needs the bottom half of the egg (the operational role). People have to learn to work in split egg ways—and that includes those in the HR function. Unless they have the big picture of dualistic tensions in mind through their work on broader organizational and societal projects, HR managers will always be followers rather than leaders in the vital task of realigning the constantly changing basics of HRM. And unless they are focused on the tangible practices of operational human resource management, they will be out of a job.

What is our scenario for the future of HRM? Whither HRM? There are many different scenarios. At the corporate level, the convergence between IT, planning, learning and knowledge management, and HR—and the tensions between these functions—may well lead in the near future to the emergence of new functional labels that relegate the HRM function to the history books. Alternatively, the HR function may play a spearheading role in the management of tensions. The future, as an interplay between these different forces, is unpredictable.

We ourselves are strong advocates of the role that HRM in general and the HR function in particular can play in this era of tension and paradox. But we are reminded of the words of Georges Doriot. The late General Doriot was one of those remarkable sages. He was French born but a U.S. citizen, quartermaster general for the American armed forces during World War II, a legendary professor of production management at Harvard Business School, one of the first venture capitalists in the United States, and a co-founder of one of Europe's leading business schools.

Like most sages, Doriot was careful with his words, and his advice was usually to be heeded. We remember vividly a discussion with him at a time when HRM was in the process of becoming very fashionable. "Watch out," he said. "The term 'human resource management' is important but ephemeral. Don't get hung up on the label. People are *not* resources, they are people."

TAKEAWAYS

1. New roles have developed for HR managers, focusing on change, requiring new skills in business leadership and influence. But there is sometimes a risk of neglecting the vital HR basics. HR professionals have to learn to work in "split egg" ways.

2. The foundations of HR need to be focused on competitive performance, including the question "What's the value added to the *external* customer?" The role of HR is also to enable strategy to happen. This may sometimes require some reconfiguration of the HR foundations, involving the skills of the change agent.

3. Competitive advantage does not come from copying others. It comes from being different. If HRM is clearly focused on performance, it leads organizations to differentiate themselves.

4. The HR umbrella embraces many different activities that require different delivery mechanisms. These need to be organized by assessing the degree to which they require differentiation by business or country and the degree to which they should be globally integrated.

5. Parent functions at worldwide or regional headquarters have to know how to add value through network leadership. This requires awareness of trends, the ability to mobilize the appropriate resources, and a good sense of timing.

6. Many corporate HR managers espouse globalization without having deep international experience, which can be dangerous. The HR function also needs to attract good people, which means providing clear exit routes out of the function.

7. Creating behavioral context is the task of social architecture. Three aspects of social architecture are building competitive culture, balancing dualities such as stretch and support, and contention management. One of the challenges for transnational firms may be creating a context for constructive debate.

8. HR has to be proactive, fighting for the long-term perspective (as well as taking care of the basics). In today's environment, this involves anticipation rather than planning. It also means ensuring that explicit values provide the necessary coherence to the elements of HRM.

9. Globalization and market competition have brought immense benefits to the world's people, including the poor. But the continued presence of widespread poverty and misery, combined with the widening global inequalities between rich and poor, mean that there is a risk of a backlash that would compromise further progress.

10. HR cannot provide solutions to complex global problems, but it has a social responsibility to ensure that future leaders are sensitive to such challenges and equipped to respond to them. This is one of the many instances of the role of HRM in tension management.

NOTES

1. T. A. Stewart, "Taking On the Last Bureaucracy," *Fortune,* January 15, 1996.
2. A good edited volume on this theme is Ulrich, Losey, and Lake (1997). Moreover, the division chair for the HR Division of the Academy of Management, supposedly the hub of the world's scholarly network, noted recently that "we are still viewed by many as being too myopic and functional, dissecting what we do into the traditional domains of selection, training, compensation and so forth" (L. Gomez-Mejia, "Moving Forward," HR Division Newsletter, *Academy of Management* 24, no. 1 (2000).
3. Yeung, Woolcock, and Sullivan, 1996. For other assessments of the competencies needed by HR professionals, see Kochanski (1996); Ulrich (1997).
4. This framework is discussed in Chapter 2.
5. The Apple story can be found on p. 78.
6. The approach of the SAS Institute is described by O'Reilly and Pfeffer (2000).
7. The "split egg" role concept is explained in Chapter 2.
8. Hansen and von Oetinger, 2001. Their concept of the T-shaped manager, drawn from McKinsey research back in the 1970s, parallels our "split egg" concept.
9. HR's role in faciliating change processes is discussed in Chapters 2 and 9.
10. See the discussion of Cisco's acquisition strategy in Chapter 6. See also O'Reilly and Pfeffer (2000) for a discussion of Cisco and how HRM contributes to strategy and performance in firms such as AES, Men's Warehouse, and Southwest Airlines; and Bunnell (2000) and Stauffer (2000).
11. Hunt and Boxall, 1998, p. 770.
12. The quote is from Brewster (1999, p. 45), who provides a good summary of the competing universalist and contextualist paradigms in HRM. This issue is discussed in Chapter 4.
13. We thank Dr Markus Pudelko for this F-1 image.
14. See the box on p. 51 for a summary of critical and postmodernist views on HRM. Ulrich's employee champion role is described in Ulrich (1997).
15. Guest, 1999.
16. Buchanan, Claydon, and Doyle, 1999.
17. See Hale and Whitlam (1997) for a discussion of the HR implications of virtual organization.
18. Ulrich, 1997, ch. 4.
19. Evans, Lank, and Farquhar, 1989; Evans and Lorange, 1989. The theoretical underpinning for this argument comes from basic economic theory underlying the resource-based view of the firm, notably Penrose (1959). These issues are discussed in Chapter 8.
20. Scullion and Starkey, 2000.
21. These arguments are outlined in Chapters 7 and 9.
22. Hodgetts, 1996.
23. See Schütte (1998) and De Konig, Verdin, and Williamson (1997) for a discussion on the merits of regional structures.
24. See Ulrich (1997, ch. 4) for a more detailed assessment of service centers and the pros and cons.
25. For a more extended discussion on cross-boundary project groups, see Chapter 7, where global process management is also explored at some length.

26. See McGovern (1997) for a discussion on the dangers of excessive devolvement to line managers of HR responsibilities.
27. Global process management is discussed at length in Chapter 7, taking performance management as an example. International leadership development is another such process, discussed in Chapter 8.
28. GE's CAP is described on p. 408.
29. The role of mobility in leadership development is discussed in Chapter 8.
30. Leaving volatility or flexibility out of the picture, an economist would point out that profitable growth (the aim of most business organizations aside from enterprises such as some family businesses and Chinese entrepreneurial firms) boils down to a simple formula: (Price − Cost) × Quality.
31. A lot of research on mentoring was undertaken in the early 1980s. See Kram (1985) for a review. For a practitioner's overview on a related matter, namely coaching, see Goldsmith, Lyons, and Freas (2000).
32. Research being undertaken by Ibarra—see Ibarra (1999); Ibarra (2000).
33. Ghoshal and Bartlett, 1997.
34. Ibid., p. 159.
35. See the box on p. 51 "Critical Views of HRM."
36. Sisson, 1994.
37. The point is cogently argued by Guest (1999).
38. The original HP Way was well adapted to its instruments business but ill suited to the computer world that Hewlett-Packard was forced into when instruments became computerized. The struggle to adapt the HP Way is described in Beer and Rogers (1995).
39. The tension between competition and teamwork is at the heart of recent coevolutionary theories of international organization (see, for example, Eisenhardt and Galunic, 2000, discussed in Chapter 9).
40. Ghoshal and Bartlett, 1997.
41. Other successful configurations based on capitalistic principles are discussed in Chapter 2, including two European configurations, the Japanese model, etc.
42. Normative integration is discussed in Chapter 7.
43. Quoted by Pascale (1990, p. 79).
44. For a review of research on conflict, see Tjosvold (1991); Brown (1983); Amason, Thompson et al. (1995).
45. Kakabadse, 1991; Kakabadse, 1993. Kakabadse found that 30% of British teams were divided, 34% of German teams, 39% of the French and 46% of the Spanish teams.
46. Eisenhardt, Kahwajy, and Bourgeois, 1997a. See also Eisenhardt and Zbaracki (1992); Brown and Eisenhardt (1997); Eisenhardt, Kahwajy, and Bourgeois (1997b); Brown and Eisenhardt (1998).
47. Tichy and Sherman, 1993, p. 60.
48. Laurent, 1983. The question that Laurent put to executives of different nationalities was strongly worded: "Most organizations would be better off if conflict could be eliminated forever." Only 4% of Swedish managers and 6% of U.S. managers agreed or tended to agree, in contrast with 24% of the French, 27% of the Germans, and 41% of the Italians. However, since Laurent's data is somewhat dated, some caution is needed. The Italian results may reflect the turbulent Italian social and labor environment of the early 1970s and early 1980s. More research is needed.
49. The dualistic value system and contention culture of l'Oréal is described on p. 86.
50. One should not stereotype Japan, or any culture, however.
51. The Sony story, where this quotation appears, is told by Nathan (1999).
52. See Evans and Bartolomé (1979); Bartolomé and Evans (1980).

53. For this data and assessment, see R. Wade, "Global Inequality: Winners and Losers," *The Economist,* April 28, 2001.

54. For example, should income be measured using purchasing power parity (PPP or the purchasing power over comparable bundles of goods) or actual exchange rates? The latter typically accentuates that gap.

55. Toynbee, 1946.

56. Handy, 1998.

57. See the lead article on "Does Inequality Matter?" *The Economist,* June 16, 2001, pp. 11–12.

58. Micklethwait and Woolridge, 2000.

59. Feagin, 2001.

60. "Does Inequality Matter?" *The Economist,* June 16, 2001.

61. Handy, 1998.

62. There is also a growing literature on organizational citizenship, focusing on behaviors such as helping, sportsmanship, individual initiative, and civic virtue. See Podsakoff, MacKenzie et al. (2000) for a review.

63. As Evans and Génadry (1998) point out, the analysis of dualistic tensions poses considerable challenges for statistical and data analysis. Conventional statistical methods are based on bipolar measurement scales where one end represents the low point and the other the high point. Conventional methods of data analysis assume a Gaussian normal distribution of data points. However, in tension analysis both ends of the scale are "low points" whereas the healthy point is the midpoint of the scale—for example, when a person recognizes that both "local" and "global" perspectives are equally valid (sometimes one must prevail, sometimes the other). However, tension itself is easy to measure. Using conventional statistics, tension is simply the variance. If the tension is high, the variance in views will be high; if the tension is low, then the variance will be low. On the other hand, the interpretation of tension scores measured on dualistic scales is more problematic (see Evans and Génadry, 1998).

64. Hedburg, Nystrom, and Starbuck, 1976.

Bibliography

Abrahamson, E., and G. Fairchild (1999). "Management fashion: Lifecycles, triggers, and collective learning processes." *Administrative Science Quarterly* 44(3): 708–40.

Adler, N. J. (1981). "Re-entry: Managing cross-cultural transition." *Group and Organization Studies* 6(3): 341–56.

——— (1984). "Women in international management: Where are they?" *California Management Review* 26(4): 78–89.

——— (1986). "Do MBAs want international careers?" *International Journal of Intercultural Relations* 10: 277–99.

——— (1987). "Pacific basin manager: A Gaijin, not a woman." *Human Resource Management* 26(2): 169–91.

——— (1991). *International dimensions of organizational behavior.* Boston: Kent.

——— (1997). *International dimensions of organizational behavior.* Cincinnati: South-Western.

Adler, N. J., and S. Bartolomew (1992). "Managing globally competent people." *Academy of Management Executive* 6(3): 52–65.

Adler, N. J., and F. Ghadar (1990). "Strategic human resource management: A global perspective." *Human resource management: An international comparison.* R. Pieper, ed. Berlin and New York: de Gruyter.

Adler, P. S. (1993). "The learning bureaucracy: New United Motor Manufacturing, Inc." *Research in Organizational Behavior* 15: 111–94.

——— (1999). "Hybridization: Human resource management at two Toyota transplants." *Remade in America: Transplanting and transforming Japanese management systems.* J. K. Liker, W. M. Fruin, and P. S. Adler, eds. New York: Oxford University Press.

Adler, P. S., and B. Borys (1996). "Two types of bureaucracy: Enabling and coercive." *Administrative Science Quarterly* 41(1): 61–79.

Afuah, A. (1998). *Innovation management: Strategies, implementation, and profits.* Oxford: Oxford University Press.

Alavi, M., and D. E. Leidner (1997). "Knowledge management systems: Emerging views and practices from the field." Working Paper 97/97/TM. INSEAD, Fontainebleau.

Allen, D., and S. Alvarez (1998). "Empowering expatriates and organizations to improve repatriation effectiveness." *Human Resource Planning* 21(4): 29–39.

Alvesson, M., and S. Deetz (1996). "Critical theory and postmodernism approaches to Organizational Studies." *Handbook of organization studies.* S. R. Clegg, C. Hardy, and W. R. Nord, eds. London: Sage.

Amason, A. C. (1996). "Distinguishing the effects of functional and dysfunctional conflict on strategic decision making: Resolving a paradox for top management teams." *Academy of Management Journal* 39(1): 123–48.

Amason, A. C., K. R. Thompson, W. A. Hochwarter, and A. W. Harrison (1995). "Conflict: An important dimension in successful management teams." *Organizational Dynamics* (Autumn): 20–35.

Amit, R., and P. J. H. Schoemaker (1993). "Strategic assets and organizational rent." *Strategic Management Journal* 14(1): 33–46.

Ancona, D. G., and D. F. Caldwell (1992). "Bridging the boundary: External activity and performance in organizational teams." *Administrative Science Quarterly* 37: 634–35.

Angwin, D. (2001). "Mergers and acquisitions across European borders: National perspectives on preacquisition due diligence and the use of professional advisers." *Journal of World Business* 36(1): 32–57.

Angwin, D., and B. Savill (1997). "Strategic perspectives on European cross-border acquisitions: A view from top European executives." *European Management Journal* 15(4): 423–35.

Antonacopoulou, E., and L. FitzGerald (1996). "Reframing competency in management development." *Human Resource Management Journal* 6(1): 27–48.

Argote, L. (1999). *Organizational learning: Creating, retaining and transferring knowledge.* Boston: Kluwer.

Argyris, C. (1967). "Today's problems with tomorrow's organizations." *Journal of Management Studies* (February): 31–55.

Arrow, K. (1973). "Social responsibility and economic efficiency." *Public Policy* 21(3): 300–17.

Arthur, J. (1994). "Effects of human resource systems on manufacturing performance and turnover." *Academy of Management Journal* 37: 670–87.

Arthur, M. B., and D. M. Rousseau (1996). "The boundaryless career as a new employment principle." *The boundaryless career.* M. B. Arthur and D. M. Rousseau, eds. Oxford: Oxford University Press.

Arthur, W., and W. Bennet (1995). "The international assignee: The relative importance of factors perceived to contribute to success." *Personnel Psychology* 48: 99–113.

Arvidsson, N. (1999). "The ignorant MNE: The role of perception gaps in knowledge management." Published PhD dissertation. Institute of International Business, Stockholm School of Economics, Stockholm.

———— (2000). "Knowledge management in the multinational enterprise." *The flexible firm: Capability management in network organizations.* J. Birkinshaw and P. Hagström, eds. Oxford: Oxford University Press.

Asakawa, K. (1997). "Multinational tensions in R&D internationalization: Strategic linkage mechanisms of distant contextual knowledge in Japanese multinational companies." INSEAD, Fontainebleau.

Ashby, W. R. (1956). *An introduction to cybernetics.* New York: Wiley.

Ashkenas, R. N., and S. C. Francis (2000). "Integration managers: Special leaders for special times." *Harvard Business Review* (November–December): 108–16.

Ashkenas, R. N., L. J. DeMonaco, and S. C. Francis (1998). "Making the deal real: How GE Capital integrates acquisitions." *Harvard Business Review* (January–February): 165–78.

Ashkenas, R. N., D. Ulrich, T. Jick, and S. Kerr (1995). *The boundaryless organization: Breaking the chains of organizational structure.* San Francisco: Jossey-Bass.

Au, K. Y. (1999). "Intra-cultural variation: Evidence and implications for international business." *Journal of International Business Studies* 30(4): 799–812.

Audia, P. G., E. A. Locke, and K. G. Smith (2000). "The paradox of success: An archival and a laboratory study of strategic persistence following radical environmental change." *Academy of Management Journal* 43(5): 837–53.

Autio, E., H. J. Sapienza, and J. G. Almeida (2000). "Effects of age at entry, knowledge intensity, and imitability on international growth." *Academy of Management Journal* 43(5): 909–24.

Bacon, N. (1999). "The realities of human resource management?" *Human Relations* 52(9): 1179–87.

Baden-Fuller, C., and H. Volberda (1997). "Strategic renewal: How large complex organizations prepare for the future." *International Studies of Management and Organization* 27(2): 95–120.

Bae, J. (1997). "Beyond seniority-based systems: A paradigm shift in Korean HRM?" *Asian Pacific Business Review* 3(4): 82–110.

Bae, J., S. Chen, and J. Lawler (1998). "Variation in human resource management in Asian countries: MNC home-country and host-country effects." *International Journal of Human Resource Management* 9(4): 653–70.

Bae, J., and J. J. Lawler (2000). "Organizational and HRM strategies in Korea: Impact on firm performance in an emerging economy." *Academy of Management Journal* 43(3): 502–17.

Bahrami, H. (1992). "The emerging flexible organization: Perspectives from Silicon Valley." *California Management Review* 34(4): 33–52.

Baker, W. (1994). *Networking smart: How to build relationships for personal and organizational success.* New York: McGraw-Hill.

Baker, J. C., and J. Ivancevich (1971). "The assignment of American executives abroad: Systematic, haphazard, or chaotic?" *California Management Review* 13(3): 39–44.

Barham, K., and C. Heimer (1998). *ABB: The dancing giant.* London: Financial Times/Pitman.

Barham, K., and D. Oates (1991). *The international manager.* London: Economist Books.

Baritz, L. (1960). *The servants of power: A history of the use of social science in American industry.* Middletown, CT: Wesleyan University Press.

Barkema, H. G., J. H. Bell, and J. M. Pennings (1996). "Foreign entry, cultural barriers and learning." *Strategic Management Journal* 17: 151–66.

Barkema, H. G., O. Shenkar, F. Vermeulen, and J. H. J. Bell (1997). "Working abroad, working with others: How firms learn to operate international joint ventures." *Academy of Management Journal* 40(2): 426–42.

Barkema, H. G., and F. Vermeulen (1999). "Sloughing the old: The learning process of internationalizing firms." Working Paper. Department of Business Administration, Tilburg University, Tilburg, Holland.

Barley, S. R., and G. Kunda (1992). "Design and devotion: Surges of rational and normative ideologies of control in managerial discourse." *Administrative Science Quarterly* 37(3): 363–99.

Barnett, W. P., and R. A. Burgelman (1996). "Evolutionary perspectives on strategy." *Strategic Management Journal* 17: 5–19.

Barney, J. (1991). "Firm resources and sustained competitive advantage." *Journal of Management* 17(1): 99–120.

Baron, J. N., and D. M. Kreps (1999). *Strategic human resources: Frameworks for general managers.* New York: Wiley.

Barsoux, J. L., and C. D. Galunic (2000). "Bertelsmann: Corporate structures for value creation." INSEAD case 4907. INSEAD, Fontainebleau.

Bartlett, C. A. (1997). "McKinsey & Company: Managing knowledge and learning." Case No. 9-396-357. Harvard Business School, Boston.

Bartlett, C. A., and S. Ghoshal (1989). *Managing across Borders : The transnational solution.* Cambridge, MA: Harvard Business School Press.

———— (1990). "Matrix management: Not a structure, a frame of mind." *Harvard Business Review* (July–August): 138–45.

———— (1992). "What is a global manager?" *Harvard Business Review* (September–October): 124–32.

———— (1997). "The myth of the generic manager: New personal competencies for new management roles." *California Management Review* 40(1): 92–116.

———— (2000). "Going global: Lessons from late movers." *Harvard Business Review* (March–April): 133–42.

Bartlett, C. A., and A. Nanda (1990). "Ingvar Kamprad and IKEA." Case No. 9-390-132. Harvard Business School, Boston.

Bartlett, C. A., and J. O'Connell (1998). "Lincoln Electric: Venturing Abroad." Case No. 398095. Harvard Business School, Boston.

Bartlett, C. A., and H. Yoshihara (1988). "New challenges for Japanese multinationals: Is organization adaptation their Achilles' heel?" *Human Resource Management* 27(1): 19–43.

Bartolomé, F., and P. A. L. Evans (1980). "Must success cost so much?" *Harvard Business Review* (March–April): 137–49.

Bateson, G. (1972). *Steps to an ecology of mind: Collected essays in anthropology, psychiatry, evolution, and epistemology.* London: Intertext Books.

Beamish, P. W. (1985). "The characteristics of joint ventures in developed and developing countries." *Journal of World Business* 20(3): 13–19.

Becker, B., and B. Gerhart (1996). "The impact of human resource management on organizational performance." *Academy of Management Journal* 39(4): 779–801.

Becker, B. E., M. A. Huselid, P. S. Pickus, M. F. Spratt (1997). "Human resources as a source of shareholder value: Research and recommendations." *Tomorrow's HR management.* D. Ulrich, M. R. Losey, and G. Lake, eds. New York: Wiley.

Beckhard, R., and R. T. Harris (1977). *Organizational transitions: Managing complex change.* Reading, MA: Addison-Wesley.

Beer, M., R. Eisenstat, and B. Spector (1990). *The critical path to corporate renewal.* Boston: Harvard Business School Press.

Beer, M., and N. Nohria (2000). "Cracking the code of change." *Harvard Business Review* (May–June): 133–41.

Beer, M., and G. C. Rogers (1995). "Human resources at Hewlett-Packard (A)(B)." Case No. 9-495-051. Harvard Business School, Boston.

Beer, M., B. Spector, et al. (1984). *Managing human assets.* New York: Free Press.

Beer, M., and A. E. Walton (1987). "Organization change and development." *Annual Review of Psychology* 38: 339–67.

Beer, M., and N. Nohria (eds.) (2000). *Breaking the code of change.* Boston: Harvard Business School Press.

Belbin, R. M. (1981). *Management teams: Why they succeed or fail.* London: Heinemann.

Bell, D. (1976). *The coming of post-industrial society.* New York: Basic Books.

Bennis, W., and B. Nanus (1985). *Leaders: The strategies for taking charge.* New York: Harper & Row.

Bennis, W. G., and D. A. Heenan (1999). *Co-leaders: The power of great partnerships.* New York: Wiley.

Berg, N. A., and N. D. Fast (1983). "Lincoln Electric Co." Case No. 376028. Harvard Business School, Boston, Mass.

Bettenhausen, K. (1991). "Five years of groups research: What we have learned and what needs to be addressed." *Journal of Management* 17(2): 345–81.

Birkinshaw, J. (1999). "Acquiring intellect: Managing the integration of knowledge-intensive acquisitions." *Business Horizons* (May–June): 33–40.

Birkinshaw, J., and N. Hood (2001). "Unleash innovation in foreign subsidiaries." *Harvard Business Review* (March): 131–37.

Björkman, I., and J. Gertsen (1993). "Selecting and training Scandinavian expatriates: Determinants of corporate practice." *Scandinavian Journal of Management* 9(2): 145–64.

Björkman, I., and C. D. Galunic (1999). "Lincoln Electric in China." Case No. 09/1999-4850. IN-SEAD, Fontainebleau.

Black, J. S. (1988). "Work role transitions: A study of American expatriate managers in Japan." *Journal of International Business Studies* 19(2): 277–94.

Black, J. S., and H. B. Gregersen (1991a). "When Yankee comes home: Factors related to expatriate and spouse repatriation adjustment." *Journal of International Business Studies* 22(4): 671–94.

——— (1991b). "The other half of the picture: Antecedents of spouse cross-cultural adjustment." *Journal of International Business Studies* 22(3): 461–77.

——— (1991c). "Antecedents to cross-cultural adjustment for expatriates in Pacific Rim assignments." *Human Relations* 44(5): 497–515.

——— (1999). "The right way to manage expats." *Harvard Business Review* (March–April): 52–63.

Black, J. S., H. B. Gregersen, and M. E. Mendenhall (1992). *Global assignments: Successfully expatriating and repatriating international managers.* San Francisco: Jossey-Bass.

Black, J. S., H. B. Gregersen, M. E. Mendenhall, and L. K. Stroh (1999). *Globalizing people through international assignments.* Reading, MA: Addison-Wesley.

Black, J. S., M. Mendenhall, and G. Oddou (1991). "Toward a comprehensive model of international adjustment: An integration of multiple theoretical perspectives." *Academy of Management Review* 16(2): 291–317.

Black, J. S., and G. K. Stephens (1989). "The influence of the spouse on American expatriate adjustment in overseas assignments." *Journal of Management* 15: 529–44.

Bleeke J., D. Ernst, J. Isono, and D. D. Weinberg (1993). "Succeeding at cross-border mergers and acquisitions." *Collaborating to compete: Using strategic alliances and acquisitions in the global marketplace.* J. Bleeke and D. Ernst, eds. New York: Wiley.

Bleeke, J., and D. Ernst, eds. (1993). *Collaborating to compete: Using strategic alliances and acquisitions in the global marketplace.* New York: Wiley.

Bloom, M., and G. T. Milkovich (1999). "A SHRM perspective on international compensation and reward systems." *Strategic human resources management: Research in personnel and human resources management.* P. M. Wright, L. D. Dyer, J. W. Boudreau, and G. T. Milkovich, eds. Stamford, CT: JAI Press.

Boam, R., and P. Sparrow (1992). *Designing and achieving competency: A competency-based approach to developing people and organizations.* London: McGraw-Hill.

Bognanno, M., and P. Sparrow (1995). "British Petroleum (BP)." *European casebook on human resource and change management.* J. M. Hiltrop and P. Sparrow, eds. London: Prentice Hall.

Bonache, J., and J. P. Barber (2000). *When are international managers a cost effective solution? An exploratory study in a sample of Spanish MNCs.* 15th Workshop on Strategic Human Resource Management. INSEAD, Fontainebleau.

Bonache, J., and J. Cervino (1997). "Global integration without expatriates." *Human Resource Management Journal* 7(3): 89–100.

Borkowski, S. C. (1999). "International managerial performance evaluation: A five country comparison." *Journal of International Business Studies* 30(3): 533–55.

Bower, J. L. (2001). "Not all M&As are alike—and that matters." *Harvard Business Review* (March): 92–101.

Boxall, P. (1992). "Strategic human resource management: Beginnings of a new theoretical sophistication?" *Human Resource Management Journal* 2(3): 60–78.

——— (1996). "The strategic HRM debate and the resource-based view of the firm." *Human Resource Management Journal* 6(3): 59–75.

Boyatzis, R. E. (1982). *The competent manager: A model for effective performance.* New York: Wiley.

Bray, D. W., R. J. Campbell, and D. L. Grant (1974). *Formative years in business: A long-term AT&T study of managerial lives.* New York: Wiley-Interscience.

Brett, J. M., and L. K. Stroh (1995). "Willingness to relocate internationally." *Human Resource Management* 34(3): 405–24.

Brewster, C. (1991). *The management of expatriates.* London: Kogan Page.

——— (1995). "Towards a 'European' model of human resource management." *Journal of International Business Studies* 26(1): 1–21.

——— (1999). "Strategic human resource management: The value of different paradigms." *Management International Review* 39(Special Issue): 45–64.

Brewster, C., and A. Hegewisch, eds. (1994). *Policy and practice in European human resource management: The Price Waterhouse Cranfield Survey.* London: Routledge.

Brewster, C., and H. H. Larsen (1992). "Human resource management in Europe: Evidence from ten countries." *International Journal of Human Resource Management* 3(3): 409–34.

Brewster, C., and H. Scullion (1997). "A review and agenda for expatriate HRM." *Human Resource Management Journal* 7(3): 32–41.

Brim, O. G. (1966). "Socialization through the life cycle." *Socialization after childhood.* O. G. Brim and S. Wheeler, eds. New York: Wiley.

Briscoe, J. P., and D. T. Hall (1999). "Grooming and picking leaders using competency frameworks: Do they work?" *Organizational Dynamics* (Autumn): 37–51.

Brown, L. D. (1983). *Managing at organizational interfaces.* Reading, MA: Addison-Wesley.

Brown, S. L., and K. Eisenhardt (1997). "The art of continuous change: Linking complexity theory and time-paced evolution in relentlessly shifting organizations." *Administrative Science Quarterly* 42: 1–34.

——— (1998). *Competing on the edge: Strategy as structured chaos.* Boston: Harvard Business School Press.

Buchanan, D., T. Claydon, and M. Doyle (1999). "Organisation development and change: The legacy of the nineties." *Human Resource Management Journal* 9(2): 20–37.

Buller, P. F., and G. McEvoy (1999). "Creating and sustaining ethical capability in the multinational corporation." *Journal of World Business* 34(4): 326–43.

Bunnell, D. (2000). *Making the Cisco connection: The story behind the real Internet superpower.* New York: Wiley.

Burgelman, R. (1984). "Designs for corporate entrepreneurship in established firms." *California Management Review* 26(3): 154–66.

Burgelman, R. A., and A. Grove (1992). "Strategic dissonance." *California Management Review* 38(2): 8–28.

Burns, T., and G. M. Stalker (1961). *The management of innovation.* London: Tavistock.

Burt, R. S. (1987). "Social contagion and innovation: Cohesion versus structural equivalence." *American Journal of Sociology* 92(May): 1287–1335.

——— (1992). *Structural holes: The social structure of competition.* Cambridge, MA: Harvard University Press.

——— (1997). "The contingent value of social capital." *Administrative Science Quarterly* 42(2): 339–65.

Burt, R. S., R. M. Hogarth, and C. Michaud (2000). "The social capital of French and American managers." *Organization Science* 11(2): 123–47.

Byham, W. C. (2000). "Bench strength." *Across the Board* (February): 35–41.

Caligiuri, P. M., M. M. Hyland, A. Joshi, and A. S. Bross (1998). "Testing a theoretical model for examining the relationship between family adjustment and expatriates' work adjustment." *Journal of Applied Psychology* 83(4): 598–614.

Caligiuri, P. M., and R. L. Tung (1999). "Comparing the success of male and female expatriates from a US-based multinational company." *International Journal of Human Resource Management* 10(5): 763–82.

Calori, R., and P. De Woot (1994). *A European management model.* Hemel Hampstead: Prentice Hall.

Calori, R., G. Johnson, and P. Sarnin (1994). "CEOs cognitive maps and the scope of the organization." *Strategic Management Journal* 15: 437–57.

Cameron, K. (1994). "Strategies for successful organizational downsizing." *Human Resource Management* 33(2): 189–211.

Campbell, A., and M. Goold (1998). *Synergy: Why links between business units often fail and how to make them work.* Oxford: Capstone.

Cannon, T. (1996). *Welcome to the revolution: Managing paradox in the 21st century.* London: Pitman.

Cappelli, P. (1999). "Career jobs *are* dead." *California Management Review* 42(1): 146–67.

Cappelli, P., and A. Crocker-Hefter (1996). "Distinctive human resources *are* firms' core competencies." *Organizational Dynamics* 24(Winter): 7–21.

Carlos, A. M., and S. Nicholas (1988). "Giants of an earlier capitalism: The chartered trading companies as modern multinationals." *Business History Review* 62 (Autumn): 398–419.

Cascio, W. F., and M. G. Serapio, Jr. (1991). "Human resources systems in an international alliance: The undoing of a done deal?" *Organizational Dynamics* 19(3): 63–74.

Cerdin, J.-L., and J.-M. Peretti (2000). "Les déterminants de l'adaptation des cadres français expatriés." *Revue Française de Gestion* (July–August): 58–66.

Chadwick, C., and P. Cappelli (1999). "Alternatives to generic strategy typologies in strategic human resource management." *Strategic human resources management in the twenty-first century.* L. D. Dyer, P. M. Wright, J. W. Boudreau, and G. T. Milkovich, eds. Stamford, CT: JAI Press.

Chandler, A. D. (1962). *Strategy and structure.* Cambridge, MA: MIT Press

——— (1977). *The visible hand.* Cambridge, MA: Harvard University Press.

——— (1986). "The evolution of modern global competition." *Competition in global industries* M. Porter, ed. Cambridge, MA: Harvard University Press.

——— (1990). *Scale and scope: The dynamics of industrial capitalism.* Cambridge, MA: Harvard University Press.

Chaudhuri S., and B. Tabrizi (1999). "Capturing the real value in high-tech acquisitions." *Harvard Business Review* (September–October): 123–30.

Cheng, M. T. (1991). "The Japanese permanent employment system." *Work and Occupations* 18(2): 148–71.

Cheng, Y., and A. H. Van de Ven (1996). "Learning the innovation journey: Order out of chaos." *Organization Science* 7:6: 593–614.

Chi-Ching, Y. (1998). "HRM under guided economic development: The Singapore experience." *Human resource management in the Asia Pacific region.* C. Rowley, ed. Portland: Frank Cass.

Child, J. (1969). *British management thought: A critical analysis.* London: Allen & Unwin.

——— (2000). "Theorizing about organization cross-nationally." *Advances in international comparative management,* vol. 13. J. L. C. Cheng and R. B. Peterson, eds. Stamford, CT: JAI Press.

Child, J., and D. Faulkner (1998). *Strategies of cooperation: Managing alliances, networks, and joint ventures.* New York: Oxford University Press.

Child, J., D. Faulkner, and R. Pitkethly (2001). *The Management of international acquisitions.* Oxford: Oxford University Press.

Child, J., and Y. Yan (1998). "National and transnational effects in international business: Indications from Sino-foreign joint ventures." Working Paper 31/98. Judge Institute of Management Studies, Cambridge, U.K.

Chu, W. (1966). "The human side of examining a foreign target." *Mergers and Acquisitions* (January–February): 35.

Chusmir, L. H., and N. T. Frontczak (1990). "International management opportunities for women: Women and men paint different pictures." *International Journal of Management* 7(3): 295–301.

Clark, T., ed. (1996). *European human resource management.* Oxford and Cambridge, MA: Blackwell.

Clark, T., and G. Mallory (1996). "The cultural relativity of human resource management: Is there a universal model?" *European human resource management.* T. Clark, ed. Oxford: Blackwell.

Coase, R. H. (1937). "The nature of the firm." *Economica* 4 (November): 386–405.

Cohen, J. (1992). "Foreign advisers and capacity building: The case of Kenya." *Public Administration and Development* 12(5).

Cole, R. E., and D. R. Deskins, Jr. (1988). "Racial factors in site location and employment patterns of Japanese auto firms in America." *California Management Review* 31(1): 9–22.

Coleman, J. S. (1990). *Foundations of social theory.* Cambridge, MA: Harvard University Press.

Collins, J. C., and J. I. Porras (1994). *Built to last.* New York: HarperBusiness.

Conference Board (1996). "Managing expatriates' return: A research report." The Conference Board, New York.

——— (1997a). "Strategic alliances: Institutionalizing partnering capabilities." The Conference Board, New York.

——— (1997b). "HR challenges in mergers and acquisitions." *HR Executive Review* 5(2).

Conner, D. R. (1992). *Managing at the speed of change.* New York: Villard Books.

——— (1998). *Leading at the edge of chaos: How to create the nimble organization.* New York: Wiley.

Conner, J., and D. Ulrich (1996). "Human resource roles: Creating value, not rhetoric." *Human Resource Planning* 19(3): 38–49.

Constant, D., L. Sproull, and S. Kiesler (1996). "The kindness of strangers: The usefulness of electronic weak ties for technical advice." *Organization Science* 7(2): 119–35.

Contractor, F. J., and P. Lorange (1988). "Why should firms cooperate? The strategy and economics basis for cooperative ventures." *Cooperative strategies in international business.* F. J. Contractor and P. Lorange, eds. Lexington, MA: Lexington Books.

Corporate Leadership Council (2000). *M&A talent management: Identification and retention of key talent during mergers and acquisitions.* Washington, DC: Corporate Executive Board Washington, DC.

Crichton, A. (1968). *Personnel management in context.* London: B. T. Batsford.

Cropanzano, R. G., and J. Greenberg (1997). "Progress in organizational justice: Tunneling through the maze." *International Review of Industrial and Organizational Psychology,* vol. 12. C. R. Cooper and I. T. Robertson, eds. New York: Wiley.

Cyr, D. J. (1995). *The human resource challenge of international joint ventures.* Westport, CT: Quorum Books.

Cyr, D. J., and S. C. Schneider (1996). "Implications for learning: Human resource management in East-West joint ventures." *Organization Studies* 17(2): 207–26.

Czikszentmihalyi, M., and K. Sawyer (1995). "Creative insight: The social dimensions of a solitary moment." *The nature of insight.* R. J. Sternberg and J. E. Davidson, eds. Cambridge, MA: MIT Press.

Daft, R. L., and R. H. Lengel (1986). "Organizational information requirements, media richness and structural design." *Management Science* 32(5): 554–71.

Davidson Frame, J. (1987). *Managing projects in organizations.* San Francisco: Jossey-Bass.

Davis, S. M., and P. R. Lawrence (1977). *Matrix.* Reading, MA: Addison-Wesley.

———— (1978). "Problems of matrix organizations." *Harvard Business Review* (May–June): 131–42.

de Bettignies, H. C. (1999). "The corporation as a 'community': An oxymoron? Can business schools re-invent themselves?" Presentation given at the Inaugural Dean F. Berry Lecture. INSEAD, Fontainebleau.

De Cieri, H., and P. J. Dowling (1999). "Strategic human resource management in multinational enterprises: Theoretical and empirical developments." *Strategic human resources management in the twenty-first century.* P. M. Wright, L. Dyer, J. W. Boudreau, and G. T. Milkovich, eds. Stamford, CT: JAI Press.

Deephouse, D. (1999). "To be different, or to be the same? It's a question (and theory) of strategic balance." *Strategic Management Journal* 20: 147–66.

DeFillippi, R. J., and M. B. Arthur (1996). "Boundaryless contexts and careers: A competency-based perspective." *The boundaryless career.* M. B. Arthur and D. M. Rousseau, eds. Oxford: Oxford University Press.

De Geus, A. P. (1988). "Planning as learning." *Harvard Business Review* (March–April): 70–74.

De Konig, A., P. Verdin, and P. Williamson (1997). "So you want to integrate Europe: How do you manage the process?" *European Management Journal* 15(6): 252–65.

Delany, E. (2000). "Strategic development of the multinational subsidiary through subsidiary initiative-taking." *Long Range Planning* 33: 220–44.

Delery, J. E., and H. D. Doty (1996). "Modes of theorizing in strategic human resource management: Tests of universalistic, contingency, and configurational performance predictions." *Academy of Management Journal* 39(4): 802–35.

De Meyer, A. (1991). "Tech talk: How managers are stimulating global R&D communication." *Sloan Management Review* 32:3: 49–66.

De Meyer, A., and A. Vereecke (2000). "Key success factors in the creation of manufacturing facilities abroad." No. 67/2000. INSEAD Euro-Asia Centre, Fontainebleau & Singapore.

Denison D., H. J. Cho, and J. Young (2000). "Diagnosing organizational cultures: Validating a model and method." Working Paper 2000-9. IMD, Lausanne, Switzerland.

Denison, D. R., R. Hooijberg, and R. E. Quinn (1995). "Paradox and performance: Toward a theory of behavioral complexity in managerial leadership." *Organization Science* 6(5): 524–40.

Derr, B. C., and G. R. Oddou (1991). "Are U.S. multinationals adequately preparing future American leaders for global competition?" *International Journal of Human Resource Management* 2(2): 227–44.

Dierickx, I., and K. Cool (1989). "Asset stock accumulation and competitive advantage." *Management Science* 35(12): 1504–11.

Donaldson, L. (1995). *American anti-management theories of organization: A critique of paradigm proliferation.* Cambridge: Cambridge University Press.

———— (1996). *For positivist organization theory.* London: Sage.

Donaldson, T. (1989). *The ethics of international business.* New York: Oxford University Press.

———— (1996). "Values in tension: Ethics away from home." *Harvard Business Review* (September–October): 48–62.

Donaldson, T., and W. Dunfee (1999). "When ethics travel: The promise and peril of global business ethics." *California Management Review* 41(4): 45–63.

Doorewaard, H., and H. E. Meihuizen (2000). "Strategic performance options in professional service organisations." *Human Resource Management Journal* 10(2): 39–57.

Dougherty, D. (1996). "Organizing for innovation." *Handbook of organization studies.* S. R. Clegg, C. Hardy, and W. R. Nord, eds. London and Thousand Oaks, CA: Sage.

Dowling, P. J., and R. S. Schuler (1990). *International dimensions of human resource management.* Boston: PWS-KENT.

Dowling, P. J., D. E. Welch, and R. S. Schuler (1999). *International human resource management: Managing people in a multinational context,* 3d ed. Cincinnati: South-Western.

Doz, Y., C. A. Bartlett, and C. K. Prahalad (1981). "Global competitive pressures and host country demands." *California Management Review* 23(3): 63–74.

Doz, Y., and G. Hamel (1998). *Alliance advantage: The art of creating value through partnering.* Boston: Harvard Business School Press.

Doz, Y., and C. K. Prahalad (1984). "Patterns of strategic control within multinational corporations." *Journal of International Business Studies* (Fall): 55–72.

——— (1986). "Controlled variety: A challenge for human resource management in the MNC." *Human Resource Management* 25(1): 55–71.

——— (1988). "A process model of strategic redirection in large complex firms: The case of multinational corporations." *The management of strategic change.* A. M. Pettigrew, ed. Oxford: Basil Blackwell.

Doz, Y., and J. Santos (1997). "On the management of knowledge: From the transparency of colocation and co-setting to the quandary of dispersion and differentiation." Working Paper No. 97/110/SM. INSEAD, Fontainebleau.

Doz, Y., J. Santos, and P. Williamson (2001). *From global to metanational: How companies win in the knowledge economy.* Boston: Harvard Business School Press.

Drucker, P. (1973). *Management: Tasks, responsibilities, practices.* New York: Harper and Row.

——— (1992). "The new society of organizations." *Harvard Business Review* (September–October): 95–104.

——— (1996). "Foreword." *The leader of the future.* F. Hesselbein, M. Goldsmith, and R. Beckhard, eds. San Francisco: Jossey-Bass.

Duarte, D. L., and N. T. Snyder (1999). *Mastering virtual teams.* San Francisco: Jossey-Bass.

Dunning, J. H. (1988). *Explaining international production.* London: Unwin Hyman.

Dunphy, D. C., and D. A. Stace (1988). "Transformational and coercive strategies for planned organizational change: Beyond the O.D. model." *Organization Studies* 9(3): 317–34.

Dyer, L. (1984). "Linking human resource and business strategies." *Human Resource Planning* 7(2): 79–84.

Dyer, L., and T. Reeves (1995). "Human resource strategies and firm performance: What do we know and where do we need to go?" *International Journal of Human Resource Management* 6(3): 656–70.

Earley, P. C., and E. Mosakowski (2000). "Creating hybrid team cultures: An empirical test of transnational team functioning." *Academy of Management Journal* 43(1): 26–49.

Eccles, R. G., and D. B. Crane (1987). *Doing deals: Investment banks at work.* Boston: Harvard Business School Press.

Economist Intelligence Unit (1996). "The reluctant expatriate." *Business China,* Report No. 20, September 20.

Edström, A., and J. R. Galbraith (1977). "Transfer of managers as a coordination and control strategy in multinational organizations." *Administrative Science Quarterly* 22: 248–63.

Egelhoff, W. G. (1988). "Strategy and structure in multinational corporations: A revision of the Stopford and Wells model." *Strategic Management Journal* 9: 1–14.

Eisenhardt, K. M. (2000). "Paradox, spirals, ambivalence: The new language of change and pluralism." *Academy of Management Review* 25(4): 703–5.

Eisenhardt, K. M., and D. C. Galunic (2000). "Coevolving: At last, a way to make synergies work." *Harvard Business Review* (January–February): 91–101.

Eisenhardt, K. M., and M. Zbaracki (1992). "Strategic decision making." *Strategic Management Journal* 13: 17–37.

Eisenhardt, K. M., J. L. Kahwajy, and L. J. Bourgeois (1997a). "How management teams can have a good fight." *Harvard Business Review* (July–August): 77–85.

——— (1997b). "Conflict and strategic choice: How top management teams disagree." *California Management Review* 39(2): 42–62.

Eneroth, K., and A. Malm (2001). "Knowledge webs and generative relations: A network approach to developing competencies." *European Management Journal* 19(2): 174–82.

Epstein, M., and J.-F. Manzoni (1998). "Implementing corporate strategy: From *tableaux de bord* to balanced scorecards." *European Management Journal* 16(2): 190–203.

Evans, P. A. L. (1974). "The price of success: Accommodation to conflicting needs in managerial careers." Unpublished doctoral dissertation, Alfred P. Sloan School of Management, MIT, Boston.

——— (1984). "On the importance of a generalist conception of human resource management: A cross-national look." *Human Resource Management* 23(4): 347–64.

——— (1992). "Developing leaders and managing development." *European Journal of Management* 10(1): 1–9.

——— (1994). "The paradoxes of a world where solutions are looking for problems." *EFMD Forum* 94(3): 67–74.

Evans, P. A. L., and F. Bartolomé (1979). *Must success cost so much?* London: Grant McIntyre; New York: Basic Books.

Evans, P. A. L., and Y. Doz (1989). "The dualistic organization." *Human resource management in international firms: Change, globalization, innovation.* P. A. L. Evans, Y. Doz, and A. Laurent, eds. London: Macmillan.

——— (1992). "Dualities: A paradigm for human resource and organizational development in complex multinationals." *Globalizing management: Creating and leading the competitive organization.* V. Pucik, N. M. Tichy, and C. K. Barnett, eds. New York: Wiley.

Evans, P. A. L., and A. Farquhar (1986). "Marks & Spencer (A) and (B)." INSEAD Case series, Fontainebleau.

Evans, P. A. L., E. Lank, and A. Farquhar (1989). "Managing human resources in the international firm: Lessons from practice." *Human resource management in international firms: Change, globalization, innovation.* P. A. L. Evans, Y. Doz, and A. Laurent, eds. London: Macmillan.

Evans, P. A. L., and P. Lorange (1989). "The two logics behind human resource management." *Human resource management in international firms: Change, globalization, innovation.* P. A. L. Evans, Y. Doz, and A. Laurent, eds. London: Macmillan.

Evans, P. A. L., and N. Génadry (1998). "A duality-based prospective for strategic human resource management." *Research in personnel and human resources management, Supplement 4: Strategic human resources management in the twenty-first century.* L. D. Dyer, P. M. Wright, J. W. Boudreau, and G. T. Milkovich, eds. Stamford, CT: JAI Press.

Evans, P. A. L., and A. Wittenberg (1986). "Apple Computers Europe." INSEAD Case series, Fontainebleau. Reprinted in *Transnational management: Text, cases, and readings in cross-border management.* C. A. Bartlett and S. Ghoshal. Homewood, IL: Irwin, 1992.

Feagin, J. R. (2001). "Social justice and sociology: Agendas for the twenty-first century." *American Sociological Review* 66(February): 1–20.

Feldman, M. 1995. "Disaster prevention plans after a merger." *Mergers and Acquisitions* 30(1): 31–36.

Ferencikova, S., and V. Pucik (1999). "Whirlpool Corporation: Entering Slovakia." Case Study No. GM 796, IMD, Lausanne, Switzerland.

Ferner, A., P. Edwards, and K. Sisson (1995). "Coming unstuck? In search of the 'corporate glue' in an international professional service firm." *Human Resource Management* 34(3): 343–61.

Ferner, A., and J. Quintanilla (1998). "Multinationals, national business systems and HRM: The enduring influence of national identity or a process of 'Anglo-Saxonization.'" *International Journal of Human Resource Management* 9(4): 710–31.

Fey, C., P. Engstrom, and I. Björkman (1999). "Effective human resource management practices for foreign firms in Russia." *Organizational Dynamics* (Autumn): 69–80.

Fine, C. H. (1998). *Clockspeed: Winning industry control in the age of temporary advantage:* Perseus Books.

Flannery, T. P., D. A. Hofrichter, et al. (1996). *People, performance, and pay: Dynamic compensation for changing organizations.* New York: Free Press.

Fletcher, J., and K. Olwyler (1997). *Paradoxical thinking: How to profit from your contradictions.* San Francisco: Berrett-Koehler.

Fombrun, C., N. M. Tichy, and M. A. Devanna (1984). *Strategic human resource management.* New York: Wiley.

Ford, R., and W. Randolph (1992). "Cross-functional structures: A review and integration of matrix organization and project management." *Journal of Management* 18(2).

Forster, N. (1997). "The persistent myth of high expatriate failure rates: A reappraisal." *International Journal of Human Resource Management* 3(4): 414–34.

Fukuyama, F. (1995). *Trust: The social virtues and the creation of prosperity.* New York: Free Press.

Gabor, A. (1990). *The man who discovered quality.* New York: Times Books.

Galbraith, J. R. (1977). *Organization design.* Reading, MA: Addison-Wesley.

——— (2000). *Designing the global corporation.* San Francisco: Jossey-Bass.

Galbraith, J. R., and D. A. Nathanson (1979). "The role of organizational structure and process in strategy implementation." *Strategic management.* D. E. Schendel and C. W. Hofer, eds. Boston: Little Brown.

Galunic, C. D., and E. Andersen (2000). "From security to mobility: Generalized investments in human capital and commitment." *Organization Science* 11(1): 1–20.

Galunic, C. D., and K. M. Eisenhardt (2002). "Architectural innovation and modular corporate forms." *Academy of Management Journal* (Forthcoming) (Working Paper No. 97/93/OB. INSEAD, Fontainebleau).

Galunic, C. D., and S. Rodan (1998). "Resource recombinations in the firm: Knowledge structures and the potential for Schumpeterian innovation." *Strategic Management Journal* 19(12): 1193–1201.

Galunic, C. D., and J. Weeks (1999). "Managing knowledge at Booz-Allen & Hamilton: Knowledge on-line and off." Case No. 09/1999–4846. INSEAD, Fontainebleau.

Garette B., and P. Dussauge (2000). "Alliances versus acquisitions: Choosing the right option." *European Management Journal* 18(1): 63–69.

Gargiulo, M., and M. Benassi (2000). "Trapped in your own net? Network cohesion, structural holes, and the adaptation of social capital." *Organization Science* 11(2): 183–96.

George, C. S. (1968). *The history of management thought.* Englewood Cliffs, NJ: Prentice Hall.

Gerhart, B. (1999). "Human resource management and firm performance: Measurement issues and their effect on causal and policy inferences." *Strategic human resources management in the twenty-first century.* P. M. Wright, L. D. Dyer, J. W. Boudreau, and G. T. Milkovich, eds. Stamford, CT: JAI Press.

Geringer, M. J., and C. A. Frayne (1990). "Human resource management and international joint venture control: A parent company perspective." *Management International Review* 30(Special Issue): 103–20.

Ghoshal, S. (1991). "Andersen Consulting (Europe): Entering the business of business integration." Case series, INSEAD, Fontainebleau.

Ghoshal, S., and C. A. Bartlett (1997). *The individualized corporation.* New York: Harper-Business.

——— (1998). *Managing across borders: The transnational solution,* 2d ed. London: Random House.

——— (2000). "Rebuilding behavioral context: A blueprint for corporate renewal." *Breaking the code of change.* M. Beer and N. Nohria, eds. Boston: Harvard Business School Press.

Gilbert, J. A., and J. M. Ivancevich (2000). "Valuing diversity: A tale of two organizations." *Academy of Management Executive* 14(1): 93–105.

Gittell, J. H. (2000). "Paradox of coordination and control." *California Management Review* 42(3): 101–17.

Glanz, E. F., and L. K. Bailey (1993). "Benchmarking." *Human Resource Management* 31(1 and 2): 9–20.

Godard, J., and J. T. Delaney (2000). "Reflections on the 'high performance' paradigm's implications for industrial relations as a field." *Industrial and Labor Relations Review* 53(3): 482–502.

Goffee, R., and G. Jones (1998). *The character of a corporation: How your company's culture can make or break your business.* New York: HarperBusiness.

Golden, K. A., and V. Ramanujam (1985). "Between a dream and a nightmare: On the integration of human resource management and strategic business planning processes." *Human Resource Managment* 24(4): 429–52.

Goldsmith, M., L. Lyons, and A. Freas (2000). *Coaching for leadership.* San Francisco: Jossey-Bass/Pfeiffer.

Gomes-Casseres, B. (1988). "Joint venture cycles: The evolution of ownership strategies of U.S. MNEs, 1945–75." *Cooperative strategies in international business.* F. J. Contractor and P. Lorange, eds. Lexington, MA: Lexington Books.

Gomes-Casseres, B., and K. McQuade (1992). "Xerox and Fuji Xerox." Case No. 391156, Harvard Business School, Boston.

Goodall, K., and M. Warner (1997). "The evolving image of HRM in the Chinese workplace: Comparing Sino-foreign joint ventures and state-owned enterprises in Beijing and Shanghai." Paper presented at the LVMH Conference, February 7–8. INSEAD, Fontainebleau.

Gooderham, P. N., O. Nordhaug, and K. Ringdal (1999). "Institutional and rational determinants of organizational practices: Human resource management in European firms." *Adminstrative Science Quarterly* 44(3): 507–31.

Goold, M., and A. Campbell (1987). *Strategies and styles: The role of the centre in managing diversified corporations.* Oxford: Basil Blackwell.

——— (1998). "Desperately seeking synergy." *Harvard Business Review* (September–October): 131–43.

Goold, M., A. Campbell, and M. Alexander (1994). *Corporate-level strategy: Creating value in the multibusiness company.* New York: Wiley.

Goss, T., R. Pascale, and A. Athos (1993). "The reinvention roller coaster: Risking the present for a powerful future." *Harvard Business Review* (November–December): 97–108.

Granovetter, M. S. (1976). "The strength of weak ties." *American Journal of Sociology* 78(3): 1360–80.

Gratton, L. (2000). *Living strategy: Putting people at the heart of corporate purpose.* London: Financial Times/Prentice Hall.

Gratton, L., V. Hope-Hailey, P. Stiles, and C. Truss (1999a). *Strategic human resource management.* Oxford: Oxford University Press.

———— (1999b). "Linking individual performance to business strategy: The people process model." *Human Resource Management* 38(1): 17–31.

Gregersen, H. B. (1992a). *Coming home to the cold: Finnish repatriation adjustment.* Paper presented at the The Academy of International Business, Brussels, Belgium.

———— (1992b). *Organizational commitment during repatriation: The Japanese and Finnish experience.* Paper presented at the Academy of Management, Las Vegas.

———— (1992c). "Commitments to a parent company and a local work unit during repatriation." *Personnel Psychology* 45: 29–54.

Gregersen, H. B., and J. S. Black (1995). "Keeping high performers after international assignments: A key to global executive development." *Journal of International Management* 1(1): 3–31.

Gregersen, H. B., J. S. Black, and J. M. Hite (1995). "Expatriate performance appraisal: Principles, practices, and challenges." *Expatriate management: New ideas for international business.* J. Selmer, ed. Westport, CT: Quorum Books.

Gregersen, H. B., J. M. Hite, and J. S. Black (1996). "Expatriate performance appraisal in U.S. multinational firms." *Journal of International Business Studies* 27(4): 711–38.

Gregersen, H. B., A. J. Morrison, and S. Black (1998). "Developing leaders for the global frontier." *Sloan Management Review* (Fall): 2–32.

Greiner, L. E. (1972). "Evolution and revolution as organizations grow." *Harvard Business Review* (July–August).

Greller, M., and D. M. Rousseau (1994). "Guest editors' overview: Psychological contracts and human resource practices." *Human Resource Management* 33(3): 383–84.

Groh, K., and M. Allen (1998). "Global staffing: Are expatriates the only answer?" *HR Focus* 75(3).

Grote, D. (2000). "The secrets of performance appraisal: Best practices from the masters." *Across the Board* (May): 14–20.

Guest, D. E. (1990). "Human resource management and the American dream." *Journal of Management Studies* 27(4): 377–97.

———— (1999). "Human resource management—The worker's verdict." *Human Resource Management Journal* 9(3): 5–25.

Guest, D. E., and K. Hoque (1996). "National ownership and HR practices in UK greenfield sites." *Human Resource Management Journal* 6(4): 50–74.

Gupta, A. K., and V. Govindarajan (2000). "Knowledge flows within multinational corporations." *Strategic Management Journal* 21: 473–96.

Haasen, A. (1996). "Opel Eisenach GMBH—Creating a high-productivity workplace." *Organizational Dynamics* 24(4): 80–85.

Hailey, J. (1993). "Localisation and expatriation: The continuing role of expatriates in developing countries." Working Paper 18/93. Cranfield School of Management, UK.

———— (1996). "The expatriate myth: Cross-cultural perceptions of expatriate managers." *The International Executive* 38(2): 255–71.

Hale, R., and P. Whitlam (1997). *Towards the virtual organisation.* Berkshire: McGraw-Hill.

Haleblian, J., and S. Finkelstein (1999). "The influence of organizational acquisition experience on acquisition performance: A behavioral learning perspective." *Administrative Science Quarterly* 44(2): 29–57.

Hall, D. T. (1976). *Careers in organizations.* Glenview, IL: Scott, Foresman.

Hall, D. T., and Associates (1996). *The career is dead—Long live the career.* San Francisco: Jossey-Bass

Hall, E. T., and M. R. Hall (1990). *Understanding cultural differences: Germans, French, and Americans.* Yarmouth, ME: Intercultural Press.

Hall, L., and D. Torrington (1998). "Letting go or holding on—The devolution of operational personnel activities." *Human Resource Management Journal* 8(1): 41–54.

Hambrick, D. C., D. A. Nadler, and M. L. Tushman, eds. (1998). *Navigating change: How CEOs, top teams, and boards steer transformation.* Boston: Harvard Business School Press.

Hamel, G. (1991). "Competition for competence and inter-partner learning within international strategic alliances." *Strategic Management Journal* 12(Summer Special Issue): 83–103.

Hamel, G., Y. Doz et al. (1989). "Collaborate with your competitors—and win." *Harvard Business Review* 67(1): 133–39.

Hamel, G., and C. K. Prahalad (1994). *Competing for the future.* Boston: Harvard Business School Press.

Hampden-Turner, C. (1990). *Charting the corporate mind: From dilemma to strategy.* Oxford: Basil Blackwell.

Hampden-Turner, C., and F. Trompenaars (1993). *The seven cultures of capitalism.* New York: Currency Doubleday.

——— (2000). *Building cross-cultural competence.* New Haven: Yale University Press.

Handy, C. (1994). *The empty raincoat: Making sense of the future.* London: Hutchinson.

——— (1998a). "A better capitalism." *Across the Board.* 35(4): 16–22.

——— (1998b). *The hungry spirit: Beyond capitalism—A quest for purpose in the modern world.* London: Arrow Books.

Hanna, D. P. (1988). *Designing organizations for high performance.* Reading, MA: Addison-Wesley.

Hansen, F. (1999). "Currents in compensation and benefits." *Compensation and Benefits Review* 31(6).

Hansen, M. T. (1999). "The search-transfer problem: The role of weak ties in sharing knowledge across organization subunits." *Administrative Science Quarterly* 44(1): 82–111.

Hansen, M. T., N. Nohria, and T. Tierney (1999). "What's your strategy for managing knowledge?" *Harvard Business Review* (March–April): 106–16.

Hansen, M. T., and B. von Oetinger (2001). "Introducing T-shaped managers: Knowledge management's next generation." *Harvard Business Review* (March): 107–16.

Harel, G. H., and S. S. Tzagrir (1999). "The effect of human resource management practices on the perceptions of organizational and market performance of the firm." *Human Resource Management* 38(3): 185–200.

Hargadon, A. B. (1998). "Firms as knowledge brokers: Lessons in pursuing continuous innovation." *California Management Review* 40(3): 209–27.

Harrigan, K. (1988). "Strategic alliances and partner asymmetries." *Management International Review* 28(Special Issue): 53–72.

Harris, H., and C. Brewster (1999). "An integrative framework for pre-departure preparation." *International HRM: Contemporary issues in Europe.* C. Brewster and H. Harris, eds. London: Routledge.

Hart, S. L., and R. E. Quinn (1993). "Roles executives play: CEOs, behavioral complexity, and firm performance." *Human Relations* 46(5): 543–74.

Harvey, M., C. Speier, and M. M. Novicevic (1999a). "The role of inpatriation in global staffing." *International Journal of Human Resource Management* 10(3): 459–76.

——— (1999b). "The role of inpatriates in a globalization strategy and challenges associated with the inpatriation process." *Human Resource Planning* 22(1): 38–50.

Harzing, A-W. (1995). "The persistent myth of high expatriate failure rates." *International Journal of Human Resource Management* 6(2): 457–74.

———— (1999). *Managing the multinationals: An international study of control mechanisms.* Cheltenham: Edward Elgar.

Haspeslagh, P. C., and D. B. Jemison (1991). *Managing acquisitions: Creating value through corporate renewal.* New York: Free Press.

Hastings, D. F. (1999). "Lincoln Electric's harsh lessons from international expansion." *Harvard Business Review* (May–June): 162–78.

Hauschild, P. R. (1993). "Interorganizational imitation: The impact of interlocks on corporate acquisition activity." *Administrative Science Quarterly* 38: 564–92.

Hays, R. D. (1974). "Expatriate selection: Insuring success and avoiding failure." *Journal of International Business Studies* 5(1): 25–37.

Hedberg, B. L. T. (1981). "How organizations learn and unlearn." *Handbook of Organizational Design.* P. C. Nystrom and W. H. Starbuck, eds. London: Oxford University Press.

Hedburg, B. L. T., P. C. Nystrom, and W. H. Starbuck (1976). "Camping on seesaws: Prescriptions for a self-designing organization." *Administrative Science Quarterly* (21): 41–65.

Hedlund, G. (1986). "The hypermodern MNC: A heterarchy?" *Human Resource Management* (Spring): 9–35.

Hedlund, G., and A. Knerveland (1984). "Investing in Japan—The experience of Swedish firms." Institute of International Business, Stockholm School of Economics, Stockholm, Sweden.

Hedlund, G., and I. Nonaka (1993). "Models of knowledge management in the West and Japan." *Implementing strategic processes: Change, learning and co-operation.* P. Lorange, B. Chakravarthy, J. Roos, and A. Van de Ven, eds. Oxford: Blackwell Business.

Hedlund, G., and J. Ridderstraale (1995). "International development projects: Key to competitiveness, impossible or mismanaged?" *International Studies of Management and Organization* 25(1, 2): 158–84.

Heifetz, R. A. (1994). *Leadership without easy answers.* Cambridge, MA: Belknap Press of Harvard University Press.

Hendry, C., and A. Pettigrew (1990). "Human resource management: An agenda for the 1990s." *International Journal of Human Resource Management* 1(1): 17–43.

Hennart, J-F. (1991). "Control in multinational firms: The role of price and hierarchy." *Management International Review* 31(Special Issue): 71–96.

Hergert, M., and D. Morris (1988). "Trends in international collaborative agreements." *Cooperative strategies in international business.* F. J. Contractor and P. Lorange, eds. Lexington, MA: Lexington Books.

Hill, L. A. (1992). *Becoming a manager: Mastery of a new identity.* Boston: Harvard Business School Press.

Hinings, C. R., and R. G. Greenwood (1989). *The dynamics of strategic change.* Oxford: Basil Blackwell.

Hitt, M. A., R. E. Hoskisson, R. D. Ireland, and J. J. Harrison (1991). "Are acquisitions a poison pill for innovation?" *Academy of Management Executive* 5(4): 22–34.

Hitt, M. A., J. J. Harrison, and R. D. Ireland (2001). *Mergers & acquisitions: A guide to creating value for stakeholders.* Oxford: Oxford University Press.

Hodgetts, R. M. (1996). "A conversation with Steve Kerr." *Organizational Dynamics* (Spring): 68–79.

Hofstede, G. (1980a). *Culture's consequences.* Beverly Hills and London: Sage.

———— (1980b). "Motivation, leadership and organization: Do American theories apply abroad?" *Organizational Dynamics* (Summer): 42–63.

——— (1999). "Problems remain, but theories will change: The universal and the specific in 21st century global management." *Organizational Dynamics* (Summer): 34–44.

Hsieh, T., J. Lavoie, and R. A. P. Samek (1999). "Are you taking your expatriate talent seriously?" *McKinsey Quarterly* 3: 71–83.

Hunt, J., and P. Boxall (1998). "Are top human resource specialists strategic partners? Self perceptions of a corporate elite." *International Journal of Human Resource Management* 9(5): 767–81.

Huselid, M. (1995). "The impact of human resource management practices on turnover, productivity, and corporate financial performance." *Academy of Management Journal* 38(3): 635–72.

Huselid, M., S. E. Jackson, and R. S. Schuler (1997). "Technical and strategic human resource management effectiveness as determinants of firm performance." *Academy of Management Journal* 40(1): 171–88.

Ibarra, H. (1992). "Structural alignments, individual strategies, and managerial action: Elements toward a network theory of getting things done." *Networks and organizations.* N. Nohria and R. G. Eccles, eds. Boston: Harvard Business School Press.

——— (1999). "Provisional selves: Experimenting with image and identiy in professional adaptation." *Administrative Science Quarterly* 44: 764–91.

——— (2000). "Making partner: A mentor's guide to the psychological journey." *Harvard Business Review* (March–April): 146–55.

Ichniowski, C., K. Shaw, and G. Prennushi (1997). "The effects of human resource management practices on productivity: A study of steel finishing lines." *American Economic Review* 87(3): 291–313.

Ilinitich, A. Y., R. A. D'Aveni, and A. Y. Lewin (1996). "New organizational forms and strategies for managing in hypercompetitive environments." *Organization Science* 7(3): 211–20.

Imai, M (1986). *Kaizen: The key to Japan's competitive success.* New York: Random House.

Inkpen, A. C. (1997). "An examination of knowledge management in international joint venture." *Cooperative strategies: North American perspectives.* P. W. Beamish and J. P. Killing, eds. San Francisco: New Lexington Press.

——— (1998). "Learning and knowledge acquisition through international strategic alliances." *Academy of Management Executive* 12(4): 69–80.

Inkpen, A. C., A. K. Sundaram, and K. Rockwood (2000). "Cross-border acquisitions of U.S. technology assets." *California Management Review* 42(3): 50–71.

Itami, H. (1987). *Mobilizing invisible assets.* Cambridge, MA: Harvard University Press.

Jackson, S. E., and R. Schuler (1995). "Understanding human resource management in the context of organizations and their environments." *Annual Review of Psychology* (46): 237–64.

——— (1999). *Managing human resources.* Cincinnati: South-Western.

Jacoby, S. M. (1985). *Employing bureaucracy: Managers, unions and the transformation of work in American industry, 1900–1945.* New York: Columbia University Press.

Jacques, E. (1989). *Requisite organization.* Arlington, VA: Cason Hall.

Jaeger, A. (1982). "Contrasting control modes in the multinational corporation: Theory, practice, and implications." *International Studies of Management and Organization* 12(1): 59–82.

Janger, A. H. (1980). *Organization of international joint ventures.* New York:

Jarvenpaa, S. L., and D. E. Leidner (1999). "Communication and trust in global virtual teams." *Organization Science* 10(6): 791–815.

Jay, A. (1967). *Management and Machiavelli: An inquiry into the politics of corporate life.* New York: Holt, Rinehart and Winston.

Jermier, J. M. (1998). "Critical perspective on organizational control." *Administrative Science Quarterly* 43(2): 235–56.

Johansen, R., D. Sibbet et al. (1991). *Leading teams: How teams can use technology and group process tools to enhance performance.* Reading, MA: Addison-Wesley.

Johanson, J., and J. E. Vahlne (1977). "The internationalization process of the firm: A model of knowledge development and increasing foreign market commitment." *Journal of International Business Studies* 8(Spring–Summer): 23–32.

Johne, F. A. (1984). "How experienced product innovators organize." *Journal of Product Innovation Management* (4): 210–23.

Johnson L., and J. Rich (2000). "Dealing with employee benefit issues in mergers and acquisitions." *SHRM's Legal Report* (March–April), Society for Human Resource Management, Arlington VA.

Jones, G. (1996). *The evolution of international business.* London: Routledge.

Jones, G., and P. Wright (1992). "An economic approach to conceptualizing the utility of human resource management practices." *Research in personnel and human resource management.* G. R. Ferris, ed. Greenwich, CT: JAI Press.

Kakabadse, A. (1991). *The wealth creators: Top people, top teams and executive best practice.* London: Kogan Page.

——— (1993). "The success levers for Europe: The Cranfield Executive Competencies Survey." Working Paper. Cranfield School of Management, UK.

Kanter, R. M. (1985). *Change masters: Innovation for productivity in the American workplace.* New York: Simon & Schuster.

——— (1989). "Becoming PALs: Pooling, allying, and linking across companies." *Academy of Management Executive* 3(3): 183–93.

——— (1994). "Collaborative advantage: The art of alliances." *Harvard Business Review* (July–August): 96–108.

——— (1995). *World class: Thriving locally in the global economy.* New York: Simon & Schuster.

——— (2001). *Evolve: Succeeding in the digital culture of tomorrow.* Boston: Harvard Business School Press.

Kanter, R. M., and R. G. Eccles (1992). "Making network research relevant to practice." *Networks and organizations.* N. Nohria and R. G. Eccles, eds. Boston: Harvard Business School Press.

Kanter, R. M., B. A. Stein, and T. D. Jick (1992). *The challenge of organizational change: How companies experience it and leaders guide it.* New York: Free Press.

Kaplan, R. S., and D. P. Norton (1992). "The Balanced Scorecard: Measures that drive performance." *Harvard Business Review* (January–February): 71–79.

——— (1996). *Translating strategy into action: The Balanced Scorecard.* Boston: Harvard Business School Press.

Katzenbach, J. R., and D. K. Smith (1993). *The wisdom of teams: Creating the high performance organization.* Boston: Harvard Business School Press.

Kay, I. T., and M. Shelton (2000). "The people problems in mergers." *McKinsey Quarterly* 4: 29–37.

Kayworth, T. R., and D. Leidner (1999). "The global virtual manager: A prescription for success." Working Paper No. 99/67/TM. INSEAD, Fontainebleau.

Kearney, A. T. (1999). *Corporate Marriage: Blight or Bliss—A Monograph on Post-Merger Integration.* A. T. Kearney report, Chicago.

Keenoy, T. (1997). "HRMism and the languages of re-presentation." *Journal of Management Studies* 34(5): 825–41.

Kennedy, C. (1989). "Xerox charts a new strategic direction." *Long Range Planning* 22(1): 10–17.

Kenney, M., and R. Florida (1992). "The Japanese transplants: Production organization and regional development." *Journal of the American Planning Association* 58(1): 21–38.

———— (1993). *Beyond mass production: The Japanese system and its transfer to the U.S.* New York: Oxford University Press.

Kerr, S. (1995). "An academic classic: On the folly of rewarding A, while hoping for B." *Academy of Management Executive* 9(1): 7–14.

Kets de Vries, M. F. R. (1989). "Leaders who self-destruct: The causes and cures." *Organizational Dynamics* (Spring): 5–17.

———— (1994). "Percy Barnevik and ABB." Case No. 05/94-4308. INSEAD, Fontainebleau.

———— (1995). *Life and death in the executive fast lane.* New York: Wiley.

Kets de Vries, M. F. R., and D. Miller (1984). *The neurotic organization: Diagnosing and changing counterproductive styles of management.* San Francisco: Jossey-Bass.

Killing, J. P. (1982). "How to make a global joint venture work." *Harvard Business Review* (May–June): 120–27.

———— (1997). "International joint ventures: Managing after the deal is signed." *Perspective for managers.* IMD Report, Lausanne, Switzerland.

Kim, C., and R. Mauborgne (1991). "Implementing global strategies: The role of procedural justice." *Strategic Management Journal* (12): 125–43.

———— (1997). "Fair process: Managing in the knowledge economy." *Harvard Business Review* (July–August): 65–75.

———— (1998). "Procedural justice, strategic decision making, and the knowledge economy." *Strategic Management Journal* (19): 323–38.

———— (1988). "Expatriate reduction and strategic control in American multinational corporations." *Human Resource Management* 27(1): 63–75.

Kochanski, J. T., ed. (1996). "Special issue on human resource competencies." *Human Resource Management* 35(1).

Kogut, B. (1988). "Joint ventures: Theoretical and empirical perspectives." *Strategic Management Journal* 9(4): 319–32.

Kogut, B., and H. Singh (1988). "The effect of national culture on the choice of entry mode." *Journal of International Business Studies* 19: 411–32.

Kogut, B., and U. Zander (1992). "Knowledge of the firm, combinative capabilities, and the replication of technology." *Organization Science* 3(3): 383–97.

———— (1993). "Knowledge of the firm and the evolutionary theory of the multinational corporation." *Journal of International Business Studies* 24(4): 625–45.

———— (1996). "What firms do? Coordination, identity and learning." *Organization Science* 7(5): 502–18.

Kolb, D. A. (1984). *Experiential Learning: Experience as the source of learning and development.* Englewood Cliffs, NJ: Prentice Hall.

Konovsky, M. A. (2000). "Understanding procedural justice and its impact on business organizations." *Journal of Management* 26(3): 489–511.

Kopp, R. (1994). "International human resource policies and practices in Japanese, European, and U.S. multinationals." *Human Resource Management* 33(4): 581–99.

Kossek, E., and S. A. Lobel (1996). *Managing diversity: HR strategies for transforming the workplace.* Oxford: Blackwell Business.

Kostova, T. (1999). "Transnational transfer of strategic organizational practices: A contextual perspective." *Academy of Management Review* 24(2): 308–24.

Kotter, J. P. (1982). "What effective general managers really do." *Harvard Business Review* (November–December): 156–67.

———— (1988). "The leadership factor." *The McKinsey Quarterly* (Spring).

———— (1996). *Leading change.* Boston: Harvard Business School Press.

Kotter, J. P., and J. L. Heskett (1992). *Corporate culture and performance.* New York: Free Press.

KPMG (1999). "Mergers and acquisitions: A global research report—Unlocking shareholder value." Report, KPMG, New York.

Kraatz, M. S. (1998). "Learning by association? Interorganizational networks and adaptation to environmental change." *Academy of Management Journal* 41(6): 621–43.

Krackhardt, D., and J. R. Hanson (1993). "Informal networks: The company behind the chart." *Harvard Business Review* (July–August): 104–11.

Kram, K. E. (1985). *Mentoring at work.* Glennview, IL.: Scott, Foresman.

Krug, J., and W. H. Hegerty (1997). "Postacquisition turnover among U.S. top management teams: An analysis of the effect of foreign versus domestic acquisition of U.S. targets." *Strategic Management Journal* 18(8): 667–75.

——— (2001). "Predicting who stays and leaves after an acquisition: A study of top managers in multinational firms." *Strategic Management Journal* 22: 185–96.

Kruger, J., and D. Dunning (1999). "Unskilled and unaware of it: How difficulties in recognizing one's incompetence lead to inflated self-assessments." *Journal of Personality and Social Psychology* 77(6): 1121–34.

Kuin, P. (1972). "The magic of multinational management." *Harvard Business Review* (November–December): 89–97.

Kurland, N. B., and D. E. Bailey (1999). "The advantages and challenges of working here, there, anywhere, and anytime." *Organizational Dynamics* (Autumn): 53–68.

Lane, C. (1989). *Management and labour in Europe: The industrial enterprise in Germany, Britain and France.* Aldershot, UK: Edward Elgar.

Larsson, R., and S. Finkelstein (1999). "Integrating strategic, organizational, and human resource perspectives on mergers and acquisitions: A case survey of synergy realization." *Organization Science* 10(1): 1–26.

Lasserre, P., and P. S. Ching (1997). "Human resources management in China and the localization challenge." *Journal of Asian Business* 13(4): 75–96.

Lasserre, P., and H. Schütte (1995). *Strategies for Asia Pacific.* London: Macmillan.

Laurent, A. (1981). "Matrix organization and Latin cultures." *International Studies of Management and Organization* 10(4): 101–14.

——— (1983). "The cultural diversity of Western conceptions of management." *International Studies of Management and Organization* 13(1,2): 75–96.

Lawler, E. E. (1992). *The ultimate advantage: Creating the high involvement organization.* San Francisco: Jossey-Bass.

Lawler, E. E. (1994). "From job-based to competency-based organizations." *Journal of Organizational Behavior* 15: 3–15.

Lawrence, P. R., and J. W. Lorsch (1967). *Organization and environment.* Boston: Harvard Division of Research.

Lazonick, W., and M. O'Sullivan (1996). "Organization, finance, and international competition." *Industrial and Corporate Change* 5(1): 1–49.

Leana, C. R., and H. J. Van Buren III (1999). "Organizational social capital and employment practices." *Academy of Management Review* 24(3): 538–55.

Leavitt, H. J. (1965). "Applied organizational change in industry." *Handbook of organizations.* J. G. March, ed. New York: Rand McNally.

Legge, K. (1995). *Human resource management: Rhetorics and realities.* London: Macmillan.

——— (1999). "Representing people at work." *Organization* 6(2): 247–64.

Lei, D., J. W. Slocum, Jr., et al. (1997). "Building cooperative advantage: Managing strategic alliances to promote organizational learning." *Journal of World Business* 32(3): 203–23.

Leidner, D., T. R. Kayworth, and M. Mora-Tavarez (1999). "Leadership effectiveness in global virtual teams." Working Paper No. 99/68/TM. INSEAD, Fontainebleau.

Lengnick-Hall, C. A., and M. L. Lengnick-Hall (1988). "Strategic human resources management: A review of the literature and a proposed typology." *Academy of Management Review* 13(3): 454–70.

Leonard, D. (1995). *Wellsprings of knowledge: Building and sustaining the sources of innovation.* Boston: Harvard Business School Press.

Leonard, D., and S. Sensiper (1998). "The role of tacit knowledge in group innovation." *California Management Review* 40(3): 112–32.

Leonard-Barton, D. (1992). "Core capabilities and core rigidities: A paradox in managing new product development." *Strategic Management Journal* 13(Special Issue): 111–25.

Leonard-Barton, D., and S. Conner (1996). "Hewlett-Packard: Singapore (A), (B), (C)." Case Nos. 694-035, -036, and -037. Harvard Business School, Boston.

Lepak, D. P., and S. A. Snell (1999). "The human resource architecture: Toward a theory of human capital allocation and development." *Academy of Management Review* 24(1): 31–48.

Levy, A., and U. Merry (1986). *Organizational transformation.* New York: Praeger.

Levy, O., S. Beechler, and N. Boyacigiller (1999). "What we talk about when we talk about 'global mindset': Managerial cognition in MNCs." Paper presented at the Annual Meeting, Academy of Management, Toronto.

Lewis, M. W. (2000). "Exploring paradox: Toward a more comprehensive guide." *Academy of Management Review* 25(4): 760–76.

Lindholm, N. (1998). *Performance appraisal in MNC subsidiaries: A study of host country employees in China.* EIASM Workshop on Strategic Human Resource Management, Brussels.

Lindqvist, M., O. Sölvell, and I. Zander (2000). "Technological advantage in the international firm: Local and global perspectives on the innovation process." *Management International Review* 40(1): 95–126.

Loewendahl, B. (1997). *Strategic management of professional service firms.* Copenhagen: Handelshojskolens Forlag.

Lorange, P. (1996). "A strategic human resource perspective applied to multinational cooperative ventures." *International Studies of Management and Organization* 26(1): 87–103.

Lorange, P., and J. Roos (1990). "Formation of cooperative ventures: Competence mix of the management teams." *Management International Review* 30(Special Issue): 69–86.

Loveridge, R. (1990). "Footfalls of the future: The emergence of strategic frames and formulae." *The strategic management of technological innovation.* R. Loveridge and M. Pitt, eds. Chichester: Wiley.

Lovett, S., L. C. Simmons, and R. Kali (1999). "Guanxi versus the market: Ethics and efficiency." *Journal of International Business Studies* 30(2): 231–48.

Lowe, K. B., M. Downes, and K. G. Kroeck (1999). "The impact of gender and location on the willingness to accept overseas assignments." *International Journal of Human Resource Management* 10(2): 223–34.

Lu, Y., and I. Bjorkman (1997). "MNC standardization versus localization: HRM practices in China-Western joint ventures." *International Journal of Human Resource Management* 8(5): 614–28.

Mabey, C., D. Skinner, and T. Clark, eds. (1998). *Experiencing human resource management.* London: Sage.

MacDuffie, J. P. (1995). "Human resource bundles and manufacturing performance: Organizational logic and flexible production system in the world auto industry." *Industrial and Labor Relations Review* 48: 197–221.

Maister, D. H. (1993). *Managing the professional service firm.* New York: Free Press.

March, J. G. (1991). "Exploration and exploitation in organizational learning." *Organization Science* 2(1): 71–87.

March, J. G., and H. A. Simon (1958). *Organizations.* New York: Wiley.

Marks, M. L., and P. H. Mirvis (1998). *Joining Forces: Making one plus one equal three in mergers, acquisitions, and alliances.* San Francisco: Jossey-Bass.

Martinez, J. I., and J. C. Jarillo (1989). "The evolution of research on coordination mechanisms in multinational corporations." *Journal of International Business Studies* (Fall): 489–514.

Maruca, R. F. (1994). "The right way to go global: An interview with Whirlpool CEO David Whitlam." *Harvard Business Review* (March–April): 135–45.

Mastenbroek, W. (1996). "Organizational innovation in historical perspective: Change as duality management." *Business Horizons* (July–August).

Maurice, M. (1979). "For a study of 'the societal effect': Universality and specificity in organisation research." *Organizations alike and unlike.* C. J. Lammers and D. J. Hickson, eds. London: Routledge and Kegan Paul.

Maurice, M., A. Sorge, and M. Warner (1980). "Societal differences in organizing manufacturing units: A comparison of France, West Germany, and Great Britain." *Organization Studies* 1(1): 59–86.

Mayer, M., and R. Whittington (1999). "Euro-elites: Top British, French and German managers in the 1980s and 1990s." *European Management Journal* 17(4): 403–8.

Mayo, A. (1991). *Managing careers: Strategies for organizations.* London: Institute of Personnel Management.

McCall, M. W. (1998). *High flyers: Developing the next generation of leaders.* Boston: Harvard Business School Press.

McCall, M., and M. Lombardo (1990). *Off the track: why and how successful executives get derailed.* Center for Creative Leadership, Greensboro, South Carolina.

McCall, M., M. Lombardo, and A. Morrison (1988). *The lessons of experience.* MA: Lexington Books.

McGovern, P. (1997). "Human resource management on the line?" *Human Resource Management Journal* 7(4): 12–29.

McGregor, D. (1960). *The human side of enterprise.* New York: McGraw-Hill.

McKenzie, J. (1996). *Paradox: The next strategic dimension.* New York: McGraw-Hill.

McMahan, G. C., M. Virick, and P. M. Wright (1999). "Alternative theoretical perspectives for strategic human resource management revisited: Progress, problems, and prospects." *Strategic human resources management in the twenty-first century.* P. M. Wright, L. D. Dyer, J. W. Boudreau, and G. T. Milkovich, eds. Stamford, CT: JAI Press.

Mee, J. T. (1964). "Matrix organization." *Business Horizons* 7(2): 70–72.

Melvin, S., and K. Sylvester (1997). "Shipping out." *China Business Review* (May–June): 30–34.

Mendenhall, M. E., E. Dunbar, and G. R. Oddou (1987). "Expatriate selection, training and career-pathing: A review and critique." *Human Resource Management* 26(3): 331–345.

Mendenhall, M., and G. Oddou (1985). "The dimensions of expatriate acculturation: A review." *Academy of Management Review* 10(1): 39–47.

——— (1986). "Acculturation profiles of expatriate managers: Implications for cross-cultural training programs." *Columbia Journal of World Business* 21(4): 73–79.

Meshoulam, I., and L. Baird (1987). "Proactive human resource management." *Human Resource Management* (26:4): 483–503.

Micklethwait, J., and A. Woolridge (1996). *The witch doctors: Making sense of the management gurus.* New York: Times Books.

——— (2000). *A future perfect: The challenge and hidden promise of globalization.* London: Heinemann.

Middelhof, T. (1998). "Bertelsmann in transition." Published version of speech delivered at the 5th Bertelsmann Management Congress, Gütersloh, Germany.

Miles, R. E., and C. C. Snow (1978). *Organizational strategy, structure, and process.* New York: McGraw-Hill.

Miles, R. E., C. Snow, and G. Miles (2000). "TheFuture.org." *Long Range Planning* 33: 300–32

Milkovich, G. T., and J. W. Boudreau (1997). *Human resource management,* 8th ed. Chicago: Irwin/McGraw Hill.

Milkovich, G. T., and J. M. Newman (1996). *Compensation,* 5th ed. Homewood, IL: Irwin.

Miller, D. (1990). *The Icarus paradox: How exceptional companies bring about their own downfall.* New York: HarperBusiness.

——— (1996). "Configurations revisited." *Strategic Management Journal* 17(7): 505–12.

Miller, D., and J. O. Whitney (1999). "Beyond strategy: Configuration as a pillar of competitive advantage." *Business Horizons* (May–June): 5–17.

Mills, D. Q. (1994). *The GEM principle: Six steps to creating a high performance organization.* Essex Junction, VT: Oliver Wight.

Mills, T. (1975). "Human resources: Why the new concern?" *Harvard Business Review* (March–April): 120–34.

Mintzberg, H. (1979). *The structuring of organizations: A synthesis of the research.* Englewood Cliffs, NJ: Prentice Hall.

——— (1984). "Power and organization life cycles." *Academy of Management Review* 9(2): 207–24.

——— (1989). *Mintzberg on management: Inside our strange world of organizations.* New York: Free Press.

——— (1994). *The rise and fall of strategic planning.* Englewood Cliffs, NJ: Prentice Hall.

Mintzberg, H., and J. A. Waters (1985). "Of strategies, deliberate and emergent." *Strategic Management Journal* (6): 257–72.

Mintzberg, H., and F. Westley (1992). "Cycles of organizational change." *Strategic Management Journal* 13: 39–59.

Mirvis, P. M., and M. L. Marks (1994). *Managing the merger: Making it work.* Englewood Cliffs, NJ: Prentice Hall.

Misa, K. F., and J. M. Fabricatore (1979). "Return on investment of overseas personnel." *Financial Executive* 47(4): 42–46.

Mitroff, I., and H. Linstone (1993). *The unbounded mind: Breaking the chains of traditional business thinking.* New York: Oxford University Press.

Mohrman, A. M., S. A. Mohrman et al. (1989). *Large-scale organizational change.* San Francisco: Jossey-Bass.

Moore, K., and J. Birkinshaw (1998). "Managing knowledge in global service firms: Centers of excellence." *Academy of Management Executive* 12(4): 81–92.

Moore, K., and D. Lewis (1999). *Birth of the multinational.* Copenhagen: Copenhagen Business Press.

Moore, L. F., and P. Devereaux Jennings, eds. (1995). *Human resource management on the Pacific rim.* Berlin and New York: de Gruyter.

Moore, W. E. (1969). "Occupational socialization." *Handbook of socialization theory and research.* D. A. Goslin, ed. Chicago: Rand McNally.

Moran, Stahl, and Boyer Inc. (1988). "Status of American female expatriate employees; Survey results." Report, Boulder, CO.

Morgan, G. (1986). *Images of organization.* Newbury Park, CA: Sage.

Morgan, G., and R. Ramirez (1983). "Action learning: A holographic metaphor for guiding social change." *Human Relations* 37(1): 1–28.

Moriguchi, C. (2000). Implicit contracts, the Great Depression, and institutional change: The evolution of employment relations in US and Japanese manufacturing firms, 1910–1940. Working Paper, Harvard Business School, Boston.

Morosini, P. (1998). *Managing cultural differences: Effective strategy and execution across cultures in global corporate alliances.* Oxford: Pergamon.

Moxon, R. W., T. W. Roehl et al. (1988). "International cooperative ventures in the commercial aircraft industry: Gains, sure, but what's my share?" *Cooperative Strategies in international business.* F. J. Contractor and P. Lorange, eds. Lexington, MA: Lexington Books.

Mueller, F. (1994). "Societal effect, organizational effect and globalization." *Organization Studies* 15(3): 407–28.

Muller, H. (1970). "The search for qualities essential to advancement in a large industrial group." Royal Dutch/Shell publication, The Hague, Holland.

Murtha, T. P., S. A. Lenway, and R. P. Bagozzi (1998). "Global mind-sets and cognitive shift in a complex multinational corporation." *Strategic Management Journal* 19: 97–114.

Myers, P. S., and R. M. Kanter (1989). "Banc One Corporation, 1989." Case No. 9-390-029. Harvard Business School, Boston.

Nadler, D. A., and M. L. Tushman (1988). *Strategic organization design.* Glenview, IL: Scott, Foresman.

Nahapiet, J., and S. Ghoshal (1998). "Social capital, intellectual capital, and the organizational advantage." *Academy of Management Review* 23(2): 242–66.

Nathan, J. (1999). *Sony: The private life.* New York: Houghton Mifflin.

Neal, J. A., and C. L. Tromley (1995). "From incremental change to retrofit: Creating high performance work systems." *Academy of Management Executive* 9(1): 42–54.

Nelson, R., and S. Winter (1982). *An evolutionary theory of economic change.* Cambridge, MA: Harvard University Press.

Ngo, H., D. Turban, C. Lau, and S. Lui (1998). "Human resource management practices and firm performance of multinational corporations: Influences of country of origin." *International Journal of Human Resource Management* 9(4): 632–53.

Nicholson, N. (1984). "A theory of work role transitions." *Administrative Science Quarterly* 29: 172–91.

Noe, R., J. Hollenbeck, P. M. Wright, and B. Gerhart (1999). *Human resource management.* New York: McGraw-Hill/Irwin.

Nohria, N. (1992). "Is a network perspective a useful way of studying organizations?" *Networks and organizations.* N. Nohria and R. G. Eccles, eds. Boston: Harvard Business School Press.

Nohria, N., and R. G. Eccles (1992). "Face-to-face: Making network organizations work." *Networks and organizations.* N. Nohria and R. G. Eccles, eds. Boston: Harvard Business School Press.

———, eds. (1992). *Networks and organizations.* Boston: Harvard Business School Press.

Nohria, N., and S. Ghoshal (1997). *The differentiated network: Organizing multinational corporations for value creation.* San Francisco: Jossey-Bass.

Nonaka, I. (1988a). "Creating organizational order out of chaos: Self-renewal in Japanese firms." *California Management Review* (Spring): 57–73.

——— (1988b). "Towards middle-up-down management: Accelerating information creation." *Sloan Management Review* (Spring): 9–18.

——— (1991). "The knowledge-creating company." *Harvard Business Review* (November–December): 96–104.

Nonaka, I., and M. Konno (1998). "The concept of 'Ba': Building a foundation for knowledge creation." *California Management Review* 40(3): 40–54.

Nonaka, I., and H. Takeuchi (1995). *The knowledge-creating company: How Japanese companies create the dynamics of innovation.* Oxford: Oxford University Press.

Nord, W., and D. Durand (1978). "What's wrong with the human resources approach to management?" *Organizational Dynamics* (Winter): 13–25.

O'Connor, E. (1999). "Minding the workers: The meaning of 'human' and 'human relations' in Elton Mayo." *Organization* 6(2): 223–46.

Oddou, G. R. (1991). "Managing your expatriates: What the successful firms do." *Human Resource Planning* 14(4): 301–8.

O'Dell, C., and C. J. Grayson (1998). *If only we knew what we know: The transfer of internal knowledge and best practice.* New York: Free Press.

O'Grady, S., and H. W. Lane (1996). "The psychic distance paradox." *Journal of International Business Studies* 27(2): 309–33.

O'Hara-Devereaux, M., and R. Johansen (1994). *GlobalWork: Bridging Distance, Culture and Time.* San Francisco: Jossey-Bass.

Ohmae, K. (1992). *The mind of the strategist.* New York: McGraw-Hill.

Orchant, D. (2001). "Expatriate taxation." *Guide to global compensation and benefits.* C. Reynolds, ed. San Diego: Harcourt.

O'Reilly, C. A. (1998). "New United Motors Manufacturing, Inc. (NUMMI)." Case study, Stanford University, Palo Alto, CA.

O'Reilly, C. A., and J. Pfeffer (2000b). "New United Motor Manufacturing Inc.: Transforming people and systems." *Hidden value: How great companies achieve extraordinary results with ordinary people.* Boston: Harvard Business School Press.

——— (2000a). *Hidden value: How great companies achieve extraordinary results with ordinary people.* Boston: Harvard Business School Press.

Orrù, M. (1997). "The institutional analysis of capitalist economies." *The economic organization of East Asian capitalism.* M. Orrù, N. W. Biggart, and G. G. Hamilton, eds. Thousand Oaks, CA: Sage.

Osterman, P. (1994). "How common is workplace transformation and who adopts it?" *Industrial and Labor Relations Review* 47(2): 173–88.

Ostroff, F. (1999). *The horizontal organization.* New York: Oxford University Press.

O'Toole, J. (1985). *Vanguard management.* New York: Doubleday.

Ouchi, W. G. (1981). *Theory Z: How American business can meet the Japanese challenge.* Reading, MA: Addison-Wesley.

——— (1989). "The economics of organization." *Human resource management in international firms: Change, globalization, innovation.* P. A. L. Evans, Y. Doz, and A. Laurent, eds. London: Macmillan.

Oxley, G. M. (1961). "The personnel manager for international operations." *Personnel* 38(6): 52–58.

Packard, D. (1995). *The HP Way : How Bill Hewlett and I built our company.* New York: HarperBusiness.

PA Consulting (2001). "Realising the value of acquisitions: A comparative study of European post-acquisition integration practices." PA Consulting, London.

Paik, Y., and C. M. Stage (1996). "The extent of divergence in human resource practice across three Chinese national cultures: Hong Kong, Taiwan and Singapore." *Human Resource Management Journal* 6(2): 20–31.

Parkhe, A. (1991). "Interfirm diversity, organizational learning, and longevity in global strategic alliances." *Journal of International Business Studies* 22: 579–601.

——— (1993). "Partner nationality and the structure-performance relationship in strategic alliances." *Organization Science* 4(2): 301–24.

Pascale, R. T. (1990). *Managing on the edge: How successful companies use conflict to stay ahead.* New York: Viking.

Pascale, R., M. Milleman, and L. Gioja (1997). "Changing the way we change." *Harvard Business Review* (November–December): 127–39.

Pauly, L. W., and S. Reich (1997). "National structures and multinational corporate behavior: Enduring differences in the age of globalization." *International Organization* 51(1): 1–30.

Pelled, L. H., K. M. Eisenhardt, and K. R. Xin (1999). "Exploring the black box: An analysis of work group diversity, conflict, and performance." *Administrative Science Quarterly* 44(1): 1–28.

Penrose, E. (1959). *The theory of the growth of the firm.* New York: Wiley.

Perlmutter, H. V. (1969). "The tortuous evolution of the multinational corporation." *Columbia Journal of World Business* 4: 9–18.

Peters, T. J., and R. H. Waterman (1982). *In search of excellence.* New York: Harper & Row.

Peterson, M. F., T. K. Peng, and P. B. Smith (1999). "Using expatriate supervisors to promote cross-border management practice transfer: The experience of a Japanese electronics company." *Remade in America: Transplanting and Transforming Japanese Management Systems.* J. K. Liker, W. M. Fruin, and P. S. Adler, eds. New York: Oxford University Press.

Pettigrew, A. M. (1985). *The awakening giant: Continuity and change in organizations.* Oxford: Basil Blackwell.

——— (2000). "Linking change processes to outcomes." *Breaking the code of change.* M. Beer and N. Nohria, eds. Boston: Harvard Business School Press.

———, ed. (1988). *The management of strategic change.* Oxford: Basil Blackwell.

Pettigrew, A., and R. Whipp (1993). "Managing the twin processes of competition and change: The role of intangible assets." *Implementing strategic processes: Change, learning and cooperation.* P. Lorange, B. Chakravarthy, J. Roos, and A. Van de Ven, eds. Oxford: Blackwell Business.

Pfeffer, J. (1994). *Competitive advantage through people.* Boston: Harvard Business School Press.

——— (1998). *The human equation: Building profits by putting people first.* Boston: Harvard Business School Press.

Pfeffer, J., and R. I. Sutton (1999). "Knowing 'what' to do is not enough: Turning knowledge into action." *California Management Review* 42(1): 83–108.

Pieper, R., ed. (1990). *Human resource management: An international comparison.* Berlin and New York: de Gruyter.

Pil, F. K., and J. P. MacDuffie (1999). "What makes transplants thrive: Managing the transfer of 'best practice' at Japanese auto plants in North America." *Journal of World Business* 34(4): 372–91.

Podsakoff, P. M., S. B. MacKenzie, J. B. Paine, and D. G. Bachrach (2000). "Organizational citizenship behaviors: A critical review of the theoretical and empirical literature and suggestions for future research." *Journal of Management* 26(3): 513–63.

Polanyi, M. (1966). *The tacit dimension.* London: Routledge and Kegan Paul.

Porter, M. E. (1980). *Competitive strategy: Techniques for analyzing industries and competitors.* New York: Viking.

——— (1985). *Competitive advantage: Creating and sustaining superior performance.* New York: Free Press.

——— (1986). *Competition in global industries.* Boston: Harvard Business School Press.

——— (1990). *The competitive advantage of nations.* New York: Free Press.

——— (1996). "What is strategy?" *Harvard Business Review* (November–December): 61–78.

Porter, M. E., H. Takeuchi, and M. Sakakibara (2000). *Can Japan compete?* New York: Palgrave.

Powell, W. (1998). "Learning from collaboration: Knowledge and networks in the biotechnology and pharmaceutical industries." *California Management Review* 40(3): 228–40.

Powell, W. W., and P. J. DiMaggio, eds. (1991). *The new institutionalism in organizational analysis.* Chicago: University of Chicago Press.

Prahalad, C. K., and Y. Doz (1987). *The multinational mission: Balancing local demands and global vision.* New York: Free Press.

Prahalad, C. K., and K. Lieberthal (1998). "The end of corporate imperialism." *Harvard Business Review* (July–August): 69–79.

Prescott, R. K., W. J. Rothwell, and M. Taylor (1999). "Global HR: Transforming HR into a global powerhouse." *HR Focus.* 76(3): 7–8.

Price Waterhouse Change Integration Team (1996). *The paradox principles: How high performance companies manage chaos, complexity, and contradiction to achieve superior results.* Chicago: McGraw-Hill/Irwin.

Price Waterhouse Europe (1997). *International Assignments: European Policy and Practice.* Report by Price Waterhouse International Assignments Services Europe, London.

Pucik, V. (1984). "White-collar human resource management in large Japanese manufacturing firms." *Human Resource Management* 23(3): 257–76.

——— (1985a). "Promotion patterns in a Japanese trading company." *Journal of World Business* 20(3): 73–79.

——— (1985b). "Strategic human resource management in a multinational firm." *Strategic management of multinational corporations.* V. Pucik, ed. New York: Wiley.

——— (1988a). "Strategic alliances with the Japanese: Implications for human resource management." *Cooperative strategies in international business.* F. Contractor and P. Lorange, eds. Lexington, MA: Lexington Books.

——— (1988b). "Strategic alliances, organizational learning, and competitive advantage: The HRM agenda." *Human Resource Management* 27: 77–93.

——— (1992). "Globalization and human resource management." *Globalizing management: Creating and leading the competitive organization.* V. Pucik, N. M. Tichy, and C. K. Barnett, eds. New York: Wiley.

——— (1994). "The challenges of globalization: The strategic role of local managers in Japanese-owned US subsidiaries." *Japanese Multinationals: Strategies and Management in the Global Kaisha.* N. Campbell and F. Burton, eds. London: Routledge.

——— (1997). "Human resources in the future: An obstacle or a champion of globalization?" *Human Resource Management* 36(1): 163–68.

Pucik, V., and C. Duffy (1999). "Developing a global mindset at Johnson & Johnson—1998." Case No. GM791. IMD, Lausanne, Switzerland.

Pucik, V., M. Hanada, and G. Fifield (1989). "Management culture and the effectiveness of local executives in Japanese-owned U.S. corporations." Report by Egon Zehnder International, Ann Arbor, MI.

Pucik, V., and N. Hatvany (1981). "An integrated management system: Lessons from the Japanese experience." *Academy of Management Review* 6(3): 469–80.

Pucik, V., and T. Saba (1998). "Selecting and developing the global versus the expatriate manager: A review of the state-of-the-art." *Human Resource Planning* 21(4): 40–54.

Pucik, V., and E. van Weering (2000). "American Diagnostic Systems." Case No. GM870. IMD, Lausanne, Switzerland.

Punnett, B. J., and J. Clemens (1999). "Cross-national diversity: Implications for international expansion decisions." *Journal of World Business* 34(2): 128–38.

Purcell, J. (1999). "Best practice and best fit: Chimera or cul-de-sac?" *Human Resource Management Journal* 9(3): 26–41.

Quinn, R. E. (1988). *Beyond rational management: Mastering the paradoxes and competing demands of high performance.* San Francisco: Jossey-Bass.

Quinn, R. E., and K. S. Cameron, eds. (1988). *Paradox and transformation: Toward a theory of change in organization and management.* Cambridge, MA: Ballinger.

Quinn, R. E., and J. Rohrbaugh (1983). "A spatial model of effectiveness criteria: Towards a competing values approach to organizational analysis." *Management Science* (29:3): 363–77.

Quinn, R. E., G. M. Spreitze, and S. L. Hart (1992). "Integrating the extremes: Crucial skills for managerial effectiveness." *Executive and organizational continuity: Managing the paradoxes of stability and change.* S. Srivastva and R. Fry, eds. San Francisco: Jossey-Bass.

Raelin, J. A. (1999). "The design of the action project in work-based learning." *Human Resource Planning* 22(3): 12–28.

Ramirez, R. (1983). "Action learning: A strategic approach for organizations facing turbulent conditions." *Human Relations* 36(8): 725–42.

Ratiu, I. (1983). "Thinking internationally: A comparison of how international executives learn." *International Studies of Management and Organization* 13(1,2): 139–50.

Redding, G. (1990). *The spirit of Chinese capitalism.* Berlin and New York: de Gruyter.

——— (2001). "The evolution of business systems." Euro-Asia Centre Report No. 72. INSEAD, Fontainebleau and Singapore.

Reich, R. B., and E. D. Mankin (1986). "Joint ventures with Japan give away our future." *Harvard Business Review* (March–April): 78–86.

Revens, R. W. (1980). *Action learning: New techniques for management.* London: Blond and Riggs.

Reynolds, C. (1995). *Compensating globally mobile employees.* Scottsdale, AZ: American Compensation Association.

——— (2001). *Guide to global compensation and benefits.* San Diego: Harcourt.

Reynolds, C., and R. Bennett (1991). "The career couple challenge." *Personnel Journal* 70(3): 46–48.

Rhinesmith, S. H. (1993). *A manager's guide to globalization: Six keys to success in a changing world.* Homewood, IL: ASTD & Business One Irwin.

Rogers, G. C., and M. Beer (1995). "Human resources at Hewlett-Packard (A)(B)." Case No. 9-495-051. Harvard Business School, Boston.

Ronen, S. (1989). "Training the international assignee." *Training and Development in Organizations.* I. Goldstein & Associates, ed. San Francisco: Jossey Bass.

Rosenzweig, P. M. (1997). "Mercedes-Benz: Setting up in Alabama." Case No. GM719. IMD, Lausanne, Switzerland.

Rosenzweig, P. M., and N. Nohria (1994). "Influences on human resource management practices in multinational corporations." *Journal of International Business Studies* 25(2): 229–51.

Rosenzweig, P. M., and B. Raillard (1992). "Accor (A)." Case No. 9-393-012. Harvard Business School, Boston.

Rousseau, D. M., and S. L. Robinson (1994). "Violating the psychological contract: Not the exception but the norm." *Journal of Organizational Behavior.* 15(3): 245–60.

Rowley, C., ed. (1998). *Human resource management in the Asia-Pacific region.* Portland: Frank Cass.

Royle, T. (2000). *Working for McDonald's in Europe: The unequal struggle?* London: Routledge.

Rudlin, P. (2000). *A History of Mitsubishi Corporation in London: 1915 to present day.* London: Routledge.

Sainsaulieu, R. (1977). *L'identité au travail.* Paris: Presse de la Fondation Nationale des Sciences Politiques.

Sampson, A. (1975). *The seven sisters: The great oil companies and the world they made.* London: Hodder and Stoughton.

Santos, J. (2001). "Virtual teams and metanational innovation." INSEAD Working Paper. INSEAD, Fontainebleau.

Sawhney, M., and E. Prandelli (2000). "Communities of creation: Managing distributed innovation in turbulent markets." *California Management Review* 42(4): 24–54.

Schein, E. H. (1968). "Organizational socialization and the profession of management." *Industrial Management Review* 9: 1–16.

————— (1978). *Career dynamics: Matching individual and organizational needs.* Reading, MA: Addison-Wesley.

————— (1985). *Organizational culture and leadership: A dynamic view.* San Francisco: Jossey-Bass.

————— (1996). *Strategic pragmatism: The culture of Singapore's Economic Development Board:* Cambridge, MA: MIT Press.

Schisgall, O. (1981). *Eyes on Tomorrow: The Evolution of Procter & Gamble.* New York: Doubleday.

Schlesinger, L. A., and J. L. Heskett (1991). "The service-driven company." *Harvard Business Review* (September–October): 71–81.

Schneider, S. C. (1988). "National vs. corporate culture: Implications for human resource management." *Human Resource Management* 27(2): 231–46.

Schneider, S. C., and J. L. Barsoux (1997). *Managing across cultures.* Hemel Hempstead, UK: Prentice Hall.

Schuler, R. S. (2000). "HR issues in international joint ventures and alliances." *Human resource management.* J. Storey, ed. London: International Thomson.

Schuler, R. S., and S. E. Jackson (1987). "Linking competitive strategies with human resource management practices." *Academy of Management Executive* 1(3): 207–19.

Schuler, R. S., and I. C. MacMillan (1984). "Gaining competitive advantage through human resource management practices." *Human Resource Management* 23(3): 241–55.

Schütte, H. (1998). "Between headquarters and subsidiaries: The RHQ solution." *Multinational corporate evolution and subsidiary development.* J. Birkinshaw and N. Hood, eds. London: Macmillan.

Scott, J. (1991). *Social network analysis.* London: Sage.

Scott Myers, M. (1970). *Every employee a manager.* New York: McGraw-Hill.

Scullion, H. (1994). "Staffing policies and strategic control in British multinationals." *International Studies of Management and Organization,* 24(3): 86–104.

————— (1995). "International Human Resource Management." *Human resource management: A critical text.* J. Storey, ed. London: Routledge.

Scullion, H., and K. Starkey (2000). "In search of the changing role of the corporate human resource function in the international firm." *International Journal of Human Resource Management* 11(6): 1061–81.

Segalla, M., L. Fischer, and K. Sandner (2000). "Making cross-cultural research relevant to European corporate integration: Old problem—new approach." *European Management Journal* 18(1): 38–51.

Selznick, P. (1957). *Leadership in administration: A sociological interpretation.* Evanston, IL.: Row, Peterson.

Semler, R. (1993). *Maverick: The success story behind the world's most unusual workplace.* New York: Warner.

Shaffer, M. A., D. A. Harrison, and K. M. Gilley (1999). "Dimensions, determinants, and differences in the expatriate adjustment process." *Journal of International Business Studies* 30(3): 557–81.

Shenkar, O., and Y. Zeira (1990). "International joint ventures: A tough test for HR." *Personnel* 67(1): 26–31.

Shimada, H., and J. P. MacDuffie (1999). "Industrial relations and 'humanware': Japanese investments in automobile manufacturing in the United States." *The Japanese Enterprise.* S. Beechler, ed. London: Routledge.

SHRM (2000). "Making Mergers Work: Strategic Importance of People." Report by SHRM (Society for Human Resource Management), Alexandria, VA.

Sigiura, H. (1990). "How Honda localizes its global strategy." *Sloan Management Review* (Fall): 77–82.

Simon, H. A. (1981). *The sciences of the artificial.* Cambridge, MA: MIT Press.

Simon, H. (1996). *Hidden champions: Lessons from 500 of the world's best unknown companies.* Boston: Harvard Business School Press.

Simonin, B. L. (1999). "Ambiguity and process of knowledge transfer in strategic alliances." *Strategic Management Journal* 20(7): 596–623.

Sisson, K. (1994). "Personnel management: paradigms, practice and prospects." *Personnel management,* 2d ed. Oxford: Blackwell.

Skinner, W. (1981). "Big hat, no cattle: Managing human resources." *Harvard Business Review* (September–October): 106–14.

Slater, R. (1999). *The GE Way fieldbook.* New York: McGraw-Hill.

Smith, K., and D. Berg (1987). "Paradoxes of belonging." *Paradoxes of group life.* San Francisco: Jossey-Bass.

Snell, S. A. (1999). "Social capital and strategic HRM: It's who you know." *Human Resource Planning* 22(3): 62–65.

Snell, S. A., D. P. Lepak, and M. A. Youndt (1999). "Managing the architecture of intellectual capital: Implications for strategic human resource management." *Research in personnel and human resources management: Strategic human resource management in the twenty-first century.* P. M. Wright, L. D. Dyer, J. W. Boudreau, and G. T. Milkovich, eds. Stamford, CT: JAI Press.

Snell, S. A., M. A. Youndt, et al. (1996). "Establishing a framework for research in strategic human resource management: Merging resource theory and organizational learning." *Research in personnel and human resources management.* G. R. Ferris, ed. Stamford, CT: JAI Press.

Snow, C., R. E. Miles, and H. Coleman (1992). "Managing 21st century network organizations." *Organizational Dynamics* (Winter): 5–20.

Snow, C., S. A. Snell, S. C. Davison, and D. C. Hambrick (1996). "Use transnational teams to globalize your company." *Organizational Dynamics* 24(4): 50–67.

Solomon, C. M. (1995). "HR's helping hand pulls global inpatriates onboard." *Personnel Journal* 74(11): 40–49.

———— (1998). "Today's global mobility." *Workforce* 3(4): 12–17.

Sonnenfeld, J. A., and M. A. Peiperl (1988). "Staffing policy as a strategic response: A typology of career systems." *Academy of Management Review* 13(4): 588–600.

Sorge, A. (1991). "Strategic fit and the societal effect: Interpreting cross-national comparisons of technology, organization and human resources." *Organization Studies* 12(2): 161–90.

Sparrow, P. (1999). "International recruitment, selection and assessment." *The global HR manager: Creating the seamless organisation.* P. Joynt and B. Morton, eds. London: Institute of Personnel and Development.

Sparrow, P., and J.-M. Hiltrop (1994). *European human resource management in transition.* New York: Prentice Hall.

Sparrow, P., R. Schuler, and S. Jackson (1994). "Convergence or divergence: Human resource practices and policies for competitive advantage worldwide." *International Journal of Human Resource Management* 5(2): 267–300.

Spector, B. A. (1995). *Taking charge and letting go: A breakthrough strategy for creating and managing the horizontal company.* New York: Free Press.

Spekman, R. E., T. M. Forbes III, et al. (1998). "Alliance management: A view from the past and a look to the future." *Journal of Management Studies* 35(6): 747–72.

Spencer, L. M., and S. M. Spencer (1993). *Competence at work: Model for superior performance.* Chichester: Wiley.

Spreitzer, G., M. W. McCall, and J. Mahoney (1997). "The early identification of international leadership potential: Dimensions, measurement and validation." *Journal of Applied Psychology* 82(1): 6–29.

Springer, B., and S. Springer (1990). "Human resource management in the US: Celebration of its centenary." *Human resource management: An international comparison.* R. Piper, ed. Berlin: de Gruyter.

Sproul, L., and S. Kiesler (1991). *Connections: New ways of working in the networked organization.* Cambridge, MA: MIT Press.

St. John, C. H., S. T. Young, and J. T. Miller (1999). "Coordinating manufacturing and marketing in international firms." *Journal of World Business* 34(2): 109–27.

Stace, D. A., and D. C. Dunphy (1991). "Beyond traditional paternalistic and developmental approaches to organizational change and human resource strategies." *International Journal of Human Resource Management* 2(3): 263–84.

Stahl, G. K. (2000). "Between ethnocentrism and assimilation: An exploratory study of the challenges and coping strategies of expatriate managers." Proceedings of the Annual Conference of the Academy of Management, Toronto.

Stalk, J. G. (1988). "Time—the next source of competitive advantage." *Harvard Business Review* (July–August): 41–53.

Stalk, G., P. Evans, and L. E. Schulman (1992). "Competing on capabilities: The new rules of corporate strategy." *Harvard Business Review* (March–April): 57–69.

Stauffer, D. (2000). *The Cisco Way: Secrets of the company that makes the Internet.* Oxford: Capstone.

Steger, U. (1999). "The Transformational Merger." *Financial Times Mastering Management Review* (Issue 30): 46–50.

Stening, B. W., J. E. Everett, and P. A. Longton (1981). "Mutual perception of managerial performance and style in multinational subsidiaries." *Journal of Occupational Psychology* 54(4): 255–63.

Stephens, G. K., and S. Black (1991). "The impact of spouse's career orientation on managers during international transfers." *Journal of Management Studies* 28(4): 417–28.

Stewart, T. A. (1997). *Intellectual capital: The new wealth of organizations.* New York: Doubleday.

Stinchcombe, A. L. (1965). "Social structure and organizations." *Handbook of Organizations.* J. G. March, ed. Chicago: Rand McNally.

Stopford, J. M., and L. T. Wells (1972). *Managing the multinational enterprise.* London: Longman.

Stroh, L. K. (1995). "Predicting turnover among repatriates: Can organizations affect retention rates?" *International Journal of Human Resource Management* 6(2): 443–56.

Stroh, L. K., and P. M. Caligiuri (1998). "Increasing global competitiveness through effective people management." *Journal of World Business* 33(1): 1–16.

Stroh, L. K., A. Varma, and S. J. Valy-Durbin (2000). "Why are women left at home: Are they unwilling to go on international assignments?" *Journal of World Business* 35(3): 241–55.

Sullivan, J. J., and I. Nonaka (1985). "The application of organizational learning theory to Japanese and American management." *Journal of International Business Studies* (Fall): 127–47.

Suutari, V., and C. Brewster (1999). "International assignments across European borders: No problems?" *International HRM: Contemporary Issues in Europe.* C. Brewster and H. Harris, eds. London: Routledge.

Szulanski, G. (1994). "Intra-firm transfer of best practice: Executive summary." Research Report, American Productivity and Quality Center, Houston, Texas.

——— (1996). "Exploring internal stickiness: Impediments to the transfer of best practice within the firm." *Strategic Management Journal* 17: 27–43.

Tahvanainen, M. (1998). "Expatriate performance management: The case of Nokia Telecommunications." Helsinki School of Economics and Business Administration, Helsinki, Finland.

Takeuchi, H., and I. Nonaka (1986). "The new new product development game." *Harvard Business Review* (January–February): 137–46.

Tallman, S., and K. Fladmoe-Lindquist (1999). "The evolution of multinational strategy: A dynamic capabilities perspective." Research paper, Cranfield School of Management, Cranfield, U.K.

Taylor, F. W. (1911). *Principles of scientific management.* New York: Harper.

Taylor, S., S. Beechler, and N. Napier (1996). "Toward an integrative model of strategic international human resource management." *Academy of Management Review* 21(4): 959–85.

Tead O., and H. C. Metcalf (1920). *Personnel administration.* New York: McGraw-Hill.

Teece, D. J. (1987). *The competitive challenge.* Cambridge, MA: Ballinger.

Teigland, R. (2000). "Communities of practice in a high-technology firm." *The flexible firm: Capability management in network organizations.* J. Birkinshaw and P. Hagström, eds. Oxford: Oxford University Press.

Thill, G., and D. Leonard-Barton (1993). "Hewlett-Singapore (A)(B)(C)." Cases 694035-037. Harvard Business School, Boston.

Thorsrud, E. (1976). "Democratization of work as a process of change towards nonbureaucratic types of organization." *European contributions to organization theory.* G. Hofstede and M. S. Kassem, eds. Amsterdam: Van Gorcum.

Tichy, N. M. (1983). *Managing strategic change: Technical, political and cultural dynamics.* New York: Wiley.

Tichy, N. M., M. I. Brimm, R. Charam, and H. Takeuchi (1992). "Leadership development as a lever for global transformation." *Globalizing management: Creating and leading the competitive organization.* V. Pucik, N. M. Tichy, and C. K. Barnett, eds. New York: Wiley.

Tichy, N. M., and E. Cohen (1997). *The leadership engine: How winning companies build leaders at every level.* New York: HarperCollins.

Tichy, N. M., and S. Sherman (1993). *Control your destiny or someone else will.* New York: HarperBusiness.

Tjosvold, D. (1991). *The conflict-positive organization: Stimulate diversity and create unity.* Reading, MA: Addison-Wesley.

Torbiörn, I. (1982). *Living abroad: Personal adjustment and personnel policy in the overseas setting.* New York: Wiley.

Tornow, W. (1998). *Maximizing the value of 360 degree feedback: A process for successful individual and organizational development.* San Francisco: Jossey-Bass.

Torrington, D., and L. Hall (1995). *Human resource management.* London: Prentice Hall.

Townley, B. (1994). *Reframing human resource management: Power, ethics and the subject at work.* London: Sage.

Townsend, A. M., S. M. deMarie, and A. R. Henrickson (1998). "Virtual teams and the workplace of the future." *Academy of Management Executive* (August): 17–29.

Toynbee, A. (1946). *A Study of History,* vols. 1–6. Oxford: Oxford University Press.

Trepo, G. (1973). "Management style à la française." *Euopean Business* (Autumn): 71–79.

Trist, E. L., and K. W. Bamforth (1951). "Some social and psychological consequences of the Longwall method of coal-getting." *Human Relations* 4: 3–38.

Trompenaars, F. (1993). *Riding the waves of culture: Understanding cultural diversity in business.* London: Nicholas Brealey.

Tulgan, B. (2001). *Winning the talent wars.* New York: Norton.

Tung, R. L. (1981). "Selection and training of personnel for overseas assignments." *Columbia Journal of World Business* 16(1): 57–71.

———— (1982). "Selection and training procedures of US, European, and Japanese multinationals." *California Management Review* 25(1): 57–71.

———— (1988). "Career issues in international assignments." *Academy of Management Executive* 2(3): 241–44.

———— (1995). "Women in a changing global economy." Paper presented at the Tenth Annual Conference of the Society for Industrial and Organizational Psychology, Orlando, FL.

———— (1997). "Canadian expatriates in Asia-Pacific: An analysis of their attitude toward and experience in international assignments." Paper presented at the meeting of the Society for Industrial and Organizational Psychology, St. Louis, MO.

Tushman, M. L., and C. A. O'Reilly (1996). "Ambidextrous organizations: Managing evolutionary and revolutionary change." *California Management Review* 38(4): 8–30.

Tushman, M. L., W. H. Newman, and E. Romanelli (1986). "Convergence and upheaval: Managing the unsteady pace of organizational evolution." *California Management Review* 29(1): 29–44.

Tyson, S., and A. Fell (1986). *Evaluating the personnel function.* London: Hutchinson.

Ulrich, D. (1997). *Human resource champions: The next agenda for adding value and delivering results.* Boston: Harvard Business School Press.

Ulrich, D., M. R. Losey, and G. Lake (1997). *Tomorrow's HR management: 48 thought leaders call for change.* New York: Wiley.

Ulrich, D., J. Zenger, and N. Smallwood (1999). *Results-based leadership.* Boston: Harvard Business School Press.

Ungson, G., R. Steers, and S. Park (1997). *Korean enterprise: The quest for globalization.* Boston: Harvard Business School Press.

Vance, C. M., S. R. McClaine, D. M. Boje, and D. H. Stage (1992). "An examination of the transferability of traditional performance appraisal principles across cultural boundaries." *Management International Review* 32: 313–26.

Van de Ven, A. H., D. E. Polley, R. Garud, and S. Venhataraman (1999), *The innovation journey.* New York: Oxford University Press.

Vandenbosch, B., and M. J. Ginzberg (1996). "LotusNotes and collaboration: Plus ça change." *Journal of Management Information Systems* 13(3): 65–82.

Van Maanen, J., and E. H. Schein (1979). "Toward a theory of organization socialization." *Research in organizational behavior,* vol. 1. B. Staw, ed. Greenwich, CT: JAI Press.

Varma, A., R. W. Beatty, and C. Schneier (1999). "High performance work systems: Exciting discovery or passing fad?" *Human Resource Planning* 22(1): 26–37.

Vaupel, J. W., and J. P. Curhan (1973). *The world's largest multinational enterprises.* Cambridge, MA: Harvard University Press.

Venkatraman, N. (1989). "The concept of fit in strategy research: Toward verbal and statistical correspondence." *Academy of Management Review* 14(3): 423–44.

Vernon, R. (1966). "International investment and international trade in the product cycle." *Quarterly Journal of Economics.* 80: 190–207.

———— (1977). *Storm over the multinationals: The real issues.* Cambridge, MA: Harvard University Press.

Vernon, R., L. T. Wells, and S. Rangan (1997). *The manager in the international economy.* Englewood Cliffs, NJ: Prentice Hall.

Vogel, D. (1991). "Business ethics: New perspectives on old problems." *California Management Review* (Summer): 101–17.

Volberda, H. W. (1998). *Building the flexible firm: How to remain competitive.* Oxford: Oxford University Press.

Volmer, H. M., and D. L. Mills, eds. (1966). *Professionalization.* Englewood Cliffs, NJ: Prentice Hall.

von Keller, E., and V. von Courière (1996). *In search of Homo Bertelsmannensis: A collection of essays in honor of Reinhard Mohn.* Gütersloh, Germany: Bertelsmann.

Walker, J. W. (1980). *Human resource planning.* New York: McGraw-Hill.

Walker, J. (1998). "Do we need succession planning anymore?" *Human Resource Planning* 21(3): 9–11.

Watson, W. E., K. Kumar, and L. K. Michaelsen (1993). "Cultural diversity's impact on interaction process and performance: Comparing homogenous and diverse task groups." *Academy of Management Journal* 36(3): 590–602.

Watson Wyatt (1999). "Watson Wyatt Worldwide's 1998/99 Mergers & Acquisitions Survey." Report by Watson Wyatt, Washington DC.

Waxin, M., A. Roger, and J. L. Chandon (1997) "L'intégration des expatriés dans leur nouveau poste, une analyse contingente et quantitative, le cas des expatriés français en Norvège." *GRH face à la crise: GRH en crise?* B. Sire and M. Tremblay, eds. Montreal: Presse HEC.

Weick, K. E. (1979). *The social psychology of organizing.* Boston: Addison-Wesley.

Weick, K. E., and F. Westley (1996). "Organizational learning: Affirming an oxymoron." *Handbook of organization studies.* S. R. Clegg, C. Hardy, and W. R. Nord, eds. London and Thousand Oaks, CA: Sage.

Weiss, S. E. (1994a). "Negotiating with 'Romans'—Part 1." *Sloan Management Review* 35(2): 51–61.

——— (1994b). "Negotiating with 'Romans'—Part 2." *Sloan Management Review* 35(3): 85–99.

Welbourne, T., and A. Andrews (1996). "Predicting performance of initial public offering firms: Should HRM be in the equation?" *Academy of Management Journal* 39: 891–919.

Westney, D. E. (1988). "Domestic foreign learning curves in managing international cooperative strategies." *Cooperative strategies in international business.* F. J. Contractor and P. Lorange, eds. Lexington, MA: Lexington Books.

Westphal, J. D., R. Gulati, and S. M. Shortell (1997). "Customization or conformity: An institutional and network perspective on the content and consequences of TQM adoption." *Administrative Science Quarterly* 42: 161–83.

Westwood, R. I., and S. M. Leung (1994). "The female expatriate manager experience: Coping with gender and culture." *International Studies of Management and Organization* 24(3): 64–85.

Whipp, R., R. Rosenfeld, and A. Pettigrew (1988). "The management of strategic and operational change: Lessons for the 1990s." Paper presented at the Eighth Annual Strategic Management Society Conference.

Whitfield, K., and M. Poole (1997). "Organizing employment for high performance: Theories, evidence and policy." *Organization Studies* 18(5): 745–64.

Whitley, R. D. (1990). "The societal construction of business systems in East Asia." *Organization Studies* 11(1): 47–74.

——— (1999). *Alternative systems of capitalism.* Oxford: Oxford University Press.

———, ed. (1992). *European business systems: Firms and markets in their national contexts.* London and Beverly Hills: Sage.

Whittington, R., A. Pettigrew, et al. (1999). "Change and complementarities in the new competitive landscape: A European panel study, 1992–1996." *Organization Science* 10(5): 583–600.

Wilkins, M. (1970). *The emergence of multinational enterprise.* Cambridge, MA: Harvard University Press.

——— (1988). "European and North American multinationals, 1870–1914: Comparisons and contrasts." *Business History* 30(1): 8–45.

Wilkinson, B., and C. Leggett (1985). "Human and industrial relations in Singapore: The management of compliance." *Euro-Asia Business Review* 4(3): 9–15.

Williams, K., and C. A. O'Reilly (1998). "Demography and diversity in organizations." *Research in organizational behavior,* vol. 20. B. M. Staw and R. M. Sutton, eds. Stamford, CT: JAI Press.

Williamson, O. E. (1975). *Markets and hierarchies: Analysis and antitrust implications.* New York: Free Press.

Womack, J. P., D. T. Jones, and D. Roos (1990). *The machine that changed the world.* New York: Rawson Associates.

Wong, C. S., and K. Law (1999). "Managing localization of human resources in the PRC: A practical model." *Journal of World Business* 34(1): 26–40.

Wren, D. A. (1994). *The evolution of management thought.* London: Wiley.

Wright, P. M., L. D. Dyer, J. W. Boudreau, and G. T. Milkovich (1999). *Strategic human resources management in the twenty-first century.* Stamford, CT: JAI Press.

Wright, P. M., and G. C. McMahon (1992). "Alternative theoretical perspectives on strategic human resource management." *Journal of Management* 18: 295–320.

Wright, P. M., and W. S. Sherman (1999). "Failing to find fit in strategic human resource management: Theoretical and empirical problems." *Research in personnel and human resources management: Strategic human resource management in the twenty-first century.* P. M. Wright, L. D. Dyer, J. W. Boudreau and G. T. Milkovich, eds. Stamford, CT: JAI Press.

Wright, P. M., and S. A. Snell (1998). "Toward a unifying framework for exploring fit and flexibility in strategic human resource management." *Academy of Management Review* 23(3): 756–72.

Yang, M. (1994). *Gifts, favors and banquets: The art of social relationships in China.* Ithaca, NY: Cornell University Press.

Yergin, D., and J. Stanislaw (1998). *The commanding heights: The battle between government and the marketplace that is remaking the modern world.* New York: Simon & Schuster.

Yeung, A., and D. Ready (1995). "Developing leadership capabilities of global corporations: A comparative study in eight nations." *Human Resource Management* 34(4): 529–47.

Yeung, A., P. Woolcock, and J. Sullivan (1996). "Identifying and developing HR competencies for the future: Keys to sustaining the transformation of HR functions." *Human Resource Planning* 19(4): 48–57.

Yoshino, M., and U.S. Rangan (1995). *Strategic alliances: An entrepreneurial approach to globalization.* Cambridge, MA: Harvard Business School Press.

Yoshihara, H. (1999). "Global operations managed by Japanese." (In Japanese.) Discussion Paper Series No. 108. Research Institute for Economics and Business Administration, Kobe University, Kobe, Japan.

Youndt, M. A., S. A. Snell, J. W. Dean, and D. P. Lepak (1996). "Human resource management, manufacturing strategy, and firm performance." *Academy of Management Journal* 39: 836–66.

Zahra, S. A., R. D. Ireland, and M. A. Hitt (2000). "International expansion by new venture firms: International diversity, mode of market entry, technological learning, and performance." *Academy of Management Journal* 43(5): 925–50.

Zbaracki, M. J. (1998). "The rhetoric and reality of total quality management." *Administrative Science Quarterly* 43(3): 602–34.

Zeira, Y., and O. Shenkar (1990). "Interactive and specific parent characteristics: Implications for management and human resources in international joint ventures." *Management International Review* 30(Special Issue): 7–22.

Zucker, L. (1988). *Institutional patterns and organizations: Culture and environment.* Cambridge, MA: Ballinger.

Zuckerman, M. R. (1989). "Quality, the American way." AT&T Report, presented at EFMD Annual Conference on Managing across Boundaries, The Hague, Netherlands.

Name Index

Subject Index